The Family Book
of Preventive Medicine

The Family Book
of Preventive Medicine

HOW TO STAY WELL
ALL THE TIME

by *Benjamin F. Miller*, M.D.
and *Lawrence Galton*

Weathervane Books • New York

To
Judith W. Miller
and
Barbara Galton
our wives
who gave us the time
and encouragement
to complete this book

THE AUTHORS GRATEFULLY ACKNOWLEDGE
THE ASSISTANCE THEY RECEIVED FROM
DR. HENRY ROSENBERG, OF THE UNIVERSITY
OF PENNSYLVANIA HOSPITAL, IN THE
PREPARATION OF THE FINAL SECTION
OF THIS BOOK, AND ALSO THE
HELPFUL DISCUSSIONS WITH DR. SILAS WARNER
AND DR. MARC HOLLENDER.

PART ONE

The Promise and Nature of
Preventive Medicine

1

THE PROMISE

THERE WAS a time when preventive medicine was—and could be—only a hope. It was expressed in the custom of the ancient Chinese who paid their doctors to keep them well; when they became patients, they refused to pay. It was implicit in the adage of ancient Greek medicine: "Help your patients to die young—as late as possible."

The exciting thing about the quest for preventing disease and its ravages is that we know more about how to go about it than ever before; it is no longer an unrealistic quest.

Recent decades have seen great strides in curative medicine. But the most significant developments now are not magic new drugs and surgical procedures that cure but new insights into how disease arises and progresses and how it may be prevented from arising and, if present, prevented from progressing.

The use of a mechanical kidney to save a patient with advanced kidney disease; the transplantation of organs, including even the heart; the rehabilitation, even partial, of a stroke victim; the easing of pain for an arthritic and sometimes even replacement of an arthritically destroyed joint—these, of course, are proud accomplishments.

But how much better, all of us would agree, if the need for such measures could be avoided.

Treatment never equals prevention. Treatment, the best that can be devised, must be used when disease exists. But treatment does not always work; even when it does, it may eliminate the disease but not the damage already done. It is prevention that must be counted upon to make the big inroads against both death and disability.

And it is prevention that has done this to date to an extent that may surprise many of us. Since the turn of the century, the death rate in the United States has been reduced from approximately 17 per 1,000 persons per year to about 9.5. If mortality rates for certain diseases prevailed as in the year 1900, almost 400,000 Americans would lose their lives to tuberculosis, almost 300,000 to gastroenteritis, 80,000 to diphtheria, and 55,000 to poliomyelitis. Instead, the toll from all four diseases this year will be less than 10,000 lives.

For this a major share of the credit must go to the sanitary engineer, the agriculturist, the public health officer, the pediatrician, and the family physician practicing preventive medicine. Nearly all the gains against the once-great killers—which also included typhoid fever, smallpox, plague —have been made as the result of improvements in sanitation, in nutrition, in immunization procedures, and in early diagnosis through mass disease screening campaigns—all techniques of disease prevention.

Therapeutic measures, including the antibiotics and other wonder drugs, have helped but not nearly as much as preventive measures. In fact, it has been observed that only two major diseases in the United States today—appendicitis and lobar pneumonia in the young—are being controlled rather completely by treatment alone. Prevention has much more to offer.

Even as death rates from infectious diseases have fallen dramatically, those for the chronic diseases have mounted. Cancer mortality, for example, rose from 65 per 100,000 people in 1900 to more than 150 by 1960. Where once 2 out of 10 Americans were felled by heart, blood vessel, and kidney diseases, now 5 out of 10 die from them. There are also the chronic disorders that do not necessarily kill but do incapacitate —mental, nervous, circulatory, arthritic, many more.

The fact is, too, that as deaths in the early years of life from infectious diseases have declined, the other disorders—often called degenerative diseases and once regarded chiefly as consequences of aging—have become important killers and cripplers of people in the middle years and even earlier. No longer, for example, are the heart attack and the stroke solely the unwelcome companions of retirement; they are now threats to life to people at the height of their careers.

As a result, there has been a change of attitude about these diseases —from one of passive acceptance of their inevitability to one of determined attack. Part of the attack, of course, is a search for cures and palliative measures. But the best hope for eliminating these disorders lies in preventing their occurrence. And the most promising aspect of the attack is the emergence of a new kind of preventive medicine, broader-based but also individualized.

THE THREE STAGES OF PREVENTION

The new preventive medicine makes use of a rapidly increasing array of remarkable new test techniques. It also uses a growing body of knowledge about risk factors in disease. And it more and more combines the two to go even beyond early diagnoses and to identify in the presently healthy any tendency to develop serious illness later and, with this knowledge, to institute changes, sometimes relatively simple, to reduce the risk.

The ideal is to prevent disease, if possible, from happening. But the new preventive medicine, on a realistic basis, also includes secondary prevention: the prevention, if a disease is already present, of progression. It also includes tertiary prevention: the holding in check of even far-advanced disease so that radical measures, such as organ substitution when applicable, may be used.

Implicit, too, in the new preventive medicine is a positive aspect: an improvement in the quality of living as well as length of life, a building of physical, mental, and emotional health.

We Americans, a warmhearted people, like to rally round to "help the handicapped"—and we think of the handicapped as the blind, crippled, mentally deficient. Yet many of us, although free of such obvious deficits, belong among the handicapped.

If not outrightly sick, we are never fully healthy. We live in "second gear." One dramatic and large-scale demonstration of this came in World War II when many relatively young men, in their early thirties and even twenties, had to be rejected by the Armed Forces as unfit. We have current reminders of our state of non-first-class health in the daily barrages of "remedy" advertising on television—all the concoctions offering relief for tired feelings, stomach upsets, heartburn, acid indigestion, insomnia, tension, a multitude of aches and pains.

Is vigorous health impossible? It should be the rule rather than the exception—and at older ages as well as earlier in life.

Man may or may not have the capacity for living to 150 or 200 years of age; there is considerable debate about this in medical circles. And there is not yet in sight any medical ability to bring a halt to aging. But with knowledge now available, the aging process can be slowed. Indeed, a good deal of what is passed off as deterioration due to aging is not that at all; it is deterioration due to insult or neglect. And preventive medicine has much to offer in showing how the insult and neglect can be eliminated.

The goals are ambitious, and certainly much more research is needed before they are fully—and universally—attainable and their necessity generally accepted. But already enough research has been done, enough tools have been developed, and the tactics have become sufficiently clear to make the new preventive medicine a practical matter for you and your family.

To help make it so is, of course, our aim in writing this book. We have tried to provide in it a detailed guide to the concepts and practices of preventive medicine—how the physician uses them and how the individual can apply them.

2

THE TACTICS

"To CURE sometimes, to relieve often, to comfort always"—so the physician's role was described in the fifteenth century. So it remained until this century. Comfort he did because there was little else he could do.

Twentieth-century medicine has undergone fundamental changes, with more progress made in a few decades than in thousands of years before. And while some of this progress has been dramatically obvious—heart surgery, brain surgery, antibiotics, hormonal treatments—even more basic advances were being made at the same time.

Medicine began to penetrate the mysteries of psychic disease and to gain understanding of the interrelationships of mind and body. It explored the influence and mechanisms of heredity in disease. It established the mechanisms of body chemistry and of inborn chemical error. It allied itself with many other sciences—drawing, for example, from physics and biochemistry new electronic equipment and test tube procedures for detecting and monitoring disease.

The crystal ball may seem less glamorous than the wonder drug and the miracle in the operating room. But medicine has been developing a kind of scientific crystal ball that promises to make far greater inroads on disease, that can be rubbed to see the portents for the individual patient and used to help guide him around the health hazards he faces.

CALCULATING RISKS

First, it became evident not only that people vary in susceptibility to disease but that increased risk depends upon many factors and that it is possible to calculate risks.

Breast cancer, for example, occurs in 5 percent of white women over age 40 in the United States—and so, on the average, there is a 1 in 20 risk. But a woman with a positive family history of breast cancer—one whose mother or sister or aunt developed the disease—has triple the risk of other women. (Let us say, at once, that if this increased hazard because of hereditary influences stood by itself, it would be only a morbid statistic. But it stands with increasingly sensitive methods of detecting cancer at earlier and earlier—and therefore more curable—stages, and underscores the wisdom of special emphasis on breast cancer detection for such a woman.)

Other factors, racial and social, help to identify special pronenesses. The Japanese have a high risk of stomach cancer but relatively low risk of breast cancer; the Chinese and Malaysians have a high risk of nose and throat cancer. In unskilled American workers and their wives, the incidence of cancer of the stomach and uterine cervix is three to four times higher than among people in the professional fields. On the other hand, cancer of the breast and leukemia are substantially more common in the higher economic classes.

There are occupational factors to be considered. For example, urinary bladder cancer has an increased incidence among aniline dye workers, and in that industry programs have been started for annual tests of urine.

Medicine also has been establishing other characteristics associated with high risk of specific diseases as a means of permitting preventive measures to be used. For coronary heart disease, which may lead to heart attack, the characteristics include excessive levels of certain fats in the blood, high blood pressure, high pulse rate, cigarette smoking, physical inactivity, and premature cessation of ovarian activity in a woman. The incidence of the disease, in men aged 40 to 59 for example, increases from 9 per 1,000 when one of these factors is present to 77 per 1,000 when any three of them are present.

DISEASE SCENARIOS

Another important development has been the discovery that death is really a slow intruder, that diseases do not suddenly spring up full-blown but often have long scenarios.

In the Korean War, autopsies of young American soldiers revealed that in 54 percent of these youths, many of whom had only very recently attained manhood, coronary heart disease was already starting. No longer could the disease be considered degenerative, a part of aging. If the seeds of the disease germinate in the early years and the ultimate heart attack is the end result of a long process in time, then here is a problem that can be combatted, for there is time to combat it. And since there is evidence of what factors are involved, there are means to fight, to retard, and perhaps even to prevent it from getting started.

Some of the most impressive preventive work recently has been the result of advances in the understanding of body chemistry—and of chemical abnormalities that may be inborn. It has now become possible to detect early in life, even almost immediately after birth, such inborn errors as phenylketonuria and galactosemia. They involve inability to properly handle certain specific food elements, and simply by avoiding such elements it has become possible to prevent development of mental retardation, growth failure, and other serious problems.

Understanding of the chemistry of disease is expanding rapidly, and there is growing confidence that the principles of early detection and treatment of diseases due to inborn chemical errors can be extended to many common chronic diseases. That can make it possible for the doctor in his practice to have to deal less with severe complications triggered while a disease smoulders under the surface before calling attention to itself with obvious symptoms, and he can be concerned instead with early detection of the still symptom-free but predisposed patient and correction of the basic problem before complications have a chance to develop.

Already, for example, promising work is being done in detecting people with prediabetes—those who have no symptoms of diabetes but do have changes in body chemistry that may forecast eventual onset of overt diabetes. Early results of treating such patients with antidiabetic agents are regarded by some investigators as promising, suggesting it may be possible to prevent the development of diabetes and such complications as visual disturbances, circulatory disturbances, and increased risk of coronary heart disease.

As we have noted earlier, kidney machines can be lifesavers for patients with kidney failure—but it would be far better to prevent the failure. And there is growing hope now that in many cases failure may be prevented by attention to asymptomatic bacteriuria. Asymptomatic bacteriuria simply means the presence of sizable numbers of bacteria in the urine without causing symptoms. The condition may occur at any age and in either sex but is especially frequent in females, affecting 1.2 percent of schoolgirls and 6 percent of pregnant women. There is evidence that if left untreated bacteriuria may eventually cause the kidney disease pyelonephritis, which in turn may result in kidney failure.

Bacteriuria can be treated effectively once detected, and newer tests now make its detection simpler and more practical. Today, as the next chapter will show, many testing procedures are available to make it possible for the physician increasingly to anticipate and prevent disease rather than wait for it to appear.

How does a preventively minded physician function?

You can expect that in working with you he will get to know you thoroughly—past medical history, family medical history, job, working habits, living habits—so he can weigh any possibility that you—as a member of a specific group based on heredity, environment, age, sex, color, personal habits—may face certain specific health hazards.

In his regular periodic examinations, he will follow your health progress in general and will be alert for the slightest early indication of anything wrong in any area of special risk for you. He may, in fact, from time to time use special tests to make certain all is going well in a special risk area.

During your visits, he will be concerned, of course, with any physical complaints and also with any mental or emotional problems (job, marital, and others), since these can affect health.

He will be interested in any changes in your habits and their possible effects, for good or ill, on your health. From time to time, he may have suggestions for an alteration, perhaps minor, of diet, exercise pattern, sleep, relaxation, etc.

As he regularly checks you, alert for earliest indications, even preindications, of possible trouble, he will be prepared to intervene without delay. Rather than wait, say, for obvious symptoms of diabetes to develop—especially if you belong to the group with greater than average probability of developing the disease—he will intervene to try to correct, if they appear, the very first changes that could possibly lead to diabetes.

As medicine has been practiced generally to now, it has been the patient who, in effect, has turned up after making a self-diagnosis. It has been the patient who has decided, "I think I am or may be sick or becoming sick," and then has sought help.

Now it will be the preventively minded physician who increasingly will be able to tell the patient, "You are about to become sick and we are going to take a few measures in advance so you won't actually develop the sickness."

3

THE TOOLS

HARDLY A month now passes without a report of a promising new test for early detection of disease or for revealing a possible propensity for disease.

It is not essential that you have a detailed knowledge of modern examining and testing procedures. But some awareness of the basic, long-established methods and tests and the newest x-ray and laboratory tools, and what they can do, will be useful.

THE CASE HISTORY

The patient's history, always an invaluable guide in disease diagnosis, is equally valuable in prevention.

We have mentioned earlier, in passing, some of the reasons. Occupational data—facts about the work you do and possibly the circumstances under which you do it—may reveal some hazards, physical or psychological, to which you are exposed. An account of family health—the illnesses of parents and grandparents, their longevity, the state of health of brothers and sisters—can provide clues to hereditary strengths and weaknesses.

Your own past illnesses are an important part of the record. Some childhood episodes of illness, if severe, may have left a mark. Rheumatic fever, for example, may strike a child at 15 or earlier and may produce some heart damage. Yet, very often, the effects of the heart damage are not felt until age 35, 40, or even later. A record of the rheumatic fever incident may be of vital importance in accurate diagnosis of a heart condition.

The case history—which includes what the patient reports about present problems—sometimes provides the first indication of onset of a serious illness. For example, angina pectoris (chest pain) is associated with coronary heart disease. In coronary heart disease, the coronary arteries feeding the heart muscle become narrowed. There are sophisticated techniques now—including x-ray movies of the coronary arteries —to show up the narrowing. But in some early cases, angina may occur before there are sufficient changes to show up on the x-ray studies.

If in taking the history the physician determines that there have been angina episodes—perhaps after some sudden unusual exertion, perhaps upon leaving the house on a particularly cold morning—he can confirm the angina diagnosis by giving the patient some nitroglycerin tablets to take when the next incident occurs; and if there is immediate relief of pain, the diagnosis is virtually 99.9 percent certain.

During history taking, be accurate, don't make wild guesses, but do report things you may think are only minor, like a sense of just not feeling well. It's important to indicate any change because it may be an early warning of something potentially serious. One patient who experienced a slight change in urination—dribbling a little during the night— passed it off as a joke, kidding with his wife that somehow, though he was still a young and vigorous man, he had entered second childhood. He had actually developed an enlargement of the prostate gland. A year of delay made the operation he needed more difficult and led to a complication, kidney infection, caused by backing up of urine.

In reporting symptoms to the doctor, don't grope for medical words; use simple English. Many diseases have strong psychological aspects, and symptoms may recede the moment you are in the doctor's office. Still, tell the doctor you have the symptoms even though it may seem silly to talk about them when they are not immediately present. You can be certain the doctor will understand the phenomenon.

THE PHYSICAL EXAMINATION

Even as he shakes hands with you, an alert physician may pick up some clues. Are your hands warm and moist, with a fine tremor? These characteristics may suggest overactivity of the thyroid gland. If the hands are cold and the skin is coarse and puffy, the thyroid could be underactive. Red fingertips may signal some abnormal flow of blood in the heart; flushing of the nail beds in time with the heartbeat may indicate another type of heart problem called aortic regurgitation.

As he observes the body, the physician can learn a great deal. The color of lips and ears may indicate possible anemia. He may note that one leg is slightly shorter than the other—enough in some cases to account for a backache problem. He may note leg swellings traceable to a heart problem, and any enlarged glands, tumors, or abnormal pigmentation resulting from internal disease.

In his examination, the physician will be looking to see if the body is symmetrical. Lack of symmetry is almost always a sign of some disability or disease. If the left side of the neck looks different from the right, it may be because of a tumor which is pushing out on that side. If the thyroid is not symmetrical, it may be because of a benign tumor which has enlarged one lobe of the gland.

In the retina at the back of the eyes, small blood vessels—arteries and veins—lie almost naked, devoid of covering material. And there, very quickly, with an instrument called the ophthalmoscope, the physician by looking through the pupil of the eye can detect any blood vessel changes which may provide clues to diabetes or kidney disease.

Women need a breast examination for any tenderness, abnormal lump, or nipple discharge. During a vaginal examination, a smear of cells for the "Pap" test is usually taken; this is a test to detect early cancer in the area.

Both men and women should have a rectal examination to detect any local disturbances. With an instrument, the sigmoidoscope, the physician can see and check the lower portion of the colon for any growths.

As a patient, you can help greatly by insisting that the physician do a thorough inspection, by reassuring him that you have no squeamishness. Some doctors feel that patients are resistant to rectal and genital examination and omit these vitally important checks.

PERCUSSION

Percussion—a simple procedure in which the physician lays one hand flat on the chest and raps on it with fingers of the other hand—can provide useful information about some internal organs.

With it, the approximate size and shape of the heart may be established, for example. The chest is largely occupied by the lungs which, because they are filled with air, produce a hollow sound when the chest wall above them is tapped. Over the heart, which is filled with fluid, the sound changes to a dull note.

The physician can begin percussing at a point on the chest known to be over the lungs, moving in the direction of the heart until a dull sound tells him he has reached it. That establishes one point of the heart's position. Other points can be determined by starting the percussion elsewhere on the chest and moving in toward the heart again.

STETHOSCOPIC EXAMINATION

The stethoscope has a small cone which concentrates and slightly amplifies internal body sounds while excluding external noise. One of its major uses is in the detection of heart problems.

The heart produces two distinct sounds—lubb-dup, lubb-dup, lubb-dup—which are related to the closing of the valves inside the heart. The rate, rhythm, pitch, and intensity of these sounds, which can be studied with the stethoscope, provide indications of the health of the heart.

The stethoscope can pick up any abnormal sounds—for example, a rubbing scratchy noise which may indicate pericarditis, an inflammation of the outer coating of the heart. With it, too, the physician can detect murmurs—audible vibrations produced by blood flow—and can distinguish among various types of them.

There are murmurs associated with different kinds of congenital heart defects. Others are produced by overactivity of the thyroid gland and disappear when the gland condition is corrected. A fever or anemia may produce a murmur which disappears when the anemia or fever is overcome.

In addition—and worth special note here—there are innocent murmurs. Unfortunately, many people worry needlessly after being told at some point, perhaps during an insurance examination, that they have a murmur even though reassured it is "innocent."

The fact is that innocent murmurs are unrelated to any physical problem and are quite common. They can be found in as many as 15 percent of normal healthy adults and in an even higher percentage of normal healthy children. Such murmurs are more readily detectable in children because they have thinner chest walls. And some authorities are convinced that if there were sensitive enough instruments, slight and innocent murmurs could be found in all people.

Your physician has been trained to understand the significance of various types of murmurs, to distinguish carefully among them, and to heed those which tell him of existing or possibly brewing trouble. Let him examine you and if he finds a murmur tell you exactly what it means. If he can report that it is innocent and no reason for worry, that is exactly what he means.

In addition to its value in studying the heart, the stethoscope often is useful in revealing characteristic sounds of asthma and of the lung disorder emphysema. Applied to the abdomen, it is often helpful in gastrointestinal problems; it may, for example, aid in diagnosis of intestinal obstruction. With the stethoscope, too, it is sometimes possible to detect blood vessel problems—the existence and location of an obstruction in an artery, for example.

BLOOD PRESSURE DETERMINATION

Measuring blood pressure is an even more important part of the medical check today than it was in the past. For one thing, we know now how common elevated pressure is, affecting at least 17 million Americans. For another thing, we know now that high blood pressure, or hypertension, is an important factor in stroke, heart disease, and kidney disease. And best of all, hypertension today almost invariably can be controlled.

Blood pressure is simply the push of blood against the walls of the arteries. It is highest when the heart contracts and pumps blood into the arteries, and this peak pressure is called systolic. It is lowest when the heart relaxes between beats, and this lower pressure is the diastolic.

To measure pressure, a basically simple, though not simply named, device, the sphygmomanometer, is used. It's an inflatable cuff attached to a mercury or other type of meter. When the cuff is wrapped around the arm above the elbow and inflated, the inflation does two things: it drives the mercury column up to near the top of the gauge and it compresses an artery in the arm so no blood flows through.

With his stethoscope placed on the artery, the physician listens as he gradually lets air out of the cuff. At some point, as the air is released, the pressure of blood in the artery will begin to exceed the pressure of air in the cuff, and the blood will begin to flow again in the artery. The beginning of flow produces a thudding sound the physician can hear through the stethoscope, and at this point the mercury gauge shows what the systolic pressure is. Then, as more air is released from the cuff there comes a point when the thudding sound no longer can be heard, and at this point the mercury gauge shows the diastolic pressure.

It is normal for pressure to vary somewhat from day to day, even minute to minute. It goes up with excitement, which is why in an examination a physician may wish to take your pressure several times. In some people, however, the pressure is nearly always higher than it should be (see page 596 for discussion of the disease high blood pressure).

SUPPLEMENTARY TESTS

A chest x-ray to disclose abnormality of the lungs is commonly made. X-ray studies are also used, when considered necessary, to check on heart size and, with the help of barium either taken by mouth or given by enema, to study the upper and lower gastrointestinal tract.

In addition, with the aid of injections of special dyes, x-rays today can be used to study the chambers within the heart and the condition of blood vessels. There is a method of using x-ray, after injection of a dye into an artery leading to the brain, to detect a brain tumor; this technique shows the blood vessel architecture of the brain and where tumor growth has pushed one or more vessels out of normal position.

Blood studies have many values. For a blood count, blood is drawn from a vein in the arm or fingertip, mixed with a diluting fluid, placed in a glass chamber so the number of red and white blood cells can be counted. Red pigment (hemoglobin) in the blood can be determined by comparison with color standards. The proportion of red cells in relation to the rest of the blood can be established by whirling the blood in a centrifuge so that heavier red cells settle in the bottom of a small measured tube called an hematocrit.

Any departures from normal—such as too little hemoglobin indicative of anemia, too few white cells indicative of inability to combat infection, too many white cells indicative of body response to an infection not otherwise apparent—can be noted quickly.

Blood, usually taken from a vein in small amounts, also may be checked for sugar content as a test for diabetes and for the level of a substance, uric acid, as a test for gout.

And sophisticated new blood tests often are valuable for heart problems, supplementing the information provided by the electrocardiogram. The electrocardiogram, a record of the electrical activity of the heart, is useful for analyzing any disturbances of heart rhythm, detecting inflammation, showing damage to the heart muscle, and making other determinations. An electrocardiogram, taken in good health, is of value because it provides a baseline for the future; it establishes what is normal for the individual and allows better interpretation of any changes that occur later.

When a heart attack occurs—and many heart attacks are silent—an electrocardiogram will show that it has occurred. But it may not show accurately how much of the heart has been damaged. Today there are sensitive blood tests for this; they measure the amounts in the blood of certain chemicals, called enzymes, released when the heart is damaged.

Urine tests are helpful in detecting kidney disease and other urinary tract disorders and may provide clues to problems elsewhere in the body, such as diabetes.

Today, radioactive isotope scanning is a sophisticated and vast new area of testing, useful for the detection of disorders in many different organs. Such scanning is based on the fact that certain chemical elements tend to be deposited in specific organs, and these elements can be made slightly and briefly radioactive; then their distribution in the body can be established with scanning instruments that can pick up their radioactivity and record it on film or paper. Abnormalities become visible as areas of increased or decreased radioactivity.

Scanning now can be used to pick up thyroid problems; brain tumors and abscesses; liver cancer, cysts, and abscesses; lung clots; bone tumors; kidney tumors, cysts, and abscesses; and many more abnormalities including those of the pancreas, spleen, parathyroid glands, and the heart as well.

Judicious use of tests has always distinguished the best physicians. It would be a simple matter, of course, for the physician to just order, indiscriminately, a whole battery of tests—at considerable cost of time and money for the patient. Rather than this, good physicians have been selective, using the patient's case history and their personal examinations as guides, determining from them what problems if any the patient might be likely to have, and, when justified, using supplementary tests to explore these problems.

AUTOMATED MULTIPHASIC SCREENING

One of the relatively recent developments that is almost certain to bring striking changes in the practice of medicine, adding further to the emphasis on and practicality of preventive medicine, is automated multiphasic screening.

The idea is to link electronic detection devices, large numbers of chemical tests, and computer science together to screen or check, at low cost, large numbers of apparently healthy people, looking for the most subtle signs of early disease and even of predisease states, doing far more routine testing than physicians have time for, providing them with the results of the tests, and giving them more opportunity to counsel patients and practice preventive medicine.

In a periodic checkup that may run two to three hours, a patient moves from one station to another for checks of hearing, visual acuity, respiration rate, lung capacity. An electrocardiogram is made; a measurement of pressure within the eye is quickly made for detection of glaucoma, a major cause of blindness. A chest x-ray is taken and, in the case of women, a three-dimensional breast photograph (mammography). Pulse and blood pressure measurements are included. The patient answers a self-administered questionnaire on health history. And blood and urine samples are taken and automatically checked for indications of infection, gout, diabetes, and other diseases and also for a variety of biochemical values that may give some indications of predisease changes.

A computer summarizes the findings and produces a printed record for the patient's personal physician to evaluate.

Automated multiphasic screening is moving rapidly out of the experimental phase. Much of the pioneering work in its development was done by physicians at the Kaiser Foundation Health Plan in northern California with some financial assistance from the U.S. Public Health Service.

The Public Health Service has awarded funds to set up pilot programs in Milwaukee, New Orleans, Brooklyn, and Providence—some affiliated with health centers in poverty areas, others with universities, and still others with city health departments.

Already, some large industries are planning automated multiphasic screening facilities as part of their occupational health programs. And there are plans for forming medically directed private companies which would provide automated screening service for patients referred by physicians.

Automated screening facilities may not be available in your community yet. Ask your doctor about them. Tell him you are interested. If the facilities are not available, you will be doing a public service by encouraging your doctor to push for their establishment in the near future.

4

YOUR ROLE

You AS the patient in preventive medicine have a role to play that goes far beyond cooperating in regular checkups. You can build and maintain your health, taking advantage of the latest knowledge in such areas as nutrition, weight control, physical activity, rest and relaxation (to be covered in later sections of this book). You can be alert, too, between checkups for any danger signals.

CHECKUP FREQUENCY

Just a word here about this. How often periodic medical checkups should be carried out is best determined by the physician on the basis of what is most suitable for you as an individual rather than on the basis of a general rule.

Age is one determinant. The elderly and the very young generally need more frequent examinations than those in between. But other factors must be considered—present state of health, past medical history, family medical history, occupational hazards if any, etc. Your physician will take these into account in deciding what is most appropriate for you —a checkup once a year, or twice a year, or perhaps once in two years.

BETWEEN CHECKUPS

Manifestations of illness or impending illness take the form of signs or symptoms, or both. Signs are objective evidence: for example, a change in skin color or the swelling of a body part. Symptoms are subjective: for example, nausea or pain.

They can vary greatly, of course, from mild and fleeting to severe and persistent. All deserve attention, though it is likely that if they are mild and transient the reason for them is inconsequential.

Any persistent or recurring sign or symptom deserves action. Even if mild it should not be ignored. Passing it off as something not worth notice except by a hypochondriac is dangerous. You may become so habituated to its presence that you regard it as something "normal" for you—until the underlying problem reaches a stage where it is irreversible or leads to serious consequences.

The following discussion is intended to help you interpret the significance of signs and symptoms that may appear between checkups, as a guide to when to consult your physician without delay.

FEVER

Fever most commonly signals infection or inflammation somewhere in the body. The temperature is likely to be highest during a bacterial or severe viral infection. With a mild infection such as a cold, temperature elevation may be slight and fleeting. When fever is high, there is usually no hesitancy about calling the physician. But there may be other occasions when the physician should be consulted.

First, a few facts about taking temperature. Aspirin and aspirin-containing medications bring down elevated temperature and tend to keep it down for as long as four hours. So for accurate determinations, temperature should be taken before use of such medications or four or five hours afterward. Remember, too, that if temperature is taken immediately after smoking, it may be higher than normal; and conversely, if taken by mouth just after a cold drink, it may be lower than normal.

Before taking temperature, rinse the thermometer in cool water and shake it until the mercury falls below the 95-degree mark. If you use an oral thermometer, hold it under the tongue, with mouth shut, for at least three minutes. A rectal thermometer, after lubrication, should be inserted up to the 98.6-degree line while the patient lies on his side. It should remain in place for three to five minutes. For the average person, mouth temperature normally is 98.6 degrees, and rectal tends to be about one degree higher.

When fever is mild—under 100 degrees orally or 101 rectally—and the only other symptom is nasal congestion, a slight cough, or a scratchy throat, there is no urgency about calling the physician. But take the temperature every three or four hours and note the severity of symptoms. If symptoms become worse or if the temperature moves up to 101 orally or 102 rectally, then notify your physician.

Always when fever is present it is important to note the accompanying symptoms. If there is a severe chill or a rash, then no matter how mild the temperature elevation, medical help is needed. A stiff neck, even if the fever is slight, may be an early indication of meningitis. A fever that develops after an accidental cut or other injury which could have become infected may mean blood poisoning (septicemia). When a fever, even mild, is accompanied by nausea and pain in the abdomen, especially in the lower right part of the abdomen, the problem could be appendicitis. Appendicitis often progresses rapidly, and whereas it can be treated effectively early in its course, it may become a major problem if neglected for even a few hours.

One final note about slight fever: If you have a chronic disorder such as rheumatic heart disease, asthma, diabetes, or nephritis, your physician may warn you to let him know the minute you discover a fever or even a common cold coming on.

PAIN

All of us have occasional headaches. And there are mild and fleeting aches and pains from unaccustomed exertion and even family arguments and business or other anxieties. These are certainly no medical emergencies.

But any new or unusually acute pain in the chest or abdomen should call for medical consultation. Pain in the chest accompanying exertion may be due to heart trouble—but not invariably. Pain at its worst when you take a deep breath may be due to pleurisy. Chest pain that develops upon bending over after eating may be due to a hernia of the diaphragm.

Many relatively mild abdominal pains are associated with gas in the bowel; some stem from constipation; some are associated with fatigue, depression, or anxiety. Sometimes, aches and pains that appear to be originating inside the abdomen or chest are actually coming from the abdominal or chest wall as the result of fibrositis of muscles. Peptic ulcer pain usually comes with hunger and is relieved by food or an acid-neutralizing agent. Gallbladder pain often starts under the lowest right ribs in front and runs up under the right shoulder blade.

WEIGHT CHANGE

Rapid weight gain in some cases may reflect a need to alter the diet, and this can be important enough to call for medical aid. In some cases, rapid gain may be the result of fluid accumulation in the body because of a heart or kidney disturbance or improper functioning of the thyroid gland.

If weight loss occurs on an adequate nonreducing diet, sickness must be suspected. The body may not be utilizing food properly or may be burning it up too fast. Diabetes and hyperthyroidism (overactivity of the thyroid) are among the possibilities the physician will check.

SHORTNESS OF BREATH

This can be an important symptom. It is not always easy to evaluate. In climbing stairs or running, almost everyone, of course, becomes short of breath. Unless breathing difficulty occurs at rest or with only minor activity, you may have only an impression that you are puffing more than you used to do when performing certain activities. This may be an indication that you have become too sedentary, are not as fit or perhaps as light in weight as you once were. But shortness of breath also may serve to indicate the beginning of heart trouble, lung disorder, chest disease, anemia, some forms of cancer, and other conditions.

BLEEDING

Bleeding without obvious explanation requires investigation without delay.

Blood in the urine may indicate urinary infection, kidney tumor, or wartlike growths in the bladder, for example. The blood may or may not look like blood; blood can impart anything from a faint pink tinge to a mahogany brown color in the urine.

Blood in the stool may appear bright red if the bleeding is low in the intestinal tract or from hemorrhoids. But if the bleeding is from the stomach or upper intestinal tract, bowel movements may be colored black.

The coughing or vomiting of blood calls for prompt action. The fact is that the body sometimes provides only one warning. Don't wait for a repetition of the bleeding. Consult your physician immediately, and the chances are he can establish what is wrong and treat it effectively.

Similarly, the woman who experiences unexpected vaginal bleeding between menstrual periods or after menopause should see her physician at once. The problem may be nothing more than a harmless polyp, but it may also be early, still curable cancer.

OTHER SIGNALS

Coughing may indicate only a minor temporary throat irritation. But a persistent cough may mean infection, obstruction, or accumulation of fluid in the air passages or lungs, and so it deserves medical attention.

So does a cough that developed during a respiratory infection but then persists long afterward.

Urinary changes: We have already noted that blood in the urine requires investigation. Frequent urination may be the result of infection or, in some cases, nervous irritability of the bladder. Frequent and voluminous urination may be an indication of a relatively rare type of diabetes, diabetes insipidus. In older men, the need to get up several times a night for urination may indicate an enlarging prostate. Difficulty in starting urination may indicate sufficient prostate enlargement to require treatment to prevent backup of urine and impairment of kidney function. Actually, any marked change in the urine—in its volume, color, or number of times it must be passed—calls for medical study.

Nausea may stem, of course, from a gastrointestinal disturbance, but it may also arise from an infection almost anywhere in the body or from disturbance of the balance mechanism in the ear. If the nausea is mild, you can delay a little before consulting a physician, for it may disappear in a short time and not return. But severe and persistent nausea, or nausea that keeps recurring, calls for medical attention.

Jaundice, or yellowing of the skin, may be due to a viral infection and is especially likely to be seen in younger people. It may signal gallstones, and this is especially likely to be the case for middle-aged women. In older people, it sometimes is due to cancer of the pancreas or to cancer that has spread into the liver from elsewhere. The safe rule is always to regard jaundice as a signal calling for immediate medical attention. In some people with sallow complexion, jaundice may not be readily discernible on the basis of the appearance of the skin; in such cases, look at the whites of the eyes—if they are distinctly yellow, jaundice is present.

CANCER SIGNALS

Some signs and symptoms are commonly associated with cancer. They include:

Any lump or thickening in the breast or elsewhere
Any sore that does not heal
Any persistent change in bowel or bladder habits
Persistent hoarseness or coughing
Persistent indigestion or difficulty in swallowing
Any change in a wart or mole
Any sudden weight loss

Actually, none of the foregoing constitutes proof of cancer—only that cancer is a possibility which should be investigated without delay.

No sign or symptom—either severe or mild but persistent or recurring —should be neglected, it bears repeating here, on the grounds that it may not mean anything or that the doctor may say it's "just nerves." The preventively minded physician whom you see regularly for your checkups will welcome being consulted about such signals, will not pass them off lightly as "just nerves," will check thoroughly, and, if it should be just a matter of "nerves," will help you do something about the "nerves."

YOUR OWN HEALTH INVENTORY

In addition to regular periodic checkups by your physician and your alertness for danger signals, there is an additional line of defense, an extra safeguard, you can put to use in maintaining health.

It consists of a simple inventory of your health, a checklist of statements. Taking the inventory at home will require only a few minutes once a month. Mark your calendar now to remind you to refer to this chapter and the following statements on some convenient date each month, perhaps the first or fifteenth.

If you cannot say "True" to any one of the statements that follow, you should see your doctor as soon as possible. If you have a perfect "True" score, it is quite likely that your health is being maintained satisfactorily, and you need not see your physician again until your next scheduled examination.

1. I have noticed no sore on skin, lips, or tongue that doesn't seem to heal.
2. I am not aware of shortness of breath when walking on level ground or when performing any type of activity that never before made me short of breath.
3. I am not bothered by indigestion, nausea, appetite loss, abdominal pain or cramps, or the recent sudden appearance of constipation or diarrhea.
4. I have noticed no blood in bowel movements or urine.
5. I am not steadily losing or gaining weight, and I am satisfied that my weight is suitable for me.
6. I do not feel myself becoming nervous, irritable, or depressed. I have had no crying spells and no feelings of overwhelming sadness, worthlessness, mental apathy. I have no persistent feeling that anybody is against me. I do not feel a nervous breakdown coming on.
7. I do not feel unduly fatigued after little effort, mental or physical. I have no feeling of being rundown.
8. I have no pallor; my skin color has not changed.

9. I have no cough that has persisted longer than a month. I have coughed up no blood.
10. I have had no persistent hoarseness.
11. My hearing remains as good as it has ever been.
12. My eyesight, too, remains good; I have had no dimming or fogging of vision.
13. I have no persistent headaches.
14. I have felt no chest discomfort without obvious cause.
15. I have had no prolonged aches in back, limbs, or joints.
16. There has been no swelling of my feet or ankles.
17. I have noticed no urinary changes.
18. I sleep well. I have no tendency to wake up during the night and have difficulty falling asleep again.
19. I have no new persistent pain or any other new symptoms.
20. I am not worried about the possibility of having a venereal disease.

Special for women:

21. I have noticed no vaginal bleeding at unexpected times.
22. I have felt no lump in my breast, and I have not been worried about the possibility of cancer or tumor there or in any other part of my body.
23. I am not troubled with hot flashes.

Special for men:

21. My urination has not been abnormal in any way recently—particularly in terms of difficulty in starting, stopping, dribbling, pain.
22. I am not ruptured and have no thoughts that I may be.
23. I do not believe that I may have picked up some disease overseas during the war which may now be coming to the surface.

Important Note: If you cannot say "True" to one or more of the preceding statements, it does not necessarily mean that you have a serious problem. There may, indeed, be a clue to something serious—and because it is likely to be an early clue, the problem is very likely to be amenable to effective treatment. On the other hand, the problem may be mild, possibly even temporary. But let your physician make the diagnosis for you. He will almost certainly agree that it is good preventive medicine, in the best interests of your continued good health, for him to check up on the lead provided when you cannot say "True" to a statement.

5

A SPECIAL WORD ABOUT
MEDICINE TAKING

THE HISTORY of modern medicines is one of major successes, but it also includes disasters. Tremendous benefits have followed the discovery of insulin for diabetes, agents for controlling high blood pressure, antibiotics and other antibacterials that kill or impede the growth of bacteria, cortisone and other steroid compounds that combat inflammation, tranquilizers and antidepressants for nervous and mental disorders, and drugs that slow the wild growth of some cancer cells.

But there have been tragedies traceable to indiscriminate use and abuse of such powerful agents and of others. For one thing, no medication yet developed is foolproof—universally useful for even the condition for which it was developed, free of undesirable effects. Virtually every drug, just as virtually every food, may produce unpleasant effects for at least a few individuals, and so it must be used with care.

We hope in this chapter to provide a useful guide to medicine taking, one that will be helpful to you both in more effective treatment of any health problems that arise and also in preventing many problems.

PRESCRIBING FOR YOURSELF

A recent survey of a small but typical group of households carried out by a major university research institute found that the number of medications on hand varied from 3 to 88, with a mean of 30. Of the 2,539 medications observed, only 445 were prescription drugs.

Each month in the United States, 750 out of every 1,000 adults 16 years of age and over experience a cold, headache, or other illness or injury for which only 250 will consult a physician. Thus, people control their own care in terms of whether and when to seek medical aid and when to prescribe for themselves. Virtually everyone on occasion does his own prescribing—and that can be a practical matter. Certainly every minor ache or pain does not require that a doctor be called. Nobody wishes to become a habitual patient.

The medicines—variously known as "patent," "proprietary," and "over-the-counter" or "OTC"—which you can purchase in drugstores without a doctor's prescription are generally milder and have fairly broad safety margins. They serve a purpose and very often can provide relief for minor problems. In themselves, they are generally safe as long as the dosage recommendations on the package are not exceeded.

It's important to keep in mind, however, that such medications, as any others, may produce undesirable effects in relatively small numbers of people who happen to be particularly sensitive to them. So if you notice any such side effects as rash, nausea, dizziness, visual disturbances, or others, which seem to follow use of a particular medication, you may well have a sensitivity to that particular medication, and no matter how popular it is with other people, it is not for you. If in doubt, you should check with your physician.

Absolutely vital when you prescribe for yourself is the need to keep in mind that you may be making a mistake in diagnosis, treating the wrong illness, or masking minor and superficial symptoms while an underlying serious problem gets worse. For example, a "simple" head cold may really not be simple when there is fever, sharp pain in the chest, sputum discoloration, rapid breathing, or nausea; it may, in fact, be a serious bronchial infection or pneumonia.

If you do treat yourself, never continue to do so for more than a day or two unless you are certain there is steady improvement—and if your symptoms get worse or change, don't wait even that long before consulting your physician.

REACTIONS TO MEDICINES

It may seem unbelievable but there are more than 250 diseases that can be caused by the very medicines designed to treat and cure illness. You may well ask, "Why is this possible?" The reasons are not difficult to understand.

Over the past twenty-five years or so, many hundreds of new compounds have been developed for treating and preventing disease. Many are powerful and complicated substances. Their very effectiveness depends upon their great potency and complexity.

In some instances, trouble has come unexpectedly because a powerful new agent was not tested fully under every conceivable circumstance. Thus, for example, thalidomide seemed to be an excellent and harmless tranquilizing agent in most people, but when it was used by pregnant women it had terrible effects on their unborn children.

Another reason for drug-induced illness is that human beings do have tendencies to develop allergic or sensitivity responses. These vary considerably, just as they do for foods. One person may eat eggs until the hens scream for mercy—and enjoy them with impunity; another person, allergic to them, cannot eat one without developing some upset. And so with other foods.

Because of sensitivity problems, a medicine that is highly beneficial for 95 percent of the population may cause trouble, even potentially serious trouble, for the remaining 5 percent. A good example is penicillin, clearly a lifesaving drug. It has, indeed, probably saved well over a million lives since its discovery. But it also has caused severe sensitivity reactions in scores of thousands of people and has taken the lives of thousands. As you may have noticed, physicians today inquire carefully about possible previous sensitivity reactions to penicillin before administering or prescribing it.

Just as some people, after repeated exposure, become allergic to ragweed pollen or to poison ivy, so some, after being helped once or even several times by an antibiotic, may develop allergic reactions to the compound. Usually the problem is mild—skin rash, hives, or slight fever— and disappears once the drug is stopped. Occasionally, however, there are anaphylactic, or shocklike, reactions which are life-threatening, and these can be overcome only if heroic measures—adrenaline and other injections—are used in time.

Still considered the single most valuable antibiotic, penicillin is a major allergy producer because it has been so widely used. It is estimated that 10 percent of Americans have become sensitized to the drug. (See Allergy, page 516, and Anemias, page 526, for more information on reactions to the many different substances we are exposed to.)

Still another reason for undesirable reactions is that no drug is 100 percent specific—hitting the bull's-eye, so to speak. In the course of countering the problem for which it is being used, it may produce other effects, and these have to be reckoned with.

Consider, for example, the gastrointestinal upsets—cramps, diarrhea, sore mouth, rectal itch—which may occur after use of many antibiotics. They can come about because of an upset in the natural germ balance in the body. Many harmless bacteria are always present in the gastrointestinal tract. Some, in fact, are essential to digestion; some manufacture vitamins. When a potent antibiotic is introduced to fight infection, it may also decimate this normal bacterial population.

Moreover, these friendly bacteria serve another purpose in the body economy: they keep under control harmful organisms that also are natives of the digestive tract. When friendly bacteria are killed off in large numbers, there is less competition for the harmful residents and they have a chance to multiply. The result may be superinfection—a new and different infection that develops as a result of another's being treated. Again, the superinfection is often mild and disappears once antibiotic treatment stops. But superinfection sometimes can be severe.

What it comes down to is this: use of potent modern medications, not only antibiotics but many others, involves a calculated risk and alertness. Ideally, the physician uses them after careful consideration and upon arriving at the decision that the good to be gained outweighs any risks along the way—and uses them with caution, keeping alert to the earliest indications of any new trouble from the drugs which he may be able to overcome by change of dosage, switch of medication, addition of other medication, or when necessary discontinuance of treatment.

One of the major problems, though, has been the insistence of many patients upon willy-nilly prescription of medication. They may demand penicillin, for example, for a cold or any fever. They have the feeling that a visit to the doctor is not complete unless the doctor "gives" them something. Too often, this has put physicians on the spot; and to please patients, some have prescribed medication against their better judgment.

So far as your own health is concerned, you can do much to preserve it not just by seeking timely medical advice but by taking it—by avoiding insistence upon medications, by indicating to your physician that you are aware of the values and also limitations of medications, the need to use them wisely not indiscriminately, to use them when they are required and not otherwise.

DOSAGE PROBLEMS

A man who took double the prescribed dose of an anticoagulant—a drug that, in effect, acts to thin the blood to prevent clot formation—found himself in the hospital a few days later with severe nosebleeds and vomiting of blood. A woman with bronchial asthma was admitted to the hospital with heart palpitations after she had used, contrary to instructions, an isoprenaline (isoproterenol) spray repeatedly for several hours. Another patient, a 29-year-old man, who had decided to take 50 percent more than his prescribed dose of a cortisonelike drug, came to the hospital with changed personality, considerable weight gain from fluid retention, and other effects.

These are just a few cases of adverse drug reactions from overdosage. One of the big complicating problems in connection with the use of potent modern medications is the hangover of an old idea in the minds of many people that if a little is good, more is better. With potent agents, excessive dosage can produce real trouble.

Similarly, underdosage can cause problems. Inadequate antibiotic dosage, for example, carries its own risk. One common example is the patient with a "strep" throat who takes penicillin, improves, stops treatment, then gets the sore throat back again. Once more, he takes some penicillin but not the full prescribed amount. Again the sore throat disappears only to recur after a short time. And so a disease that can be eradicated by continued administration of penicillin for eight to ten days is converted into one that drags on with repeated remissions and relapses.

Physicians have, in fact, long suspected that many failures of antibiotic treatment stem simply from failure of patients to keep taking medication as prescribed. A recent study uncovered disturbing evidence that many parents may be risking their children's health by failing to make certain they take their medication as long as necessary. Actually, in acute "strep" infections, penicillin treatment for 10 days is considered essential to prevent rheumatic fever. Yet in a follow-up of 59 children for whom a 10-day course of penicillin had been prescribed, investigators found that 56 percent of the youngsters had stopped taking the drug by the third day, 71 percent by the sixth day, and 82 percent by the ninth day.

When a doctor prescribes medication, the first thing to do is to get the prescription filled immediately. The value may be lessened, or even lost completely, if you delay.

Then follow directions of the doctor to the letter. If you are not certain you understand them, ask him for clarification—even for instructions in writing as to exactly what you are to do. Take all the medicine prescribed, not some amount you arbitrarily settle on. Don't decide, if you begin to feel better, that you can stop or reduce dosage.

Sometimes, illnesses require several prescriptions. Very much worth noting here is an old principle taught to nurses: read every label three times. You can use that principle to advantage at home. First read the label when you take the drug container from the medicine cabinet; read it again when you take the drug itself; and finally, read the label a third time when you put the container away. That last reading is an extra check to make certain you read the label properly the first two times. If you did happen to make a mistake, you have a chance to do something about it at once.

LITTLE TRICKS FOR PROPER DOSAGE

Most medicines today are made by machines that produce attractive capsules and pills of perfect roundness and purity. Such machine-made medications, for the most part, are more attractive-looking and less expensive than those that were made individually by a druggist to a special prescription of a physician.

The trouble with machine-made articles of medicine, as with mass-produced clothes, is that tailoring to each individual's needs cannot be built in. Thus, it's known that the amount of medicine required varies almost directly with the weight of a person. Most machine-made capsules and pills are made for a standard person of about 150 pounds so they are apt to contain just a bit too much for most women, a bit too little for most men.

Doctors have learned how to adjust dosages even with the limitations of machine-made medicines. For example, consider pills of phenobarbital often prescribed for nervousness, tension, headaches with a psychogenic component. Phenobarbital is commonly available in 1/8, 1/4, and 1/2 grain sizes. Suppose phenobarbital in 1/4 grain dosage is prescribed for a woman and it helps her tension but makes her just a bit too forgetful and drowsy to do her work properly. The doctor tries 1/8 grain, but that doesn't help her tension enough. The solution lies in going back to the 1/4 grain dosage and proper use of a fingernail file. The patient is instructed to consider a tablet as a circle, and to gently file away one fourth of the circle, to get a tablet that is just halfway between 1/8 and 1/4 grain sizes. Usually, the patient "plays around" a bit and finds just the right tailormade size for her needs.

When it comes to capsules—especially of sleeping medicines such as Nembutal, Seconal, and Amytal—it's a help to learn how to take apart a capsule gently and pour out a portion to adjust the dosage to individual needs, then rejoin the capsule. Many people find a standard 1-1/2 grain capsule ineffective; on the other hand, when they take two capsules, they may experience hangovers. One full capsule and half of another may be the right dosage. With many common sleeping medicines, it is possible to get a 3/4 grain size as well as 1-1/2 grain so that one of each may be used. For Amytal there is also a 1 grain size, which many women find is just the right amount. Some men like to take two of the 1 grain capsules and find that this dosage gives them a pleasant night's sleep.

Delicate assaying of dosage is often possible with liquid medications —for instance, tincture of belladonna, an old standby for stomach cramps and indigestion. Some doctors say, arbitrarily, take 15 or 20 drops. The expert therapist uses a different approach. His instructions to a patient may go something like this: "I want you to get the full effect, which is just short of the beginning of toxic symptoms which are dryness of the mouth and blurring of vision. So start with 15 drops just before each meal and at bedtime. Then, each day, increase by 1 drop so that you will be taking 16 drops four times a day the second day, 17 drops the third day, and so on. Keep increasing until you notice one of the toxic symptoms. Then drop back by 1 drop each day until there are no toxic manifestations. You may settle on 18 drops or you may need 22, or some other amount. The strength of the tincture may vary slightly from drugstore to drugstore, and sometimes the size of the drops varies too. Once you have standardized the dosage you need, keep it and use the same bottle and get the prescription refilled by the same drugstore."

Thus, what seemed like a simple prescription turns out to be something of a scientific experiment. But for you such experimenting to find exactly the right dose you as an individual need may mean the difference between having and not having disagreeable dyspeptic symptoms.

OUTDATED MEDICINES

If your physician has prescribed a drug for you and instructs you to discontinue its use before the supply is all gone, don't save what is left over for another time. Discard it. It may seem like a waste to throw away expensive medication; actually, it is an important safety precaution.

Some drugs lose potency with time; some gain potency. Either way, their use after a lapse of time can be dangerous. Moreover, it has become clear that some drugs, in the process of aging, not only change in potency; they undergo marked chemical changes that can make them dangerous.

Not long ago, for example, physicians at three New York hospitals reported on several patients who had suddenly experienced nausea and vomiting and then developed symptoms like those of diabetes. The trouble in each case was traced to chemical deterioration of an antibiotic, a tetracycline, taken long after it should have been thrown away.

DRUG INTERACTIONS

When one medication is being used, the addition of another sometimes can be helpful but sometimes can be harmful. When two agents used in concert do not harmonize, the interaction or interference can cause trouble. Moreover, even effects on dosage requirements must be considered when two or more medicines are being used.

Recently, for example, a patient who had had a heart attack and recovered from it was released from the hospital. Ten days later, an alarming condition developed. While in the hospital the patient had received an anticoagulant medication as part of treatment—a compound aimed at preventing clotting. At home, he continued as directed to take the same compound in the same dosage. But now the drug was thinning the blood too much. Something had changed. It had indeed: in the hospital, the patient had been given phenobarbital upon retiring. The sedative, in the course of its activity in the body, had stimulated certain liver chemicals which broke down the anticoagulant faster. At home, without the phenobarbital, the anticoagulant activity continued longer and was more potent. In effect, without the sedative, the patient was getting an overdose of the anticoagulant. The matter, once understood, was quickly adjusted. But it illustrates what is coming to be virtually a new science in medicine, concerned with understanding and taking into account interactions between medicines.

This, of course, is not the place to go into complex technical details. But as indications of how important interaction can be, here are some recent findings:

When a patient is taking aspirin, addition of an anticoagulant drug may lead to bleeding. If a patient is receiving a medication such as amitriptyline for mental depression and is also given guanethidine for high blood pressure, the antihypertensive activity of the latter is lost. If a patient is receiving hydrocortisone and then is given either an antihistamine or a barbiturate, the hydrocortisone effect is lessened. If a patient is taking an antihistamine for an allergy and uses alcohol, the result may be central nervous system depression. If a patient is using alcohol and takes a barbiturate, there is a marked increase in the effect of the barbiturate, which has been responsible for many deaths.

An understanding of the complex details of drug interaction is something for a doctor to be aware of and make use of, not for a patient to worry about. And the point of mentioning the subject here is simply this: If you are already taking one or more drugs for a condition, when you see a physician about a new condition let him know what you are taking. If you are taking drugs under a physician's direction, get his advice even on such a seemingly simple matter as whether it will be all right, if you develop a headache or a cold, to take aspirin or other agents to make yourself more comfortable.

PROPER USE OF MEDICATION

Although most sick people benefit from their contact with the treasure chest of modern medications, the experience is unhappy for too many. Much of the unhappiness could be avoided by common sense procedures based on awareness of the realities of diseases and medications.

The rules are simple and few:

1. Take medications on your own only for the most minor conditions, and seek medical advice if there is no clear improvement within a day or two.

2. If you are using a medication prescribed by a physician, do not take any medications on your own for some other problem unless you have been informed they will cause no trouble.

3. When you seek medical help for a problem, leave it up to the physician to determine whether you really need medication or whether it may be wiser, in a particular situation, to let the body use its defenses to overcome the problem—for the body often can do exactly that. Don't be in a rush to take something, to pressure the physician to give you something. Make it clear to him that you understand that sometimes no medicine is the best medicine.

4. Follow the physician's instructions to the letter when he gives you a prescription. Get it filled immediately. Take exactly as directed—in the prescribed dosage, for the prescribed length of time.

5. If you notice any untoward reactions while taking a medication, let your physician know immediately. A side reaction may not be serious —or it may be. If it's the latter, prompt measures can ameliorate it.

6. Do not save leftover drugs.

7. Ask your physician to instruct the druggist to label the bottle or other container of any medication prescribed with the name of the medication. You will find that more and more doctors today believe strongly in this. It can be a safety measure, helping you to avoid mistakes in taking medication. And if trouble should arise during the course of taking the medication, if there should be an accidental overdose, if a child should happen to get hold of the medication and use it, the immediate identification of the compound may well help to prevent fatality. Moreover, your knowledge of what you are taking can come in handy if you have to consult another physician while your own is away.

8. Safeguard medication. Never leave any, including aspirin, standing around on a dresser or a table. Return it to the medicine cabinet immediately after use. A medicine cabinet should be kept closed and locked. It's a good idea, especially in any household with children, to have a medicine cabinet equipped with a combination padlock, or a drug safe or chest with combination lock. Your druggist can advise you about obtaining one at reasonable cost.

9. Teach your children to properly respect medications. Do not tell a child that medicine is like "candy" because it tastes good. Instead, even at a very early age, teach him that medicine is to help overcome illness, and that it doesn't matter whether he likes it or not, it is something he must have when sick to make him well, and never at any other time.

PART TWO

Building General Health
as Preventive Therapy

6

THE FOOD YOU EAT

Is THERE some one food or class of foods with special value for preventing disease? The science of nutrition has much to offer for health but it does not take the form of a panacea food or food combination. The one fact that stands out most clearly as new advances are made is that except for certain specific problems—disease states for which special diets have been definitely established as helpful—the healthiest diet has two basic characteristics: it is *balanced* and it is *varied*.

NEW REASONS FOR BALANCE AND VARIETY

One of today's most exciting research stories has to do with investigations into the role of trace elements in health and disease.

It has long been known that an amount of iron that would bulk up no bigger than a couple of nails stands between us and suffocation, for iron is an essential part of the blood substance hemoglobin, which carries oxygen to body tissues.

But it now seems that many other elements in minute amounts—each constituting at most 1/10,000 of body weight and very often far less—may play significant roles.

Recent studies have suggested that lack of adequate zinc in the diet can delay wound healing and may be a factor in diseases of the arteries.

In one investigation, zinc supplements were given to some Air Force men who had undergone surgery. Their surgical wounds healed in less than half the time required in other men who had had the same surgery but did not receive zinc supplements. The results not only demonstrated zinc's role in speeding healing; they suggested that the diet of these airmen may well have been zinc-deficient.

In a later study, investigators treated with zinc supplements a group of patients who had skin sores that refused to heal. Of the 17 patients in the group, 11 were found to be deficient in zinc, and in all 11 the chronic skin ulcers healed with zinc treatment. The remaining 6 were not zinc-deficient, and although they received the same treatment, their wounds still did not heal.

Although the relationship between zinc deficiency and hardening of leg arteries that can block circulation and cause gangrene is not clearly established, some patients who were deficient in zinc and had advanced degeneration of the arteries have shown improvement with zinc therapy.

Currently, scientists are investigating the influence on human health of many other trace elements, including chromium, manganese, cobalt, cadmium, copper, selenium, molybdenum, vanadium, nickel, and fluorine. Some preliminary evidence suggests that a deficiency of chromium may play a part in diabetes and, on the other hand, an excess of cadmium may adversely affect blood pressure. Even arsenic may be needed by the human body in these trace amounts.

Trace materials occur in water and in soils, find their way into foods, and may be present in relatively large amounts in some foods, relatively small amounts in others. Existing knowledge is still inadequate; there is enough to suggest the importance of trace materials but far from enough yet to provide a reliable guide to how much of them the body needs, how much of them can be dangerous, and their concentrations in various foods.

Earlier, the discovery of the role of vitamins in human health underscored the need for a balanced diet that would provide the vitamins. Now the work with trace materials underscores the need even more.

WHAT IS A BALANCED DIET?

Nearly 50 nutrients—including amino acids (the constituents of proteins), carbohydrates, vitamins, and minerals—are now known to be essential for health. A balanced diet is one that can supply all the essentials. It is almost certain that as time passes still other essential elements in foods will be isolated. This is added reason why a balanced and varied diet makes sense; if it is balanced and varied, it can supply all known requirements and others still unknown.

The currently known essential nutrients have their specific functions. Briefly, because muscles, heart, liver, kidney, and other organs are composed chiefly of proteins, proteins are needed for development and growth of these organs during childhood and adolescence. After growth is over, body tissues, which are continually being worn out, must be replaced by new materials. So ample dietary protein is essential at all times. Meat, fish, milk, and eggs are among the main sources of protein.

Bones are composed chiefly of mineral substances such as calcium and phosphorus which are required both for original bone formation and for maintenance. Milk—fresh, canned, dried, skim, or whole—is a major source. Calcium also is supplied by American and Swiss cheese, molasses, turnip tops, dandelion greens. And cereals, meat, and fish contain phosphorus.

The fuel of life—what the body burns for energy—is sugar. Carbohydrates, which include both sugars and starches, provide the fuel most readily, for in the body starches are quickly converted to sugar. Fats and proteins also supply the fuel for metabolism—not as quickly, but they can be stored by the body as reserves, for use as needed.

Vitamins help to convert foodstuffs into body tissues—skin, bones, muscles, nerves. Although required only in minute amounts, their role is obviously vital, and it is suspected that trace elements and perhaps still other materials yet to be isolated may perform similar functions.

A well-balanced diet—for young and old, active or sedentary, tall or short—can be supplied daily from four basic food groups:

Milk and milk products—

2 servings for adults; 3 to 4 for children; 4 or more for teen-agers. One serving equals an 8-oz. glass of whole or skimmed milk; 1 oz. (1 slice) of hard cheese; or 1/2 cup of cottage cheese.

Cereals and breads—

4 servings of enriched or whole grain cereals and breads. One serving equals 1 slice of bread; 1 small biscuit or muffin; 1 cup of potatoes, pasta, or rice; 3/4 to 1 cup of flaked or puffed cereal; or 1/2 cup of cooked cereal.

Fruits and vegetables—

4 servings, including one of citrus fruit or tomatoes and one of dark green or leafy vegetable. One serving equals 1/2 cup of canned or cooked fruit; 1 fresh peach, pear, etc.; 1 cup of fresh berries or cherries; 1/2 cup of cooked vegetables; or 1 cup uncooked leafy vegetables.

Meat and protein-rich foods—

2 servings of meat, fish, poultry, eggs, or cheese. Occasionally nuts, dried beans, peas may be substituted for the meats. One serving equals 3 oz. of lean, cooked meat; or 3 eggs; or 3 slices (ounces) of cheese.

Foods selected each day from each of the four groups provide balance; and by varying the choices within each group, you can expect to achieve a desirable averaging of intake of trace elements as well as other essential nutrients. For the same reason, it is a good idea, we suggest, for you to sample unusual foods whenever you can—internal organs such as liver, kidney, heart, sweetbreads, seafoods, Italian and Chinese vegetables, and other national dishes.

ABOUT CHOLESTEROL

Cholesterol has become a household word because of evidence indicating that excesses of it in the blood may play a part in producing coronary atherosclerosis, the narrowing of the coronary arteries which may lead to heart attacks. Cholesterol is present as such in some foods. It is also produced by the body.

Actually, the soft, waxy, yellowish substance is an essential part of every body cell. It plays a basic role in the passage of substances through cell walls. One example of how cholesterol does this is readily observable: when you put your hand into a basin of water, little of the water soaks into the skin. The reason: cholesterol in the outer layer of skin cells makes the skin impermeable to water.

Since the material is essential, the body is equipped to produce a supply as well as use what comes in, ready-built, in food. The liver can make cholesterol from molecules of acetyl coenzyme A, a chemical derived from fats, carbohydrates, and proteins.

It is not cholesterol per se but an excess of it in the blood which is the danger factor. And while an excess can be traced to some extent to a diet heavy in foods rich in cholesterol, a high-fat diet may raise blood cholesterol levels abnormally. This appears to be due to increased deposits of fat in the liver, providing an increased source of acetyl coenzyme A for liver manufacture of cholesterol.

Moreover, it is the nature of the fat in the diet that is significant. Some types of fat, known as saturated, increase blood cholesterol levels. Others, called unsaturated and polyunsaturated, do not—and, in fact, tend to slightly decrease cholesterol levels. The difference between saturated and unsaturated, from a chemist's viewpoint, is a matter of hydrogen atoms: saturated fats are saturated with, or full of, hydrogen atoms; unsaturated fats have room for more hydrogen atoms.

In everyday terms, the primary saturated fats are milk fat, meat fat, coconut oil, and cocoa fat. Milk fat includes the fat in butter, most cheeses, and ice cream as well as whole milk. Meat fat means primarily the fat of beef, pork, and lamb; veal has less fat, and chicken and turkey are low in fat and the fat they contain is less saturated.

Polyunsaturated fats are the liquid vegetable oils such as safflower, soybean, corn, and cottonseed.

SENSIBLE CHOLESTEROL RECOMMENDATIONS

An unequivocal answer to whether lowering cholesterol levels will reduce heart attacks will require long-term studies involving large numbers of people. But there is enough evidence at hand to make it seem wise, many authorities agree, to encourage changes in the typical American diet, which tends to include excessive amounts of cholesterol and fats.

Desirable changes have been recommended by the American Heart Association. Where the average daily diet in the United States contains about 600 milligrams of cholesterol, the Heart Association recommends that this be cut to less than 300. Also called for: a decrease in intake of saturated fats and an increase in intake of polyunsaturated. This, the Association is convinced, will lower abnormal concentrations of cholesterol in most people. The ideal quantity of fat needed in the diet is not known, but an intake of less than 40 percent of calories from fat is considered desirable. And of this total, polyunsaturated fats probably should make up twice the quantity of saturated fats.

To follow these recommendations, you may have to change some eating habits but you will not have to give up all your favorite dishes. To control cholesterol intake, you will need to eat no more than three egg yolks a week, including eggs used in cooking. You will also need to limit your use of shellfish and organ meats.

To control the amounts and types of fats:

1. Use fish, chicken, turkey, and veal in most meals for the week. Limit beef, lamb, pork, and ham to five moderate-sized portions a week.
2. Choose lean cuts of meat; trim any visible fat; and discard any fat that cooks out of meat.
3. Avoid deep-fat frying. Instead, use cooking methods that help to remove fats: baking, broiling, boiling, roasting, stewing.
4. Restrict use of fatty "luncheon" and "variety" meats such as sausages and salami.
5. Instead of butter and other cooking fats that are solid or completely hydrogenated, use liquid vegetable oils and margarines that are rich in polyunsaturated fats.
6. Instead of whole milk and cheeses made from whole milk and cream, use skimmed milk and skimmed milk cheeses.

HOW MUCH TO EAT

"A word about food. It is better to eat no more than eighty per cent of your capacity. A Japanese proverb has it that eight parts of a full stomach sustain the man; the other two sustain the doctor." So one of the Zen masters is quoted in the book *Three Pillars of Zen* (Beacon Press, Boston, 1967). The advice is relevant. That Americans generally consume too many calories for the amount of physical energy they expend is a matter of record and of increasing concern as the energy expenditure tapers off even more.

Every five years, the National Research Council, which serves as scientific adviser to the United States government, publishes recommended dietary allowances. After recommending, in 1963, a cut of 100 calories per day for men and women, it recommended another 100-calorie reduction in 1968. In its calculations, the Council uses a "reference" man and woman—each 22 years old, weighing 154 pounds and 127 pounds respectively, living in a mean temperature of 68 degrees, and engaging in light physical activity. Such a man, the Council now figures, needs 2,800 calories a day; the woman 2,000. The Council also recommends that caloric intake be cut below these levels with age—by 5 percent between ages 22 and 35, by 3 percent in each decade between 35 and 55, and by 5 percent per decade from 55 to 75. This brings the figure for the woman, for example, to 1,900 by age 35, to 1,843 by age 45, to 1,788 by age 55, to 1,699 at 65 and to 1,614 at 75.

These, of course, are general guidelines, leaving room for individual variations, and your physician may well have suggestions of value for you.

It is a measure of good health, and a contribution toward maintaining it, to reach and keep a desirable weight. For that, an effective balance between food intake and energy output is needed. If you are currently at ideal weight (see table on page 61), your intake and output are in balance—which is fine if you are getting adequate amounts of exercise. Exercise, of right kind and in adequate amounts, is a vital element in health for many reasons (see Chapter 8). If you should need to increase your physical activity, you will need to increase intake to maintain desirable weight.

WHEN TO EAT

Meal patterns generally are dictated by custom, work schedule, and personal preference. Most people eat a light breakfast, moderate lunch, and hearty evening meal. If you have a preference, however, for more but smaller meals, there is certainly nothing wrong with eating that way. In fact, we believe that, where feasible, more but lighter meals are desirable since they are easier to digest and put less load on the body.

The fact is that there is a limit to what the body's chemistry can take on at any one time. One can add to a fire a reasonable amount of wood or coal and have a vigorous flame. But if too much fuel is added, the fire huffs and puffs, smokes and smoulders inefficiently. So, too, with the body when it is burdened with dealing with a big evening meal, for example. Quite possibly, too, if a large amount of fat or cholesterol is consumed at one sitting, the body may not be able to metabolize it completely, and it may overflow into vital areas such as the arteries.

When obesity is a problem, the practice of eating five or six small meals daily may be helpful. There is less tendency to overeat when smaller portions are taken more often—and less tendency to indulge in snacks. When you know you will be eating again in two hours or so, the temptation to snack is not so great.

VITAMINS

About $1.5 billion is spent yearly for vitamins, much of it by healthy people convinced by high-powered advertising that they need extra vitamins. While essential, vitamins are required only in minute amounts, and a fully adequate supply is provided by a balanced, varied diet. To be sure, some people, relatively few, may need vitamin supplementation because they do not absorb certain vitamins properly when they are on vigorous reducing diets. In such cases, medical advice is required.

Vitamins in excess cannot restore the vigor of youth or perform other assorted health miracles. If diet is poor, vitamin-deficiency diseases may result: scurvy, with its gum bleeding, muscle aching, general weakness caused by deficiency of vitamin C; rickets with its bone deformities from deficiency of vitamin D; pellagra with its mental deterioration from deficiency of one of the B vitamins (niacin). Correction of a deficiency when it exists may produce near-miraculous changes.

But unless there is an actual deficiency, increasing vitamin intake with supplements—adding more to what is already adequate—can be useless, needlessly expensive, and in the case of some vitamins such as A and D can be harmful, since these two vitamins can accumulate in the body to poisonous levels.

Some interesting, though not definitive, reports on the possible value of large doses of vitamin C taken early during a common cold have appeared recently (see page 567).

The following table lists excellent sources of principal vitamins:

Vitamin E

Vegetable greens: beets, kale, chard, mustard, spinach, turnips
Yellow vegetables: carrots, yellow squash, sweet potatoes
Beef liver
Cod-liver oil, halibut-liver oil

Vitamin B (several vitamins, including niacin and thiamine, make up the
   B family)

Liver, pork, beef, salmon
Whole-wheat bread, enriched bread, oatmeal and other cereals
Peanuts, peanut butter

Vitamin C

Citrus fruits: oranges, lemons, grapefruits, limes
Tomato juice (fresh or canned)
Strawberries, raspberries, gooseberries, currants

Vitamin D

Halibut-liver oil and other refined fish-oil preparations
Vitamin D milk
Exposure of the skin to sunlight

THE IRON-DEFICIENCY PROBLEM

A deficiency of iron in the diets of young girls and women is a cause of
growing concern. Iron deficiency can produce anemia, and the need for
iron is universal. Generally, there is no problem in men, who require only
10 milligrams (1/3,000 of an ounce) of iron a day to maintain adequate
body stores. But menstruating and pregnant women require 18 milligrams a day, and dietary analyses indicate that many adolescent girls
and menstruating women have an iron intake of only 10 milligrams a
day. Some studies reveal iron-deficiency anemia in as many as 60 percent
of pregnant women.

   The problem centers around the fact that overall iron content of foods
on the market runs around 10 milligrams for every 2,000 calories. Thus,
unless she is paying particular attention to iron, a woman consuming
2,000 calories a day will not be getting adequate amounts of the mineral.

   The fact is that 50 to 60 percent of iron in the diet comes from cereals
and meats, with nearly equal contributions from each, but the proportion
of cereals and meats consumed by women varies widely. Whenever
weight is a problem, too, the tendency is to reduce consumption of
cereal products. Most meats provide 2 to 3 milligrams of iron per 3-ounce
serving. Dry beans and nuts provide about 5 milligrams per cup. Most
leafy green vegetables contain from 1 to 4 milligrams per cup. Egg yolk,
whole grain and enriched bread, potatoes, oysters, dried fruits, and peas
are other good sources. There are on the market a number of prepared
breakfast foods fortified with high levels of iron; some provide 8 to 10
milligrams per one-ounce serving. The use of iron-fortified food items
when necessary to achieve adequate iron intake can be an important aid
to health. For some women with high iron requirements—during preg-

nancy or because of abnormal menstrual losses—physicians may need to prescribe supplemental iron preparations.

SUGAR AND THE HEART

Can consumption of large amounts of sugar be as much of a factor in coronary heart disease as cholesterol? So British investigators led by Dr. John Yudkin of the University of London maintain. They note that over the past 200 years in Great Britain sugar consumption has gone up almost 25-fold, from an average of 5 pounds per person in 1760 to 25 in 1860 and to 120 pounds in 1960. A sizable increase in sugar consumption in the United States also has been noted by American investigators.

The British workers note that increasing affluence anywhere is accompanied by increased incidence of heart attacks and by diet changes which include greater consumption not only of fat but of sugar. They point to studies showing that recent Yemeni immigrants to Israel have little coronary thrombosis but those who have been in Israel 20 years or more become prone to the disease—and the major change in their diet is increased sugar consumption.

Among their own studies, Yudkin and his co-workers report one covering three groups of men, aged 45 to 66. Twenty had recently suffered first heart attacks, 25 had hardening of leg arteries, and 25 others had no health problems. The sugar intake of the first two groups customarily had been roughly twice that of the healthy group.

Not all doctors agree with Dr. Yudkin. Much work remains to be done to identify the mechanism by which sugar in excess may produce artery disease. And a big question to be answered is whether reduction of sugar intake will reduce risk of artery disease. Still, even the possibility that sugar may be involved in this major disease adds another reason why moderation in its use appears warranted.

Ordinary refined sugar is what nutritionists call an "empty calorie" substance. It provides energy—but no protein, no vitamins, no minerals. It can add to body weight but does not help the body repair itself. Sugar, as contrasted, say, with cereal, puts the body at a nutritional disadvantage.

VEGETARIAN DIETS

There are three types. The strictest excludes all animal products as well as animal flesh and organs. The second allows use of such animal products as milk, cheese, and eggs. The mildest allows fish and shellfish in addition to dairy products.

Some people adhere to them and may be lean, but there is no scientifically discernible special virtue in vegetarian diets. There are vegetarianists who attribute their long life and healthy old age to their diet, but there are equally healthy old people who credit daily meat eating.

One possible hazard in vegetarian diets, particularly the strictest, may be lack of sufficient protein. We learned recently of a 78-year-old physician-patient who developed a huge enlargement of the liver, estimated to weigh 15 pounds instead of the usual 3. Biopsy showed cirrhosis. He had never used alcohol *but* from the age of 10 had never eaten meat and had reduced other sources of the complete proteins (see page 49). Specialists in liver disease who were called in finally concluded that the many years of a diet inadequate in rich, complete proteins had caused damage to the liver. The prescription: beefsteaks, filet mignon, roast beef. The patient is having the time of his life at meals.

NATURAL FOODS

Many health food and natural food stores in the country offer a wide range of "unprocessed" or "organic" foods. The foods, for the most part, are good and nutritious. They often cost more than foods available at regular food stores and supermarkets. Claims made in their behalf are that they are grown in soil that has not been impoverished and they are not spoiled by processing.

Arguing against the idea that generally available foods are grown in poor soil, nutritionists note that commercial agriculture in this country treats soil as a precious commodity and keeps it rich through crop rotation and fertilization. Even if soils were widely impoverished, they add, this would not necessarily mean that foods grown in them would be nutritionally inferior. Infertile soil may lead to reduced yield per acre but no inferiority in the makeup of the plant grown. Many nutritionists also observe that the nutritive value of a given crop, such as corn or wheat, is influenced more by the kind of seed planted than by the fertility of the soil. Thus, corn can be bred to contain more niacin or more starch, tomatoes to contain more vitamin A or vitamin C, through development of new strains and seeds.

As for food processing, leading nutritionists argue that commercially canned and frozen foods—in terms of practical nutrition if not of taste —are not inferior to fresh. According to Food and Drug Administration studies involving regular market basket sampling, foods available at ordinary groceries and supermarkets contain ample quantities of vitamins.

Many food additives are now in use. Times and distances involved in getting products from farm to consumer are often great, and additives are used by processors to maintain quality. In some cases, they are used to improve quality or add some advantage not found in the natural state. Thus, some foods are fortified with vitamins and minerals. Flavoring agents may be employed to add taste appeal. Preservatives have to be used for some foods that would otherwise be spoiled by organisms or would undergo undesirable chemical changes before use. Emulsifiers may be added to bakery goods to achieve fineness of grain; and stabilizers and thickeners, such as pectin and vegetable gums, may be used for maintaining texture and body.

A federal food additives law requires that additives be tested and proved safe for consumption before they may be used. Much remains to be learned about additives—and much, too, about safe use of pesticides, but on a realistic basis, with a growing population, we need both additives and pesticides and must learn to use them to best advantage.

FADS AND FALLACIES

Perhaps no other area of human concern is as surrounded with fads and fallacies as nutrition. We have had blackstrap molasses and wheat germ offered as virtual panaceas and, more recently, vinegar and honey. Although no food has any special health virtue all its own, it would be hard to find any that at some time or other has not been touted as such.

Do oysters, raw eggs, lean meat, and olives increase a man's potency? Hardly. They have their nutrient values but confer no special potency benefits.

Are fish and celery brain foods? The idea could have arisen because brain and nerve tissue are rich in phosphorus, and fish provides phosphorus-containing materials. But so do meat, poultry, milk, and eggs. And celery, it turns out, has relatively little phosphorus.

Are white eggs healthier than brown? The fact is that the breed of hen determines eggshell color, and color has nothing to do with nutritive value.

Some magical powers once attributed to foods have been explained by scientific research. For example, lemons and limes were once considered panaceas for scurvy; it is their vitamin C content, of course, which did the work. Rice polishings were indeed fine for preventing beriberi, but solely because of their vitamin B_1 content. Goiter was once treated with sea sponge, and the seeming magic stemmed not from something unique about sponge, but from its content of iodine.

Food myths arise, too, from distortions of scientific fact. Thus, carrots are commonly considered to be good for the eyes. They are—in cases of vitamin A deficiency. The yellow pigment of carrots, carotene, is converted by the body into vitamin A, which is needed to produce a pigment for the retina of the eye. Incidentally, carotene is plentiful, too, in green vegetables where the yellow color is masked by chlorophyll.

Food fads and fallacies might be amusing were it not for the danger that they can interfere with the selection of a proper diet.

SPECIAL DIETS

Special diets can be of value for certain specific health problems. For example, a protein-free diet may be prescribed in some cases of severe kidney damage; a high-protein diet in some cases of hepatitis; a high-residue diet in cases of atonic constipation; a low-fat diet in certain diseases of the liver and gallbladder; a low-purine diet in gout; a low-sodium diet in high blood pressure, congestive heart failure, and toxemia of pregnancy; a bland diet for ulcer, gastritis, and hiatus hernia; a gluten-free diet for celiac disease and sprue. Special dietary treatment is also an important part of the overall therapy in many cases of diabetes.

Whenever a special diet may be of value, it should, of course, be prescribed by a physician on the basis of the patient's individual needs.

WHAT SCIENCE STILL DOES NOT KNOW ABOUT FOODS

Every physician and scientist concerned with nutrition knows well that despite all that has been learned, much more remains to be. At any time, some fundamental new finding—of a previously unknown vitamin or other essential nutrient—may be made.

At the risk of being repetitious, we would like to emphasize again that every advance to date has underscored the one fact: except in special instances, the best and healthiest diet is a balanced and generously varied diet. Nature distributes her largesse. We can be most certain of benefitting from it by making use of many rather than limited numbers of foodstuffs. Almost certainly, if we do this, we will be enjoying the values of still-undiscovered vital elements.

7

WEIGHT CONTROL

WHILE THERE are nutritional diseases due to deprivation—rickets, scurvy, and others—by far the most common nutritional disease in this country is one that results from abundance. Overweight, affecting one in every five Americans, is a mammoth, chronic, frustrating problem. It can be called, justly, the number-one health hazard of our time. It's a remediable problem—but not, unfortunately, the way most of us choose to go about attacking it. To a much lesser extent, underweight constitutes a health problem. And the correction of both is an important function of preventive medicine.

WEIGHT DOES MAKE A DIFFERENCE

It would be a fallacy to say that obesity is ever the one and only cause of a death. But the association between overweight and excessive death rates is unmistakable. Among overweight men, mortality from all causes is 150 percent that for other men; among overweight women, 147 percent that for other women. As for individual diseases, insurance statistics show that overweight men and overweight women, respectively, have these excesses of mortality as compared with the general population: 142 and 175 percent for heart attacks; 159 and 162 percent for cerebral hemorrhage; 191 and 212 percent for chronic nephritis (kidney disease); 168 and 211 percent for liver and gallbladder cancer; 383 and 372 percent for diabetes; 249 and 147 percent for cirrhosis of the liver; 154 and 141 percent for hernia and intestinal obstruction; 152 and 188 percent for non-cancerous gallbladder diseases.

Obesity is associated with many diverse types of health hazards. There may be breathing difficulties, since the greater the weight in the chest wall, the greater the work involved in breathing. With their increased difficulty in breathing, obese people have less tolerance for exercise. They have a higher rate of respiratory infection than do people of normal weight. They may experience two complications related to their breathing problem: lethargy may develop because of accumulation of carbon dioxide in the blood from decreased ventilation; and as the result of reduced levels of oxygen in the blood, the body, trying to compensate, may produce increased amounts of red blood cells. The latter condition, called polycythemia, often is responsible for the ruddy complexion of obese people. It may lead to blood-clotting problems. Heart enlargement and congestive heart failure attributable to obesity have been reported. Many studies have established that more hypertension, or high blood pressure, exists among the obese than among the nonobese, that the obese hypertensive experiences a greater risk of coronary heart disease than the nonobese hypertensive, and that mortality rates for obese hypertensive persons are greater than for others with obesity alone or hypertension alone.

Obese people often have impaired carbohydrate tolerance that may be sufficient in degree to be classified as diabetes. Difficulties during anesthesia and surgery have been associated with obesity. In women with significant degrees of obesity, menstrual abnormalities and abnormal hair growth (hirsutism) have been observed with some frequency. For pregnant women, obesity can be a hazard in several ways: it is associated with a greater incidence of toxemia, of complications during delivery, and of stillbirths.

Some skin problems are related to obesity. Thus, the extra surface area of the skin in the obese person may lead to excessive perspiration, and the juxtaposition of moist skin areas in adjacent folds may lead to boils, fungal infections, and other inflammatory conditions.

It has been well established that in many health problems, significant benefits often follow loss of weight. Among such conditions are hypertension, angina pectoris, congestive heart failure, varicose veins, rupture of intervertebral disks, osteoarthritis, and many other varieties of bone and joint disease. And certainly not to be omitted from even a partial list, many foot aches and backaches may be relieved to a significant extent, sometimes even completely, by weight loss.

DOES THIS MEAN YOU?

By definition, an obese person is anyone who weighs 30 percent or more over what he or she should weigh. Even if you are not that much overweight, it can be important to lose the first 10 pounds or so of excess, because the chances are that if you are overweight at all, you will gain more in the future, and it is easier to lose 10 pounds than 20, 30, 50, or 100.

Usually, your mirror provides you with a fairly good clue about whether you are too heavy. You can consult the accompanying table to determine whether your eyes have deceived you.

DESIRABLE WEIGHTS FOR MEN AND WOMEN
Weight in pounds, according to frame, as ordinarily dressed, including shoes

HEIGHT (WITH SHOES ON) FT. IN.	SMALL FRAME	MEDIUM FRAME	LARGE FRAME
Men			
5 2	116–125	124–133	131–142
5 3	119–128	127–136	133–144
5 4	122–132	130–140	137–149
5 5	126–136	134–144	141–153
5 6	129–139	137–147	145–157
5 7	133–143	141–151	149–162
5 8	136–147	145–160	153–166
5 9	140–151	149–160	157–170
5 10	144–155	153–164	161–175
5 11	148–164	157–168	165–180
6 0	152–164	161–173	169–185
6 1	157–169	166–178	174–190
6 2	163–175	171–184	179–196
6 3	168–180	176–189	184–202
Women			
4 11	104–111	110–118	117–127
5 0	105–113	112–120	119–129
5 1	107–115	114–122	121–131
5 2	110–118	117–125	124–135
5 3	113–121	120–128	127–138
5 4	116–125	124–132	131–142
5 5	119–128	127–135	133–145
5 6	123–132	130–140	138–150
5 7	126–136	134–144	142–154
5 8	129–139	137–147	145–158
5 9	133–143	141–151	149–162
5 10	136–147	145–155	152–166
5 11	139–150	148–158	155–169

You will note that this table, unlike some others, gives desirable rather than average weights. Average people tend to become fat with the passing of the years, and this is not desirable. Average weight tables reflect the fatties who make up the upper part of the average. Note that in each ideal weight group there is an allowance or range of about 10 pounds. If you have lost or gained a few pounds outside the limits for your height and frame, discuss the matter with your physician at the next visit. If you vary 15 or more pounds from the limits, make an appointment for an immediate checkup.

There are several simple tests, too, by which you can assess your actual fatness. One, the ruler test, is based on the fact that if there is no excess of fat, the abdominal surface between the flare of the ribs and front of the pelvis normally is flat. If you lie flat on your back and place a ruler on the abdomen, along the midline of the body, it should not point upward at the midsection. If it does, you need to slim down.

The skinfold, or pinch, test simply calls for grasping a "pinch" of skin with thumb and forefinger—at your waist, stomach, upper arm, buttocks, and calf. At least half of body fat is directly under the skin. Generally, the layer beneath the skin—which is what you measure with the pinch since only the fat, not muscle, pinches—should be between one-fourth and one-half inch. Since, with your pinch, you are getting a double thickness, it normally should be one-half to one inch. A fold much greater than one inch indicates excess body fatness; one much thinner than half an inch indicates abnormal thinness.

GLANDULAR VERSUS ORDINARY OVERWEIGHT

Some 50 years ago, when hormones were discovered, there was a common notion that obesity must be due to some hormone problem. When this turned out to be rarely the case, there was a shift to the idea that obesity is never due to hormonal disturbances but is always the result of overeating. Today, some physicians think that the reasonable view is that to become obese it is always necessary to eat more than you need for the energy you expend, and how often this may be due to some shift in hormone functioning, even within the so-called normal range of such functioning, is simply unknown.

What is known is that in those relatively few cases where a hormone problem can be detected and corrected, it is most commonly the thyroid gland that is at fault. Located at the side and in front of the windpipe, just below the "Adam's apple," the one-ounce thyroid gland acts somewhat like a thermostat, regulating the rate at which body organs function and the speed with which the body uses food. With an overactive thyroid, body functions speed up noticeably. There may be a perceptibly faster heartbeat, nervousness, difficulty in sleeping at night, and weight loss. With an underactive thyroid producing inadequate amounts of thyroid hormone, there is a tendency to be lethargic and to gain weight.

When thyroid dysfunction is suspected in an overweight person, or anyone else, there are tests—basal metabolism and others—that can determine whether, in fact, there is a problem. If underactivity is established, thyroid extract may be used to supplement the thyroid's secretion, and weight will return to normal—if the patient is not overeating on his own.

But the fact of the matter is that in the vast majority of overweight people no thyroid dysfunction or other physical cause is detectable and treatable.

There is an old story about a rotund person who used to claim that he wasn't overweight at all—merely too short for his weight. And, of course, he was right—by the charts, he should have been 12 feet tall.

And there are, of course, many people who insist that they never eat too much; indeed, they claim, they eat like birds. But if they do, it is like inactive birds. According to all the available scientific evidence—and overweight has had a considerable amount of scientific scrutiny—the problem of excess poundage is a problem of too much intake for too little outgo.

WHY DO PEOPLE EAT TOO MUCH?

Overweight is a common problem in this country not just because of affluence but because of our inventiveness and way of life. For most of us, eating is no longer something done for survival; it's a social function, and everywhere around us are invitations to eat. In addition to family meals, there are coffee breaks with doughnuts or Danish; candy counters and peanut, soft drink, and other types of vending machines in office buildings; business and club luncheons; popcorn and soft drinks in movie houses; and on ad infinitum.

And while we have thrust upon us opportunities galore for consuming calories, we have to make opportunities for calorie expenditure. The way we live—riding in elevators, riding to work, being bused to school, even riding golf carts—discourages exercise. We are, we might well say, victims of the system. Clearly the only way to lose weight or to keep from gaining it is to outsmart the system. And that includes the whole of the system, including the fad diet part of it.

THE FAD DIETS

Of the total of 40 million overweight Americans, pollsters have found, 30 million have made some attempt, however halfhearted, to control their weight, and at any one time 20 million people in this country are on some reducing diet or other. Dieting, in fact, has been called the number-one national pastime. And the dietary regimens followed are as numerous as they are almost incredibly bizarre and even self-defeating and health-impairing.

There are magic-pair diets: lamb chops and grapefruit, eggs and spinach, or bananas and skim milk, which have their share of fanatic followers. There are reducing formulas that concentrate on a single food —six to nine eggs a day, for example, until the chickens or the reducers beg for mercy.

Crash diet formulas include grapefruit and coffee for days on end; celery and virtually nothing else; cottage cheese and little more; purges of lemon juice and nothing in the way of solid food. The intent seems to be to make oneself miserable and hope to melt away a lot of fat in little time. Yet acute malnutrition and even worse may develop. Not long ago there was considerable publicity when a young New Jersey woman died following a crash diet, and there have been reports since of others who failed to survive similar diets.

There are high-protein diets which, through restricting intake to steak, eggs, and other high-protein foods, are purported to reduce. But any single-category diet can be dangerous because it omits other necessary food groups. And few people actually can stick with them long enough anyhow to lose appreciable amounts; even those who do very often quickly return to obesity.

There is an "eat fat" diet which supposedly puts the fats you eat to work somehow melting away fat deposits in the body. But while Americans have spent millions of dollars on books advocating such a diet, there is no evidence that any one type of food stimulates the burning off of fat stores.

There is a low-carbohydrate diet, sometimes called the "Air Force Diet" though the Air Force disclaims it. It calls for counting and restricting the intake of "carbohydrate units" but allows eating just about anything else you wish. But there is some possibility that restricting carbohydrates can upset both digestion and the body's fluid balance. Moreover, the diet tends to concentrate on foods high in fats, especially saturated fats, which may be harmful to the coronary arteries and the heart.

When they are not outrightly dangerous, unscientific diets, however attractive they are made to sound, are self-defeating. While they may appear to be initially successful in taking off weight, such loss usually is the result of (1) water loss rather than loss of body fat, (2) decrease in appetite and thus caloric intake due to radical changes in eating practices, or (3) both reasons.

Because they differ from family meal patterns, such diets are not acceptable for long periods—and so weight is regained once the original faulty eating habits are resumed. And on-again-off-again dieting can be dangerous.

THE DANGERS OF UPS AND DOWNS

The frequent weight gains and losses indulged in by the many obese people who practice what one writer calls the "rhythm method of girth control" may actually be more harmful than maintenance of a steady excess weight. For example, it has been shown that serum cholesterol is elevated during periods of weight gain, thus increasing the risk that it will be deposited on artery walls? *We have no evidence to show that once cholesterol is deposited it can be removed by weight reduction.* And it is possible that a person whose weight has fluctuated up and down a number of times has been subjected to more atherogenic (artery-hardening) stress than a person with stable though excessive weight—and such stress increases the danger of heart attack and stroke.

Animal experiments have shown that animals of normal weight have a longer life expectancy than obese animals. They have also shown that if an animal has been obese and has been repeatedly reduced, it will have a shorter life expectancy than the obese animal that has never been reduced. Such evidence adds further question to the advisability of undertaking weight reduction that cannot be sustained.

THE ONLY SCIENTIFIC WAY TO REDUCE

There is nothing complicated about the principles for safe, sound, and effective weight reduction, and they are principles that rest on solid scientific study. There are no healthy substitutes for them, and any attempts to circumvent them are only invitations to frustration and failure. Without any equivocation but rather as forcibly as we can, we wish to emphasize that all else is bunk, junk, profitable only to the purveyors and never truly so to the believer-buyers—and this is the set of principles upon which you must, and can reliably, pin your hopes for safe and effective weight control:

If the number of calories you eat averages more than the number your body uses, you gain. If calorie intake totals less than calorie use, you lose weight.

If you are to lose one pound of fat, you will have to take in 3,500 calories less than you expend.

And while a sound reducing diet should, of course, lead to weight loss, it must, in addition, have three basic characteristics:

1. It must produce loss of weight at a safe pace.
2. It must offer variety so that it maintains health and provides some pleasure in eating as well as some satisfaction of hunger.

3. It must teach new, and enjoyable, eating patterns so that you do not promptly slip back into old, weight-gaining eating habits.

And, in most cases, coupled with a good reducing diet having such characteristics there must be a sound program of exercise or other physical activity that will increase the calorie expenditure level, ease the dieting regimen, and contribute to general health in the process.

IS A DOCTOR NECESSARY?

Weight reduction on a sound basis calls for the special knowledge of a physician. He will make certain that you do not lose your health while losing excess weight; that you do not reduce too rapidly and thereby put a strain on your heart and circulation; that you do not find yourself with a cosmetic problem because you have lost weight but have not regained skin tone and end up with flabby masses of pendulous skin.

He will suggest proper exercise. He will also prescribe vitamins, minerals, and other substances, if necessary, to prevent weakening of bones and organs and to maintain resistance to disease. For example, if you use a "no-calorie" salad dressing made of mineral oil, your doctor may want you to take some vitamins, because mineral oil tends to prevent adequate absorption of some of the vitamins your diet would ordinarily provide.

Moreover, it helps considerably if you can have your diet suitably adjusted to your eating habits. You may be one of those who will be miserable if deprived of a bedtime snack. You may prefer a substantial dinner and be willing to cut down on lunch to have it. A physician can help you establish a sound diet and one best suited to your needs. He may, if necessary, prescribe sedatives for your use during the toughest phase of dieting. The psychological aspects of a relationship with a sympathetic, encouraging physician also can be of great importance during dieting and later on in maintaining low weight. *A doctor's encouragement and praise of a patient's efforts in reducing, we have found, can be of major value.*

PILLS AS PROPS

Should you take drugs to reduce? Without a doctor's supervision, never. If, in an individual case, a physician feels that an antiappetite drug as a temporary prop is justifiable, he will prescribe it—and it should be taken exactly as prescribed. Most physicians, however, prefer to have a patient rely on willpower and determination rather than on drugs and to adjust the diet so this is feasible.

In the past, medicines for weight reduction generally were based on amphetamine and so stimulated patients that physicians were reluctant to use them. Now, a number of appetite-reducing agents are available, free of the side effect of overstimulation. These apparently safer agents are available only on prescription.

Over-the-counter reducing preparations are big business. At worst, they can be risky business because of the possibility of side effects; at best, the money is foolishly spent because in and of themselves the medicines are not to be relied upon for effective permanent weight reduction.

The problem with even safe reducing agents is that they are only supports that help temporarily. It makes much more sense—and has far greater chance of permanent success—to regulate your diet by a healthy change in eating habits which, once desired weight reduction is achieved, can be continued with some upward shift in calorie intake, to maintain you at proper weight.

THE EXERCISE FACTOR

For years, the role of exercise in reducing has been misinterpreted. Today, regular exercise is known to be essential for maintaining good health and preventing many diseases as well as being a vital adjunct to diet for weight control. As some put it, diet is half the battle for weight control; it helps you on your way. Exercise provides the vitality and the drive; it helps take you where you want to go.

There are still two widely prevalent misconceptions about exercise and weight control. One is that it takes great amounts of time and effort to use up enough calories to affect weight significantly. The other is that exercise increases the appetite and the end result is increase, not decrease, in weight.

The misconception about time and effort stems from the impression that any exercise has to be accomplished in a single uninterrupted session. To be sure, it takes an hour's jogging to use up 900 calories, but one does not have to do all the jogging in one stretch. One must walk 35 miles to lose a pound of fat, but walking an additional mile a day for 35 days will take off the pound. And so one can lose 10 pounds in a year by walking an extra mile a day.

In one dramatic demonstration of the value of exercise, the daily food intake of a group of university students was doubled, from 3,000 calories daily to 6,000. At the same time, exercise each day was stepped up. There was no gain in weight.

Another fact about exercise that deserves consideration: Body weight affects the amount of energy expended whatever the activity may be —walking, jogging, tennis playing, or anything else. For example, a 100-pound individual walking 3 miles per hour will burn about 50 calories in 15 minutes; someone weighing 200 pounds would use up as many as 80 calories in the same period.

As for appetite and exercise, while it is true that a thin person in good condition may eat more after increased activity, his exercise will burn up the extra calories. But the overly fat person does not react the same way; only when he exercises to excess will he experience an appetite increase, since he has large stores of fat, and moderate exercise in his case is not likely to stimulate appetite. This difference between the response to exercise of fat and thin people is an important one.

There are many opportunities to be found throughout the day for using up calories through little extra bits of activity. You can, for example, use up 100 calories with 20 minutes of gardening, 30 minutes of ironing, or 30 minutes of playing with the children. Any time you get up from behind a desk, walk about the room, perhaps just bend and stretch for a few times, you will not be burning up great quantities of calories— but do this every hour or two, and at the end of the week you will have burned a significant number.

IS MASSAGE A REDUCING AID?

No. Massage may tone up the skin and muscles and help the body adjust to its new, slimmer contours. Your doctor will know when to recommend massage if it would help.

CAN HOT BATHS OR SWEATING HELP?

Only temporarily, since they serve merely to eliminate water, which is almost immediately regained. Not only do these methods achieve no permanent results of value but they may put a strain on heart and circulation. Sauna baths, recently fashionable, expose the body to high temperatures to bring about violent sweating. This is a shock to the body, sometimes doubling the pulse rate, as much of a shock as sudden and violent exercise. To be sure, saunas have long been popular in Finland, but the Finns use saunas over a lifetime rather than starting suddenly in flabby middle age, and they dash water on heated stones, producing a more humid and more tolerable (and possibly safer for the lungs) type of heat than electrically heated American saunas.

CALORIE COUNT

How do you determine the proper calorie level per day for you? Your physician can help, taking into account your present weight, desired weight, state of health, and normal activities. He may suggest perhaps as few as 1,200 calories per day if you are an adult woman, 1,500 to 1,800 if you are an adult man. These levels are about half those of nondieters. Within these limits, you can diet reasonably happily on a wide variety of foods and obtain all essential nutrients. Or your physician may suggest a reduction of intake level by as little as 300 or 400 calories. It is usually not considered wise to depend upon a reduction of less than 300 or 400, since one or two miscalculations or indulgences may mean no weight loss at all.

Remember that the objective is permanent weight loss, not a flashy quick cutdown, promptly followed by a return of the excess pounds. So what if it takes several months or even a year to reach your ideal weight —as long as you will be using a tolerable diet, one you can sustain, retraining your eating habits so you can enjoy the new habits and the desired weight level for the rest of your life. Always remember that only one-half pound of weight loss per week means 26 pounds for the year, and 1 pound a week means over 50 pounds lost.

In setting up your diet, your physician most likely will move in the direction of a little of everything, to assure balance and variety. He will make certain you get something from each of the four basic food groups (see page 49). He will be thinking in terms not merely of reducing but of general health, of reducing without risk of malnutrition or risk of fomenting heart disease.

As an example, sample menus for a 1,200 calories a day diet might go like this:

Breakfast: 1/2 small grapefruit; 1 poached egg; 1 slice of toast; 1 small pat of butter or margarine; coffee or tea.

Lunch: A 3-ounce cooked serving of lean meat, poultry, or fish; 1 serving of vegetable; 1 serving of fruit; 1 slice of bread; 1 small pat of butter or margarine; 1 glass of skim milk.

Dinner: A large broiled beef patty; 1/2 cup of asparagus; 1/2 to 1 cup of tossed green salad with vinegar dressing; 1 slice of bread; 1 small pat of butter or margarine; 1/2 cup of pineapple; 1 glass of skim milk.

Snacks, if desired, may consist of bouillon or consommé, tomato juice, raw vegetables, coffee or tea, or food saved from meals.

You may find it convenient to use a mini-pocketbook calorie counter available in pharmacies and food stores. For your general guidance, the following table lists the calorie content of many commonly used foods and beverages.

CALORIE CONTENT OF FOODS AND BEVERAGES

FOODS	AMOUNT	CALORIES
Soup		
Bouillon or consommé	1 cup	30
Cream soups	1 cup	150
Split-pea soup	1 cup	200
Vegetable-beef or chicken	1 cup	70
Tomato	1 cup	90
Chicken noodle	1 cup	65
Clam chowder	1 cup	85
Meat and fish		
Beef steak	4" × 2-1/4" × 1", 3 oz.	300
Roast beef	average portion, 3 oz.	300
Ground beef	1 patty, 3 oz.	245
Roast leg of lamb	average portion, 3 oz.	250
Rib lamb chop	1 medium	130
Loin pork chop	1 medium	235
Ham, smoked or boiled	2 slices	240
Bacon	2 strips	100
Frankfurter	5-1/2" × 3/4"	125
Tongue, kidney	average portion	150
Chicken	average breast, 6 oz.	190
Turkey	3 slices or 3-1/2 oz.	200
Salami	2 slices or 2 oz.	260
Bologna	4 slices, 4-1/2" × 1/8", or 4 oz.	260
Veal cutlet (unbreaded)	1 piece, 4" × 2-1/2" × 1/2", 3 oz.	185
Hamburger patty (regular ground beef)	5 patties per pound of ground meat, 3 oz.	245
Beef liver, fried	1 thick piece, 3" × 2-1/2", 2 oz.	130
Bluefish, baked	1 piece, 3-1/2" × 2" × 1/2", 3 oz.	135
Fish sticks, breaded (including fat for frying)	5 fish sticks, 4 oz.	200
Tuna fish, canned, drained	2/5 cup	170
Salmon, drained	2/3 cup	140
Sardines, drained	10 sardines, or 4 oz.	260
Shrimp, canned	4 to 6	65
Trout	average portion	250
Fish (cod, haddock, mackerel, halibut, whitefish, broiled or baked)	average portion	190
Whole lobster	1 lb.	145
Vegetables		
Asparagus	6–7 stalks	20
Beans, green	1/2 cup	15
kidney	1/2 cup	335
lima	1/2 cup	80
Beets	1/2 cup	30
Broccoli	1 large stalk	30
Cabbage, raw	1/2 cup	12
cooked	1/2 cup	20
Carrots	1 medium or 1/2 cup	25

CALORIE CONTENT OF FOODS AND BEVERAGES

FOODS	AMOUNT	CALORIES
Vegetables		
Cauliflower	1/2 cup	15
Celery	1 large stalk	5
Corn	5" ear or 1/2 cup	70
Cucumber	1/2 medium	5
Eggplant	2 slices or 1/2 cup	25
Green pepper	1 pepper	20
Lettuce	3 small leaves	3
Peas	1/2 cup	55
Potato, sweet	1 medium	200
white	1 medium	100
Potato chips	10 chips	100
Radishes	2 small	4
Spinach	1/2 cup	25
Squash, summer	1/2 cup	15
winter	1/4 cup	45
Tomatoes, raw	1 medium	30
canned or cooked	1/2 cup	25
Fruits		
Apple	medium	75
Applesauce, unsweetened	1/2 cup	50
sweetened	1/2 cup	95
Apricot, raw	2 to 3	50
canned or dried	halves, 4 to 6	85
Avocado	1/2 small	250
Banana	1 medium	85
Cantaloupe	1/3 medium	35
Cherries, fresh	15 large	60
canned, syrup	1/2 cup	100
Cranberry sauce	1/2 cup	250
Fruit cocktail, canned	1/2 cup	90
Grapefruit	1/2 medium (4-1/4" diameter)	55
Olives	1 large	8
Orange	1 medium	70
Peach, fresh	1 medium	45
canned, syrup	2 halves, 1 tbsp. juice	70
Pear, fresh	1 medium	45
canned, syrup	2 halves, 1 tbsp. juice	70
Pineapple, canned (with syrup)	1 slice	90
Plums, fresh	2 medium	50
canned, syrup	2 medium	75
Prunes, cooked with sugar	5 large	135
Raisins, dried	1/2 cup	200
Tangerine	1 large	45
Cereal, bread, and crackers		
Puffed wheat	1 cup	45
Other dry cereal	average portion	100

CALORIE CONTENT OF FOODS AND BEVERAGES

FOODS	AMOUNT	CALORIES
Cereal, bread, and crackers		
Farina, cooked	3/4 cup	100
Oatmeal, cooked	1 cup	135
Rice, cooked	1 cup	200
Macaroni or spaghetti, cooked	1 cup	200
Egg noodles, cooked	1 cup	100
Flour	1 cup	400
Bread, white, rye, or whole wheat	1 slice	70
Ry-Krisp	1 double square	20
Saltine	1 cracker 2″ sq.	15
Ritz cracker	1 cracker	15
Biscuit	1 biscuit, 2″ diameter	110
Hard roll	1 average	95
Pancakes	2 medium	130
Waffles	1 medium	230
Bun-cinnamon with raisins	1 average	185
Danish pastry	1 small	140
Muffin	1 medium	130
Dairy products		
Whole milk	1 cup	160
Evaporated milk	1/2 cup	170
Skim milk	1 cup	90
Buttermilk (from skim milk)	1 cup	90
Light cream, sweet or sour	1 tbsp.	30
Heavy cream	1 tbsp.	50
Yoghurt	1 cup	120
Whipped cream	1 tbsp.	50
Ice cream	1/6 qt.	200
Cottage cheese	1/2 cup	100
Cheese	1 oz. or 1 slice	100
Butter	1 tbsp.	100
	1 pat	60
Egg, plain		80
fried or scrambled		110
Cake and other desserts		
Chocolate layer cake	1/12 cake	350
Angel cake	1/12 cake	115
Sponge cake	2″ × 2-3/4″ × 1/2″	100
Fruit pie	1/6 pie	375
Cream pie	1/6 pie	200
Lemon meringue pie	1/6 pie	280
Chocolate pudding	1/2 cup	220
Jello	1 serving (1/5 pkg.)	65
Fruit ice	1/2 cup	145
Doughnut, plain	1 doughnut	130
Brownie	2″ sq.	140
Cookie, plain	3″ diameter	75

CALORIE CONTENT OF FOODS AND BEVERAGES

FOODS	AMOUNT	CALORIES
Miscellaneous		
Sugar	1 level tbsp. or 3 level tsp.	50
Jam or jelly	1 level tbsp.	60
Peanut butter	1 tbsp.	100
Catsup or chili sauce	2 tbsp.	35
White sauce, medium	1/4 cup	100
Brown gravy	1/2 cup	80
Boiled dressing (cooked)	1 tbsp.	30
Mayonnaise	1 tbsp.	100
French dressing	1 tbsp.	60
Salad oil, olive oil, etc.	1 tbsp.	125
Margarine	1 tbsp.	100
Herbs and spices		0
Chocolate sauce	2 tbsp.	90
Cheese sauce	2 tbsp.	65
Butterscotch sauce	2 tbsp.	200
Beverages		
Ice-cream soda	1 regular	250
Chocolate malted	8 oz. glass	300
Chocolate milk	8 oz. glass	185
Cocoa made with milk	1 cup	175
Tea or coffee, plain		0
Apple juice or cider	1/2 cup	65
Grape juice	1/2 cup	90
Cola drink	8 oz.	95
Ginger ale	8 oz.	70
Grapefruit juice, unsweetened	1/2 cup	40
Pineapple juice	1/2 cup	55
Prune juice	1/2 cup	85
Tomato juice	1/2 cup	25

SOME DIETING SUGGESTIONS

FATS.   Rather than whole milk, use skim or powdered milk for your beverages (hot skimmed milk is enjoyed by some people in breakfast coffee) and in cooking soups, mashed potatoes, gravies, etc. Powdered milk is quite good for gravies. You can separate out your portion and then add cream or butter or margarine for the rest of the family. The cream you save can be used to convert your low-calorie gelatin or fruit desserts into higher-calorie desserts for others in the family.

Use plain cottage cheese instead of butter or margarine. It is especially good with chives, or onion or celery salt, on thin dry (melba) toast. Cook finely chopped spinach and other greens in very little water to which you add a bouillon cube, and you are not likely to miss the butter.

Avoid fried foods, especially those that are French fried. It is difficult to determine just how many calories these foods contain, since they absorb varying amounts of fat, but it is always a great deal.

Boil or poach eggs; you won't mind unbuttered toast if you serve your egg on it. Try cooking eggs on a griddle or the type of pan that does not require greasing. If you cook stews ahead of time and let them cool, you can remove the hardened fat, at least from your portion—and stews often are even better when rewarmed. Trim fat from your meat, and omit rich gravy.

SWEETS.   An artificial sweetener, in tablet, powdered, liquid, or crystal form, can be used in many ways in addition to sweetening beverages. It can be used with skim milk on cereal and on strawberries or other fruits, cooked or uncooked. (If you serve fruit stewed in sugar, give the syrup to someone who needs the calories.) Sponge and angel cake are not very high in calories if you separate out your portions before adding icing for others in the family or before adding jam or fruit syrup. Make your own gelatin desserts so you can use saccharin for your portion, sugar for the rest. Take very small portions of any dessert, and avoid soft drinks unless you use the low-calorie types.

STARCHES.   Undoubtedly you are accustomed to getting bulk from starches. You can get it instead from leafy green vegetables. Don't munch on bread and butter. In restaurants, ask the waiter not to bring the bread until he serves the main course. In some areas, salads are served first—a good idea because salads take the edge off your hunger before you get to the higher-calorie foods. Use wine vinegar with herbs or lemon juice on your own salad while serving richer dressings to others.

Good gravies can be made without flour; one way is to use powdered milk which is fat-free. Vegetables, either dried ones or fresh ones cooked down, and herbs will thicken stews.

Chinese restaurants serve bulky, low-calorie dishes—if you avoid the rice. Many Chinese vegetables can be purchased in stores.

Avoid restaurants that have a strictly enforced "no substitutes" rule. Many restaurants will give you an extra vegetable or an extra serving of the one on your dinner, or a salad, in place of potatoes.

When serving soups such as minestrone or chowder, take mainly the clear part for yourself, leaving most of the macaroni, potatoes, and so on, for the others.

OTHER SUGGESTIONS

Don't taste while cooking and don't lick the bowl when finished cooking. It has been said jokingly, but not without a grain of truth, that half the overweight housewives in this country have tasted or licked themselves fat.

Snacks add a great deal in calories. Are they worth it? If you happen to be a "snacker," you can study the snack chart (see table on page 76) and decide. Consider that a cup of tea or coffee, without cream, with one teaspoonful of sugar, contains only 16 calories; it may satisfy your hunger or at least take the edge off it, and provide the quick energy you need. On the other hand, a chocolate sundae will run between 300 and 400 calories, and half a brick of plain ice cream is 200 (and even low-calorie ice cream is 100).

Nibbling between meals does help some people to diet by decreasing their appetite at mealtime. If you try this, keep careful count of calories so you will know whether or not it is really helping you. Nibbling also may be suggested by a physician for some heart patients, since the body can manage five or six very small meals daily more easily than the customary three, one or two of which may be fairly heavy.

The idea that you are helping your children when you sample their dinners or finish their portions is one that ought to be dropped. It helps neither them nor you—and can become a fattening habit.

EATING BINGES.   Some dieters are able to go off their diets occasionally without ill effect. Their morale may even benefit from knowing they can do this every month, which is better than constant "cheating." But remember that you probably have a great tendency to eat more than you need or you wouldn't be dieting in the first place, so be very careful.

TALKING ABOUT YOUR DIET.   If you do talk about it, some people may consider you a bore; some may try to get you to break your diet; some will help you to keep it. You have to know which kind you are with before you start discussing your diet. Sometimes, it may be just as well simply to say that your physician has asked you not to eat certain foods. As a general rule, the best social technique is to avoid calling attention to your problem. Simply eat very little of fattening foods placed before you.

BREAKFAST.   A reasonably hearty, high-protein meal in the morning often keeps people from being hungry in the midmorning and from eating too much at noon.

ALCOHOLIC BEVERAGES.   As you can see from the listings in the accompanying table, alcoholic beverages are high in calories. They don't satisfy hunger except perhaps when taken in excess. Three glasses of beer, at 120 calories per 8-ounce glass, will supply as many calories as a fairly substantial breakfast. An evening of cocktails can provide almost as many calories as a full day's reducing diet. Even more serious is the fact that the calories supplied by alcohol are empty ones, without necessary food values such as proteins or minerals.

MODERATION. It took time to put on the excess weight you want to be rid of. Take time to reduce. Moderate loss, at the rate of one-half pound to one pound a week, is healthier loss and the fat lost is more likely to stay off than fat lost in a hurry. And a pound a week adds up to 52 pounds a year. When you lose weight slowly, your skin adjusts and you don't get that deflated-balloon look.

CALORIE CONTENT OF SNACK FOODS

FOOD	AMOUNT	CALORIES
Chocolate bar	1 small bar	155
Chocolate creams	1 average size	50
Cookies	1 medium size	75
Doughnut	1 plain	135
Banana	1 large	100
Peach	1 medium size	50
Apple	1 medium size	75
Raisins	1/2 cup	200
Popcorn	1 cup popped	55
Potato chips	8–10 or 1/2 cup	100
Peanuts or pistachio nuts	1	5
Walnuts, pecans, filberts or cashews	4 whole or 1 tbsp. chopped	40
Brazil nuts	1	50
Butternuts	1	25
Peanut butter	1 tbsp.	100
Pickles	1 large sour	10
	1 average sweet	15
Olives	1	10
Ice cream	1/2 cup	200
Chocolate-nut sundae		270
Ice cream soda		255
Chocolate malted milk	1 glass	450
Eggnog (without liquor)	1 glass	235
Carbonated beverages	6 oz. or 1 bottle	80
Alcoholic Beverages		
Beer	8 oz. glass	120
Wine	1 wine glass	75
Gin	1 jigger	115
Rum	1 jigger	125
Whiskey	1 jigger	120
Brandy	1 brandy glass	80
Cocktail	1 cocktail glass	150

DIET CLUBS

In recent years, many people have turned to weight-reducing clubs where they can join with others wishing to reduce. The clubs are helpful in providing motivation. But medical authorities have reservations about the medical supervision provided.

The clubs vary considerably in their programs, but all emphasize diet coupled with lectures, literature, and experience-sharing. Some prescribe particular exercises. Many require an initial medical certificate for membership, but few have continuing medical supervision. Physicians have reported that, because of the lack of medical supervision in some clubs, the condition of their heart and diabetic patients worsened as a result of diet advice given.

If you are considering joining some diet club you may have read or heard about, the best policy is to check with your physician about that particular club and its standing and whether he advises that you join it.

OBESITY STARTS IN CHILDHOOD

The problem of overweight in adults may well have its roots in infancy and childhood. There has long been a tradition—certainly no longer valid in an age of modern medicine—that the plump child is better equipped to withstand disease. The practice of actually encouraging fatness in babies to help them withstand tuberculosis and other diseases is not only unnecessary; it is potentially dangerous.

Recent scientific work provides some tentative new insights into how overfeeding of children in infancy and the preadolescent years may build up fat cells (adipose tissue) that may remain with them a lifetime. The studies suggest that once these cells are laid down, they never disappear. When weight is lost, the cells shrink, but still remain. At times, they may send out signals demanding to be fed. This demand may help explain why many people find it difficult to keep their weight down after dieting. A constant craving for food may not be wholly psychological, as many have thought; it may be at least partly based on biological demand from deprived fat cells.

A lean adult may have about 27 trillion fat cells in his body; an obese person may have 77 trillion.

Obesity, when it exists, can be overcome. But its prevention is far more desirable—and that involves establishing reasonable eating habits in childhood, even in early infancy.

IF YOU NEED TO GAIN WEIGHT

If you are markedly underweight or are losing weight, medical advice is important. A chronic underweight condition or a sudden loss of weight is an indication of poor health. It may signal the presence of onset of disease—for example, diabetes, overactivity of the thyroid gland or, especially in children, intestinal worms. Chronic infections and other problems also may lead to weight loss.

Finding the cause is the job of a physician. Your responsibility is to watch your weight—and your children's—and seek medical advice when there is a definite abnormality of weight.

DETERMINING IF YOU ARE UNDERWEIGHT

Usually, the advice of a physician is necessary in deciding whether you are really underweight. Quite possibly, if you are 10 to 15 pounds under the figures given in the chart on page 61, if your bones stick out all over your body, if the muscles don't cover the back, thighs, and buttocks with resilient protection, or if your face is thin and drawn, you are underweight. However, you may be the long lean type whose weight normally runs below the given figures. Your physician, by considering results of his physical examination, including observations of the size and bony framework of your body, can decide fairly accurately whether you are underweight.

If your extreme thinness is due to ill health, it is, of course, the physician's responsibility to determine what the problem is and to correct it. You will respond well when a chronic infection is the cause and is eliminated, or when thyroid gland functioning is at the root of the problem and is corrected.

If the problem lies with failure to eat enough of the right food, your doctor can help you plan a diet that will add needed weight. Depending upon your individual problem and needs, your physician may suggest some or all of the following aids:

Time. It takes time to eat properly and to enjoy food. Pleasant company may help you to prolong your mealtime so you can eat more without feeling stuffed. If it is necessary for you to eat alone, you may find it helpful to listen to the radio, particularly to music, or even to read to keep from being bored. It can also be helpful to relax before meals. It is difficult to eat well when you are tired.

Substitute High-Calorie for Low-Calorie Foods. It can be helpful to substitute high-calorie vegetables such as peas, potatoes, and lima beans for bulky low-calorie ones. Within the bounds of moderation, you can eat somewhat more of desserts, cream soups, bread, nuts and olives, oils and salad dressings. You can get into the habit of adding an extra pat of margarine to your vegetables and to many soups.

EAT MORE.   You can do it. Another piece of bread, a second helping, soon become matters of habit.

SNACKS.   You can learn to enjoy them, finding ones that do not spoil your appetite.

SWEETS.   Although they have a role in the diet, sweets present a problem. Candy, jellies, pastry, cake, and ice cream are concentrated sources of energy. But they may satiate the appetite for more valuable foods. They may also, particularly in children and young adults, increase the decay of teeth. If they do not interfere with your appetite and do help you to gain weight, be sure to have frequent dental checkups.

SMOKING.   There is no doubt that smoking, particularly when excessive, can interfere with enjoyment of good food and may dull the appetite somewhat. It may help, if you are a heavy smoker, to at least cut down and, if possible, to avoid cigarettes just before and at mealtimes. Best of all, stop completely.

ALCOHOLIC BEVERAGES.   Many people find that a drink, such as a glass of sherry, when sipped in leisurely fashion before dinner helps bring about relaxation and has a stimulating effect on the appetite. Alcohol should not be substituted for food, but its moderate use may be helpful.

8

PHYSICAL ACTIVITY

PERHAPS NOTHING else is more important as a means of maintaining health and even warding off some major diseases than a reasonable level of physical activity. It is no exaggeration to say that exercise is good for almost everybody and everything—that virtually no one but a bed-ridden person doesn't stand to benefit from it.

There is a curious irony. New discoveries are constantly revealing the deep need of the body for activity, the values (some not even dreamed of just a few years ago) of activity in restoring health after serious illness, the values for mental and emotional as well as physical well-being. Yet, at the same time, most of us have less and less routine opportunity for activity in our daily lives unless we deliberately seek it, and few of us seek it.

On the job and off, most of us today lead soft lives. Progress—as represented by power tools and automation, elevators and cars, TV sets and electric toothbrushes—contributes to an ever-continuing reduction of physical expenditures. We need to search out opportunities for activity, to understand the basic principles involved, and to apply them. It is very clearly worth the effort.

BENEFITS

The person who gives proper attention to exercise and other physical activity can expect to derive a long list of benefits. Muscles, of course, if they have been weak and sagging, will become strong. So will the heart, and the lungs and circulatory system. Along with strength, there will be increased endurance, coordination, and joint flexibility, and there may well be a reduction of minor aches and pain. Postural defects, too, may be corrected, and there is likely to be an improvement in general appearance. Feelings of listlessness and fatigue are likely to be replaced by sensations of alertness and energy. Sleep will be more restful. And there is likely to be improved ability to relax and to voluntarily reduce tension.

FITNESS, FATIGUE, AND TENSION

Emotional tension and chronic tiredness are among the most common complaints today. There may, of course, in some instances be an actual physical illness to account for them. But in many people the cause lies in gradual deterioration of the body for lack of enough physical activity.

The human body, it has been observed, is capable of generating 14 horsepower with maximum effort; it generates only 0.1 horsepower at rest. In many of us who lead sedentary lives, there is some muscular atrophy, or wasting away; we become undermuscled for our weight, and so we may lack the strength and endurance needed even for our sedentary jobs. But, in addition, it may well be that in many who lead sedentary lives, the unused horsepower, so to speak, goes into the building up of tension, with the tension then becoming a factor in producing fatigue and, sometimes, other complaints as well.

Physicians encounter many cases like that of a relatively young man, in his late thirties, who had moved along well in his career and should have been happy and at the height of his powers. Instead, he complained of chronic fatigue, sleeping problems, growing difficulty in concentrating effectively and handling work he once would handle with little effort. He suffered from frequent headaches and many vague complaints that made him feel constantly under par.

Tests disclosed no underlying disease process. And the prescription given to him by his physician involved no medication of any kind, only a program of activity, of regular exercise beginning at a leisurely pace and progressing gradually, and of sports. Within a few months, he was sleeping well, feeling vigorous and relaxed, turning out better work in less time, finding time to have more fun, as he put it, than he had had since his college days.

ACTIVITY AND MANY KEY PHYSICAL HEALTH PROBLEMS

There is increasing evidence that exercise is of value in preventing many key diseases such as heart disease, stroke, and peripheral vascular disorders which affect circulation in the extremities. It is good for most lung diseases; an aid in the prevention of backaches and foot problems; a help too in the prevention of hernias; and a means of maintaining good skin tone.

For many years, vigorous physical activity was considered a hazard for the healthy heart, let alone the diseased. Today, there is mounting evidence that regular activity not only is essential for optimal maintenance of heart health but also, with certain precautions, can be of great value in heart patients formerly doomed to inactive existence.

ACTIVITY AND THE HEART

In one of the pioneering studies concerned with exercise and the heart, British investigators found that the frequency of coronary heart disease in London bus conductors was about 30 percent lower than in the less active bus drivers. Since then, an inverse relationship between physical activity and coronary heart disease—the more of the former, the less of the latter—has been found by many other investigators in this country and elsewhere in the world.

In a study carried out by Harvard scientists, 700 Bostonians of Irish descent were compared with their brothers who stayed in Ireland. Coronary heart disease deaths in the Boston group (ages 30 to 60) were two times those in the Ireland group. The men in Ireland ate more eggs, more butter, and more of other saturated fats—yet had lower serum cholesterol levels. They consumed 400 calories more per day on the average than their Boston counterparts but weighed 10 percent less. They were getting more exercise and their lower cholesterol levels showed that physical activity does more than just burn off calories.

Somewhat to their amazement, American scientists who recently made a special trip to study Masai tribesmen in Africa found that these people, despite a diet containing enough cholesterol to send the ordinary worried American fleeing in panic from the dinner table, never seem to get heart trouble. They live almost exclusively on meat and on milk with a butterfat content that soars to 6.5 percent. Yet they have lower blood cholesterol levels on the average than do Americans.

It is possible that it is exercise which protects Masai hearts, keeping cholesterol levels in their blood low despite the high dietary intake. The Masai are known to walk as much as 50 to 60 miles a day—and to do it without strain.

In a study covering 120,000 American railroad employees, the heart attack incidence among sedentary office workers was found to be almost twice that of men working in the yards.

Investigators have noted that activity trains the heart to beat slowly, to function more economically, to require less oxygen for a given amount of work. In addition, the well-exercised body requires a smaller amount of heart muscle activity for a given physical performance than the untrained body.

Many studies indicate not only a lower incidence of heart attacks among the physically active than among the sedentary but also a greater likelihood, when a heart attack does occur, for the physically active person to recover. One possible reason is that exercise appears to promote the development of supplementary blood vessels which can take over the burden of nourishing the heart muscle when a coronary artery is blocked in a heart attack.

In a recent study to try to explain why physical exercise may ward off heart attacks, investigators at the University of Oregon Medical School fed radioactively tagged cholesterol to animals. Because of the tagging, they could follow what happened to the cholesterol. (It is a high level of blood cholesterol that is thought to foster development of atherosclerosis, the pile-up of fatty deposits on blood vessel walls that may shut down blood flow to the heart muscle, producing a heart attack.) The Oregon workers found that the more the animals exercised, the more cholesterol was broken down; the less exercise, the higher the levels of cholesterol in the blood.

In Israel recently, a special program of activity has been set up for men who have had actual heart attacks. In the program, exercise is gradually intensified until it becomes quite vigorous, including jogs along the Mediterranean Sea. The program is carried out under close medical supervision. Dr. Daniel Brunner, its director and Associate Professor of Physiological Hygiene at Tel Aviv University, reports that many of the patients now are more fit than before their heart attacks—and more fit than nontrained people of their age who have not had coronary artery disease.

ACTIVITY AT ANY AGE

That even elderly people, men in their 70's, can regain much of the vigor and physical function of their 40's through carefully planned physical activity has been demonstrated by a University of Southern California investigator. In the program, in which exercise is prescribed with the same care as a physician prescribes medications, 69 men aged 50 to 87 have been working out one hour three times a week. Their closely supervised regimen includes calisthenics, stretching, swimming, and jogging.

At the end of one year, these were the results expressed in terms of group averages: blood pressure improved by 6 percent; body fat decreased by 4.8 percent; oxygen consumption increased by 9.2 percent;

arm strength increased by 7.2 percent; and nervous tension reduced by 14 percent.

It would be an invitation to disaster for older people—and, for that matter, for younger people—to rush pell-mell into vigorous activity after long years of sedentary living without having a thorough physical checkup first and without undertaking activity on a gradual, progressive basis under medical supervision. But there is growing support now for the concept that proper physical activity can help the aged and can even delay the aging process, prolonging the active years, retarding and possibly helping to avoid some degenerative diseases.

DO YOU NEED EXERCISE?

The chances are that, like most of us, you are getting too little daily exercise. If you need specific clues to the fact that you can benefit from more activity, here are some: heart pounding or hard breathing after relatively slight exertion; a long time required for your heartbeat to return to normal after heavy exertion (you can measure the heart rate by the wrist pulse); stiffening of legs and thighs after climbing stairs; aching muscles after such activities as gardening or furniture moving; waking up from sleep as tired as before; frequent restlessness.

Your physician, as part of his preventive medicine program for you, will be glad to determine with you, on the basis of your specific present condition, daily activities, and other personal factors, whether you need more exercise, how much time you need to devote to it, what kinds of activities would be best suited for you.

OPPORTUNITIES FOR ACTIVITY

Undoubtedly you will benefit from a soundly planned regular exercise schedule, even if it occupies no more than just a few minutes a day—and more on this shortly. Along with such a schedule, you can, and should, find other opportunities for increasing your activity. For one thing, it is possible to find opportunities for physical recreation that can supplement scheduled exercises and provide enjoyment. The list is almost endless: fishing trips, family outings, evenings of dancing, bowling in an office or neighborhood league, walking, etc. For another thing, there are opportunities for stepping up daily activities—and little bits of action add up in their good effects.

It's a matter of attitude, of recognizing that it is good to use the body as much as possible and of seeking chances to do so. Walk up a flight or more of stairs instead of relying entirely upon the elevator; walk part or much or sometimes all the way to the market, to the office. Interrupt sedentary work with little bursts of activity, even if no more than getting up out of the chair and bending, stretching, moving about, flexing the arms, squatting, imitating a few golf swings.

EXERCISE TIME

Exercise should become part of your daily routine. That means setting aside 30 minutes to an hour a day about five times a week. The daily activity period, or periods, should be considered as being as essential a part of your life as eating, sleeping, bathing, and dressing. Pick a time, or times, most suitable for you. If it is convenient for you to carry out much or all of your activity in one period each day, fine; divided periods of activity can also serve the purpose. Some people, early starters, like to exercise before breakfast. For others, this is impossible. Many men find it convenient to exercise late in the afternoon or before lunch. Never perform any exercise sooner than one hour after a meal.

GADGETS

Keep equipment to a minimum. It's a good idea to avoid complicated apparatus and overreliance on weights, pulleys, and other devices.

BASIC PRINCIPLES

Whatever program of activity you propose to engage in, check with your physician to be certain it is suitable for you. And your physician may have valuable suggestions for activities particularly suited to you.

Start slowly. Rush in without preparation and lift 200 pounds over your head—or even try to—and it may be your last act on earth. Take on a routine of mild setting-up exercises and you may feel a bit better, but this is far short of what you can get out of well-planned activity.

What is needed is a program that follows certain key principles.

Tolerance is one. There should be no sudden demand on your body for a burst of tremendous effort. Excessive straining beyond the level your body is ready for accomplishes nothing and may produce injury.

Overload is another. Easy workouts continued endlessly day after day have value—but it is limited value. You have to push yourself just a bit. Start easily, then gradually begin to work a little harder, working just slightly beyond the first feeling of tiredness, but still within your limits of tolerance. Your body has more capacity than it is called upon to use. Give it a bit more load than usual and it can handle it. Progressively, it will become able to handle more.

Progression is another important principle. As you maintain a regular schedule of exercise and your strength and endurance grow, your activities will become easier for you. Continue them at the same level and you will maintain the improvement. To go beyond, you can make the workouts progressively more strenuous, if your physician indicates this is desirable, until you arrive at a level of fitness you want to achieve.

A BALANCED PROGRAM

Your exercise program should be balanced, just as diet should be balanced. You need one or more activities to exercise the heart and lungs and to build endurance. Brisk walking, jogging, and swimming relatively long distances are good for this. Other parts of the program should be aimed at improving strength, agility, flexibility, and muscle tone. Suggestions for a home exercise program to achieve these objectives can be found in such publications as these:

Adult Physical Fitness. President's Council on Physical Fitness. Washington, D.C., Supt. of Documents, U.S. Government Printing Office.
Physical Fitness. Department of Health Education, American Medical Association, 535 N. Dearborn, Chicago, Ill.
Seven Paths to Fitness. Department of Health Education, American Medical Association, 535 N. Dearborn, Chicago, Ill.

Most people understand how specific exercises for various muscles and parts of the body can develop strength. These are certainly worthwhile. For some reason, one particular area of relative neglect is the abdominal muscle area. Another is the muscles of the back. Both are important in terms of good posture; both are important, too, as aids in avoiding sagging waistlines and backaches. We give exercises for these in this chapter along with another exercise for the muscles of the buttocks; and the four exercises, in addition to their general value, are helpful in restoring muscle tone in these areas in people who are slimming down.

But we think it important to go on at once to emphasize here the activities that exercise the heart and lungs and build endurance. When you are at rest, all the muscles in your body use only about one thirtieth of the oxygen they can use during maximum effort. The more oxygen they use, the more the heart will respond, pumping harder to get more oxygen-carrying blood into circulation. Over a period of time, as a result of this, heart pumping efficiency will increase. The heart will become able to pump much more blood with each stroke. At the same time, lung capacity, much of it never used in sedentary living, will increase to absorb and feed more oxygen into the bloodstream. The higher oxygen content of the blood will aid muscle nutrition.

As circulation improves in both quality and quantity throughout the body, the total effect is admirable: Muscles are strengthened; so is the whole supporting system. It appears, too, that there may be a double effect on the heart itself: It becomes more efficient in its pumping not only during activity but at other times as well, thus reducing the strain on it at all times; in addition, it appears that activity which builds endurance also stimulates the development of new and extra blood vessel pathways to feed the heart muscle. Thus, if there should be trouble in the future, if a coronary artery should become choked by atherosclerosis and a heart attack occurs, that attack is likely to be less severe because of the extra circulation available. Because of the extra circulation, much less damage to the heart muscle is likely to occur, and chances of survival are greatly increased.

The best activities for exercising the heart and lungs and for building endurance are those that are continuous in nature—brisk walking, jogging, swimming, for example.

The effectiveness of walking is not fully appreciated by most people. It brings many muscles into play. It is a continuous activity. It lends itself to putting a healthy progressive load on the body. Start with a relatively easy mile walk. Gradually lengthen the walk and increase the pace. Keep doing this until, for example, you are up to a three-mile walk as fast as you can get your legs to carry you, and you are getting great benefits every step of the way.

Jogging, too, has its merits, as a simple and practical aid in developing both muscular strength and endurance. It is inexpensive, requires no special skill, can be done outdoors and, in inclement weather, indoors. Start with a jog that is only a little faster than a brisk walk. Jog until you begin to puff. Then walk. Then jog again. Your body should be upright, not bent forward. Keep the buttocks in, not protruding; the back straight, not arched; bend the elbows; breathe through nose and mouth.

The objective is to start at a comfortable level and gradually exert yourself more and more. At first, you may jog for 50 yards, walk for 50 yards, keep alternating, and cover about a mile. As you keep working out, you will find you can increase the distance, jog more and walk less, jog faster, even perhaps interspersing some sprints, running as fast as you can for 50 yards, then dropping back to a jog or walk. Over a period of months, you may progress until you can cover as much as three miles at a good pace, walking very little of the time. Be sure you obtain your doctor's approval before you start jogging as an exercise.

ISOMETRICS VERSUS ISOTONICS

For some years, the virtues of *isometrics* have been trumpeted, often in advertising which promises an isometric system that "will put you in top shape in a minute a day—and no sweat."

Isometrics involve muscular contractions without movement. The system is based on the principle that when a muscle is required to work beyond its usual intensity, it will grow. In isometrics, one set of muscles may be pitted against another or against an immovable object such as a doorway or floor. Put your palms together and push your hands against each other as hard as you can, without moving either hand. Or push against a closed door which does not move. These are isometrics.

On the other hand, *isotonics* involve movement. Running, lifting, push-ups, sit-ups, virtually all sports are isotonic.

Isometric exercises can be useful—for example, in correcting specific deficiencies such as building arm muscles or putting back into condition a leg that has been in a cast. They may be useful, too, as a supplement to isotonics for further development of specific major muscles and muscle areas.

But it is important to realize that your objective in exercising is not simply to build muscular strength. Strength is the ability to work against a resistance. Additionally, you need muscular endurance, the ability of a muscle to respond repetitively for a relatively long period of time; flexibility or muscular elasticity so you can use the muscle effectively throughout its whole range of motion; and cardiovascular-pulmonary efficiency—the adaptive response of heart, blood vessels; and lungs to work and exercise.

Isometrics can help develop strength. But for the other needs, you have to get down on the floor and do push-ups and sit-ups and other isotonic exercise; you have to walk and jog or swim; you have to work the muscles through their whole range and work them repeatedly; and you have to sweat at the job and give the heart and blood vessels and lungs a workout. There is no shortcut.

WARMING UP AND COOLING OFF

Any time you are going to work out hard—when you have reached the stage where that is advisable as well as appealing to you—it is important to warm up gradually first. Light warm-up—easy stretching, bending, twisting, slow running in place—limbers up the muscles, prepares the heart and lung for exertion, and tunes up the nervous system.

There is some controversy among athletic coaches as to whether warming up ever actually improves athletic performance, but there is evidence that it is valuable as a safety measure, a means of reducing risk of injury.

As important as warming up at the beginning of a hard workout is tapering off properly afterward. During active exercising, the heart pumps blood out faster to keep the muscles supplied. And the muscles, as they contract, produce a kind of pumping action on the veins that helps return blood to the heart and lungs.

If you stop exercising suddenly, the heart will continue for a while to pump extra blood but the muscles, especially those in the legs, no longer active, no longer squeeze on the veins. As a result, some pooling of blood may occur in the muscles, causing a temporary shortage elsewhere in the body, making you feel faint. Also, it appears that cramps and stiffness are less likely to develop if you taper off.

To taper off, just keep moving about, in relaxed fashion. Instead of sitting down, walk about, lazily bend and stretch. A few minutes of this will suffice.

Do not rush into a hot tub or shower immediately after a workout or even after tapering off. Give yourself another 5 to 10 minutes to cool off. You need this time to radiate some of the heat you have worked up. If you jump right into a tub or shower, your body temperature will be above normal and the hot water will impede heat dissipation, so you will come out of the bath still sweating.

EXERCISES FOR ABDOMEN, BACK, AND BUTTOCKS

Exercise 1 for muscles of lower abdomen: Lying flat on the floor, exhale, then raise one leg slowly without bending; hold it up at about a 45-degree angle while counting to 10 (about 10 seconds); lower it slowly; inhale. Repeat with the other leg. To strengthen the muscles without straining them, begin by repeating the exercise 2 or 3 times, and increase gradually until you can repeat about 20 times without straining. *Note:* Exhaling helps to protect the diaphragm from the pressure generated by some exercises.

Exercise 2 for muscles of upper abdomen: Lying flat on the floor, exhale; with arms folded over chest, raise head and shoulders slowly, keeping legs on the floor; hold for about 10 seconds; relax and inhale. Repeat 2 or 3 times. As muscles grow stronger, increase gradually to about 20 times.

Exercise 3 for muscles of buttocks: While lying flat, tighten the buttocks as much as possible; hold for about 10 seconds before relaxing. Repeat 2 or 3 times and increase gradually to about 20 times.

Exercise 4 for muscles of back: Lying on your stomach, keep arms at sides and legs on the floor, and slowly raise chest and shoulders. Hold for about 10 seconds. Lower slowly. Increase gradually from 2 or 3 times to about 20 times.

9

SLEEP

SLEEP IS fundamental to good health and yet, it would appear, many of us need a refresher course in sleeping. According to recent surveys, about half of all men and women in the United States have trouble sleeping at night, and about one fourth of the population use some form of sleeping medicine.

Before considering how sound, healthy sleep may best be encouraged, let's get some basic understanding of this long-mysterious process which has come in for scientific exploration only in recent years. How much sleep do you need? Have you ever really tested yourself over a period of time? What is the nature of sleep? Are sleeping patterns inborn or acquired habits? What happens in sleep?

THE SLEEP PROCESS

As you have discovered when you do not get adequate sleep, sleep is necessary for both physical and psychological well-being. Even now, however, scientists are unable to explain why about one third of our lives must be spent in sleep and why in our sleep we dream.

In trying to get sound insights into the mysteries of sleep, investigators in many sleep laboratories use volunteers to whose scalp they tape electrodes to detect tiny currents in the brain. Amplified many hundreds of thousands of times, the impulses are registered on graph paper as an electroencephalogram (EEG). In addition, equipment records pulse, eye movements, breathing, body movements, and muscle tensions while the subjects sleep.

Sleep, it is now known, is not a state of oblivion, of complete unconsciousness. Rather, it is a progression of rhythmic cycles.

With their equipment, scientists have been able to establish that sleep is an acquired habit; that a newborn baby alternates between sleep and wakefulness at about hourly intervals; that gradually, as the child grows older, the cycles stretch out until eventually they become 90-minute cycles in adulthood. These 90-minute cycles are beyond conscious control.

It used to be thought that we fall into deeper and deeper sleep during the night until we arrive at a turning point, and then sleep lightens progressively until we wake up. But it is now clear that this is not so. Instead, throughout the night, we shift from one gradation of sleep to another and are even awake several times during the night without necessarily remembering the wakefulness.

Based upon distinct changes in the EEG and upon another phenomenon—the appearance of rapid eye movements (REM) at some points —sleep investigators divide sleep into a series of stages:

In stage 1, light sleep begins. There are slow EEG waves, 4 to 6 cycles a second. In stage 2, medium deep sleep, slower waves appear and voltage increases. In stage 3, deeper sleep, voltage increases still more. And in stage 4, deepest sleep, very large slow waves of high voltage appear on the EEG.

But when deepest sleep is reached, it is not maintained long. Instead, there is a return to stage 1 sleep. And with the return to stage 1, REM or rapid eye movements appear. And the progression through the various stages occurs about every 90 minutes.

Thus, however much you may think so upon full awakening in the morning, you never sleep through a night "like a log." In fact, many changes take place. There are muscle movements at various stages of sleep, less often during stage 1, quite often during moving from one stage to another. Actually, in stage 1, the heart beats faster, breathing quickens, muscles tend to relax, as if, some investigators suggest, you were settling down to dream much as you would settle down in your seat before the curtain goes up in the theater.

It is in stage 1, with the appearance of REM, that you dream. And you dream whether you remember the dreaming or not. Investigators, after many thousands of studies, know enough to realize that, for whatever reason dreams are needed, all people dream just as all people sleep, and the dreams are not haphazard but appear at regular times in the sleeping cycle. The need for dreaming has been demonstrated by investigators who have awakened subjects from sleep every time REM began, depriving them of their dreaming periods, allowing them to sleep at other times. The result: impaired functioning, both physical and psychological.

The EEG has established that some of the older ideas of sleep, such as the popular notion that sleep is always deepest and soundest at the beginning of the night and lightest in the morning near awakening time, are false.

From work in the sleep laboratory, you can reconstruct what happens to you during a night's sleep in this fashion: As you relax and close your eyes, your pulse is steady and even, your body temperature gradually begins to fall, and your brain waves show an even frequency of about 9 to 13 per second, called alpha rhythm. You are awake but relaxed, ready to move into sleep. It is quite normal now for a sudden body spasm to occur, perhaps awakening you for a fraction of a second. And then you move into stage 1 sleep; voltage from your brain is small, changing rapidly; pulse is slowing, muscles relax.

You enter stage 2 sleep as brain waves rapidly grow larger. If at this point you were to be awakened, you might well believe you had not been asleep at all, though you have been for about 10 minutes.

In about half an hour, you are in stage 3 sleep. Brain wave voltage is higher, the waves slower. You are breathing evenly, muscles relaxed, with temperature and blood pressure still falling. It would take a loud noise now to wake you.

Soon you move into stage 4 sleep, with large slow brain waves. This is the very deep sleep that most people may think of as real sleep, but it is only a small fraction of the total. After about 20 minutes of stage 4 sleep, you start to move upward into lighter sleep.

Now you may turn in bed or make some other movement; you are almost at the consciousness level. But instead of waking, your eyes move under closed lids, much as if you were watching a movie. Your heartbeat is now irregular and your blood pressure fluctuates. You are dreaming and if awakened at this point you can describe the dream in detail—but if you are not awakened then, you may or may not remember the dream in the morning. After about 10 minutes of REM or dream sleep, the cycle starts again.

This, then, is the sleep process.

There are still many unknowns. For example, there is no clear answer to the natural question: which sleep is better, deep or light? Nature apparently considers both necessary and oscillates between them.

Also, there has long been a theory that sleep is needed in order to allow the body to get rid of "fatigue toxins." The idea is that during an active day, with constant contraction of muscles, certain chemicals are produced which are disposed of as waste. But during activity the disposal rate is not sufficient to prevent some buildup of the materials and fatigue results. It has been thought, therefore, that as this fatigue linked to undisposed wastes builds up, sleep results. Yet, if this were the case, the "toxins" should disappear during the night and we should leap out of bed in a state of exuberance in the morning. But this rarely happens.

In any case, with or without adequate explanations of why, we do know that adequate sleep is necessary. Without it, not only do we feel physically fatigued; we also feel emotionally drained. Studies at the

Walter Reed Army Institute of Research in Washington have demonstrated that the longest a person can go without sleep is about 240 hours, or 10 days. And volunteers who went through the experience found it much like torture. Even after 65 hours of sleeplessness, one volunteer was discovered in a washroom, frantically trying to wash "cobwebs" from his face, believing he was covered with them. Sleep is needed for emotional stability as well as physical refreshment.

HOW MUCH SLEEP?

Sleep is essential, but the amount required varies. The usual sleeping time for the adult is eight hours, but some people need less, some need more. Everyone has heard the story of Thomas A. Edison sleeping only two hours a night—and the romantic picture of Edison working on through the night to invent the electric light bulb suggests that any of us, strongwilled enough, could cut down on sleep and have more time to become famous and rich. The fact is that Edison, though protesting that sleep was a loss of time and opportunity, was concerned about getting his own quota of sleep, according to his own diaries. He napped often, and frequently drifted back to sleep for another hour or so after waking in the morning.

Some physicians are firmly convinced that if shortchanging yourself on sleep does not catch up with you quickly, it will eventually, and there will come the day when you suddenly appear to lose your energy, become prone to ailments, and suffer a general deterioration of health.

There is no simple answer to the question of how much sleep is best. The essential test is whether you feel rested in the morning and have enough energy to carry on the day's activities. Eight hours, as we have noted, is an average figure. If you do very heavy physical work or extremely exacting mental work, you may need more. Children need more sleep than adults since they are growing fast and are very active. Old people often have been thought to need less sleep; this is not necessarily true. They may need more, depending upon their activity and health.

It could be a most worthwhile exercise to make your own investigation into your sleep needs, on the simple basis of experimenting to determine how much sleep makes you feel good, how much less makes you feel out of sorts, irritable, fatigued.

MYTHS

Many myths and misconceptions have grown up about sleep, and it would be impossible to cover them all here. But it does seem to us to be important to discuss a few, still widely prevalent ones. Among them is the idea that an hour of sleep before midnight is worth two hours after midnight. The fact is that when you sleep is less important than that you do sleep. Some people prefer to work late and get up late; others prefer to get up early in the morning and go to sleep early at night. Sir William Osler labeled the former "owls" and the latter "larks." It doesn't matter which you are except that if you know which you are and can arrange your life and work around the fact, you probably will be more effective and happier. When sleep takes place is not important; the proper amount of good sleep is what counts.

Another misconception: five or six hours, even just three or four, of sound sleep are worth more than eight hours of restless sleep. The fact is that while sound sleep is desirable, so is enough sleep.

A third myth: sleep, to be good, must be consecutive; you need to get your seven or eight or nine hours at one time. Actually, there is no inviolate rule. If you feel well after sleeping three, four, or five hours and taking naps during the day, as Edison did, this is satisfactory for you though it may not be for someone else.

INSOMNIA

There is certainly no question about many people having problems with sleep. They can be very real problems but it is worth looking at some new insights sleep research provides on imaginary insomnia.

Everyone has heard of arguments between husband and wife, one complaining that the night was sleepless, the other that the spouse slept soundly and snored so much that the other was kept awake.

In one experiment in a sleep laboratory, investigators worked with people who claimed they could not sleep at all. As part of the study, each insomniac was required to press a bedside button whenever during the night he heard a buzzer. More often than not, when the buzzer was sounded, there was no response. And yet in the morning, the self-convinced insomniacs greeted investigators with their usual protest of never having slept a wink.

That people who honestly believe they get no sleep at all do, indeed, sleep has been demonstrated repeatedly in laboratories. A confusion between sleep and waking may arise because some people consistently overestimate the time it takes them to fall asleep. They may do so because it is possible to fail to distinguish between dreams and waking thought, and because light sleep and waking may become intermixed in the mind, leaving an impression of a long stretch of sleeplessness.

It should be emphasized that imaginary insomnia is not a laughing matter. Even if the insomnia is only imaginary, sleep that is not refreshing is a problem. But realizing that some sleep does occur even on seemingly sleepless nights is reassuring in the sense that it can eliminate any worries about the possible harmful effects of total sleeplessness.

Realizing this has another value. The causes of sleeping problems are many, ranging from hunger and pain to excessive worry over business or other problems. Tensions can interfere with sleep—and there are many possible tensions. But one that bothers many people is the tension associated with the conviction that sleep is not just difficult but impossible. However bad an insomniac you may seem to be, you can be virtually certain that you are getting far more sleep than you honestly think you are getting.

Aware of the cycles of sleep, of how much dreaming you do, of how you move from dream state to other stages of sleep, you can understand and take some comfort in the knowledge that your honest conviction that you do not sleep as much as you should may be founded on the fact that you often confuse dreaming and waking states.

None of this, of course, means that you do not have a sleeping problem and that you may not benefit from a "refresher course" in sleeping.

FOR BETTER SLEEP

If you have trouble with insomnia, if you are not sleeping now so that you feel refreshed in the morning, there are many things you can do to overcome the problem.

One of the most important is to start by changing your attitude if it is now a fretful, worrisome one. It is now possible for you to draw reassurance from many scientific studies that you undoubtedly sleep much more than you honestly think you do, that you are not in any acute danger of suffering a mental or physical breakdown for lack of sleep. You need not be afraid of staying awake. Some people have sleeping difficulties largely because they do worry nightly about their ability to fall asleep.

If you have any leeway, if your work allows you some choice of sleeping hours—a choice between going to bed a bit earlier and getting up earlier, or going to bed later and getting up later—and if you haven't ever experimented, or haven't done so for years, it may be helpful to experiment now, trying various times for going to bed and getting up.

Sleep in a dark room, of course, and one as quiet as possible. If you live in a noisy neighborhood and find the noise bothersome, you might try overcoming the nuisance noise with "white" noise—the steady hum from an air conditioner or window fan, for example, which many people find soothing.

Is your bed really comfortable? The American double bed is ordinarily not equal to two single beds; it is smaller. If you are a fairly large individual and prefer a double bed, a king-sized bed may be in order.

Keep the room comfortable—for you. Some people sleep best in a cool environment; for them, snuggling down under a mountain of covers is a comfortable, relaxing experience. If you are one of them, by all means keep your room cool; if you wish a window open, open it without worry. If you're at the other extreme, there is nothing wrong with a warmish room if it makes for better sleeping for you.

Make every effort to relax mentally before retiring. That could well mean making it a rule to stop brain work at least an hour before going to bed.

Similarly, make every effort to relax your body physically. A leisurely walk outdoors or some other moderate exercise may do the trick. Sometimes a tepid bath before bedtime is a help.

Should you have a snack or drink before bedtime? You might try and see if it works for you. It does for many people. For some, warm milk is effective; for others, a glass of beer or wine helps bring relaxation; and for others, small portions of high-protein foods work.

As part of a mental slowdown process to prepare yourself for sleep, avoid TV just before retiring; it tends to be stimulating for most people. Reading is usually better. And certainly if you find that some activities —chess, bridge, or anything else—tend to key you up, it would be wise to avoid them for a time until you have a chance to reestablish good sleeping patterns.

When you get into bed, relax physically. Try to let your muscles "go," to go limp, to feel yourself sinking into the mattress.

Relax mentally. It usually is not possible to let your mind go completely blank, but you can try to find something relaxing to think about. Sheep counting, time-honored though it is, does not work for many people. Find something you enjoy imagining—perhaps it is sitting in a boat with a fishing rod, watching the water, waiting for a bite.

Leave your worries outside the bedroom. This may seem difficult to achieve. But there is a bit of basic philosophy which the poet Robert Frost wrote about and which all of us could use, a philosophy that is perhaps most opportune in preparing for bed:

"I've been licked. We all have. I've been thoroughly licked when I didn't think I could be. It was a terrible blow sometimes. But still, most of life is like that. . . . Anybody with an active mind lives on *tentatives* rather than on tenets. You've got to feel a certain pleasure in the *tentativeness* of it all, the unfinality of it. . . . Every general who goes into battle wishes he had more information before he goes in. But each crisis you go into is on insufficient information." Of course, you have problems; but you won't solve them by stewing over them in bed.

If you vow to keep problems out of the bedroom and they still intrude, try amusing reading. If that doesn't help, pick something you feel you have a duty, but no great desire, to read and go at it for a few minutes; the boredom may help. Have a pad and pencil handy, and if you get ideas you think are important, jot them down so you can forget them for the night.

Don't try to force yourself to sleep. Don't approach the bed with grim determination. Remember that lying quietly in bed for several hours, even if sleep does not come, is restful; and very often sleep will come. If you don't get to sleep and lying quietly disturbs you, begin again by reading for a while or listening to soothing music.

ABOUT MEDICINES

If your insomnia fails to yield to any of these measures, by all means see your physician. He can help. He can do so by determining whether any physical problem may be causing the trouble; if so, he can correct it. He may prescribe some medication to relieve a minor discomfort which is keeping you awake. Or, if necessary, he may prescribe medication designed to help you reestablish sound sleeping habits. If he does prescribe such medication, follow his instructions carefully.

Taken indiscriminately for extended periods, sleeping pills can be dangerous—in many ways. Habitual use can lead to the development of tolerance, which means that larger doses will be required. There may be side effects—hangover reactions next day, skin rashes, other undesirable reactions.

Many pills that put you to sleep do not provide normal sleep. They may cause trouble, with extended use, because they actually inhibit the REM stage of sleep during which dreaming occurs. Laboratory studies have established that people kept from dreaming tend to become irritable, anxious, and hostile. People who take pills that interfere with dreaming though they promote sleep may find that they have horrible nightmares when they try to stop taking the medication, a reaction that may cause them to return to habitual use.

Barbiturates in particular, when taken indiscriminately over long periods, have a serious potential for physical as well as psychological addiction. Some experts report that barbiturate addiction can be more difficult to cure than narcotic addiction. If the drug is stopped suddenly, the user may experience such symptoms of withdrawal as cramps, nausea, headache, delirium, convulsions, and in some cases sudden death. Withdrawal has to be medically supervised, usually in a hospital, over a period of several weeks, and it may take several months for the body to return to normal.

Barbiturates, when used in precise fashion, under medical supervision for a limited period, can be valuable. There are other sleeping medications, nonbarbiturates, which the physician can prescribe, ranging from an old and effective standby, chloral hydrate, to newer agents such as Quaalude.

Other medicines are sometimes used. Tranquilizers, or relaxing drugs, help some people over a crisis. Relatively safe when taken in small doses, they can also be addictive and otherwise dangerous when misused.

Antihistamines are ingredients in some products which are available without prescription as sleep inducers. Antihistamines, often used for allergies and relief of some cold symptoms, have drowsiness as a side effect. These compounds should not be used as sleeping pills on a regular basis unless a doctor so recommends.

Also available without prescription are compounds containing such ingredients as scopolamine and bromides. Scopolamine and bromides can be toxic and may be particularly hazardous for people with certain health problems.

It comes down to this: A sleeping medication, when properly prescribed and used, can be helpful—when it is really needed because of sudden shock, grief, or other crisis. Occasional use does no harm; occasional interruption of the dream stage of sleep is not more harmful than loss of a night's sleep now and then.

Trouble develops when the individual begins to use such medication regularly in an effort to solve sleep problems. Then the medication covers up the problems, prevents solving them, and may introduce new and even more serious problems.

If you have chronic sleeping difficulty and if the measures suggested in this chapter, after being given a fair trial, do not help adequately, see your physician. Your problem, however serious it may seem, is not a hopeless one; it deserves, and is most likely to be solved by, expert treatment.

10

RELAXATION

FATIGUE, ESPECIALLY when it becomes chronic, can be a major factor in hastening the onset, and may even be a major cause, of many illnesses, both organic and emotional. And while sleep, obviously enough, is essential for overcoming fatigue, hardly any less so is relaxation.

Fortunate people who have learned the art of relaxation almost never are candidates for a long list of diseases. They have a vital measure of protection against such health problems as migraine headaches, irritable bowel, heartburn, colitis, and possibly even pulmonary tuberculosis, ulcerative colitis, and other serious organic maladies which are rarely observed in the completely relaxed.

It is difficult to imagine a relaxed person becoming a candidate for a "nervous breakdown." He or she tends to be free of neurotic fatigue and to be capable of consistently good work output. We would make the guess, too, that the relaxed individual has less probability of developing malignant emotional disorders such as manic-depressive states and schizophrenia.

Rest and relaxation also are of major importance in secondary prevention—in keeping already-present disease from advancing. They are far more important than generally realized. For example, consider rheumatoid arthritis, which affects millions of Americans. Few specialists in the disease would be happy if in treating patients with active arthritis they had to rely only on presently available medicines. They know, however, that when they have relaxed patients, or when they can convince their patients of the need for rest and relaxation, they have a far greater chance of arresting, or at least retarding, the progress of this potentially crippling disease. A woman we know has arthritis, and although the crippling element in her disease has been arrested by medical treatment, she still experiences pain and stiffness in several important joints. As part of her overall treatment, she follows this schedule: ten hours' sleep, and rest in bed in the morning when her pain and stiffness are most troublesome; breakfast in bed whenever feasible; then four hours of activity followed by one or two hours of bed rest during which, if she cannot sleep, she reads or does light work such as correspondence or her bookkeeping. Of course, this schedule is varied when she has guests or goes out for an evening. But then she makes up for the lost rest time the following day. Her doctor is convinced that this schedule of rest and relaxation not only helps to make her more comfortable but also is contributing materially to preventing severe damage and possible crippling of her joints.

At one time, before powerful modern medicines became available, rest and relaxation in sanatoriums or at home were all that doctors could offer pulmonary tuberculosis patients. And patients often finished their year or two of rest and relaxation with either cure or arrest of their lung disease.

Many physicians urge patients with angina pectoris, the chest pain associated with coronary artery disease, to rest and relax for 30 to 45 minutes after any sizable meal. Such patients—perhaps because more blood goes to the intestinal tract to aid digestion—often are more sensitive to chest pain after meals. At other times, they may be encouraged to walk for miles or to jog and run.

People who have experienced heart attacks have a much better outlook if they can learn the art of relaxation and achieve comfortable, easeful rest periods several times a day. In addition to the physical rest that takes a strain off the heart, emotional relaxation is important. The nonrelaxed, excitable person is pouring adrenalin into his bloodstream, speeding up the heart, raising blood pressure, and thus doing the already-injured heart a disservice.

Similarly, people with diabetes get better regulation of blood sugar when they are relaxed because adrenalin causes big jumps in blood sugar and depletes stores in the liver. Also, since diabetics are more prone to heart disease than others, relaxation is valuable for them because of its protective effect on the heart.

That applies no less to people with high blood pressure. Nervous tension can lead to an outpouring of adrenalin which further increases blood pressure. Peptic ulcer is another problem for which relaxation is of great value, for emotional tension increases the output of stomach acid, the chief enemy of the patient with an ulcer.

THE MANY VALUES OF RELAXATION

"If more of us were concerned with the art of living than with the quest for longevity," one distinguished physician remarked recently, "we'd live more happily and productively, and perhaps longer, too."

Many things enter into the art of living, and relaxation is certainly one of them. It is valuable not only in and of itself for the enjoyment of life but also as a means of preventing undue physical fatigue, boredom, and tension, and for actually making work easier and more enjoyable.

Ours is an age of rapid change, of increasing complexity in social and industrial organization. We are more and more busy with mental and less with physical work. We live at a faster pace. There are more and more challenges and opportunities—and perhaps, more and more stresses, pressures and, deadlines.

How people react to stress depends, of course, upon very many things, and certainly included among them are general health, physical fitness, fatigue, and emotional well-being. And relaxation is an important influence on all of these.

Almost everyone knows from experience that pronounced tiredness from day to day can, if extended, produce chronic fatigue. When this occurs, the weariness sensations are intensified, appearing not only at the end of a day but during the day and even early in the morning. Along with the weariness, there may be increased irritability, a tendency to lapse into depression or blue moods, a general lack of drive and loss of initiative.

Many people have the idea that they can't afford to take time for rest and relaxation, that in the modern world it's essential to work long and hard or you won't keep up. But this is to overlook, for one thing, the relationship between performance and working hours.

While more studies are needed of the relationship between mental work performance and working hours, there are guidelines to be found in the many investigations carried out in factories. They have shown repeatedly that when working time is shortened, hourly performance improves, whereas lengthening the work period has the opposite effect. In many cases it has been observed that after more than ten hours of work, overall performance falls off decidedly, because the slowing down of working speed due to fatigue is not compensated for by the longer period worked.

Longer working schedules are frequent in wartime and boom conditions. But the overtime worked often proves of little value because productivity fails to increase to the extent that was expected. Various studies have shown that overtime work not only cuts down on performance per hour but also leads to a characteristic increase in absence due to illness and accidents.

A better understanding of the importance of rest and relaxation has been made possible by advances in neurophysiology providing new insights into what happens in the central nervous system. Investigators have been able to establish—by actually picking out the structures in animals and stimulating them with electric currents—that there are certain brain structures which have a damping or inhibitory effect and are involved in fatigue, and there are other structures which make up an activating system.

If we sum up the vast amount of neurophysiological research, we arrive at this picture: An individual's mood—his ability to perform—at any given time depends on the degree of activity of the two systems. If the inhibitory system dominates, the individual is in a state of fatigue; if the activating system dominates, he is ready to step up performance.

This concept of fatigue helps to explain many symptoms otherwise difficult to understand. All of us know, for example, that a feeling of tiredness can often disappear immediately if something unexpected happens or if a piece of intelligence or train of thought produces an emotional change. In such cases, the activating system is being stimulated. But if the surroundings are monotonous, if we are bored by what we are doing, the pitch of the activating system is lowered and the inhibitory system is in the ascendancy. And it is this that explains the fatigue that can occur in monotonous situations even when there is no stress.

Monotony, by definition, is a wearisome sameness, a lack of change and variety. And whatever the work we do, it can be considered monotonous work if it goes on without pause or change of pace all through the day.

We all are aware of the need for a good night's sleep, but too few of us recognize the need for rest and relaxation during the day. Many of us —businessmen, professional people, and others—who not only work hard but are under heavy stress could live more comfortably without sacrificing efficiency—indeed, with increased efficiency—and probably live longer if we managed to take breaks during the day and take them without guilty consciences.

HOW TO ACHIEVE RELAXATION

Someone has remarked that the doctor who tells a tense, nervous, high-strung person to relax might just as well tell him to stop breathing. But the art of relaxation can be learned. If the guidelines we give you here do not work, then some form of treatment is required. It may consist of a few talks with your sympathetic physician or, in extreme cases of compulsive inability to relax, may require psychotherapy.

Any medical advice must take account of individual differences. No two people react precisely the same way to a prescription for digitalis or other medicine. Similarly, there is a tremendous difference in the way people relax, in what makes them relax, in how much relaxation they need, in how much of a toll work takes from them.

We know two surgeons who work the same long hours from 8:00 A.M.

to 7:00 P.M. with some night calls. Yet one ends the week rested, happy, and ready to enjoy a fun weekend; the other ends the week a bundle of nerves, with a body so tired that it takes until Monday morning before he has recovered his stamina for the week ahead. We know two business partners, one of whom returns from a month's vacation perfectly rested while the other returns from his vacation more fatigued than when he left.

To achieve suitable relaxation, each person must take an inventory of need. One chronically fatigued person we know did so and learned that his really effective work span—the time he could work at peak efficiency and without fatigue—was only four hours. He rescheduled his life, put a couch in his office, and with an hour's rest every four hours has increased his work output and become thoroughly relaxed.

Consciously or unconsciously, a relaxed person has carried out an inventory and knows when rest and change of pace are needed during his daily work. Some men like to spend part of their lunch hour at a gym or athletic club, taking a swim or engaging in other physical activity; others prefer a nap or a book; still others thrive on luncheon with friends. There is an almost endless variety to activities that can provide restful, relaxing change of pace during the day. It's the change that is important—and at the end of the day as well. The sedentary worker may benefit from a long walk or some jogging or other physical activity; on the other hand, the person whose work is physically demanding may need a quiet hour, stretched out, perhaps napping briefly, or listening to the radio or watching TV. Some fathers find relaxation with their children; others need to be insulated from the demands of the children—and possibly from any of the wife—when they arrive home.

The housewife, too, is entitled to, and no less needs, change of pace. And it doesn't matter what the change involves, so long as it is restful and relaxing to the individual woman. A break for coffee or tea? Fine. A pause to watch a favorite TV program, call a friend, read a magazine or book—all good if the individual finds them rewarding. No less than the man who works away from home, the woman who works at the demanding job of running a home and caring for children needs to make her inventory of need and find activities that diminish her fatigue and renew her zest.

And for both man and woman, important elements in relaxation are recreational activities, sports, and vacations.

HOBBIES AND OTHER RECREATION

Recreation—refreshment of the strength and spirit after toil—is an extremely broad term. It covers physical activities which can be as vigorous as one likes, on the one hand, and, on the other hand, quiet activities such as reading. It covers solitary activities and group activities. It covers educational and cultural activities which can be considered creative and worthwhile; it also covers activities that some may consider trivial—except that any activity which provides recreation cannot be dismissed as a triviality. It is a common observation among physicians that patients who have developed hobbies and learned to enjoy recreational activities tend to be healthier as well as happier. And there is nothing trivial about that.

Ideally, each individual should have an indoor hobby and an outdoor one, both capable of providing genuine satisfaction. Some people prefer to change hobbies every year or two and even to relate their indoor and outdoor activities—so that, for example, one year archery may be the outdoor hobby and Indian art the indoor diversion, the next year the combination may be sailing and ship models. Others prefer to be casual about choosing and staying with their hobbies.

Hobbies need not be expensive. Some, such as gardening and refinishing old furniture, may, in fact, more than pay for themselves.

In selecting hobbies, look for those you will really enjoy. Don't be like a businessman who, years ago, because his doctor had advised taking up a hobby, began to collect stamps. Dutifully he kept on collecting them though for him it was a bore. It took many years for him to realize that what he really wanted to do was to paint and that he had been mistaken in thinking that painting would be no suitable hobby for a man in his position. Today he belongs, with great enjoyment, to a growing group of amateur "Sunday artists."

Pick your hobby without regard to what others like or dislike, without regard to what may be fashionable or to what may seem to have some kind of "status." It should be something you like and want to do, something interesting, satisfying, relaxing for you.

It is worth noting here that adult education is increasingly popular. It provides for some people opportunity to complete degree requirements. For others, it offers opportunities for learning about hobbies and even for acquiring new knowledge or skill for its own sake, as a hobby in itself. Newspapers and magazines are full of advertisements and notices of adult education courses in colleges and universities. Your local public school board may also offer adult evening courses, ranging from arts and crafts to languages, current events, science, philosophy, and psychology. One of them is almost certain to appeal to you.

SPORTS

Properly chosen, with the advice of your physician as to suitability in terms of your health, sports can be relaxing and at the same time can contribute to your physical well-being.

Too many young people become proficient only in sports that cannot be carried into later life. Football, baseball, basketball, crew, and track may be too strenuous in the middle and later years or require too many participants. A busy adult with job and family responsibilities rarely has time to set up a neighborhood football or baseball game.

But such activities as swimming, golf, tennis, handball, canoeing, hiking, badminton, squash racquets, horseback riding, skating, cycling, bowling, rowing, and swimming can be carried into middle and later life. They can be mentally relaxing, physically stimulating, require only one or two people, lend themselves to weekend relaxation. Married couples can enjoy them together; children can participate in them.

Many of these activities can be taken up at any time of life. Badminton, for example, is popular because it can be played with pleasure by beginner as well as expert, the court is relatively small, the player does not have to cover so much ground, yet the fast action builds wind, strengthens leg and shoulder muscles, and provides a feeling of exhilaration. Canoeing, rowing, and sailing in season provide healthful, relaxing outdoor exercise.

Millions of Americans bowl. Bowling exercises the muscles of arms, shoulders, and back. And although it is not vigorous enough to offer more than mild exercise of heart and lungs, it is suitable for people of all ages and for many for whom other sports may be too vigorous.

Bicycling, before the automobile made it dangerous, was once the most popular recreational activity. It is now becoming increasingly popular again as cycle paths appear. While it exercises the leg muscles principally, it does provide some workout for back and shoulders, and is excellent for building endurance.

Golf, enjoyed by millions, primarily provides walking exercise, with the average golfer covering about six miles on an 18-hole course.

Some five million Americans now play handball. Many modern playgrounds include a cement court with one wall; many gyms have four-wall handball facilities. Handball develops both speed and endurance, while also strengthening leg and shoulder muscles.

Roller skating maintains its popularity. Ice skating has increased in popularity as indoor ice rinks have become more common and made the sport an all-season one. Skating provides exercise similar to, but less vigorous than, running.

Such four-wall court games as squash racquets, squash tennis, racquets, and paddle racquets enjoy popularity because they are fast, emphasize skill, and can be played year-round. They are excellent conditioners for both men and women.

About seven million Americans play some version of tennis on grass, clay, wooden, or composition courts indoors and out. Tennis provides good general conditioning activity if played regularly, and although speed and agility are essential for competitive tennis, the game can be modified and played even by the elderly.

VACATIONS

Vacations are not luxuries; they are necessities. From the viewpoint of big business, the chairman of the board of a major corporation not long ago remarked: "We regard the rest period as a vital component of a year's total work situation, and I constantly remind our people that they are not scoring points with the corporation by refusing to take their vacations."

Physicians have observed that nonvacation-takers often are plagued by poor mental and physical health, family conflict, and inefficient work performance. A consultant in psychiatry and neurology at one of the largest corporations in the country recently reported that "Between 85 and 90 percent of the problems that psychiatrists see at work are the results of off-the-job troubles, and many of these could at least be lessened by more frequent recreation and regular vacations."

For both man and woman, a proper vacation is important for both physical and mental health. And the essence of a proper vacation, at least for most people, is a complete change from the usual routine.

It is possible to stay home and have a vacation—doing things in the garden, the workshop, and the library, going to ball games, golf links, theater, beach. This can save money and avoid some of the frustrations and disappointments sometimes involved in going away. But generally you can have a better and more rewarding time by going away; a complete change of scene and of people usually helps to improve morale.

Should a family vacation together or separately? There is no hard-and-fast rule. If tastes differ markedly, the family that is together all year long may well profit most by taking separate vacations. When tastes are much the same, the joint vacation may be more enjoyable. And there are families who enjoy vacations on the basis of compromise, doing this year what one member enjoys most, next year what another does.

There are no clear-cut guidelines for how long a vacation should last. For some people, a two- to four-week vacation once a year works well. More and more now, there is a trend toward dividing up vacation periods and taking two or more vacations a year. This, too, has its advantages for many people. Still others benefit by arrangements that allow them to enjoy a series of four-day or five-day vacations, taken perhaps four times or more each year.

If it is possible for you to have such flexibility, it could be well worthwhile, after consultation with your physician and your family, to experiment until you discover what vacation arrangements work out best for you.

Before You Go on Vacation

It's a good idea to see your doctor before you go off on an extended vacation—so you won't have to see him after it is over. In fact, just before a vacation can be an especially suitable time for having your regular periodic checkup. For one thing, your doctor can tell you how much and what kind of exercise you should undertake. If he finds you are not in condition to climb mountains or play tennis, you can select a place where you won't be tempted to engage in such activities. You will have more fun perhaps lying on a beach or sitting in a boat pulling in fish.

Deciding where to go on your vacation can be important if you have a health problem such as hay fever, for example. Your doctor can advise about avoiding certain places at certain seasons. If you have a heart or lung problem, he can advise about altitudes and their possible effects.

Tell your physician not only where you plan to go but how you will get there—by train, plane, ship, or car. If you have any tendency to motion sickness, your physician can prescribe medication to help prevent it (see page 626 on motion sickness).

Depending upon where you plan to go and the availability there of medical facilities, your physician may suggest that you take along a first-aid kit. A minimum one, under some conditions, might include the following items, and your physician can provide prescriptions for those that require them:

Aspirin—for headache, fever, muscle aches and pains
Antiseptic—such as hydrogen peroxide, tincture of iodine, or benzalkonium chloride
Skin lotion—to protect against sunburn and windburn
Antinauseant—for motion sickness
Antacid—for mild stomach upset
Sedative—for emotional upset, overstimulation, or nervous upset
Broad-spectrum antibiotic—effective against a wide range of bacteria, in case of serious illness; to be selected by your physician and used precisely as he instructs
Container of small bandages
Sterilized gauze squares
Roll of adhesive tape, one-half inch wide
A pectin-kaolate compound such as Kaopectate, or paregoric, or Lomotil —for diarrhea and "tourist trots"
An ointment for itching bites and sunburn

Rules for Vacationists

Remember that your vacation is not for the purpose of overexertion, for making up for year-round sedentary living, for acquiring a copper skin. It is for "re-creation"—for change of scene and change of pace that can help wipe away ennui and mental fatigue. It is to restore your zest. And you should return from it with zest restored instead of with vacation weariness and even vacation illness.

Don't plunge immediately into a heavy program of physical activity. You can virtually count on immediate collapse if you go from a sea-level city to high altitude, promptly indulge in a few highballs and a set or two of tennis. You are likely to have trouble, in fact, at any altitude if you overdo. Take it easy for the first day or two. Play ball or swim for only an hour or so; work up to increased activity gradually. In this way, you can avoid exhaustion and muscular cramps.

Don't overeat. Chances are you will be tempted to do so when you sit down to a hotel or restaurant dining table lavishly laden with food. Certainly you are paying for it and you may be even more hungry than usual because of all the activity. But you are likely to pay in other ways for overeating. The extra food may put more strain on your heart, which will be pumping fairly hard as you dash around the tennis court later. Never stuff yourself to the point where your stomach feels distended. Avoid, during vacations, those rich foods that give you indigestion at home.

If you are plagued by the unpleasant problem of diarrhea—which may develop because of an overly rich diet, eating strange foods, or drinking contaminated water—change to the softest, blandest foods possible: boiled or poached eggs, custard, rice with milk and sugar. After each movement, drink something hot—soup, tea or milk—to compensate for fluid loss. (See page 108 for medicines to use for diarrhea.)

Sunburn

An attractive skin tan is not anything that can be acquired in a day or two. If you try to tan quickly, you are likely to get a burn that reddens and blisters your skin and may even put you in a hospital. You can prevent painful and ugly sunburn if you are careful about just a few things:

Watch out for the noonday sun. When the sun is high overhead, its rays are short, direct, more burning. Late afternoon is the safer time to start your sunbathing.

Remember that when the sky is overcast, the sun can still burn cruelly, so be careful on hazy as well as bright days.

Know your own type of skin and how it burns. Skins differ. A child's burns more quickly than an adult's. Among adults, people with fair skins are quicker to burn than brunettes. And some people never develop a tan but burn every time they stay out in the sun, and some others merely freckle.

Fifteen minutes, for most people, is long enough for the first sunbath. Each day after that, exposure time can be gradually extended, perhaps by as much as 15 minutes. Time your sunbaths.

Use a suntan preparation. Such a preparation can help guard your skin against burning, but even the best one will not provide complete protection—so watch the clock. If you want to stay in the sun without tanning or freckling, you will need a heavier preparation than the usual commercial ones. Your druggist can make up a cold cream containing 15 to 20 percent zinc oxide, or titanium oxide, or calamine. A heavy cream of this type may be helpful for people with skin troubles that are exacerbated by sunlight, but should be used only on their own physician's recommendation.

Drink plenty of water when suntanning, to make up for fluid you lose. Even though you do not realize it, you can perspire profusely on a dry, sunny day. It's wise to replenish salt, too, by taking salt tablets or salty crackers, or tomato juice with salt added to it.

If you are called upon to help a person badly burned by the sun, don't hesitate about calling a doctor. Extensive, large blisters always need medical attention; there is danger of infection. In mild cases where the skin turns red, use a dusting powder containing equal parts of zinc oxide, boric acid, and talcum. For moderately bad burns, where the skin is red and slightly swollen, apply wet dressings of gauze dipped in a solution of aluminum acetate, 1 part in 500 parts of water. Another soothing dressing is made by soaking gauze in cold white mineral oil. After the swelling goes down, replace the dressings with a soothing cream containing cold cream, 88 parts; methyl salicylate, 10 parts; and benzocaine, 2 parts. Any druggist will make these preparations for you.

Being Wise About the Water

It's essential today to make certain any body of water in which you are going to swim is not polluted. A clear blue lake or silver brook may be contaminated by germs capable of causing typhoid fever or dysentery. A swimming pool may be too crowded or its water changed too infrequently to protect you against many diseases. The local health department will know about the safety of pools and bathing beaches in its territory. Feel free to check with it.

Don't venture into the water immediately after meals or when overheated or tired from other activities. Always come out before you become tired or chilled. A swim should leave you relaxed and comfortable; if it does not, you have stayed in the water too long. Take a shorter swim next time.

On a long swim, have someone row along beside you or go with another good swimmer. And be sure both of you know lifesaving techniques. The most expert swimmer can get a cramp—and if he does, he can drag you down unless you know how to avoid desperate clutches and how to tow him to shore.

No matter how well you swim, stay close to shore if you are swimming in an isolated spot. Any races you may have won in high school or college will not protect you against cramps.

Don't try to swim a long distance the first few times out. Your swimming muscles may have lost strength through inaction; give them time to get strong again before you tackle rapid currents, heavy seas, or long distances.

Before diving in a new place, test the water for depth and hidden logs or rocks. Lakes and rivers change in depth depending upon rainfall; and in salt water, high and low tides have to be considered. Find out for yourself whether your dive should be a shallow one—rather than risk a broken neck.

If you have trouble with sinuses or ears, give up diving and underwater swimming. Excessive water in the nose may wash away secretions that help protect against infection. In addition, infections may wash into the sinuses through the nose or may even reach the middle ear through the eustachian passage from the throat.

Poison Ivy

Poison ivy is responsible for about 350,000 cases of skin poisoning each year. The best protection is to be able to recognize and then to stay away from the plant. If you are not certain you can recognize poison ivy, don't hesitate to ask about it. The plant grows in the form of clinging vines, shrubs which trail on the ground, and erect shrubbery. It clings to stone and brick houses, climbs trees and poles, flourishes along fences, paths and roadways, and may be partially hidden by other foliage.

The leaves, one to four inches in length, are green and glossy in summer, red or russet in spring and fall. The leaves always grow in clusters of three; this is the one constant characteristic that makes poison ivy easy to recognize even though it assumes many forms and leaf colorings. "Leaflets three, let it be" is an old jingle and a good one to remember.

The irritating substance in poison ivy is the oily sap in leaves, flowers, fruit, stems, bark, and roots. Most cases of ivy poisoning are due to direct contact with the plant—at any time, even in winter. Some come from handling clothing, garden tools, and pets contaminated by the oily sap.

If you realize that you have accidentally handled poison ivy, wash your skin as soon as possible, preferably with yellow laundry soap. Lather several times and rinse in running water after each sudsing. This removes or makes less irritating any oil that has not already penetrated the skin.

Ivy poisoning manifests itself first in burning and itching. A rash and swelling follow, and there may be blisters, large or small. The interval between contact and first symptom can vary all the way from a few hours to a week.

If there are large blisters, severe inflammation or fever, or if the inflammation is on face or genital area, a doctor's help is needed. He will be able to relieve discomfort and guard against secondary infections until the attack subsides, as it eventually does.

When there are only a few small blisters on hands, arms, or legs, apply compresses of very hot plain water for brief intervals. Or apply a compress soaked in dilute Burow's solution (1 part to 15 parts of cool water). Your druggist can supply Burow's solution. If these measures do not help, consult a physician.

Insects

Insects can ruin vacations. Spraying with insecticides will help get rid of most insects, and among the most effective are the space sprays such as Flit Aerosol Bomb, Special Gulfspray, Raid, Black Flag, and Slug-a-Bug. All insecticides contain material poisonous to human beings so use them with care, following directions exactly.

Commerical insect repellent preparations are available. Some can be applied directly to the skin.

The U.S. Department of Agriculture has carried out studies of the most effective means of keeping insects from biting humans. Department scientists have developed formulas which can repel insects for about two hours. The following materials have been found to be safe and generally effective. They can be used separately, although combinations of them provide more protection against a larger variety of pests. The materials:

Dimethyl phthalate
Dimethyl carbate
Indalone
2-Ethyl-1, 3-hexanediol (Rutgers 612)

Most druggists can supply dimethyl phthalate. They may also be able to provide the following combination which is sometimes referred to as "5-22": dimethyl phthalate, 60 percent; Indalone, 20 percent; dimethyl carbate, 20 percent.

Always try these materials on a small area of your arm or leg before using them liberally, to make certain that you are not unduly sensitive to them. As a rule, they do not cause irritation. Some people object to the oily consistency of these repellents, but most people find that a small price to pay for protection against black flies, gnats, mosquitoes, and other pests.

When Your Vacation Ends

You took it for change of pace, relaxation, rejuvenation. Don't spoil it by extending it to the last possible minute if that means having to fight heavy Sunday traffic so you arrive home tense and exhausted. Give yourself time to take it easy on the way home, to arrive in time to unpack, read your mail, make any phone calls you must attend to before getting to bed. By so doing, you will get the full benefit of what ought to have been some of the healthiest weeks of your life—sustenance for a return to regular daily life with new zest.

11

SMOKING

No HEALTH problem in our time has commanded more attention than smoking. The issuance of the official Surgeon General's Report in 1964 constituted a major scientific and medical event and began a public and medical concern that continues.

Despite the concern, however, one third of the women and half the men in the United States still smoke cigarettes. Deaths from diseases associated with cigarette smoking continue. A large proportion of health resources and money must be devoted to trying to treat such diseases.

But there are encouraging events. As many as 1.5 million people a year recently have been abandoning smoking. Among them, fortunately, are young and middle-aged men who are at particularly high risk of premature death from lung cancer and coronary heart disease. Also hopeful is evidence from a Public Health Service survey indicating that while 29 percent of boys and 15 percent of girls at age 17 are regular smokers, this represents a significant reduction in the proportion of young people taking up smoking. And school systems across the country are emphasizing educational programs on smoking and health in the hope of creating a "smokeless generation."

The evidence about the dangers of cigarette smoking to health is now overwhelming. In the words of the Surgeon General of the U.S. Public Health Service, smoking "is the greatest preventable cause of illness, disability and premature death in this country."

A conviction shared by medical and health agencies has been expressed by the New York State Commission of Health: "No other single factor kills so many Americans as cigarette smoking. . . . Bullets, germs and viruses are killers; but for Americans, cigarettes are more deadly than any of them. No single known lethal agent is as deadly as the cigarette."

ORIGINS OF SMOKING

There is a certain irony in the history of tobacco use. American Indians, as early explorers discovered, smoked tobacco in pipes for ceremonial purposes, and believed it had some medicinal values. And it was mainly for the latter reason that explorers took the custom back to Europe. In the seventeenth century, there was even a book authored by a London physician on smoking, *Panacea, or the Universal Medicine*. The book advocated a drop of tobacco juice in each ear to cure deafness, a leaf on the head to cure headache, a leaf on a tooth for toothache. And, in the form of ointments, powders, leaves or concoctions, tobacco was suggested as a cure for burns, wounds, cancers, sciatica, diseases of the liver, spleen and womb, worms, colic, warts, corns, and mad dog bites.

The smoking of tobacco in paper wrappers as small cigars or cigarettes began in Spain in the seventeenth century and gradually spread. But the really tremendous spurt in cigarette smoking came during World War I with free distribution of cigarettes to soldiers, followed not long afterward by acceptance of cigarette smoking by women.

Even a century ago, Dr. Oliver Wendell Holmes, author, poet, and distinguished physician and Harvard Medical School professor, was writing: "I think tobacco often does a great deal of harm to health. I myself gave it up many years ago. I think self-narcotization is a rather ignoble substitute for undisturbed self."

Early in this century some reports began to appear in medical journals suggesting an apparent relationship between smoking and specific diseases. In 1927, Dr. F. E. Tylecote in England reported that in virtually every case of lung cancer he had seen or known about, the patient was a regular smoker.

But striking evidence of the effects of smoking was yet to come.

THE MODERN INDICTMENT

In 1938, Dr. Raymond Pearl of Johns Hopkins University published a study on smoking and length of life based on findings in 2,094 men who did not use tobacco, 2,814 moderate smokers, and 1,905 heavy smokers. Dr. Pearl concluded that smoking is unquestionably associated with a reduction in length of life. For example, between the years of 30 and 50, the chances of dying are 15 percent greater for a moderate and 98 percent greater for a heavy smoker than for a nonsmoker.

By 1965, studies of mortality rates of smokers and nonsmokers had become extensive enough for Dr. Luther Terry, then Surgeon General, to report that 240,000 men would die that year prematurely from diseases associated with cigarette smoking. About 138,000 of the premature deaths would be from diseases clearly associated with smoking, such as cancer of the lung, larynx, oral cavity, esophagus and bladder, as well as bronchitis, emphysema, and coronary heart disease. Another 102,000 deaths would result from diseases in which the relationship to cigarette smoking, while not so obvious, is nevertheless well indicated. These figures did not include women.

By 1967, there was evidence that, including women, there were on any average day 800 deaths in the United States attributable to cigarette smoking: 175 due to cancer, 375 to diseases of heart and circulatory system, 250 to chronic bronchitis, emphysema, peptic ulcers, and other diseases.

Cigarette smoking is the major villain, but studies do show some relationship of cigar and pipe smoking to coronary heart disease and circulatory system disease, and to cancers of mouth, pharynx, and larynx. The noninhaling mouth smoker, which is what the usual cigar and pipe smoker tends to be, must realize that there is still 25 to 50 percent absorption of nicotine from the mouth (compared to 90 percent from the lungs when smoke is inhaled) and for the heavy mouth smoker this can be a real hazard. But the overall death rate is much less influenced by cigar and pipe smoking. For example, for men smoking only cigars the death rate is 22 percent higher than for nonsmokers between ages 45 and 64, and 5 percent higher after 65. For pipe smokers, it is 11 percent higher than for nonsmokers between 45 and 64, 2 percent higher after 65.

THE HARMFUL SUBSTANCES

Tobacco smoke is made up of gases, vapors, and chemical compounds with the proportions varying depending upon the type of tobacco, how it is smoked, and the burning temperature. While a cigarette is being puffed, the burning zone temperature reaches about 1580°F (water boils at 212°F).

One of the potentially harmful gases in cigarette smoke is a powerful poison, hydrogen cyanide. Another is carbon monoxide, which is present in a concentration 400 times greater than what is considered a safe level in industry.

Carbon monoxide combines with hemoglobin, the oxygen-carrying substance in red blood cells. Studies indicate that as much as 6 percent of the hemoglobin in the blood of an average smoker is taken up and inactivated by carbon monoxide; in a heavy smoker, 8 percent. Taking the place of oxygen, carbon monoxide leads to shortness of breath on exertion.

In smoke, too, are millions of tiny particles, called particulate matter, per cubic centimeter. It is this matter which, upon condensation, forms the brown mass called tar. Tar contains nicotine and more than a dozen chemicals known to trigger cancer when applied to the skin or breathing passages of laboratory animals. The chemicals are called carcinogenic because of their cancer-producing activity. In studies in which one of the chemicals, benzpyrene, has been diluted 1,000 times and placed in paraffin pellets implanted in the cheek pouches of hamsters, 90 percent of the animals have developed mouth cancer within 25 weeks.

Nicotine, a colorless oily compound, occurs in cigarettes in a range of 0.5 to 2 milligrams. In concentrated form, nicotine is a potent poison and 70 milligrams, which form about one drop, will if injected kill an average man.

Among the other chemicals in cigarette smoke are phenols, which interfere with the action of the cilia, the hairlike projections which line the respiratory tract and have a protective action. Other chemicals are irritants contributing to cigarette cough, and some are believed to be involved in the gradual deterioration of the lungs in emphysema.

The person just beginning to smoke experiences symptoms of mild nicotine poisoning, such as rapid pulse, faintness, dizziness, nausea, and clammy skin. Sometimes even long-experienced smokers develop one or more of the symptoms.

IMMEDIATE SMOKING EFFECTS

Smoking tends to reduce the appetite. There is also a dulling of taste and smell, and because of the tar the breath tends to become odorous.

Because of the nicotine, smoking produces an immediate feeling of stimulation which is followed by depression. The physical base for this is clear enough: nicotine causes the adrenal glands to discharge epinephrine (adrenaline), which stimulates the nervous system and other glands, producing release of some sugar from the liver. The result is a kind of "kick" and even some relief of fatigue—but this is followed by return of fatigue as the nervous system becomes quickly depressed again.

With smoking, the heart rate increases. Occasionally, the heartbeat may become irregular, producing chest pain. Blood pressure usually rises somewhat. Smoking also tends to constrict smaller arteries, reducing blood flow, and lowering skin temperature. Studies have revealed an average drop of about 5°F in finger and toe temperatures after the smoking of one cigarette.

It is well known, of course, that excessive smoking causes cough, hoarseness, bronchitis, all of which usually disappear when smoking is abandoned.

Physicians have little trouble identifying a smoker by one look at the inflamed mucous membranes of the nose and throat.

The cilia lining the passages to the lungs play an important protective rule. The mucous membranes in these passages secrete a sticky fluid which serves to trap dust and other particles in inhaled air; and the cilia, through a continuous whiplike motion, carry the sticky fluid upward so it can be swallowed or expectorated. Thus the lungs are kept clean. Cigarette smoking slows, then stops, ciliary action and, if continued long enough, destroys the cilia.

There have been studies with carefully controlled populations—in boarding schools, for example, where observations could be carried out over an extended period—showing that regular smokers have nine times as high an incidence of severe respiratory infections as do nonsmokers.

SMOKING AND CANCER

Smoking today stands indicted as a significant factor in many types of cancer, most notably cancer of the lung. Most researchers believe that there are multiple causes, rather than some single cause, for cancer. Many believe that certain human cancers will be proved to be due to viruses which already are known to produce some cancers in animals.

No matter what the cause may be, the basic cancer process involves a change in DNA or RNA, chemicals that are part of the reproductive mechanism of cells. As a result of the change, the cells no longer reproduce in orderly fashion but divide rapidly and, upon dividing, each cell may produce three or more new cells instead of the normal two.

Whether a virus is the cause or chemical disturbances are involved, the effect is upon the cell reproductive system. And many contributory factors may open the way for cancer by disturbing the balance between viruses and cells or by upsetting chemical processes in cells. Thus, sunlight, soot, and other irritating substances are known to be factors in provoking skin cancer; radiation is known to be involved in leukemia; and cigarette smoke in lung cancer.

Lung cancer today is the leading cause of death from malignancy in the United States. Before World War I, 371 deaths in the United States were attributed to lung cancer. By 1940, there were 7,121; by 1950, 18,313; by 1960, 36,420; and recently the rate has reached 55,300 a year. The increase has been epidemic in its proportions.

The association between smoking and lung cancer has been established by many studies. One of the largest involved a follow-up of more than one million men and women for a four-year period. The study determined that the risk of dying from lung cancer for men aged 35 to 84 who smoke less than a pack a day is 6 times as great, and for men smoking two or more packs 16 times as great, as for nonsmokers. And for women smoking a pack or more a day the risk is more than 4 times as great as for other women.

Inhaling is a significant factor. Every smoker gets some smoke into his lungs, but purposeful inhalation multiplies the amount. Men who think they do not inhale or inhale only slightly have 8 times the risk and men who inhale deeply have 14 times the risk of lung cancer as against non-smokers. Women who do not inhale or who inhale only slightly have 1.8 and women who inhale moderately or deeply 3.7 times the risk in comparison with those who do not smoke.

The earlier smoking starts, the greater the risk. Men who begin before 15 years of age have nearly 5 times as much risk as those who start after 25; women who start before 25 run twice the risk of women who start later.

Although lung cancer sometimes does occur in nonsmokers, this is so relatively rare that it is estimated by authorities that at least 90 percent of lung cancer deaths would not occur if there were no smoking of cigarettes.

Other cancers are associated with smoking. The incidence of cancer of the larynx is 6 times as great and that of cancer of the esophagus 4 times as great in men cigarette smokers, aged 45 to 64, as in nonsmokers. Similarly, cancer of the pancreas is 2.7 times as great, cancer of the liver and biliary passages 2.8 times, cancer of the urinary bladder 2 times, cancer of stomach and kidney 1.4 times, and leukemia 1.4 times as great. Women smokers have death rates 1.8 times as high as nonsmokers for cancer of the mouth, larynx, esophagus, and pancreas.

Pipe and cigar smokers have rates for lung cancer twice as high as nonsmokers; for cancer of the oral cavity, 4.9 times as great; for cancer of esophagus and larynx, 3 to 4 times as high.

While the cancer death rates associated with smoking are not as high in women as in men, it seems likely that they will catch up because of the great increase of smoking by women in recent years.

RESPIRATORY DISEASES

Chronic bronchitis is an inflammation of the bronchial tubes. As the cells that line the tubes become irritated, they secrete excessive amounts of mucus, whereupon a chronic cough develops as part of the body's effort to get rid of the excess mucus and the irritants. The persistent deep coughing and the thick mucus make breathing difficult.

Emphysema, which is often associated with chronic bronchitis, involves loss of lung elasticity. As a result, the lungs are less able to expand and contract in normal fashion. Gradually, with progression of the disease, air sacs in the lungs are destroyed. The lungs now are less able to obtain adequate amounts of oxygen and get rid of carbon dioxide, causing the heart to work harder in the effort to circulate blood so as to get enough oxygen to body tissues. Heart failure is the most common immediate cause of death.

Between 1945 and 1965, deaths from chronic bronchitis and emphysema in the United States shot up from 2,038 to 22,686—a more rapid increase than for any other cause of death.

Lung cancer patients die relatively quickly. Those with chronic bronchitis and emphysema are disabled, partially or completely, for many years. As one chest specialist has remarked: "I make my living taking care of patients with chest diseases. I agree about the seriousness of lung cancer but I want to add that the person who gets lung cancer from smoking is lucky in comparison to the patient who gets emphysema, because lung cancer is usually of short duration while patients with emphysema spend years of their lives gasping and struggling for breath."

Many factors can be involved in the development of bronchitis and emphysema: repeated infections, asthma, air pollution. But cigarette smoking is more important, involving intensely polluted air.

A 10-year British study shows that the death rate for bronchitis and emphysema is 6.8 times as high for those smoking 1 to 14 cigarettes a day as for those who do not smoke; 12.8 times as high for those smoking 15 to 24 cigarettes; 21.2 times as high for those smoking 25 or more. A United States study found death rates for men aged 45 to 64 to be 6.6 times as high for smokers; in the age group 65 to 84, 11.4 times as high. For women smokers, it is, overall, 4.9 times as high as for nonsmokers and 7.4 times as high for the heavier smokers.

CARDIOVASCULAR DISEASE

The most common cause of death in the United States is coronary heart disease, and over the past 20 years many studies have shown an association between this disease and smoking.

In coronary heart disease, the coronary arteries which nourish the heart muscle itself become narrowed by deposits. When one of the coronary arteries becomes obstructed, usually by a clot that forms in the narrowed, roughened vessel, a heart attack results.

Certainly many factors may enter into the development of coronary artery disease. Sedentary living is one. Diet, particularly diet heavily laden with fats, is another. Excess weight may be involved. High blood pressure is an important factor.

But cigarette smoking has been found to be associated with the disease to the point that, as far back as 1965, in testimony before a congressional committee, American Heart Association authorities stated that about 125,000 preventable deaths each year are associated with cigarette smoking.

In a study published by the National Cancer Institute, "Smoking in Relation to the Death Rates of One Million Men and Women," the following conclusions were reached: In the 45 to 54 year age group, death rates from coronary heart disease are 2.8 times as high for men and 2 times as high for women smoking a pack or more of cigarettes daily as for nonsmokers. The greater the number of cigarettes smoked, the greater the inhalation, and the earlier the age when smoking starts, the greater the death rate. And autopsies of people dying from diseases other than coronary heart disease show more plaques, or roughened spots, on which clots can develop and much more extensive atherosclerosis in the coronary arteries of smokers than nonsmokers.

Many studies show that smokers have larger amounts of cholesterol in the blood than nonsmokers. Other studies indicate that smoking speeds the clotting of blood, which increases risk of clot formation in the coronary arteries. Smoking also increases the work load of the heart, forcing it to pump more blood more rapidly because the carbon monoxide from smoke reduces the oxygen-carrying capacity of the blood and impairs the elasticity and gas-exchange capacity of the lungs.

There is evidence, too, of an association betwen cigarette smoking and strokes, which annually kill 200,000 Americans. An American Cancer Society study found that stroke death rates are 74 percent higher among women and 38 percent higher among men who smoke cigarettes than among nonsmokers.

THE REWARDS OF STOPPING

It is better, of course, never to start smoking. But the rewards of stopping are great. Recent studies show that if smoking is stopped before lung cancer has actually started, lung tissue tends to heal itself. Even for those who have smoked long and heavily, the lung cancer risk begins to decrease about one year after the habit is abandoned and then continues to decrease progressively until after ten years it is very little higher than for people who have never smoked regularly.

One recent study compared the lung cancer death rate among British physicians, a large proportion of whom have stopped smoking, with that of the population in general. The physicians' death rate from the disease declined 30 percent while the lung cancer rate for British men in general increased 25 percent.

The death rate from coronary heart disease decreases rapidly with cessation of smoking. And while some people who stop smoking gain weight, and overweight is a factor in heart disease, it has been calculated that a man of average weight who has customarily smoked 40 cigarettes a day and stops would have to gain at least 75 pounds to offset the added years of life he can expect from no smoking.

In chronic bronchitis and emphysema, for which immediate cessation of smoking is an essential part of treatment, elimination of the habit reduces cough and other symptoms within a few weeks. While lung tissue destroyed by emphysema is not replaced, usually the progress of the disease is slowed down and may even be arrested.

According to Dr. Donald Frederickson, Director of New York City's Smoking Control Program, who has had considerable experience with people who wish to give up smoking, a major reason for the desire, even among the young, is to avoid not just possible death from lung cancer or heart disease but to minimize the risk of early disability. Dr. Frederickson reports that many smokers tell him: "Dying doesn't bother me—after all, once you're dead, you're dead. And I calculate my chances of developing lung cancer to be relatively small. But the idea of spending fifteen or twenty years with a chronic disease that interferes with the enjoyment of life and reduces my ability to function—well, that's too much. Smoking just isn't worth it."

There are, in addition, many other rewards of abandoning the habit: a better taste in the mouth and a better taste of foods; reduced fatigue and shortness of breath; sounder sleep; amelioration and even disappearance of cough and nasal stuffiness; fewer headaches; reduced tensions; greater safety. Cigarette breath will disappear. There will be no more cigarette burn holes in clothing, furniture, rugs, tablecloths. And there will be money savings, a significant amount in the course of a year.

There are, at this writing, 19 million ex-cigarette smokers in the country. About one of every five adult men has dropped the habit. And those who give it up report a great sense of satisfaction, a tremendous pride in being able to do it.

HOW TO QUIT

Some find the quitting process relatively easy; many do not. But it would be a mistake to believe that if you have tried to quit in the past and have failed, you are doomed to go on smoking. If you have failed before, that in itself does not mean that you are hopelessly weak-willed. Beyond determination alone, you need insight, a plan, a constructive attitude.

One of the most important factors in quitting is to view the process positively. If you look upon it as simply giving up something of value, you may feel sorry for yourself. Rather, you have to view the process as one of teaching yourself—because of knowledge that it will represent a tremendous gain—a more rewarding behavior pattern.

There have been many methods suggested for quitting, and the American Cancer Society has compiled the recommendations of recognized experts in cigarette-withdrawal programs. To begin with, set a date when you plan to quit. Call it Q day; that will be complete quitting day. You may want to give yourself as much as a month to get ready for Q day. And getting ready can involve a gradual reduction in the number of cigarettes you smoke day by day.

A good system is to determine that you will smoke only once an hour or that you will stop smoking between the hours of 9 and 10, 11 and 12, 12 and 1, 1 and 2, 3 and 4, etc. And then extend the nonsmoking time by half an hour, an hour, and more.

You may find it helpful, too, to smoke just half of each cigarette.

Deliberately, make it an effort to light a cigarette. If you habitually carry your pack in a certain pocket, now start using another pocket so you have to do some fumbling for a smoke. If you habitually use your right hand to bring a cigarette to your mouth, determine to use the left hand.

Wrap your pack in several sheets of paper so it becomes an involved process to get at a cigarette.

Shift from a brand you like to one you don't like.

Each time before actually lighting up, make it a point to ask yourself a direct question: Do I really want this cigarette right now, or am I just lighting up out of habit? For whatever else it is, cigarette smoking is a habit, and anything you can do to put even small crimps in the automation involved can be a help.

Undertake something else preparatory to Q day. Along with determination to break the habit, you need deep motivation to sustain your determination. Think carefully and then write out for yourself a list of reasons why you smoke, and another list of reasons why you should give up cigarettes.

Another Aid

Get to know yourself—in terms of smoking behavior. You may well be able to place yourself in one of four categories of smoking behavior suggested by Dr. Silvan Tomkins:

1. HABITUAL SMOKING. If you are basically a habitual smoker, you may hardly be aware many times that you even have a cigarette in your mouth. Perhaps you once thought of smoking as a status symbol; now it is automatic. If you fall into this category, it is important for you to be-

come aware of when you are smoking; and knowledge of your smoking pattern will be a significant first step toward change.

2. POSITIVE EFFECT SMOKING.   For this type of smoker, smoking seems to serve as either stimulant or relaxant. He or she may most enjoy handling of a cigarette or the sight of smoke curling out of the mouth. If you fall into this category and can persuade yourself to make the effort, you may find abandoning cigarettes relatively easy.

3. NEGATIVE EFFECT SMOKING.   This is smoking to reduce feelings of distress, fear, shame, or disgust. If you are this type of smoker, you may not smoke at all when things go well—on vacations, at parties, etc.—but you reach for a cigarette when there are problems and when you are under tension. If you are, indeed, this type of smoker, you may find it relatively easy to give up smoking—only to reach for a cigarette on a tough day. For you, a strong substitute, such as nibbling ginger root, may be helpful.

4. ADDICTIVE SMOKING.   If you are this type of smoker, you are invariably aware any time you are not smoking. The lack of a cigarette even briefly builds need, desire, discomfort. You may enjoy a cigarette only very briefly, if at all, but suffer for lack of one. Tapering off may not work. The only solution may be to quit cold. Once you have gone through the pain of breaking your psychological addiction, you are not likely to go back to smoking again. Some addictive smokers find it helpful to do just the reverse of tapering off during the week before Q day, actually doubling their smoking, forcing themselves to smoke until their bodies revolt against the double dose of tar and nicotine.

That Last Week

In the week before Q day, go over your reasons for not smoking: the disease risk, the cost, the cough, the bad breath, the bad taste, etc. Each evening, before falling asleep, concentrate on one dire result of smoking: repeat and repeat that fact, and another the next night, etc.

Remind yourself all during the week of some clearly established facts: that if you keep on smoking, you risk losing six and a half years of life; if you smoke heavily, you have twice the chance of dying between 25 and 65 as a nonsmoker. Are the six minutes of pleasure, if such they really be, in a cigarette worth six fewer minutes of life? Consider that 100,000 American doctors have quit cigarette smoking.

Q day

On Q day, you get up—and don't smoke. You may find it helpful to drink water often; to nibble fruit, celery, carrots; to suck candy mints or chew gum. You may resort—and good if it helps—to chewing bits of fresh ginger or biting a clove when you start reaching for a cigarette.

Exercise. Strenuous physical activity, if your physician says you are up to it, can help work off irritation from not having a cigarette in your mouth. Even mild calisthenics and stretching exercises and walks can help relax you.

Breathe deeply from time to time. Deep breathing can have a calming effect.

The time after meals can be difficult. Instead of a cigarette, try a mouth wash. Change habit patterns that have gone with after-meal smoking. Immediately after eating, if you are used to relaxing in one chair, use another; if you are used to reading a newspaper, read a magazine or book instead, or try a puzzle.

Reward yourself. Have your favorite meal on Q day. Treat yourself to things you like best—except cigarettes. After saving some money from not smoking, reward yourself with a present: a new record, book, trinket.

IF YOU CAN'T QUIT SMOKING ENTIRELY

If you have tried to quit before and failed, you may be surprised this time. You may, indeed, succeed now. Circumstances, motivation, willpower, and ability to break a habit do not remain stationary forever.

If you must smoke, smoke cigarettes with less tar and nicotine. Don't smoke a cigarette all the way down; leave at least the last third, which yields twice as much tar and nicotine as the first third. Take fewer puffs on each cigarette. Reduce inhaling; don't consciously inhale. Smoke fewer cigarettes each day.

Cigarette users, unable to stop smoking entirely, should shift to a pipe or cigars. While there still is some risk of mouth cancer, overall mortality of cigar and pipe smokers is only a little higher than among nonsmokers if the smoke is not inhaled. A good trick is to use an *unlighted* pipe to get the feeling of something held in the mouth or hand.

12

DRINKING

THIS IS not a Prohibition treatise.

If you drink alcoholic beverages—and it is certainly possible to do so intelligently and, in our opinion, rewardingly—it is important from the standpoint of preventive medicine to understand certain facts. Drinking can begin moderately and remain moderate, and all will be well. But the number of people who fall into the trap of excessive drinking, who end up as alcoholics with a disease serious in itself and serious because of other grave health problems it can trigger, has been increasing.

Alcoholism ranks today as the fourth most important health problem in the United States, afflicting between 5 and 6 million persons, and exceeded in importance only by heart disease, mental illness, and cancer. One of every 13 adult males over 20 years of age is an alcoholic. There are many women alcoholics—an unknown number because they come less to medical and public attention. Only 3 percent of the total alcoholic population is on a Skid Row. Alcoholics are to be found in every walk of life, in all occupations, races, and social strata.

Drunkenness is only the most obvious manifestation of alcoholism. A slow, insidious, malignant disorder, alcoholism is a major cause of death in the 35 to 65 age group. The life expectancy of alcoholics is 10 to 12 years less than that of others. Common causes of death include liver and heart failure, gastrointestinal hemorrhage, accident, suicide, and acute intoxication itself.

Many if not most heavy drinkers are poorly nourished. One reason is that alcohol may dull the appetite so that food is forgotten after several drinks. In addition, alcohol can irritate the stomach lining, and the resulting pain may make the thought of eating repulsive. Drinking heavily and failing to eat properly, the alcoholic suffers malnutrition though taking in several thousand calories daily (each fluid ounce of alcohol has an energy content of 150 calories—"empty" calories which provide no sustenance for body tissues).

Delirium tremens may follow an excessive siege of drinking. This can be a temporary disorder, lasting several hours to a week, during which the victim talks incoherently and usually has visual and aural hallucinations, sleeps with difficulty, experiences nightmares. But for a person already seriously weakened by malnutrition, the DT's can be fatal.

Chronic alcoholics are about eight times as likely to fall victim to cirrhosis of the liver as other people. The liver degenerates, sometimes so seriously that function ceases completely and the victim dies.

Excessive drinking can have nervous system effects, producing painful nerve inflammation as well as impairing memory and intellectual powers. Resistance to infection is impaired, so that lobar pneumonia, for example, is more often fatal among drinkers than among nondrinkers. Alcoholic psychosis—serious mental disturbance—constitutes about 5 percent of all mental illness.

Unhappily, too, alcoholism affects not only the victim but spouse and children as well, often leading to emotional or psychosomatic illnesses among the latter.

INTELLIGENT DRINKING

There are some people who believe that to touch alcohol at all, to take even the first drink, is to invite possible disaster. But there are many, including knowledgeable physicians, who believe that intelligent drinking has much to recommend it.

Intelligent drinking is a matter of timing as well as moderation. The time to drink is at the end of the work day, not at lunch and not after dinner. Cocktail time, provided it involves an unhurried drink or two, can be a pleasant time. It can foster relaxation, especially if the atmosphere is quiet, peaceful. It can ameliorate some of the tensions of the day —in effect, ringing down the curtain on the work day, opening the way for a relaxed dinner and relaxed evening.

Intelligent drinking of this sort, if your regular preventive medical checkups indicate that you have no health problem, is not likely to be a health hazard.

UNINTELLIGENT DRINKING

It has been said that the road to alcoholism is an easy one to travel. And, indeed, some rules, *seemingly facetious* but not really so, have been suggested:

1. Start each day right—by taking a drink as soon as possible after you get up.
2. Whenever you feel depressed or have a problem, take a drink or two. If you are alone, take more; who will know?
3. If you take one drink and then feel like having another, and then another, you are on the right track. Keep it up.
4. When you serve drinks to guests, be sure to sneak a few snorts for yourself between regular servings.
5. If you want to get up nerve or bolster your self-confidence, take a drink to get rid of your inferiority complex.
6. Don't just take a cocktail or two before dinner; keep it up after dinner.
7. No matter how many drinks you have had, if you can lie flat on the floor without holding on, you can regard yourself as OK.

Despite their seeming facetiousness, these rules make an important point: It *is* easy for some people to slip into uncontrolled drinking and to delude themselves that it is still intelligent drinking or harmless drinking.

WHAT HAPPENS IN DRINKING?

There is still a widespread misconception that alcohol is a stimulant. Actually, it has exactly the opposite effect. The gay chatter of a cocktail party, for example, is not the result of drinking-induced stimulation but rather of the depressant effect alcohol has on the nervous system which, in terms of behavior, may remove inhibitions.

Alcohol dulls the cerebral cortex, an area of the brain that is involved in judgment, motor coordination, and self-control. As a result of the dulling—which, of course, will vary in degree depending upon the rate and quantity of alcohol consumption—judgment and self-control are reduced, and feelings and emotions may be expressed more freely.

As muscular control decreases, reaction time becomes greater, so that a driver, for example, who has had several drinks is unable to stop or swerve in an emergency as quickly as he would normally. With heavy drinking, speech becomes slurred, vision is affected, hearing is impaired, equilibrium is lessened. Continued intake of alcohol slows the breathing rate and heart action and lowers blood pressure. When concentration in the blood goes beyond 0.4 per cent, there may be coma and eventually death.

Alcohol acts very quickly to affect thought, feeling, and behavior because it can enter the bloodstream and begin to circulate within two minutes. Unlike food, alcohol does not have to go through the process of digestion. Some of it is absorbed even by the stomach walls; the rest is quickly absorbed into the bloodstream through the intestinal walls. Alcohol taken on an empty stomach is especially fast-acting; when it is mixed with food, the absorption rate is less rapid.

In whatever form it may be consumed—as beer, cider, whiskey, straight, mixed—alcohol's effects on the body are the same. The potency of an individual drink is, of course, determined by the percentage of alcohol it contains. Commonly, alcoholic content is measured by "proof," a term indicating concentration by volume. The proof number is actually twice the percentage of alcohol—so that 86 proof Scotch, for example, is 43 percent alcohol.

While there are variations between individuals, generally these are the effects of various blood concentrations of alcohol:

0.01%—Sensory organs in the mouth and digestive tract are stimulated; blood circulates more rapidly; and there may be feelings of well-being.

0.02%—Bodily warmth is experienced; inhibitions begin to disappear; the drinker talks freely.

0.03%—Some dizziness may be felt; judgment and memory now are affected.

0.04%—Reaction time has slowed considerably; the drinker may be gay but somewhat wobbly.

0.05%—There may be some boisterousness, lack of self-control, unjustified confidence in the ability to drive and do other tasks.

0.1%—In some states, this is considered legally to be drunkenness. At this level, the drinker has little if any conscious control left.

0.15%—For the average drinker, this level is induced by 6–7 ounces of whiskey. It produces incoherence, confusion, inability to walk normally.

0.2%—If the drinker is still conscious, he needs help even to stand up; bladder control is lost.

0.3%—The drinker now may alternately sleep and wake to vomit, is unable to understand what is said to him when he is awake.

0.4%—When this level of blood alcohol is reached, the drinker is unconscious.

While it is possible to become drunk quickly, sobering up takes much longer. Most of the alcohol in the body is handled by the liver. There it goes through a chemical process, oxidation, in which its energy is released as heat. A feeling of warmth is experienced at first but the heat is quickly lost through the skin. Some alcohol also is oxidized or burned off in the lungs; and some is removed through sweat and urine.

WHY SOME PEOPLE DRINK EXCESSIVELY

A drink or two can help to create an aura of relaxation and contentment, allowing cares and responsibilities to be forgotten temporarily, and encouraging sociability. Most people find this desirable—and recognize that it is desirable only as a temporary state.

Some people, however, want to extend the state, cling to it, accentuate it. When they yield to the desire, drinking more and more and even almost continuously, they become alcoholics, addicted to drink.

Addiction involves an accommodation by the body to the presence of a drug. With the accommodation comes dependence. Details of the mechanism are not entirely clear, but it appears that the cells of the body may shift their metabolism. They depend, of course, upon circulating blood for their nourishment. As they are exposed to alcohol in the blood, they accommodate to the presence of the alcohol. Once they have made the accommodation, they have, in effect, become as dependent upon alcohol being there as they once were upon it not being there. At this point, it is difficult to stop drinking. If an addict's alcohol supply now is taken away suddenly, he reacts with distressing symptoms which may include violent tremors, nausea, and headaches.

There is still no definitive answer to the question of what causes alcoholism. Both physical and psychological factors have been cited. Studies have failed to establish any one specific type of prealcoholic personality. People who become excessive drinkers may or may not be immature or neurotic. Some, in early life, may have been well-adjusted only to regress, as the addictive process takes over, to immature behavior.

As their addiction takes hold, all alcoholics, whatever their backgrounds, tend to become much alike in behavior. It is as though the disease of alcoholism remolds them into a stereotype. The procurement of alcohol becomes their chief concern, superseding other interests, producing a deterioration in their work, social life, and relationships with their families.

One physician specializing in the treatment of alcoholics has reported that a battery of psychological tests given to 300 consecutive patients showed gross disturbance in every case. The patients did not conform to any single personality type and yet showed markedly similar character traits. All had low frustration tolerance and inability to tolerate tension or anxiety. All gave evidence of mental depression, withdrawal, low self-esteem, and a sense of isolation. In all cases, there was marked hostility. Almost all had sexual problems.

Whatever the causative factors of alcoholism may turn out to be, one thing is clear from a practical preventive standpoint: without excessive consumption of alcohol there cannot be alcoholism. Perseverance at heavy drinking is required to establish the addiction. Alcoholism is no sudden visitation. The person who becomes alcoholic builds up to it, and often does so quite gradually, unaware that he really is beginning to drink to excess and then that he is drinking more and more to excess.

Significantly, there have been surveys of highly intelligent, heavy-drinking business executives to determine what they consider excessive drinking—and always, it appears, the definition of excessive drinking turns out to be several drinks more than the heavy drinker personally consumes. Some of these men have indicated that they see nothing excessive in drinking as much as a fifth of whiskey a day.

Unless they have specific guidelines to follow, it would appear that even intelligent people who have moved far along the road to alcoholism may not recognize the fact. In an effort to provide such guidelines, the Life Extension Foundation in New York, a nonprofit organization devoted to improving the health of business executives through preventive measures, has produced the following for its executive clients which deserve repeating here. Any drinker, the Foundation suggests, can consider that alcoholism is approaching:

1. If two or three years ago a half hour before dinner was set aside for a drink and now this has stretched to two hours and four drinks.
2. If two or three years ago dinner was anticipated with pleasure and now there is little interest in food and sometimes dinner is completely omitted.
3. If two or three years ago cocktails at lunch were for business entertaining only and now one or two are routine.
4. If two or three years ago weekend consumption was little more than that of weekdays but now drinking is started in the morning and continues more or less all day.

Dr. Harry J. Johnson, President of the Foundation, goes on to urge, very soundly, that every heavy drinker should give himself a test to determine whether or not he is becoming an alcoholic.

It's a simple test. It merely requires that the heavy drinker declare a semiannual alcoholic abstention period of not less than one week. If he can get through the week without unpleasant withdrawal symptoms, without a feeling of martyrdom, and with no obsessive desire to return to drinking when the rest period is over, alcoholism is not yet present. If, when time for the test period arrives, the drinker rationalizes and justifies a postponement for any reason whatever, he is entering the twilight zone of alcoholism and the point of no return may be near.

Alcoholism is preventable. Even the heavy drinker, alert to the danger that he is traveling the road to alcoholism, often may have time to prevent development of the full-blown addiction and disease by limiting alcohol intake.

HELP FOR THE ALCOHOLIC

Once alcoholism has developed, the problem is difficult but not hopeless. It can be solved—and must be solved if permanent damage and possibly death to the alcoholic, and incalculable damage to spouse and family as well, are to be prevented. If it is to be solved, it must be approached in no simplistic fashion. It must not be regarded as simply a form of neurosis. Every aspect of the problem, which means virtually every aspect of the alcoholic's life, must receive attention.

An important part of the physician's job is to help the patient recognize, accept, and understand his illness. He must be made to feel not an outcast, a pariah, but a worthwhile person who has a definite sickness. Treatment—more properly, rehabilitation—must be multifaceted: physical, psychological, social, and spiritual. On the physical side, for example, because an alcoholic often drinks instead of eating and may be seriously malnourished, lacking in essential vitamins, minerals and other basic nutrients, his diet must be carefully supervised.

Many forms of treatment for alcoholism have been tried. There are medications which in some cases have stopped the abuse of alcohol and have prevented the complications of alcoholism. For example, for some well-motivated alcoholics, Antabuse, a drug that leads to uncomfortable reactions upon drinking, has proved useful. It may eliminate preoccupation with drinking, freeing the mind for other things, and giving the patient a lift through the feeling that he can live without alcohol. Although hypnosis has been found of limited usefulness in producing aversion to alcohol, it sometimes may help in teaching the nervous, anxious patient to relax and develop greater self-esteem. Psychoanalysis as a rule has produced disappointing results with alcoholics.

In the view of many distinguished authorities, Alcoholics Anonymous is of first importance in the rescue and rehabilitation of alcoholics. "AA," says Dr. Ruth Fox, medical director of the National Council on Alcoholism, "is a pragmatic, simplified, spiritual approach to life, a prescription for living. For patients who can and will accept it, it may be the only form of therapy needed. There can be an immediate amelioration of symptoms as the isolated alcoholic feels that there is hope for him."

Alcoholics Anonymous is an organization of individuals who have conquered or are trying to conquer their own habitual drinking and to help others with their problems. From their own personal experiences, they have learned how to encourage and stimulate others in their desire to stop drinking. Meetings and discussions provide opportunities to air problems, and this is a most useful form of psychotherapy. The organization has branches in many communities across the country and members are welcomed wherever they may travel. A call to a local branch can bring immediate help. The national headquarters is P.O. Box 459, Grand Central Annex, New York, N.Y. 10017.

If abused, alcohol can be extremely dangerous. If used intelligently, it can have a place in the life of the healthy, well-balanced individual. A good and simple rule for intelligent drinking is to restrict daily intake to one or two drinks, preferably long ones, at the end of the day.

If alcohol is consumed at other times, it should be selective, not routine, consumption. By all means, limit the practice of lunchtime drinking and after-dinner drinking to special occasions. Count your drinks; limit their number; if you lose count, stop drinking. Don't order "doubles." Don't stop for "quickies" on the way home. Don't sneak drinks in the kitchen. Drink moderately, leisurely, not alone but with family or friends, to promote relaxation, sociability, a pleasant interlude after a day's hard work.

13

DRUGS

RELATIVELY FEW readers of this book will have had any personal experience with illicit drug use. Yet it has become important for every concerned person—in terms of children and other contacts—to be informed about that problem and what can be done to prevent serious consequences.

Until fairly recently, illicit drug use and addiction were largely confined in the United States to the Skid Rows—to the hopeless, helpless, and disadvantaged of society. But in recent years, the scene has shifted dramatically to better neighborhoods and schools, to the respected and well-educated who, in increasing numbers, especially the adolescents, have been "turning on."

College and university students have been tempted to try drugs since 1962 when a Harvard instructor and some graduate students enthused over the virtues of a then little-known drug, LSD. Soon LSD became an "in" drug. It has also become an illegal drug, and even aside from its illegality, after a first surge of use it has become much less popular as it has become clear that taking LSD is playing a chemical Russian roulette.

But the use of other drugs—marijuana, amphetamines, barbiturates, opiates—is widespread. And the penalties may be multiple. There are the legal punishments which may ruin the life of an offender. There are the possible threats of impaired development and alienation from life and society. And there are the risks to physical health.

What scientific information is there available about the various drugs, their effects, and their hazards? Recently, pediatricians, psychiatrists, and other physicians, and the National Institute of Mental Health and other government and private agencies have been working to bring together all known facts.

LSD

LSD, lysergic acid diethylamide, is a man-made chemical first synthesized in 1938 from ergot alkaloids. Often called "acid" by its users, it is a mind-altering drug, classed legally as a hallucinogen. A single ounce of LSD is enough to make 300,000 of the usual doses, each amounting to a speck, usually taken in a sugar cube or on a cookie or cracker.

LSD, in an average dose, has effects that last eight to ten hours—increase of pulse and heart rate, rise in blood pressure and temperature, dilation of the pupils of the eyes, flushing or paleness of the face, sweaty palms, chills, irregular breathing, nausea, and distortion of the physical senses.

Actually, the first effects of the drug may be on the physical senses. There are visual phenomena: walls appear to move, colors become more brilliant, unusual patterns unfold, flat objects become three-dimensional. There may be a sharpening of other senses—taste, smell, hearing, touch. And often various sensory impressions may appear to merge, so that colors, for example, may seem to have taste.

Users report many other strange experiences, including simultaneous opposite emotions, being at once happy and sad, elated and depressed, tense and relaxed. At different times, there may be different effects for the same individual. Responses cannot be predicted, which is why users often describe their experiences as "good trips" and "bad trips."

Some LSD users believe that since LSD heightens their senses, it makes them more creative. But this is not supported by the paintings, writings, and other creative efforts of drug users; in fact, in many cases, the works produced after drug use are poorer than before.

How LSD works in the body is not yet thoroughly understood. There is some evidence that it affects the amounts or levels of certain chemicals in the brain and changes brain electrical activity. Experiments with animals suggest that the drug may block a normal filtering process in the brain which then becomes flooded with myriad unscreened sights and sounds.

The dangerous effects of LSD are many. Hospitals report that some users, in a panic over their inability to cut off the effects of the drug, fear they are losing their minds. Some become paranoiac, developing increasing suspicions that people are out to harm them and control their thinking. Weeks and even months after LSD use has been stopped, some people have recurrences of the same experiences they had while using the drug and fear they are going insane. Accidental deaths have been reported—instances of users walking in front of moving cars, convinced they were impervious to harm, and even leaping out of high windows because of a conviction they could fly.

Medical experts report that the overwhelming fears and worries that may accompany an LSD experience can sometimes be disturbing enough to produce acute and even long-lasting mental illness.

Changes in chromosomes—the tiny threads in the nucleus of all cells which carry genetic information and guide reproduction—have raised concern. The changes found are actual breaks in the chromosomes, and the fear is that this may lead to birth defects in children of users.

MARIJUANA

This is a drug found in the flowering tops and leaves of a hemp plant which grows in mild climates in countries around the world. Known variously as pot, tea, grass, weed, Mary Jane, hash, and kif, marijuana is smoked in short cigarettes or pipefuls made up of the leaves and flowers of the plant. The smoke has an odor resembling burnt rope or dried grass.

Marijuana produces certain clear-cut physical reactions: increase in heartbeat, lowering of body temperature, reddening of the eyes. In addition, the drug affects blood sugar levels, stimulates appetite, and tends to dehydrate the body.

The effects on emotions and senses vary considerably not only with the quantity and strength of the drug used but also with the circumstances, including the social setting and the expectations of the user. Beginning about fifteen minutes after inhalation of the smoke and for as long as four hours, some users feel excited, some depressed, some experience no mood change. Often, the sense of time and distance becomes distorted so that a minute may seem as long as an hour, a nearby object may seem far off. The drug affects ability to perform any task requiring clear thinking and good reflexes.

Marijuana is an extremely controversial drug. There is a prevailing belief that it is harmless, but some investigators are convinced it is not. A recent survey of 2,700 doctors and other professionals in mental health practice disclosed that they had seen 1,887 patients with adverse reactions to marijuana in a period of eighteen months.

As some scientists note, "The very unpredictability of marijuana on different individuals and on the same individual at different times and under different conditions increases the risk to the user."

Much still remains to be learned about the long-term effects and possible dangers of marijuana; and aided now by the recent synthesis of the drug's active ingredient, tetrahydrocannabinol, investigations are being carried out.

HASHISH

Only very recently has hashish, a drug known for centuries, become a major element in what has been called "America's drug subculture."

Both hashish and marijuana come from the same plant. While marijuana is made from the tops and leaves, hashish is the dried resin of the plant. Hashish is often sold in chunks about one-inch square and one-quarter-inch thick and looks much like a clod of dirt. It has little taste —a hint of the household spice thyme.

Users may put a tiny pebble of it in a pipe or sprinkle a few crumbs of it onto a cookie. Reactions are varied. Some users feel nothing but a slight drowsiness. At the other extreme, some go into panic and scream that they are losing their minds. Some authorities report that if there is a psychological disability, the drug tends to aggravate it and that large doses can cause the same kind of psychotic breakdown as LSD can produce.

No one really knows the long-term effects of the drug. Users claim that there will be no permanent effects upon body or mind. On the other hand, doctors in countries with long histories of hashish usage suggest that the user will become lethargic, apathetic.

As this is written, plans are being formulated for the first United States scientific studies of hashish.

STIMULANT DRUGS

Amphetamines—stimulants for the central nervous system—were first introduced in the 1920's. Best known for their ability to combat fatigue and sleepiness, they have many medical uses. Under some circumstances, they may be employed as an aid in weight reduction because of their appetite-suppressing effect. They are sometimes used in the treatment of mild mental depression. In some children—who tend to be overactive and irritable, behavior problems in school and at home—the amphetamines have what seems to be a paradoxical effect: though basically stimulants, in these children they have a valuable calmative effect.

Stimulants have been widely abused. There has been a heavy illegal traffic in such agents as Benzedrine, Dexedrine, and Methedrine, commonly called pep pills, bennies, and speed. While these drugs produce no physical dependence, a tolerance to them does develop and increasingly large doses are required to achieve the same results.

Their effects are many: increased heart rate, elevated blood pressure, palpitations, dilation of the pupils, dry mouth, sweating, headache, diarrhea, paleness. The drugs stimulate the release of norepinephrine, a neurohormone ordinarily stored in nerve endings. Norepinephrine becomes concentrated in higher brain centers. When seriously abused, the stimulants can produce exhaustion and temporary psychosis which may require hospitalization.

When used for long periods for "kicks" or for staying awake, the drugs have another danger: they may lead people to try to do things beyond their physical capacity, leaving them seriously exhausted at best and, at worst, leading them into serious and even fatal accidents.

"Speeding," the injection of Methedrine into a vein, has still other dangers. An unaccustomed high dose can kill. And injections may lead to critical serum hepatitis.

Heavy chronic users of stimulant drugs tend to become irritable and unstable and, like other chronic drug users, may suffer social, intellectual, and emotional breakdown.

In our heavily medicated society, the abuse of stimulants is not limited to young people and thrill seekers. Many otherwise intelligent persons get on a kind of pill-go-round, using sedatives to calm themselves down and fall asleep and stimulants to wake themselves up and keep going.

SEDATIVES

Sedatives constitute a large family of compounds with relaxing effects on the nervous system. Dating back to 1846, the barbiturates are the best known. Many barbiturates with different types of action are available. Some, such as pentobarbital and secobarbital, are fast-starting and short-acting, exerting their effects quickly but for a relatively short period. Others, phenobarbital, amobarbital, and butabarbital, are slow-starting but long-acting.

Most often abused are the short-acting compounds, commonly called goofballs and barbs.

In normal, medically prescribed doses, barbiturates mildly slow the heart rate and breathing, lower blood pressure, and mildly depress nerve activity. In larger doses, they may cause confusion, slurred speech, staggering, deep sleep—symptoms much like those of alcoholic inebriation.

Sedatives not only produce tolerance so that increasingly greater doses are needed to achieve the same results; they also produce physical dependence. Their abrupt withdrawal can lead to cramps, nausea, delirium and convulsions, and, in some cases, sudden death. Withdrawal must be carried out in a hospital over a period of weeks with gradual reduction of dosage.

It isn't only large dosage that can be fatal. Even a small dose may produce slowing of reaction and some distortion of vision. Barbiturates are a major cause of automobile accidents. The combination of barbiturates and alcohol is especially dangerous; the two substances have a synergistic effect in which each greatly increases the effects of the other.

Barbiturates are frequently implicated in suicides, but they also cause many accidental deaths which only appear to be suicides. A major problem with barbiturates is that a user may react more strongly at one time than another; and with a strong reaction, there may be some confusion about how many pills have been taken and the user may groggily go on to take more, sometimes a fatal overdosage.

NARCOTICS

Narcotic drugs include opium and its pain-killing derivatives such as heroin, morphine, and codeine, which are obtained from the juice of the poppy fruit. In addition, there are synthetic, or man-made, narcotics such as Demerol and nalorphine.

Most used by addicts is heroin, also called junk, snow, stuff, and smack. Heroin is a brain and nervous system depressant. It reduces hunger, thirst, and sex drive as well as pain feelings. Typically, heroin produces an easing of fear and a relief from worry as a first emotional reaction. It provides self-confidence and, as some addicts describe it, a kind of imperviousness to troubles which "roll off the mind." After this first reaction, there may be a period of inactivity that verges on a stuporous state.

Heroin and other narcotics produce tolerance, so that increased dosages are needed to achieve effects, and physical dependence. When an addict stops taking heroin, withdrawal sickness may include such symptoms as sweating, chills, shaking, diarrhea, nausea, sharp abdominal and leg cramps.

HOW VALID ARE THE REASONS FOR DRUG TAKING?

Typically, many youngsters today defend their use of drugs on the grounds of adult use of alcohol. Their thrust to anxious parents is: "Well, you drink, don't you?"

Perhaps as good an answer to this as any has been made by Dr. Stanley F. Yolles, director of the National Institute of Mental Health.

"The analogy," he points out, "is pale. In the first place, the use of alcoholic beverages by persons over 21 is not against the law. Secondly, the immoderate use of alcohol as a crutch by some people does nothing to recommend this or other chemical means of 'copping out.' To the contrary, problem drinking and alcoholism are currently subjects of intensive medical and social research. Thirdly, the acceptability of moderate social drinking assumes that adults are mature enough to make mature decisions as to their behavior. And, finally, there is the irrefutable fact that the fresh young years of personality growth and development are dangerously inappropriate for any chemical means of confounding reality.

"As authorities well recognize, neither laws nor awareness of the medical facts can themselves secure drug abuse prevention. Nor can we stop people from using alcohol or cigarettes as support or as a bandage for their psychic wounds. Ours is a drug-oriented culture. From aspirin to sleeping pills, from tranquilizers to the 'pill,' Americans of all ages are ingesting drugs in greater variety and number than ever before.

"It is not so much the phenomenon of use, however, but the misuse and abuse of drugs that bears close investigation. Why do people choose to distort or to ward off reality through chemical means? Perhaps we deal with deep-rooted feelings of alienation. Alienation among the young has been characterized as 'rebellion without cause . . . rejection without a program . . . refusal of what *is* without a vision of what *should be*.' As scientists we are left to probe whatever reasons can be found for this sad anomaly."

SUSPECTING DRUG USE

Rehabilitation of a chronic drug user can be a long, hard process. Prevention and intervention—turning youngsters off when they start turning themselves on—are problems of parental concern.

How can a parent begin to suspect that a child may be taking drugs? It's important to note any unusual changes from normal behavior. If a child who has always been friendly and outgoing suddenly becomes withdrawn and hostile, something is wrong though it may not necessarily be drug use. Some experts suggest that a youngster who keeps to himself for long periods in his room or in the bathroom, who is often on the phone and who is called by persons who will not identify themselves to parents, may be taking drugs. Other possible indications include a sharp slide in school grades, disappearance of clothing and personal belongings and thievery at home (used to pay for drugs), alienation from old friends, and taking up with strange companions.

There are physical indications. A person smoking marijuana has a strong odor of burnt leaves on both his breath and clothes which persists for hours after use of the drug. Marijuana dilates the pupils of the eyes and sometimes reddens and inflames the eyes. Other symptoms include sleepiness, lack of coordination, wandering mind, increased appetite, and craving for sweets. There may be a tendency to laugh and giggle excessively.

If a person is high on LSD or another hallucinogen, the symptoms are almost unmistakable: severe hallucinations, incoherent speech, cold hands and feet, strong body odor, laughing and crying jags, vomiting.

Symptoms of amphetamine usage include aggressive behavior, rapid speech, giggling and silliness, confusion of thinking, extreme fatigue, shakiness, loss of appetite. Those for the barbiturates are stupor, dullness, blurred speech, drunk appearance, vomiting.

If pills are found on children who deny they are illicit drugs, the pills can be identified by a druggist or physician. If cigarette papers and possibly small seeds are found in clothing pockets, they may well indicate marijuana usage.

When a child is sniffing glue or drinking cough medicine containing narcotics for kicks, he may have a dreamy blank expression and a drunk appearance. Heroin or morphine use may be spotted by watery eyes, appetite loss, stupor, needle marks on the body.

HOW A PARENT CAN HELP

What can be done if a child is believed to be taking drugs? Certainly, a parent has no more important function than to keep a child from harming himself. But there must be no panic and the situation must be handled with tact.

Some experts who have dealt often with the problem suggest that the parent talk quietly with the youngster, telling him that his behavior has caused concern and that the parent has wondered if he might be taking drugs and might be too frightened to say so. The parent might add that his or her prime concern is the child's health and happiness, and that while it's true that the parent is invading the youngster's privacy and the child has the right to be angry about that, the seriousness of the situation justifies the invasion. There should be an effort then to find out whether the child has only experimented briefly or is taking a drug regularly.

In discussing drugs with a child, the parent can, and should, use an intelligent, reasonable approach. It is far more likely to be successful than an authoritative pronouncement. A youngster can be reminded that LSD usage is extremely dangerous risk-taking; that it has caused hundreds of victims to end up in mental institutions or to suffer injuries such as three University of California at Santa Barbara students suffered when, on an LSD trip, they stared so long at the sun while holding a "religious conversation" that they never again will be able to read.

A youngster may resist any argument that marijuana is as addictive or as dangerous as heroin. But a parent can remind him that marijuana can be habit-forming, cause listlessness with prolonged use, and temporarily alter vision enough to make driving extremely dangerous. And, of course, too, it may lead to possible arrest and conviction of a felony, barring the individual from the practice of many professions and from obtaining a passport.

Barbiturates, it can be explained, can be as addictive as heroin. Strong doses of amphetamines are dangerous, too, and even hippies have been known to post signs warning that "Speed Kills."

A child tempted by drugs or already experimenting with them is not a hopeless case by any means. And with wise rather than hysterical action on the part of parents, there is a good chance he may "turn off" rather than "turn on."

Where, if needed, can a parent turn for help? A good place to start is with the family physician. In most communities help is also available through psychiatric clinics and outpatient services. Virtually every major city has a center that will refer a parent to the best agency for a particular problem. Hospitals, child-guidance centers, voluntary health and social organizations, and many law enforcement agencies which are anxious to protect rather than prosecute, unless prosecution is absolutely essential, can tell parents what to do.

HELP FOR ADDICTS

Addiction is a disease. It is not an easy one to overcome—but it is curable in many instances. In fact, as authorities point out, many addicts, when they reach the age of 30 or 35, often suddenly lose the need for heroin, for example. They withdraw on their own and never go back to the habit. Why this maturing-out process, as it is known, occurs is a mystery; addicts themselves are unable to explain it. "Our problem," says one authority, "is to keep them from dying of heroin addiction before they get to be 30 or 35 and to replace their 10-year to 15-year period of drug abuse with years of useful activity."

There are three major approaches to treatment in the United States. One is civil commitment, used in some states, with emphasis on education, job rehabilitation, and careful follow-up. Another is a methadone maintenance program which substitutes the milder drug methadone for heroin and includes schooling, job training, and other rehabilitative activities. There are also group therapy programs, typified by organizations such as Synanon and Day Top, which are regarded by many authorities as promising.

14

YOUR WORK AND YOUR HEALTH

Is YOUR job good for you? This is no rhetorical question. First of all, obviously enough, a job should provide reasonably adequate earnings to enable you and your family to afford good diet, good housing, health care, recreation, and other essentials. It should do more. Ideally, it should be interesting to you, should offer some challenge, should provide opportunities for advancement, and should provide an emotionally healthy rather than emotionally toxic environment.

Physicians are increasingly aware that how a person feels about himself or herself heavily influences health as well as recovery from illness —and that high on the list of important feelings is self-esteem. As one wise physician has put it: "The man who is able to regard himself highly believes himself capable of mastering the vicissitudes of life. He adapts by attacking his environment constructively and shaping it to his needs. He who has low self-esteem struggles valiantly but pessimistically, sometimes passively accepting fact, sometimes destructively attacking. Self-esteem is the partner of hope, and hope is the chief agent of occupational mental health."

More and more men and women now earn their livelihoods in organizations—companies, government agencies, educational and other institutions. And as their social and economic status becomes more dependent upon their roles in their work organizations, how they feel about themselves is related to a significant extent to what happens to them in those organizations.

It is not always possible to fully achieve an ideal. Yet many of us could come much closer to it in our work than we do if we took real inventory —a hard look at our work, its satisfactions and dissatisfactions, specific possibilities for improving the job we have or finding something more satisfactory.

If your job does not pay you enough for your needs, is it possible for you to get a raise in salary? Are there courses you might take or other things you might do that could lead to promotion? If not, is it possible that you might find a job that has more to offer? Is there helpful information—and possibly sound advice and guidance—you might get from a foreman or supervisor? In particular, perhaps these people or others could help you with an objective view of your situation, capabilities, and opportunities.

Some cities have job counselors or provide other means to help you determine how to fit yourself for a better position. Vocational guidance has made considerable progress in studying the "square peg in the round hole" problem. You might write the U.S. Employment Service, Bureau of Employment Security, U.S. Department of Labor, Washington, D.C. 20210, asking for the nearest local office where you can obtain counseling, testing, and job placement services. Veterans may obtain similar help from the Veterans Administration.

If your job brings you sufficient income but leaves you frustrated, bored, or otherwise unhappy, vocational guidance agencies may help solve the problem. It could be worthwhile, too, for you to have a frank talk with your physician who, knowing the importance of job satisfaction as a factor in good preventive medicine, may himself be able to help with some guidance or refer you to a psychologist or psychiatrist for help in discovering whether you should try to adjust yourself to your present job—whether there are things you can do to make a satisfying adjustment—or find another.

A good job, too, should be as safe as modern technology and your own alertness, ingenuity, and awareness of potential hazards can make it. If you are frequently ill or have had accidents at work, it may be that you do not observe proper precautions, or it may be the result of poor conditions in your place of employment. After reading this chapter, you may be able to decide better which it is. If it is the latter—poor work conditions—you can bring the fact to the attention of your employers, either directly (perhaps through a suggestion box) or through your foreman, supervisor, or union. If this fails to produce improvement, the matter should be reported to the proper authorities, such as the department of labor in your state or the local or state health department.

The fact is that while much has been done to improve occupational safety in this country, in any year on-the-job accidents kill 14,000 and partially or completely disable 2,200,000 of the nation's 82 million workers. Another 5 million suffer lesser work injuries or illnesses. Beyond the toll in pain and suffering, job-related accidents and ailments cost workers $1.5 billion in lost wages and deprive industry of $5 billion in production. This record is an improvement over 50 years ago when industrial accidents killed nearly twice as many people in a work force half the size of today's, but it leaves much to be desired.

STAYING WELL ON THE JOB

Many companies today have highly organized safety programs and preventive industrial health programs. They employ both physicians and safety experts to direct these programs. Many also employ industrial hygienists to study the hazards of all jobs and develop criteria for safe operation. Safety equipment is specified for new machines and often added to existing ones. Workers are provided with safety goggles, safety shoes, and other protective devices.

Still, even in these industries as well as in others which have not yet fully caught up with new trends in improvement of conditions of employment, preventable accidents and illnesses occur. Different jobs, of course, have their individual health problems, and we will take these up after a look at some important basic rules that apply to virtually all work.

BASIC GUIDELINES

Come to work rested. Fatigue has been shown repeatedly to be a major factor in accidents on the job. Plan your late-hour entertainment—dances, card parties, etc.—as much as possible for the nights before your days off from work. It's a good idea to avoid drinking alcoholic beverages after dinner any night, and especially on nights before work days. It doesn't take an outright hangover, just a feeling of moderate or slight upset and sluggishness, to invite trouble on the job. If you have a drinking problem, be sure to read Chapter 12.

Beyond reasonable hours, regular periods of rest and relaxation are important. A day or two off each week, with a change of pace, is essential for avoiding mental and emotional as well as physical rundown. So is an annual vacation. Coming to the job fresh and invigorated—mentally, emotionally, and physically—helps not only to greatly reduce the likelihood of accident and illness but also makes it possible for you to do a better job and create a better impression. It's important to note here that you should not ruin your days off by doing things to overtire yourself or otherwise affect your health.

Don't have any fears about being considered "prissy" if you make a point, as you certainly should, of finding out and following all safety rules that apply to your particular job. If you start on a new job, don't hesitate to do the obviously sensible thing: discuss precautions with your employer, foreman or other supervisor, and older workers. Ask questions, especially about any particular hazards.

If a fellow worker is a danger to you or to others, take up the problem with those in authority. There is no room in any job, and especially a job involving any risks, for the practical joker. Every year, people are rushed to hospitals, dying or seriously injured, because "jokers" playfully but cripplingly pushed a compressed air jet against them, worked a "hot foot" gag, or carried out some other "innocent" practical joke. Workers who insist on practical jokes or who don't know how to handle dangerous equipment properly are frequent causes of industrial accidents and deaths.

Find out the location of the first-aid station or other nursing or medical facility. Many big plants now have full-time nursing and even medical staffs. Smaller ones have first-aid stations and safety or other personnel trained in first aid. A squad of workers can and should be organized and trained to treat minor burns, shock, and cases requiring artificial respiration. Such measures can save lives and help avoid serious disabilities.

Electrical hazards can crop up almost anywhere. Exposed wires, crossed circuits, and carelessness can lead to serious shocks and burns. If you become aware of any wiring that is defective, waste no time calling it to the attention of someone who can correct it. We would like to stress this here: If someone is unconscious from electric shock, do not give up; artificial respiration and heart massage, continued over a period of hours, have been known to save people who appeared beyond hope of reviving.

Be particularly careful about floors and staircases wetted by chemicals or other liquids. If there is any danger of slipping, handholds should be provided; if they are not, notify the proper authorities.

Any job, from that of a miner to an office worker's, can be made unpleasant and even dangerous if lighting is poor. If your eyes feel strained after a day's work, if they are inflamed or puffy, you may need glasses or a change of glasses—but the problem also could be due to poor lighting. See your physician. If he says the lighting is to blame, and the company for which you work seems disinclined to do anything about it, have your physician write a letter urging that the lighting of your work area be inspected and improved. Sometimes, simply keeping windows and light bulbs clean will help considerably. Walls of light-pastel shades help make a room light, and flat paint reduces glare.

Rest rooms or lavatories usually are inspected regularly by the health department. If yours are not sanitary, or not adequately equipped with soap, etc., find out whether health inspections are being performed. Dusts, fumes, and mists are hazards in some jobs. Their dangers can be minimized by proper ventilation and other measures such as those discussed later in this chapter.

KNOW THE SPECIAL HAZARDS OF YOUR WORK

No job is completely free of hazards, and each job may have its own special ones. Even sedentary occupations such as those of clerks and office workers are not entirely safe. Women who work at home should carefully read Chapter 40, in which we discuss danger spots in the home and how to avoid accidents which cripple and kill many people each year.

In addition, salespeople, teachers, librarians, and others who deal with large numbers of people in the course of their work should know and do as much as possible about the increased danger of exposure to colds and other respiratory ailments (page 566).

SPECIAL FARM AND RURAL WORKING PROBLEMS

Although it is commonly thought that working on a farm or in a rural area is healthier than urban work, statistics indicate that this is not so, that illness and disability have much the same incidence in both places. In some rural areas, moreover, where doctors are few and hospitals poorly equipped, residents may have more health problems than do city dwellers.

If you live and work in a rural area, you should know the facts about certain diseases that may occur in some rural areas: brucellosis (undulant fever), tularemia, typhoid fever, tuberculosis of bones and joints, dysentery, malaria, hookworm (see Index).

Rural living provides no particular protection against tuberculosis and, indeed, farmers need to take every precaution listed and some extra ones as well. For example, milk in cities almost invariably is pasteurized, a precaution that helps prevent tuberculosis of the glands and bones, and other diseases such as undulant fever and septic sore throat. Unless a farmer goes to the trouble of pasteurizing the milk from his own cow, he and his family are in danger from these diseases. Many wise farmers set an example all might well follow: they either do their own pasteurizing or buy back some of the milk they sell to dairy plants after it has been pasteurized. Home pasteurization is described elsewhere in this book.

Farm Accidents

The accident toll among rural Americans is high. While there is less danger than in the city from traffic, this is counterbalanced by the frequency of accidents during operation of farm machinery and by other hazards.

Because the accident rate is high and medical care may not be very close by, every farmer should have a good working knowledge of first aid, and all farm vehicles should carry first-aid kits, including instruction booklets. Even small wounds need immediate treatment because of the danger of infection. Any animal bites should be promptly washed with soap and water and treated, and they should also be reported to a physician and the animal should be checked for rabies.

Tetanus (lockjaw) organisms thrive in the intestines of horses and other grass-eating animals and are therefore found around barns and in soil fertilized by manure. This disease, which can develop as the result of any deep wound such as one produced by stepping on a nail, is a constant threat to people in rural areas. It can be prevented by inoculations, and everyone, from childhood on, should be protected against tetanus by such inoculations. No deep wound, however trivial it may seem, should be neglected; an immediate injection of protective serum may make the difference between life and death. Be sure to read further on tetanus elsewhere in this book (see Index).

New agricultural chemicals are being introduced frequently. They are of value in killing weeds, enriching the soil, eradicating insects and rodents, and cleaning animal areas. But they must be used with care, following manufacturers' directions to the letter. In case of any question, however seemingly unimportant, your county agricultural agent or health department can advise and help. Be especially careful about handling or breathing chemicals. If you have to dispose of any unused portions, bury them in containers. Don't burn them, since they may release harmful fumes; and don't bury them in the ground unpackaged, since they may contaminate water supplies.

Rural Medical Facilities

Comprehensive hospital facilities, specialized medical equipment, and the advice of medical and surgical specialists are not readily available in most farming communities. Your own physician, like any other physician, cannot be expected to handle every conceivable type of medical and surgical problem. He will advise consultation with a specialist when necessary. For serious illness he will also help arrange for you to be admitted to the nearest medical center when necessary. And when he deems it essential, you should make every effort to get the best specialized medical care even if it means taking a trip of several hundred miles to the nearest medical center or specialist.

The fact is, as emphasized throughout this book, that good medical care today, when begun at the proper time, can do much not only to provide relief for a problem but also can include measures which, even if they are unable sometimes to cure, can retard or arrest a disease process so it does not progress relentlessly. This is a major function of preventive medicine.

INDUSTRIAL JOB HAZARDS

Certain types of jobs in industry, of course, involve more hazards than others—for example, those requiring the mixing of chemicals or use of blowtorch, drilling equipment, baking, meat handling, construction, lumbering, mining, and work with radioactive materials. Often, several sources of danger are involved, some peculiar to the particular job and others common to many types of work.

Yet, no matter how many sources of danger there are, it is possible to take precautions against them. A good example of the fact that precautions can be taken and there is little excuse for many industrial accidents is welding. Here is an occupation that carries with it four major threats to health and life: electrical shocks and burns; burns from gas flames and splashes of hot metal; damage to eyes and skin from the rays of powerful arc lights; and bad air produced by chemical fumes. Yet, during World War II when it became essential, women without any previous experience at all in heavy industry and new workers without previous experience in welding were quickly and effectively trained to weld—and to weld safely.

Your employer should supply you with equipment and instructions needed to reduce or eliminate risks you face. Your union may have further information to provide. You should acquaint yourself with any and all dangers you may be up against—and never become lax.

MAIN OCCUPATIONAL HAZARDS

1. Dust. Whether it comes from grinding, crushing, cutting, or drilling, or from other sources, dust can be a serious problem. One type of dust encountered in industry is organic—from substances whose source is plant or animal life, such as coal, leather, flour, sugar, feathers, cotton. Many such dusts are not harmful, since the particles are too large to reach finer and more delicate body tissues; many are not composed of poisonous compounds. Organic dusts, however, may produce allergies, skin irritations, or asthma. Miners of both soft and hard coal may develop a disabling shortness of breath because of the effects of coal dust on the lungs.

Inorganic dusts, the second major type, generally are from metals and minerals. Most dangerous is silica, which causes silicosis. Silica dust may lead to formation of fibrous nodules in lung tissue; it also encourages development of tuberculosis, which can be severe enough to be fatal. Asbestos dust also causes a lung inflammation, asbestosis. Workers such as diamond cutters, rock drillers, asbestos-products workers, foundry and furnace men, abrasive-soap makers, and packers are among those who may be exposed to silica and asbestos dust.

Most likely, workers exposed to such dangerous dusts will be protected by exhaust systems or suction devices which catch the dust at the point of origin, or by the use of oil or water to cover the dust and keep it from rising, and by good ventilation and the use of respiratory masks. Even so, they should have regular, periodic chest x-rays to detect any early presence of silica or asbestos in their lungs. They should be constantly alert for colds that do not seem to get completely better, for prolonged coughs, and for other symptoms of tuberculosis (see Index).

2. SKIN DISEASES.   These are among the most widespread industrial health problems. Almost anything—chemicals, dirt, and oil, as well as germs—can irritate the skin. Chief troublemakers are petroleum products, such as machine oil, naphtha, and cutting oil compounds; solvents which include degreasers such as kerosene, gasoline, and trichlorethylene; alkalis, such as lime, caustic soda, and strong yellow soap; and plants, including poison ivy, sumac, and poison oak. Florists are particularly subject to skin irritation from plants. Furriers may be affected by para-phenylene-diamine. Workers who use chromium in electroplating may develop chrome ulcers.

While the list of possible skin afflictions that may develop in connection with work is an almost endless one, there are several important precautions you can use to avoid trouble. Immediately after finishing any dirty or oily job, and also before eating lunch and leaving for the day, apply soap and water generously. Special soaps may be required to remove some substances that cling stubbornly or penetrate into the skin. Don't try to rub away oils that get on hands and face; this may only force them into the skin, clogging the pores, causing irritation and pimples. Wash off oil with soap and water, using repeated applications if necessary; then dry with a clean towel. Special ointments are available to cover the skin before contact with offending substances, providing protection and greatly simplifying the removal of some otherwise difficult-to-remove materials.

Gloves, sleeves, and aprons can afford protection. Pull sleeves over the cuffs of gloves to make certain no skin is exposed. Keep protective clothing clean; change it often.

Do not use advertised ointments for any skin problems you may develop. Let your physician diagnose and prescribe, for your problem may require a special prescription. The fact is that many skin problems are compounded by self-treatment. The self-treatment—actually overtreatment by a worried victim—may produce skin problems of its own. Overtreatment dermatitis is a common problem that confronts dermatologists —skin specialists to whose care serious victims often must be referred.

If you have used the precautions mentioned above and still suffer because of certain oils or chemicals, you may have developed an allergy to them. See your physician, who may be able to help with special desensitization treatment designed to increase your tolerance for specific materials. If this does not help, it may be essential that you move to another job. But let your doctor decide this. (See Allergy, page 561.)

3. POISONS.   In some industries, poisonous materials have long been used and recognized to be potential hazards. But hazards today are increasing as the result of technical advances and introduction of many new chemicals and synthetic materials. We can consider here the more common industrial toxic materials, but there are far too many to be dealt with in a book of this nature. Workers, however, can, and should, familiarize themselves with materials they are using and find out whether they contain poisonous ingredients.

There are certain general precautions of value in many situations involving the handling of toxic materials. Masks, gloves, and respiratory devices should, of course, be used whenever necessary and feasible. Against carbon monoxide and other poisonous gases, good ventilation is the best protection. If the work is such that fumes are produced, an airline respirator and safety line should be worn.

It's important to be on the alert for such symptoms as headache, vomiting, dizziness, and flushing of the face, which may warn of the beginning of a toxic condition.

Do not eat in rooms where poisonous substances are handled.

Cleanliness is vital: use plenty of soap and water, especially prior to eating and before going home.

Be sure to have regular medical checks, preferably on the job by a plant physician.

These are the more common industrial poisons and some of the jobs in which they may be involved:

Lead poisoning can menace color and dye makers, electroplaters, painters and paint makers, petroleum refiners, automobile workers, storage-battery workers, varnish makers, sheet-metal workers, lithographers, insecticide makers, explosives workers, rubber workers, and zinc miners. Most dangerous are soluble forms of lead which may form deposits in drinking cups. Slow lead poisoning can result from small daily inhalation of lead dust over a period of time. The poison affects stomach, brain, and nervous system. It may produce paralysis of frequently used muscles, such as those of a painter's right hand. The precautions previously noted

—proper clothing, good ventilation, regular medical checks—are of critical importance.

Carbon monoxide poisoning can be a hazard for blast furnace workers, firemen, airplane pilots, cooks, petroleum refinery workers, plumbers, welders, miners, compressed-air workers, and others. Early symptoms include abdominal pains, headaches, nausea, and dizziness. In severe cases, carbon monoxide poisoning can be fatal. Efficient ventilation is essential for preventing accumulation of carbon monoxide fumes. The gas affects the hemoglobin of the blood, usurping the place of vital oxygen and depriving tissues of adequate oxygen supply. For first aid, fresh air and, if necessary, an oxygen tank and artificial respiration can be effective.

Benzol and carbon tetracholoride are used in such industries as lacquer making, leather processing, dry cleaning, soap making, electroplating, dye making, and the manufacture of paint and paint removers. Benzol (or benzene) is a colorless liquid with penetrating odor. It evaporates quickly but gives off a poisonous vapor. It is possible to develop benzol poisoning by breathing concentrated fumes for only a few minutes although gradual poisoning is more common. For protection, the worker should wear an air-line respirator and safety belt. All machinery containing benzol should be shut down regularly and checked for leaks. Adequate ventilation is essential and regular medical checkups are needed. Any unusual bleeding, especially a sudden nosebleed, calls for immediate medical attention. People who have heart disease, anemia, tuberculosis, or a tendency to bleed easily should not work in plants where benzol is used.

In addition to causing such symptoms as nausea, headaches, and nose and throat irritation, carbon tetrachloride is a serious threat because of the injury it can inflict on liver and kidneys. If you work with carbon tetrachloride, be sure to take all the precautions described above for benzol.

4. INFECTIONS. Workers handling cattle may be exposed to undulant fever (brucellosis). Those handling hides may develop anthrax. Slaughterhouse workers, as well as farmers, have to guard against tetanus. Dogpound workers must be wary of rabies. Barbers and beauticians have to guard against ringworm (fungus infection).

These are just a few of many infections that may be acquired in various occupations. Frequent washing of exposed body areas and the use of gloves provide valuable protection. Cuts, even slight ones, should be washed immediately with soap and water, then treated with the mild form of tincture of iodine or other safe antiseptics. If your job involves the handling of living or dead animals, it is wise to get your physician's advice on the best precautions against specific infections you may face.

5. RADIATION HAZARDS. Devices and materials that give off potentially harmful radiation are in increasing use. Fortunately, increasingly effective controls have been developed so workers can be protected.

One type of irradiation, x-ray, has been used for years in medicine for viewing internal body structures and more recently for treating cancer and certain other problems. The same rays, however, if absorbed in excessive dosage, can cause cancer. In industry and in scientific laboratories, where x-rays may be used for quality control and other purposes, they must be carefully monitored and controlled; so, too, other types of radiation which can be harmful. It is possible for an individual to receive an excessive amount of radiation, as from atomic fallout, without being aware of it for years. The effects on his genes, which control heredity, may not affect him at all but may seriously damage his children.

X-rays, radium, and other radioactive substances emit different types of radiation which require different types of protection. These are some of the ways you can be protected if your job requires working with or near radioactive materials:

Film badge: This widely used personal protective device measures the amount of radiation to which you are exposed. It is developed regularly and the type and energy of the radiating source can be determined.

Dosimeter: Of the many kinds of dosimeters, the most common is a pocket-type device about the size and shape of a fountain pen. It can be held up to the light, and the user at any time can determine whether he has received a sudden or heavy dose of radiation or is getting close to his maximum allowable exposure.

Glove box: This is an enclosure with its own air supply, exhaust system, and lighting which allows some industrial operations on radioactive materials to be carried on directly, instead of with remote-control devices.

Bioassay: This is an analysis of breath and urine which determines the amount of radioactivity absorbed by the body. Two or three assays a year are recommended.

Instrumentation: Human senses cannot detect radioactivity but special instruments are available which can detect, measure, and record different types of radiation.

Decontamination: If an accident occurs—if radioactive substances are spilled or if an exhaust system breaks down—properly trained safety personnel can deal with the situation quickly. Their job includes getting rid of the contaminant at once; getting affected workers, their clothing and equipment clean; and testing workers for physical reactions.

In addition to causing cancer or leukemia (malignancy of the bone marrow), radiation can do other damage. It can have harmful effects on the skin, including "burns," loss of hair and fingernails, darkening of the skin. It can affect organs producing blood, thus leading to anemia and insufficient white cells to combat infection. It can lead to hemorrhages—bleeding from gums, in stools, and under the skin—by affecting certain substances that play a role in normal blood clotting. It can produce sterility in both sexes.

Such effects do not usually become manifest until some time after exposure. In some cases—development of cancer, for example—they may not appear for years. Therefore, very great precautions must be taken, since there is no warning of danger by immediate symptoms such as pain.

6. DAMPNESS: Tankmen, vatmen, coal miners, and washers are among those who have to work exposed to almost constant dampness. As a result, they may suffer from coughs, respiratory troubles, rheumatic diseases, and skin changes. Such workers should be as completely protected as possible by waterproof clothing, rubber boots and gloves. In addition, efforts should be made to control dampness by drain channels through which excess water can be carried away.

7. ABNORMAL AIR PRESSURES: Tunnel workers and divers do their jobs under unusually heavy air pressures. In going underground, tunnel workers travel in a chamber which descends slowly so there is a gradual increase in air pressure. If the descent is fast, the change in pressure is distressing. The first sensation is felt in the eardrums and can be relieved by swallowing. Extremely rapid decrease in pressure can produce the "bends" in which blood supply from different parts of the body is blocked off by small air bubbles. Decompression sickness is dangerous and can be fatal. It may develop several hours after a diver has returned too rapidly to the surface. Treatment usually requires recompression and then gradual decompression.

Rising rapidly to a high altitude, which means entering a lower air pressure situation, can be just as harmful. Ascent as well as descent should be gradual. Pilots who ascend too rapidly or take sudden dives may become dizzy, and the change in pressure may be violent enough to burst their eardrums. Commercial airliners are pressurized to avoid the effects of high altitudes.

8. ABNORMAL TEMPERATURES: Steelworkers, welders, furnace men, blacksmiths, and others may be exposed to very high temperatures which may lead to heatstroke, heat exhaustion, and cramps. Very low temperatures may cause frostbite, gangrene, or death. Insulation or air conditioning and protective clothing can help protect against temperature extremes and their effects. Additional salt, which can be taken in the form of tablets, is needed to make up for large amounts lost in perspiration. Re-

lief periods—providing opportunity to return to normal temperature—are extremely important. Workers should be on the alert for symptoms and should ask for relief the moment any symptoms appear. They should also report any colds or other disturbances to the company doctor or their own physician.

9. NOISE AND VIBRATION: In use in industry today are many new machines that produce high levels of noise and vibration. Excessive noise can damage hearing and can cause pain. The use of protective devices—ear plugs and others—can help prevent discomfort and disability.

Vibration, when excessive, can have much the same effect as motion sickness. Excessive vibration may damage the heart, lungs, abdominal organs, and brain. Injuries from overexposure to excessive vibration may not be immediately apparent.

Many studies have been made to establish tolerable limits of noise and vibration, both to protect worker health and to make the industrial operation as efficient and productive as possible. There is clearly room for better methods of minimizing both noise and vibration.

Much has been done in industry and much more remains to be done to make working conditions healthier and safer. Everyone concerned with the problem of occupational disorders—management, workers, doctors, government, and union officials—would do well to consider carefully these statements from the excellent book *Medicine,* edited by Hugh G. Garland, M.D.:

No field of medicine . . . offers greater scope for prevention than the industrial medical field. . . . The late Sir Thomas Legge . . . after much practical experience in the field of prevention enumerated the following now famous axioms:

1. Unless and until the employer has done everything—and everything means a good deal—the workman can do next to nothing to protect himself, although he is naturally willing enough to do his share.

2. If you can bring an influence to bear external to the workman (i.e., one over which he can exercise no control), you will be successful; and if you cannot or do not, you will never be wholly successful.

3. Practically all industrial lead poisoning is due to the inhalation of dust and fumes; and if you stop their inhalation you will stop the poisoning.

4. All workmen should be told something of the danger of the material with which they come into contact, and not be left to find it out for themselves—sometimes at the cost of their lives.

Although these axioms were based on experience in the lead industry, they have wide applicability.

PART THREE

Preventive Body Care

15

THE BASIC STRENGTHS
OF THE HUMAN BODY

A FASCINATING case in medical records is that of an 80-year-old man who some years ago stepped off a curb in Boston, was hit by a truck and taken to Massachusetts General Hospital where, within an hour, he died. Upon autopsy, even the physicians were astonished by what they found.

The man had had almost every known major disease, including several that, individually, might have been potentially deadly. His blood pressure had been grossly elevated, so much so that his heart had almost doubled in size under the burden. He had generalized arteriosclerosis, or hardening of arteries. Tuberculosis had left marks on both lungs. Chronic kidney disease had destroyed large portions of both kidneys. He had had severe cirrhosis of the liver.

Even more astonishing was the report of the man's wife: He had been no invalid; instead, he had been active until the day he was killed and had complained of nothing.

His is an extreme and encouraging example of the reserve powers and adaptability of the body.

There are many other examples: The 7-year-old boy who survived a plunge over the 160-foot-high Horseshoe Falls at Niagara after the boat in which he was a passenger capsized in the river above the cataract. The workman who fell 150 feet from a chimney scaffold, landing on his left side near the base of the chimney, creating an impression 8 inches deep in the earth, bouncing over a 30-degree slope toward a concrete retaining wall, then dropping another 10 feet to a lower level. He fractured his jaw, both ankles, complained of chest pain for less than 36 hours, recovered rapidly—surviving an impact that might well have crushed an airplane.

There was also the hammer thrower, a world record holder, who while warming up to compete for a place on the U.S. Olympic team pulled a back muscle. Desperate, he persuaded a physician to give him an injection of novocaine and let him compete; he whirled out a 212-foot throw to finish second and get his place on the team. In Olympic team trials, too, a swimmer won a place by qualifying in the 800-meter relay while still sore and still bandaged six days after an appendicitis operation.

It is also reassuring to view the spare capacity of the body—what one can live without if necessary and, in some instances, even live without comfortably.

Half the brain is a spare. This has been shown in cases of serious brain damage caused by strokes and head injuries, with loss of memory, language, speech, even understanding. Although damaged areas remain damaged, other areas can be trained to take over their function. During World War II, a marine lieutenant on Okinawa received four shell fragments that ripped through the whole left side of his brain, leaving him paralyzed on one side of his body, unable to read, write, talk, or even understand what was said to him. Two years later, he was in college, his paralysis largely overcome, his ability to read, write, and talk restored.

If necessary, the stomach can be removed completely—and has been to save the lives of cancer patients—with part of the large intestine transposed to become a kind of new stomach. Eighty percent or more of the small intestine—the organ that normally does most of the work of digesting food—can be dispensed with. More than three quarters of the liver can be removed. One kidney, if necessary, can support life. So can one lung. Virtually every organ can be removed from the pelvic area, and life can go on. In fact, a super-radical operation has prolonged life in otherwise hopeless cases when cancer of the vulva, uterus, ovaries, vagina, bladder, or rectum has spread to adjacent organs. The operation involves removal of all organs, nerves, and blood vessels in the pelvic region; nothing is left there.

The body has been known to survive extremes of hunger, thirst, temperature. A South Barre, Massachusetts, seaman lived after floating on a raft at sea for 83 days without food and, during the last 12 days, without water. At Memorial Hospital, New York, a 100-pound woman survived a fever of 114 degrees, possibly the highest on record. At the other extreme, a young Chicago woman survived a body temperature of 60.8 degrees.

On a November day some years ago, a young woman in Newcastle, England, gave birth to a child. The previous May she had been struck on the head by a log falling from a truck and had lost consciousness. She had remained unconscious for 169 days. For seven days, too, she had been in a state approaching hibernation when, as part of treatment, cooling had brought her temperature down to well below normal. She recovered in time to give birth without complications to a husky 8-pound son.

But capable as the body is of demonstrating remarkable powers in emergencies, it is obviously the better part of wisdom to avoid the need. The purpose of this section is to consider the various systems of the body, to provide what we hope will be practical, useful insights into how they are organized and their functioning, how nature has provided for their protection, and what you can do to add to the protection.

Total health represents the summation of the health and efficient functioning of the individual parts of the body. If lungs, heart, liver, kidneys, skin, and other organs and tissues work at maximum efficiency—and if, to this, is added a healthy mind free of excess nervous tension, anxiety, or depression—then the basis for full enjoyment of the body and of life is complete. The complex and wonderful human mind will be covered in the next section. The body, as you will see in this section, is no less complex and wonderful.

16

THE SKIN, HAIR, AND NAILS

THE SKIN is the body's largest organ, having an area in an average 150-pound person of 17 to 20 square feet and weighing about 6 pounds, twice as much as either liver or brain. It extends into the nose and other body cavities in the form of thin mucous membrane which secretes lubricating fluids.

The skin is an enormously versatile and protective organ. It serves to keep body fluids in and foreign agents out, to shield against harmful rays, to help regulate body temperature. It forms the body's shape, contains the sense of touch, is a main organ of sexual attraction. The skin even reflects much about the state of health of the body, as you may have noticed in sick people, and also about the state of mind, as is evident when someone blushes with embarrassment or pales with fear. And although beauty is a composite of many things, physical and mental, there is no doubt that an attractive, healthy skin contributes greatly to beauty.

The more knowledge you have about the skin, the better able will you be to prevent disturbances to it and maintain its integrity, beauty, and protective values.

STRUCTURE

Although it appears to be just a simple covering, a single square inch of skin may contain some 70 feet of nerves, 650 sweat glands, 15 to 20 feet of blood vessels, 65 to 75 hairs and associated muscles, 100 oil glands, and hundreds of nerve endings for detecting pressure, pain, heat, cold.

Three layers of tissue form the skin: the epidermis, dermis, and subcutaneous layer. The epidermis is the outer layer, and because living cells cannot survive exposure to air, the outermost portion of the epidermis, the visible surface, is actually made up of dead rather than living cells. Microscopic layers of cells from the outer epidermis are constantly being lost through bathing and rubbing against clothing. They are replaced from underneath by new cells formed in the malpighian layer of the epidermis. Here, in this deeper layer, where new cells are formed, the skin may be colored by a pigment called melanin, which has as its purpose the prevention of tissue damage from the more dangerous rays of the sun. Skin color is also influenced by another pigment which is yellow and by the presence of blood vessels in the dermal layer.

Beneath the epidermis is the dermis, sometimes called the "true skin." At the top of the dermis is a layer of tiny, rounded ridges called papillae, which project outward, perhaps 150 million of them throughout the body. The cell layers of the epidermis grow down around the papillae. On the fingertips, the papillae form the lines and whorls called fingerprints.

The dermis carries the skin's blood supply. Through microscopically thin walls of tiny capillary vessels in this layer of skin, the blood supply of the body can be brought close to the surface. When the body becomes overly warm, these blood vessels dilate. When dilated, the capillaries have more surface area, permitting an increase in the rate of evaporation and cooling. When the body becomes cool, the capillaries constrict, reducing heat loss through the skin.

Along with blood vessels, bundles of nerve fibers enter the skin and branch out in profusion. The supply of nerve endings makes the dermis highly responsive, especially in such areas as the fingertips where the nerve endings are in particularly heavy supply.

There are involuntary muscles in the skin which dilate and contract the capillaries. There is also an erector muscle connected to the side of each follicle, or hair pocket. When erector muscles contract, hairs stand upright. It is this that makes furred animals appear larger when they are in danger; it also provides an insulating air layer between the hairs as protection against cold. Some investigators believe that the action of erector muscles in man, which produces "goose pimples," stems from the days when our ancestors had hairy bodies.

The subcutaneous layer under the skin is attached loosely to inner body structures such as bones and muscles. Along with blood vessels and nerves, the subcutaneous layer contains fat globules which serve both to insulate the body against heat and cold and to cushion inner organs against bumps and jolts. If fatty tissues become too thick, graceful movement of muscles may be hindered. As people grow older, the fatty tissue in the subcutaneous layer may be absorbed, causing the outer skin layers to form uneven folds, or wrinkles.

Hair ·

Hair, which is part of the skin, varies considerably in texture from the soft, almost invisible type on the forehead to the long scalp hairs and the shorter, stiff hairs on the eyelids.

The root of each hair is anchored at the bottom of a follicle, or tiny shaft. The follicle passes through the epidermis, deep into the dermal layer, and the follicle of a long hair may penetrate into the subcutaneous layer. Emptying into the follicles are sebaceous, or oil, glands.

Each hair has a shaft which extends past the top of the follicle and is covered with microscopic overlapping scales. Cells in an inner layer of the shaft contain pigment that determines hair color. In white hair, these cells contain air rather than pigment. Attached to each hair follicle, too, is a small bundle of muscle fibers which, under influence of cold or emotions, causes the hair to become erect and produces "goose flesh."

The average scalp has about 100,000 hairs. Blonds generally have about 20,000 more and redheads about 20,000 less. Hereditary influences determine color, texture, and distribution of hair over head and body. Hairs can grow only so long as follicles are alive. Sometimes follicles wear out or are destroyed by illness. Baldness indicates that the follicles have stopped functioning. If the baldness is caused by disease, the hair may grow back. Most often, however, baldness is a hereditary condition and there is no known way to renew the hair follicles.

Like baldness, the tendency for hair to turn gray is inherited. There is no evidence that graying is caused by a vitamin deficiency or a sudden emotional crisis.

Hair follicles follow a cycle: they are active for a period, then wither, then rest, then become active again. Withering lasts several weeks and during this period hair shafts fall out. About 30 to 60 hairs are lost daily from the scalp but the follicles are not lost. After a resting period of several months, the hairs begin to grow again and continue to grow for several years.

Hair growth during the active period varies according to body location. Scalp hair growth has been measured at about .012 inch daily, beard growth at .15 inch. Elsewhere on the body, growth is slower.

Nails

Like hair, the fingernails and toenails are a specialized form of skin. As fingers and toes develop, a thin layer, known as the stratum lucidum, which separates dermis and epidermis, thickens and hardens. The fully developed nail overlays a modified part of the dermis that is the nail bed. At its base, the nail is covered by epidermis.

The root of the nail grows outward from pockets in the epidermis much as hair grows from a follicle. The nail is made up of living cells as far as the pale lunule, visible at the base of the nail. The rest of the nail, virtually all the visible portion, is made up of dead cells.

Nail growth rate varies, depending upon such factors as age and season of the year. Nails tend to grow faster in young people and during summer months.

SKIN CARE

Regular cleaning of normal skin with soap and water is desirable for both health and cosmetic reasons. Cleaning removes oily secretions, sweat, dead skin, and bacteria as well as any dirt present. There is no particular mystique about the cleaning process. A clean washcloth or complexion brush serves the purpose. Soap need not be massaged into the skin. It should always be rinsed off thoroughly.

Normal skin tends to become dry with middle age, and a plain cold cream or oily lotion can be helpful. If the skin tends to be excessively oily, washing with a moderately drying soap two or three times daily and use of a nongreasy cleanser often will help. If the oiliness still persists, an astringent may be used two or three times a day on such oily areas as nose, chin, and forehead. If, however, any redness or unusual irritation develops, such preparations should be discontinued.

Germicidal soaps and antiseptics are not essential. Healthy skin is not bothered by germs that land on it. You should, of course, take proper care of cuts and scrapes.

SHAVING

Most men develop their own individual routines of shaving—and if they work well, if there are no problems of frequent cuts or infections, they need no change. For those, however, who do have troubles, a few guidelines may be helpful. It is not commonly appreciated but actually the most effective beard softener in preparation for shaving is water. Two minutes' contact with warm water hydrates and softens bristles—and the warmer the water, the shorter the time needed. Soap or cream helps to accentuate and maintain the softness achieved with water. Apply the soap or cream after the water exposure, employ a sharp blade in a good quality safety razor, stretch the skin ahead of and in the path of the blade, and a good shave should result.

After shaving, it is helpful to wash the face completely with warm water, and follow with an after-shave lotion. If you don't react well to perfumed lotions, ask your druggist to supply pure 70 percent alcohol. Finish the job with powder, especially over any areas that appear chafed.

For cuts: Usually a small cut will stop bleeding if treated with cold water and some clean tissue paper. By the time you have finished shaving, you should be able to remove the tissue gently with cold water and there should be no further problem. If there is, however, use a styptic.

For infections: If there is any infection of the face, shave around it. With infection present, discontinue using a shaving brush. Use a new blade for each shave, and shave noninfected portions of the face first. If infection covers a wide area, your physician may want you to continue shaving daily, even over the infection, in order that medicine he prescribes may penetrate more thoroughly into infected hair follicles.

Electric razors: Men who use them insist that anyone who gives them a fair try will be converted. For men with heavy beards whose work requires freedom from "five o'clock shadow," keeping a spare electric razor at work may be advisable. An often-useful procedure for men with excessively tough beards is to shave quickly with an electric shaver to remove 80 to 90 percent of the obvious stubble, then finish with lather and safety razor. This often produces an elegant result even with the toughest type of beard.

EXCESS HAIR IN WOMEN

Excess hair can be unattractive and it is certainly understandable to want to be rid of it. But consider trying a bleach first, using ordinary peroxide to which a drop of ammonia has been added. Avoid bleaches containing sodium perborate.

If you still find that the excess hair must be removed, the simplest method is to shave. An electric razor—and there are some, of course, made specially for women—will not toughen the skin. And despite what you may have heard, shaving does not encourage growth of hair or make the hair coarse. It is easier and better to shave than to rub hair off with an abrasive such as pumice, and far less painful than pulling out many hairs with tweezers.

Be careful about use of a chemical depilatory on the face. Waxes, though painful, are safer. If you do use a chemical depilatory on the body, be careful not to get it in the eyes; and always try it on a small spot of skin to make certain that it is not irritating for you. Don't use a chemical depilatory more often than once every two weeks, and discontinue promptly if the skin itches or becomes inflamed.

No depilatory removes hair permanently. The only permanent hair removal method is electrolysis, which involves insertion of a tiny needle into the hair follicle and passing an electric current through the needle to destroy the root. This is a tedious, difficult method and is useful only for removal of hair from small areas. Some women have had hair successfully removed this way from upper lip or cheek. Keep away from quacks or people who advertise miraculous methods of hair removal. Your physician can help you find an expert who can do the work well and safely, avoiding scarring and pitting.

WRINKLES

Many skin specialists place a large share of blame for wrinkles on excessive sunshine. Total avoidance of the sun is not necessary, but care in the amount of direct or reflected sunlight you expose yourself to is warranted.

Another cause of wrinkles is excessive exposure to soap and water. Many housewives rinse their hands automatically before touching almost anything. Without realizing it, they may rinse several dozen times a day. Cleanliness is not to be forsaken but it is a good idea to do some housework wearing rubber gloves or to rub on a good hand lotion from time to time. Bath oils have become popular because women have noticed how attractive the skin looks after being anointed with oil.

It is important, we think, to note here, too, that when an overweight person takes off weight too quickly—more than three or four pounds a week—the skin may become loose and wrinkled. Weight loss should be undertaken at a moderate pace, for the sake of both general health and skin appearance. If careful reducing is combined with exercise, the skin will not become loose and wrinkled.

Skin massage cannot prevent wrinkles; it may make you feel good but accomplishes little else. "Skin foods" won't do any good either. Like any other organ, the skin is fed by the body and needs no special foods of its own. Wearing "wrinkle eradicators" or "masks" to bed nightly won't help either. Actually, once wrinkles or lines have appeared, only skillful plastic surgery can eliminate them.

There is, we believe, a place for wrinkle removal through surgery—for anyone, such as an actress, for whom a youthful appearance may be a professional necessity. For the average woman, we would suggest: Why not just avoid frowning and, instead, smile, so that when wrinkles or lines appear, they add to, rather than detract from, the appearance.

Exaggerated wrinkle-removing and rejuvenating claims are made for many lotions, creams, muscle oils, astringents, skin conditioners, etc. If you find yourself sorely tempted to use one, consult your local Better Business Bureau or write to the American Medical Association, 535 North Dearborn Street, Chicago, Illinois 60610.

COSMETICS

Most cosmetics on the market today may improve appearance without harming the skin. Lipstick, powder, rouge are usually harmless unless you happen to have a special allergy or sensitivity to the preparations themselves or perfumes they contain. Some lipsticks dry the lips, but with a little experimenting most women can find a suitable one. Pancake makeup and powder bases may clog the pores, and it is important to wash them off or remove them with cleansing cream every night.

There is usually no significant difference, aside from odor and attractiveness of packaging, between expensive and inexpensive cosmetics, though it is sometimes difficult for women to believe this.

BODY ODOR AND DEODORANTS

Perspiration itself is essentially odorless. When odor does develop, it is the result of bacterial action on the secretions from the skin's glands. Thus, bathing is the primary method of body odor control. When a full bath cannot be taken, body odor can be largely controlled by bathing armpits and genital area with soap and warm water.

Deodorants are formulated to mask or diminish body odor. They do not affect the flow of perspiration. Antiperspirants contain compounds to reduce the amount of perspiration. Their effectiveness varies depending not only upon ingredients but on such factors as the individual's normal perspiration rate and activities that may encourage perspiration.

CREAMS

Cold cream, a cleansing agent, generally is a water-in-oil emulsion. The mineral oil in it helps dissolve fatty skin secretions and loosen grime particles. The cream's suspending effect helps in removing dirt with tissue or soft towel.

A variation, the so-called liquefying cleansing cream, may contain mineral oil that is not emulsified but rather is solidified with paraffin or petrolatum to a consistency that allows it to melt upon contact with the warmth of the skin. This oily film is intended for the same purpose as emulsified cold cream.

Cold creams and other cleaners should remain on the skin only briefly, since the actual cleaning operation requires removal of the cream together with the secretions and grime.

On the other hand, other creams—lubricating, moisturizing, conditioning, and "night" creams—have a different purpose and require longer contact, generally overnight. Their objective is to help make the skin smoother by overcoming drying and roughness. For this, they provide a lubricant, emollient (softening) or humectant (moisture-attracting or -retaining) action. The film of cream, when applied to the skin, closes out air, and the water in the cream—sometimes aided by ingredients such as glycerine and sorbitol—has a moistening effect.

Foundation cream has similar ingredients for moistening and is used prior to makeup to provide a thin film that becomes a base for powder and rouge while providing some protection against grime.

Although many manufacturers add to creams certain mystic ingredients—ranging from royal jelly to orchid pollen, mink or turtle oil, placenta extract, and assorted hormones and vitamins—claiming that they make it possible for women to keep or regain youthful appearances, many medical authorities believe that the claims have not been substantiated on a scientific basis, and the buyer is getting perhaps a good cold cream but at a high price.

COMMON SKIN PROBLEMS

Skin variations among individuals—for example, in the amount of pigment, number of sweat and lubricating glands—can be considerable. Sometimes extremes of these give rise to problems.

SKIN SPOTS AND FRECKLES. The less pigment the skin contains, the lighter the color. Those rare people who have virtually no pigment are called albinos. Much more common are less extreme cases of people with skins that tend to produce relatively little pigment; for them, sunburn must be guarded against.

Many individuals have skins that freckle on exposure to the sun. If you happen to be a freckler who must spend considerable time in the sun, expose your skin as little as possible. A heavy suntan lotion or face powder will help. Some lotions contain perfume oil which may cause dark brown spots to develop, and so you may find it necessary to use a lotion without perfume.

Avoid "freckle removers." Any preparation strong enough to be effective may produce inflammation unless used under medical supervision. Usually, the best thing to do for freckles is to cover them with face powder or, if necessary, with a preparation such as Covermark. If the freckles are so disfiguring as to present a very real problem not otherwise solvable, it is best to ask your physician to refer you to a dermatologist or a skin clinic for a trial of more intensive treatment.

What holds for freckles does, too, for "liver spots"—marks that may occur in dark-skinned people, and actually have nothing to do with the liver but are simply increases in pigmentation.

White areas that appear on the skin are usually due to loss of pigment in specific areas (vitiligo). If the areas are conspicuous, the best thing to do about them is to cover them—and, certainly, to avoid tanning, which makes them more conspicuous.

EXCESSIVE PERSPIRATION. While this in some cases may be due to the menopause or to actual poor health—night sweats, for example, are characteristic of some diseases—excessive perspiration is not uncommon in people in excellent health. If you're in good health and perspire excessively, especially under the arms, you can probably control it with a commercial antiperspirant-deodorant preparation of your choice. A common ingredient in such preparations is aluminum chloride, which is usually perfectly safe, unless you happen to be allergic or sensitive to the chemical. It is always wise to test any preparation cautiously a few times, using very little, until you are certain it is all right for you. If it is not, if repeated applications produce irritation, stop using it.

Deodorants, as already noted, mask odor but do not check perspiration. Antiperspirants, commonly combined with deodorants, tend to reduce the amount of perspiration. It does no harm to check perspiration in the armpits, hands or feet, since the rest of the skin is large enough to do the work of sweating. But never apply an antiperspirant preparation to the entire body.

Offensive body odor (bromhidrosis) is rare. It can often be overcome by bathing and use of a deodorant or antiperspirant under the arms. No special soap is needed. Men may prefer to wash under the arms with soap, follow with an application of rubbing alcohol which, upon drying, can be covered with an absorbent powder such as an ordinary baby talcum preparation.

DRY SKIN. An insufficient flow from the sebaceous glands causes dry skin. This is not uncommon in middle and older age, and tends to encourage wrinkling. If your skin is dry, avoid frequent washing with soap and water; instead, use a cleansing cream or oil, or a soap substitute. At bedtime, apply an emollient cream which usually contains lanolin or cholesterol (which is derived from lanolin) blended with vegetable oils and fats. Do not use plain lanolin. Olive oil or a commercial product such as Nivea cream is satisfactory. Apply more frequently if necessary.

Dry skin often tends to chap during cold weather or in very dry air. If chapping occurs, treat as just indicated for dry skin. A lotion or hand cream may be used for chapped hands.

CHAFING. This is the result of friction, usually from clothing or the rubbing together of body surfaces such as the thighs, which may be damp from perspiration. By keeping the areas dry and by using a good plain talcum powder, you can usually clear up the irritation.

PRICKLY HEAT. Common in infants, this is due to overheating of the skin. Keep the skin as cool as possible and use a light powder rather than a heavy one which will block perspiration and accentuate the condition.

FROSTBITE. The result of severe cold, frostbite usually affects nose, ears, fingers, or toes. Warm the parts gradually. Do not rub on snow or massage a frostbitten area, since this may damage the skin. For severe frostbite, a physician should be seen as soon as possible so effective treatment may be started and gangrene prevented.

OILY SKIN. Sometimes more distressing than dry skin, oily skin often can be corrected by use of plenty of soap and water, avoidance of creams and greasy lotions. Go easy, too, on heavy powder or pancake makeup, always washing it off thoroughly at night. The main problem faced by many people with oily skin is acne.

ACNE

Acne, with its pimples, blackheads, and whiteheads, is a disorder that affects almost all teen-agers and some adults. Severity varies greatly. Acne may sometimes take the form of only a few blackheads. On the other hand, there may be many blackheads plus pustules and cysts or inflamed sacs deep in the skin.

The exact cause of acne is still not clear, although much is known about the problem. As sexual maturation approaches in both sexes, glandular activity increases, and, as part of this, there is a stepping up in the outpourings of the sebaceous glands of the skin. In girls, this may be particularly pronounced at the time of menstrual periods.

The sebaceous glands, which keep the skin moist and soft, pour an oily substance, sebum, onto the skin surface through hair follicles. Normally, the sebum is liquid and passes readily through the follicles. However, if the flow is hampered—through some obstruction of the pathway or through overthickening of the sebum itself—an inflammation may follow.

Acne can be looked upon as a disorder of body chemistry, even though its manifestations appear on the skin. Adolescent acne accompanies a natural but sudden increase in the production of sex hormones and other glandular changes. Activity of the sebaceous glands is stepped up, too.

Usually, acne disappears in later adolescence or early adulthood, even though sex hormone activity continues. The sebaceous glands function more efficiently after the rapid adolescent glandular changes have passed.

Blackheads, or comedones, develop when excess oil accumulates in the pores. Their blackness represents not so much dirt as the discoloring effect of air on the fatty material in the clogged pore. If inflammation occurs, as it often does, a pimple results.

Acne is a problem that, in effect, often feeds on itself. An unsightly pimple is something the owner wishes to have disappear. The seemingly simple and beguiling solution is to squeeze the pimple. But the squeezing, while it may reduce, immediately, the size of the elevation, breaks a membrane—a kind of inner capsule around the pimple below the skin surface. As a result, infectious material, previously contained within the pimple through the good offices of the membrane, now may spread to surrounding tissue. And, of course, infectious material squeezed out of the pimple spreads over the skin surface. One consequence may be more pimples. There is considerable risk, too, that the rough breaking of the membrane and the disturbances that follow may produce scar tissue and pits.

There is no 100 percent effective way to prevent acne. But there are measures that can be used to minimize the immediate unsightly effects of acne and the risk of an aftermath of scars and pits.

For one thing, certain foods are known to increase sebaceous gland activity; in effect, they feed the glands and encourage production of sebum. Their avoidance, and the resulting reduction of sebum production, can be of value. The foods include nuts, chocolate, fried items, pastries, and candies with high butterfat content. It is not necessary to eliminate all desserts and fats. Do go easy on rich foods, greasy foods, and chocolate; and carry on an intelligent search for any other foods that you may find have a particularly irritating effect on your skin.

Especially in the acne years, keep the skin scrupulously clean. This can help reduce plugging of pores and start-up of blackheads. Wash often and thoroughly with warm water and plain soap. Scrub the skin with a clean washcloth, but not so hard as to produce irritation. Follow with a cold rinse. Have your own washcloth and towel; change both at least once a day.

Avoid all creams and greasy lotions. Do not contribute to pore plugging with heavy makeup or "pore-closing" beauty aids; this is the last thing in the world you want to do.

Do remove blackheads—but do so properly. Soak in warm sudsy water to help loosen them. Never use your fingers to squeeze out a blackhead. At most drugstores, you can buy an inexpensive little device, a comedone extractor. Press the extractor gently over a blackhead. If the blemish comes out readily, fine; after its removal, touch the spot with rubbing alcohol (70 percent). If it doesn't come out readily, leave it alone for a while until it is ready to come out more easily.

If you watch your food intake, keep your skin clean, take care of blackheads properly, there is likely to be a minimum of pimples. This is about the limit of primary prevention of this important, widespread ailment. There is no vaccine for prevention. Yet, by employing the primary and secondary preventives we advise, you should escape the major problems of acne.

Some pimples may appear, and these too can be handled properly. Do not squeeze; this will take willpower, but it is worth exerting. Apply a compress wetted with hot water. This will encourage healthy drainage and healing. Hide the offending spot with Acnomel cake, which will also help to heal the pimple.

If you have severe acne, your physician can help bring it under control with medication he can prescribe, including antibiotic agents that are taken internally. Topical applications of special medicated preparations may also be of value. Medical attention for a severe case of acne not only can help to improve appearance but also can root out any serious infectious process and greatly reduce risk of scarring.

Even if acne has scarred your face, medical science can help. "Planing" with a rotary high-speed brush is often effective in scar eradication. In the process, the outer layer of pitted skin is removed, leaving the part containing glands and hair follicles. New skin, rosy at first, then fading to normal color, grows in from the bottom up. Planing has been used successfully even in removing some types of birthmarks and disfigurations due to accidents.

Remember that planing is a surgical operation, though not a major one. But it must be performed by a competent physician with the same care used during and after any operation. Never let a beauty shop employee or any other nonmedical person treat acne.

ACNE ROSACEA

Although somewhat similar in name to common acne, acne rosacea bears no resemblance to it in appearance or mechanism. Popularly, it is often termed "whiskey nose," which could hardly be more erroneous. Rosacea occurs in people who have never touched alcohol.

It involves excessive flushing of the blood vessels of nose and cheeks. A nervous reflex may be a factor in such excessive flushing, and drinking alcohol may encourage the reflex, but the alcohol is not essential. With long-continued abnormal flushing, the blood vessels become more apparent, and nose size may increase.

Even the worst case of acne rosacea can be cured. And, in mild or early stages, the problem often can be controlled by simple measures: frequent application of cold water, witch hazel, or ice to help contract the blood vessels. Pat or rub on gently; do not massage. It is also often helpful to minimize intake of alcohol and of hot and spicy foods.

SKIN ALLERGIES AND SENSITIVITIES

The skin, if a tough organ, is also a sensitive one. It can mirror emotions; it can also mirror internal allergic states. People have long been familiar with one form of allergy manifested in the skin—hives. In hives, superficial areas filled with a watery fluid appear and disappear on the skin, often itching quite severely. Hives may pop up after a particular food is eaten. Nettle rash, drug rash, and urticaria are other names for similar conditions.

Itching from allergic reactions can be relieved by application of calamine lotion available in any drugstore or by bathing in water containing a cupful of bicarbonate of soda per bathtub of water.

Of course, the best thing to do, when possible, is to identify and avoid the substance that produces the reaction. Sometimes, this is not difficult. Many people have been able to determine for themselves that they get hives or "break out" after eating strawberries, for example, or after using a perfumed soap, wearing certain types of fabric, or taking a certain medication. It is certainly not difficult to discover that one is allergic to poison ivy or poison oak. There are instances, however, when it requires the detective skill of a specially trained physician—a dermatologist or allergist—to determine whether, in fact, a condition is really due to allergy and, if so, what the culprit substance or substances may be.

Skin sensitivity is not the same thing as allergy. For example, if your hands become irritated after repeated use of a strong cleansing agent, but not irritated after repeated use of the same agent in a weaker solution, you are sensitive rather than allergic to it. The allergic individual reacts to very tiny amounts of materials to which he is allergic.

Skin sensitivity varies greatly among individuals. Some skins are sensitive to a multiplicity of things; others to few if any. (See Allergy, page 567.)

SKIN INFECTIONS

Exposed as it is, the skin is subject to invasion by many types of microorganisms, including bacteria that may be harmless and other bacteria that may cause boils or impetigo; viruses that cause fever blisters; parasites responsible for scabies; fungi that cause such problems as athlete's foot; and the organism of syphilis, the spirochete, which produces syphilitic lesions.

A boil is a swollen, inflamed area on the skin produced by bacteria—bacteria that often are present on the skin but unable to do any damage unless resistance has been lowered by such things as irritating friction, cuts, poor health, bad nutrition, or diabetes. A carbuncle, which may be produced by the same type of bacteria involved in boils, is more serious than a boil because it involves inflammation not only of the skin but of deeper tissues and is accompanied by a general feeling of illness.

Boils and carbuncles respond readily to medical treatment, which may include use of penicillin or another antibiotic and/or incision and drainage if necessary. In addition, the physician will try to determine the basic cause and treat or eliminate it if possible. (Diabetes may be heralded by the appearance of boils and other skin infections.)

Anyone with a carbuncle should see a doctor. So should anyone who has a number of boils at one time or suffers from repeated outbreaks. Boils and carbuncles can be serious matters. Organisms from a boil or carbuncle may enter the blood, with grave and even fatal consequences. This is particularly true of a boil or carbuncle on the nose or upper lip, because in these areas there is an easier access route for the organisms to reach the brain.

If you have a small boil that is not on nose or upper lip, it is usually safe for you to try the following:

Wash the boil and surrounding area with soap and water several times a day. Lightly dab on 70 percent alcohol afterward. Cover, not too tightly, with an antiseptic gauze pad to prevent irritation. In addition, hourly for ten minutes at a time, apply hot compresses. Make the compresses by soaking an antiseptic gauze pad in hot water containing as much table salt as will dissolve in it. This not only helps relieve pain but stimulates the boil to come to a head and drain. Cover with a fresh dry pad. If the boil does not get better within a few days, see your physician. Do not attempt to open a boil yourself or let an amateur surgeon friend try.

Impetigo, which is caused by bacteria, is a contagious skin infection, especially in infants. It is characterized by yellowish crusts, often on the face, that look as though they had been deliberately pasted on the skin. A doctor can easily cure impetigo before complications have a chance to develop.

Folliculitis is similar to impetigo except that the infection affects the hair follicles or the pore openings of the skin. *Barber's itch* is a special case of folliculitis which involves the beard and makes shaving a problem for men afflicted with this frequently stubborn infection. The medical name for barber's itch is *sycosis vulgaris.* It may take some time to cure even a mild case of folliculitis. You may need one visit to the physician for instruction in removing infected hairs.

Fever blisters (herpes simplex) are virus-caused and usually occur with a fever or cold, appearing around the mouth and nose. Sometimes the blisters follow exposure to sun and wind. Usually they clear within a week or so. A drying lotion such as 1:500 aluminum acetate in cold water is comforting when applied with bits of cotton. Spirit of camphor is a helpful application in mild cases. Cold cream may help to bring relief during the onset period. Troublesome, recurrent fever blisters should be seen by a physician who may be able to eliminate the cause.

Shingles (herpes zoster) is also virus-caused and actually involves infection of a nerve, along with the eruption that appears on the skin. Once it was commonly believed that shingles could be fatal if the infection completely encircled the body and "met." This has no basis in fact. There are potentially serious complications from shingles in the eyes and nerves. Shingles should be treated promptly by a physician.

The itch (scabies), caused by a tiny mite, is extremely contagious. Fortunately, it yields quickly to treatment. While almost any part of the body may be affected, favorite areas for the mite to burrow into the skin include hands, genitals, and skin folds. It is not always easy to determine whether or not one has scabies, and a physician should be consulted for a diagnosis. The remedies used for scabies can aggravate other skin troubles that may be confused with it. A physician will tell you how to kill the parasites in bed linen and clothes.

Athlete's foot, also called *ringworm of the foot,* should have medical attention if it persists. It is caused by a fungus, a microscopic plant growth, which thrives on dead cells of the foot, particularly under warm and damp conditions that may be found on the skin between the toes. Swimming pool walkways, locker rooms, and public showers are sources of infection. For primary prevention, shower slippers should be worn whenever possible. Other means of prevention include keeping the feet clean and dry. If you have a tendency toward athlete's foot, dust the feet with talcum powder after washing and drying. Wear clean socks daily. Persistent athlete's foot, if untreated or inadequately treated, may lead to more serious bacterial infection (streptococci); so if you have a persistent problem, let a physician help you to eradicate it and prevent recurrence.

Other ringworm diseases may develop under the nails, on the scalp, on the skin, and in the genital area. All may be spread by way of contaminated clothing, an infected pet, a barber's unsterilized tools, or dirty combs and brushes. Personal cleanliness and refusal to use anyone else's unwashed clothing, towels, or toilet articles offer the best protection against ringworm ailments.

SKIN GROWTHS

A *wart*, produced by virus invasion, is a small growth of epidermal skin cells. Don't attempt to treat a wart yourself. There are satisfactory methods of getting rid of warts, including application of chemical substances or painless burning off of the growths with a special needle. These methods are not safe unless employed by a skilled physician.

Birthmarks include pigmented moles and the vascular types such as "strawberry marks." Never attempt to remove either kind yourself. Your physician can advise you about the precise nature of the mark, whether it may be expected to disappear spontaneously on its own (as some do), whether and when any special treatment may be needed, and when it is simply most practical to conceal the mark with a cosmetic preparation such as Covermark. Your physician may feel that it is best to remove moles located on the palms, soles, or genitals. Any mole that starts to grow or bleed should be seen promptly by a physician.

Keloids are tumors that do not become malignant. They appear in scars, and should not be cut out, as they usually will reappear in the new scar tissue forming after the cutting out. A physician can remove them with dry ice or radium.

Harmless yellow tumors, called *xanthomas*, are caused by deposits of fat in the skin. If unsightly, they can be removed by your physician.

Keratoses are soft brown spots that may appear in middle age. Later, they become hard, in which case it is usually good practice to have them examined by your physician. They may need to be removed, as they may turn into malignant growths.

Cancer of the skin can be much less serious than cancer in any other part of the body because it can be diagnosed readily and early and removed early—provided no time is wasted on dangerous home treatment. Always make certain that any new or changing growth or lesion —a lump, sore, or wart—is harmless by having your physician check it rather than by "waiting to see." Waiting can represent dangerous loss of time. (See page 556 for more on cancer.)

OTHER SKIN DISEASES

Syphilis may be the reason behind any sore appearing in the genital region between three days to three months after sexual intercourse with an infected person. It may manifest itself again about six weeks later in the form of a measles-like rash, accompanied by symptoms somewhat like those of a cold. Although it is not true that many skin diseases stem from syphilis, there is no time to waste if a sore or rash should be syphilitic in nature. Your physician can cure the disease immediately or set your mind at ease by making a test that can prove you do not have it. Syphilis does not cause pimples and itching. (See page 657 for fuller discussion of syphilis.)

Erysipelas, also known as St. Anthony's fire, is an infection of the skin and underlying tissue caused by streptococcal bacteria. The affected skin becomes swollen, painful, burning, itching, and red, with a glazed, shining surface. It must be treated by a physician, who can cure it with available modern medications.

Glanders, anthrax, and *tularemia* are serious ailments contracted from animals with these diseases. Skin lesions can be important symptoms.

Rashes can be caused by many contagious diseases such as smallpox, meningitis, measles, and other common diseases of childhood. It is important to note that any rash or abnormal skin condition that is accompanied by a fever or a general feeling of illness is a danger signal. A physician should be consulted for prompt diagnosis and necessary treatment.

Lupus erythematosus, pemphigus, and *scleroderma* are potentially dangerous skin diseases. Lupus erythematosus is manifested by a red eruption of the nose and cheek, which takes the shape of a butterfly. It may follow exposure to the sun. The disease frequently remains in its mild form, especially if the patient follows the physician's recommendations. Pemphigus usually begins as a number of blisters, most commonly starting around the nose and mouth and gradually involving the rest of the body. Scleroderma, a hardening of the skin, is usually preceded by changes in the circulation of the skin, especially in the hands and feet, which become bluish and cold. These diseases today, with prompt treatment, have a far better outlook than only a few years ago. They are rare diseases and are mentioned here as a reminder that the skin is an important organ of the body and can be affected by more than minor ailments.

NEVER NEGLECT A SKIN PROBLEM

It is important to understand that there are literally hundreds of skin ailments, both minor and major; that a skin condition can mirror an internal disorder—a disease of lungs, liver, heart, or other organs of the body; that it may also indicate general poor health, or a vitamin or other nutritional deficiency.

Without years of study, you cannot learn all the skin ailments and all the possible meanings of changing skin conditions. Some, in fact, are difficult for physicians to identify and may require special study by specialists. For this reason, and because the significance of skin changes varies greatly, it is important to consult a doctor if anything unusual happens to your skin. He may be able to quickly relieve your mind of worry; and if it is a serious or potentially serious problem, the opportunity you give him for early diagnosis and early treatment is likely to be of great help in preventing complications and making possible eradication and cure.

NAILS

Generally, fingernails need little special care. In fact, most infections such as abscesses, whitlows, paronychias, or "runarounds" are caused by excessive care—too much manicuring of the cuticle. Push the cuticle back gently. Do not use a sharp instrument for this or for nail cleaning.

Generally, any nail polish you happen to like can be considered safe to use if it does not produce irritation because of allergy or sensitivity. It's a good idea to try out any new polish on a single nail at bedtime and make certain it is safe to use on your other fingers in the morning.

Excessive dryness encourages the development of hangnails, and plain oil or a hand cream can be helpful in correcting the condition. If a hangnail develops, it will heal over in a few days if protected by a small bandage.

Brittleness of the nails does not, as many people still believe, stem from a deficiency in proteins, vitamins, or any other recognized nutrient. Brittleness can be caused by external factors such as detergents, solvents, and manicure preparations. To some extent, brittleness increases with age.

Nails tend to be plastic when moist, brittle when dehydrated. It is possible that frequent use of nail polish removers containing solvents produces some decrease in water-holding capacity. Some investigations suggest that gelatin in large daily doses may be helpful, although, in general, physicians are convinced that no significant improvement is to be expected from gelatin. In some instances, brittleness can be traced to impaired thyroid gland functioning, a circulatory disturbance, or other systemic disorder. If you are bothered by persistent brittleness without obvious external cause, your physician may well be able to help.

The problem of ingrown toenails is discussed in Chapter 27.

HAIR AND SCALP

Hair, which grows from the skin, can reflect, as the skin does, the general state of health. For example, dry, coarse hair may be an indication of underactivity of the thyroid gland. While hair performs no indispensable function—and countless numbers of bald people live long and healthy lives—attractive, well-groomed hair can be psychologically important. Also, proper hair and scalp care can be important in the control of skin problems.

Care of the Hair

Hair, of course, should be kept clean. That requires a washing no less often than every ten days—more often if the hair tends to be oily. Plain toilet soap is excellent for the purpose, dissolved in a little water if you find it easier to use in liquid form. Good shampoos usually contain little, if anything, more of consequence than soap or detergent, along with some perfume to which you may happen to be allergic. Poor shampoos may contain an alkali or borax that may irritate the scalp. Washing removes both natural oil and dirt, and no shampoo we are aware of actually fulfills any claim that it restores oil while washing the hair.

For oily hair, a tincture of green soap is satisfactory. For dry hair, a castile shampoo is good.

Don't forget to wash comb and brush at least as often as you wash your hair. After washing, rinse hair thoroughly. If your water supply is hard, soap is apt to leave a deposit on the hair. Some hard water can be softened by boiling; in other cases, distilling is necessary, but a nuisance. If you have very hard water and soap doesn't rinse off properly, you may want to use a soapless detergent.

While drying the hair, do not rub too hard. Sunlight or a hair dryer that blows air on the hair is good. So is gentle brushing during the drying. A little massage is helpful—but don't be too rough; just press the scalp with your fingers and move it about a little to stimulate the fatty tissue under the scalp. Do this once a day. One hundred daily strokes with a hairbrush is an old custom that deserves continuing; it is excellent for the hair, giving it a sleek and glossy look, and stimulating the glands that supply the natural oil.

If your hair is dry, rub in a little pure olive oil or other oil after shampooing, or more often if necessary. Lanolin, somewhat overrated, works no magic. Brilliantines and similar pomades usually are made of mineral oil and keep the hair in place but nothing more. Sometimes the pomades are so heavy that they clog gland openings. It is generally best to avoid them. If your hair is oily after shampooing, a little alcohol, quickly rubbed off after application so it does not evaporate on the hair, will help.

Your hair does not require singeing although you may have been told that singeing "seals up the ends, keeping in the oil, coloring, and other vital fluids." It does none of this. Sunlight is good for the hair in moderation, but will not make it grow. Nor will cutting the hair or shaving increase the growth rate. Keeping hair clean and brushed is the best procedure.

Creme rinses are designed to help make hair more manageable and give it a feeling of softness after shampooing and rinsing. A creme rinse leaves a light film which may improve hair gloss.

While egg shampoos and other protein rinses have been put forth as highly beneficial, there is no scientific evidence to support the claims. In fact, many investigators doubt that shampoos or rinses can penetrate the hair shafts, which are essentially lifeless structures. They may, however, have much the same effect as a creme rinse in influencing hair behavior by coating the outer surfaces of hairs.

Dandruff

A certain amount of dead cells, oil, bacteria, and dirt accumulating in the hair is natural and readily controllable with regular shampooing and rinsing. In dandruff, however, there are excesses and complications. The outer layer of scalp peels off in little white scales. The flakes become large, greasy, yellowish. They may block sebaceous gland openings so the hair becomes dry, but more often dandruff is associated with increased activity of the glands and the hair becomes oily. This latter condition is called oily seborrhea. And the scalp condition may be accompanied by greasy patches of skin on face, neck, and body.

A number of factors can be responsible for dandruff: lowered resistance because of poor physical condition or nervous tension, infecting organisms, lack of absolute cleanliness.

You may be able to clear dandruff by giving some attention to nutrition and general care of the body. Keeping hair and scalp scrupulously clean by shampooing and rinsing every few days may help. It's important to keep comb and brush clean. A moderate amount of sunlight is helpful.

For mild dandruff, you can use a lotion which your druggist may have in stock or your physician can prescribe:

Mercuric bichloride 0.26 gram
Euresol 8.0 cc
Spirit of formic acid 30.0 cc
Castor oil 8.0 cc
Alcohol sufficient to make 240 cc

Apply the lotion two or three times a week, rubbing it into the scalp.

For persistent dandruff, an ointment can be used, either Pragmatar, which is made by Smith, Kline & French Co., or one your druggist can compound:

Sulfur 2 grams
Salicylic acid 2 grams
Water 10 grams
Aquaphor sufficient to make 30 grams

Massage a small amount of either ointment into the scalp at night and remove the following morning by shampooing and rinsing. Use only a small amount so the ointment will not cling to the hair and be difficult to remove.

Oily dandruff can be more difficult to clear up. Apply a pure oil such as olive oil a short time before shampooing, to help loosen scales. Add a drop or two (no more) of ammonia to the rinse water, and rub a little vegetable or mineral oil into the scalp afterward.

Again, it is important to use great care to prevent reinfecting yourself with your comb and brush; cleanse them thoroughly and often. And be sure any beauty parlor or barber shop you visit uses only sterilized combs and brushes.

Almost every type of dandruff, including the severe type accompanied by itching, crusting, or inflammation (seborrheic dermatitis), will improve when treated with a selenium sulfide preparation (Selsun). You will need a prescription from your physician to obtain it. Alboline, Sebulix, Silicare, and Silicote are useful nongreasy preparations, but no preparation we know of actually cures dandruff. The main value of an effective preparation is that it keeps the dandruff under control and makes you wash and brush your hair regularly. Some people like to finish up with a plain shampoo after using a medicated preparation.

Gray Hair

Pigment, of course, determines hair color. And hair grays because, for some reason still not understood completely, air spaces form in the hair shaft replacing pigment—usually in middle age, though it may happen prematurely. Graying, despite the stories you may hear, does not happen overnight, although illness has been known to cause rapid onset of graying. As yet, there is no solid evidence that vitamins or anything else can prevent graying or restore original color to hair which has turned gray.

Hair Bleaching

Hair can be bleached by ordinary hydrogen peroxide to which a drop of ammonia has been added. Sodium perborate bleaches can be harmful. And all bleaching, in fact, tends to alter hair texture. It is to be expected that new hairs, and new portions of hair round the roots, will grow in with the original color.

Hair Dyes

Hair can also be tinted or dyed. An important precaution, if you wish to have your hair dyed, is to have a small lock tested first to find out whether the dye will irritate your scalp or cause a general illness; some people have been made seriously ill by hair dye. Always repeat the test process each time you have your hair dyed, because you can develop a sensitivity as you go along.

Henna is safe but produces only reddish tones and it may make the hair somewhat brittle. There are rinses and tints you can buy in reliable stores; they are generally satisfactory. They do not wash off your hair should it get wet but do come off during shampooing—an advantage if you change your mind or decide that you like your hair gray after it has turned completely so. It is worth remembering, too, that in many cases white hair may make a person look younger rather than older.

Never dye either eyelashes or eyebrows because of the extreme sensitivity of both the eyes and the skin about them. There have been cases of blindness due to eyelash dyeing. A temporary darkener such as mascara is relatively safe but should be used with caution because it may produce irritation.

Permanent Waving

Because the intrinsic structure determines whether hair is curly or straight, its character cannot be changed permanently. But hair is pliable and can be stretched and made curly by hot iron or hair curlers. Too much heat dries it out or scorches it. Hair that is too curly can be stretched and straightened.

Is permanent waving safe? In the process, chemicals are used to make the hair more pliable so it will take the shape of the curler; another chemical is used to make it hold the new shape. While these chemicals may do little harm to the hair, this is not the vital issue, since hair grows fairly regularly under ordinary circumstances. More important is allergy or sensitivity. Always have a "test curl" made first to be certain you will have no severe reaction. Extreme care should be taken to keep waving lotions from the eyes and from any cuts or sores, and to remove them promptly if they touch any sensitive areas. Don't have permanents more often than absolutely essential, and make certain your beauty parlor operator knows her business, since too strong a solution can injure the hair.

Home permanents operate on much the same principle as those used in beauty parlors. There may be greater danger, however, in home permanents because too often a test curl is neglected and there may be some carelessness about keeping the lotion from the eyes and face and from the reach of children. All the lotions are potentially dangerous, so it's important not to grow careless even though you have not yet had any trouble.

Nonneutralizing home permanent kits depend for their action on the oxidation that takes place when the waving lotion is exposed to air as it dries. So far there is no indication that this can cause any more damage to the hair than would occur if a neutralizer were used, but it may not produce so long-lasting a wave.

Baldness

We are sorry to have to report that there is no cure for ordinary baldness—at least, not thus far. Any miraculous cures you may hear about have nothing to do with ordinary baldness, only with special types. For example, in a condition called alopecia areata, the hair suddenly falls out, often in clumps. The disease, not fully understood, appears to be connected with tension and other emotional factors. In many cases, the hair will grow back again after the illness has subsided; and if the sufferer has been using a "hair restorer," he may sign a testimonial in good faith crediting it with his new hair growth.

Baldness can stem from general ill-health, scalp infections, emotional problems, and diseases such as typhoid fever. The ordinary baldness of men, however, is the result of a combination of being male, one's age, and inheritance and, in medical terms, it is called "male pattern alopecia."

Frankly, we do not have available yet a full understanding of ordinary baldness. We know well enough that the tendency to it runs in certain families; that certain racial groups are more susceptible than others; that it is often associated with aging, perhaps because the fat layer between scalp and skull tends to disappear in men with advancing years. We know that the male sex hormone has something to do with it, as it has with the growth of body hair. And here we think it important to warn you never to take or use any preparation containing hormones or any preparation supposed to stop the action of a body hormone without your physician's advice. Such a preparation, if it actually does what it is supposed to do, may endanger the endocrine gland system.

There are some things that may be helpful in retarding ordinary baldness. Control of dandruff is one. Avoidance of excessive hair wetting is another. It can be helpful, too, to avoid lotions and tonics, to protect the general health of the body, and to give the hair proper, but not excessive, attention and care. Once baldness has arrived, it cannot be cured. If it should be particularly distressing because of your business or profession, we strongly urge that you do not waste money on "hair restorers" but rather spend it on a hairpiece which, if carefully made and fitted, cannot be distinguished from your own hair.

Other Hair and Scalp Problems

The hair and the scalp may be affected by many of the same conditions that affect other parts of the skin. Protect your head from irritating chemicals. Don't remove growths of any kind on your own; these should have the attention of a physician.

Scalp infections can become serious, affecting glands, even entering the blood to produce blood poisoning. They can usually be avoided by proper care of scalp and hair, but if an infection does occur, let your physician see, diagnose, and treat it.

Head lice (pediculosis capitis) are a common problem in children, readily transmitted from youngster to youngster. While there are many old methods of eliminating them, including laborious use of a fine-tooth comb, new medications are so effective that it is worthwhile having your physician prescribe one and direct you in its safe use. Care should be taken to avoid reinfection by keeping comb and brush clean through boiling or dipping in alcohol. Children also are quite susceptible to ringworm infections of the scalp. Your physician can cure such infections with little difficulty after he has determined the fungus involved and the medication most suited to eradicating it.

17

THE SKELETAL SYSTEM

BONES FORM the basic framework—the skeleton or chassis—of the body. The primary purpose of the framework is to provide support for the rest of the body through a combination of strength to resist great pressure and flexibility to absorb some shock without shattering. By means of rib cage and skull such vital organs as the heart and brain are guarded.

Obviously, the skeletal system is important. Obviously, too, it is a source of much trouble—witness spinal disk problems and the proneness some people have toward easy bone fracture. Yet it is possible to use simple preventive measures to help maintain a healthy skeletal system. Much of the trouble people have is avoidable trouble.

THE BONES

Generally, there are 206 bones in the body, although about 5 percent of people have an extra, or thirteenth, pair of ribs, and a much smaller percentage have only 11 pairs. At birth, there are actually about 350 bones, some of which later fuse. The fusion is usually complete by the end of the growth period.

Each arm has 32 bones: a collarbone, shoulder blade, humerus, radius, ulna, 8 wristbones, 5 metacarpals in the palm, and 14 phalanges (3 to each finger, 2 to the thumb). Each leg has 31: hipbone, femur, kneecap, tibia, fibula, 7 tarsals in instep and heel, 5 metatarsals in the foot, and 14 phalanges (3 to each toe except for 2 to the biggest toe, the hallux).

The axial skeleton has 80 bones: there are 29 in the head, of which 8 are in the cranium, 14 in the face, 6 in the ears, and 1 in the throat between lower jaw and upper larynx; the spine has 33 bones in all—7 cervical, 12 dorsal or thoracic, 5 lumbar, 5 sacral vertebrae forming 1 bone, and 4 coccygeal vertebrae which, with the sacrum, are fused into one bone (thus, everyone is born with 33 vertebrae but in later life has only 26); there are also the 25 bones in the chest: the breastbone and 24 ribs.

THE STRUCTURE AND STRENGTH OF BONE

About one fifth of the weight of bone is water. Of the rest, about two thirds is mineral and one third organic matter. The minerals are chiefly compounds of calcium and phosphorus, with some of magnesium and other elements, while the organic matrix is chiefly a kind of protein fiber, collagen, which also is found in skin and connective tissue.

The organic and inorganic components of bone along with a cement-like substance are combined in a way that is sometimes compared to reinforced concrete. Bone is so strong that there are areas along the outside of the femur, the long bone between hip and knee, which have been known to resist pressure of over 1,200 pounds per square inch.

There are long bones like the femur (thigh bone), short ones like those in the wrist, flat ones like the shoulder blade, and irregular types like the vertebrae in the spinal column. All, however, have an outer layer of compact bone and an inner meshwork of less dense, actually porous material. Even the inner layer, sometimes called spongy because of its appearance, is remarkably strong.

Far from being inert, the bones contain living cells and blood vessels. There are in fact three types of cells: the osteoblasts, which function in the construction of new bone material and repair of broken bones; the osteoclasts, which dissolve bone bits that are not required; and the osteocytes, which maintain the health of bone around them, using materials obtained from blood.

The long bones, ribs, and vertebrae are the sites, too, where the red blood cells of the body are produced. Each minute, millions of these vital elements are developed in the spongy area from red marrow, since the body requires billions and their lifetime is only a few months.

Thus, the bony framework is not at all comparable to the framework of a building. It is a living framework. And while it has rigidity, it also has flexibility. Muscles are anchored to bone, and the anchoring must be strong. But there has to be movement, too. And it has been said aptly that man is a mixture of stiffness and relaxation, restriction and freedom, joints without movement and joints with great versatility.

THE SKULL

The skull is made up of 22 flat or irregular bones. Fourteen are facial, including those for cheeks, jaw, and upper bridge of the nose. Air spaces, or sinuses, in many of the facial bones serve to reduce the weight of the skull. Eight bones form the cranium, which protects the brain.

There are additional bones in the head area: the hyoid, to which are attached the muscles that move the tongue; and the auditory ossicles in the middle ear—hammer, anvil and stirrup—which respond to sound waves hitting the eardrum with a lever action that transmits the waves to the inner ear.

THE SPINAL COLUMN

The spinal column—a flexible stack of vertebrae—serves to support the head and trunk and also to protect the spinal cord, which extends downward from the brain. Each vertebra is shaped like a circle with the back side of the circle made up of a solid cylinder of bone. Running through the hollow part of the circle, the spinal cord shoots out branches of nerves that go to various parts of the body.

As they stack toward the skull, the vertebrae gradually decrease in size. The vertebra just above the sacrum at the base is a heavy, large bone with large projections on each side and at the back, to which muscles and ligaments are attached. At the base of the skull, the top vertebra is a delicate bony ring with small protuberances.

Between each vertebra and the next is a spinal disk—a circular cushion of connective tissue and cartilage about one-half-inch thick. Each disk has several layers of tough, fibrous rings and a softer nucleus in the center.

THE DISKS

The spinal disks absorb the impact of body weight and movements. Normally, they serve as efficient shock absorbers for a long lifetime. But some of us give them more load or shock than they can bear—through excessive body weight, excessive or improper load lifting, and neglect of good tone in the muscles of both back and abdomen which help to maintain good posture.

There is no such thing as a "slipped" disk, although you hear the term often. What has happened to the victim of a so-called slipped disk is that the disk has been crushed or has worn out and a portion of it has been extruded. The ligaments and fibrous layers of the disk have weakened, and the nucleus has been pushed out from the center into the spinal canal, compressing the nerve roots that branch from the spinal cord at this level. The disk most commonly undergoing such herniation is the one between the fourth and fifth lumbar (lower back) vertebrae. When this disk is affected, pain is usually felt down the back of the leg and even into the side of the foot.

Disk herniation can occur gradually over a period of many years of strenuous jarring activity, or it can be caused by an accident like a fall. Effective treatment for disk herniation is available. It may be conservative, relying upon removal of pressure from nerve roots, use of a firm bed or bed board, traction, and medication. In some cases, surgery may be required.

The wise thing, of course, is to prevent disk problems. One sensible measure is to keep body weight at the proper level. Another is to be careful in picking up heavy weights. And very much worthwhile is the maintenance of physical fitness through regular moderate exercise and the use of special exercises (see page 89) for strengthening back and abdominal muscles.

CARE OF THE BONES

In addition to the measures just mentioned to help protect the spinal disks, and precautions against accidents (see page 501), proper nutrition is extremely important for bone health. Vitamin D is essential for bone production, and other vitamins are required to nourish the bone marrow. These are to be obtained in a balanced diet. Calcium, too, is vital. Most of the calcium in the body is in the bones, but calcium is also needed for muscle contraction, for heartbeat, and for blood clotting. In a remarkable automatic process, when the amount of calcium immediately available for the heart and other parts of the body falls below a certain level, some of the calcium from bone is carried by the blood to these areas. This is normal and healthy, but it underscores the need for adequate intake of calcium to maintain the bone stores. Milk contains plentiful amounts of calcium, which is one reason why it is such a basic item in the diet of growing children and in pregnant and nursing mothers. All through life there is need for adequate calcium intake, and this can be assured by a balanced diet. Calcium is contained in many food items. It is plentiful in dairy foods such as cheeses and in skim or fat-free as well as whole milk.

After the menopause, bones in women need special care. See our discussion of the menopause on page 618.

JOINTS, LIGAMENTS, AND BURSAS

Joints and ligaments connect bones to each other. At the ends of bones are smooth, gliding joint surfaces which make possible easy, painless movement. A joint consists of a fibrous sheath attached to the smooth ends of the bones. Nature also provides, for the ends of those bones that take part in body movements, a special material, cartilage, which has a resiliency and smoothness that enable fingers, arms, and legs to move many thousands of times daily without making us conscious of their activities. To bind bones together and strengthen the joints, there is a special type of tough "binding cord" called tendon. Tendons are so firmly attached to the bones that only an exceptional strain will tear them away. A final element in the smooth, effective movement of joints is the bursa. This is a sac or bag with smooth surfaces which contains a small amount of lubricating material.

Everyday care of the joints, ligaments and bursas is important. An injured joint, torn ligament, or inflamed bursa—as anyone who has ever suffered one knows—can interfere seriously with enjoyment of life and may even be incapacitating. It's essential that you work with, not against, nature so you impose no extra stress on joints, ligaments, and bursas. For one thing, that means maintenance of normal weight; gross overweight overloads the joints of knees and feet every time you stand or walk. Good posture also is important for keeping joints in good condition, distributing weight as nature engineered the body to handle it. And good physical condition, which helps to assure good muscle tone, helps to avoid undue strain.

We suggest that, in connection with proper care of joints, ligaments, and bursas, you read sections of this book dealing with posture and exercise (page 80) and weight reduction (page 59) if you are overweight. Everyone should know the proper technique for lifting objects —by bending the knees and bringing into play the leg muscles to help with the lifting rather than relying entirely upon the muscles of the back.

There are many injuries and diseases that can affect the bones, joints, ligaments, and bursas. These are discussed later in this book—e.g., arthritis and rheumatism, fractures, backaches, bursitis, bone diseases.

18

THE MUSCLES

BONES FORM the framework; joints permit movement; and it is the muscles that do the moving when they pull on bones. The hundreds of voluntary muscles in the body weigh two and one-half times as much as all the bones together. They constitute the flesh that gives the body its basic shape.

An understanding of muscles and how they function is very much worth having, since it can help you to use your muscles most effectively, prevent injuries to them, prevent progressive deterioration if an injury should occur. As noted in the preceding chapter, good muscle tone is an important element in preventing skeletal problems, and as we will point out in this chapter, tone is also important in maintaining good circulatory function.

Muscles always work by pulling, never by pushing. Muscle fibers contract and as they do so the muscle pulls a bone toward it. The body is so engineered that where one muscle acts to pull a bone in one direction, there is another muscle that can be contracted to pull the bone in the opposite direction. Thus, for example, the bulge that can be felt in the front of the upper arm when the lower arm is drawn up is the body of the biceps muscle. The mate to the biceps, called the triceps, lies on the opposite side of the arm and when this muscle contracts it straightens the elbow and stretches the biceps into position for another contraction.

Muscle tissue is formed before birth, and a baby's supply of muscle fibers is his supply for life. The fibers, of course, grow as the child grows. Strength develops as the fibers do their work of contracting. The arms of a blacksmith, prizefighter, or weightlifter contain about the same number of fibers as do those of a little girl but are much stronger and thicker through use.

TYPES OF MUSCLES

Each muscle is made up of a bundle of fibers, each of which is about the size of a hair and capable of supporting 1,000 times its own weight. All told, there are something more than 6 trillion fibers in the muscles throughout the body.

There are three types of muscle tissue. One, when viewed under a microscope, has dark and light bands across the fibers, and is known as striped muscle. It is also called skeletal muscle because it is attached to some part of the skeleton. And it is classed as voluntary muscle because it is under the control of the conscious part of the brain. This is the type of muscle used to walk, write, lift, throw—to perform any movement we actually will to be done.

A second type of muscle, called smooth or involuntary, lacks the dark and light bands. This type of muscle handles the functions of all internal organs except the heart. It is involved in the vital movements of the stomach and intestine, for example. It is called involuntary since we do not have direct control over its action. Its workings are automatic, freeing us from concern over it, allowing us opportunity to concentrate on other matters.

The third type of muscle, that of the heart, is called cardiac. It is striped like the voluntary type but has no sheaths as the voluntary does. It, too, is involuntary.

Muscle fibers vary considerably in length, from as little as 0.04 inch or even less to 1.5 inch or more. The diameter, of course, is very small, as little as 0.004 inch or even less. When a muscle contracts, it becomes shorter by as much as one third to one half, and as it shortens, it thickens.

Most skeletal muscles are linked to a bone either at one end or at both ends. The tendons, or sinews, which do the linking, vary considerably in size, ranging up to more than a foot in length. Ligaments, like the tendons, are made up of strong fibrous tissue, but their function is to bind bones together. Tendons join muscle to bone; ligaments join bone to bone. Ligament fibers stretch. Tendons are so strong that a bone may break before the tendon attached to it gives way.

When muscles join bones, one of the bones usually functions as an anchor to help move the other bone. The point where the muscle attaches to the anchor bone is known as the point of origin. The attachment to the bone that does the moving is called the insertion.

Before a muscle can contract, it must receive a contract signal. In the case of voluntary muscles, the signal comes from the brain via the central nervous system and is relayed instantly through tiny nerves that reach each of the fibers involved.

Involuntary muscles get their signals from the autonomic nervous system, which is concerned with the regulation of body functions that do not have to be under conscious control.

To be sure, even in the case of voluntary muscles, you are not required to give a direct order—to take the time to stop and think and issue a command for a particular muscle to contract. You simply decide to bend an elbow, move a finger, throw a ball—and the brain and nervous system translate the decision into orders which go to the proper muscle fibers.

Since muscle fibers exert pull when they contract, they use energy. The energy comes from food supplied to them through the blood. A muscle works by converting chemical energy into mechanical energy. Actually, only about one fourth of the chemical energy is converted properly into mechanical energy; the remaining three fourths is lost as heat, raising the temperature of anyone doing strenuous work. This efficiency of 25 percent is similar to that of an automobile engine, which also loses much of its energy as heat.

There have been calculations which suggest that the maximum energy output for man is about 6 horsepower and that as much as 0.5 horsepower output can be sustained almost indefinitely.

SOME MAJOR MUSCLES

Skeletal muscles are of many shapes and sizes suited to their particular jobs—and they have many jobs.

The sternomastoid muscles, which are on either side of the head, serve two purposes. When you nod your head, it is because both of the sternomastoid muscles contract simultaneously. You turn your head to one side or the other depending upon which of the two you contract.

Among muscles at the shoulder are the trapezius, which shrugs the shoulder when it contracts, and the pectoralis major, which spreads over the chest and attaches to the humerus and helps sweep the arm across the chest.

On the forearm are muscles that divide into tendons extending down to the fingertips; they help move the fingers.

Among the big muscles of the lower extremity are the gluteal muscles on the buttocks, which, with their contraction, move you from sitting to standing position and are involved in walking; the sartorius, in the thigh, the longest muscle in the body, which pulls the thigh into cross-legged position; the quadriceps in the thigh used for balance during standing and for kicking; and the gastrocnemius and soleus in the calf which enable you to stand on tiptoe and provide the push from the ground for walking, running, dancing.

Along each side of the spinal column are muscles which help to maintain an erect posture, to bend the body, and to help turn it to one side or the other.

Inside the body is the major muscle for breathing, the diaphragm, which is attached through tendons to the spinal column, ribs, and lower tip of the breastbone. The contraction of the diaphragm helps fill the lungs with air. And the diaphragm, incidentally, is also used in laughing, sneezing, and coughing. Its spasmodic contractions occasionally produce hiccuping.

Among the many additional muscles are those of expression—small bundles of fibers around the eyes, mouth, and nose which we use to look angry or surprised, to wink, sneer, smile, frown.

In the gastrointestinal system, there are voluntary muscles at the top, in the upper part of the esophagus. But in the walls of the lower esophagus as well as most of the stomach and intestines are involuntary muscles that help push food along. Actually, there are two layers of such muscles which work in concert: one, a circular layer, contracts to narrow the gastrointestinal tract; the other, longitudinal, contracts to widen the tract again and make way for further narrowing.

Between the esophagus and the stomach, and at other points in the digestive tract, are thick muscular rings, called sphincters, which contract at intervals and can remain contracted for extended periods if necessary to regulate the flow of food and liquid.

MUSCLE TONE

Imagine for a moment that you have a rope fastened to a small wagon. In effect, the rope is a tendon and the wagon is a movable bone. If you pull on the rope, the wagon will move toward you. But if the rope is lying slack on the ground, you first must pull it tight before the wagon can begin to move. If the rope is kept taut, the wagon will move as soon as you pull.

Most voluntary muscles of the body keep their ropes tight, so to speak. They are partly contracted at all times. Rarely, for example, does the jaw sag, and you can hold your head and shoulders erect for hours without fatigue. This ability to maintain partial contraction is muscle tone. Tone may be maintained, and the muscles prevented from becoming slack and deteriorated, by regular exercise and proper nutrition.

MUSCLE CARE

The voluntary muscles are the only ones that require your everyday care. Muscles remain in good condition only when they are used. If they fall into complete disuse, they atrophy or waste away. Short of this, if they are used relatively little, they lose strength and vigor and their tone diminishes.

Healthy vigorous muscles are important for many reasons: for good posture, graceful movement, and a sense of well-being. The spring in the step of a healthy vigorous man isn't simply a matter of well-developed muscles, but of the contribution that good muscular health makes to overall body health and even to mental outlook. Also, strong muscles protect the bones, joints, and internal organs more effectively against injury.

In our increasingly sedentary way of life, unless we resort to special measures, our muscles are victimized by disuse. Actually, when muscles are not used, they have relatively little need for blood and nourishment; and as a result most of the capillaries, the tiniest blood vessels which supply them, collapse and remain collapsed, out of business most of the time. The greater the activity of muscles, the more the capillaries open up and, in fact, the more capillaries may be developed by the body to supply the need. With sedentary living, there is little demand.

One famed experiment by Dr. Hardin Jones of the University of California has shown that the average sedentary American man is, in terms of muscle circulation, middle-aged by the time he is 26. Using Geiger counter tests to follow blood flow through muscles in teen-agers and in 500 industrial workers, Dr. Jones established that between the ages of 18 and 25, the flow drops 40 percent; by the age of 35, it is down 60 percent, at which point, in the sense of physical vigor, the average sedentary man is less than half the man he used to be.

Because of our sedentary living, deliberate exercise is essential—and this applies to all of us, women and children as well as men.

The objective of the exercise should not be the development of big muscles, for muscle size is not a true measure of fitness. A well-founded exercise program should aim at strengthening muscles and also the circulatory system in the interest of endurance—the ability to sustain activity and keep going without quick fatigue.

When you are at rest all the muscles of the body use only about one thirtieth of the oxygen they can use during maximum effort. With a well-rounded exercise program, they can be made to use much more. When they do, the heart will respond, pumping harder to get more oxygen-carrying blood into circulation, and over a period of time, heart pumping efficiency will increase; the heart will pump more blood with each stroke.

At the same time, lung capacity—much of it never used in sedentary living—will enlarge to absorb and feed more oxygen into the bloodstream. The higher oxygen content will aid muscle nutrition.

As circulation improves in both quality and quantity throughout the body, the capillaries penetrating into muscles will open and become more effective.

A good exercise program also will help to strengthen the muscles around the veins in the lower part of the body, and this is of considerable importance. When you stand, the veins in the legs expand and there may be a tendency for them to become distended with blood which pools in them so that less blood is available for circulation through the rest of the body. As less blood returns to the heart from the veins in the lower part of the body, the heart, with less blood to eject with each beat, tries to compensate by increasing its beat rate. But this is not always effective and does impose added stress on the heart. The amount of blood that can pool in the lower veins depends considerably on the amount of pressure by the muscle tissues around the veins. If the tissues are tight and firm, the expansion of the veins is limited. Soft muscles without tone do not provide much external support to the veins to prevent their expansion.

Thus, a good program of exercise can have many admirable effects throughout the body—in terms of health of heart, lungs, muscles, blood vessels. We suggest that you read, in connection with this discussion, the contents of Chapter 8 on exercise.

A word here about nutrition: It, too, is vital in the proper care of muscles. A good diet containing the sources of protein described in Chapter 6 will help you build and maintain strong, healthy muscles.

COMMON MUSCLE PROBLEMS

Almost everyone has experienced a painful muscle cramp or "charley horse." When a muscle is exercised too violently, especially one that has had relatively little use, it may react by going into painful cramp. It contracts—and does not relax. A charley horse will clear up if the involved muscle is rested. Warm baths will help. Two tablets of aspirin by mouth every four hours will also be useful in relieving the pain.

Muscle twitchings can stem from varied causes, usually minor, such as temporary fatigue, overwork of a group of muscles, nervousness, or insomnia. If the twitches become frequent or painful, or if they involve the face and produce grimaces, you should discuss them with your physician without delay. Consult your physician, too, if you experience frequent or painful muscle cramps, especially cramps at night, which sometimes wake people from sleep as they produce intense pain in the calf of the leg or elsewhere.

The most common muscle injury is strain, caused by the overworking of muscles. This is the type of muscle soreness that may follow a long bicycle ride or an afternoon of working in the garden. The muscles become sore and the tendons ache. Usually, no real damage is done and a warm bath and good rest will provide relief.

OTHER MUSCLE PROBLEMS

Muscles may be affected by various diseases. Some are intrinsic ailments of the muscles themselves, such as muscular dystrophy (page 630). Muscles waste away if the nerves connecting them with the brain are damaged, as happens in polio and other afflictions of the nerves and spinal cord. If a stroke damages a part of the brain controlling an arm or leg, then the muscles of the limb may atrophy from disuse. Similarly, in severe diseases of the joints or bones, there may be inability to move a limb, which then causes secondary wasting of the muscles. These problems are discussed in connection with various diseases in later sections of this book.

19

THE CIRCULATORY SYSTEM

ALL LIVING cells of the body must have a supply of fuel, water, and oxygen brought to them and must have their waste products removed. This is the function of the remarkable circulatory system, consisting of the heart and a vast network of blood vessels. In recent years, much knowledge has been acquired about the functioning of the human heart and circulatory system and about factors critical for the health and welfare of the system. There have been significant developments in the area of prevention of disturbances, and there are many measures which you can take quite readily.

THE HEART

Weighing less than a pound when full grown and only a little larger than your fist, the human heart ranks as perhaps the world's most fantastic machine. Despite its small size, it beats an average of 72 times a minute, 100,000 times a day, nearly 40 million times a year. Each day it pumps the equivalent of some 5,500 quarts of blood weighing 6 tons through more than 60,000 miles of the circulatory system. The work done by the heart is comparable to the effort you would have to expend to lift a ten-pound weight three feet off the ground twice a minute for the whole of your life.

A hollow organ, the heart perches in the front part of the chest, under the breastbone in the center, with its apex pointed to the left. It has a muscular wall, the myocardium, which is surrounded by a fiberlike bag, the pericardium, and is lined by a strong, thin membrane, the endocardium.

The heart is actually a double pump. It has four chambers—two at the top called atria and two at the bottom called ventricles. The atrium and ventricle on the right are separated from their counterparts on the left by a wall of muscle, called a septum.

Into the right atrium comes "used" blood returning from coursing through the body, during which trip it has given up its oxygen to body cells in exchange for cell wastes. It now needs freshening and it flows from the atrium through a valve into the right ventricle. The valve, the tricuspid, is there to prevent blood from being pushed back into the atrium when the ventricle contracts. The contraction of the ventricle pushes the bluish "used" blood into the pulmonary artery toward the lungs. Thus the right side of the heart is a pump devoted to moving blood toward the lungs for oxygenation.

When the blood, freshened in the lungs, returns through the pulmonary veins to the heart it enters the left atrium. From here it goes, through the mitral valve, to the left ventricle. And it is the contraction of the left ventricle that sends a surge of fresh blood into the aorta, the great artery which comes out of the heart and from which branches run to all parts of the body. Valves to prevent backward flow of blood are also located where the aorta and pulmonary artery emerge from the heart.

THE HEARTBEAT

The beat of the heart—on the average, 72 times a minute—starts in a knot of tissue called the sinoatrial node located in the atria. The node contains nerve cells and fibers and muscle cells and is called the heart's pacemaker because it gives rise to the impulse, or spark, that starts a wave of contraction. The wave spreads over the muscle of the atria and, upon reaching another node near the junction of atria and ventricles, produces an impulse which leads to contraction of the ventricles.

As already noted, the heart does not lie entirely on the left side, despite a popular notion to that effect. Rather it is near the midline with about one third of its bulk on the right and two thirds on the left. The flatter base of the heart faces backward, and the sharper apex faces out and downward. It is the apex that reaches to the left, and because it pulses with each beat, the heart appears to be centered at that spot rather than stretching toward it.

THE PULSE

You have undoubtedly noted physicians—and perhaps you have done the same yourself—place a finger on the radial artery at the wrist to "take" the pulse. The pulse is caused by the impact of the pressure of blood on the arteries as the heart beats. It provides useful information about the strength and regularity of blood flow.

Generally, for a person in good health, the pulse may speed up from around 70 a minute to more than 120 after vigorous exercise, but then, within three minutes, should return to the original value. There may be some quite normal deviations from average beat, deviations too from the beat with vigorous exercise, and deviations from the average interval required for return to the preexercise rate. If you have any doubt in your own case, you should check with your physician.

BLOOD PRESSURE

Blood pressure is the force exerted against the walls of arteries as blood flows through. With each contraction of the ventricles, which is called a systole, there is a spurt of blood and this increases blood pressure. During the part of the cycle when the ventricles are not contracting, called the diastole, the pressure decreases. Thus, there is always pressure of blood, highest during systole and called the systolic pressure, lowest during diastole and called diastolic pressure.

These pressures can be readily measured with an instrument, the sphygmomanometer (see page 24). And, as the discussion under high blood pressure indicates (page 596), measurement of pressure is an important means of determining the health of the heart and circulatory system.

BLOOD DISTRIBUTION

The circulation of blood—so often dismissed as "blood from the heart into the arteries, to the tissues, then back to the heart through the veins" —is, in the human body, a really intricate and marvelous process. For it is remarkably adaptable.

When blood moves from the heart into the aorta, it is at a speed of about 15 inches a second. Almost immediately, distribution around the body begins through arteries branching off from the aorta. From the smallest arteries, even smaller vessels called arterioles branch out. From the arterioles, blood flows to the smallest of all vessels, the capillaries.

The capillaries transport blood to individual cells; and through microscopic spaces in the capillary walls, oxygen and other supplies are diffused to the cells and, in return, waste materials move into the bloodstream. The capillaries connect with venules, tiny vessels of the venous return system, which run into veins. The veins carry the blood to the great venae cavae, large vessels which empty into the right atrium of the heart.

By the time blood reaches the capillaries, its speed—originally 15 inches a second in the aorta—has slowed to about one fiftieth of an inch a second. The capillaries are so tiny that red blood cells have to move through them in single file—and the red cells are so small that you could cover four or five dozen of them with a single period, such as the one right here.

But small as the capillaries are, the capillary system is so extensive—many thousands of miles, all told—that if all the capillaries were open to the flow of blood at any one time, they could hold the entire five-quart supply of the body. This is where the adaptability of the circulatory system comes in. All the capillaries are never open at one time. They open and close, first in one area, then in another, depending upon need.

When, for example, you are exercising vigorously, the muscles need more blood. The heart responds; from over a gallon of blood per minute, it can pump as much as five and a half gallons a minute. And much of this flow now goes to the muscles which need it, diverted from other organs which do not have such pressing need at the moment. In times of extreme exertion, even though the heart is pumping only five times as much blood, the muscles may receive eighteen times as much, as the capillaries in various organs shut down to allow diversion. The digestive system, for example, will get only one fifth of its normal supply during extreme exertion. Blood flow to the muscles goes up from about two pints a minute to about forty. At rest, the muscles ordinarily get about 20 percent of the heart's output; with extreme exertion, they may get as much as 88 percent. It is only from the brain that blood is never diverted this way. The brain gets its required one and a third pints a minute whether the body is at rest or furiously active.

THE HEART'S OWN SUPPLY

The heart, being a muscle, and a hard-working one, needs nutritious blood. And nature has seen to it that it gets it by special means. The heart's special system begins at the aorta, from which branch off two arteries, the coronaries, each about the size of a thick knitting needle. One enters the heart muscle on the right side; the other, on the left. And the two together form a kind of wreath about the heart. The coronaries divide and divide to feed every part of the heart muscle. And after the blood has deposited its oxygen supply and picked up waste, it is carried by a system of veins to the right atrium to be passed, along with blood returning from other parts of the body, to the lungs.

As we have noted, the heart has remarkable ability to adapt to demands of the body—to beat faster, contract more completely, and thus pump much more blood when necessary. In turn, the coronary circulation has remarkable ability to adapt to the heart's needs when they increase. When the heart must work harder, it needs more nourishment —and the coronary circulation accommodates. Ordinarily, the coronary arteries take only a small fraction of the blood moving through the aorta. But when the heart is working harder, the arteries will take more, even up to half of the total flow through the aorta.

An unusual feature of the coronary circulation is the presence of extra capillaries, many of which form connections between the two coronary arteries. These extra tiny vessels lie unused and empty except when you are exerting yourself to the point of putting bigger demands on the heart. Then they go to work to bring more blood and oxygen to the heart muscle. These same capillaries help, too, if some of the regular blood channels no longer function effectively because of disease. Then the spare capillaries go into regular use as substitute pathways.

There is another safeguard in the fact that each coronary artery doesn't supply only its own side of the heart. Branches extend over to the other side so that many heart areas have blood supplied from both coronary arteries. Thus, if one of these vital vessels should become diseased and narrowed, all is not necessarily lost.

BLOOD

Blood, the body's transport medium, consists of about equal parts of a watery fluid called plasma and a mixture of red cells, white cells, and platelets.

The red cells give blood its color and there are some 25 trillion of them. Each lasts about four months, wearing out and breaking up. And new cells to replace the old are produced in the bone marrow at a rate of about one million a second.

The red color of the cells comes from hemoglobin, a combination of protein and an iron pigment. It is the hemoglobin that actually carries oxygen from the lungs to the capillaries and then carries carbon dioxide to the lungs, where it is exhaled. Hemoglobin is a substance with an ability to hold very large quantities of oxygen. If it didn't exist, and if oxygen had to be dissolved in blood plasma, the body would require 300 quarts of blood instead of 5.

White cells are less numerous than red but still there are 20 to 50 billion of them. Typically, in a pinprick of blood there may be some 10,000 white cells and as many as 5 million red cells. There are several kinds of white cells. One type, the granular leukocyte, is produced in the bone marrow along with red cells. Another, the lymphocyte, is produced in the lymph nodes, tonsils, and adenoids.

White cells have an important role in the body's defense against invasive bacteria. Unlike the red cells, the white ones can move. They usually move along the sides of blood vessels rather than being pushed along with the red cells in the middle. They move by pushing out part of themselves ahead, then sliding the rest into the advanced area. They can flow around and engulf bacteria. The battle, however, is not all one-sided. White cells can be destroyed by bacterial poisons, and pus is an accumulation of dead white cells and bacteria. But while bacteria sometimes can overwhelm the white cells, much more often the outcome is the other way, and most bacterial invasions (and they occur almost constantly) are repulsed.

The blood platelets, which are smaller than the red cells, help blood to coagulate or clot. They collect at the site where a blood vessel is cut or otherwise injured, and they produce tiny fibrin threads, which lead to clot formation, helping to minimize blood loss.

Plasma, which constitutes about half of whole blood, and is the part without cells, is itself about 91 percent water. The remainder is made up of such minerals as sodium, calcium, potassium, and phosphorus, plus fats, sugars, plasma proteins, and antibodies.

Antibodies are another part of the body's defense mechanism. Micro-organisms entering the body stimulate the production of antibodies which then, in very specific fashion, lock on to and incapacitate them. And it is by causing the body to produce antibodies specific against a particular disease organism that vaccines work. After use of a vaccine, the antibodies are in the plasma, ready and waiting to attack immediately if the disease organism should appear.

PROTECTIVE CARE

There is much you can do to guard the health of your heart and circulatory system. Contrary to what many people believe, the heart is a tough rather than delicate organ. Surgeons have successfully closed stab and other wounds of the heart; they have repaired the valves within the heart and corrected malformations. Protected by the tough ribs, the overlying lungs, and its own surrounding membrane, the heart is rarely damaged by a blow. This fact should be reassuring to parents of football players, boxers, and other athletes.

Guarding the health of the heart does not mean trying unduly to spare it. Like any other healthy muscle—even more so than most—the healthy heart needs exercise and is not damaged by it. Exercise maintains the health of the pump, actually makes it work more efficiently. And there is increasing evidence that exercise serves protectively, too, by increasing the vessel network that supplies the heart muscle, thus reducing the risk that if a heart attack occurs it will have fatal consequences.

So fast have come the discoveries about the value of exercise for the heart that a practice now accepted as a safeguard—a gradual return, after an actual heart attack, to active, even strenuous exercise—would, only a decade ago, have been considered medical malpractice if a doctor had prescribed it. Today, many cardiologists advise patients after heart attacks to get moving—to begin slowly, with extreme caution, gradually increasing their activity. With a gradual, well-tailored, well-supervised program, there is little or no danger of overstraining the heart. Many ex-heart cripples now are even playing strenuous games such as handball.

It is now realized that such slow, gradual, progressive physical training can help the heart develop an increased network of blood-supplying vessels, sometimes a greater network than it may have had before the heart attack, and there is increasing evidence that such training may substantially reduce the risk of another attack.

However, there are limits to the amount of strain that should be placed on a middle-aged, old, or damaged heart, particularly sudden strain. If you have been leading a sedentary existence, and now, wisely, you decide you need to increase your physical activity and overall physical fitness, you should by all means check with your physician first and, with his guidance, based on the health of your heart and whole circulatory system, map out a program which will lead gradually to your goal.

You can guard your heart, too, by avoiding obesity and, if now overweight, by sensible reducing. If you are overweight, your heart has to work harder routinely, day in and day out, minute after minute.

Take your heart seriously—but don't worry about it. If this sounds contradictory, it is really not. Fear can injure the heart; and too many people are more afraid of heart trouble than of anything else. Because of their fear and anxiety, they may actually be contributing to the development of heart trouble. Not worrying about your heart simply means this: Have your heart examined at regular intervals by your physician. If he says your heart is sound, get your mind off it and on to other advice he may have for you on proper nutrition and exercise.

We should like to emphasize very strongly here that only a physician can tell whether or not there is really anything wrong with the heart. Pounding of the heart (palpitation) can be alarming, but it is more likely to be caused by nervousness than by a serious organic condition. When your heart suddenly seems to "flop over" in your chest, you may be frightened, but needlessly, for the phenomenon often is due to nothing more than the fact that you have been smoking too many cigarettes or drinking too much coffee.

Between medical checkups, you can help yourself and your physician keep your heart in good shape by avoidance of excessive smoking. If you must smoke (see the chapter on that subject), cut down as much as possible or, preferably, switch to a pipe or mild cigar.

Good diet, with regular spacing of relatively small meals, helps the heart to work at its best, and, as noted in the chapter on nutrition, there is evidence that sound diet may well reduce the likelihood of clogging of the arteries feeding the heart. Good diet also can reduce the likelihood of arterial damage elsewhere in the body, helping to maintain the integrity of the whole circulatory system.

Keep your work and social life under reasonable control so that you are not chronically fatigued. If you feel tense and "driven" in our competitive world, talk to your physician. He may have advice that will be helpful; he may suggest little patterns of physical activity to be used at particularly tense moments to reduce the tension; if necessary, he may prescribe medication that may help tide you over a tense period; he may, if advisable, have you talk with a psychotherapist. You may be able, by any or all of these measures, to reduce nervous tension to the point where you can avoid trouble with your heart in later life.

There is much talk these days about "iron-poor" blood. You will recall that it is hemoglobin—a combination of protein and iron—which carries oxygen. When the number of red cells in the blood is not adequate or the cells do not contain adequate amounts of hemoglobin, the body is not able to get its proper supply of oxygen. Without the oxygen, the muscles and other tissues are not able to burn all their supplies of fuel. The body is unable to get sufficient energy. The condition is called anemia.

If anemia is the result of inadequate hemoglobin, the problem may be overcome by good diet—and may be avoided the same way. As noted previously, foods rich in iron include meats, particularly liver, heart, and kidneys; also leafy green vegetables; enriched bread and cereal; egg yolk; potatoes; oysters; dried fruits; peas; beans. And since hemoglobin also contains protein, good-quality protein foods in the diet help.

It should be emphasized, too, that there are other types of anemia and other possible causes. And if you feel unduly fatigued and suspect that you have anemia, don't guess that it may be for lack of enough iron or enough protein or anything else. Find out—let your physician test to determine—exactly what, if any, kind of anemia it is and what should be done about it.

There are certain diseases that are great enemies of the heart and circulatory system. They include high blood pressure, hyperthyroidism, rheumatic fever, hardening of the arteries, diabetes, nephritis, and syphilis. Read the detailed accounts of these diseases elsewhere in this book so you will be alerted to their hazards and will know that medical science has learned about their prevention as well as control.

20

THE RESPIRATORY SYSTEM

MAN CAN survive for weeks without food, for days without water, but for only a few minutes without air. Air must reach the lungs almost constantly so that oxygen may be extracted there and distributed via the blood to every body cell.

Even in a relaxed state, you breathe in and out 10 to 14 times a minute, with each breath lasting 4 to 6 seconds. In the space of a minute, you take in 9 to 12 pints of air. The fact is that the body has small reserves of oxygen, all of it consumed within less than half a minute after the start of vigorous exertion. And with such exertion, the need for air increases manyfold so that your breathing rate may speed up to one second per breath and a total intake of 20 gallons of air a minute.

You can figure roughly that in a normal day you will breathe in some 3,300 gallons of air—enough to occupy a space about 8 feet by 8 feet by 8 feet—and, in a lifetime, you will consume a prodigious quantity, enough to occupy 13 million cubic feet of space.

The respiratory system is one, of course, that you will want to understand well. It is a system in particular that you can do much to guard through knowledge of how it functions, what can go wrong, and the preventive techniques available for you to use.

THE NOSE

Respiration begins with the nose, which is specially designed for the purpose, although there will be times when you breathe through the mouth as well. As you read this, you are quietly, with little or no awareness, breathing lightly through your nose. When you race for a bus or train, or perform any vigorous activity, and begin to puff and pant, you

206

are breathing rapidly through the mouth to provide the blood with the extra oxygen needed.

The mouth, however, is not designed for breathing. You may have noticed this on cold days when you make a deliberate effort to keep your mouth tightly closed, because if you take air in through the mouth you can feel its coldness. Cold air passing through the mouth has no chance to become properly warmed. But cold as the air may be, you can breathe comfortably through the nose. The nose, acting somewhat like an air conditioning system, regulates the temperature and humidity of air passing through and filters out foreign particles as well.

Air enters, of course, through the nostrils. Hairs around the nostril openings catch dust and other impurities. The nostrils are separated by a partition, the septum, which is made of cartilage—a flexible kind of bone —in the lower part of the nose, and of real bone in the upper part. Thus, while you can pull the bottom part of the nose from side to side, the top part is immovable.

On both sides of the septum are rounded ridges, called turbinates, outgrowths of soft bone covered with mucous membrane. Air is warmed and moistened in the turbinates, and the sticky surface of mucous membrane catches any foreign particles that have gotten by the nostril hairs. The mucus, which is continuously secreted by the membranes covering the turbinates, drains into the throat. In addition to the mucus, the membrane contains hairlike filaments, called cilia, which wave back and forth a dozen times a second, helping to clean incoming air and move foreign particles trapped in the mucus down the back of the throat and into the stomach where impurities are inactivated by gastric acid.

Extending into the nasal cavity from the base of the skull are large nerve filaments which are part of the sense organ for smell. From these filaments, information on odors is relayed to the olfactory nerve which goes to the brain.

THE SINUSES

The sinuses are cavities lined with mucous membranes which are continuous with those lining the nose. There are eight sinuses: the frontal on each side of the forehead; the maxillary in the cheekbones on each side; the ethmoidal in the walls between nasal cavity and eye sockets; and the sphenoidal behind the nasal cavity.

Filled with air, the sinuses lighten the head bones. They help equalize air pressure in the nasal cavity, aid in warming and moistening air, and serve as sounding chambers to give resonance to the voice.

Many of us undoubtedly would be happy to do without the sinuses if we could be spared the pain of sinus infections—for, linked as closely to the nasal cavity as they are, the sinuses can be affected by infection spread from the nose. It is worth noting here that excessively hard nose blowing is a factor in spread of infection to the sinuses. (See Sinus Infections, page 650.)

THE PHARYNX (THROAT)

From the nasal cavity, air moves into the pharynx, or throat, which ranks as one of the most complex parts of the human body. Seven tubes enter the pharynx: the two from the nasal cavity, called the internal nares; the eustachian tubes which lead to the ears; the mouth cavity; the opening of the esophagus; and the glottis, the opening of the windpipe. Traffic in the pharynx becomes complex during the eating process. Food and water go down one opening; air must pass through another. Fortunately, the traffic control is automatic and things usually go where they should.

Tonsils, masses of soft tissue, are located on each side of the pharynx, behind the mouth cavity. There is also tonsil tissue at the base of the tongue. And adenoids are tonsil-like masses of tissue that grow on the back wall of the pharynx behind the internal nares. It appears that the function of tonsil tissue is to trap and destroy disease organisms, helping to guard the body against infections that may develop from germs entering through the nose or mouth.

Tonsils become infected rather easily. In some cases, the tonsils may become so diseased that tonsillitis, sore throat, and other respiratory infections become frequent. Then a physician may recommend tonsil removal, although such removal, once extremely popular, today is not done on a routine basis, but only where there is strict need. Mere enlargement of tonsils is no reason for removal. Tonsils are normally larger in children than in adults. Only when they interfere with breathing and swallowing may it be necessary to remove them because of size.

Enlarged adenoids may block the openings of the eustachian tubes and interfere with normal pressure changes in the middle ears, causing discomfort and hearing impairment. When enlarged adenoids happen to block the internal nares, they force mouth breathing. Fortunately, adenoid removal, when necessary, is a simple operation.

THE LARYNX

The larynx, or voice box, is at the top of the windpipe, or trachea, which takes air to the lungs. But while incoming air passes through the boxlike larynx, it is actually air expelled from the lungs that makes voice sounds.

In the front of the larynx, two folds of membranes, the vocal cords, are attached and held by tiny cartilages. Muscles attached to the cartilages move the vocal cords, which are made to vibrate by air exhaled from the lungs. The vibrations are carried through the air upward into the pharynx, mouth, nasal cavities, and sinuses, which serve as resonating chambers. The greater the force and amount of air from the lungs, the louder the voice. Pitch differences result from variations in the tension on the cords. The larger the larynx and the longer the cords, the deeper the voice. The average man's vocal cords are about three fourths of an inch long. Shorter vocal cords give women higher-pitched voices.

THE WINDPIPE

The windpipe, or trachea, is a tube about four and a half inches long and one inch in diameter. It extends from the bottom of the larynx through the neck and into the chest cavity. At its lower end it divides into two tubes, the right and left bronchi. The bronchi divide and subdivide many times into smaller branches that penetrate deep into the lungs. The esophagus, which carries food to the stomach, is immediately behind the trachea.

Rings of cartilage hold the trachea and bronchi open between breaths. The windpipe wall is lined with mucous membrane, and there are many hairlike cilia fanning upward toward the throat, moving dust particles that have been caught in the sticky membrane, thus preventing them from reaching the lungs.

Respiratory infections such as colds and sore throats may sometimes extend down into the trachea and bronchi; they are then called tracheitis and bronchitis. Inflammation of the walls of these passages cause harsh breathing and deep cough.

THE LUNGS

The two human lungs weigh about two and a half pounds. They have an area forty to fifty times greater than the total surface area of the body's skin—equivalent, some investigators have noted, to the area of a tennis court.

Within a lung, the bronchi divide and subdivide, becoming smaller and smaller, until the branches reach a very fine size at which they are called bronchioles. Each bronchiole ends in a microscopic air sac, called an alveolus. It has been estimated that human lungs contain more than 750 million alveoli. Filled with air, these tiny sacs give the lungs their characteristic appearance of large sponges.

A vast network of capillaries penetrates the lungs. Tiny capillaries contact each alveolus. Air in an alveolus is separated from the blood by two thin membranes—the wall of the alveolus and the equally thin wall of a capillary. These thin walls permit ready exchange of gases between blood and air.

The lungs are covered by a double membrane. One, the pleural membrane, lies over the lungs; the other lines the chest cavity. Separating the two is a thin layer of fluid which, during breathing, prevents the two membranes from rubbing against each other. Inflammation of the pleura can cause roughness and irritation, the condition called pleurisy. When it is present, the physician, with an ear against the chest, can hear the membranes rubbing each other with each breathing motion.

MECHANICS OF BREATHING

Breathing is accomplished by changes in the size of the chest cavity. Surrounding—and guarding—the lungs are twelve pairs of ribs. They are joined to the spine at the back and curve around the chest to form a cage. In front, the top seven pairs are connected to the breastbone. The next three pairs are connected to the rib above. The last two pairs, unconnected in front, are called floating ribs. The entire cage is flexible and can be expanded readily by special muscles.

In addition to the rib cage, which forms the wall of the chest, there is the dome-shaped diaphragm, which forms the floor of the chest cavity. The diaphragm is attached to the breastbone in front, the spinal column in back, and the lower ribs on the sides.

The lungs do not suck in air; all the work is done for them by the diaphragm and muscles of the rib cage. When you inhale, muscle fibers of the diaphragm contract and the sheet of tissue is drawn downward; at the same time, rib muscles pull the ribs upward and outward. This expands the chest cavity and lowers the pressure within it to below that of the atmosphere. This causes the lungs to expand, too; and the tiny air sacs in the lungs also become a little bigger. Air then rushes into the lungs to fill the extra space.

When you exhale, just the opposite series of events occurs. Muscles of the diaphragm relax; so do those of the rib cage. The chest becomes smaller; the elastic tissue of the lungs returns to its original shape, making the air sacs smaller; and the air is driven out.

The rate of breathing varies with age. In a baby the rate is about 45 times a minute; by age 6, it is down to about 25; between ages 15 and 25, it drops to about 18. There is some tendency for it to increase again with advanced age.

The rate of breathing is also influenced by the carbon dioxide content of the blood. If you hold your breath, carbon dioxide accumulates in the blood until, finally, it so strongly stimulates the respiratory control center of the brain that you are forced to breathe again. The length of time the breath can be held varies from 25 to 75 seconds. Mothers sometimes become alarmed when children hold their breath during crying spells or temper tantrums. There is no real danger of suffocation; when the child really needs air, he will be forced to inhale.

In any condition leading to elevation of body temperature, the respiration rate is always increased.

CHOKING, COUGHING, SNEEZING

Large particles of undesirable substances bring, fortunately, an immediate response from the respiratory system. If food accidentally starts down the wrong way, into the lungs rather than the stomach, there are explosive protests from the lungs.

Normally, swallowing blocks off the glottis, halts breathing briefly, and assures correct division of air and food. It should be noted, however, that this automatic activity may be lacking in an unconscious person, and if a drink is poured through clenched teeth it may proceed straight into the lungs. The automatic system is not 100 percent perfect even during consciousness, and many a fruit pit, bite of food, or other object has gone into the windpipe and has had to be coughed up or, in some cases, forcibly retrieved. The protective reflex becomes sluggish after heavy alcohol intake.

A cough can be a very powerful force. Involved in it are a slight breathing in, closing of the glottis, buildup of pressure, and a sudden release of the trapped air—at speeds of as much as 500 feet per second.

A sneeze can be even more explosive. And attempts to muffle a sneeze, to quiet it down, to make it polite, or to avoid it can sometimes lead to nosebleed, ringing in the ears, or sinus trouble.

HICCUPS (SINGULTUS)

Hiccups are short, sharp inspiratory coughs involving spasmodic lowering of the diaphragm. They may be due to indigestion, overloaded stomach, irritation under the surface of the diaphragm, alcoholism, and many other possible causes. There are many home remedies, any one of which may work in simple cases: warm applications to the diaphragm region, protrusion of the tongue, holding of the breath, drinking water, applications of cold to the spine, exhaling and inhaling into and from a paper bag. In severe persistent cases, medical attention is required.

PREVENTIVE CARE

It goes almost without saying that the most common respiratory problem —in fact, the most common disease in the world—is the common cold. You will undoubtedly want to read the special discussion of this (page 566). Other conditions, as well as the common cold, may produce nasal congestion. They include hay fever and other allergies (see page 516), chronic infections, nasal polyps, sinusitis (page 650), and a deviated or crooked septum. Enlarged adenoids may also be a cause of nasal congestion in children (page 471). Your physician, or a specialist to whom he may wish to refer you, can do much now not only to provide relief for such problems but very often to use preventive techniques that will avoid recurrences and possible progression to more complicated problems.

Ozena is a disease of the nose involving the turbinates and mucous membranes. It is accompanied by considerable crusting and discharge and a very offensive odor. It should have medical attention as soon as possible. Actually, a persistent, foul-smelling discharge in children is much more often caused by some foreign object such as a bean or pencil eraser lodged deep in a nasal passage. Always have a physician take care of this.

An occasional minor nosebleed is no cause for alarm. It may stop by itself—and often does. Cold compresses to the nose and back of the head, and pressure on the soft portion of the nostril on the bleeding side for five minutes, may help. Or the bleeding may stop if the affected nostril is plugged with sterile cotton.

Frequent nosebleeds deserve medical attention. They may simply mean that a particular small blood vessel in the nose is at fault, and the physician may be able to attend to it in a few minutes. On the other hand, nosebleeds in children sometimes may indicate rheumatic fever. They may also herald onset of typhoid fever. Contrary to a popular notion, they rarely stem from high blood pressure. If your nose bleeds frequently without apparent cause, your physician will try to determine exactly what is involved and then use suitable treatment. (See page 590 on bleeding diseases.)

Should an unsightly nose be changed by plastic surgery? Perhaps. This is a matter to talk over with your physician. If he advises an operation for cosmetic reasons, he will refer you to a surgeon specializing in this type of surgery. Surgery may be appropriate, too, when an abnormal shape of either the external nose, the septum, or the turbinates causes obstruction.

The ordinarily healthy nose needs little special care. Avoid the use of nose drops, sprays, or sniffers unless your physician prescribes them for a specific purpose. Their continued use can cause irritation or injury. They will not cure postnasal drip.

Actually, the nose normally is moist inside, kept so by mucus and a thin watery secretion produced by small glands in the lining of the membranes. There is a continuous healthy process of flowing and drying and sweeping backward to the throat of any excess fluids and mucus. It's this process that accounts for a normal amount of mucus in the throat termed postnasal drip. Thus postnasal drip is a normal process. If the drip becomes excessive and unpleasant, it may be because of infection, allergy, vitamin deficiency, excessively dry, heated wintertime environment, or other problems. Nose drops and sprays will not help under these circumstances and may, in fact, add to the problem if your postnasal drip excess is due to overly sensitive membranes.

If you have a disturbing postnasal drip problem, the best thing to do is to see your physician for definitive diagnosis and treatment, with emphasis on preventive treatment. If you won't see a physician, the next best thing to do is leave the drip alone. Despite what you may have heard, we can assure you that mucus which accumulates is *not* "full of dangerous germs" and will *not* "poison you or ruin your digestion if you swallow it." It is quite harmless.

Your mouth does not need and may actually be harmed by "medications" that claim to cure halitosis and other conditions. Mouthwashes, antiseptic lozenges, and gargles come in contact with only the surface of the mouth and do not reach any germs that are more deeply entrenched when infection is present.

Halitosis, or bad breath, accompanies gum disease. It can also be caused by teeth and gums that are not kept properly clean. However, it may be due to inflamed tonsils, infections in or behind the nose, and conditions of the stomach or intestines. Certain foods, of course, cause odorous breath. Some diseases such as uremia produce foul breath. It is not always easy to tell whether or not one has a mild case of halitosis. It is sometimes possible to find out for oneself whether marked halitosis is present by forced expiration into your cupped hands held over mouth and nose. In any case, there is no need to worry endlessly about halitosis or spend time and money on remedies that do little good, since your dentist or physician will be glad not only to determine whether you do have halitosis but also, if you do, to help you find cause and cure.

Like the nose and mouth, the throat does not need sprays, gargles, or lozenges to keep it healthy. Avoid them because their regular use may produce irritation.

Sore throats are almost as common as colds, since a certain amount of throat inflammation may accompany a cold. A sore throat also may be due to irritation from excessive smoking. If cutting down on smoking and a trial of gargling every two or three hours using a third of a glassful of warm water containing two crushed aspirin tablets do not help, if the sore throat persists for more than a few days, you should see your physician. Serious conditions may begin with a sore throat. Any acutely sore throat accompanied by fever in either adult or child may mean trouble. It may indicate early stages of diphtheria, scarlet fever, septic sore throat, or serious infection of the tonsils. If these conditions are treated promptly by your physician, they can be cured quickly and serious complications can be avoided.

In some individuals, even moderate use of cigarettes may produce irritation in the throat and larynx, leading to a hacking cough. There is no magic medicine for this. The problem can be solved only by greater moderation or even complete discontinuation of smoking.

Hoarseness is a sign that something may be wrong with the larynx. If you have been cheering at a football game the day before, the reason is obvious enough. But if hoarseness or a change in your voice appears without apparent cause and lasts longer than a few days, it may indicate a tumor, tuberculosis, or some other potentially serious condition, and immediate medical attention is essential.

What commonsense precautions should you take to care for your lungs? First, considering what we now know about the effects of smoking on the lungs—in terms not only of lung cancer but of emphysema and chronic bronchitis (see discussions of smoking and of these diseases in other chapters)—you should give up smoking or at least switch from high-risk cigarettes to lower-risk mild cigars or a pipe.

The moist, warm air passages of the lungs provide ideal growing conditions for many types of bacteria and viruses. This is the reason nature has provided so many barriers to these organisms, in the form of sticky mucous membrane secretions and cilia. But it is impossible to keep the passages 100 percent free of microorganisms. Fortunately, they do not attack when body resistance is high. When, however, resistance is lowered—by fatigue, poor nutrition, emotional turmoil, or another infection—a lung infection can strike suddenly. The most common lung infections are pneumonia and tuberculosis. Today, they can be treated effectively with medications chosen to combat the involved organisms. But much can be done to prevent their development through following the rules of good nutrition, reasonable everyday living with a balance of work, rest, and relaxation, and by paying attention to prompt and proper treatment of minor infections.

If you are a worker in any industry where dust, gases, and smoke are inhaled, you should recognize the possibility of harm. By all means, check to determine whether increasingly stringent health laws aimed at minimizing or eliminating risk are being followed to the letter by your employer. If they are not being followed, it is a matter that should be brought to the employer's attention and, if necessary, to the attention of health authorities. If they are being followed and yet some risk remains, if you even suspect that you may be suffering some ill consequences, it is imperative to see your physician. It may be necessary, particularly if you happen to be especially sensitive to any specific materials, to change your job if your health is to be protected (see Chapter 14).

We would like to emphasize here, too, that the moisture content (humidity) of air can influence health. There is considerable individual variation. Some people feel well in cold weather areas where the indoor air is extremely dry because of heating. Other people notice that this dry atmosphere irritates nose and throat. They react very much better when using humidifying devices now available commercially in many forms.

21

THE DIGESTIVE SYSTEM

FOOD SERVES two important purposes for the body. It is a source of materials for the growth and replacement of tissue and a source of fuel for energy. And it is digestion that bridges the gap between what we enjoy as food and what must enter the bloodstream to supply the body with its needs.

The digestive process, which takes place in the 30-foot tube called the alimentary canal, involves both mechanical and chemical changes. It requires the squeezing and pushing of muscles and the action of a series of digestive juices. It is interesting; it is understandable; and it is very much worth understanding, for understanding can do much to avoid disturbances and prevent useless anxieties, some of them stirred up by commercial interests in behalf of digestive aids and remedies which, perhaps as often as not, are gulped at considerable expense by those who have no real need for them.

START OF THE PROCESS

The alimentary canal has five major divisions: (1) mouth; (2) esophagus, or gullet; (3) stomach; (4) small intestine; and (5) colon, or large intestine.

The mouth, though many people are not aware of it, has an important role to play in digestion. Here, of course, chunks of food are reduced to small particles as the tongue, itself a bundle of muscles, rolls them around while the incisors and canine teeth in front cut and tear and the molars in back grind. In the mouth, too, during chewing, the first digestive chemical change takes place.

A pair of salivary glands, known as the parotid glands, lie in the sides of the face, in front of and slightly below the ears. Saliva from these glands reaches the mouth through parotid ducts which open on the inner surfaces of the cheeks opposite the second molar teeth. There are also a pair of submaxillary glands in the angles of the lower jaws and a pair of sublingual glands under the tongue. Ducts from these glands open into the floor of the mouth beneath the tongue.

Saliva mixes with food in the mouth and softens and lubricates it. Saliva, too, contains a digestive enzyme, ptyalin, which acts to convert cooked starch to sugar. This is why, even as you are chewing them, bread and potatoes dissolve. Ptyalin, however, is unable to reach and work on starch grains that are still wrapped in their natural cellulose containers, and this is why starches should be cooked before being eaten.

A word here about enzymes, since these are substances very much involved in the whole process of digestion. Anyone who has ever used a test tube in a high school laboratory, or even used a frying pan, knows that the more heat applied, the faster a chemical reaction can be expected to take place. Yet the body, in all of the chemical processes carried on in digestion, does its work at the ordinary temperature of the human body, 98°F—less than the temperature of bath water. It is able to do so at a good pace in large part because of enzymes—catalytic substances that promote biochemical reactions without themselves being used up in the process.

When food has been chewed and salivated in the mouth, it is swallowed and enters the esophagus. This division of the alimentary canal has no digestive function. It carries food downward from the mouth a distance of nine or ten inches to the stomach. In the esophagus, food is moved by peristaltic action, which is achieved as two sets of muscles work together. One set is circular and squeezes inward when it contracts; the other is longitudinal and pushes food toward the stomach. It is because of peristaltic action that you can swallow food in any body position.

THE STOMACH

The stomach, which resembles a bag, is about a foot long and six inches wide. Its capacity is about two and a half pints, and a heavy meal may take as long as six hours to pass through it.

The stomach wall has three layers of muscles—circular, longitudinal, and oblique. Each contracts in a different direction, permitting the stomach to squeeze, twist, and churn its contents, actions that are important for the mechanical breaking up of food and thorough mixing with digestive secretions.

The thick mucous membrane lining of the stomach serves as a chemical factory. In addition to mucous glands, it contains other glands which secrete hydrochloric acid and several enzymes.

One enzyme, rennin, acts on casein, a protein in milk, forming a curd to be digested by other enzymes. Lipase, an enzyme which splits some fats, including those in cream and egg yolk, plays a small role in the stomach, a larger one in the intestine. Hydrochloric acid helps in the digestion of proteins and has other useful chemical effects. Another enzyme produced by the stomach, pepsin, helps digest the milk curd resulting from the action of rennin.

What emerges from the stomach after the activity there is a semifluid material called chyme. It takes little time, a matter of minutes, for fluids —water, beverages of various kinds—to pass through the stomach. But the rest of a meal spends from three to as much as six hours in the stomach. The time is affected somewhat by the nature of the food. Carbohydrates pass through most quickly; proteins take longer; fats require the most time. Some fats, in fact, slow the digestive process in the stomach for other foods by slowing secretion of gastric juices, thus somewhat prolonging stomach emptying time.

At both ends, stomach muscles form sphincters, ringlike valves. At the junction of stomach and esophagus, there is the cardiac sphincter. A similar but stronger valve, the pyloric sphincter, lies at the lower end of the stomach where it joins the small intestine. The two valves close the stomach during digestive activities. When chyme is ready to move on to the intestine, the pyloric sphincter opens and closes several times to allow the stomach to gradually empty.

One phenomenon associated with the stomach is worth noting here. Somehow, the stomach, which secretes hydrochloric acid to digest proteins in foods, is not itself digested by the acid. How it resists the action of an acid that is capable of dissolving even iron is not fully understood. Yet it does resist, and it is normal to have a usual quota of acid in the stomach—this, despite the concern of millions of Americans who, with the help of constant reminders from the manufacturers of various antacids, spend about $100 million a year to neutralize stomach acid.

THE SMALL INTESTINE

The intestines, small and large combined, form a continuous tube from stomach to anus. The small intestine, so called because of its lesser diameter, plays important roles in both digestion and absorption. It is about 20 feet long, roughly four times as long as the large intestine, and resembles a coiled tube about one inch in diameter.

The first part of the small intestine, the duodenum, begins at the pylorus of the stomach and extends about 12 inches, making several bends in the upper region of the abdominal cavity. The duodenum joins the jejunum, a second region extending about 8 feet and less coiled than the other regions. The final, much coiled, region of the small intestine, is the 12-foot-long ileum.

As chyme enters the duodenum, more digestive juices are added, not only by the intestine itself but also by the pancreas and the liver. Several enzymes in pancreatic fluid act upon all types of food—breaking down proteins into their amino acid constituents, converting large and complex sugar molecules into simple sugars, and changing fats to fatty acids. (Insulin is also secreted by the pancreas, but it goes directly into the bloodstream rather than into the intestine, where it would be destroyed by digestive juices; this is the reason why insulin, when required by diabetics, cannot be taken by mouth but must be injected.) A discussion of oral drugs (not insulin) for use in the treatment of diabetes can be found on page 569.

Bile enters the duodenum either directly from the liver where it is produced or from the gallbladder where it is stored. It serves to emulsify fatty foods, so they become easier to absorb, and to reduce the acidity of the chyme. Bile also functions as a carrier for the pigments of red blood cells that have been destroyed. These pigments, which undergo chemical changes in the intestinal tract, give the characteristic yellow-brown color to feces.

While a limited amount of actual absorption of digested materials occurs in the stomach, it is in the small intestine that the bulk of absorption takes place. For this purpose, the walls of the small intestine are lined with tiny, fingerlike projections, the villi. Millions of villi give the mucous membrane lining the small intestine a velvety appearance. In constant motion, the villi keep the chyme mixed with digestive juices while carrying on absorption through two types of vessels. Tiny, branching capillaries, smallest of blood vessels, form a network in each villus to absorb sugars and amino acids. Other vessels, lacteals, contain lymph, a fluid present in the spaces between body cells. Fat products generally are absorbed by the lacteals. Indigestible food remains in the intestine.

THE LARGE INTESTINE

By the time a meal has spent several hours in the stomach and another five hours or so in the small intestine, all that remains to enter the large intestine is a combination of water and indigestible waste, and it enters through a valve that prevents backflow.

The large intestine, or colon, is about two to three inches in diameter. Upon entering, material travels upward through the ascending colon along the right side of the body, then through a sharp curve under the liver on the right and via the transverse colon across the top of the abdomen just below the diaphragm. Another sharp curve carries the material to the descending colon along the left side. The lower end of this part leads into an S-shaped section, the sigmoid colon. The colon ends in the rectum. Waste is held in the rectum by a sphincter muscle until it is discharged through the anal opening.

Peristaltic movements in the colon are normally slower than elsewhere in the digestive tract. Waste often requires 12 to 24 hours to pass through. The colon has no digestive function but it does serve a vital purpose in absorbing water into the blood to maintain the water balance of the body. Indigestible material, which enters the colon in a watery mixture, becomes nearly solid, because of the water absorption, by the time it reaches the lower end of the colon.

Even with the absorption of large quantities of water, feces still consist of two-thirds water. The remainder is made up of small amounts of food residue, bacteria, intestinal secretions, and intestinal cellular remains—the reason why feces are produced even during starvation.

Under normal conditions, the amount of feces may vary considerably. On the average, about 12 ounces of chyme may enter the colon daily (somewhat more on a rich vegetable diet), and from this will be derived about 4 ounces of feces.

Intestinal gas, or flatus, is natural. It is a mixture of swallowed air and gases produced by intestinal bacteria. The bacteria quite normally occupy the digestive tract; some contribute materially to health by producing vitamins.

While waste products are excreted in the form of semisolid feces, some, including salts and proteins, are filtered from the blood, along with excess water, by the kidneys and excreted as urine.

The materials absorbed from the intestinal tract and deposited in the blood go to the liver.

THE LIVER

If you place your left hand over the lowermost ribs on the right side of your chest, it will cover the liver, the largest internal organ in the body. In a baby, the liver makes up about one twenty-fifth of total body weight and occupies more than one third of the abdominal cavity, giving the child a pudgy appearance. In an adult, it weighs three to four pounds. It's a remarkably versatile gland, with dozens of functions.

In its role as a digestive organ, the liver secretes bile, as already noted. Bile flows from the liver through tubes which join to form the hepatic duct. This duct joins the cystic duct, which leads upward to the gallbladder. Between periods of digestion, bile backs up in the gallbladder and is stored there. As food passes from stomach to duodenum, the gallbladder contracts and bile flows out the cystic duct, through the common bile duct, to an opening into the duodenum.

The liver serves as a storehouse for digested food—fats, proteins, and carbohydrates. It manufactures proteins, absorbs fat products, processes carbohydrates, and makes these available as fuel. It processes iron for the blood. It filters the blood, rendering harmless many poisons that may have entered the bloodstream. It is the liver that modifies various medicines, drugs, and poisons to make them innocuous.

The liver can replace its own tissues. If nine tenths of the organ is removed, the remaining one tenth will undergo such active cell division that the original size will be restored within six to eight weeks.

GALLBLADDER, PANCREAS, AND SPLEEN

The gallbladder, already discussed, is a kind of "side pocket" in the channel through which bile flows from the liver into the intestine, serving as a storage place.

The pancreas, which weighs about three ounces, lies high up in the abdomen, deep behind the stomach. The pancreatic duct carries the digestive secretion, pancreatic fluid, through a common opening with the bile duct, into the duodenum. The fluid contains three important enzymes: amylase acts on carbohydrate foods; lipase functions in fat digestion; and trypsin is a protein-digesting agent.

Equally important are the islets of Langerhans which are contained in the pancreas and produce insulin, a lack of which causes diabetes.

The spleen, although often bracketed in people's minds with the pancreas, is not an organ of digestion. Roughly fist-shaped and about six inches long, it lies high up behind the stomach. In the unborn baby, the spleen plays an important role in producing red and white blood cells. After birth, it no longer manufactures red cells but still makes white cells. In adult life, it makes neither but does serve by doing the opposite—destroying old blood cells.

The spleen is not vital; it can be removed without harm. While it is a useful organ, its functions can be performed elsewhere in the body. Normally, the spleen cannot be felt from outside unless it enlarges considerably. It usually does so when affected by disease, and in extreme cases may increase fiftyfold in size. Enlargement may carry some hazard since the spleen, when engorged with blood, may produce severe internal bleeding after a bump or knock that ordinarily would be trivial.

APPENDIX

The appendix is a wormlike appendage at the junction of small and large intestines. Its reason for existence is not clear. The apparently useless structure, unfortunately, can be the source of serious illness. No age group is immune to appendicitis, an inflammation of the appendix (page 531). Its prompt diagnosis can lead to effective removal of the inflamed organ before serious complications can occur. The operation is comparatively simple and safe when performed early by a competent surgeon.

The one thing you can do about your appendix is to realize that if it is inflamed, you may cause it to rupture if you take a laxative or apply a hot water bottle over it.

CARE OF THE DIGESTIVE SYSTEM

Unlike the chest with its rib cage, the abdomen offers relatively little protection for its organs. Liver, spleen, and kidneys may be ruptured by accidental injuries. The abdominal muscles should be kept strong to help protect adjacent organs, a need recognized by all coaches of athletic teams.

Disorders of the gastrointestinal system are among the most commonly encountered in medical practice. Almost everyone has some degree of difficulty at one time or other. The disorders can be functional. Because of the extensive nerve connections involved in the digestive system, fear, anger, and other nervous upsets can readily set off attacks of nausea, cramps, diarrhea, and other symptoms.

Perhaps the most famous stomach of all time belonged to a French-Canadian, Alexis St. Martin, who, in 1822, when he was 18, was accidentally wounded by musket fire. His stomach was pierced, and although in those days a wounded man was virtually a dead man, William Beaumont, a U.S. Army surgeon, was able to save St. Martin's life. The one problem: the stomach wound refused to heal completely.

St. Martin refused any kind of operation that might close the stomach wall, preferring instead to get along with bandages in place of an intact wall. He did get along remarkably well, and cooperated with Beaumont, who decided to take advantage of the unfortunate situation to make some observations. It was this work that led to the isolation of hydrochloric acid in the stomach. And from it came many other findings. Beaumont was able to note, for example, that the stomach became flushed with blood when St. Martin became angry and that it also moved about with considerable energy during anger.

Organic diseases—including ulcer, cancer, virus infection, food poisoning, and many others—can, of course, affect the digestive system. You can protect the digestive system by taking many simple, sensible precautions.

For one thing, you can be sensible about the food you eat. If you know that some particular food does not agree with you, you should avoid it. If you happen to be a person with a sensitive colon, it may be that raw vegetables or fresh fruits trouble you. Some people are bothered unduly by such gas-forming foods as radishes, cabbage, cucumbers, and eggs. Alcoholic beverages may cause great difficulties for some sensitive people, leading to diarrhea or cramps in some and belching in others. Excessive smoking can upset the stomach. The list of possible trouble-makers is long; individual sensitivities vary greatly. You need to, and can, be your own "alimentary tract detective."

You should, of course, eat a balanced diet. Since such a diet will contain well-proportioned amounts of proteins, carbohydrates, and fats, without an excess of any, it will put less of a strain on any one particular digestive function. Avoid rapid eating; the stomach works overtime in trying to handle a meal you did not take time to eat properly—and it may start sending out distress signals.

None of us can be entirely free of tension. We're all subject on occasion to "nerves." But we can see to it that we make mealtime a reasonably pleasant, relaxed time, as an aid to both enjoyment of food and its better digestion. Those of us who are victims of chronic tension can, and should, take the tension problem to a physician who practices preventive medicine. It's a problem that usually can be solved, quite frequently with simple measures.

You can protect your digestive system by precautions against infectious disease. Habits of cleanliness by all members of the family should be encouraged. The washing of hands after going to toilet—and especially before eating or handling food—should be a habit as automatic as breathing. Cleanliness is all the more vital because contamination can be spread by people who are not themselves ill.

All milk that comes to the table should be pasteurized. In most cities, water coming from the faucet is safe to drink. But if you live in the country or go there on vacation, check on the safety of the drinking water.

Pork, it must always be emphasized, should be thoroughly cooked since it may contain the parasite that produces trichinosis.

Dangers may be lurking in bakery goods, especially those with custard fillings, such as eclairs, on which bacteria thrive. It is important to buy pastry from a clean, reliable bakery and to put it in the refrigerator as soon as you reach home. Make sure the pastry has not been standing around in the bakery for a long time.

Perhaps no less important in guarding the health of your stomach and intestines is to leave them alone. Don't indulge in enemas to "clean out the colon and get rid of germs." The germs belong there and many people would have far better digestions if they had never heard of the term, "autointoxication." You will do best to remove it from your vocabulary; it is a meaningless, and potentially harmful, concept. So, too, are the terms "acid stomach," "alkaline stomach," and "heartburn." You can't cure these nonexistent diseases by taking stomach "sweeteners" or "aids" to digestion, which can do real harm.

It is unfortunate that there are so many so-called simple remedies for indigestion on the market. Indigestion is by no means a simple disease. In fact, it is not a disease at all but a condition or group of symptoms which can be caused by any number of problems, ranging from migraine (page 582) and heart disease (page 585) to impending influenza or a dinner bolted when you're tense and tired.

Even a skilled physician often finds it a long and difficult task to determine the cause and hence the proper treatment, of chronic indigestion. If you have the problem, don't object if your doctor asks you to have a complete set of x-rays so that he can determine whether the indigestion is caused by gallstones, ulcer, or tumor. He may need to examine the stomach with an instrument called the gastroscope. Such tests, and others that sometimes may be needed, are well worthwhile. Almost every disturbance of the gastrointestinal tract that makes itself known by indigestion can be helped if identified in time. It is reassuring to know that tumors are rather rare causes of the tremendous number of cases of chronic indigestion.

On the other hand, a disease can progress to a serious, even fatal stage while you are engaged in "treating" your indigestion—for example, if you take a cathartic for indigestion which is caused by appendicitis. Let your physician decide whether or not you should take any medicine.

Realistically, we know that few people will consult a physician for every mild stomach upset. If it is, indeed, only a mild upset, we recommend one of the following remedies: a level teaspoonful of bicarbonate of soda in water or, if you prefer, in fruit juice; or 10 to 20 drops of essence of peppermint taken either on a lump of sugar or in a teaspoonful of sugar, and chewed slowly; or a teaspoonful or two of iced crème de menthe, or other liqueur or brandy, sipped slowly; or a little wine such as sherry.

For nausea or cramping, tincture of belladonna is helpful. Adults require 15 to 20 drops in water. Each person must find his proper dosage. Usually, an effective amount will cause some dryness of the mouth or slight blurring of vision. The dosage can be repeated in four to six hours. For more intense abdominal cramps, one to two teaspoonsful of paregoric may be used (see Appendicitis, page 531). Lomotil, two tablets four times a day, is prescribed by many physicians for tourist cramps and other gastrointestinal complaints.

A persistent "nervous" stomach may be helped by mild sedatives such as phenobarbital, especially if given in combination with tincture of belladonna. However, this medication should be prescribed only by a physician.

Aspirin, taken for headache, cold, or rheumatism, sometimes produces stomach distress. This can be alleviated by a teaspoonful of bicarbonate of soda in water or by use of a buffered type of aspirin. If you are truly sensitive to aspirin, you may find Tylenol a useful substitute.

If you are occasionally, not habitually, constipated, it is safe to take a mild laxative such as a teaspoonful or two of milk of magnesia. Avoid regular dosing with any laxative or cathartic.

Be certain to see your physician if you find yourself beginning to suffer persistently or repeatedly from any of the following symptoms: nausea, vomiting, excessive belching, fullness or burning sensations in the abdomen, cramps, constipation, or diarrhea. Be certain to see him *immediately* if you pass stools that are blood-streaked, blackish, colorless, or foul-smelling.

The liver in a healthy body requires no particular care. It certainly does not need to be "stimulated" by such medicines as those claiming to "increase the flow of bile." But there are several things you can do to prevent damage to the liver. You can protect it from the harm that can result from excessive intake of alcoholic beverages and from poisons such as carbon tetrachloride to which you may be exposed at work or in the course of hobbies requiring use of solvents. Remember that glue sniffing, engaged in by youngsters seeking a "thrill," can harm the liver. Both normal weight and balanced diet are necessary to keep the liver healthy.

Liver damage, such as that from a virus infection, may produce jaundice—a yellowing of the skin and particularly of the whites of the eyes. Jaundice should be reported immediately to your physician. Some viruses that cause liver infection are transmitted by blood on syringes or needles. That is why drug addicts who share equipment have a high rate of liver disease. Alcohol and ordinary boiling do not kill the viruses; the very high temperature of an autoclave type of sterilizer is needed. Do not use someone else's injection equipment in administering insulin, for example. Other viruses affecting the liver are transmitted hand to mouth, and so it is vital to wash hands with soap and water after passing a stool, before each meal, and after trips and contacts on buses, trains, and other public conveyances and places.

Infection may affect the gallbladder. Gallstones sometimes cause considerable pain and may block the flow of bile, leading to jaundice and infection of the liver and gallbladder. Fortunately, the gallbladder can be surgically removed when necessary; the body can get along well without it.

Except for keeping your weight normal, there is nothing you need do about the everyday care of the gallbladder. Obesity increases the tendency toward gallbladder disease. Women who have had more than one or two children are somewhat more likely to suffer from gallstones; and in general, after age 40, about twice as many women as men have this problem. Once stones form, they cannot be dissolved; sometimes, however, they pass spontaneously into the intestines. Your physician has methods of stimulating bile flow and of decreasing infection in the gallbladder, and these measures may reduce the formation of additional stones.

The best thing you can do for your pancreas is to avoid overweight, which predisposes people to diabetes.

CONSTIPATION

Many people suffer from constipation that is nonexistent, except in their imagination, or self-induced, or could be corrected or prevented with relatively simple measures.

It is a fact—and this deserves emphasis—that constipation *can* be organic, that is, the result of some physical change. It can be caused by a tumor that obstructs the intestines, a stricture that narrows them, or some disease such as a hypothyroid condition. That is why it is important to consult your physician if you have constipation, especially if it has developed fairly suddenly. This is essential for middle-aged and older people to make certain that if a cancer does exist, it is discovered in the early, curable stage.

Here is the medical definition of *real* constipation: A person has constipation when bowel movements are too hard to pass easily or are so infrequent that uncomfortable symptoms result. Constipation does not mean failure to pass a stool daily; this may be imaginary constipation.

Hard movements that require straining can bring about rectal troubles such as hemorrhoids and fissures or may aggravate a hernia or the tendency to hernia. Constipation may cause uncomfortable symptoms such as nausea, heartburn, headache, or distress in the rectum or intestines, continuing until the stool is passed. Notice that we say uncomfortable rather than harmful symptoms; that is because these symptoms stem from nerve impulses to various parts of the body when the rectum is distended by retained fecal matter. They are not due to "autointoxication," or absorption of poisons from the fecal matter. It has actually been established that similar symptoms can be brought on when cotton is placed in the rectum after all fecal matter has been removed. Some people suffer more than others from these symptoms, not because of their imagination but because they are actually more sensitive.

In *imaginary* constipation, the bowel movements are not difficult to pass; they cause no unpleasant symptoms; they simply do not take place as often as the individual thinks they should. Often, it is a mother or other relative who insists the movements should be more frequent. The fact is that bowel movements can be normal without being "average." While the "average person" has a movement daily, usually immediately after breakfast, countless people are normal even though they have more than one movement a day, or a movement only every second day, or every third, fourth, fifth, or even eighth day. People vary markedly in body makeup, type of intestine, eating habits, physical activity, and custom.

By *self-induced* constipation, we mean the kind caused by one or more of the following: improper diet (eating the wrong things or eating too little); the use (that is, *abuse*) of laxatives, cathartics, etc.; irregularity in habits of elimination.

Modern living, with its strains, stresses, and sedentary habits, helps promote constipation; indeed, in some primitive languages there is no word such as constipation because the need for it does not exist.

Functional constipation can also be caused by "sluggishness." As we have seen, after food has been digested in the stomach and intestines, the residue, a watery material, enters the colon. Water is absorbed in the colon; that is why the feces may become hard and difficult to pass if they remain too long in the colon. The stools are propelled along by a series of wavelike, peristaltic movements. Usually the waves are strongest in the morning, which is why it may be easiest to have a bowel movement before or just after breakfast.

In some people, peristalsis is weak. This may happen with increased age, and some elderly people may require an aid to elimination. Mineral oil is the best remedy. But we think it wise to accept as helpful virtually any method that an elderly person has long used and found satisfactory —whether it is hot lemon water early in the morning or the enema that some elderly people believe has magical virtues. In such cases, the important thing is to watch for any sudden change in established bowel habits.

How to Cure—and Prevent—Functional Constipation

If you now do have constipation, there are certain things you can safely do to cure it, and these same methods will also prevent you from becoming constipated.

1. DEVELOP REGULAR HABITS OF ELIMINATION. Choose a time, shortly before or after breakfast every morning, for going to toilet, and attempt

to defecate whether or not you have "the urge." Allow ten minutes. Relax, be comfortable, read if you like—the important thing is not to feel tense or hurried. Prop your feet on a footstool so your knees are close to your chest. If you choose to go before breakfast, it will help to drink a glass or two of fluid upon getting out of bed; it can be warm or cool water, fruit juice, tea, or coffee.

Teaching your bowels to move regularly is a little like training yourself to wake up at a given hour every morning; it can be done, with patience, and once acquired the habit persists.

2. DIET. The residue of foods you eat is easier to eliminate if it contains some roughage in the form of fibers, lubricants in the form of fats or oils, and fluid. These should be included in the diet of healthy people. (In some disease states, there may be an inability to tolerate roughage; in such cases, a physician will so advise.)

To cure or prevent constipation, make certain your diet includes:

For breakfast: 1/2 to 1 glass of tomato, grapefruit, prune, or orange juice. Also include one item from each of the following, (a) through (e):
  (a) Mixed dried or stewed fruits—prunes, apricots, figs
  (b) Cooked, whole-grain cereals with milk—barley, brown rice, oats, wheat
  (c) Margarine
  (d) Whole-grain bread
  (e) Beverage

For lunch, dinner or supper, some of the following:
  Green leafy vegetable—beet greens, spinach, escarole, lettuce, turnip greens, dandelion greens, mustard greens
  Baked potatoes (eat the skins)
  Margarine, salad oils
  Dried or stewed fruits—especially for dessert at evening meal

Take two glasses of fluid between meals and at least eight all told during the day. Drink an extra amount of water in summer because part of it is lost in perspiration.

3. EXERCISE. Strong abdominal muscles help elimination. If you do not have a firm, well-toned abdominal wall, start the exercises described on page 89. If your job requires much sitting and very little physical activity, you should indulge in regular sports or other forms of exercise. You will feel better generally as well as have less tendency toward constipation.

4. LIVE SENSIBLY. Try as much as you can to avoid the stresses and

strains of modern living. Get relaxation to help temper those stresses and strains. *Don't worry about constipation.* If your physician gives you a clean bill of health on your regular visits, and you follow our suggestions for home checkups (page 33), constipation is not going to harm your health. Usually, these suggestions are enough to prevent or cure constipation. If they are not, and failure to move the bowels causes real discomfort, you may:

5. TAKE AN ENEMA.   Use a pint of warm water containing a level teaspoonful of table salt. If you use an enema bag, hold it about two feet above the toilet seat; if you use a bulb, do not press it too hard—the water should flow under gentle pressure. This should help soften the stool so it can be passed easily. You may take an enema every day—but remember that this is a crutch and the sooner you discard it, the better. If an enema does not help, your physician can show you how to insert olive oil into the rectum at night through a catheter, which will soften the stool and make it easier to pass in the morning.

6. LAXATIVES.   If you cannot take an enema, use a mild laxative such as petrolatum and agar, aromatic cascara sagrada, or milk of magnesia. Do not do this until you have given your bowels a chance to work by themselves. An important step in curing constipation may be to stop taking all laxatives and cathartics. Strange as it seems, laxatives are frequently the *cause* of constipation and seldom are necessary in its cure. As noted above, mineral oil may be of value.

A final warning: Don't give a laxative to a child, and don't take one yourself, if there is any fever, nausea, pain, or general feeling of illness associated with the constipation. It can cause fatal consequences if the condition is caused by appendicitis (see page 531).

22

THE GENITOURINARY SYSTEM

EVERY BODY cell not only must build its substance and obtain its energy from nutrients supplied in the food you eat; it must get rid of wastes. And all cells deliver their waste products continuously to the blood. In turn, the blood carries them to various centers for excretion. Thus, carbon dioxide and some water in the form of vapor are removed from the blood in the lungs. Salts and additional water pour out through the skin's sweat glands. Other wastes—including water, salt, urea, and uric acid—leave the blood in the kidneys.

Blood enters the kidneys through the renal arteries and leaves through the renal veins and, in circulating within the two kidneys, goes through a fabulous filtering system.

The kidneys—each about 4-1/2" long, 2-1/2" wide, 1-1/2" thick, and weighing 5 ounces—are located deep in the abdomen at about the level of the lowest ("floating") ribs. Essentially, they are filters containing intricate plumbing—a system of tiny tubes called nephrons whose combined length in each kidney is about 140 miles.

To the naked eye, a single nephron would resemble a grain of sand. Under a microscope, it has the look of a twisted worm with a huge head. The head, called the glomerulus, is covered with a network of capillaries that carry blood continuously into the glomerulus. The tail is the tubule.

In a healthy kidney, as blood enters a glomerulus, a fluid is separated from it. The fluid contains neither red nor white blood cells and only a trace of large protein molecules. The fluid passes along the tubule, and about 99 percent of the water, amino acids, proteins, glucose, and minerals needed by the body are returned to the bloodstream. The remaining fluid, with its content of waste materials, is eliminated from the body as urine.

Every 24 hours, the kidneys filter about 200 quarts of fluid and salts.

One or two quarts of the waste go to the bladder and are flushed out of the body. Actually, the kidneys have a tremendous reserve capacity; they could clean nine times more fluid than they are called upon to do, and for this reason one healthy kidney can readily serve the body's needs.

The kidneys function to maintain the correct balance between the salts and water of the body, to get rid of any toxic substances, and to keep the body in correct mineral balance. For example, too much potassium in the blood could stop the heart quite as effectively as a bullet.

THE BLADDER

A tube, or ureter, leads from each kidney to the urinary bladder. The bladder empties through the urethra, a tube leading to an external opening called the meatus.

The bladder, which functions as a collecting and temporary storage point for urine, expands to accommodate increasing amounts. With the accumulation of about half a pint, reflex contractions lead to a desire to urinate, or micturate. The contractions stimulate pressure receptors in the muscles of the bladder wall, from which nervous impulses go to the brain. When it is convenient to urinate, the brain sends out signals which cause the bladder's external sphincter to relax. The signals also set up a whole series of other events, including holding of the breath, forcing of the diaphragm down, and contraction of the abdominal wall, which increase pressure on the bladder and help it void its accumulated urine. Such is the complexity of the process that it is hardly any wonder that most children are walking before they become able to urinate with controlled competence.

Normal daily production of urine may range from two to three pints. In some diseases, such as diabetes insipidus, the quantity is increased; in others, fever and diarrhea decrease it. Tea, coffee, alcohol, excitement, and nervousness increase urine output; hot water decreases it. Whatever the actual liquid output, a day's urine generally contains about two ounces of solids.

CARE OF THE URINARY SYSTEM

Your kidneys do not require "flushing," "stimulation," or any of the things that patent medicines may claim to achieve. Kidney disorder may produce low back pain, and this symptom, together with any changes in the urine, should always be reported immediately to your doctor. Contrary to claims made for certain "kidney medicines," they cannot cure chronic pain in the back, which is seldom caused by a kidney disorder. Don't take any medication for your kidneys except on a doctor's orders.

Some causes of kidney stones (renal calculi) are beyond control. But prevention or prompt treatment of infection is helpful in avoiding stone formation. Another important preventive measure is maintenance of adequate urine flow. When the urine becomes highly concentrated because of excessive perspiration during hot weather or exertion, there is increased tendency to form stones and to develop infection. Drink plenty of water if you perspire heavily. (See page 605 for more on kidney stones.)

A floating (movable) kidney is usually not serious, although it may cause discomfort. Bright's disease (also called nephritis) is a potentially serious illness (page 601). Whenever the urine appears bloody, wine-colored, smoky, or at all unusual, it may be a sign of Bright's disease which, as a rule, causes no pain. Always see your doctor immediately if you notice any such urine changes. See him immediately, too, if the urine should appear to be cloudy or pus-laden. Inflammation of the kidneys is called pyelitis (page 604). If treated early, this and many other kidney disorders can be completely cured. If not cured, kidney infections can slowly damage these vital organs, leading to high blood pressure and uremic poisoning.

The bladder is subject to infection (cystitis) and inflammation. These conditions usually yield to treatment with a suitable antibiotic prescribed by your physician. Never use a "bladder pacifier" or other home remedy. Infections can be the cause of incontinence, the inability to control urination. Frequency of urination can be a symptom of a disorder such as diabetes. Difficult urination may be caused by a urethral stricture or narrowing. Always consult a physician if you experience frequent, difficult, or painful urination; don't attempt to treat the condition yourself. It often is traceable to an easily cured inflammation, but it may stem from a disease such as prostate gland enlargement in men (page 639). Stones can also form in the urinary bladder; never take any home remedy to "dissolve" them. If necessary, stones can be removed by surgery.

THE MALE GENITAL SYSTEM

Sperm are produced in the testicles, each of which is about two inches long, one inch wide, and less than one inch thick. In man, unlike many animals, sperm production is continuous. Each spermatozoon, when formed, is complete with head, neck, middle piece, and tail. It is jostled along by the production of other sperm until it reaches the epididymis. Within this lump of tissue, which sits astride the testicle, sperm mature and gain motility. The motility and ability to fertilize endure for several weeks, after which a sperm cell, if it has not been emitted, degenerates and liquefies.

In emission, sperm travel up a tube, the vas deferens. Seminal vesicles produce a yellow fluid which mixes with sperm and constitutes much of the semen; the prostate also contributes a secretion. The mixture is ejaculated down the urethra along the penis. In an ejaculation, there may be 300 million or more sperm.

Prior to birth, the testes of a boy baby lie within the abdominal cavity. At birth, they descend through the inguinal canal into the scrotum. (If they fail to descend, as sometimes happens, they can usually be surgically placed in the proper position.) It is because of this passageway, the inguinal canal, that rupture (hernia) occurs so much more often in men than in women. You should consult your physician if you notice a bulge in the groin toward the upper part of the scrotum or in the lowest part of the abdomen just above the tight cord that separates it from the thigh. Don't listen to people who may tell you to wear a truss. Only a physician is capable of deciding between the relative merits of an operation and a truss in a particular case of hernia.

Is circumcision necessary? This operation removes the skin fold called the foreskin or prepuce. It may be necessary if the fold covers the entire end of the penis (the glans) and obstructs passage of urine, or is so tight that irritation results. Otherwise, circumcision is a matter of choice. Some groups have used it for millennia. The Egyptians practiced circumcision before the Hebrews made it a part of their religious customs. Circumcision is safe and simple when performed in accordance with principles of modern aseptic surgery. It can be performed late in life but is best done when a boy is seven or eight days old and will experience no physical or emotional discomfort. Talk the matter over with your family physician or pediatrician.

Circumcision does not alter the sexual act or its enjoyment. Some believe that the greater freedom of married Jewish women from cancer of the womb is due to circumcision of their mates and resulting increased cleanliness of the penis. For the uncircumcised, healthy practice is to scrupulously wash foreskin and glans of the penis regularly, and especially before intercourse.

Routine Care

The genitals should be kept clean, free from infection. For this, an uncircumcised male can gently pull back the foreskin and wash off any secretions with soap and water as often as required to keep the penis clean. The genitals should be protected from blows and other injuries during football and other strenuous sports. No special food is needed for genital development and health. No medicines are required, and none should be taken except under a doctor's orders. Masturbation causes no organic damage or harm; it may, however, give rise—because of feelings of guilt often associated with this practice—to emotional conflicts which may lead to phobias about syphilis or to impotence.

Venereal Disease

Five venereal diseases may affect the male genital system. Syphilis is the most serious. Syphilis can be cured, and we urge you to read the section on this disease so you will not fail to seek medical advice if you have any reason to suspect you may have contracted syphilis. (Women, too, should understand venereal diseases.) No one except a competent physician is capable of treating the disease properly. You would be running grave risk if you depended upon a quack to even diagnose the condition. The fact that syphilis can be cured is no reason for carelessness, smugness, or delay. Syphilis cases in the United States and in many other countries have been increasing rapidly. One reason seems to be that many people assume they have nothing to worry about—but, left to smoulder, syphilis can have serious consequences.

Gonorrhea is a common venereal disease. Prior to the development of effective antibacterial agents, it was a serious problem. Now it can usually be cured with one injection of penicillin. Every person, female as well as male, should read the section on gonorrhea. Even children are susceptible. Gonorrhea can be transmitted in ways other than sexual contact. If you understand the facts thoroughly, you will know how to prevent gonorrhea.

The other venereal diseases—less common and less important—are chancroid, lymphogranuloma inguinale, and veneral warts. These are made evident in men by sores on the penis or enlarged lymph nodes in the groin. (Women, too, may contract these diseases.) They respond to treatment while in early stages and no time should be lost in consulting your physician.

Venereal diseases can be prevented. The simplest and most effective prophylactic is the condom, or rubber sheath. Some men think this diminishes the pleasure of intercourse. But anyone who has seen really severe cases of venereal disease comes away convinced that if a man must expose himself to the dangers of VD, he can well afford to reduce slightly the physical pleasure in return for protection and freedom from worry.

The testicles are not often affected by disease. They are not, however, immune to involvement and may be affected by mumps, undulant fever, or gonorrhea. The cord that supports them may be invaded by an extension of a hernia, or there may be enlarged veins. The epididymis may become diseased. If you notice a swelling, lump, or congestion of the scrotum or testicles, be sure to see your physician as soon as possible.

It may be an indication of early cancer or other potentially serious problem, curable if treated early. The skin in and around the scrotum may be infected by ringworm fungus causing so-called jockstrap itch. Keeping the area clean and dry—with a simple drying powder such as used for babies—will help prevent such infections.

The prostate gland can be affected by cancer and by infections. In men of about 50 and older, the prostate often enlarges for reasons that are still not fully understood. This is called benign hypertrophy of the prostate gland (page 639).

THE FEMALE GENITAL SYSTEM

The reproductive anatomy in the female takes the form of the letter "Y." At the ends of the two top arms are the ovaries. The arms themselves are formed by the fallopian tubes, also called oviducts, thin passageways through which eggs released from the ovaries travel. At the Y's center is the uterus, or womb, the muscular pear-sized organ which will house and nourish a fertilized egg from earliest stages through all phases of fetal development, enlarging greatly in the process. The cervix is the neck of the uterus, which seals off the uterine cavity until, in the last hours prior to birth of a baby, it changes its shape. The cervix leads into the vagina, the receiver of sperm during intercourse and the exit passage for the baby at birth.

Elsewhere in this book, as the Index indicates, are discussions of menstruation, menopause, pregnancy, childbirth, and sterility.

Hygiene

Douches are not essential to feminine hygiene, although many women have been persuaded to take frequent douches with commercial preparations because of advertisements implying that no woman can be clean or dainty without them. Actually, nature has provided for the cleansing of the internal passages. If you wish to take an occasional douche, it should be of the mildest type, imitating nature's own secretions. You can use a physiological salt solution: add two level teaspoonfuls of table salt to a quart of moderately warm water. Administer the douche under gentle pressure.

Whether a woman, during the menstrual period, should use an internal absorptive pad (tampon) or an external sanitary pad is entirely a matter of personal preference. Either is safe. Each woman can decide for herself, based upon which she finds more effective and comfortable. An unmarried woman can wear an internal pad if her hymen happens to be well perforated—and this may be the case, contrary to some opinion, whether or not she has ever had sexual relations. Certain kinds of exercise may cause rupture of the hymen in a virgin. If the hymen is completely lacking in perforation—a condition called imperforate hymen—there may be interference with menstruation, and a minor surgical procedure may be needed to create an opening.

Any irregularity in menstruation, once menstruation has become well established, should be checked with your physician.

Infections

Syphilis, gonorrhea, and nonvenereal infections can seriously damage the female reproductive system. A sudden, profuse, odorous, colored, or painful discharge may indicate an infection that may not only affect the vaginal passage but could spread into the uterus, tubes, and ovaries. If such a discharge is accompanied by chills and fever, serious trouble may be developing. Such infections usually can be eradicated like magic by penicillin or other medicines, if you give a competent physician a chance to help you without delay.

It is important to remember that infections that are readily curable with prompt, knowledgeable treatment can progress to cause sterility if neglected or if treated by a quack or on the advice of a well-meaning friend or neighbor. If they advance far enough, they may cause problems requiring surgery, including possible removal of a reproductive organ. Remember, too, that gonorrheal vulvovaginitis in young girls can be contracted without sexual intercourse, so be certain not to neglect any discharge in a young daughter.

What can a woman do to prevent venereal infection? While this is often regarded as too delicate a subject even for a book on health, the medical profession is pledged to treat and prevent disease in all people, regardless of moral status. For those women who for any reason are exposed to the risk of venereal disease, there is only one safe preventive measure to recommend: Insist that the male employ a condom during the entire time of the sexual act. Obviously, if the sheath is put on only just prior to male orgasm to prevent conception, there will be no protection from syphilis if the male organ has a syphilitic sore, nor will there be protection if the male has gonorrhea and his germs are present in the lubricating secretion produced at the earliest moments of male erection.

In case of rape, see your doctor *immediately*, or go to a hospital emergency room. Prompt medical care can help prevent danger of pregnancy and also of venereal disease.

It is important to note that vaginal discharge, leucorrhea, is not always serious. Normally, a certain amount of fluid is produced to keep tissues moist. It is virtually odorless and colorless and nonirritating. Congestion, tension, and minor inflammations can increase the discharge. Germs far less dangerous than those responsible for syphilis and gonorrhea can produce infections which may become troublesome unless eradicated. Your physician must establish the cause of the infection before he can prescribe suitable treatment. That is why you should not use an antiseptic or germicidal solution as a douche unless you are under a physician's orders; you may be eradicating some, but the wrong, germs.

Tumors

The female reproductive organs are subject to tumors and cancers and should be examined at regular medical checkups. At such times, your physician may well decide to take a "Pap smear," a simple, painless procedure that can establish the presence of early cancer and even a precancerous condition. Scores of thousands of women today owe their lives to the fact that their physician included this test as part of routine checkups.

Any change in menstruation and any unexpected bleeding or discharge, especially after the menopause, should be reported immediately to your physician. These symptoms may or may not stem from a malignant growth; when they do, the cure rate is very high if the growth is detected and treated early.

23

THE BRAIN AND NERVOUS SYSTEM

EVERYTHING YOU do in, and every awareness and impression you have of, life is the result of activity in the brain and nervous system. To call it a remarkable system is to understate the obvious. It is so complex that scientists are only making a beginning at penetrating its mysteries. And yet enough has been determined, and it is now possible to understand sufficiently the broad outlines of the makeup and functioning of the system in health and disease, to permit you to do much to preserve its health.

THE BRAIN

Of all things known in the universe, the human brain is, by far, the most intricate. Although it weighs only about 12 ounces on the average at birth and in an adult only about 3 pounds, its storage capacity is phenomenal. It has been estimated that the brain can store more facts, impressions, and total information than are contained in all the 9 million volumes in the Library of Congress.

It's another indication of the brain's complex organization that, if necessary, you can get along with only half of it. The fact is that after removal of much of one side of the brain because of tumor, doctors, lawyers, and others have been able to carry on with their regular work. And in one study with 62 soldiers who suffered penetrating head wounds during World War II, the men, upon being retested for intelligence, showed little or no change in scores they had made in the Army General Classification Test upon first entering service.

Although at various times there has been some belief that the brain is compartmentalized, with specific areas for specific functions, the evidence from many studies is that when some brain area is damaged, another area may be able to take over its functions.

The brain has 15 billion nerve units which permit storage of memory images and all the learning we accumulate. In addition, it has huge numbers of connections which control the more than 600 muscles in the body. Other connections into the brain from the eyes, ears, and nerves in the skin permit us to record and remember what we see, hear, feel, smell, and taste.

The brain is made up of several parts. The cerebrum, largest and most familiar, takes the form of two hemispheres divided by a groove. The surface, or cortex, of the cerebrum is the gray matter we hear about, formed by the cell bodies of nerve cells. Fibers from these bodies lead inward and form the white matter of the cerebrum. Some of these fibers lead to the center of the brain; others extend from front to back and from side to side; and deep in the brain, complicated junctions are formed. Actually, most of the fibers cross over so that one entering the brain from the left side of the body crosses to the right side of the brain, which is why the right lobe of the cerebrum controls most of the left side of the body, while the left lobe controls the right side.

At the base of the cerebrum are three structures: pons, medulla, and cerebellum. The pons, a saddle-like mass of coarse fibers, connects the medulla with the higher brain centers. The medulla, or spinal bulb, just below the pons and at the upper end of the spinal cord, is a switching center for nerve impulses to and from higher brain centers. It also contains centers which, as we will see, work through the autonomic nervous system to control heart action, changes in artery walls, breathing, and other activities that go on without our conscious effort.

The cerebellum, or little brain, is divided into hemispheres like the cerebrum. The front and back areas control muscle tone. Equilibrium is the concern of an area behind the back lobe. The two main hemispheres coordinate voluntary movements. It is characteristic of the intricate organization of brain and nervous system that the cerebellum receives nervous messages from the balance mechanism of the inner ears, from the muscles and joints, and from centers deep in the brain, and then sends impulses to the muscles adjusting their tone and coordinating their action.

Are you able, with eyes closed, to touch the tip of your nose? Can you both rub your stomach and pat your head simultaneously? Then your cerebellum is still at work.

Protection for the Brain

The brain is an excellent example of built-in protection provided by nature for a vital organ. Despite the delicacy of emotion and thought processes in the brain, brain tissue itself is quite sturdy stuff, tough and resilient. It is protected against injury in a number of ways.

A tough bony cage, the skull, surrounds the brain completely. It takes a very strong blow to break the skull. The skull itself is protected by the scalp, which can absorb some tough blows. The scalp is made up of five layers which medical students remember by an acrostic: S is for skin (and hair,,which in women constitutes considerable protection), and the skin of the scalp is the thickest in the body; C is for the cutaneous tissue, a layer under the skin; A is for the aponeurosis, a tough layer of fibrous tissue which helps the scalp slide around; L is for some loose tissue; P is for the periosteum which covers the bone of the skull.

Still more protection is provided. Inside the brain are four reservoirs, the ventricles, which contain cerebrospinal fluid. This fluid circulates around the brain. Thus, the brain practically floats on and in fluid. And engineers will tell you that this is an ideal "shock absorber" system. Finally, inside the bone of the skull the brain is wrapped in layers of tissue. One of these layers, the dura mater, is particularly tough and helps protect the brain against blows.

But nature cannot provide infinite protection, and it has not foreseen the demands of modern society. It did not anticipate that man would ride motorcycles at 100 miles an hour, and might hurtle over the handlebars. Or that children would go out on hard turf and play football. Or that workmen would walk under skyscraper construction projects where a bolt falling from the fortieth floor would develop the speed of an artillery projectile. So we need additional protection: adequate helmets for motorcyclists and athletes, steel hats for workmen exposed to possible head injuries. Parents must realize, too, that babies fall off beds and, at some stage, jump out of cribs. These must be guarded against and a baby doctor can advise.

Beyond protecting the brain from injuries, you can protect it so there is no interference with its efficient operation.

Sleep is essential not alone for the body in general but for resting and revitalizing the brain in particular. Good sleeping habits (page 94) are well worth developing. Both overstimulation of the brain through excessive use of caffeine in coffee, tea, and soft drinks and depression of the brain through frequent use of sedatives such as barbiturates and bromides are best avoided.

The brain works most effectively when freed from anxieties and mental conflicts. We suggest that a reading of the next section of this book, Preventive Mental Care, may provide you with insights you will find useful in keeping your psyche—the functional part of the brain—in the best possible condition.

Are special "brain foods" and "brain tonics" necessary? Not at all. As it will for all the rest of the body, a well-balanced and varied diet will provide the brain with all the nourishment it requires. Fish, a good food, is not any better for the brain, despite its reputation for being so, than any other protein food. There is no magical brain food.

It bears emphasizing that the mind reacts to distress elsewhere in the body. Headaches, dizziness, fainting, impairment of memory, and other "brain" symptoms may, of course, stem from disturbances in and around the brain (for example, sinusitis or tumor). But they can also be the results of, for example, the circulation of poisons because of failure of damaged kidneys to remove toxic materials from the blood. In short, brain symptoms call for a complete medical checkup.

Can the effects of aging on the brain be prevented? Some of the most harmful effects of hardening of the arteries can be prevented or considerably diminished by following the suggestions given in the sections of this book devoted to nutrition, obesity, high blood pressure, and aging.

There is every reason to be optimistic about your brain function as you get on in years. You may recall that Michelangelo produced some of the greatest art of all time when he was more than 80 years old, and Arturo Toscanini at 87 directed symphonies without reference to musical scores. Many people in everyday life continue to have alert, active brains long beyond the age of 70.

Actually, a study made for the Office of Naval Research indicates that, contrary to what has been commonly thought, mental ability does not invariably decline with age but may, in fact, be greater at and after 50 than at 20.

The ONR study avoided a pitfall of other studies in the past. In the latter, the same tests were given to various age groups, and the results suggested that a peak of intelligence comes at 20 and thereafter declines. But such studies, many scientists have thought, were faulty. In recent years, young people have been receiving more and more formal education, and it has been demonstrated that generally the more formal education, the higher the score on mental tests. Therefore, older people, who generally had had less formal education, were handicapped in test competition with younger ones.

In the ONR study, 127 men who had taken the Army Alpha Examination upon entering Iowa State College after World War I were retested 30 years later. They were competing against their younger selves. The results showed them to be intellectually more able at mean age 50 than they had been at mean age 19 when they had been college freshmen.

THE NERVOUS SYSTEM

If the brain is likened to a control center, then the nervous system can be thought of as a two-way communications network through which informational messages flow to the control center and command messages are transmitted from the center. The informational, or sensory, messages come from the outside world through the sense organs (eyes, ears, etc.); they also come from within the body itself—there are billions of receptors all over the body concerned with various functions.

The nervous system is organized to give you essential voluntary control over many actions. It is also set up to relieve you of concern with routine matters. Thus, for example, you eat dinner and decide whether you like or dislike a certain dish and wish to finish it. On the other hand, you walk along, stumble on an object; without thought on your part, the muscles of the legs are automatically commanded to react, and one leg is extended and the other flexed so you maintain your balance.

How Nerves Work

Messages travel along nerves, at speeds of as much as 250 miles an hour, as the result of both electrical and chemical action.

A nerve cell, or neuron, when viewed under a microscope, looks like a tiny blob, rounded or irregular in shape, with one or more threads extending from it. The blob is the actual nerve cell body; the threads are nerve fibers. Shorter fibers, called dendrites, bring messages to the cell body; they may range from a very small fraction of an inch to several feet in length. One fiber, longer than the others and called the axon, transmits messages away from the cell body.

A nerve impulse, going through the nerve network, travels over the fibers of many cells. As it reaches the end of one fiber, it jumps a gap, called a synapse, to the next fiber. Chemicals produced and stored around synapses can help the impulse to jump the gaps or can block the impulse. Some drugs that act in the nervous system—some of those for high blood pressure, for example—accomplish their tasks by affecting the chemicals at the synapses.

Nerve cells are so specialized that they have lost the ability to reproduce themselves. When a neuron dies, it cannot be replaced. However, when an axon is damaged, if the damage is at some distance from the cell body, the neuron will not wither away. The damaged section of the axon may perish but often the remaining section will grow. The growth may be slow, although studies in some animals show a growth rate as fast as an inch a week. Even when a neuron is completely destroyed, all is not necessarily lost; sometimes other pathways may come into use to serve the function of the destroyed unit.

Man's endowment of neurons is vast. For example, the ant, often considered to be a remarkably wise little insect, capable of constructing cunning houses and leading a relatively complex social life, has some 250 neurons. Man has billions, and the number can be looked upon as an indication of his tremendous potential if he chooses to use them all, and wisely.

Actually, man has two nervous systems, not just one.

The Central Nervous System

The central nervous system includes the brain and spinal cord. The spinal cord is suspended in a cylinder formed by the bones of the spine. The meninges, which cover the brain, also continue down to serve as protective coverings for the cord. And cerebrospinal fluid, between middle and inner membranes, cushions the cord, just as it does the brain, from shock.

The central nervous system connects to every part of the body by means of 43 pairs of nerves. Twelve of these, the cranial nerves, go to the eyes and other sense organs, the heart, and other internal organs. They are called olfactory, optic, oculomotor, trochlear, trigeminal, abducens, facial, auditory, glossopharyngeal, vagus, accessory, and hypoglossal.

The 31 other nerve pairs go to skeletal muscles throughout the body. They branch off the cord between the bones of the spine. One of a pair goes to the right side of the body, the other to the left. Outside the cord, each nerve splits. One branch carries sensory-type fibers—for incoming messages—to the cord; the other carries motor-type fibers.

The central nervous system works in more than one way. There are simple reflex actions and there are reactions at higher levels. Consider, for example, what happens when you unexpectedly touch a hot object. Instantly, your hand is jerked away. The pain stimulated the receptor endings in a sensory nerve in the skin. Nerve impulses immediately flowed along a fiber, passed through a sensory branch of a spinal nerve and into the cord. There then followed a quick transfer across a synapse of a central nerve in the cord, another transfer across another synapse to a motor nerve, which then passed impulses out of the cord and along a motor fiber of a spinal nerve through the body to the muscles. The muscles reacted; your hand was jerked away. It took just a fraction of a second for the entire reflex—an involuntary process, requiring no thought, assuring immediate helpful action.

But there was another reaction, too—at higher levels. Although you were not consciously aware of the reflex as it happened, you very quickly learned about it through another transfer in the cord, this one from the sensory nerve coming from the affected skin area to another sensory nerve traveling up the cord to nerve endings in the cerebrum. As a result, you felt pain, looked at your finger and at the hot object, and associated the two. Then knowledge stored in the cerebrum's memory centers directed you to shove the finger quickly under cold tap water, motor areas sent messages to your muscles, and you moved to the tap. And, as you probably realize, while all this was going on, your emotional centers entered the picture and you had some feelings—perhaps of anger, or disgust, or both—about the event.

The Autonomic Nervous System

A second nervous system, the autonomic, provides for control, on an automatic basis, of vital internal organs. The autonomic system has two nicely balanced parts—the sympathetic and the parasympathetic—which oppose each other, much like accelerator and brake of a car. In so doing, they make possible a precise balance.

The sympathetic system begins at the base of the brain and runs along both sides of the spinal column. The nerves extending out from the system go to glands such as salivary, sweat, liver, and pancreas, and to muscles such as those in the iris of the eyes, heart, stomach, intestines, and bladder. They also go to muscles in the walls of blood vessels.

The parasympathetic system consists of two major nerves. One, the vagus, comes from the medulla and sends branches through the chest and abdomen. The other, the pelvic, arises from the spinal cord in the area of the hip and sends branches to organs in the lower part of the body.

As examples of how the two systems work: The sympathetic dilates the pupil of the eye, while the parasympathetic constricts the pupil. Sympathetic nerves speed up the heartbeat; parasympathetic slow it down. The sympathetic constricts blood vessels and raises blood pressure; the parasympathetic expands the vessels and lowers pressure.

The autonomic nervous system is influenced strongly by emotions. For example, when you experience a dry mouth and goose pimples because of fear, the sympathetic system is at work.

Preventing Nervous System Damage

Diseases such as multiple sclerosis and parkinsonism affect the brain and/or spinal cord. These are discussed elsewhere in this book.

Other maladies affect the peripheral nerves which connect the brain and spinal cord with the muscles, organs, skin, eyes, etc. When a peripheral nerve is affected, the condition is called neuritis or neuralgia. And since a peripheral nerve usually contains both pain and motor fibers, painful symptoms plus some paralysis of muscle power may occur.

Certain toxic materials such as lead, arsenic, and mercury may produce a generalized poisoning of the peripheral nerves, with pain, tenderness, and paralysis of the limbs. There are many other causes of generalized neuritis, including alcoholism, vitamin deficiencies, some types of allergy, diabetes, severe vomiting of pregnancy, thallium toxicity, and some viral and bacterial infections.

While some attacks of generalized neuritis begin with fever and other symptoms of acute illness, on the other hand, neuritis caused by lead and alcohol toxicity comes on very slowly over a course of weeks or months. In most instances, an attack of generalized neuritis will subside when the toxic substance is eliminated. Rest and good diet containing extra vitamins, especially of the B group, are helpful. Physiotherapy may relieve the pain or paralysis. Effective prevention of generalized neuritis is based on knowledge of the danger of poor nutrition, chronic alcoholism, industrial hazards, and infections—all discussed elsewhere in this book.

Frequently, instead of a generalized irritation of the nerves, only one nerve is afflicted. For example, if you sleep in a cold draft which blows on one side of the face, next morning the facial nerve on that side may be temporarily paralyzed. When produced by drafts, the paralysis clears up after some days or weeks. After such an episode revealing your sensitivity to drafts, you will want to take steps, of course, to avoid recurrence.

Peripheral nerves may be cut, bruised, or torn by fractured bones or blows. A torn or cut nerve should be treated by a specialist in such work. If your doctor advises it, by all means go even hundreds of miles for such treatment as a means of preventing permanent paralysis and other serious consequences of nerve injuries.

It will be apparent that you can do much to help guard the health of your nervous system by observing commonsense precautions to avoid accidents and injuries and by following suggestions made in many pages of this book about maintaining general good health. In addition, you can best influence the nervous system, including the autonomic, to exercise effective control over body functions by maintaining good mental health and by making use of suggestions given in the next section of this book on coping with the tension and stresses that all of us must expect to encounter.

24

THE SENSE ORGANS

THE EYE

The human eye, which presents us with a world of space and depth and a continual variety of sights, packs into a single cubic inch of space more than 150 million light receptors.

The eye is often compared to a camera. The outermost layer of the eyeball forms the white of the eye and at the front becomes the completely transparent cornea. The next layer is the iris, which has an adjustable aperture, the pupil, which becomes larger or smaller depending upon the amount of light entering.

Just behind the iris and its pupillary opening is the oval-shaped and elastic lens, which bulges out when its muscles contract, and flattens when they relax, thus adjusting to properly bend and focus light rays on the retina. (The lens muscles are the fastest and best-coordinated in the body.)

The retina, which lines the eye and serves as the "film," contains the light receptors that react to incoming images. The responses of the receptors are transmitted along a million nerve fibers which form one outgoing cable, the optic nerve, at the back of each eye. The exit of the optic nerve leaves a "blind" spot—an area without receptors.

It has been estimated that 85 percent of everything we learn comes to us through our eyes.

It's the brain that does the actual seeing; the eyes are light-transmitting machines. This is the process: Light rays strike an object and are reflected to the eyes. The rays pass through the cornea, the clear front window, the aqueous humor (a watery liquid behind the cornea), the pupil, and the lens. The lens bends and focuses the rays on the retina. As the rays impinge on light-sensitive pigments in the retina, chemical reactions take place that send impulses through the optic nerve to the brain. Actually, images are received upside down because the lens inverts them, but the brain has learned to interpret them in accord with reality.

Central vision—what you use when you look straight at an object—is sharpest. But you also have side, or peripheral, vision. And while peripheral vision is not very acute, it is important; without it, you would bump into things and be unaware of objects approaching from the side. You can demonstrate side vision with a simple experiment: With both eyes open, hold your right thumbnail 16 inches in front of your face. Have someone hold a wrist watch at arm's length to your left and gradually move it toward your thumb. Without moving your eyes, you will be able to identify the watch as a watch probably when it is about 15 inches away from your thumb. Chances are, though, that you will not be able to tell time until the watch is about two inches away.

Interestingly enough, each of us has his own individual view of the world. That's because, for one thing, the eyes can transmit millions of impulses per second but the brain chooses details on the basis of individual past experience, mood, and interests at the moment.

How we see things also can be affected by their meaning for us. In one experiment, when subjects were asked to estimate the size of coins and cardboard disks that were exactly the same size, they guessed, on the average, that the coins were one-fourth larger than the disks—and the poorer off financially a subject was, the more he overestimated coin size.

The eyes even serve a purpose beyond seeing. They have a marked effect on taste, as shown by studies at a U.S. Air Force medical laboratory where volunteers were fed in a completely darkened room. Unable to see the food, they could detect no difference in taste between white and whole-wheat bread or between various canned foods.

Eye Problems and Their Prevention

Defects and diseases to which the eyes are susceptible account, in part, for the fact that there are nearly half a million people in the United States who are totally blind and two million more who are partially blind. But in part, too, this unpleasant fact is the result of misunderstanding, neglect, and delay in seeking aid, for many potentially blinding disorders can be prevented, or arrested, or even cured with prompt attention. In addition, of course, about 40 percent of the population wears glasses, indicating that the vision of almost one of every two people leaves something to be desired.

Three common eye defects—farsightedness, nearsightedness, and astigmatism—are the result of simple optical aberrations in the eye. If the lens is to focus light rays directly on the retina, it must be at the proper distance. When the eyeball is too short, the lens will be too close;

conversely, if the eyeball is elongated, the lens will be too far away. Moreover, to accommodate to both near and far objects, the lens must change its curvature to maintain proper focus.

At birth, the average baby has foreshortened eyeballs and is farsighted. From about age 6 to age 20, the eyeballs elongate. After about age 45, people tend to become farsighted again because the lens, going through a normal hardening process, loses some of its ability to change curvature to focus on near objects.

Nearsightedness is usually due to a lengthening of the eyeball, an increase in curvature of the cornea, or a change in refraction of the lens. Astigmatism is usually caused by an irregularity of the shape of the cornea. When the cornea does not have a perfect curve, images are distorted. The effect can be similar to that of looking through a dirt-streaked pane of glass.

Fortunately, nearsightedness, farsightedness, and astigmatism are readily corrected with eyeglasses. And it is important that these conditions be corrected, for both comfort and good eye health. If, for example, one eye is more effective than the other, the good eye may do all the work, which could be bad for it and also for the one that is not being used. This is why children's eyes should be checked at an early age, even before school, and why you should mind your own eyesight, remembering that changes do occur with time. Have your eyes examined as soon as you find yourself holding things off at a distance to see them, or when you notice that you no longer see as well as you once did in poor light. Always have an eye doctor examine your eyes and prescribe any necessary lenses.

It is true, of course, that eyeglasses are an expense and possibly a bit of a nuisance. But what a joy it is to see properly and to know you are protecting your precious sight. Fortunately, glasses have become so "glamorized" that resistance to them is disappearing.

For people in special occupations—actresses and others—who would find ordinary glasses a handicap, contact lenses which fit directly over the eyeball are often useful. They are expensive, not always easy to insert, and may be tolerated for only limited periods. Contact lenses, however, are constantly being improved, and your eye doctor can advise about their suitability for you.

Exercises for the eyes may be helpful under some circumstances. They should not, however, be used without first consulting an eye doctor. There can be grave danger when exercises are used indiscriminately to try to correct vision difficulties that in reality may stem from glaucoma or some other potentially serious disorder that needs attention without delay.

An ophthalmologist—an eye specialist who has had medical school and additional postgraduate training in the field—has the background to check not only for eye defects and problems per se but also for any systemic problems that may show up through the eyes. It is usually important to see such a specialist whenever you believe you have an eye problem. His examination and diagnosis can make a valuable contribution to maintaining your general health as well as improving your eye health. He can prescribe not only suitable glasses but also, when appropriate, helpful corrective eye exercises.

Eyes That Cross

The belief that crossed eyes in a child will straighten themselves is a tragic misconception; a child does not outgrow crossing.

If an infant's eyes "float," momentarily turning in or out, there is usually nothing to worry about. It may take the first three months of life for eyes to become coordinated. After that, however, crossing (strabismus) warrants immediate attention. Without attention, there may be loss of vision in the turned-in eye.

When eyes cross, each views an object from a different angle. The brain then receives two different images. Since seeing double is highly disturbing, the cross-eyed child will squint and tilt his head in an effort to combine the two images. Finally, he will give up, resort to using just one eye, and the sight in the other will deteriorate for lack of use. When a child is helped early, simple treatment may be effective.

One cause of crossing is farsightedness, which may lead to such excessive use of the eye muscles that the eyes overconverge. Sometimes glasses alone, to correct the farsightedness, may be enough to straighten the eyes.

A qualified orthoptic technician in an eye doctor's office can help many children by teaching them eye exercises and how to use them at home. Special devices allow each eye to see only half a scene; the eye muscles are strengthened while the child practices fusing the two images into a whole picture—for example, putting the dog he sees with one eye into the doghouse he sees with the other.

Even when surgery is necessary, the operation to bring the eye muscles into proper balance is virtually free of risk. A muscle that does not pull enough may be shortened; or excessive pull may be reduced by reattaching the muscle at a different point on the eyeball. In most cases, the child experiences little or no pain, is up the day after operation, and goes home in another day or two.

Lazy Eye

Lazy eye, or amblyopia, affects children who are cross-eyed and also those who have one normal and one nearsighted or farsighted eye, or one nearsighted and one farsighted eye. Here again the brain gets two dissimilar images and may shut out one.

Even when sight in one eye has deteriorated to a considerable extent, there is a good chance it can be restored. But it has been estimated that as many as 100,000 children a year in this country are on the way to joining the untreatable ranks. Amblyopia is a major reason why every child should have a thorough examination of the eyes by the age of four, for the learning ability of the eye is at its height up to age seven, then falls off.

Treatment for lazy eye before age seven—and in some cases, later —can be effective. Eyeglasses and a patch over the good eye may be needed. The patch forces use of the weak eye so that, with increased work, its vision builds up.

Glaucoma

Often insidious, glaucoma is a leading cause of blindness. The most common form develops when the fluid that normally fills the eyeball, the aqueous humor, fails to drain properly. Ordinarily, the fluid is produced continuously within the eye, and excess amounts drain off through a small duct near the iris. But aging, infection, a tumor, congenital defects, and other causes can constrict or block the drain. Fluid pressure then builds up and the pressure, if great and of long duration, may damage the optic nerve.

In the acute type of glaucoma, vision may dim suddenly, the eyeball becomes painful, and the victim feels quite ill. But the insidious type of glaucoma causes no pain, injuring vision very slowly. Sometimes it may make itself known by the appearance of colored rings and halos about bright objects or by dimming of side vision.

Much can be done to preserve vision in most cases, provided glaucoma is diagnosed in time. Surgical enlargement of the drainage ducts may be used, or medicine may be effective in constricting the pupil enough to allow the canals to open by themselves.

Glaucoma is easily recognized by an eye doctor. And it is foolhardy not to have regular examinations of the eyes—once a year after age 50, somewhat less often at younger ages. More and more now, examinations for glaucoma are being included in preventive medicine checkups.

Cataracts

Cataracts are opaque spots that form on the lens and impair vision of many elderly and some younger people. There is no primary preventive method known. If you suspect you have cataracts, don't delay going to a doctor. Cataracts can be removed surgically at any time and at practically any age. There is no need to wait for a cataract to become complete, or "ripe," as was once believed. Depending on the condition of the lens, the retina, and other factors, an occasional cataract will be treated without surgery.

Eye Infections

Today, even such severe chronic eye infections as trachoma can be cured with antibiotics and other medicines.

Don't decide for yourself that an eye infection is nothing to worry about. Of course, there are minor eye infections. Most common is conjunctivitis, or pinkeye, which causes the eyes to redden and the lids to swell and usually stick together in the morning. Many home remedies are used. We think the best approach is: (1) Wash the eye with warm water using a disposable tissue or cloth (otherwise the infection may be spread to the other eye or another person). (2) Apply yellow oxide of mercury *ophthalmic ointment* generously on the lids, and close the eye. Use the ointment morning and night. (3) Apply hot compresses, moistened with clean water, for five minutes, three or four times daily. If the eye does not improve quickly, see your physician.

But if you may, on occasion, treat a mild case of pinkeye, it is unwise to diagnose and self-treat any other form of eye infection. Your eyes are simply too precious to be toyed with. If you can't reach a doctor and you find your eyes are severely inflamed or have pus in them, use this emergency measure: Put a generous amount of ophthalmic ointment containing penicillin or some other antibiotic on the inner lids, then close the eyes so the ointment gets at the eyeballs. Repeat every three hours until you can get medical help. If your physician is not available, go to his hospital's emergency room.

It is safe for you to treat an occasional stye—a pimple-like formation in the tiny glands of the eyelid. Apply hot compresses every two hours for 15 minutes at a time. If the stye does not open and drain and heal in a few days, be sure to see your doctor. See him, too, if you have styes repeatedly.

Cleaning the Eyes

When the eyelids become irritated by wind or dust, you can relieve them by washing them with a warm salt solution, a level teaspoonful of salt to a pint of water. Be sure the utensils you use have been thoroughly cleaned and scalded. You may use an eyedropper or eyecup, as you prefer.

It is not necessary to routinely wash the eyes, since nature has provided for cleaning through the tear glands. So don't use eyedrops or wash your eyes daily with any solution. Incidentally, boric acid does not deserve its reputation as an antiseptic for the eyes. All you need do to keep your eyes clean is to wash the skin around them, using a clean personal washcloth. Avoid rubbing your eyes with your fingers.

Eye Injury

You can't be too careful in guarding your eyes against accidents at home, work, and play. Impress the need on children. And always see a physician immediately if an eye has been hurt, since delay can mean blindness.

One serious injury is that resulting from sun eclipses. There are still too many adults as well as children who are unaware of the danger, and many eyes continue to be damaged because of failure to view an eclipse properly. For proper viewing, let the sun shine through an opening in one piece of cardboard onto another piece, where it will produce an image you can observe in safety. Keep the sun at your back.

Commonly, of course, dirt, cinders, and other bits of foreign material get into the eyes. Remember that in children, especially in the excitement of play, a foreign body in the eye is often quickly forgotten, but some hours later there may be sensitivity to light, beginning redness, and a tendency to keep the lids closed. It's important to suspect a foreign body even though a child may not remember it.

Blindly trying to wash out a foreign body may do little good. The object may be trapped in small folds which the washing fluid does not reach. Pull the lower lid down and have the child look upward. This tends to open folds in the lower part of the eye and may reveal the object. To find an object under the upper lid can be more difficult. Have the child look downward while you hold the lashes of the upper lid and turn it inside out over an index finger. When objects lodge on the cornea, they may be more difficult to locate. If there is obvious irritation and yet no object can be found, it is advisable to have the child seen at once by your physician.

Eyestrain

Eyestrain may result from a need for eyeglasses or from use of outgrown glasses. It may also result from unfavorable conditions under which the eyes are used. Improper lighting, especially for reading or close work, is a frequent cause of strain. Do not face the light; it should come from in back of you and from the side so you are not in shadow. Be sure light bulbs are strong enough (75 to 100 watts) and free of dust. Hold a book or paper about 16 to 18 inches away from you and slightly below eye level. Reading when lying on your back in bed or propped up on an elbow may strain the eyes, and so will reading for long periods in a vibrating vehicle. Avoid glare, of course. And rest your eyes from time to time by shifting focus, looking off into the distance.

Night Blindness

Inability to see well or at all in dim light can mean something wrong not alone with the eyes but with the entire system. Night blindness, as it is called, is a threat to safety, particularly on the highway, because a driver may have 20/20 vision and not realize that his vision is somewhat impaired at night. The condition produces no discernible changes in eye tissues, so it cannot be diagnosed unless the patient tells the physician that he has difficulty in reading road signs at night or has trouble picking out objects in dimly lighted streets. It is not normal to have trouble seeing in dim light after a brief period, two to three minutes, of adjustment. If you become aware of such a problem, discuss it with your physician. It can be treated, sometimes simply by addition of vitamin A to the diet.

Sunlight

Good sunglasses can protect your eyes if you are in bright sunlight. Poor ones may only add to your troubles if you wear them for long. Don't wear glasses with scratches or irregularities. Some glasses are too lightly tinted to do much good. It's true that good sunglasses are expensive. The best have ground and polished lenses, and are worth the investment. Even though you wear sunglasses, do not look directly into the sun. Don't wear the glasses indoors and at night no matter how fashionable it may seem because accidents result from the reduced visual perceptiveness. If you use regular glasses, it is worthwhile to have a pair of sunglasses ground to your prescription rather than clip a pair of possibly inferior sunglasses over your carefully made regular glasses.

Television Viewing

Television will not hurt the eyes if you have a fairly large screen, do not keep the room in total darkness, do not sit too close to the set or at an angle, and do not watch steadily for extended periods. It can be wise to be arbitrary about children's viewing, setting an hour as the limit for any one session, with a good long rest period before another session. It is wise, too, to make a mark about six feet away from the set, and that far, no closer, may youngsters go; otherwise they tend to sit practically on top of the screen.

THE EARS

The ears are vital organs in more ways than one. Without them, of course, we would live in a silent world. The ears also are involved in providing us with a sense of equilibrium, balance, and orientation.

A human ear is made up of three parts. The outer ear consists of lobe and ear canal. The canal leads to the eardrum and the middle ear in which lie the "bones of hearing," called the hammer, anvil, and stirrup because of their resemblance to these objects. The bones relay the vibrations of the eardrum—set up by sound waves entering through the outer canal—to the fluid-filled cavity of the inner ear. The middle ear is connected by a tube, the eustachian, to the rear part of the throat. The tube serves to adjust pressure of air in the middle ear to outside pressure.

In the inner ear is the cochlea, which contains the organ of Corti, consisting of specialized nerve cells with hairlike projections. It is the organ of Corti that transforms the incoming vibrations into nerve impulses which the brain interprets as sound.

A good ear has remarkable sensitivity. It can respond to sound waves that deflect the eardrum by only 0.00000001 millimeter. It can assess some 1,600 frequencies from high to low, some 350 intensities from quietest to loudest. It can measure the intensity and frequency of sound waves oscillating between 20 and 20,000 cycles per second.

Also within the inner ear is the organ of equilibrium or balance. It consists of three semicircular canals and two small sacs next to the cochlea. The canals are set in different planes and contain a gelatin-like material along with nerve receptors. The movement of the gelatin in the canals as the head is moved causes the nerve receptors to flash to the brain the information that the head is changing position. A somewhat similar system in the sacs next to the cochlea transmits the messages which, in effect, always let you know which way is up.

Prevention of Ear Problems

Infections of the ear are common. Those involving the outer ear may be caused by fungi or bacteria. Eczema also frequently affects this area. If these conditions—which can usually be cleared by medical measures

—are ignored, they may travel inward and involve the eardrum and middle ear.

Infections that may harm hearing also can stem from foreign objects, such as beads and pencil erasers, that very young children sometimes push into the ear canal. Such objects should be kept away from them. Adults can cause similar trouble by "cleaning" the ears with hairpins, matchsticks, and other long objects. There is much sense in the old axiom commanding, "Never put anything smaller than your elbow into your ear." A safe rule for cleaning the ear canal is to use your little finger after thoroughly cleaning the finger with soap and water, and anything you cannot remove with the finger should be left for a physician or nurse to remove.

If excess wax accumulates and becomes embedded, a physician can wash it out with an ear syringe; and if you have such trouble frequently, he can show you how to use a syringe for the purpose. For a child, ordinary washing of the external ear with soap and water is usually all that is necessary; never try to go beyond this in cleaning a child's ears unless a doctor or nurse has given you instructions.

Middle ear infections usually arise from infections in the nose and throat transmitted via the eustachian tubes. That is why inflamed tonsils and adenoids, severe colds, and sore throats are often accompanied by a sense of pressure or pain in the ears. Especially in children, infection may spread readily into the middle ear via the eustachian tubes. Your physician can prevent this, which is one reason for calling him whenever you or a family member has a sore throat, severe cold, or sinusitis.

One important precaution you can take is to avoid vigorous nose blowing. This always carries with it some risk, and the risk increases when the nose is obstructed or when pus or nasal secretions fill the nasal passages so that forceful blowing may force these materials into the middle ear through the eustachian tube.

If the middle ear becomes seriously infected and is not promptly treated, hearing may be affected. Infection may lead to rupture of an eardrum. It may spread into the mastoid cells and, unless checked, can enter the nearby brain. Before the development of sulfa medicines and antibiotics, mastoiditis was a common, and dreaded, disease. Now a physician, if called early, can control infections. Operations for infected middle ears and mastoids, once common, fortunately are seldom necessary today.

Some people have the mistaken idea that a chronic running ear cannot be helped. The fact is that it is possible to cure almost every case of chronic infection of the ears. Sometimes it may be necessary for your physician to send you to a specialist or to a clinic or hospital at some distance, but it is worthwhile clearing up a condition that can ruin hearing.

Swimming

Rarely does swimming cause ear trouble unless there is a nose, sinus, or throat infection. Learning how to breathe in through the mouth and out through the nose during swimming is a helpful preventive measure. In the case of a perforated eardrum, however, you should have your doctor's permission and advice before going swimming. Once in a while, an eardrum may be perforated by the pressure of high diving; pain, and sometimes bleeding, will result. If you see a doctor immediately, there will probably be no permanent harm from such an accident.

Deafness

There are many degrees of hearing impairment. Mild hearing loss may go unnoticed. When the loss is great enough to produce some difficulty in communication, the condition is commonly called "hard of hearing." When so much hearing ability is lost that a loud voice, even a voice amplified by a hearing aid, cannot be heard, the condition is called deafness.

Hearing impairment may stem from an inner ear problem; essentially, this is nerve deafness. Often, the impairment is of the conductive type in which there is no nerve involvement but rather some defect in the conduction of sound waves in the outer ear canal or the middle ear.

An infection, injury, or congenital deformity may close the ear canal, and the canal may need surgical reconstruction. If an eardrum has been partially destroyed by infection, plastic surgery may repair it. If the middle ear bones are damaged by infection, corrective surgery may help.

Otosclerosis, a common form of impairment, involves the stapes, one of the middle ear bones. Because of overgrowth of bone, the stapes cannot vibrate properly and so is unable to transmit sound waves. An operation to mobilize the stapes has restored hearing for many people. And other surgery may be used when the mobilization operation is not suitable.

Many types of hearing impairment can be overcome to a marked degree, even almost completely, with hearing aids. It is tragic to think of all the people who lead handicapped lives because they believe that others will make fun of them if they wear an aid. If this was ever true —and we doubt it—it is certainly no longer true with aids that bear no resemblance to trumpets. Modern devices are well designed and effective when properly chosen. Since various hearing impairments differ, it is important to find an instrument suited to the wearer's specific needs. An ear specialist, not a salesman, can give you the right advice.

The most important measures you can use to prevent hearing impairment consist of having your own and your children's hearing tested at regular intervals and of seeing your doctor the moment you or a child feel any pain, note any ear discharge, experience any unusual buzzing, ringing, or pressure in the ear, or become aware of any seeming diminution of hearing acuity.

THE OTHER SENSES

Man has about 3,000 taste buds. They are mainly on the tongue, although there are a few on the palate, tonsils, and pharynx. There are four primary or basic taste sensations—sweet, bitter, sour or acid, and salt. You can't taste all flavors on all parts of the tongue. Sweet flavors register near the tip, sour on the sides, bitter on the back, and salty all over.

The sense of smell is located in odor receptors in the upper passage of the nasal cavity. The size of the membrane containing the odor receptors is only about one-fourth square inch in man as against an area 40 times as great in the dog. The organ of smell, which can detect things at a distance, is obviously more important as a danger warning system in animals than in man.

It's because of the location of the receptors that you may not smell delicate odors at first. It takes several whiffs to get the odor into the upper nasal passage.

Before you can taste anything, the substance must be moistened, and the salivary glands supply the moisture. And to be smelled, an odor must be dissolved in the mucus secreted by the nasal membranes. Smell receptors in man, although they do not have the same capacity as in lower animals, still are sensitive enough to allow you to detect a substance diluted to as much as one part in 30 billion.

No special care is required to guard the senses of taste and smell. You may wish to read, in connection with these senses, the section dealing with care of the mouth and the nose.

Touch, sometimes called the fifth sense, is actually five senses: touch, pressure, pain, heat, and cold. Skin sensations are registered in nerve endings all over the body. Nerve fibers carry them as impulses to the spinal cord and then to the brain where all these feelings register.

If you place your hand lightly on any object, the first sensation is touch. Press harder and you sense pressure. And if the object has a rough surface and you press hard enough, you may feel pain. The senses are closely related though distinct from each other. Also in the skin are separate nerve endings to register heat and cold, which is absence of heat.

A discussion of sense organs could go much further but would serve no useful purpose here. For example, you can feel the pain of a stomach-ache, but you can also feel hunger, which is quite different. You can also feel thirst, which is not among the sensations classically classified. Some investigators have suggested that the senses might well be divided into a dozen or more categories. In addition to the usual five—sight, hearing, taste, smell, and touch—pressure, heat, cold, and pain deserve individual categories, and so, too, the ability to sense vibration, position, and equilibrium.

25

THE ENDOCRINE GLANDS

UNTIL ABOUT a century ago, the nervous system was generally credited with being the one controlling force for complex body processes. But then it became evident that some other influence must be at work. Too many phenomena appeared to have no relationship to the nervous system. It was difficult to explain—in terms of the nervous system alone—the differences in size among people, body changes of puberty, variations of vigor and energy.

The explanation was to be found in certain glands, the *endocrines*, which are not at all like the salivary, sweat, and other *exocrine* glands. The exocrines are glands of external secretion. They pour their products through ducts or tubes, and the secretions have purely local activity. Indeed, the ducts carry them to the sites where they serve self-evident purposes.

The endocrines are glands of internal secretion. They have no ducts. Instead, their secretions go into the bloodstream, and their effects are felt in areas far removed from the sites of the glands.

The existence of some of these glands was long known. It was long clear, for example, that there was a connection between the sex glands —testes and ovaries—and secondary sexual characteristics such as male beards and female breast development. It had been apparent enough for centuries that when a boy's testes were destroyed, he failed to develop masculine characteristics.

Now much more is known about the sex and other endocrine glands and the activities of the substances they secrete, called hormones, as powerful chemical regulators. Hormones control the size, shape, and appearance of the body; influence emotions and mental state; team up with the nervous system in determining, essentially, the kind of individual you are and even to some extent how you live.

The exact chemical composition of many of these hormones has been established. They have been extracted in pure form from the glands—in many instances, from equivalent animal glands—for medical use. Some have been created synthetically in the laboratory.

Much has been learned about the exact functions of the various hormones and the consequences when a specific gland fails to function properly, creating too much or too little of its hormone or hormones. Endocrinology is still a young science with much to learn, but some of the most remarkable advances in medicine have come as the result of advances in endocrinology.

THE ENDOCRINE SYSTEM

The endocrine glands differ markedly in appearance and are widely separated in the body.

The pituitary is a round mass about the size of a large greenpea, attached by a stalk to the brain stem. The thyroid, deep in the throat, has been likened to a small oyster, though it is beefy red in color. Attached to the thyroid are the parathyroids—generally four, although there may be more or less—which somewhat resemble BB shots. The adrenals, rising like mushrooms from atop the kidneys, are two in number. Each consists of a core, the medulla, and a casing, the cortex. The pancreas, lying against the back wall of the abdomen, might appear at first glance to be no endocrine gland at all, since it has a duct leading into the intestine. But in the tail and elsewhere it also has a few tiny segments, called islets, which form an endocrine gland, pouring their secretions into the bloodstream. The gonads, or sex glands, consist of testes in men and ovaries in women. In addition, there are the pineal gland in the upper back part of the brain, and the thymus which is found below the thyroid in young people and withers away. Very little is known as yet about the pineal and thymus.

The hormones these glands send through the blood to various parts of the body act like messengers (the word hormone comes from the Greek word meaning to excite or stir up). The hormones do not actually create processes; instead they give the orders for certain processes to speed up or slow down.

And the endocrine glands form an interdependent system. In a sense, they can be likened to a family in that what happens to one affects the others. If one gland is removed, the functioning of all others is altered. Similarly, if the functioning of one increases so its secretions increase, others are affected. This is one reason why it can be dangerous to dose oneself with a hormone, glandular tissue or extract, or whatever it may be called, for the purpose of reducing weight, getting rid of excess hair, developing the breasts, becoming more virile, or for any other reason.

As an example of how the glands work together, the pituitary secretes a hormone that moves through the blood to the adrenals to stimulate the latter. In turn, the adrenals secrete a hormone that travels to the pituitary and signals the latter to slow production of the adrenal-arousing hormone.

Actually, the pituitary secretes hormones to stir up each of the other endocrine glands, and each gland responds in the same way. Until recently, it was thought that the pituitary was the "master" gland. But it is now evident that the pituitary is no all-powerful monarch on its own. It is connected to the floor of one of the ventricles in the brain called the hypothalamus. The hypothalamus produces secretions—and here, as some endocrinologists put it, is what might be considered a two-way chemical bridge between "body" and "mind."

Certainly, it is now clear that the endocrine system and the autonomic nervous system work together closely. Consider, for example, what happens when, for any reason, you experience an alarm reaction. From the nervous system, a message is transmitted to the cores of the adrenals which then secrete into the blood a hormone that increases heart action and narrows blood vessels so blood is pushed through them with more force; the hormone also relaxes and enlarges airways so more air can reach the lungs more quickly; in addition, the hormone reaches the pituitary which then secretes hormones to cause adrenal cortex, thyroid, parathyroids, even the gonads (which are not exclusively sexual in function) to secrete hormones. All these hormones complete the almost instantaneous mustering of body and mind to deal with stress—and account for some of the superhuman feats of thinking, action, and muscular accomplishment which humans often exhibit under stress.

There is no simple, neat categorization for the endocrine system, its functionings, and its relationships with the nervous system.

The pituitary, if not the master, is a critical link in a delicate check-and-balance system, and all endocrine glands are involved in the checking and balancing. If one becomes overactive or underactive, it influences all the rest. Some may speed up activities; others may slow them down. A new balance is set up, but it may not always be a healthy balance. For this reason, glandular disorders can be very complex.

The relationship between endocrine system and nervous system is two-way. Nerve impulses influence glands; and glands influence nerves. Emotions affect the autonomic nervous system, which in turns affects gland activity. And glands work through the nervous system and influence emotions. One example of the latter is evident in the hyperthyroid person whose thyroid is excessively active; he or she is tense, easily excited, stirred up by the slightest disturbance, nervous, irritable.

Many hormones are secreted by the endocrines. The pituitary alone is known to pour out a dozen or so; the adrenals more than 30. The following table shows a number of the hormones and some of the diseases resulting when a gland is too active or not active enough:

| | | Disease Caused by | |
GLAND	HORMONE	OVERACTIVITY	UNDERACTIVITY
Thyroid	Thyroxin	Exophthalmic goiter (also called Graves' disease or hyperthyroidism)	Myxedema, cretinism (in infants)
Parathyroid	Parathormone	Hyperparathyroidism (osteitis fibrosa cystica)	Parathyroid tetany
Islets of Langerhans (pancreas)	Insulin	Hyperinsulinism	Diabetes mellitus
Adrenal Cortex	Cortin, cortisone, etc.	Cushing's syndrome, adrenal hypercorticism, adrenal virilism	Addison's disease
Medulla	Adrenaline	Hyperadrenalism, pheochromocytoma	May contribute to symptoms of Addison's disease
Gonads Female (ovary)	Estrogen (estrin)	Menstrual irregularities	Menopause
Male (testis)	Androgen (testosterone)	Excessive virilism	Eunuchism
Pituitary anterior lobe	Corticotropin, thyrotropin, gonadotropins, lactogenic hormone, prolactin	Cushing's syndrome (hyperadrenalism), gigantism (acromegaly)	Dwarfism, Simmonds' disease
posterior lobe	Vasopressin, oxytocin		Diabetes insipidus

ROLL CALL OF THE GLANDS

The Islets of Langerhans

Diabetes is the most familiar of the diseases caused by endocrine gland disorder.

The islets of Langerhans of the pancreas secrete insulin. This hormone enables the body to use, or burn, sugar and starch after they have been converted by digestive juices into glucose. The body must utilize glucose (sugar) to provide heat and energy and to help in utilization of other foods. Any sugar the body does not immediately need is stored in the tissues to be drawn on later, like money in the bank.

When the islets fail to provide insulin to spark this process, the sugar passes unused into the blood and is eliminated in the urine. The quantity of urine increases, causing the diabetic to become thirsty and to drink more fluid, which in turn is quickly eliminated.

Not all reasons why the islets may fail to produce enough insulin are known. A disease of the pancreas may be involved. Diabetes tends to run in families. Some authorities on this disease believe diabetes is present at or shortly after birth, although it does not necessarily show up for many years. They suspect that a person destined to develop diabetes undergoes continuous abnormal and hidden body changes until, finally, the symptoms become apparent. Diabetes occurs most frequently in overweight people; the islets, trying to make enough insulin for the large amounts of sugar and starch that fat people consume, may be unequal to the task and so falter on the job.

An additional discussion of diabetes will be found elsewhere in this book. This much can be said here: Until about 1923, when insulin was introduced, the only thing that could be done for diabetics was to use diet. Today, with insulin, diabetics can live virtually normal, active lives. More recently, too, other agents, taken by mouth, have been employed for some diabetics.

The Thyroid Gland

The thyroid, in front of the throat below the Adam's apple and just above the breastbone, is roughly U-shaped, each end of the U flaring out to a lobe about the size of a big toe. The gland is extremely important for all-round health of the body. It regulates the rate at which the body utilizes oxygen; it also controls the rate at which various organs function and the speed with which the body utilizes food.

In effect, the thyroid, through its secretions, acts as a kind of thermostat. Every cell in the body is like a tiny power plant, burning food and setting energy free, some of the energy coming off as heat. Thyroid hormone can be said to determine how hot the fires get in the cells. The term "metabolism" refers to the fires—the speed of activity in the cells.

An overactive thyroid is a thermostat set too high. Food is burned up almost as fast as it is eaten, and even some body tissue may be burned up. Loss of weight with excessive appetite is a symptom. Too much thyroid secretion produces a general speed-up so that the patient becomes overactive and nervous, the heart may palpitate, there may be sleeping difficulty. In some cases, the eyes bulge and have a staring look. Today, of course, several methods of treatment are available for hyperthyroidism. Part of the gland may be removed surgically. In some cases, medications that block thyroid activity may be used. In others, radioactive iodine may be employed; it is picked up by the thyroid, and the radioactive particles destroy some of the gland to reduce the secretions.

With too little thyroid activity, hypothyroidism, food is not burned fast enough, much of it is changed to fats causing weight gain. A sluggish thyroid also makes the patient drowsy, slow moving, easily fatigued.

MYXEDEMA. In this condition produced by thyroid underfunctioning, the patient is sluggish physically and mentally, cannot stand the cold, sometimes develops a tongue so large and thick that it sticks out of the mouth. Treatment, by administration of thyroid hormone, usually brings marked improvement.

Some babies are born with thyroid deficiency. Any child who seems to be developing too slowly—for example, in following objects with his eyes or holding his head erect—should be checked by a physician for thyroid deficiency. The earlier such a child is treated, the better the chances for normal development.

SIMPLE GOITER. To function normally, the thyroid must have iodine. Lacking sufficient iodine, it cannot produce the normal quantity of hormone. In an effort to compensate, the gland enlarges until a noticeable lump may appear in the throat. The swelling, or goiter, may become large enough to interfere with breathing or swallowing.

Thyroid hormone consists of about 65 percent iodine, but the amount of iodine needed in food to avoid goiter is small. Iodized table salt—an amount no more than ordinarily used with meals—is enough, even in areas where the soil is completely lacking in natural iodine. Too much iodine may cause a skin eruption. Although consuming iodine does not cure a simple goiter, it will prevent one and will stop an existing goiter from enlarging further. Anyone with even a small goiter should have medical attention for it.

It is especially important for expectant mothers who live in regions such as the Rocky Mountain States, the Great Lakes Basin, and the Upper Mississippi River Valley, where the soil is lacking in iodine, to follow doctor's orders about the amount of iodine they need. Insufficient iodine in the diet may cause a mother to produce a child with thyroid deficiency. However, most pregnant women develop a slight enlargement of the thyroid, and this should cause no undue worry. Children whose diets lack iodine may show signs of goiter when they reach adolescence.

A physician, of course, should check on any suspected case of thyroid disturbance. Tests are not simple; several may be needed, especially when a disturbance is relatively mild.

One frequently employed test is the basal metabolism, which records the amount of oxygen used. In hyperthyroidism, the amount is increased; in hypothyroidism, it is decreased. Another test uses radioactive iodine as a tracer. Severity of the disease can be established by the amount of the iodine taken up by the thyroid; an underactive gland will take up less, an overactive one more. The protein-bound iodine (PBI) test involves an examination of the blood taken from a vein to determine whether the amount of PBI normally produced in the body is elevated as in hyperthyroidism or low as in the opposite condition.

Thyroid tumors occur. Most are benign, or harmless; some are malignant. Surgery is the usual procedure in cases of thyroid cancer but radiation is sometimes used, particularly if the malignancy has begun to spread.

The Parathyroid Glands

These tiny glands, usually found in clusters of four, are embedded near the thyroid base. They are so much smaller than the thyroid that before surgeons were certain of their presence they were sometimes removed with the thyroid when excision of the latter was necessary. The location and significance of the parathyroids are well known today, and there is little danger of accidental removal.

The hormone of the parathyroids, called parathormone, has much to do with the balance in the body, and the excretion in the urine, of calcium and phosphorus which are derived from milk and other foods and are necessary for bone growth and maintenance. If the parathyroids become underactive, the calcium level in the blood falls and muscles develop painful spasms, called tetany. In severe cases, convulsion and death may result. Administration of parathyroid hormone, or certain synthetic compounds with similar actions, or a potent vitamin D preparation, will usually keep calcium output normal and stop the spasms. Feeding calcium is helpful in such cases.

Hyperparathyroidism, caused by tumors, can deplete the bones of calcium and may cause kidney stone formation as well. Some patients have duodenal ulcer. A rare disorder, hyperparathyroidism is curable if diagnosed early.

The Adrenal Glands

Each of the adrenal glands, one atop each kidney, has a cortex, or outer portion, and medulla, or central section. The cortex secretes about 30 hormones and regulates many metabolic processes. The medulla produces the hormone epinephrine, more commonly called adrenaline. Adrenaline output is stepped up when you become fearful, angry, or excited—leading to a speed-up of heartbeat and many chemical changes that prepare the body for action.

Among the major functions of the adrenal cortex and its hormones are the control of salt and water content of the body, and the control of sugar and protein metabolism. The cortex also secretes a hormone similar to that put out by the testes. In some tumors of the cortex, women develop masculine characteristics such as a deep voice and facial hair, and menstruation may slow or cease. In men with such tumors, the masculine secondary sex characteristics become more pronounced.

Underfunctioning of the adrenal cortex produces a rare disorder, Addison's disease, discussed elsewhere. With cortisone and other preparations, Addison's disease can be controlled and the afflicted person can lead a normal life.

Both cortisone, an adrenal hormone preparation, and various derivatives of it, can replenish the body's supply when the adrenals function improperly. In addition, these medications may bring about favorable results in such diseases as arthritis, asthma, sarcoidosis, and rheumatic fever. The reason is not yet clear, for people with such diseases do not appear to be deficient in adrenal hormones and yet additions to the normal output sometimes produce striking improvement.

The Pituitary Gland

If you think of one line drawn through the head from ear to ear and another drawn backward from between the eyes, the pituitary lies at the spot—at the base of the brain—where the two lines cross. It consists of an anterior or front lobe; an intermediate part; and a posterior or back lobe.

The secretions of the pituitary are many and perhaps still more remain to be discovered. From the anterior lobe come powerful agents that influence other endocrine glands as well as various body regions. ACTH, adrenocorticotrophic hormone, stimulates the adrenal cortex. Thyrotrophic, or thyroid-stimulating hormone, often called TSH, regulates size and activity of the thyroid gland. Also from the anterior pituitary comes a hormone called the growth hormone, which has an important influence on height. During the years when a child is moving toward adulthood, the anterior pituitary secretes gonadotrophic hormone which stimulates the reproductive organs. After childbirth, the anterior lobe secretes lactogenic hormone which causes milk to flow.

One of the posterior pituitary hormones, vasopressin, helps regulate water balance in the body. Another, oxytocin, stimulates smooth muscles such as those of the digestive organs and the uterus.

Research is constantly revealing new facts about the pituitary and the relationship among the various glands of the endocrine system. Scientists are trying to unravel the mysteries of the thymus and pineal glands. When such problems are solved, it can be expected that many more diseases may become not only curable but preventable.

Pituitary gland diseases are rare. Inadequate pituitary secretion causes some types of dwarfism; excessive secretion stimulates growth to gigantic proportions. Pituitary tumors may press on the optic nerves and produce some loss of vision and headaches. Acromegaly, in which bones increase in size, particularly the bones of face, hands and feet, is caused by an overactive pituitary. Cushing's disease also is sometimes caused this way. Underactivity of the anterior lobe of this complex gland leads to a thin, malnourished condition, Simmonds' disease. Pituitary insufficiency can cause children to become excessively fat. In some cases, a condition called Frohlich's syndrome develops; children who have it are excessively obese and sexually underdeveloped. If given an extract of pituitary gland in time, they become normal and are spared unhappy lives. If pituitary secretion decreases after puberty, fat may accumulate around certain portions of the body, particularly the hips. When the back lobe of the pituitary fails to function properly, excessive urination results—as much as 30 quarts a day. This rare malady is diabetes insipidus, not to be confused with "ordinary" diabetes mellitus.

While effective replacements for all pituitary hormones are not available, treatment of the organs affected by specific hormones is often possible. Thus, cortisone, thyroid, and sex hormones are often employed for patients suffering from specific pituitary hormone problems. For patients affected by dwarfism, human growth hormone has become available; it is effective only in specific cases and only if administered before the normal growth period has ended.

The Sex Glands (Gonads)

The gonads (derived from the Greek word meaning seed) consist of the testes in men, the ovaries in women. In addition to producing sperm and ova, the glands elaborate hormones that are responsible for the special male and female characteristics.

THE MALE SEX GLANDS. The two testes, which lie enclosed in the scrotal sac of skin just below the penis, secrete semen containing the male reproductive element, the sperm. They also produce the important male sex hormone, testosterone.

One of the first known hormones, testosterone's activity was deduced from the events that followed removal of the testes. It has been known for centuries that if the testes of a boy are removed or destroyed before puberty, he does not develop typical masculine characteristics. Instead, his personality is gentle, his voice high-pitched, his chest narrow and flat, his muscles underdeveloped. He lacks facial hair and pubic hair, his penis is small and underdeveloped, and he is impotent.

In addition to affecting male sex organs and secondary sexual characteristics, testosterone stimulates muscular and bone development and helps maintain muscle strength.

If testosterone is injected into a female animal, certain masculine characteristics develop and female hormonal function is inhibited as long as the testosterone injections continue. If testosterone is injected into a eunuch or a man with underactive secretion, the size of the sexual organ increases, secondary sexual characteristics develop, and there is an increase in sexual desire and potency. The effect is transitory. People who benefit from testosterone require treatment for their entire lives.

It is important to note here that while testosterone administration may be helpful in cases of hormone deficiency, injections of the hormone are ineffective for "rejuvenation" and may in fact be dangerous, sometimes leading to tumor or cancer of the prostate. The aging process is not confined to sexual function and cannot be halted by a single hormone or any combination of hormones yet discovered.

Actually, many men can reproduce at age 70 and beyond. The feeling of decline experienced by some men is more likely to be due to factors other than sex gland inadequacy—either other physical problems or psychological difficulties. A thorough medical checkup is advisable rather than costly and potentially dangerous testosterone injections.

MALE IMPOTENCE. Inability to have sexual relations is a complex problem. It may result from a disease of the testes or of the pituitary. Some nervous system disorders cause impotence. In most cases, however, the testes and entire endocrine system are normal and the problem is traceable to emotional disturbances or psychoneuroses. Such men may be helped by a family physician who understands emotional disorders. If necessary, the family physician may suggest help from a specialist in psychotherapy.

Sterility, the inability to beget children, occurs in some men who are not impotent. It may be due to failure, for many possible reasons, to produce enough sperm or sperm active enough to reach and fertilize the female cell. While only one healthy sperm is needed for fertilization, and 300 million or more are usually released in an ejaculation, the journey to reach the female cell is so hazardous that many lively ones are required to ensure that a survivor gets to the right place at the right time. Ways have been found to help many men with sterility problems, as discussed elsewhere in this book.

THE FEMALE SEX GLANDS.   Like the testes, the two ovaries have more than one function. They produce the ova, or eggs; they also secrete hormones needed for both reproduction and feminine characteristics.

The ovaries lie in the front part of the abdomen, below the navel, and each is connected with the uterus by a fallopian tube. The ovarian hormones are estrogen and progesterone. They are produced in small amounts before puberty and after menopause, and in abundance during the childbearing years, the period when a woman has her regular monthly cycles.

MENSTRUATION AND OVULATION.   Menstruation involves the discharge of the extra blood and tissue built up in preparation for conception but not used. Cycles vary among women and even in the same woman, but generally the time from one menstrual period to the next averages about 28 days.

Doctors customarily count the first day of menstruation as day 1 in a cycle. During the first 14 days of the cycle, the ovary contains a follicle, a small hollow ball about the size of a pinhead. Within the follicle is an egg. The follicle grows during the two weeks until it becomes about as large as a pea. As it grows, it produces estrogen. Follicle growth as well as the menstrual cycle in general is under pituitary gland control. On about day 14, stimulated by the pituitary, the follicle bursts and the egg is discharged from the ovary to enter the fallopian tube on its way to the uterus. If sperm are present in the tube at this time, fertilization may take place in the tube. The fertilized egg then continues its journey to the uterus where it implants itself on the wall of the uterus. Meanwhile, the ruptured follicle from which the egg came is transformed into a yellowish, solid ball, now called the corpus luteum, or yellow body. The corpus luteum produces a second hormone, progesterone.

Scientists now know how to make synthetic hormones to control ovulation. Contraceptive pills imitate the natural body processes in preventing ovulation, as discussed elsewhere in this book.

Estrogen and progesterone help build up the lining of uterus, making it thicker and providing it with a rich blood supply to feed the unborn baby. During the last 14 days of the cycle, the two hormones are produced by the corpus luteum. The fertilized egg secretes a hormone that causes the corpus luteum to persist in producing estrogen and progesterone. The hormone from the fertilized egg is necessary because at the end of the 28-day cycle, the pituitary no longer maintains the corpus luteum; so the fertilized egg must take over the job.

If pregnancy has not occurred, the corpus luteum degenerates and its secretions stop. With cessation of hormone production, the rich blood supply built up in the uterine lining sloughs off and menstruation occurs. Menstruation and menstrual difficulties are discussed in detail elsewhere in this book.

MENOPAUSE. Menopause, or change of life, is as natural for women as menstruation is. There should be no dread of it: nothing more disastrous occurs than the tapering off and cessation of the monthly cycle.

True, some changes, natural ones, occur. Estrogen secretion is reduced. The follicles no longer release eggs. Menstruation stops, suddenly or gradually. After menopause is well established, in about a year, there should be no more bleeding. Be certain to consult a physician immediately if bleeding or spotting occurs, since this may signal cancer or another disorder requiring prompt treatment.

Actually, unfounded fears are to a large extent responsible for the emotional disturbances some women experience during menopause. Certain physical symptoms may occur because of the glandular changes taking place. If they become troublesome, they may be relieved by hormone treatment. We discuss menopausal symptoms more fully elsewhere.

PREVENTIVE CARE OF THE ENDOCRINE SYSTEM

It has been said that we are what our glands make us. That, of course, is an oversimplification. Other factors enter the picture—but the glands do, indeed, have a vital role, influencing structure, function, and personality.

What everyday care is required to prevent disease of the endocrine system? Everything that contributes to good general health contributes to good health of the endocrine glands. That includes sound nutrition; it includes proper exercise and other physical activity, which have a stimulating effect on many of the glands; it includes the avoidance as much as possible of excessive stress and strain, which may debilitate glandular functioning.

If you suspect at any time that you may have a glandular problem, don't toy with the idea or attempt self-treatment. Let your physician consider the problem, make any necessary tests, arrive at an informed diagnosis—and then, using the constantly growing knowledge of endocrinology and growing stockpile of therapeutic aids, provide treatment. The sooner any endocrine disorder is discovered and properly treated, the more likely the prevention of debilitating conditions and complications.

Some specific things to do: To protect the islets of Langerhans so they will secrete insulin normally, two items are important. First, keep your weight normal; obesity promotes diabetes. Second, use as little refined sugar as possible. We urge, too, that you read our section on diabetes and make certain that at your periodic medical checkups tests for diabetes are included.

To protect the thyroid gland, use iodized salt, especially if you live away from the seacoasts.

To protect the ovaries and testes against venereal disease, see our discussion of gonorrhea (page 580).

To help assure the health of the adrenals, get reasonable amounts of physical activity which can provide normal stimulation for these glands.

There is no primary protection for the pituitary, parathyroids, and other endocrine glands. See the Index for listing of diseases of these glands and what can be done for secondary prevention.

26

THE TEETH

THE MOST exciting news in dentistry today is not any new drill, anesthetic, denture material, or other fix-it device or procedure. Just the opposite: It's a whole new concept which puts the emphasis on stopping dental disease before it can happen rather than treating it after it does. It is based on the development of simple, practical tools for calling a halt to tooth decay and gum disease. It promises, if you use it, to cut your dental pains and dental bills and could do much for your appearance and general health as well, no matter how old you are or even how much you have been ravaged by dental disease up to now. It is high time we had it.

Good teeth contribute not only to appearance but to good digestion. They are necessary, too, for good and clear speech. And teeth that are free of disease provide no portal of entry for infections that may spread to affect other areas of the body.

And yet tooth and gum troubles, which have plagued man through all recorded history, do so even now. Even though American dentistry has been the best in the world from a reparative standpoint, the American mouth is a disaster area, getting worse, not better. Right now, more than 20 million Americans have lost all their teeth; 90 million have at least 18 missing, decayed, or filled teeth; and there are more than a billion unfilled cavities in the country.

By age 35, one of every five of us needs dentures; by 55, one of every two. Fifty percent of all two-year-olds have decaying teeth; by the teens, five of every six youngsters do.

On top of this, gum disease takes a huge toll, affecting not only older people—90 percent of those over 65 and 80 percent of the middle-aged —but also two thirds of young adults. Even among 12-year-olds, four out of five have gingivitis, the precursor of most gum disease.

Dentists have been kept so busy fixing and patching that, according to a recent survey, 40.3 percent of the 90,000 dentists in the country are unable to take on any new patients. This, despite the fact that 40 percent of the population, practicing complete neglect, have never once visited a dentist.

So bad is our dental health that, according to the American Council on Education, if all the dentists in the country were lined up on the East Coast and moved westward, taking care of the needs of the population as they went along, they would get only as far as Harrisburg, Pennsylvania, before having to turn around and go back and start over again.

Such facts, coupled with insights into the why of both decay and gum disease, are galvanizing the dental profession. Its leaders and the best dental schools now are working to turn dentistry into a new kind of profession—no longer mechanical and reparative in major emphasis but rather primarily devoted to making dental disease as avoidable, in effect, as measles or smallpox. Already, the Armed Forces dental corps have developed pioneering programs which are producing dramatic results. At the U.S. Naval Academy, Rear Admiral Frank M. Kyes, Chief of the Navy's Dental Division, has reported, "Dental decay has virtually become a thing of the past."

In a recent cross-country trip to visit dentists leading in introducing the new preventive dentistry into private practice, one of us found them reporting enthusiastically that decay can be reduced by as much as 90 percent and even more in both children and adults; that gum disease also can be checked; and that the required measures are to a very great extent simply new, more effective methods of home care.

THE DECAY PROCESS

Decay, essentially, is an acid-etching process. The acid is formed when bacteria, always present in the mouth, digest food particles left in the mouth. The acid attacks the enamel, the outer layer of the teeth which, even though it is the hardest substance in the body, will dissolve in acid.

Decay is sneaky. Even a tiny hole, one you cannot see, through the enamel can be enough to allow acid to enter to start dissolving the dentin, the softer structure under the enamel. When the decay process finally reaches the pulp, the living part of the tooth containing nerves and blood vessels, you may feel pain, but not necessarily. A tooth may be almost completely rotted away and abscessed without causing pain.

It would be bad enough if the effects of decay in a tooth were limited to the tooth, but a diseased tooth can allow bacteria to enter the bloodstream to be circulated to the rest of the body. Dr. J. C. Muhler, of Indiana University, one of the country's leading dental researchers, has written:

"Dental diseases are directly responsible for general poor health, affecting patients of all ages. Rampant dental cavities in children not only result in facial deformities in adulthood but contribute significantly to bacterial contamination of the blood and may be quite important in the development of certain forms of heart disease. The elimination of decay . . . is most urgent in the treatment of bacterial endocarditis [a heart infection] and rheumatic fever. Elimination of dental disease is essential in preventing certain forms of kidney disease in children and adults."

MOVING TOWARD PREVENTION OF DECAY

The first glimmer of hope for avoidance came with the discovery some 30 years ago of the value of fluoridated drinking water. Ingested regularly during childhood while the teeth were being formed, fluoride could combine with the developing enamel· to make it more acid-resistant. It could halve the incidence of decay in children. Currently, some 3,000 communities serving about one third of the total population have fluoridated water. Many dentists in nonfluoridated areas now prescribe fluoride tablets, or vitamins with fluoride added, for children.

Another advance came about 20 years ago with the discovery that painting a sodium fluoride solution directly on the enamel could cut decay 25 to 40 percent. This, however, was true only for children up to about age 15. And the applications, which took quite some time, did not add extra protection for children in fluoridated water communities.

After some searching, scientists next turned up stannous fluoride, a combination of tin and fluorine. One application a year of stannous fluoride proved far more effective than sodium fluoride applications. It added to the protective effect of ingested fluoride. And it worked for adults as well as children.

There followed incorporation of fluoride in toothpastes—to provide, in effect, a daily topical fluoride application that could supplement periodic applications by the dentist. In 1960, for the first time, the American Dental Association established a therapeutic category for dentifrices. Where before toothpastes had been considered aids to cleaning and no more, now, with fluoride added, they could also reduce decay by one third or more.

At that point, the picture was this: Ingested fluoride could help endow youngsters with teeth better able to resist decay. Topical applications by a dentist and use of fluoridated toothpaste could increase protection. Combined, the measures could reduce decay by as much as 90 percent in children. Another important development was to come when work of the Armed Forces demonstrated dramatically that adults, too, could benefit.

The Armed Forces always had been faced with a serious dental disease problem. Entering servicemen had an average of seven decaying teeth each, and developed more while on duty; service dentists couldn't begin to cope adequately. In 1961, the Army set up a small-scale experimental program. Servicemen had their teeth cleaned in the dental chair, but instead of finishing up with the usual abrasive polishing paste to make the teeth gleam, Army dentists used a paste with fluoride added. Along with bright teeth, servicemen also got fluoride burnished into the enamel during the polishing. In the same sitting, a topical fluoride solution was dabbed on. They were then sent away to make regular daily use of a fluoridated toothpaste.

By 1963, Army dentists had expanded the program so it reached more than 300,000 men. It has been expanding since, and in the Navy and Air Force as well. Result: huge reductions in new cavity formation. A comparison study at the Navy's New London, Connecticut, base, for example, showed an 86 percent reduction in the decay rate among men on the program. After two years of experience with the program at the Naval Academy at Annapolis, Admiral Kyes could report that "midshipmen now have a caries expectancy of one new cavity in ten years," versus the average rate of university students of the same age of two new cavities each year.

The Navy has experimented further—with a "self-preparation" program. Before they go to the dental clinic, servicemen get a cup of pumice paste containing fluoride and are shown in groups how to brush it on their teeth for 10 minutes to achieve a thorough cleaning and burnishing. After that, a dentist has only to apply a fluoride solution for 15 seconds and the treatment is completed.

The self-preparation technique has been extended to children of naval personnel, and Admiral Kyes is convinced it has broad implications for the civilian community. "As Navy children scrub their teeth at home under their mothers' supervision and go to dental clinics for brief and inexpensive treatment, so schoolchildren can scrub at home and receive their topical application at home. Self-preparation is a dental Pandora's box because it breaks through dentistry's two restraining bonds—time and lack of manpower."

The Armed Forces' work has provided a clear-cut demonstration on a massive scale that decay prevention techniques are highly effective for adults as well as children and that they may be widely and inexpensively applied.

ADVANCES AGAINST GUM DISEASE

Meanwhile, gum disease—technically known as periodontal disease—has come in for hard study. And not only have effective methods to help prevent it been developed; these very same methods provide for even further improvement in reducing decay.

Gum disease progresses in stages. It starts with gingivitis, in which the gums become inflamed, swollen, and tender. Left uncontrolled, the inflammation advances and the gums begin to stand away from the teeth so that pockets are formed which harbor bacteria and pus. This is pyorrhea. As pyorrhea progresses, fibers holding the teeth in their sockets weaken and gradually the bone supporting the teeth is destroyed, and the teeth become loose and are lost.

What starts the process?

There is now evidence—thanks to the brilliant work of many investigators, notably Dr. Sumter Arnim of the University of Texas, Houston—that, just as in tooth decay, bacteria are involved. Clinging to the teeth and working on food particles to produce acid, bacteria also produce a material—a film called plaque—that covers them over, allowing them to work undisturbed.

Plaque not only furthers decay; it triggers the formation of tartar, or calculus. And it is calculus that, spreading down below the gum line, irritates the gums, starts up inflammation and gingivitis, and opens the way for pyorrhea and gum disease progression.

"Calculus cannot form unless plaque is present," says Dr. Irving Glickman, Chairman of the Department of Periodontology at Tufts University School of Dental Medicine. "It's important for a dentist to remove calculus once formed; but it's also vital for the individual to minimize formation. In no other field of medicine can the patient so effectively assist in preventing and reducing the severity of disease."

Other factors may enter into decay and gum disease. In some caries-rampant individuals—those with far more even than the bad-enough average of decay—poor nutrition or faulty saliva flow may play a role; dentists can correct both. Faulty bite may help foster gum trouble; this can be corrected.

But it is now clear that against both decay and periodontal disease, effective home care to prevent plaque formation is a prime weapon of prevention. And more and more dentists are taking time to educate patients in proper home care methods. Recently, one of us spent two and a half months visiting such men in and around more than a dozen cities and in small communities. It was gratifying to see them lift bits of plaque from patients' teeth and place them under special microscopes so the patients could see for themselves the teeming colonies of bacteria in the plaque. Plaque on the teeth is invisible, but these dentists reveal it to patients graphically with a simple tool, a disclosing wafer. It's a small tablet containing a harmless vegetable dye. Chewed up, it stains the teeth temporarily, but only where the plaque is.

These dentists take the time to show patients exactly how to break up and clean away plaque with toothbrushing methods not the same as those most of us use; and they demonstrate the use of dental floss, not as most of us use it to merely dislodge food particles from between the teeth, but also to get plaque off the sides of the teeth. They send patients home with a supply of wafers and a little dental mirror to be used for self-checking on home cleaning. They take the time to recheck with wafers in the office on subsequent visits to make certain home care is effective.

Ideally, the mouth should be cleansed immediately after a meal or snack. Practically, that is a difficult goal for many people. But these dentists emphasize that, because it takes 24 hours or more for plaque to reform, even a single thorough cleansing of the mouth at night before retiring can go a long way to minimize decay and gum disease.

And these dentists can point to patients, children and adults, with long histories of severe decay brought under control by educated home care.

Among these dentists are periodontists, specialists in gum diseases, who get only the worst cases referred to them—so far advanced that surgery to eliminate the deep gum pockets is necessary. But, typically, they will not operate until the patient is shown how to care for his mouth at home and goes on a prevention program for several weeks or even months. In virtually every case, these periodontists report, they are able to demonstrate that the patient himself, with proper home care, can bring even the most advanced periodontal disease under control so that, once surgical repairs are made, there will be no recurrence.

Under way today is a vast amount of research seeking additional preventive measures. Before long, antidecay agents may be going into foods. Recent studies with children suggest that a chemical, sodium dihydrogen phosphate, added to breakfast cereals, can help reduce decay. Other work indicates that adding phosphate to chewing gum can be similarly helpful. In a dozen laboratories, scientists are busy trying to develop a vaccine that may immunize against decay-causing bacteria. Much other research is going on.

But the preventive measures available right now can drastically reduce dental disease.

HOW CAN YOU USE PREVENTIVE TECHNIQUES?

A cardinal rule is to see your dentist for regular checkups. Get your children to him early, even at age two. Encourage your dentist to use preventive measures in the office—fluoride topical applications once or twice a year, or oftener if needed, and not only for children but for adults in the family. If your dentist is too busy or not interested, you can find one who will be interested, happy to take the time for the applications and for instruction.

Make use of the following guide for mouth care which details, step by step, the home oral hygiene measures advocated by many dentists who are leaders in the preventive approach. You can check the guide with your dentist for any special suggestions he may have that could make it even more valuable for you.

A GUIDE FOR EFFECTIVE MOUTH CARE

This is a guide to *thorough cleaning of the mouth, not just brushing of the teeth,* as a means of helping to prevent both decay and gum disease. It is important to remember that decay occurs when bacteria attack food particles and produce acid which eats away at the tooth structure. The bacteria cluster on teeth in a film called plaque. Plaque also fosters tartar formation and, in turn, gum inflammation and infection. Whenever possible, brush after eating to remove food particles. But remember: one complete cleaning of the mouth, preferably at night before retiring when you can take time to be thorough, is essential. Because it takes 24 hours for plaque to form anew, one such cleaning daily can help eliminate this prime factor in both gum disease and decay.

Tools. A toothbrush, preferably soft-bristled, never hard, since it will be used at the gumline as well as on the teeth.

Dental floss.

An irrigator, or water spray, attachable to the bathroom faucet. Many types are available. Your dentist may recommend one.

A small, inexpensive, plastic-handled mouth mirror, available from your dentist or drugstore.

Disclosing wafers, available from your dentist or drugstore. The wafers, called Xpose, are not yet widely distributed, but a store may order them for you from the maker: Amurol Products, Box 300, Naperville, Illinois 60540.

How to Proceed

Brushing. Properly used, a toothbrush can clean three of the five surfaces of the teeth—chewing, cheek side and tongue side. Note: A critical, often missed zone is the last one-sixteenth inch of the tooth at the gum margin. Plaque and bacteria near the gum as well as on the rest of the tooth must be removed.

Direct the brush bristles gently into the crevice between gum and teeth. Mildly vibrate brush handle so bristles do not travel and skip about but can dislodge material in this area. A soft-bristle brush gently used will do no damage to gum tissue; a stiff bristle brush may.

Next, move brush, applying gentle but firm pressure, so bristles travel over surface of tooth. Brush upper teeth with a downward motion; lower, with upward motion. Brush surfaces next to tongue and surfaces next to cheek. Then clean the chewing surfaces, brushing across tops of teeth. Brush at least half a dozen strokes in each area.

FLOSSING. Plaque must be cleaned away from the other two surfaces of the teeth—the sides, or interdental surfaces. Floss can accomplish this.

Cut off a piece of floss 18 to 24 inches long. Wrap the ends around the forefinger and middle finger of each hand, leaving the thumbs free. To floss between upper teeth, use thumbs as guide; hold thumbs about 1 inch apart, keeping floss taut. For lower teeth, use forefingers as guide, keeping them 1 inch apart.

Slip the floss between each pair of teeth. Do not try to snap floss through a tight area; work it gently back and forth until it passes through. Carry the floss to the base of one tooth, stopping when it is just under the edge of the gum. Scrape the floss up and down against the side of the tooth until you get a rough or "squeaky" feeling, which indicates you have broken through the plaque and are actually touching the tooth. After cleaning the side of one tooth, clean the side of the adjoining tooth.

RINSING. After brushing and flossing, vigorous rinsing will remove dislodged food particles, plaque, and bacteria. An irrigating spray also helps clean under any bridges or braces and in gum pockets where brush and floss cannot reach.

Place the spray tip in the mouth pointing toward the tongue and adjust water flow until pressure and temperature feel good. Move tip so warm water washes spaces between teeth and between gums and teeth. The spray should not be painful at any time.

DISCLOSING WAFERS. Disclosing wafers, containing a harmless red vegetable dye, are invaluable aids in helping you to establish effective cleaning habits. For the first week, you can use one before and another after each nightly cleaning. In the second week, clean first, then use a wafer to check on whether any areas have been missed. Once proper cleaning habits are established, use a wafer about once a month for checking.

Place a wafer in the mouth, chew slowly to help dissolve, then swish around as if it were a mouth rinse. You may then swallow it.

Any bright red stains you see on the teeth (use the mouth mirror to help view the tongue side of the teeth) indicates areas of plaque and bacteria. Pay particular attention to brushing and flossing these areas.

The dye will color the tongue and the lips. It is readily removed from the lips with a wet cloth. Brush it from the tongue and you will simultaneously remove bacteria that grow on the tongue's furry surface and may contribute to bad breath. As the bacteria are brushed off, much of the dye color goes with them; the rest is gone, dissolved in mouth fluids, by morning.

Cleaning the mouth thoroughly this way does take time and patience. But you will find the experience refreshing and pleasantly habit-forming. There will be a cleaner taste in the mouth and a cleaner "feel" to the teeth as plaque is kept off.

WORKING WITH YOUR DENTIST

Prevention of dental disease is a partnership proposition. You should have no difficulty using the suggested home care methods. If, for any reason, you do, your dentist can help. He may also have suggestions for adapting the techniques to make them more valuable for you if you have any special problem.

Visit your dentist regularly for checkup examinations, for topical fluoride applications, and for advice.

ABOUT BABY TEETH

Nature provides two sets of teeth in a lifetime: the 20 deciduous (baby) teeth, and the 32 permanent (second) teeth. This is no extravagance, for the jaws of an infant are hardly large enough to accommodate the teeth needed later. Make no mistake about the importance of proper care of the first teeth. Even though they are to be replaced, if they become badly diseased and fall out, the permanent teeth may not come into place properly.

A child's first set of teeth begins to form before birth, and their proper formation and structure are influenced by the diet of the mother. She need follow no special diet for her baby to have good teeth; the balanced, nutritious diet prescribed by her physician for her general health will provide for good teeth in her child.

Usually, by the age of two and a half years, the child's complete set of baby teeth will have erupted. Shedding will usually begin when the child is six or seven years old. At that age, the first permanent teeth, the first molars, also appear.

Here is a rough guide to when the different teeth may be expected —rough in the sense that there is some variation among individuals:

TEETH	BABY TEETH (AGE IN MONTHS)	PERMANENT TEETH	
		UPPER (AGE IN YEARS)	LOWER
Central incisor	5–8	7–8	6–7
Lateral incisor	7–11	8–9	7–8
Cuspid	16–20	11–12	9–10
First bicuspid		10–11	10–12
Second bicuspid	10–16	10–12	11–12
First molar	20–30	6–7	6–7
Second molar		12–13	11–13
Third molar		17–21	17–21

Proper nourishment is required for healthy development of both the first and second teeth; important, too, are cleanliness and dental supervision and, when necessary, dental treatment.

PICKING THE PREVENTIVE DENTIST

As we have indicated, dentistry today is in a new era—of prevention rather than mere mechanical repair. As in medicine, there are tremendous differences among men in the dental profession. They differ in personality, and your family needs a dentist whose personality is attractive to you and with whom you feel compatible. You need a skilled dentist, of course. But you also need one, in our opinion, whose interests are along the lines of prevention rather than merely of good treatment.

There are still some otherwise excellent dentists—men capable of remarkable repair work—who have not quite caught up with the modern trend of dentistry. But increasingly there are men dedicated to the idea that total mouth care is vital, that what has to be corrected must be corrected and, going beyond, patients must be helped to avoid need for correction.

There may well be such a man available to you even if you live in a small community. Your family doctor or your pediatrician will help you find him.

It is important in terms of dental health—and, in the end, it is economic in terms of family budget—to make regular visits to a dentist practicing prevention. And it is important to introduce your child to him at an early age, even as young as two years. At that point, he can check the child's dental development; he can, if necessary, make corrections to prevent trouble; he can provide detailed instructions for you in the care of the child's mouth and in how to introduce the child gradually to caring properly for his mouth. Chances are that no treatment will be needed and the child's first—and very important—experience with the dentist will be a pleasant one, which will stand him in good stead all his life.

ALIGNMENT OF TEETH

Teeth that are irregular, that overlap or stick out in odd directions, can present problems. Sometimes there is malocclusion—failure of upper and lower teeth to meet (occlude) properly. Heredity may account for this. Irregularity also may stem from early loss of baby teeth because of decay or accident or from failure of the baby teeth to fall out at the right time. When there are regular visits to the dentist, he can, in the case of a prematurely lost baby tooth, insert a "spacer" to help maintain the space so that permanent teeth will have the opportunity to grow in properly. And if a baby tooth is being retained too long, he can, with the help of x-ray examination, determine the presence and developmental state of the permanent tooth that is to replace it and can take appropriate measures.

Some dentists believe that irregular teeth may be the result of excessive thumb and finger sucking at the time the second teeth are coming in. Since a healthy, happy child usually has given up sucking his thumb by the time he is six, it is advisable to discuss this habit with your doctor if it persists. Another factor in irregular tooth alignment and faulty bite is insufficient chewing because the diet is overloaded with soft foods.

CORRECTING IRREGULAR TEETH

Poorly aligned teeth are likely to do more than detract from appearance. Often, food tends to collect behind them and the gums may become irritated. When only a few teeth meet properly in chewing, the force of the bite falls entirely upon them and may loosen them.

Your dentist can check to determine whether a child's bite is poor. He can detect the first signs of serious malocclusion and advise whether and when orthodontic treatment to correct it should be undertaken. The earlier a potentially serious case of malocclusion is detected and treated, the less time may be needed for its correction.

An irregular tooth or two does not necessarily mean malocclusion and may not really be disfiguring. Your dentist can tell you whether it is advisable to have treatment.

Orthodontic treatment takes time, patience, skill. It can be expensive. If your child really needs orthodontic care and you cannot afford it, discuss the matter with your dentist and investigate dental clinics.

FILLING TEETH

Once tooth enamel has been destroyed by acid, it will not be replaced; neither will the dentin of the tooth when it has been destroyed. But if the decay has not gone too far, the dentist can save the tooth by removing the diseased portion and filling the cavity. For this, he drills out the decayed area, applies an antiseptic, then inserts a well-fitted filling.

When decay has penetrated to the pulp and root canal, the tooth may ache. The nerve dies and infection spreads around the ends of the roots in the jawbone. This may lead to infections elsewhere even when the tooth itself does not hurt. The dentist tries to save most of the tooth by cleaning out the decay and the residue of pulp and nerve. He sterilizes the root canals, then fills them and the cavity to seal them and keep them sterile. Thereafter, such a tooth is examined at intervals by x-ray. If the infection continues or recurs, the tooth may have to be extracted, but there is a good chance that it can remain in place.

REIMPLANTING TEETH

Techniques of reimplanting dislodged teeth and of inducing damaged tissue to regrow are new and still not matters of routine dental practice, but they are advancing beyond the merely experimental stage. Reimplantation means that, under some circumstances, a permanent tooth that has been knocked out may be reinserted into its socket, reinforced, and encouraged to grow back into the jaw. In regeneration, the tissues and bone around teeth, after being destroyed by disease, may be induced to grow back.

TEETH AS FOCI (CENTERS) OF INFECTION

Some years ago, infected teeth got the blame for many diseases, especially arthritis, and "bad" teeth were extracted wholesale in the hope that once these "foci" of infection were removed, health would be restored.

Now infected teeth are regarded as important in disturbing general health and as accessory rather than prime factors in some disease states. The decision to have teeth pulled is a major one; and as in the case of any operation, you should feel free to tell your dentist that you wish a consultation with your physician or a specialist before proceeding. Be sure to consult with your physician before having even a single tooth pulled if you suffer from such problems as chronic heart trouble, rheumatic fever, high blood pressure, diabetes, or nephritis.

REMOTE SYMPTOMS RELATED TO FAULTY BITE

The way your teeth come together as you chew food may cause or aggravate symptoms far from the teeth. A faulty bite can displace the joints just in front of your ears·where the jaws meet (the temporomandibular joints). Their displacement may account for face or head pains, noise or blocking of the ears, and dizziness with or without nausea and vomiting. Patients usually seek their physician's advice for such conditions, but your physician may advise that your bite may be the cause of such distress and needs investigation.

ARTIFICIAL TEETH

With proper preventive dental care, including the use of effective home methods of keeping the mouth healthy, artificial teeth should become much less commonplace than they are now.

If you must use dentures, they should be removed and cleaned, and the mouth rinsed, after every meal if possible. Don't use hot water which may warp or crack them. Keeping them overnight in a glass of water helps to maintain their cleanliness. Artificial teeth should be checked regularly to make certain that they have not warped out of shape and that a change in your mouth or gums has not made them fit badly.

PERIODIC DENTAL CHECKUPS

How often should you see your dentist? As often as necessary—for you in particular. If dental decay is on a rampage in your mouth or if you are combatting a threatened case of gum disease, you may have to see him for a time as often as once a month. At other times, a visit a year or twice a year may suffice. Let your dentist decide what your checkup frequency should be.

· Have you seen him recently? If you are like too many of us, chances are you are overdue for a visit. Make an appointment now.

27

THE FEET

BECAUSE FOOT problems are so common, and because so many of them are the result of misunderstanding, improper care, neglect, and a kind of fatalistic acceptance of them as inevitable and unavoidable, the feet deserve and are here getting a special chapter of their own.

Actually, except for the common cold and tooth decay, no human ailments are more prevalent than foot troubles. As many as 80 percent of adults have one kind or another in their lifetime. And while a huge sum—some $2 billion annually—is spent on foot powders, sprays, pads, supports, and potions to correct foot ailments, much of the money is wasted.

ENGINEERING MASTERPIECES

In terms of anatomical engineering, the feet are—and, indeed, have to be —masterpieces. When you stand, your feet carry the dead weight of your body. Walk—and if you're average, you will walk some 65,000 miles in your lifetime—and you impose upon them a force of hundreds of tons a day. In walking just one mile, a 150-pound man brings down on his feet a total work load of 132 tons, or 264,000 pounds.

The feet have to absorb the impact of body weight and keep the shock from traveling up the network of nerves and joints throughout the body. In addition, they have to balance the body, propel it, and working against gravity get blood flowing up the legs back to the heart.

To accomplish all this, you have 52 bones in your feet, one fourth of the total number in the body, and they are encased in an intricate system of some 200 ligaments, 40 muscles, and millions of muscle fibers and blood vessels.

The biggest foot bone is the heel, which is one of the seven tarsal bones; the other six tarsals arch in front of it and meet five long bones, the metatarsals, whose heads make up the ball of the foot.

A major part of the body load is borne by bones in the rear of the foot; the rest is spread among the long bones in the forepart of the foot. As you walk, body weight comes down on the heel but is quickly transferred to the ball, and from there some goes to the toes which, by their spreading action, prevent turning on the ankles and aid in takeoff for the next step.

When something goes wrong with the feet, the trouble isn't necessarily confined there. Foot discomfort may cause a shift in gait or change in posture. Other parts of the body, including the spine, may be thrown out of kilter to cause other troubles. Some low back disturbances, joint complaints, and even headaches have been blamed on the feet.

EARLY PROBLEMS

About 99 percent of us are born with perfect feet and manage to quickly acquire trouble. One study carried out not long ago in seven cities found that 74 percent of children in elementary schools had foot problems; by high school, 88 percent.

There are several reasons for this. Throughout life the feet are subjected to the stress of standing on hard surfaces. Man doesn't do enough walking, which is good for the feet. Standing is an enemy of the feet in the sense that it involves 100 percent use of them; walking involves only 50 percent use since one foot rests while the other supports weight. And shoes—poorly fitted and often designed for the eyes rather than the feet —deserve a major share of the blame. Foot specialists who have examined many thousands of feet lament over what they call "man's insistence on forcing a square into a triangle."

If you take off a shoe and look straight down at your foot, you will note that the sides make roughly parallel straight lines, and even the front can be described more or less as a straight line running from big to little toe. But look at your shoes and more than likely the toes are shaped like triangles. Only when man started enclosing his feet in shoes did he have to start worrying about corns, calluses, hammer toes, bunions, and other foot ailments.

MYTHS

We are surrounded by foot myths. They range from the notion that many foot troubles stem from wearing sneakers in childhood (not really harmful) to wearing loafers, which are supposed to be bad because they let the feet spread. As one authority on the feet notes, undoubtedly the feet will grow somewhat larger and wider if not restricted by ill-shaped shoes, but this is healthy.

The biggest misconceptions center around flat feet and fallen arches. Because the Army once rejected thousands of men with flat feet, the idea that there's something inevitably wrong with flat feet persists. Dr. Dudley Morton, one of the nation's outstanding investigators of the foot, has reported that many people with arches "as flat as pancakes" never have experienced foot pain, while some of the most painful and obstinate cases involve feet with well-formed arches.

According to some authorities, only one out of 1,000 people with flat feet experiences pain because the feet are flat. The best practice for the flat-footed person—and anyone else with a painful foot problem for which there is no clear-cut, obvious cause—is to get advice and treatment from a physician or podiatrist rather than to keep buying arch supports.

A SOUND APPROACH TO FOOT PROBLEMS

If you think your feet are not normal, don't buy any kind of remedial shoes or get arch supports without consulting a physician. You may be "correcting" the wrong thing, or your troubles may be due to something entirely apart from the shoes you are wearing. Your socks or stockings may not fit properly, thus bending or cramping the toes or causing calluses and blisters. Your feet may be swelling because garters restrict circulation. You may be putting too much of a burden on the feet because of overweight.

If you have foot problems, consider whether you have to stand too much on hard surfaces. Walking around a little helps to relieve the strain of standing, and getting your feet up on a couch or footstool for even a few minutes' rest at a time often does wonders. You may not be standing or walking properly. When you stand, your feet should be parallel with each other, not toeing out. When you walk, your footprints should make tracks that would almost touch a straight line drawn between them, with the heels just a trifle farther away from the line than the toes. This is not walking pigeon-toed but it certainly is not toeing out.

Whether or not your foot trouble traces to flat feet or fallen arches is something only a doctor can really determine and cure. By all means, don't leave the diagnosis up to a shoe salesman. Flat feet may be inherited or be caused by overweight or by wearing improper shoes in childhood.

If you believe you have flat feet or fallen arches, the following exer-

288 / Preventive Body Care

cises, done in moderation, will not hurt if your diagnosis is wrong and, if right, may help:

With shoes off, sit in a chair and pretend there is sand on the floor and that you are heaping it into a pile between your feet by drawing them together in a scooping motion.

Put some marbles on the rug in front of you. Pick one up with your toes and throw it forward.

Repeat these exercises but stop if your feet become tired.

CORNS AND CALLUSES

These can cause a considerable amount of trouble, and the best way to avoid them is by wearing shoes that fit. Corns are of two varieties: hard, usually found on the outside of the little toe; and soft, between the toes. Corns are hardened or thickened skin which, unlike calluses, have a central core or point.

So many people get into trouble by using corn remedies or by cutting their own corns that we wish everybody would have them removed by a podiatrist. But common sense tells us that some of you are going to go right on attending to your own corns, so we are providing directions for the best way to do the cutting—but with the following important proviso: If you are not in good health, if you suffer from poor circulation, and, above all, if you are a diabetic, you should NEVER cut your own corns. In addition, never treat corns or warts on the soles of the feet, since they are usually the result of infection and you can do harm by treating them yourself. Injections of novocaine have been found useful in relieving pain caused by warts on the soles and in some cases apparently have caused the warts to disappear.

Now—for the directions. Don't use commercial corn removers as they are usually too strong. For hard corns, soak the toes in warm water for about 15 minutes, apply a drop or two of 10 percent salicylic acid in collodion, then cover the corn with a plain cornpad of the right size, and leave it on for three or four days. Then soak the toes again and the corn will probably lift out easily. If it does not, see a podiatrist.

For soft corns, pare down the horny rim very carefully with a razor blade or scissors (which has been thoroughly washed and scalded or immersed for a few minutes in alcohol). Take great care not to cut too far. If you should nick the skin, apply iodine and leave the corn alone. After you have pared the corn, cover it with a plain pad or piece of adhesive plaster to protect it from pressure, and keep it as dry as possible. It will probably get better; if not, see a podiatrist.

Calluses can be removed by careful paring.

BUNIONS

A bunion is a deformity of the big toe, almost always caused by the use of shoes that force the toe to turn toward the other toes. In mild cases, the pain can be relieved by heat, and the condition will correct itself after properly fitting shoes have been worn for some time. In more severe cases, a physician should be consulted, since surgery may be required for correction.

INGROWN TOENAILS

These can be prevented by the use of good shoes and by keeping the nails short, with the sides a little longer than the middle. Badly ingrown nails should always be treated by a physician or podiatrist, since a serious infection may otherwise develop. If you have a slightly ingrown nail, insert a tiny bit of cotton that has been soaked in castor oil under the ingrown edge of the nail; protect the nail from pressure by a pad of clean gauze held in place by adhesive tape.

ATHLETE'S FOOT

Athlete's foot, or dermatophytosis, often requires medical attention. It is caused by a fungus, a form of plant life, which grows on the dead cells that make up the calluses and "old skin" of the feet and thrives on warmth and dampness. It causes itching or burning spots, and often blisters, usually between the toes. In addition to discomfort, it provides sites for more serious infections.

If you insist on treating athlete's foot yourself, the following method is safe: Dry the feet thoroughly and always keep them as dry as possible. Wear socks that will absorb moisture without being so rough as to irritate the skin, and shoes that fit well without being "airtight." After drying your feet, apply a mild alcoholic solution—rubbing alcohol or toilet water. Dry again. Put some plain unscented talcum powder on the feet and in your shoes. Keep your toenails short. Gently remove all scaly, soggy, or horny material from between the toes and from the soles of the feet. Put pledgets of lamb's wool or absorbent cotton between the toes if they are too close together. And use Desenex ointment over the infected, itching areas morning and night.

You may also try the following method when the lesions are moist and oozing: Soak the feet in 1:15,000 solution of potassium permanganate (made up by a pharmacist), morning and night, 10 minutes at a time. The permanganate causes the skin to turn brown temporarily.

If the condition does not clear up, do not buy a remedy at the store; see your physician. You may not have athlete's foot at all but some other skin condition that resembles it; or you may have an allergy or sensitivity to something that contacts your feet.

Primary prevention for athlete's foot can be achieved by simple measures: (1) wearing protective sandals or slippers in the course of using public showers and swimming pools; (2) keeping the skin between the toes dry, taking pains to assure dryness especially after bathing, and for good measure applying a mild baby talcum powder.

HEEL DISCOMFORT

If severe, this is a problem that may require medical attention. If relatively mild, nightly soaks in hot water containing epsom salts and the use of a heel pad with a hole at the point of greatest discomfort may help.

EXCESSIVE SWEATING

Often, this may be relieved by applying rubbing alcohol and foot powder, especially between the toes. In more severe cases, your doctor may prescribe medication.

HAMMER TOE

Also called claw toe, this is another deformity that can be caused by poorly fitted shoes. It leads to undue pressure and corn formation. While severe cases may require surgical correction, conservative treatment—which includes use of corn plasters, new and well-fitted shoes, and toe stretching—often offers relief.

AVOIDING TROUBLES

Most common foot problems can be prevented from happening at all or from recurring.

Buy good, and properly fitted, shoes. *Buy them late in the afternoon; your feet will be bigger then.* Don't tell the salesman your size; let him measure. Make certain the shoes are wide enough to accommodate the widest part of your foot and that there is room to extend your toes fully. What should you look for in a good shoe? Soft upper, moderately broad heel, narrow waist, straight border along the inner sole.

Socks and stockings should be a quarter-inch longer than the longest toe. If you perspire profusely, wool or cotton may be preferable to synthetic material.

Keep the feet scrupulously clean. Bathe them at least once daily, drying carefully, and dusting with talcum powder. It often helps to put them in hot water for a minute or two, then into cold water for just an instant, after which they should be rubbed briskly as they are being dried. Tired feet are often relieved by massage; use a kneading rotary motion of the hands with some plain cold cream, olive oil, or cocoa butter, if the feet are dry or irritated.

To help check any unpleasant perspiration, you can use Desenex powder or a preparation made as follows:

Thymol, 0.5 gram
Salicylic acid, 2.0 grams
Talcum sufficient to make 100 grams

Apply either powder, morning and night. If excessive perspiration persists, see your doctor.

Don't neglect your feet. If any kind of trouble develops and persists for more than a few days, do what you would sensibly do if the trouble were in an arm or the throat or the chest: Get professional help to diagnose and treat it before it can get worse.

It was Abraham Lincoln who complained: "When my feet hurt, I can't think." Enough is known today so that with a little forethought, your feet aren't likely to hurt and you will be less likely to hurt elsewhere.

28

BODY DEFENSES AND
MEDICAL REINFORCEMENTS

You can be certain of one thing about your body: it is a battleground. You have had your share of colds and other commonplace infectious diseases and perhaps even a few serious ones. Much more often, hundreds upon hundreds of times, you have been threatened by infection, your body has responded, and invading organisms have been repulsed— all without your being aware of even the threat, let alone the encounter.

All of us are constantly exposed to microorganisms in the air, soil, and water. Some are harmless; many are potentially dangerous. And the body's defenses are so organized that it is usual for a quick counterattack to be mustered against invading organisms—quick and effective enough to prevent infection. It is only when invading organisms are too numerous to be fended off in time or when body defenses are impaired through injury or poor health that an infection takes hold.

You can probably expect to live a long time, because of your body's natural ability to repulse many invasions and because of the growing arsenal of weapons your physician has to help when necessary. Also of tremendous importance: the growing armamentarium that medicine now has to increase your defenses against specific disease agents in advance of attack, and the growing knowledge about natural defenses and how to help keep them intact, knowledge that you yourself can apply.

THE STEPS IN DISEASE ONSET

An infectious disease can begin when the causative organism, microscopic in size, gains entry through a wound or natural body opening.

Under suitable conditions, microorganisms can reproduce at fantastic rates. In 30 minutes, one may divide to become two; in another 30 minutes, the two double again; at that rate, it takes only about 12 hours for the multiplication process to produce an army of more than 16 million organisms.

There is no warning when a disease process begins. It takes many organisms to produce symptoms. And the incubation period—the time between entry of an organism and your awareness of being sick—may extend for several days, weeks, even months. There are great variations in multiplication rates among disease organisms and in the numbers needed to cause symptoms. For some diseases, the incubation period may be a day or two; for others, far longer. The rabies virus, for example, may multiply in some instances for several months before producing symptoms.

Organisms are specific, each producing its own kind of disease—diphtheria, tuberculosis, boil, pneumonia. They are specific, too, in terms of site of attack—lungs, brain, nervous system, kidneys, skin, etc.

In some diseases, symptoms result from destruction of tissue by the organisms. Thus, polio virus destroys nerve cells, producing paralysis. Tuberculosis bacteria destroy lung, bone, or other tissue. In other diseases, the symptoms arise from the production of toxins, or poisons, by the organisms. Thus, toxins produced by streptococcal bacteria may cause rheumatic fever, heart damage, or kidney disease even though the organisms themselves do not directly attack the joints, heart, or kidneys. Their toxins get into the bloodstream and are carried to these areas.

Five types of microorganisms cause communicable diseases. Knowing something about them will help make it easier for you to avoid trouble with them.

BACTERIA

Visible only under a microscope, bacteria are so tiny that you may best get an idea of their size through an analogy: If you can imagine for a moment that all eight million inhabitants of New York City are reduced to the size of bacteria, all eight million would fit comfortably into a single drop of water.

Different types of bacteria differ considerably in size, shape, and habits. For example, streptococci form chains like strings of beads; others, such as those that produce boils, live in clusters, like bunches of grapes.

Bacteria have a bad press, which only some of them deserve. More of them are beneficial than destructive. Bacteria, for example, are industrious workers in sewage plants, helping to dispose of waste. Bacteria, too,

294 / Preventive Body Care

help the growth of many plants on which all other plants and animals depend. But certainly life would be more pleasant without those varieties that cause syphilis, pneumonia, boils, abscesses, strep sore throats, tuberculosis, and many other diseases.

VIRUSES

Far smaller even than bacteria, viruses are not visible under an ordinary microscope, only under the far more powerful electron microscope.

Much that is known about viruses has been learned only recently. Once considered nonliving bits of matter, they are now regarded as the lowest forms of life—parasites that do not grow unless they can occupy living cells in which they set up reproductive housekeeping. If dried or frozen, they look like lifeless chemicals and remain inactive for years only to resume activity again when favorable conditions are provided.

About 500 of them have been identified by the electron microscope, which magnifies them 25,000 times or more. They look much like pearls, beautifully cut gems, bricks, or rods when seen this way.

They are extremely potent. Small numbers of them, given ideal conditions, can start a disease. They cause many diseases including polio, influenza, yellow fever, rabies, infectious hepatitis, smallpox, chickenpox, measles, mumps and the common cold.

PROTOZOA

While still microscopic in size, protozoa are much larger than bacteria. Protozoan diseases occur in this country, but they are much more prevalent in the tropics. An amoeba, a particularly dangerous protozoan, causes a severe form of dysentery. Another protozoan causes malaria. The dreaded African sleeping sickness is caused by a protozoan carried by the tsetse fly.

PARASITIC WORMS

Some of these can be seen by the unaided eye, but others can be identified only with a microscope. The smallest are roughly the size of pinheads, while a tapeworm can grow to a 30-foot length.

Many parasites, including the flukes (one of the two types of flatworms), are more prevalent in the tropics than here. The other type of flatworm, the tapeworm, is found in this country and is acquired by eating beef, pork, or fish containing the parasite. Inside the intestine, the tapeworm attaches itself to the intestinal wall and proceeds to grow.

Some roundworms are also common in this country, especially in the South. They include the pinworm, intestinal roundworm, and hookworm. Another roundworm, found in pork, causes trichinosis, a disease in which the parasites eventually get into muscles.

FUNGI

Related to mushrooms, fungi are smaller growths. It is a tiny fungus that produces the green or white mold on stale bread; another causes athlete's foot; others are responsible for various skin disorders; still others produce internal infections. There are many fungal diseases. Fortunately, most are rare in this country.

BODY DEFENSES

In the past, infectious diseases took a huge toll. Less than a century ago, every fifth child died before reaching his first birthday, and almost as many more died before reaching the age of two, most of them from dysentery and various childhood infectious diseases. Epidemics of diphtheria have been known to kill every child under 12 in an entire community. Plagues of smallpox, yellow fever, and other diseases decimated populations. Until medicine learned about microorganisms, there was little that could be done to prevent disease—other than what the body itself could do. And, fortunately, the body is not helpless against germs, else man would have ceased to exist at all long ago.

Against an overwhelming influx, body defenses, as already noted, may not suffice. But those defenses, day in and day out, serve to prevent many instances of what otherwise could be serious disease.

There are actually several lines of defense, and it is important to understand all of them.

The first line prevents organisms from gaining entrance. The skin itself is part of this vital defense. Unless broken by a wound, it is practically microbe-proof. Organisms lie harmlessly on it.

Body openings also are defended. Mucous membranes form a protective lining. In the respiratory passages, the membranes' secretions of mucus form a sticky coating that catches many organisms before they can penetrate farther. Tiny filters, such as the hair in the nose, help keep out germs. Irritation of the mucous membranes leads to coughing and sneezing which force out germs and irritating substances.

Body fluids have defense functions. Tears wash organisms out of the eyes and, being slightly antiseptic, discourage organism growth. Stomach acid kills many organisms entering with food. Vomiting and diarrhea are part of the defense mechanism, helping to get rid of invading organisms.

A second line of defense goes into action when organisms get by the first line. It consists of leukocytes (white blood cells) and tissue cells. As organisms and their poisonous products begin to damage tissue cells, the body increases the blood supply to the infected area, producing an inflammatory reaction. And as cells are destroyed, others form a wall around the invading organisms, aimed at confining them and protecting other body areas. It is this wall that surrounds a boil, infected cut, even a pimple. Fever, too, develops in many infections and sometimes helps in the destruction of some germs that are unable to thrive at a temperature much above normal body temperature.

Meanwhile, the white blood cells are at work. The number in the blood increases rapidly when they are needed to fight infections. Moving into an infected area, the white cells attack and devour the organisms. The infected area becomes a mass of living and dead organisms and white cells, forming the pus that develops in infected tissue. Lymph helps clear out the debris, moving it to the lymph nodes where it is filtered and gradually destroyed. This is why swollen lymph nodes are indicators of infection in the body.

Thus, often, infection is conquered by second-line defense in the tissues, sparing the body more general combat. But if the infection prevails, other body resources are available.

The body produces materials called *antibodies*, which can counteract germs and render their poisons harmless. There are various types of antibodies. One, *antitoxin*, is highly specific, acting against only a toxin formed by a particular kind of organism. For example, diphtheria antitoxin neutralizes diphtheria toxin but not scarlet fever or any other kind.

Other antibodies, called *agglutinins*, make certain types of organisms clump together, turning them into easier targets for white blood cells, which surround and devour them. Still other antibodies, *bacteriolysins*, make certain types of organisms dissolve in the bloodstream.

After the body has won its battle against some types of disease, antibodies remain in the blood and prevent the organisms of those particular diseases from getting footholds again. This is what happens when you have measles, chickenpox, or any of the other diseases that people do not get more than once. In such cases, the body becomes immune to the disease; this is called *acquired immunity*. Many of us are immune to one or more forms of polio because we have had an attack that was so mild we didn't even know we had it, usually mistaking it for flu. Some types of immunity can be passed from mother to child. People who are immune to a disease without ever having had it are said to have *natural immunity*. Some immunities are partial or temporary—that is, they do not completely protect an individual an entire lifetime (a notable example is the common cold).

MEDICAL ASSISTS FOR BODY DEFENSES

On a May day in 1796, an English country physician, Edward Jenner, opened a new era in combatting disease—the age of immune therapy as a preventive. A smallpox epidemic had struck, but not as hard in rural areas as in larger cities. Jenner wondered about that and about the cowpox infection many people in his village contracted from cattle. Cowpox caused only a running sore that quickly healed. But was the disease related in any way to smallpox? Did exposure to cowpox provide immunity against smallpox?

To test his theory, Jenner made a small cut in an arm of an 11-year-old boy patient and applied to it pus taken from a cowpox sore on a dairymaid's hand. The boy developed a mild case of cowpox and was soon over it. Then Jenner made the critical test, applying to another cut pus from a smallpox patient. The boy did not get smallpox; he was immune.

Here was the first use of the fact that a mild attack of some diseases may prevent full-fledged illness from occurring. It took a long time before Jenner's work was accepted. Almost a century went by before Louis Pasteur of France used much the same technique to inoculate against rabies. Since then—slowly at first, now with increasing rapidity —vaccines have been developed to protect against many diseases.

Whatever the vaccine, the principle is the same: to introduce material specially treated so that, without causing actual disease, it causes the body to develop defenses against the disease.

The immunity produced by such vaccination is active; the individual himself manufactures antibodies that will protect him. Another form of immunity, passive, involves injection of antibody material created in the body of another person or an animal. Passive immunity usually does not last very long.

Everyone should be immunized against these dangerous diseases: smallpox, diphtheria, polio, tetanus, sometimes typhoid fever, and, in the case of children, whooping cough and measles. Inoculations are readily obtainable, virtually free of discomfort, can be administered by family physician or pediatrician, and are available free, or at little cost, so lack of money should not, and must not, keep anyone from being immunized. Any public health department or hospital can provide information about low-cost or no-cost immunizations.

It is particularly important to give children the advantages of protection against diseases that could be extremely dangerous for them. Diphtheria once was a prime cause of death in youngsters; whooping cough, if it occurs, has a high fatality rate in infants. Be sure to follow this program carefully:

CALENDAR FOR IMMUNIZATION

At 2, 3, and 4 months of age	A series of 3 injections, each providing protection against diphtheria, whooping cough (pertussis), and tetanus. A series of 3 doses for polio.
Between 6 and 12 months	Smallpox vaccination.
Before 1 year	Typhoid fever inoculations (for children in rural areas or where water supply is of doubtful nature).
16 to 18 months	1st triple-shot booster; 1st polio booster.
4 years	2nd triple-shot booster.

In addition: Recently measles, long thought of as a kind of innocuous childhood disease, has been recognized to be a really dangerous one, capable of leading to pneumonia and many other possible complications, including nervous system disorders. In the past children died from such complications, but they were attributed to other causes. Happily, now an effective vaccine is available to prevent measles and its complications. Every child should receive this protection, with a first dose at nine months of age, followed at intervals by other doses.

Vaccination against smallpox should be repeated every five to seven years until there have been three successful vaccinations, and after that, whenever there is risk of exposure to smallpox.

We strongly urge adults who have not yet had the aforementioned inoculations to have them as soon as possible. While inoculation against typhoid fever is not essential under all circumstances, why not have it done to be safe? Other diseases against which adults as well as children should be inoculated under special circumstances are yellow fever, tularemia, and tick (Rocky Mountain spotted fever). Because of the effectiveness of medicines in curing spotted fever, some physicians may not consider immunization for it essential, but we think it worthwhile if you live in or visit a locality where the disease is prevalent.

Another vaccine development provides protection against German measles. This form of measles also was once thought to be innocuous—and it is virtually harmless except when it occurs during the first three months of pregnancy when it may damage the unborn child.

At the moment, no inoculations are available to provide complete protection against the common cold, some strains of influenza, and some forms of pneumonia, although flu shots are being used increasingly in the fall of the year to give some measure of protection over the winter. See the discussion of pneumonia (page 637) for more information about the place of vaccine in this disease.

Other Protection

Even after some germs have gained a foothold, immunization can be of value. For example, for rabies and tetanus, injections can be of value when administered between the time the germs start to grow and the time symptoms would appear. But remember that time is short and there should be no delay in getting treatment if you have any reason to suspect these germs have entered your body.

In some cases, injections help even after illness is under way and symptoms are present. For example, in diphtheria, antitoxin can be injected to neutralize the poisonous effects of the organisms.

Chemotherapeutic Agents

Chemotherapy is a valuable ally of immune therapy. It is the use of specific medicines capable of combatting disease organisms in the body when immunization is not available. To be used in chemotherapy, a therapeutic compound must have the facility of being harmful to micro-organisms without harming body cells.

Malaria was probably the first disease to be controlled by a specific medical substance, quinine, which was used by the Inca Indians in Peru more than 300 years ago. Paul Ehrlich, father of modern chemotherapy, discovered salvarsan, an arsenic compound helpful against syphilis. Another major development was the introduction of sulfa medicines, powerful antigerm agents. The first of the modern antibiotic compounds, penicillin, came into general use only after World War II.

Today, available antibiotics include more than half a dozen types of penicillin plus streptomycin, neomycin, bacitracin, and erythromycin—all considered "specific-target" in the sense that they have powerful effects against a limited range of disease-causing organisms. In addition, there are broad-spectrum antibiotics, so called because they combat a wide range of bacteria. Broad-spectrum agents include chloramphenicol, chlortetracycline, tetracycline, and oxytetracycline.

Antibiotics work in two ways. Some, like penicillin, actually destroy organisms. Others are bacteriostatic; they hold bacteria in check without actually killing them. The bacteriostatic compounds prevent the entrance of some essential element, such as iron, into the metabolic processes that maintain growth and reproduction of bacterial cells. The bacteria do not die, but they no longer divide and multiply. If antibiotic treatment is stopped too soon, organisms may resume growth and reproduction. A single bacterium, unchecked, can produce a billion descendants in 24 hours. The bacteriostatic antibiotics are valuable in that, as they hold bacterial populations in check, they give body defenses time to muster and to destroy the germs.

It's important to understand that different germs may produce similar symptoms—and a boil or sore throat or finger infection that earlier yielded to one kind of antibiotic may, another time, come from another type of bacteria and require another type of antibiotic. Clearly, you should not try to medicate yourself. Let your doctor treat the infections in your family, and respect him if he is not in a rush to use an antibiotic. He may judge it wiser to give the body a chance to throw off an infection, as it often can, or to wait until he can establish exactly what the problem is and then pick the right antibiotic for it.

Indiscriminate use of antibiotics, like indiscriminate use of any potent medication, can be dangerous, leading to undesirable side effects and to failure to hit the actual germs causing trouble, thus adding to problems of body defenses.

When your physician does prescribe medication, follow his directions exactly. Remember that just because you begin to feel better does not mean that the medication should be discontinued or the dosage reduced unless your physician specifically so directs. A few more days of treatment, or even just one more day, may be essential to control infection. When your physician suggests that treatment stop, then stop, and do not use any remaining pills except under his advice. In most cases, leftover medication is best thrown away.

When antibiotics are thoughtfully prescribed and intelligently taken, you need have no fear of using them. So used, when they really need to be used, these substances often turn out to be wonder workers indeed.

HOW GERMS ENTER THE BODY

Despite an excellent coat of armor in the form of the skin and defensive mechanisms at body openings, germs do find opportunities for getting into the body.

Nose, Throat, and Lungs

Many bacteria and viruses gain admission through the nose and throat. Microorganisms generally flourish in moisture; and spitting, coughing, and sneezing keep them circulating. A sneeze, as motion pictures show, consists of tiny droplets expelled several feet and carrying with them large numbers of microorganisms. Such diseases as the common cold, pneumonia, tuberculosis, whooping cough, scarlet fever, diphtheria, influenza, and meningitis are spread this way. They are circulated not only by the outrightly sick but by people who are just "coming down" with a disease and by still others who harbor or "carry" germs without themselves becoming sick.

It is not etiquette alone that demands that you cover nose and mouth when coughing or sneezing. Germs in your nose and throat relish the free ride and opportunity to spread and multiply. Never place in your mouth pencils or any other objects handled by people. And as much as possible, avoid crowds during the "sniffle" season and during epidemics.

One of the most serious diseases spread by germ inhalation is tuberculosis—and more people have tuberculosis than you may suspect. The disease does not always reveal itself with outward signs; a healthy-looking individual may have it. Any cough that persists more than six weeks calls for a chest x-ray; and, in fact, everybody should have periodic chest films to exclude tuberculosis.

Sore throats, colds, and coughs should be treated with rest and plenty of fluids until cured. Prompt care of colds is important as a means of preventing serious complications. Colds offer bacteria, especially streptococci and pneumococci, an opportunity to multiply.

Physicians have long urged avoidance of excessive physical activity or other stress during a cold or other viral infection because, somehow, stress seems to further complications. In polio-infected patients, for example, strenuous exercise has seemed to contribute to paralysis. Now recent research suggests some reason for the harmful effect of stress. In animal studies, investigators have been able to show that brain and central nervous system viral infections, including polio, are enhanced when animals are given doses of epinephrine (adrenaline) and serotonin. These hormones increase blood flow through the brain and nervous system, consequently allowing more viruses to reach these areas. The levels of both hormones are known to increase somewhat under stressful conditions. Thus, unusual stress at a time when viruses are in the blood may increase the hormone levels and their effects on blood flow enough to facilitate viral invasion of the nervous system.

It is best to stay in bed until fever is gone. Too many people with contagious diseases get out of bed too soon, risking complications for themselves and increasing the likelihood of infecting others.

Nursing mothers with colds should ask their doctor about wearing a nose-and-mouth mask when handling their baby.

Infection from Food and Water

Typhoid, amoebic dysentery, and bacterial dysentery are among diseases that gain footholds through the mouth. Typhoid germs appear in food, milk, and water that have been contaminated by fecal matter. Flies that have fed on such matter may carry the germs to food and drink. Every precaution should be taken to keep food from being exposed to flies, especially warm food. Plastic dish covers are practical.

Habits of cleanliness should be encouraged for all family members.

Washing hands after use of the toilet and before preparing and eating food should be automatic. This is important because contamination can be spread by a person not himself ill, as in the case of a typhoid carrier. Exemplifying this is the classic story of Typhoid Mary, an otherwise healthy carrier who, as a cook, went from job to job and spread typhoid to more than 100 victims.

All the milk you use should be pasteurized, not just certified. Certified milk may not be safe, because certification of the health of cattle is not foolproof; also certified milk is handled before it is bottled. Pasteurization heats milk for 30 minutes at 142°F or for one minute at 160°F. After the heat process, the pasteurized milk goes directly into sterilized bottles without being touched by human hands.

Unpasteurized milk may carry the agents not only of typhoid but also of tuberculosis, brucellosis, and other diseases. If at any time you are in doubt about milk, you can do your own home pasteurization by boiling for 3 minutes or scalding the milk for 30 minutes in a double boiler.

In cities, water supply is usually safe. In the country, be cautious. No matter how clear water may look, it may come from wells or lakes, ponds or rivers containing many disease organisms. Unless you are certain of purity, boil for 10 minutes before drinking.

Meats may carry any of several diseases. Uncooked pork sometimes contains living parasites that produce trichinosis. For protection, pork should always be cooked thoroughly; any pinkness means inadequate cooking. For roast pork, an hour to the pound at 350 degrees is safe. Brucellosis (undulant fever) may be acquired from pork, beef, or unpasteurized milk. Raw fish and raw beef may contain tapeworms. Although the U.S. Department of Agriculture inspects meats, you cannot always be certain they are still pure by the time they reach your table. Thorough cooking of all meats and fish is the best precaution.

Diseased rabbits cause tularemia, a serious disease that may be contracted not only by eating but even in the course of skinning and preparing rabbits.

Improperly canned food can be dangerous. Bacteria, growing in such food, can produce poisoning. Botulism is a severe form of food poisoning which often leads to fatal paralysis. The food and canning industries are extremely careful to avoid food contamination; botulism is usually the result of improper home canning. If you like to can food, boil for at least three hours or steam-cook it under correct pressure. Boil again for 15 minutes before eating.

It's important to buy pastries from a clean, reliable bakery and to refrigerate them promptly when you get them home. Bacteria thrive on custard fillings such as those in eclairs unless the pastry is properly handled and refrigerated.

Frozen foods can be healthy and tasty. But the home freezer can be a source of danger if food is not frozen correctly. Most meats, poultry, and fish can be quick-frozen and kept safely for extended periods. Vegetables, bread, and cake are also popular freezer items. But many foods, such as concentrated fruit juices, should be used as soon as thawed and should not be refrozen.

Some down-to-earth pamphlets about frozen foods and freezing equipment have been produced by the U.S. Department of Agriculture and are available from the Department in Washington, D.C., without charge; they are well worth having. The pamphlets include the following titles:

Freezing Combination Main Dishes
Home Care of Purchased Frozen Foods
Home Freezers—Their Selection and Use
Home Freezing of Fruits and Vegetables
Home Freezing of Poultry

Venereal Diseases

The two major ones are syphilis and gonorrhea, spread mainly by sexual contact, although syphilis has been known to be spread also by kissing. These diseases are discussed elsewhere in this book.

Insect Bites

An insect bite produces a small puncture in the skin, and infection may be introduced when the insect carries organisms in its mouth or excrement.

Tick fever, or Rocky Mountain spotted fever, which is similar to European typhus fever, is transmitted by the bites of ticks. In Mexico and southern United States, a type more closely related to European typhus is transmitted by lice, ticks, and mites living on rats. Malaria and yellow fever are carried by certain mosquitoes. While most of the United States is free of malaria, in parts of the South it has not yet been eliminated completely through destruction of mosquitoes chemically or elimination of stagnant ponds and other places where the mosquitoes breed. If you live in or visit such areas where malaria may be a threat, protect yourself against mosquitoes with a repellent salve, make certain that screening is adequate, and if necessary use mosquito netting over the bed at night. You can be immunized against yellow fever, and although the disease has been eliminated in much of the world, immunization is worthwhile if, for example, you travel to parts of South America or Africa which are near jungles where the yellow fever mosquito still flourishes.

Animal Bites

Any animal bite that penetrates the skin should be thoroughly washed with soap and water and treated by a physician.

Rabies, or hydrophobia, a viral disease affecting brain and nervous system, is transmitted by the bite of dogs and other domestic and wild animals harboring the virus in saliva. If possible, a biting dog should be caught and studied by the health department. If the dog is infected, or if it dies within 10 to 14 days, the bitten person must receive Pasteur treatment or the new serum to prevent rabies, which is a 100 percent fatal disease. If the bite is on the head, neck, or face, treatment should be started at once, without waiting to see if the dog dies, since the virus, when introduced at these sites, can reach the brain quickly. The rabies virus travels along nerves to the brain, so the farther away the bite the longer the trip to the brain. In bites on the foot, it has taken as long as a year for rabies to develop. Unless the dog is caught and found to be free from the disease, Pasteur treatment or the new serum must be given.

All warm-blooded pets—cats, dogs, monkeys—now can be vaccinated periodically against rabies by a veterinarian. No pet owner should neglect this precautionary measure.

If a dog must be shot because of viciousness, it should be shot in the body so the undamaged brain can be studied in a health department or police laboratory. Any dog that is acting queerly should be examined by a veterinarian.

Cuts, Wounds, and Scratches

Because these are potential portals of entry for infectious organisms, they should be washed promptly with soap and water and covered with sterile gauze; a Band-Aid will do if the cut is small. Any cut that penetrates deeply may heal better if sewn together. If in doubt, let your doctor or the nearest hospital emergency room decide for you; otherwise you may blame yourself later for an unsightly scar.

A serious danger from wounds and deep scratches is tetanus, or lockjaw. The tetanus germ is commonly found in soil and wherever there are horses, cattle, and manure. It is also found in the dust of city streets. A deep puncture by a nail can be serious. Although many people think it is the rust on a nail that may cause trouble, this is not true; it's the germs on the nail that constitute the danger.

The best preventive measure for tetanus is immunization. Tetanus toxoid provides immunity for several years. For anyone who has not been so immunized, a deep wound or scratch calls for use of tetanus antitoxin (TAT) as an emergency measure to prevent tetanus. It is available in hospital emergency rooms, infirmaries, and first-aid stations. While TAT provides protection, it does cause unpleasant reactions in some people, and doctors will test the patient for possible sensitivity to the horse serum with which TAT is made. Tetanus toxoid does not produce unpleasant reactions, another reason why you should take this important safety measure in advance of any possible accident.

Take Reasonable Precautions

We hope that this chapter motivates you—through understanding rather than just admonition—to take sensible precautions against infection. Make it a way of life simply not to drink out of glasses, eat out of dishes, or use the towels that others have used; to stay, as much as possible, away from sneezers and coughers; and to keep yourself and your home fastidiously clean.

There is no need to go to extremes, to become a fanatic on the subject of germs. Some people do, devoting themselves to almost constant scrubbing, boiling, sterilizing of food, home, and their own person. They spray their noses and throats and the air about them with antiseptics, shun others, wage a constant battle against contamination. This is neither necessary nor effective. It is unnecessary because, where germs are concerned, the odds favor us. Most organisms are harmless. The dangerous ones seldom live long under ordinary conditions, dying without proper food, moisture, temperature, and other requirements. Most cannot tolerate air and sunlight. Soap and water kill or remove them. Extreme methods of precaution are usually useless as well as unnecessary. Germicides, sprays, and disinfectants either do not reach germs they are intended for or provide only very brief protection, or are too weak to kill germs, on the one hand, or too strong to be used safely on the skin and other tissues.

How about household disinfectants? Many are advertised. Personally, we feel there may be a risk that such disinfectants will be used as substitutes for rather than aids to cleanliness. Sprinkling or spraying a little disinfectant around makes everything smell so antiseptic that there may be a temptation to go easy on soap and water.

Fumigation after some illnesses used to be required by law. Scientific studies, however, show it is unnecessary and ineffective, except for destroying mice and vermin, which can be destroyed more effectively in other ways. Fumigation was often used as a substitute for thorough cleaning. Soap and water, fresh air, and sunlight are the best aids in destroying germs. (Incidentally, it is probably worth mentioning here that books and magazines handled by sick people are not considered contagious.)

Take reasonable precautions for keeping germs away, keep your body and its defenses up to par, and you can expect to do quite well in the battle against infectious disease.

PART FOUR

Preventive Mental Care

In this part, you will find covered a wide range of subjects relating to emotion and disease. We discuss the close relationship between body and mind; the psychosomatic disorders; also, the normal personality and its range of variation. The neuroses and psychoses are described along with new, as well as tried, methods of treating them. There is an important section on depressions. Also, we provide some advice on how to prevent yourself from becoming "stale" or developing mental fatigue.

Finally, beginning on page 368, we attempt to show the dozens of important factors that go into the molding of secure, poised human beings; these range from nursing, toilet training, and weaning of the infant to problems of adolescence, work, marriage, and then menopause, aging, retirement, chronic illness, and fatal illness. It is of great importance, we believe, that you understand and analyze all of these factors in order to help prevent emotional disturbances in yourself and in your children.

29

MIND, BODY, MIND

THE EFFECTS of mind and emotions on physical health are, in a sense, much more widely understood today than a decade or two ago. The word "psychosomatic" has become commonplace. "Just nerves" is an often-heard expression. At every cocktail and dinner party, at least one amateur psychiatrist announces, with an air of certainty, that so and so has asthma or a backache because of a childhood emotional trauma, or that somebody else only *seems* to be suffering from arthritis and the "disease" is imaginary, an effort to gain sympathy.

Occasionally, of course, the amateur diagnostician may be right. But it is no easy matter to determine whether any physical ailment is basically a result of an emotional problem. Emotional problems can, indeed, cause physical difficulties, but the reverse is equally true: any physical problem may produce emotional difficulties. To the word *psychosomatic* in the language we should add *somatopsychic*.

Not, by any means, do all problems in either category require the intervention of a psychiatrist. And if you understand the role emotions play in health and disease, you may well be able to prevent certain ailments from occurring and others, if they do occur, from progressing.

THE EMOTIONAL BASIS OF ILLNESS

Can emotions really cause an acute emergency such as a perforated duodenal ulcer? Can guilt feelings produce sore throats? Can unexpressed resentment be responsible for elevation of blood pressure or for migraine headache? In short, is there a direct link between emotional turmoil and physical suffering? How can something as intangible as emotional disturbance be translated into body disturbance? What is the scientific evidence? The volume of research in this area has been huge, and what follows is just a sampling.

Investigators studied 2,000 Army draftees, using a blood test to determine the level of stomach secretion in each man. They also administered psychological tests. On the basis of the tests and measurements, they predicted that 10 of the men would develop duodenal ulcers during a 16-week period of basic training. They were correct in 7 cases.

In Cincinnati, student nurses were divided into two groups: those who adjusted successfully during the first six weeks of training to their separation from home, and those who failed to adjust well. The investigators then predicted that the nonadjusting girls, those complaining of feeling helpless or hopeless, would have a significantly higher frequency of physical illness during their freshman year. Their prediction was accurate.

One study covered nearly 3,000 people, Americans and Chinese. For many, life data extending back over a period of at least 20 years could be collected. Episodes of physical illness in this large sample of people, the study showed, tended to occur in clusters, and the illness risk appeared to be linked not so much to actual life stresses as to how the individual perceived difficult life situations. At certain times, some given stress—a job difficulty, a family problem, a financial reverse—produced more conflict in a given individual than at other times, and it was then that illness was more likely to occur. The researchers concluded that only occasionally is illness the result of a chance encounter with germs, or injury, or other physical environmental factor. They concluded, too, that inheritance and constitution are relatively unimportant in determining susceptibility to physical illness when compared to life situations and how the individual perceives and is able to cope with them.

When 42 children hospitalized for physical illness and 45 healthy children were studied for psychological differences, the sick children were found to have experienced significantly more personal losses and other stress situations, and usually their physical illness had followed, within one month, a social or psychological change important to them.

Evidence that intense rage may lead to serious surgical emergencies came in a study of 20 consecutive patients with perforated ulcers. Most were found to have been recently faced with situations they believed damaging to their self-esteem and to which they had reacted with rage.

It has become possible to measure, in laboratory trials, physical reactions not only to emotional stress in general but to specific stresses such as fear, frustration, and feelings of hopelessness. In one of many such studies, rats were divided into three groups: one received electroshock; the second received the electroshock preceded by warning signals; the third received neither shock nor signals. The rats exposed to the warnings first and then the shock—i.e., to emotional stress through anticipation of pain—had the highest sickness and death rates.

In one study with human subjects, topics uncomfortable to them were discussed (stress interviews) while blood pressure was monitored and heart output and blood flow through the coronary arteries were checked with radioactive tracer materials and counting devices. The study revealed that when anger was aroused during an interview, there was a marked increase in coronary blood flow, a significant blood pressure rise, and an increase in heart output. Much the same happened in interviews covering anxiety-provoking subjects.

It has long been suspected that in some societies, voodoo death is produced by creating a conviction of doom in the victim. Some indication of how this may occur comes from a study with wild rats placed in a situation—swimming in a tank from which no exit was possible—that represented a hopeless predicament. The rats died by going into a shock state, with marked slowing of heart rate and lowering of body temperature, long before they reached the stage of actual physical exhaustion.

Thus, it is clear that psychosomatic illnesses can and do result from interaction of mind and body. They usually affect parts of the body under control of the involuntary nervous system, such as digestive tract, endocrine glands, heart, lungs, urinary bladder, and skin.

Doctors have been able to observe in a patient who, as the result of a serious accident, had to be fed through an opening made directly into his stomach, that inflammation occurred when he became angry or upset.

When food is in the stomach, it stimulates a necessary flow of digestive juices. Emotional reactions also can stimulate the flow. And if no food is present, the acid juices may irritate the stomach itself, eventually causing an ulcer or open sore.

It's important to remember that an ulcer exists as an organic disease of the stomach. Unless it is treated by medicine and diet, it may cause a hemorrhage or perforate. But unless the emotional tension is relieved, the patient won't be giving his ulcer its best chance to heal. *Thus, psychosomatic diseases usually require treatment of both body and mind.*

In addition to generating ulcers, emotional factors may be important in producing migraine, mucous colitis, ulcerative colitis, asthma, hypertension, hyperthyroidism (overactive thyroid), arthritis and rheumatism, and skin allergies. Undoubtedly, many more diseases will be added to this list.

As yet, evidence is not as clear-cut for any of these diseases as it is for certain ulcers. It is not known, for example, to what extent asthma may be due to a patient having an inherited allergic constitution and to what extent it may be due to emotional problems. However, it is known that asthmatic patients generally improve more rapidly when their emotional difficulties are relieved at the same time that they are being treated for any sensitivities (to pollens or other allergens) that may be involved in their attacks.

Unfortunately, some people still equate the term "psychosomatic illness" with "imaginary illness," something a victim could readily get rid of if he so chose because "it's all in the mind." This is a serious misconception. Pain can be just as real and intense when emotionally triggered as when physically based.

It's important to remember that emotions serve purposes. Fear causes the heart to beat faster and produces other temporary reactions, designed to get the body ready for action, either to run or to fight. It's when fear or other emotional tension is prolonged or repeated very frequently that it can have a debilitating effect on body organs. It is hardly surprising that about half of all people seeking medical help—according to some estimates, even 75 percent—have ailments either produced or made worse by emotional factors.

We shall examine in the next chapter the kinds of emotional stresses that most commonly bring on physical symptoms. But it is important to emphasize something here: No patient, and no doctor, should blithely make a diagnosis of psychosomatic illness, or "nerves." No wise physician does.

Psychosomatic problems are common, but to assume that emotions explain everything in an individual case is to risk serious consequences. Even when the emotional problems seem clearly to be the kind that could produce a physical complaint, the emotions may actually be stemming from the complaint. They may, in fact, be the first indication of a developing physical disease.

Restlessness, sleeplessness, and loss of appetite may stem from an emotional disturbance, but they may also result from a yet-undiagnosed heart condition. Systemic or central nervous system infections can present themselves as severe behavior disorders. Even helpful medicines such as cortisone may produce mental disturbances.

Traditionally, a diagnosis of psychosomatic illness is a diagnosis of exclusion—a process in which other likely possibilities are carefully considered and found not applicable, leaving emotion as the culprit. The physician notes the symptoms, makes a physical examination, may order some basic and special laboratory and x-ray studies. Only when he has satisfied himself that, for example, the chest pain is not due to actual heart disease or that the episodes of abdominal pain and vomiting are not produced by gallstones or other physical causes does he feel justified in considering an emotional explanation.

There is always the danger that an organic problem—an overactive or underactive thyroid, underactive adrenal glands, diabetes, possibly even a brain tumor—may pass unnoted if a full history, thorough examination, and supporting clinical studies are not meticulously executed. In such cases, as soon as the organic problem has been solved, the emotional symptoms disappear.

What, then, can you carry away from this discussion?

First, that emotional problems are commonly involved in physical difficulties. Often, they are the cause of the physical illness. At other times, they may not be the prime cause but an accentuating factor. At still other times, the emotional disturbances may be the result of the physical problem. Thus, there should never be a blithe assumption that any physical complaint is entirely psychosomatic; there should be a medical study to determine whether it is.

Second, if the diagnosis is psychosomatic, it should be accepted gratefully, not shamefully. Much can be done about overcoming the problem, as we shall see.

Also, as we shall see, the patient often can help the physician in the diagnosis when the patient is aware of the guises that emotional disorders can assume and when he is aware, too, that physical distress may be so overwhelming that it is easy to forget the emotional problems. By making certain that he informs the physician about his tensions at work and at home, the patient can help speed diagnosis and possibly avoid a long, costly, and uncomfortable chase after a physical cause that does not exist.

It is often said that in today's world, stresses, tensions, and emotional onslaughts have replaced yesterday's big hazards of hunger and infection. We are more hurried than our parents, exposed to more stimulation than we may have been constructed to take. Ours is a fast-moving world, with values constantly changing, leaving us no stable value system to cling to and help steady us.

While some or much of this may be true, nobody would want to live, or could, without emotions. They may cause trouble but they do not necessarily have to do so. The individual can learn to handle them and to use them constructively. Medical counseling often can help. If necessary, psychotherapy—quite often, brief, simple, supportive psychotherapy—can be used. Special medicines, too, are available for wise use —for example, when they can help bring runaway, illness-producing emotions under control, buying time for the individual to learn to handle them and redirect them constructively.

30

THE GUISES OF MENTAL PROBLEMS

MENTAL AND emotional problems can have obvious enough manifestations—in an individual's behavior, feelings, outlook on life. The tense and anxious person or the depressed and apathetic person may wear his inner state, so to speak, "on his sleeve."

But an anxiety or depressive state, whether or not obvious to others, may take a physical as well as emotional toll. And sometimes, in fact often, the physical problems may loom so large to the sufferer that he may consider them his whole burden and tend to dismiss his emotional state, not even mentioning the latter when he consults a physician. This can make it difficult for the physician to help.

If you understand well the many guises that emotional disturbances can take, you will be better able to obtain help if any develop, and you may be better able to prevent their development.

ANXIETY

This is often called the age of anxiety. Tranquilizers are in common use. Each day physicians see many patients with physical problems either triggered or made worse by anxieties.

The human body, when faced with a threat, usually reacts in one of two ways: it prepares to remove the threat or escape from it. This is the basis of the familiar "fight or flight" concept of adjustment. When there is a failure of adjustment, when the body does not react one way or the other, when there is internal conflict, there is anxiety.

Anxiety is not the same as fear. Fear stems from recognition of a specific danger, but anxiety tends to be unspecific—a condition of heightened tension and apprehension that often cannot be pinned down.

314

While fear and anxiety both signal that the security of the individual is threatened, the danger signaled by anxiety is not necessarily concrete and objective.

Both fear and anxiety set protective body processes in motion. When you experience a fear, adrenal gland and other changes take place, organizing the body to meet the fear-provoking threat. The emotion of fear is no mistake of nature; it can aid survival.

Recently, for example, when a plane by accident dropped a live 200-pound bomb on an aircraft carrier deck, a sailor rushed over, lugged it to the side and threw it overboard, saving his own and many other lives. Next day, when challenged, he could not budge a similar but safely defused bomb. There have been many instances of mothers who, in behalf of threatened children, accomplished seemingly impossible feats of strength. Human energy is stimulated by a normal emotion such as fear.

Like fear, anxiety sets similar body processes in motion. But since nothing is accomplished, the body is not called upon either to fight or flee, there is no decision; and the anxiety may be prolonged, it may lead to disturbances—respiratory difficulties, heart palpitation, muscular pain, headaches, gastrointestinal problems.

Normal Anxiety

Some degree of anxiety is experienced by all of us.

Many psychiatrists believe that the major source of it is man's conscience, an internal censor that begins to develop early in life in response to real or assumed attitudes of parents and others close to the child. As the child grows up, he may accept some of these standards, reject some, and eventually he develops a system of right and wrong. When this system, or conscience, or internal censor, clashes with an individual's natural desires in some situations (for possession, vengeance, love, sex), his personality in a sense is divided, and he experiences feelings of apprehension, tension, and inner restlessness.

Anxiety has other sources, too. The conscience may take over the approval-disapproval functions of parents, teachers, and others. But the individual still has need for the approval of others. And anxiety may arise not only from a conflict with conscience but because of the disapproval, or fear of disapproval, of other people—family, friends, employers.

Normal anxiety is part of the growth process, a natural response when a child, for example, is threatened by separation from parents, or when an adult considers old age and death. But if we need a certain amount of anxiety to help give us initiative and responsiveness to changing situations, to help us think and act creatively, there is also a sick or unhealthy anxiety, an inappropriate or excessive response to a situation.

Chronic anxiety may reveal itself in abnormal behavioral patterns. A chronically anxious child may show his emotional disturbance or unrest by nail-biting, thumb-sucking, or bed-wetting. A chronically anxious adolescent may reveal it in excessive shyness or excessive activity.

Obviously, anxiety is not a pleasant emotion. As quickly as we can, we try to be free of it. For this, we may use one or more defense mechanisms. We may try to deny the anxiety or rationalize it. A particularly common mechanism is repression, by which we exclude from the mind, push down into the unconscious, any ideas or memories that might arouse painful anxiety.

But if the repressed material does not well up into the mind, it is not inactive. It exerts drive. And we may use any one or several other mental mechanisms to keep it from coming into consciousness again. We may release the anxiety indirectly and inappropriately.

This, psychiatrists point out, accounts for many cases such as that of a young woman who, for no clear reason, often became enraged with an older woman under whom she worked. Her rage was not warranted and, study revealed, it was really directed toward her own unpleasant mother; but because she could not tolerate the idea of being so angry with her own mother, she had shifted her feeling to a substitute person.

Not all mental mechanisms for handling anxiety are necessarily seriously harmful. A mother who is overly protective, for example, may be using her excessive concern to disguise from herself some unconscious hostility toward the child, and yet she may remain a reasonably happy and effective person.

Actually, many defenses we erect against anxiety may help us, contributing to our emotional equilibrium. But if they are carried to excess, they become disturbing and may lead to neuroses. Consider, for example, one way by which an obsessive-compulsive neurosis may develop. A child becomes anxious because of some hostile feelings he has toward one or both parents. He tries to repress the feelings but this is not enough. To strengthen the repression, he shifts his hostility toward an activity that disturbs his parents—soiling, for instance. But then the soiling disturbs him and to counteract the disturbance he becomes overly preoccupied with cleanliness. Eventually, this obsessive-compulsive reaction may become incapacitating, as in one patient who became so obsessed with cleanliness that she spent virtually the whole of every day washing and rewashing her hands.

Anxiety may lead to phobic reactions. For example, an individual who experiences an attack of anxiety while riding in a car, or bus, or airplane may link his anxious feeling to the vehicle and thereafter try to avoid riding in such a vehicle. If anxiety attacks develop in other situations, he may avoid these, too, until his activities become tragically limited.

Because of abnormal anxiety, some people develop problem personalities, dealing with their internal conflicts by assigning the blame to society. Some may become psychotic, unable to deal with reality at all.

Many develop psychosomatic conditions. There is virtually no system of the body that may not be disturbed to some extent by abnormal anxiety: the heart and blood vessels (high blood pressure, fainting, angina pectoris, migraine, coronary artery disease); the respiratory system (asthma, nasal stuffiness, chronic sinusitis); the gastrointestinal tract (ulcer, gastritis, colitis, constipation); the genitourinary tract (urinary disturbances, painful menses, sterility); the skin (eczema, acne); the glandular system (diabetes, pernicious vomiting of pregnancy, premenstrual tension).

Anyone who realizes he is suffering from anxiety should seek help. By doing so, he can prevent more serious anxiety or anxiety panic states and also possibly prevent the onset of a psychosomatic illness. His physician may be able to provide the help; if not, he can direct the patient to a psychiatrist. As we shall see in a later chapter, there are available today many forms of psychiatric treatment, some quite brief yet helpful.

The patient who has physical problems that may be linked with anxiety needs reassurance that they are really so linked and that no serious underlying physical disease process is at work. This can come only from expert medical examination and diagnosis.

Unfortunately, many patients who seek medical help fail to reveal anxieties. They should. There is no shame. Reporting anxieties may save needless oversearching for physical causes that may not exist and may permit quicker, more effective treatment.

This is equally true when it comes to mental depression.

DEPRESSION

In a midwestern city, a 35-year-old engineer suddenly loses his appetite, is unable to sleep, experiences splitting headaches and alarming chest pains. A thorough medical check shows nothing organically wrong. But the doctor, refusing to leave it at that, discovers that there have been several such episodes before, not quite as bad, but always coming during periods of pressure on the job and always, as now, accompanied by feelings of discouragement and "blues."

To the credit of the physician, not a psychiatrist but an alert general practitioner, the engineer doesn't get a medicine chest full of drugs, one for each symptom—only a prescription to combat mental depression and some counseling about depression. Before long, the symptoms disappear.

In a Boston suburb, a young housewife suffers from overwhelming fatigue and constant abdominal distress. She has tried vitamins, "tonics," assorted remedies. When finally she consults a doctor, he notes while examining her that there is a kind of dullness and mental withdrawal about her.

And when he finds no physical explanation for her troubles, he gently asks: Has anything happened to make her feel depressed? She had lost her mother ten months before, had grieved, and had thought she had recovered from the grief. Yet, true, her symptoms, she recalled, had come on not long after her mother's death. She, too, is treated for depression—and relieved.

These are two of the lucky people.

Mental depression is being recognized today as a critical medical problem. According to some psychiatrists, more human suffering may result from depression than from any other single disorder. Some physicians term it "the great masquerader," noting that it has many faces and often hides behind physical complaints without betraying its presence by an obviously sad or despairing mood. Is depression, in disguised form, right now affecting someone in your family or a friend or neighbor? It could be.

More Than a Mood

There is nothing unusual about a brief spell of despondency or blues now and then. All of us have our ups and downs, days when we feel on top of the world, others when we feel a bit low. But depression—a chronic change of mood, a drawn-out lowering of the spirits—is another matter. It can be triggered by the loss of a loved one, loss of money or job, failure to get a promotion. Such a depression is called reactive or "exogenous," meaning it comes from outside.

But there is another common type that develops without apparent cause. Suddenly, a person may decide that he or she is a failure in life, when that is not really true. Unaccountably, self-confidence and self-esteem vanish. Ordinary everyday problems—family problems, social problems, economic problems—once handled as matters of course may suddenly seem too much to cope with. Such a depression is called "endogenous," indicating that it comes from within, perhaps as the result of some chemical upset in the body.

Some authorities believe that many depressions are mixed, both endogenous and exogenous. And some argue that there must be some endogenous or internal factor, otherwise a death in the family or other loss would lead only to temporary, normal sadness.

When depression occurs, it is not limited to the mind. There is a lowering of general vitality as well.

In a study to determine whether depressed people may be harder hit when common illnesses strike, Johns Hopkins University researchers gave psychological tests to employees at Fort Detrick, Frederick, Maryland. The following winter, when flu broke out and many employees were affected, those who had been found to be mildly depressed by the psychological tests took three weeks or longer to recover, while the others were over their flu in three to fourteen days.

Some authorities believe depression may even open the door to many germ attacks and other illnesses. They have noted that many patients become sick for the first time, or begin to suffer from chronic disease, or decide to undergo surgery when they are depressed.

Dr. Edward J. Kollar of the University of California has reported that, "During five years' experience as chief of a large general hospital, I gradually became aware of the large number of patients who had *masked depressions*, sometimes behind a smiling, amiable facade. Anyone who is ill is entitled to react to his illness with depression. The point I wish to emphasize is that these individuals were depressed before they developed the illness."

On Top of Other Problems

Even when depression stems from illness, doctors have discovered, treating the depression sometimes may contribute greatly to successful treatment of the physical illness.

In rheumatoid arthritis and chronic ulcerative colitis, depression is frequent, and some relief of these diseases has been reported following use of antidepressant medicines. Such medication was tried in one study with asthma and eczema patients who had not responded well to usual treatment and were suffering from depression. Of 113 patients, 69 showed improvement of both depression and asthma or eczema.

At one heart clinic, some patients with angina pectoris, the chest pain associated with hardening of the coronary arteries feeding the heart, have shown some improvement after addition of treatment for depression.

British doctors have studied the depression factor in head and face pains failing to respond to usual treatment. Some patients had trigeminal neuralgia, which produces stabbing, lightning-like face pain. Others had pains for which no physical cause could be found. Some were suffering from obvious depression; others, upon careful investigation, were found to be depressed. And the response to antidepression treatment often was gratifying, the British physicians have reported.

Depression Alone—in Disguise

In addition to complicating physical illness, depression also may be the sole cause of many symptoms that mimic those of physical illness. Very often, the physical symptoms overshadow the depressed feelings.

In a four-year study, doctors at Massachusetts General Hospital found fatigue to be the single most frequent symptom in patients who proved to be depressed. It was often overwhelming fatigue, making daily activity difficult. At the same time, the victims had sleeping problems. Usually, they could doze off but woke up early in the morning and tossed for hours. In fact, any sudden tendency to wake very early may be a cardinal sign of depression.

Headache also is common. In studying 423 patients with depression, Dr. Seymour Diamond of the Chicago Medical School found that 84 percent had headache as a major complaint; in some cases, it was the only complaint. Depressive headaches, Dr. Diamond reports, are capricious, follow no definite location pattern, usually are worse in the morning than in the evening, often resist ordinary headache remedies. But once recognized for what they are, they may be relieved with antidepressant medication.

Among his patients, Dr. Diamond also found 75 percent experiencing weight loss ranging from 5 to 20 pounds. Next in order of frequency were such symptoms as breathing difficulty, dizziness, weakness, urinary disturbance, palpitations, nausea.

In a recent seminar to alert family doctors, Dr. Jack R. Ewalt, distinguished Harvard psychiatrist, reported that "depression symptoms are frequently referred to the gastrointestinal tract," and urged a check for depression in people who complain of gas or abdominal pains that are unexplained by medical examination. He also noted that changes in sex habits are likely to occur and to take the form of reduced potency in men, menstrual disturbances in women.

According to one industrial physician, Dr. Rex. H. Wilson, of the B. F. Goodrich Co., depressed people who suffer from digestive upsets, nausea, vomiting, constipation, or diarrhea too often may be thought to have ulcers or colitis. The depressed, he also notes, may develop urinary frequency or urgency, sometimes accompanied by burning and sensations of pressure in the bladder area; many feel heart palpitations, chest constriction, pain in the heart area, and may seek medical help for "heart trouble"; still others may have noises in the ears, visual disturbances, mouth dryness, numbness or tingling sensations; and some develop red blotches on the body.

Nobody knows how many elderly people thought to be hopelessly senile are really only depressed. "The depressions of the geriatric patient often remain undiagnosed," says Dr. Sidney Cohen, Chief of Psychiatry

Service, Wadsworth Veterans Administration Hospital, Los Angeles. "There is the feeling that he is too senile, too little in contact, to be depressed. Actually, depressions can contribute to or even cause senile confusion."

While depression in older people may lead to weakness, sleeping difficulty, appetite loss, and many aches and pains, Dr. Cohen reports that "another depressive syndrome in the aged consists of irascibility, irritability, indecisiveness, and inertia. These personality changes repel family, friends, and physician. It is necessary to penetrate behind the disgruntled attitude and annoying behavior to recognize the underlying depression."

Once depression is recognized, treatment for it may be rewarding.

New Treatments

Until recent years, doctors had rather limited treatment to use against depression. Now there are many medicines. Not long ago, when 170 of the nation's outstanding medical clinicians and researchers were polled on the most significant new drug developments of recent years, one major advance listed was an antidepressant medication introduced in 1959. Another major advance listed was an antidepressant introduced in 1965. There are other valuable antidepressants in addition.

No one medicine is a panacea. The therapeutic compound that helps one patient may be of little or no value for another. Careful selection is needed. Many physicians prefer to use these medicines only when psychotherapy does not work. They report that psychotherapy alone—and it may be brief psychotherapy provided by a family doctor, not necessarily a psychiatrist—often can work wonders. It may take the form of a few sessions in which the patient is told about the nature of his or her physical complaints, is encouraged to ventilate, or talk out, worries and feelings, and is given realistic reassurance.

When psychotherapy and medicines do not help, electroshock very often does. Electroshock treatment is particularly valuable in severe depression when there may be danger of suicide.

Recently, a new technique of electroshock has shown promise. Brief bursts of current are applied to one side of the brain instead of to both sides. The one-sided treatment has been reported to be fully as effective as two-sided, while minimizing or even completely avoiding the temporary confusion and memory disturbance that may sometimes follow the latter.

Solving the Major Problem

The big problem is recognition of depression, particularly when it leads, as it so often does, to distressing physical troubles. Keenly aware of their real aches and pains, people with depression often regard their blue feelings as results, not causes. Many try doctoring themselves for long periods, fruitlessly. If and when they do seek medical help, many fail to mention any feelings of dejection. Some even vehemently deny feeling depressed, many doctors find, apparently out of a belief there is something shameful about depression. There is not. It is one of the most common of all disorders and hits people in all walks of life, even the most brilliant. Now something can be done about it.

When you seek medical help for any physical complaint, a good doctor will usually want to ask many questions, get a full case history. Increasingly alert to what depression can do, to the many physical disguises it can take, he will want to probe for any clues that it may be a factor in your case.

Cooperate. You can help by answering his questions and by volunteering information. If you have experienced a change of mood—if, along with your physical troubles, you have been aware of feeling low in mind, dejected, for months or even weeks—let him know. The chances are that by doing so you will save yourself much misery and needless expense.

Suicide is a constant threat in the depressed person. Suicide and its prevention are discussed in detail on page 655.

31

COPING EFFECTIVELY

MENTAL AND emotional stress cannot be eliminated from life. Nor does it have to be. In itself it is not harmful. It is not a disease but a normal part of life.

It is not so much the amount of stress an individual is subjected to that determines whether he or she will suffer from acute anxiety or depression or psychosomatic illness as it is how the stress is perceived, understood, and handled. And there are measures we can make use of to handle stressful situations in our lives more effectively. There can, of course, be situations that seem so overwhelming that we may need medical or other professional help if we are to cope with them. Such help, as the next chapter will show, is available. But for most situations we have resources of our own that we can learn to use successfully.

HANDLING FEELINGS OF FRUSTRATION

When we have worries and cannot do anything about them, we have feelings of frustration. Long continued, frustration can take serious physical toll. In a classic experiment demonstrating the physical effects of frustration, rats were strapped to a board—for them, a most frustrating situation. As they struggled uselessly to get out of the situation, large areas of their heart muscles disintegrated and the animals died. Obviously, the one way to have saved the rats would have been to release them. Medication might conceivably have dulled the frustration for them but not released them.

Man's frustrating situations are not so obvious. But they can be no less exacting. And while there is often a temptation to regard them as insoluble and to dull the feelings they arouse by such means as drugs and alcohol, man's frustrating situations quite often can be solved. There is usually something that can be done to adapt to the circumstance or to change the seeming circumstance.

If, say, your job is a particularly frustrating one, must it remain so? Is the frustration irremovable? There are many cases like that of a man, a successful young executive, or so he had been, who became a victim of painful headaches and insomnia and began to have trouble with associates on the job and with family at home. He had recently been assigned to a responsible new position in a division of the company that was in trouble.

He worked hard and yet couldn't make as much of a dent in the many problems the division faced as he thought desirable. Increasingly anxious and tense, he put pressure on the people working with him as well as on himself, to the point where he no longer had their cooperation. He had a gnawing, ever growing fear that his superiors were dissatisfied with his work.

Only when he faced up to the fact that it was this fear which was driving him and, at the same time, was frustrating him, making him act in a self-defeating fashion, could he nerve himself for a showdown with the company president.

It was a productive showdown. Was the president dissatisfied with his work, he wanted to know. On the contrary, the president told him, he thought he had done remarkably well in a difficult situation. And, in fact, so concerned was the president over the possible loss of the young man that he insisted he take an immediate vacation and promised to assign additional personnel to help him in his work.

If you feel you are faltering in your job, that you are out of your depth, it may or may not be true. It's healthy to find out where you stand, to take action rather than suffer along. You may not be out of your depth at all but may have created frustration for yourself by demanding more of yourself than anybody could reasonably expect. If you are out of your depth, the chances are that this will be discovered by others sooner or later; and if you own up to it sooner, there may be something of an immediate wrench but you will save yourself much grief and may well find yourself a happier situation much sooner.

ARE YOU REALLY WORKING TOO HARD?

Many tense, anxious people today blame their problems on the so-called modern rat race. They argue that they are caught up in that rat race, that the demands upon them are excessive, that they simply have to work too hard.

Many investigators believe—and we agree with them—that overwork is rarely the reason for emotional problems. More often the problem lies, as one physician experienced in industrial medicine puts it, with creating a rat race of one's own.

Actually, half a century ago, people worked longer hours than now. But they also lived a different kind of life. Today, too many people only ride; they move about little on their own two feet. With food and drink readily available, they consume to excess. With TV readily at hand, they take their leisure passively and get little of the stimulation, both mental and physical, that active games and good conversation can provide.

If you find yourself tense, you may do well to consider your whole living pattern as well as job situation.

Everybody needs to get intimately acquainted with the most important person in the world—himself. He needs to know, clearly, how he reacts to various foods, to smoking, to drinking; he needs to know what actually are his own individual requirements for exercise and relaxation.

In one survey on tension among business executives, it was found that those who complained of excessive tension—13 percent of the total number—shared a long list of undesirable health habits. The tense men ate breakfast on the fly, in less than 5 minutes; bolted their lunch (15 minutes); hurried through dinner (under 30 minutes). They got no form of regular exercise; tended to have few civic, church or other extracurricular activities and interests; many had no hobby at all. Many got six or less hours sleep a night; few had weekends free for themselves and their families; and any vacations taken were much below average in length. Most were heavy smokers; many drank excessively; most used sedatives to induce sleep and tranquilizers to quiet their nerves.

Often, an overly tense person, if he can make an adjustment in his living habits on his own or with the advice and help of his physician, may need to do no more.

RELEASING MUSCLE TENSION

One important means—but not a commonly appreciated one—we have for releasing pent-up emotion is physical exercise. Actually, this is a means for releasing the tensions that we tend to store up in muscles.

Perhaps you've had the experience of hearing a telephone ring in another room. You expect somebody else to answer it, but the telephone goes on ringing, and you became tense. You are prepared to act—but don't. Your muscles are ready, some of them possibly even contracted, but you don't move and you don't relax them for a time.

When nervous tension leads to an almost continuous tensing of some muscles, contracture, or shortening of the muscles, may result. They no longer relax properly. For some years, investigators have been reporting that this is a mechanism in many common disorders. In tension headache, for example, the frontalis muscle in the forehead and the occipital muscles running up the back of the head may be involved. Often involved in painful, stiff neck are the neck muscles, the trapezius muscles lying over the shoulder blades, and the rhomboid muscles under the trapezius. In many cases of backache as well, muscles may be involved.

Sometimes injections of novocaine may be needed to relieve the pain produced by knotted-up muscles. Exercise, even if only a long walk, can help when tension builds up, not only to divert the mind but also to work off muscle tensions.

You may well find great relief from tension if you break up, even just briefly, long periods of sedentary work with interludes of physical activity. Every hour or so, get up, walk about (even just a few steps), stretch and bend, perhaps wave your arms a bit, take a few deep breaths, and sit down and go to work again. Chances are you will feel some lessening of fatigue and will be able to go back to your work a little more relaxed and with somewhat more zest.

For some people who are especially tense, special relaxing exercises may be helpful.

Some years ago, Dr. Edmund Jacobson of Chicago observed that muscles which had been made tense could be taught to relax. One of his first steps, an important one, was to teach people to identify the sensation of residual tension.

He would have a patient lie down, close his eyes, and rest his arms beside the body. Then he would ask the patient to bend one hand up and back, slowly, steadily, going as far back as possible. And, for a long minute, as the patient held the hand there, he would ask him to "observe carefully a certain faint sensation in the upper portion of your forearm. This sensation is the signal mark of tension wherever it appears in the body. Vague as it is, you can learn to recognize it." It was not unusual for a patient to take several days just to discover the sensation.

Dr. Jacobson then would remark: "When you understand what you are looking for, start afresh and bend the hand slowly back again. But this time, when it reaches its peak, relax your muscles and let it fall. Let it go completely. Let it fall limply." Eventually, after such release, there would be no tension left to feel.

If you would like to try relaxing exercises, the following may be helpful. First, check with your physician to make certain you have no possible ailment that might be affected detrimentally by exercise.

Get into as relaxed a state as you can. Sit down and, for five minutes or so, just try to relax mentally and physically. If you feel tension anywhere in the body, let it go. Try to make yourself as limp as a rag doll.

Then go on to one or more of the following exercises, working slowly, smoothly, without jerking. Start by doing them for just a few minutes a day; then work up to perhaps as long as half an hour.

Seated comfortably, raise your arms slowly overhead—and let them drop suddenly. Do the same with the legs. After each drop, pause several seconds to appreciate the relaxed effect. Breathe deeply, exhale slowly.

Lie on your back on the floor. Close your eyes. Take a deep breath. Exhale slowly. Tighten all muscles in your body. Then let go. Breathe deeply, exhale slowly.

Still on the floor, shrug your shoulders up to your ears—and then let them fall back. Turn your head far to the left, then to the front, and relax. Repeat to the right. Breathe deeply and exhale after each movement.

Lying on your abdomen, rest your head on your folded arms. Tighten buttock muscles, then let go. Repeat several times.

If you find these exercises helpful, you may wish to consult two books written by Dr. Edmund Jacobson: *Anxiety and Tension Control,* * which is primarily addressed to physicians, and *You Must Relax,*† primarily written for lay people.

Many other physicians today believe that the key to relaxing tension is muscle control. With every type of nervous stress, they note, there is muscular expression—sometimes as obvious as drumming with the fingers, sometimes as subtle as a mere flick of the eyes. If you can develop muscular control, you can help prevent buildup of tension.

For that you will need to recognize delicate sensations most people are unaware of, distinguishing the slightly different feeling of a muscle performing useful work and a muscle tensed uselessly. Then it is necessary to control the unused muscles, turning them off. The objective is differential relaxation in which muscles in constructive use stay in use while others are relaxed fully.

As an example of how to go about this, close your eyes and silently repeat to yourself the names of three states or Presidents of the United States. Though you are not speaking, notice the small, almost imperceptible tentative movements that take place in your tongue, lips, jaw, cheeks, throat. Then see if you can relax these muscles completely.

* Jacobson, Edmund, *Anxiety and Tension Control.* Philadelphia: Lippincott, 1964.
† , *You Must Relax.* New York: McGraw-Hill, 1957.

HANDLING WORRIES

All worry cannot be escaped. If you face a lawsuit, have a loved one who is dying, or a business that is failing, you can hardly be blamed for worry. But many people tend to worry over problems in advance, problems that often never actually materialize.

One of America's most distinguished psychiatrists used to teach his students two cardinal propositions about worry. One: Don't worry about something that is not *your* worry. Is a son or daughter, someone else in the family, or perhaps a friend taking what seems to you to be an inordinate amount of time to decide something, perhaps to marry someone you think highly desirable? That is not really your problem. You may have advice to offer. Offer it tactfully. Then quit worrying. The decision is not yours to make. Why worry yourself sick uselessly? The second proposition: If it isn't your worry now, let it lie. Worry only if, and when, the problem actually comes up.

There are other sound principles, too. Worry about a problem when it really faces you. Then worry in the sense of examining it carefully, considering possible alternative solutions, and coming to a decision. Then waste no more time, worry no longer over that problem. Decide what to do—and do it. Don't make yourself sick because you can't make up your mind about things. You can decide; chances are you will make some mistakes, but you will also make mistakes if you decide, undecide, and keep up a worrisome process of indecision.

If you are worried about something, invest your time and talents in trying to resolve the problem; but if you find that you can't resolve it and some expert could resolve it for you or help you resolve it, make the sound investment of getting his advice—whether it is a physician who can resolve your worry about a lump in a breast or a good lawyer who can advise about a threatened lawsuit.

One bit of advice that wise physicians also often impart to patients: If you really must worry (realistically), do it by day, not by night; use your nights for sleeping.

It's important to realize that all of us have problems; they are evidence that we are alive. And while we can rise to their challenge and develop skill in handling them, it may well be—as some physicians believe, based on their experience with many troubled patients—that if we adopt a policy of letting nothing bother us unduly, that alone would solve 80 percent of our problems.

That is not a matter of irresponsibility. But we do have to recognize that many, if not virtually all, of us quite humanly tend to exaggerate several things: first, our own importance in matters; second, other people's importance in our lives; and, not least of all, the importance of what appear to be problems.

If you think you have a problem, you may indeed have one; but often, if you examine the situation closely, you will find that there is no real problem and all you needed to realize the lack of a problem was an awareness and understanding of some facts that might not have been recognized before.

If there is an actual problem, decide whether it is really yours or someone else's. If it is your own problem, determine whether it is something you are likely to solve with the knowledge and skills you possess. If it is so, go ahead. But if it is not, put the problem into the lap of an expert who can solve it.

OTHER MEANS OF COPING WITH DAILY PROBLEMS

Can you get a better grip on your job? Jobs are not tense; people are. If your job is bothering you, it could be that you need to change jobs. But it might well be that you need rather to try to reduce tensions by changing your perspective in several ways:

If you are under tension, an ordinary workload may seem intolerable. Try tackling one thing at a time. Dispose of urgent needs, and the remaining workload may not seem so heavy.

Are you too perfectionistic? Nothing is ever perfect, and letting yourself be driven by an urge to perfection may only succeed in producing failure, frustration, and tension.

Seek diversion. It's no waste of time. Temporary respite in a book, movie, game, or hobby will let you return to work better equipped to deal with your problems.

Consider your relationships with others. Do some people rub you the wrong way? Perhaps you are being influenced more by subjective feelings than by any wrong done you. If you seem to be quarreling constantly with people, it could be beneficial—in terms of better relationships and also in terms of easing your own inner tension—if you give in occasionally, even when you think you may be right.

Don't take your work home if you can possibly help it. If you can't help it, put it away at least an hour before bedtime. Relax to sleep well— and sleep well to be more relaxed. Fatigue is a tension provoker.

Talk out your tension-provoking problems. Talking over a worrisome matter with a friend, a level-headed relative, or a clergyman can relieve your strain and may help you put things in proper perspective.

Consider well a familiar prayer based on wisdom: "God grant me the serenity to accept the things I cannot change, courage to change the things I can, and wisdom always to tell the difference."

Behind every accomplishment lies a certain amount of discontent, frustration, and worry. But by failing to channel these forces properly, some people let themselves be exhausted and made ill and ineffective by them.

HOW TO COPE WITH BEREAVEMENT AND GRIEF REACTIONS

All of us sooner or later must face bereavement. And one of the most valuable developments in modern psychiatry is new understanding of the importance of the grief process, of what it apparently must consist of, and of the suffering, physical and mental, which may occur if the process is not properly worked through.

In particular, the studies of Dr. Eric Lindemann of Harvard on the mourning process have clearly useful implications for maintaining mental and physical health. Dr. Lindemann has established that in adapting to the death of a loved one, a bereaved person goes through a well-defined process which usually takes four to six weeks to complete and involves a succession of specific psychological steps. His findings indicate that it is essential to work hard psychologically to adapt to a loss.

Starting with studies of mourners for people lost in a disastrous Boston nightclub fire some years ago, Dr. Lindemann was able to note that the majority of people do their "grief work" satisfactorily, on an instinctive basis, and recover their psychological and physical equilibrium at the end of four to six weeks. But a significant number do not, and either immediately or later show signs, sometimes extreme, of psychiatric or psychosomatic illness. They are especially likely to develop depressed mental states and peptic ulcers, ulcerative colitis, or other gastrointestinal disorders.

Dr. Lindemann has not merely theorized that there is a causative relationship between failure to go through a normal mourning process and the later development of such illnesses. He has been able to demonstrate that sometimes the illnesses can be brought under control by helping the patients revive, months and years later, their bereaved feelings and at that point do their previously undone grief work.

What constitutes a healthy mourning reaction? Among the typical manifestations of a healthy reaction are a temporary loss of interest in the usual daily affairs of life and work; feelings of loneliness and mental pain; crying; breathing disturbances, including frequent deep sighs; insomnia; appetite loss; and preoccupation with many memories about the lost one. It appears that the normally bereaved person actually loses interest in most phases of daily life in order to concentrate on remembering how his life was influenced and enriched by the lost one. It appears, too, that it is necessary for him to suffer through, detail by detail, his loss, realizing it in terms of the role the lost one played in various segments of his life. Only after he has gone through this process can he truly return to emotional stability and normal activity.

On the other hand, unsuccessful mourners who later develop illnesses depart in one or several ways from this process. Some throw themselves into more business or other activity than usual, trying in that fashion to escape the trials of mourning. They do not cry. Some show a strange cheerfulness; others merely say that they feel numb or empty. There is no preoccupation with the departed one. Often there is difficulty in recalling the image of the dead person. Overall, in effect, unsuccessful mourners are trying to deny the emotional importance of the death in their lives and are trying to get on with living without the burden of mourning. But while, in the short run, they may seem happier than active mourners, they pay, in the long run, with more suffering.

A guideline for physicians, as a means of making use of the study, may be helpful for you personally and perhaps for others in the family. It is simply this:

To help people grieve successfully, it is not essential to bring to light any deeply buried psychological reasons for their failure to start to grieve properly. What is vital is just to get them, by any possible means, to think of the image of the deceased, to avoid putting the image out of mind, to actually dwell on the image, and to go over repeatedly in their minds the many activities shared with the departed one in the past—so they can realize, once and for all during the mourning process, that he will be missing from their lives.

32

HELP FOR EMOTIONAL PROBLEMS

TODAY, NEW forms of help are available for people with critical emotional problems—psychiatric treatments which are brief, pointed, relatively inexpensive. They promise not only to provide an immediate lift for people in trouble but also to prevent more serious illness, physical or mental or both, that otherwise might develop. One of these is crisis intervention, a kind of emotional first aid.

It has been said, perhaps somewhat overenthusiastically but nevertheless with some basis in fact, that there have been three revolutions in mental health. The first was the medical discovery, less than two centuries ago, that the insane were neither criminals nor possessed by demons but rather sick people. The second was Freud's insights into the deeper levels of the mind. The third is crisis intervention.

Crisis intervention aims at dealing with a specific incident that causes a crisis. Rather than delving analytically into past events and early life experiences which might have contributed to a problem, its objective is to get the person over the hump immediately so he or she can function effectively.

As a part of psychiatry, crisis intervention developed out of the experiences of Dr. Eric Lindemann after the Boston nightclub fire we mentioned earlier. During his studies of bereavement reactions among relatives of the dead, Dr. Lindemann not only found that grief work passes through a series of steps essential for mental health; he also determined that the human capacity to cope with problems, which is not inborn but rather is gained through experience, often falters in a time of crisis.

In 1948, Dr. Lindemann and a Harvard colleague, Dr. Gerald Caplan, established the Wellesley Project, a communitywide mental health program in a town near Boston, with special emphasis on *preventive intervention*. Their idea, in essence, was that there are sound and unsound, adaptive and maladaptive, ways of meeting a range of emotional hazards during life, each of which may have important consequences for later psychological soundness and ability to cope.

Their hope was to be able to step in when a patient, up against an emotional crisis, couldn't handle it properly. They hoped to help him to handle it, and in so doing not only keep him functioning effectively but also maintain his ability to meet other, later crises, perhaps less significant ones, perhaps just as significant.

The Korean War helped buttress the idea. During that conflict it was discovered that psychiatric first aid administered on the spot to battle-shocked soldiers often quickly restored them to duty. On the other hand, those sent home for long-drawn-out institutional treatment responded slowly.

To go into a little more detail, crisis intervention rests on the concept that as an individual meets problems in daily life he may become temporarily emotionally upset. The upsets, however, are managed by techniques he has learned in the past: by tolerance of tension, by hopeful expectation that the problem will be solved (based on past successes in solving problems), and by various methods he has learned to use to discharge tension. Soon, he regains his previous equilibrium.

When, however, the problem is a greater one and previous problem-solving methods are not suitable, then the person may move from what might be called an emotionally hazardous state into a crisis state. And the word "crisis" is used not as a synonym for emergency but rather for an acute, often prolonged disturbance in an individual as the result of an emotionally hazardous situation.

The crisis period, in fact, can be divided into four phases. In the first, there is a rise of tension along with some disorganization of behavior as the impact of the hazardous situation is realized and the usual problem-meeting techniques are brought to bear. In the second phase, tension mounts as the problem remains unsolved. In the third phase, the tension reaches a point at which still more resources are mobilized. The individual is now trying even harder to solve the problem. And at this stage, the situation may improve, perhaps because the added problem-solving methods help, or the problem is seen in a new light, or certain goals are given up. In the fourth phase, the individual suffers major disorganization when the problem continues and cannot be solved, avoided, or freshly defined.

In this framework, crisis intervention makes use of several important principles. First, because the person is teetering, in painful and precarious disequilibrium, a small influence may produce a great change quickly. The intervention of another person—a physician or other professional, a family member, a sensitive friend—may significantly affect the outcome for the better. And the first six weeks are key weeks. Another principle is that the outcome of the crisis is not determined by previous experiences alone but by current psychological and situational forces. And a third principle is that if the person can be helped to find his equilibrium again, the new equilibrium may be at a better adaptive level than before; he will not only be over the hump of the present crisis but perhaps better able to deal with future crises.

Just how does crisis intervention work? Consider a seemingly extreme case. Mr. A was brought almost forcibly to a crisis clinic by his worried wife and brother-in-law; he was seemingly on the verge of complete mental breakdown. He had been acting strangely, talking agitatedly of wild business schemes, getting up in the middle of the night to make "vital business calls."

Asked by the therapist at the clinic why he was there, Mr. A said he had no idea; there was nothing wrong with him; and he insisted upon talking jovially about his business schemes. Finally, upon being pressed, he admitted that he had had a back injury recently, had lost some time from work, and that, he supposed, had worried his wife and was why she had brought him to the clinic.

But the therapist was quickly able to establish that the back injury, though not severe, had triggered emotional upheaval in Mr. A, causing him to feel that he was getting older and losing his vigor; and to try to bury such feelings, he had launched into wild overactivity.

Quietly, the therapist pointed out to him what had been going on. He needed, first, to calm down, stop feeling tense, and a sedative would help. And he was to come back in a few days for a consultation; they would then examine his problem further and try to find a solution. He returned for that consultation and for another a week later. And after the second consultation, his wife reported that he was acting normally again.

Crisis intervention does not attempt to make over an individual, to delve deeply into events that may have formed character. And yet, often, it can be helpful not only as first aid but as long-lasting aid.

In crisis intervention, an effort is made to encourage people to actually "experience" their emotions—to examine them and feel them fully—rather than to merely have vague, unexamined emotional stirrings and to try to block the stirrings.

Emotions are what move us to action. Almost always they have to do with people and what we want from or did not obtain from people. We may get angry at someone because of something he has done or failed to do. We may feel shame in connection with some person because of what we ourselves did or thought.

"Emotions," one psychiatrist puts it, "are the affective coloring of our desires (our goals) toward someone. There is only a handful of specific emotions: fear, shame, anger, guilt, sadness, joy, sexual desire, grief."

Going on to explain how he tries to help, the psychiatrist tells us: "I am interested in what the client is experiencing when he is with me, and I may put it to him just like that: 'I'm curious about what you are experiencing right now.' Then I see how well he is able to discern his own feelings. Most of us have not been taught this skill. We have learned how to keep our emotions vague. We have learned all the imprecise words for feelings: tense, nervous, upset, disturbed, bad, frustrated, bothered, agitated, aggravated, overwrought, tired, lousy, depressed, and so on.

"Either the client's present emotions are giving him distress, or the automatic constraint (repression) of these emotions is producing distress of a second order. There is a reduction in distress from both sources when he can acknowledge the constraining actions and put the emotions into thoughts and words. This starts a benign circle—thought, verbalization, sharing, new perceptions, augmented coping resources—replacing the vicious circle of increasing tension and further demoralization."

Crisis intervention today is being practiced at most general hospitals that have psychiatric units. It is available through many private psychiatrists. There are storefront clinics in many areas, an increasing number of them.

Some indication of the value of crisis intervention is to be found in the experience of Los Angeles County Hospital, which used to admit 95 percent of·patients coming in or brought in for emotional disturbances, better than 1,500 a month, and had to send many to mental institutions. Now, employing crisis intervention, the hospital helps 65 percent as outpatients, and the 35 percent admitted stay an average of 5.2 days instead of 180 days as before; very few go to mental institutions.

There is also the experience of San Francisco where the annual commitment rate to state mental institutions dropped from 2,887 to 119 in the first four years in which the city had an expanding complex of emergency treatment centers. Grady Memorial Hospital in Atlanta now treats 5,000 psychiatric emergencies a year in its crisis center; and its 36-bed mental ward, previously inadequate to meet the need, is seldom completely occupied today.

Crisis centers are staffed by teams which include nurses, social workers, lay therapists, and clergymen as well as professional psychiatrists.

Certainly, crisis intervention is no panacea for all mental illness. It often benefits people whose emotional problems seem overwhelming, but it appears to be of much less, if any, value to others with problems that are not overwhelming, including so-called normal neurotics who manage to live with their problems even though not happily.

It could be important in your life or the life of someone close to you to be aware of the availability of crisis intervention and of the likelihood that it can help in seemingly desperate situations.

33

OTHER PROBLEMS, OTHER HELPS

MENTAL ILLNESS fascinates yet bewilders most people. We are eager consumers of books, motion pictures, magazine stories, and articles about the subject. Psychological terms have entered everyday language. We talk freely of guilt complexes, neurotics, fixations, and phobias.

Yet such is the basic bewilderment that when one investigator not long ago tested 3,500 people on their ability simply to recognize mental illness when they saw it, as demonstrated in six short case histories, most failed to recognize five out of the six as mentally ill. Many if not most of us need only try to define or distinguish among psychiatrist, psychoanalyst, psychologist, and psychotherapist to realize how tenuous a grip we have on the subject of mental illness.

Adding somewhat to the confusion, too, have been conflicting reports —in the public media and from friends and acquaintances—about people who have spent months or even years in treatment and seem no better and, on the other hand, about people who, as a result of treatment, seem clearly healthier and happier in marriage, in business, and in general.

Because a knowledge of what is mental illness and what is not, of how to recognize early indications, and of what can be done, can be vitally important for preventive medicine and healthful living, let us examine the subject.

WHAT IS SOUND MENTAL HEALTH?

Sigmund Freud, founder of psychoanalysis, once said that his objective was "to substitute for neurotic misery ordinary human unhappiness." That gloomy remark added weight to an impression that good health, physical and mental, is simply the absence of overwhelming distress.

338 / Preventive Mental Care

This, to most physicians today, is much too restrictive and limited a view. To merely exist without pain is not enough. Health, physical or mental, should be measured not by whether or not something hurts but by pleasure and achievement. A person free of emotional distress cannot merely on that basis be categorized as mentally healthy.

Mental health is not simple to define. Some people consider that to be mentally healthy is to be like the majority, despite the fact that history has shown that in a decadent society such as Nazi Germany the majority can be brutal and sadistic. Some people feel that to be mentally healthy is to be happy, though some obviously insane people are "happy." "Maturity" is another word used as a synonym for mental health, though adolescents can be healthy without being mature.

Physicians think of a normal person as one who adjusts to his surroundings, the world he lives in and the people in it, and also to his own potentialities for living, which may include making realistic efforts to change the world about him for the better. By abnormal behavior, physicians mean inappropriate or ineffective methods of getting along in one's surroundings. For example, a person who is afraid of being hit by a car might refuse to go outdoors; this might relieve his fear but obviously would not be a satisfactory solution. When we examine abnormal behavior carefully, we see that it consists of techniques for adjusting to situations, techniques that are not adequate but are used because they satisfy in some way, or at least are more satisfying than anything else the individual has tried.

Among other questions physicians may want answered before deciding about an individual's state of mental health are: Is he or she capable of loving someone else? Is he or she reliable, contented, productive in his or her work? Is he or she able to appreciate the commonplace wonders of the earth?

Once, a century or so ago, only the real "madman" was recognized as being mentally ill. Now much behavior that once was considered merely unwise or the result of a vague "weakness of character" is viewed as an indication of psychological disorder. For example, even many lay people today believe that a person who has had three or four divorces is not merely unwise or weak but has problems that prevent him from choosing a marriage partner properly or from adjusting properly to married life.

People today who are interested in mental health are concerned about those of the many persons who get divorced for neurotic reasons, the 700,000 children each year who are brought into court as delinquents, the 200,000 women in any year who bear illegitimate children, the millions suffering from alcoholism, and the other millions whose symptoms of psychological stress range from colitis and migraine to friendlessness. Adding them all together, some authorities estimate that 20 million Americans, one of every ten, are emotionally disturbed.

Nor is it only the authorities who consider so many people to be mentally sick to some degree. In a survey conducted for the Joint Commission on Mental Illness and Health, 20 percent of adults reported that at one time or other they had felt that they were on the verge of nervous breakdown.

We would like to emphasize that these figures should not cause dismay. They do not necessarily mean that we are mentally sicker today than earlier generations were, but rather that we have become aware that many problems and unpleasantnesses which once were simply taken to be "man's lot" are not inevitable, not necessary, and very often can be overcome.

Actually, it has been estimated that about one fourth of those who are mentally and emotionally ill are ill enough to be seriously hampered; the remaining three fourths have problems that bother them but do not necessarily need professional treatment.

Who is normal? Before considering the basic mental and emotional disorders and how to prevent them, it may be helpful to have, as a basis for comparison, a little more detail about the personality structure of a normal, mentally healthy person.

ELEMENTS OF HEALTHY PERSONALITY STRUCTURE

1. REALISTIC ATTITUDES. An emotionally healthy adult faces facts, pleasant and unpleasant. He may, for example, enjoy driving a car but realizes there are dangers attached to driving. Because he is mature, he regularly checks brakes, tires, lights, other essential parts of his car. An immature person may say and feel that "accidents never happen to me" and may take no precautions. Or, on the other hand, he may be the type of immature individual who checks his brakes daily and then nightly loses sleep worrying about the "fact" that "accidents always happen to me."

2. INDEPENDENCE. A mentally healthy person forms and acts on reasoned opinions. He is not reckless; he seeks a reasonable amount of advice. Once he has the facts, he is capable of making a decision and is willing to face the consequences of his decisions.

On the other hand, the immature person often has difficulty making up his mind. He wants others—relatives, friends, business associates—to tell him how to proceed. When forced to make his own decisions, he may become upset, nervous, even vicious. Many immature people refuse to accept responsibility for their decisions and blame others when something goes wrong, although they may demand inordinate praise if the decision leads to success.

3. ABILITY TO LOVE OTHERS.   A healthy, mature adult derives pleasure from bestowing love upon spouse, children, relatives, friends. He is selective in his love relationships and does not require a huge circle of people to be intimate with. On the other hand, the immature person has difficulty giving love and wants always to receive it, to be fussed over, and to be the center of attention. Young children want to be loved and the center of all affection; seldom does a small child show sustained love for others. This is part of normal development in children, but when it carries over into adulthood it interferes with healthy personal relationships. A healthy adult will expect to give more love to a child than the child is able to return.

4. REASONABLE DEPENDENCE ON OTHERS.   While a mature person can bestow love and affection, he also enjoys receiving them. A good love relationship in marriage must be based on the ability of both partners to give, and receive, love and sexual pleasure. The ability to share, to give and to receive love and friendship indicates that a person is flexible, adaptable, mature.

5. MODERATE ANGER AND HATE REACTIONS.   Any normal healthy person gets angry, of course, but keeps his anger within reasonable limits and doesn't indulge in temper tantrums. In work and other situations which he may not be able to control, he may have to curb his temper in the face of petty annoyances in favor of long-term values. The normal person can get stirred to fierce anger when the occasion demands. Such anger is very different from that of the person who goes into a temper tantrum because a storekeeper is unable to provide a desired item.

6. ABILITY TO MAKE LONG-RANGE CHOICES.   A mentally healthy person can give up immediate gratification for the sake of more lasting values. For example, a mature student working hard before examinations will refuse invitations to parties, forgoing the immediate pleasures to make a good showing on his examinations. Later, when it is appropriate, he may take a vacation as well as go to parties.

Similarly, a mature young couple, with educations to be finished and other needs to be met, may decide to postpone marriage for a time. They will consider all possibilities and alternatives rather than rush into an elopement without thought of the possibly greater happiness that a delay might bring.

7. RELAXED CONSCIENCE.   A normally healthy person accepts responsibilities, does his job well, and insists on and enjoys leisure hours and vacations. He and his conscience are at ease. The poorly adjusted person feels driven to accomplish things, rarely enjoys his work or leisure, al-

lows himself no real relaxation, spends weekends and vacations worrying about how things "could have been done better." The mature person enjoys leisure in restful ways so he returns to work refreshed. He may busy himself during leisure hours, but looks upon his activities then as hobbies, not more work.

8. GOOD ADJUSTMENT AT WORK.   A healthy person usually likes his work, does not change jobs very often, and when he does make a change it is on the basis of a realistic appraisal of the job and the chances of finding something else more rewarding. He will give up a job when there are health and accident hazards which are not being corrected or when the pay is substandard. But he will not change jobs merely because a supervisor or fellow worker may be difficult to get along with. He does not indulge in constant job hopping because the other side of the fence looks greener.

9. LOVE AND TOLERANCE FOR CHILDREN.   A healthy adult likes children and takes time to understand their special needs. He can almost always take a few minutes, no matter how busy he is, to play with a 3-year-old or to answer the questions of an older child.

10. GOOD SEXUAL ADJUSTMENT.   A healthy adult is not prudish, enjoys the sex act with a loved one, does not require additional stimulation from love affairs, achieves a satisfying orgasm, and can relax completely after the sex act.

Sexual adjustment has broader implications. It means accepting oneself as a male or female without conflict about the accident of birth.

11. ACCEPTANCE OF MASCULINITY AND FEMININITY.   This includes understanding the special problems of the other sex and accepting tolerantly and sympathetically some of the emotional difficulties these problems create. We refer, for example, to the still-existing "inferior status" of women and the "breadwinner" role of men, and the tensions these produce in an excessively competitive business world. For the healthy person, this tolerance toward, and appreciation of, those who are different from oneself extends not only to the opposite sex but to people of different racial, national, and cultural backgrounds.

12. CAPACITY FOR CONTINUED EMOTIONAL GROWTH.   The ability to keep learning and growing emotionally is characteristic of the healthy individual. This makes it possible to age gracefully, for wisdom and understanding can grow even though an individual may have passed his physical prime.

Does any one person possess all these qualities? Quite likely you can think of nobody who does. No one is perfectly healthy; perfection is rarely reached by humans. But these are goals to be sought throughout life.

And let us round out the picture. To be normal is not to be untouched by fears and conflicts.

Healthy People Are Human

There are limits to what even the best-adjusted can take. During wartime, it was clear that pilots, even the healthiest, could carry out just so many bombing missions before suffering combat fatigue. They recovered quickly if relieved of the unbearable tension. Some forms of stress are difficult for anyone to endure long.

And some forms of stress can be endured by one normal person and not by another. When not long ago a distinguished physician had to face a situation he knew would be difficult for even a doctor—the fatal illness of his only child—he sought help from a psychiatrist. He wanted help so he in turn could give the best help of which he was capable to his wife.

While pressures sometimes go to dramatic extremes, routine everyday life too can be frustrating and stressful. The business executive under pressure to make a profit, the student obliged to make good grades, the worker on an assembly line pressed to meet a quota—these and other people in many situations need to find acceptable outlets for daily pressures.

Normal people aren't all alike. Obviously, they do not have the same intellectual and physical endowments. There are different personality types as well. There are people who are introverted, absorbed in what goes on inside their own minds; there are others, extroverts, more interested in external events than in their own inner experiences. Dr. Karen Horney, a distinguished psychiatrist, defined three basic character types: those who move toward people, those who move against people, and those who move away from people. These might become, respectively, successful salesmen, competitive athletes, and philosophers—or, under unfortunate circumstances, playboys, gunmen, and recluses.

Normal people are influenced by unconscious motivations. Even before Freud, people often noticed, for example, that they forgot some things they did not want to remember, even though they had supposed they wanted to remember them. They knew that one could fall in love despite a conscious intention not to do so. In short, they knew that something went on under the surface of their awareness. Even a well-adjusted person does not, for example, fall in love in completely conscious fashion, although he is not ruled by his unconscious to such an extent that he falls in love with someone he knows to be completely unworthy of his affection.

Healthy men and women are subject to human tensions but they are able to find ways to relieve them without excessive anxiety. Among the ways they use:

Talking over worries with a sympathetic friend, relative, physician, or anyone else whose judgment they respect.

Getting away for a while, even if only for a short walk.

Working off anger, preferably by discussing it openly with a trusted, mature person; sometimes in some physical activity.

Taking one thing at a time, especially when feeling overwhelmed by the pressures of too much to do.

Giving in sometimes, even when certain they are right.

Helping others, getting out of the vicious circle that preoccupation with one's own troubles can produce.

Being slow with criticism.

Cooperating, being aware that though we live in a competitive society, many situations call for cooperative effort; and aware, too, that if one competes all the time, one may be too weary and too worn to enjoy success when it is achieved.

THE BASIC DISORDERS

A useful way to classify abnormal behavior is by dividing it into four broad categories: psychosomatic disorders, neuroses, character disorders, and psychoses. Although there can be some overlapping and intermixing, these four types of ailments can be examined separately.

Psychosomatic Disorders

These illnesses, which we have discussed in earlier chapters, are understandable to anyone who has ever had a headache after a fight with spouse or employer, or experienced butterflies in the stomach before taking an important examination. Occasional mild distress of this sort is universal and harmless. But some people experience such symptoms almost constantly, and their discomfort is intense. Psychosomatic illnesses can assume many forms, including skin outbreaks, stomach upsets, high blood pressure, and asthma. These are not imaginary problems; even when there is no physical cause, pain can be authentic and illness very real.

A person with an emotionally produced physical ailment needs psychological help, but he also is as much in need of medical help as the individual whose disease has organic roots.

Many psychosomatic illnesses reflect, symbolically, the underlying emotional problem. A child traumatized because of poor feeding by his mother may, as a man, experience chronic stomach troubles; a boastful but insecure actor may develop mouth ulcers which keep him from having to perform; a wife whose husband threatens to leave her may develop crippling arthritis.

From a technical standpoint, psychosomatic illness involves a disorder of some involuntary function, such as blood pressure, heart rate, digestion, which the individual is unable to control at will. When some function of the voluntary system, which normally responds to commands, is impaired, the condition is called a conversion reaction. Examples include paralysis of limbs by deep psychological shock sometimes seen in soldiers in battle and even loss of vision when the victim sees a friend killed on the battlefield.

Neuroses

Neurotics, unlike people with psychosomatic problems, usually do not develop clear-cut, tangible physical symptoms such as headaches or palpitations. Their problems have to do with their feelings.

If, occasionally, you leave home and have a feeling that you forgot to shut off the water in the kitchen sink or to turn off lights, and if you really believe you didn't forget and yet go back to check and make certain, you are not being abnormal. But neurotics can be continually bothered by such false alarms which use up their energy, hinder their efforts to work and lead normal lives, and fill them with a nameless dread.

Typically, a neurotic person doesn't know the source of his misery. Other people may be as worried or frightened but they can usually point to understandable reasons. The neurotic cannot. He worries when no worry seems called for, frets even in circumstances that should be relaxing. His behavior is not so much bizarre as inappropriate or exaggerated. It doesn't fit the apparent circumstances.

For example, a neurotic person, upon receiving a promotion, may feel glum instead of joyful. Where a normal person may be somewhat apprehensive about looking down from great heights or riding elevators, a neurotic may have phobias about these which terrify him.

Among neurotics are fanatically neat people, inveterate worriers always dwelling on the worst that can possibly happen, uncontrollable overeaters. Most neurotics get along; they earn their livelihood, frequently a handsome one, but at the cost of great effort and pain; have a home life (often dismal); and seem normal in some activities while markedly abnormal in others.

While a full-blown neurosis can be painful and make life miserable, still it may protect some people from things they unconsciously feel would make them even more miserable. A mother who is overly concerned about her children, constantly worrying over them, may in fact resent them but hides this feeling, which she cannot tolerate, by being overattentive.

Neuroses can be broken down into more than half a dozen types.

1. ANXIETY NEUROSIS.   In this type, the person experiences episodes of anxiety which may range from mild uneasiness to panic. Sometimes physical signs develop: sweating, dizziness, diarrhea, breathing difficulty, chest pain. The victim may feel tense and irritable, may awaken in the night in a state of terror. A characteristic feeling is one of "anxious expectation," the way one normally feels when something dreadful is about to happen, except that the victim of an anxiety neurosis may have no idea as to what the dreadful thing might be.

This state often is linked with a fear of losing love—for example, when there is a conflict in the unconscious mind between a desire to hate the loved one (perhaps to get even for having been hurt) and a desire to win that person's love.

Sometimes, the anxiety is shunted off by linking it with the situation in which it was experienced. If it occurred first in an elevator, the individual may blame the elevator, which he then fears and avoids in the hope of avoiding the anxiety.

2. PHOBIAS.   These can be divided into two types: common phobias, or exaggerated fears of things most people have some fear of, such as death; and specific phobias, or exaggerated fears of things that aren't in themselves ordinarily frightening, such as open fields. Psychiatrists usually exclude more realistic fears stemming from forgotten experiences, such as an adult fear of touching an electric cord because of a forgotten experience in childhood of receiving a severe shock from a defective cord. Phobias usually are rooted in guilt feelings, in fears that, having been "bad," something is bound to "get you."

The list of phobias is almost endless. Among them: *acrophobia*, the fear of high places; *agoraphobia*, of open spaces; *aichmophobia*, of sharp and pointed objects; *anthropophobia*, of people; *claustrophobia*, of enclosed spaces; *climacophobia*, of falling downstairs; *dromophobia*, of crossing the street; *hypnophobia*, of sleep; *kleptophobia*, of stealing; *mechanophobia*, of machinery; *monophobia*, of being alone; *mysophobia*, of dirt and contamination; *necrophobia*, of the dead; *nyctophobia*, of the dark; *pantophobia*, of everything; *phagophobia*, of swallowing; *syphilophobia*, of syphilis; *topophobia*, of situations (stage fright); *zoophobia*, of animals.

3. Hypochondria. In this condition, the mind's illness is manifested through abnormal preoccupation with body organs or functions. Afraid of, or convinced he suffers from, physical disease, the patient notices many body sensations, even those of normal fatigue, which do not concern other people. There is no physical cause for the condition, but merely assuring the patient that he is all right physically does not eliminate the hypochondriacal attitude.

4. Conversion Hysteria. This differs from hypochondria in that it produces a physical manifestation which, although not real in one sense, is certainly real to the individual. One example is hysterical paralysis, which may develop in a soldier undergoing severe conflict between a desire to be brave and a desire not to be killed. Suddenly he feels his legs paralyzed. He is not faking. Pins can be stuck in his legs and he has no feeling. Yet, when the conflict is resolved, either by circumstances or by the soldier himself, the paralysis vanishes.

5. Obsessive-Compulsive Neurosis. This leads people to do things without knowing why or without wanting to do them. The impulse stems from ideas that have no relationship in the individual's conscious mind. For example, a person always puts on a certain garment inside out. It is a kind of ritual, an appeal to magic powers, much like the knock on wood some people use. But the normal person who knocks on wood does so as a kind of joke because he has been told it is a lucky thing to do; a victim of neurosis sees no joke in his rituals, performing them because he is extremely insecure. As a child, he may have turned to his own "magic" rituals in a desperate attempt to cope with problems too great for him to handle.

6. Neurasthenia. The word means, literally, nerve weakness. It was once supposed that nerves in the brain could actually tire and that brain fatigue would result. Now it's known that neurasthenia, like hypochondria and conversion hysteria, is a product of emotional conflict. The patient honestly feels too weak or tired to get out of bed or even to think coherently. He can sleep for extended periods impossible for a well person, or can lie for hours doing nothing. Yet he is not physically ill; resting will not cure him; only solving his problems can lead to cure.

7. Neurotic Depression. It is not neurotic to experience unhappiness or depression on occasion—for example, when a loved one dies. It is normal to experience grief and to mourn; in fact, as we have seen earlier, this is an essential process.

Normal people do not grieve almost endlessly and to the point of melancholia, not because they are insensitive or superficial; their grief may be even more profound than that of badly adjusted people. But when the latter suffer from neurotic depression, they feel helpless; their low self-esteem convinces them they can never cope. These neurotic depressions are so closely bound up with feelings of insecurity and inadequacy that they can be triggered by events that well-adjusted people accept matter-of-factly. Such depressions cause great suffering.

8. DISSOCIATIVE NEUROSIS. Anxiety may cause a person to forget for a time who he is and what he is doing. When he regains awareness, he has forgotten what took place during the forgetful period. An extreme example of this neurosis is amnesia.

Character Disorders

A character disorder, also called behavior disorder, involves a lack of conscience or a pattern of conduct that violates the standards of social responsibility. People with the disorder do, indeed, behave as if they did not respect standards important to most people.

A character disorder may be harmful to society as well as to the individual. At the least serious level, a person with a character disorder may flunk out of school because he can't make himself care about studying. While this may trouble his family a great deal, the problem may not be considered socially very serious, since basically he alone is the real victim and because, too, there is some likelihood he may outgrow his immature behavior.

On the other hand, a person with a more serious character disorder may cause harm to others as well as to himself. He may lie, cheat, or steal even when he has no realistic need to do so. Or he may become a drug addict, alcoholic, or sex deviate.

Unlike most other emotionally troubled people, those with character disorders often feel no great anxiety or guilt about their behavior. Those who lack any normal sense of guilt or anxiety about socially destructive acts—whose passions enjoy free rein, who can tell right from wrong but pay no attention to the distinction—are called psychopaths.

Exactly why psychopaths act as they do, rejecting social criteria, is not clear. Several reasons have been suggested. Perhaps a psychopath has not yet developed an effective conscience but remains like a child: selfish, impulsive, shortsighted. Perhaps a psychopathic personality emerges as the result of growing up in a subculture or minority group that may not have the same values as society in general. This may be the case with some juvenile delinquents who believe that violent acts indicate manhood. Because of the difficulty sometimes in determining whether an individual with a character disorder is really emotionally sick or healthy but antisocial, some authorities use the term sociopath instead of psycho-path.

Unlike the neurotic individual whose unconscious conflicts carried over from childhood may show themselves in specific symbolic symptoms such as compulsive hand-washing, the psychopath is affected throughout his entire personality. To him, everyone else may appear to be wrong. The psychopath or sociopath may really believe that anyone who tries to live honestly and to maintain good relationships with other people is stupid.

Alcoholism and Drug Addiction

Alcoholics and drug addicts are chronically ill people whose ailments are manifested in their behavior. Unlike many people with mental conflicts, they have turned to something outside themselves to find in-adequate but temporarily satisfying easement. Far from solving their conflicts, they add extra, and serious, problems that result from excessive drinking or drug taking.

Much of the progress in treating alcoholism and drug addiction has been made possible by the recognition that the victims are sick people, not criminals (although crimes often are committed by addicts in order to obtain the funds needed to maintain their habit). See the chapters on alcohol and drugs.

Sexual Deviation

Physicians do not include among deviations or perversions all forms of sexual activity that vary from the usual. Broadly speaking, physicians consider a man or woman normal if he or she derives the highest sexual pleasure and satisfaction from the insertion of the male genital organ into the organ of the female.

Deviations are emotional illnesses, maladjustments, or immaturities which reveal themselves in the individual's sexual behavior. It was once felt that such behavior indicated that the individual was too weak to use willpower. Today, it is generally believed by psychiatrists that such be-havior results from emotional difficulties which must, if possible, be corrected, while at the same time the actions of deviates must be con-trolled in order to prevent them from harming themselves or others.

It may be important here to note that mature people often carry with them certain holdovers from childhood. If you find in yourself traces of some of the sexual deviations described, don't decide, for that reason, that you are perverted. Today, many normal persons engage in oral and other forms of sexual stimulation, perfectly acceptable so long as they increase love and trust between the sexual partners.

There are true perversions of sexuality. For example, a Peeping Tom derives his greatest sexual gratification from watching a woman undressed or undressing, or watching a couple engage in sexual activity. He is undoubtedly maladjusted, perhaps because in his childhood he had a shocking experience connected with his parents' sexual relations, or perhaps because he had been so strongly convinced of the wickedness of intercourse that he cannot permit himself to be involved actively but has to get his pleasure as an "innocent bystander." This does not mean, however, that anyone is perverted if he has not entirely outgrown a childish fascination with the forbidden. Most men, no matter how mature, find the glimpse of an accidentally revealed bosom exciting—more so, in fact, than complete nudity.

Deriving the highest, or only, satisfaction from watching or peeping is one form of sexual deviation. Following are some others:

HOMOSEXUALITY.   In some instances, homosexuality, which makes deep emotional and sexual attachment possible only with a member of the same sex, may be the result of glandular malfunction. Usually, however, it is of psychic origin. While many theories have been suggested to explain homosexuality, there is fairly general agreement along the following lines:

A child normally tends to identify with the parent of the same sex. A little girl wants to be like (and to rival) her mother; a boy, his father. If, for some reason, identification is with the parent of the other sex, the child may be oriented in the direction of homosexuality at an early age.

Homosexuality may also develop another way. Usually, for a time, shortly before and during early adolescence, children prefer members of their own sex. Boys enjoy being together, have male heroes, look down upon girls; girls "detest" boys, have crushes on girls, and love some "best friend" intensely. With the advent of sexual maturity, sexual drives are directed—not always without some conflict—toward members of the opposite sex.

During this difficult period, unfortunate experiences may have a devastating effect on some young people who have emotional problems. Whether the experiences are obvious or subtle, they set up a barrier on the road to normal sexual development. Homosexuality can be looked upon as a detour on that highway, and some people never find their way back to the main road, especially if their homosexuality has brought added problems of guilt and fear to confuse them.

Homosexuals often are lonely, unhappy people. They are certainly not to be regarded as wicked or depraved.

Amateur psychiatrists have done much harm by speaking too glibly about "latent homosexuality" and "bisexuality." To avoid needless worry, let us state emphatically: (a) A homosexual experience or even several experiences, especially during adolescence, do not mean that an individual is homosexual; nor does a homosexual dream or fantasy. (b) In any normal individual, there is a certain amount of basic homosexuality as a carryover from the period during which one preferred the company of one's own sex; perhaps this was expressed about as well as it can be by a high-school girl who remarked to her mother: "I'd ever so much rather be with girls except for the fact that men are so attractive." (c) Homosexuality is a complex problem and in itself only one aspect of a maladjusted individual's personality.

EXHIBITIONISM.   The act of revealing one's body, usually the genital organ, is essentially similar to "peeping." A certain amount of "showing off" is normal and not to be confused with the exhibitionism of a maladjusted person. The maladjusted individual may be attempting to reassure himself against fears of sexual inferiority or may be expressing defiance toward a seemingly hostile world by trying to shock people with his exhibitionism.

NARCISSISM, OR SELF-LOVE.   This is considerably different from self-respect and from the satisfaction any normal person derives from looking well. The term narcissism comes from the name of a Greek youth who, according to myth, saw his own reflection in a pond and became so enamored of it that he fell in and was drowned while trying to embrace himself. Most children go through a stage of being attracted to their own images in a mirror. They may remark, "You're pretty," and even, "I love you." People who do not outgrow this stage are often so basically insecure that they feel no one else will ever love them. This preoccupation is often accompanied by a preference for masturbation rather than sexual intercourse. Such people are incapable of loving anyone else. They may marry for money to spend on their true beloved ones—themselves.

NYMPHOMANIA AND SATYRISM.   Nymphomania (excessive desire in a woman for intercourse) and satyrism (excessive desire in a man) are rare. The terms often are mistakenly applied to promiscuous or highly sexed people but should be reserved for compulsive sexuality which cannot be satisfied. Such sexuality, like compulsive eating, often springs from insecurity and may be indulged in to ward off anxiety. Unable to find hoped-for release in intercourse, such people are driven desperately to try, try again. A nymphomaniac often is unable to experience orgasm, remaining unsatisfied no matter how often she has intercourse. She may be unconsciously homosexual and unable to find what she is seeking in any man, or she may unconsciously feel that intercourse is wicked and she must not enjoy it fully. The male equivalent may be similarly maladjusted; he may be an unconscious homosexual or have intense conflicts due to guilt, fear, or inferiority feelings.

BESTIALITY. Intercourse with animals is a practice fairly common among shepherds and others who are isolated from women. It has been reported by Kinsey that about 17 percent of all males raised on farms have had some sexual experience with animals. However, actual preference for sex relations with animals is due to an emotional maladjustment involving feelings of inferiority. Even a woman who showers affection on a pet may be afraid to bestow it on a fellow human being. She may tell herself that people are unworthy of her love, but she is actually afraid they will not appreciate her because she is unworthy.

SADISM AND MASOCHISM. Sadists derive sexual pleasure from inflicting pain, usually on their sexual partners. They want to prove their strength or virility by being aggressive or, for example, by emulating domineering fathers who used to punish them. Sadism may be expressed in forms other than sexual deviation. Teasing may be one. Children may be sadistic in their drive to assert themselves, though some seemingly sadistic actions by children are due to curiosity and lack of understanding. Thus, a child who pulls the wings off insects may have no idea that he is being cruel, since he may be acting from the same impulses that make him examine rocks and other inanimate objects.

Masochists derive sexual pleasure from being treated cruelly, from being hurt physically or emotionally, or from hurting themselves. They may unconsciously wish to be punished for some "sin."

Sadism has been called neurotic aggressiveness; masochism, neurotic submissiveness. Both spring from similar maladjustments and both may exist in the same individual. Masochism actually appears as a character attitude more frequently than it does as a sexual deviation.

SEXUAL CRIMINALITY. The term sex maniac is an unscientific one used to describe people who commit violent sex crimes such as rape. These are people with serious emotional disorders, however concealed they may have been before a crime was committed. The fact is that many of us have peculiar sex impulses; they are usually fleeting and we do not actually consider acting upon them any more than we do acting upon other transient notions that pop into mind, such as jumping from the top of a tall building. In some sex criminals, however, the control mechanisms that normal people possess are defective or break down. In others, deep-rooted feelings of guilt, inferiority, or insecurity may divert sexual instincts in abnormal directions that are socially dangerous.

Psychoses

People who suffer from the neuroses and other emotional illnesses previously described usually have a grasp on reality. They live in the real world and usually are able to get along in it, even if in awkward, suffering fashion. Psychotics—those who suffer from any of the several illnesses called psychoses—are farthest removed from rational behavior. They can no longer cope with reality or can do so only intermittently. They make up the greatest portion of the more than half-million persons in state, federal, and private mental institutions. Their actions often are absurd or grotesque, occasionally dangerous.

SCHIZOPHRENIA. This is the most common psychosis. It was once called dementia praecox (early loss of mind) because it often appears between the ages of 15 and 30. Schizophrenia means split mind but the illness is not simply a mental fragmentation. It is an extensive deterioration of the personality and a breaking away from reality, a retreat into an unreal world.

Schizophrenia manifests itself gradually as a rule, but it may show up abruptly as an acute attack of confusion. The individual becomes increasingly withdrawn, his emotions become distorted or fade.

Schizophrenia takes four forms. *Simple* schizophrenics are apathetic, inattentive, detached, indifferent to their surroundings. *Hebephrenics* escape from reality through infantile devices—baby talk, thumb-sucking, incontinence. *Paranoids* experience delusions of grandeur, considering themselves to be famous figures (the President, Napoleon, even God), or they suffer from ideas of persecution, convinced that they are being hounded, that someone is out to get them. *Catatonics* may sit motionless for hours or even days, totally unreachable, much like statues, refusing food, then suddenly they may go into a wild frenzy. (See also page 645.)

PARANOIA. This psychosis also is called monomania, delusional insanity, and persecutory insanity. Although a paranoid person is extremely ill, he may seem to act fairly normally. He may have adequate memory, logical reasoning, and show no apparent confusion, although his judgment is impaired. The disorder usually strikes between the ages of 30 and 50, particularly among individuals who have been suspicious, jealous, self-centered.

A victim of paranoia suffers increasing delusions, seeing hidden meanings in many things that convince him he is being plotted against—by such means as x-ray or hypnotism. Often, he feels he must defend himself by lawsuits or antisocial acts which may even include murder. Some paranoiacs are referred to as maniacs—for example, the pyromaniac who may set fire to buildings in order to destroy the "evil people" in them.

MANIC-DEPRESSIVE PSYCHOSIS. In this illness, there are alternating extreme moods—periods of mania, with grossly exaggerated feelings of well-being and elation, and supreme overconfidence; and periods of melancholia, with equally exaggerated feelings of misery during which a sense of profound, unjustified guilt may make the victim immobile.

Normal people have ups and downs of mood. The changes may be rhythmical in nature, alternating from day to day, sometimes within the same day. But such mood variations are quite different from the wild elation and profound unhappiness of manic-depressive psychosis.

INVOLUTIONAL MELANCHOLIA. There is no manic phase, no elation, in this psychosis; only severe depression. The disorder generally is associated with middle age when physical and social changes may lead a person to conclude that his or her usefulness is over. Melancholia amounts to an extreme exaggeration of normal fears about aging. It is accompanied by the danger of suicide. (See page 618 on menopause.)

Other personality types also show traits somewhat similar to those of psychotics. The *schizoid personality* keeps to himself as much as possible, is uncomfortable and nervous in company, daydreams extensively, and may find more pleasure in his fantasies than in the real world. The *paranoid personality* is suspicious of other people, though not to the point of believing they are actually plotting to harm him. It is very difficult to decide at what point these personality traits begin to pass over to genuine psychosis.

The psychoses mentioned above are believed by one school of psychiatrists to be functional—that is, they spring from psychological not organic causes. However, there is a growing conviction among some psychiatrists, particularly in the case of schizophrenia, that some subtle metabolic or chemical disturbance may be involved and that eventually the exact disturbance may be determined, allowing schizophrenia to be treated and perhaps even prevented through specific medical therapy.

Several mental disturbances spring directly from physical causes and are known as organic psychoses. Victims may have the same symptoms as those with functional psychoses, but their problem lies with physical damage to the brain by tumor, stroke, infection, or from other sources. The most common organic psychosis is the one that may accompany senility. Even when the basic problem is organic, there are often psychological ramifications which may require treatment. (See Aging, page 514.)

WHEN TO SEEK HELP

Advanced mental illness can be obvious enough, manifested in traits and actions so far from normal that there is no room for mistake. But the more subtle manifestations of mental illness in early stages, when treatment may be most effective, frequently are missed.

Symptoms alone can be misleading since there are circumstances when temporary mental or emotional distress is normal. Only a qualified expert is capable of properly diagnosing mental disorder. Yet there are some guidelines which often can be helpful in determining when diagnosis, and proper treatment, should be sought:

1. *Is a person's behavior appropriate?* When, for example, a man cries upon hearing very bad news, the crying is not unnatural. But crying in response to a commonplace everyday frustration, or any exaggerated or inappropriate reactions to daily happenings, may signal that trouble is brewing.

2. *Has there been any major change in traits or behavior?* A man who has been a jovial extrovert grows increasingly withdrawn and silent; a once-fastidious housewife becomes slovenly; a person who has tended to be somewhat miserly becomes a heavy spender—any striking change in long-established personality patterns and habits can be a warning.

3. *Can the individual give good reasons for his behavior?* Ask any healthy person why he does something and chances are great you will get a logical explanation. When, however, anyone has difficulty explaining his acts and feelings rationally, he may not be reacting to the real world but to imaginary circumstances and may be on the verge of mental illness.

4. *Can he control his actions?* As we have seen earlier, all of us quite normally experience dangerous urges fleetingly; we know better than to give in to them; we control our "crazy" ideas without difficulty. But people with some mental illnesses lose this ability, may see no need for control, may consider they are capable of doing things impossible for others. In any case, when an individual loses control, it may be more obvious to others than to himself.

5. *Has there been a loss of emotional vigor?* All of us have to face periods of crisis, times when because of grief over a personal loss (loved one, job opportunity, possession, etc.) we feel low. But if we are basically healthy, we regain our good spirits, shake off our depression. We have the emotional vigor and resilience to do so. Thus, a temporary state of depression in itself is no cause for suspicion, but when the depression lingers beyond a reasonable time, it may be well to seek help.

6. *Is the behavior harmful, destructive?* Any time an individual—child or adult, and if a child no matter how young—exhibits a continuous tendency to do damage to people, pets, property, or himself or herself, an emotional disturbance, possibly a serious one, is likely to be at work, and expert advice is needed.

While the sickest people are the most likely to get at least some kind of treatment, among people with less severe forms of psychological illness it is estimated that as few as 10 percent are getting help. Whether all need help is a question, since some appear to cope with their problems reasonably well, but it is generally felt that even those who do not urgently need help could often benefit from it.

THE SPECIALISTS

Perhaps in no other field of health has there been so much quackery as in mental health. Self-labeled experts flourish.

If at any time you need help for a mental illness or for what you have reason to believe may be an early developing emotional problem, you can best protect yourself against outright deception and incompetence by asking your physician's advice. He can usually decide the kind of specialist who could be most helpful and provide you with the names of several he knows to be competent.

Among the kinds of specialists he may choose from are the following:

A *psychiatrist* is a physician who specializes in mental and emotional disturbances. Along with basic medical education, he has had special training, including years of internship and residency, in diagnosis and treatment of emotional disorders. Preferably, he should be certified by the American Board of Psychiatry and Neurology, indicating that he has satisfied established requirements for training, experience, and competence.

A *psychoanalyst* is a psychiatrist schooled in the procedures of psychoanalysis. He has had special postgraduate study, usually at a training institution associated with the American Psychoanalytic Association. While psychoanalysts are psychiatrists, not all psychiatrists are analysts. There are also lay analysts who are not physicians; most often they are clinical psychologists who have had analytic training at a psychoanalytic institution.

A *neurologist* is a physician with special training in brain and nervous system problems. He is often of service when mental disorders stem from physical problems.

A *psychologist* is not a physician. He may be a "doctor" as the result of earning a doctorate in philosophy after extensive postgraduate work in the field of human behavior. Some psychologists teach; some do research work. A clinical psychologist works in the field of abnormal behavior and deals with patients. One of his important functions may be to administer psychological tests that may be helpful in diagnosing mental problems.

A *psychiatric social worker* generally serves as an important aide, providing rehabilitative counseling, keeping a patient's family informed, maintaining records. Often social workers with suitable backgrounds, including college education and postgraduate work leading to a master of

356 / Preventive Mental Care

social work degree, are trained to work with patients, providing psychotherapy, usually under the supervision of a psychiatrist.

It is important to note here that often your family physician himself may be able to help you. Don't hesitate to talk about yourself—your real self and your real problems—to your doctor. More and more family physicians today are interested in emotional as well as physical problems. Medical schools increasingly have been teaching psychiatric principles as a major part of medical training. Many general practitioners have taken special postgraduate training and are qualified to provide some of the forms of psychotherapy we will discuss shortly.

Actually, psychotherapy is a broad term which covers everything from the simplest "spilling out" of troubles to a wise friend to the long, detailed process of psychoanalysis.

And the fact is that virtually every doctor has always practiced some form of psychotherapy—quite often, in the past, without realizing it. In dealing with a patient who has an exaggerated fear that he is ill, the doctor's examination, explanation, reassurance, and firmness are forms of psychotherapy. When he helps a tense, nervous patient to find a hobby—that, too, is psychotherapy.

Physicians, of course, are human. Not all are emotionally constituted to be able to help with all kinds of problems which their patients face, even if they have the time. Try to size up your doctor. It is important to find someone with whom you will be personally in sympathy. Give your doctor a chance, and if you discover that the two of you do not click, you have a perfect right to find someone else. The best psychiatrists know that it is not possible to establish a good relationship with every patient. Knowing how important such a relationship is for the success of treatment, they sometimes even suggest that a patient change to someone else if the existing relationship is not sufficiently good.

TREATMENTS

There are three principal methods of treating mental and emotional illness today—psychological, physical, and social.

Psychological Treatments

Psychotherapy is the overall term for psychological forms of treatment. While there are many definitions, essentially psychotherapy involves discussion, probing, evaluation, advice, and other treatment given through the medium of words. Psychotherapy itself does not include use of medicines or other physical treatment, though any of these may be used as an adjunct.

Usually, in psychotherapy, patient and therapist sit down in a quiet room; sometimes the patient may lie on a couch. The therapist encourages the patient to speak freely about himself and his feelings. Often, as the patient does so and the therapist interprets and makes suggestions, the patient begins to see himself and his problems more clearly; he may lose some of his inordinate fears as he understands his problems better; he may soon experience completely different feelings about old problems.

Psychotherapy may aim simply at relieving a temporary state of depression, and sometimes this may even be accomplished in as little as half an hour; or, at the other extreme, it may aim, over a period of years, at making fundamental changes in personality.

A process called ventilation may be used in brief psychotherapy. It amounts, seemingly simply, to letting a troubled person blow off steam. Yet, when it is done properly by a therapist trained in its use, ventilation alone may permit a relatively healthy person facing a minor crisis to dislodge his feelings of gloom or panic and his inability to do anything constructive and restore his usual self-control.

When emotional problems are more serious and ventilation is not enough, reassurance may be added. This is authoritative, informed reassurance. Particularly dramatic examples of how effective it sometimes can be came during the Korean conflict. Most soldiers who had to be taken out of the line because of acute combat nerves could return to action after a few brief sessions with a psychiatrist. In addition to encouraging them to talk frankly about their fears and guilt feelings, the psychiatrist could reassure them that virtually every officer and soldier is secretly afraid.

In psychotherapy, the patient—because he is aware that the therapist has no personal bias and is specially informed about psychological problems as no friend or family member is—can take advice and suggestions he would not accept from others (for example, on settling marital disagreements or problems with children).

Encouragement and support are also tools of brief psychotherapy, and when skillfully used often can be effective.

Reparative psychotherapy, as it is sometimes called, may be used when measures such as ventilation and reassurance are not enough and when some corrections or repairs of personality may be required.

Beyond helping the individual to develop a new and better perspective on problems he knows he faces, reparative psychotherapy makes an effort to look at problems the individual may not be aware of. As in ventilation, the patient is encouraged to speak out about his problems and feelings. As he does so, the therapist tries to gain some insight into what is left unspoken—the unconscious problems and motives that bother the patient.

The therapist, as he himself gains the insights, may provide the patient with interpretations and understanding, although there may be no attempt, because of the extended period that might be required, to develop full understanding on the part of the patient.

The skill comes in providing enough practical understanding for the patient to digest and sometimes, too, in helping to alter the patient's living situation. Thus, for example, a domineering and difficult woman may be directed into a job in which she can express some of her domineering qualities. The therapist may well discuss with her the fact that by taking such a job she may make life easier for her husband and children and, in so doing, for herself as well. But there may be no effort to go into, or even once discuss, the fact that her domineering characteristics may have roots in a deeply buried resentment that she is a woman instead of a man.

Group therapy is a method of treatment coming into increasing use. Four to ten patients may be treated during the same therapy period. Some psychiatrists combine group therapy with individual sessions as well; others use group therapy alone. Group sessions can be valuable because patients react to each other as well as to the doctor and because their self-confidence is increased by being with people whose problems are similar to their own. For example, obese people who overeat for psychological reasons may respond well to group therapy. Alcoholics Anonymous, which has a high success rate, uses some of the principles of group therapy. Its members encourage, advise, and exhort each other. They are kept sober by the support of the group, so that even though there may be no basic change in their personalities, there is vast change in their habits.

Group therapy is used in many kinds of institutions as well, including rehabilitation centers for adolescent boys, veterans' hospitals, and prisons. There are many variations in approach, but all forms of group therapy are based on the principle that humans are social beings, influenced greatly by groups to which they belong.

Family therapy is another method in increasing use. Just as an individual has, a family has its values, principles, goals, and problems. Perhaps only one member of a family appears to be in trouble, but the relationships within the family group may have much to do with that trouble and may have to be examined. In family therapy, the entire family may work out with a therapist its conflicts and difficulties through discussions, much as an individual does in individual therapy. Family treatment has attracted the interest not only of psychiatrists but also of social agencies and of the federal government, which supports research projects in this area.

Play therapy is a form of psychotherapy adapted to children. Anyone who has tried to help an emotionally disturbed child knows how difficult it is to get him to talk about his problems. But often the child reveals himself, far better than he could by talking, when he plays with toys and acts out his fantasies. The therapist helps him get things out of his system, accepting him warmly as he is and guiding him toward a solution of his problems. Since these are related to the way he is treated at home, play therapy is often combined with some form of therapy (frequently, group) for the parents.

Psychoanalysis, or reconstructive psychotherapy, has the most ambitious objective of any form of psychological treatment. Freud was the originator but there are now many other schools of psychoanalysis. There are differences in the number of sessions per week, their length, and the total period of treatment. But all try to help the patient examine his thought and behavior patterns, uncover his concealed problems and wounds, and rebuild his personality structure along more healthful lines.

Free association is used to help the patient bring into his conscious mind the unconscious forces that influence him. While he is with the analyst, the patient tries to speak freely of everything that comes into his mind, no matter how irrelevant or shameful it may seem. The sequence of these thoughts may reveal to the analyst the unconscious connections and help explain the source of trouble.

In the course of these sessions, transference takes place. That is, the patient tends to react to the analyst in ways he reacted or still reacts to important figures in his life, usually his parents. Since the analyst is a neutral type of figure, the patient can see his own patterns of reaction. For example, a patient might be able to rationalize his fear of a neighbor by saying the neighbor is after his job or his wife. In analytic sessions, unable to find a reason for a similar fear of the analyst, he may then discover that it springs from his unconscious mind, and later may realize that it was actually a concealed fear of his father carried over from childhood.

Day after day, month after month, as the patient acts and speaks in neurotic, immature ways, the analyst helps him examine his feelings and responses. And slowly the patient becomes aware of what is and is not rational and appropriate, and why he thinks and acts irrationally. With this, he begins to think and talk in healthier fashion and, fortified by little pieces of success, becomes increasingly able, over a period of time, to function in a more mature manner.

Psychoanalysis is expensive, often exhausting. But when, after years, it works well, it can be highly rewarding (though there is no guarantee of a completely successful result in all cases).

Medical Therapy

Since 1955, when the first two tranquilizing medicines, chlorpromazine and reserpine, were introduced int United States mental institutions, revolutionary changes have taken place. These new therapeutic compounds often changed the wild, reckless, abusive, or confused behavior of patients to such an extent that they could be given considerable liberty. Some psychotics, especially the more recently admitted, improved so rapidly that they could leave the hospital in a few weeks.

It is now apparent that a brief course of treatment with tranquilizers is seldom enough for permanent cure, but the medicines are of tremendous value in making many psychotic patients, previously unreachable, amenable to psychotherapy. And continued maintenance doses of them allow thousands of patients to function in the community.

Similarly, severely depressed patients may be treated with another type of compound—a central nervous system stimulating or mood-elevating agent. There is a whole family of such agents which have helped to cut short what could otherwise be long-drawn-out and even permanent depressive states.

As yet, exactly how the "mind medicines" accomplish their work is not understood. It may be, as some physicians suggest, that in effect they help much as do antibiotics. As we have seen earlier, when the body is injured, it tends to heal itself, unless a wound or infection is overwhelming. An antibiotic helps not by curing the disease but by changing the odds, helping to control the infectious organisms, giving the body a chance to muster its defenses and then to heal. In mental illness, the mind medicines probably produce no cures on their own, but by reducing the intensity of fears, wild ideas, and hallucinations, they may give the mind an opportunity to heal itself.

That same type of effect may explain the value of other methods of treatment. Shock treatment, for example, can be considered to produce a temporary respite which may allow self-healing to take place. Electric shock and insulin coma are the most frequently employed forms of shock therapy. The patient is rendered unconscious by a carefully controlled electric shock or dose of insulin. Shock therapy, especially when followed by psychotherapy, has been successful in severe depression, particularly involutional melancholia, and in schizophrenia.

Despite the ability of mind medicines to make psychoses recede, they are of only limited value in the treatment of neuroses. With the medicines, the neurotic patient remains what he is but doesn't feel as bad —until the medicines wear off.

Psychosurgery may be employed, usually only in otherwise unyielding cases of mental illness. Psychosurgery stems from observations that soldiers and others who had suffered head injuries of a kind that severed the connection between the two parts of the brain, without injuring either part, sometimes underwent marked improvement in personality and experienced significant lessening of tension. This is what the surgeon does—carefully sever the connections between the two parts of the brain —when he performs an operation called lobotomy.

Social Treatment

For social treatment, the patient is placed in a sheltered environment, such as a mental hospital, where there is a deliberate effort to provide him with many reassuring, friendly, useful experiences. He is drawn into games, work, other daily activities. The idea is that through many encouraging human contacts he can be rescued from his private nightmare and brought back, bit by bit, to a real world, one that, in the sheltered environment at least, is friendly, interesting, not as alarming as the one from which he fled. Like medicines, social treatment gives him some relief from the noxious thoughts that have ruled his life, helps him to rebuild himself, and helps him to visualize himself again as a person relating to other people.

To achieve this, private hospitals and public institutions provide trained people to talk, play, and work with the patient. The whole hospital becomes a therapeutic environment or milieu.

Behavior Therapy

A new technique called behavior therapy is arousing considerable interest. It is used to help people with phobias of various kinds and is, on the psychological level, a treatment somewhat akin to the desensitization treatment used for hay fever and other allergies. The objective in allergy treatment is to build up resistance by means of injections of small, gradually increasing doses of pollens or other materials to which a patient is sensitive. In behavior therapy, the patient identifies his fears and he lists, in order of increasing severity, the situations that provoke the fears. He is then taught a technique of deep muscle relaxation and, while relaxed, is presented with an imaginary situation based on the least fear-provoking item on his list. The situation is presented repeatedly at intervals of about half a minute until it no longer evokes fear. Then, progressively stronger fear-provoking situations are presented until even what were the most frightening in the past no longer cause fear. When the patient stops reacting fearfully to imaginary situations, he may be freed of fear in real situations.

Behavior therapy, which may be completed in about a dozen sessions, has been reported to be highly effective for phobias, producing apparently complete recovery or marked improvement in about 87 percent of patients.

New Facilities for Help

For centuries, victims of mental disease were treated little better, and sometimes even worse, than animals—tied in chains, hidden away in filthy institutions, with virtually no chance for recovery, released only by death. Today, the situation is entirely different. It would be too much to say that all of our public mental institutions routinely use all the modern forms of treatment that might rescue many inmates, but more and more do so.

Moreover, before tranquilizers and other medicines came along, few general and community hospitals would admit patients with emotional problems because their behavior could be disturbing and even frightening to other patients. Now most do admit them and have staff and facilities to treat them. Some have special psychiatric units for those who need inpatient care. Others admit emotionally ill patients to regular medical wards. In both cases, inpatient treatment is directed at helping the patient to get over his problem in a matter of weeks.

In addition, many hospitals now have special provisions for patients who do not require inpatient care around the clock. There are, for example, night hospital provisions which make it possible for a patient to work or go to school by day and be hospitalized and treated by night.

Psychiatric outpatient clinics and community mental health centers have been springing up. For patients who can afford it, the private mental hospital often can provide excellent treatment and care. And, of course, mental and emotional problems may be treated in a specialist's private office.

Which Treatment?

Some forms of treatment take longer than others, and it is impossible to make any valid blanket statement as to which is likely to be of most benefit to various types of people who need help. Perhaps a parallel from the field of surgery can help explain why. Lancing a boil is a simple surgical procedure compared with correcting a congenital hip dislocation. A family physician would probably feel competent to handle the first but not the second. Yet the person with the boil may be suffering acutely while the person with the dislocated hip may get along quite well. The distress caused by a condition, physical or emotional, is not always a sound indication of how long and complicated may be the method needed to relieve it.

As we have noted, soldiers with severe emotional disturbances have recovered after only a few sessions of superficial psychotherapy. As another example of how little treatment may be needed, an intelligent young college girl was visited at one point by her parents who became alarmed at what they termed a "nervous breakdown" in the girl. As it turned out, the girl had fallen in love, wanted to marry, yet that desire was in conflict with her wish to complete her education, which she knew meant a good deal to her parents. Her hesitation led to a quarrel with her sweetheart, who said things that hurt her. Angry with him, she unconsciously blamed him for the predicament she was in, yet loved him. She began to experience anxiety feelings. Fortunately, she discussed her problem with a fine clergyman at college. Because she was basically a well-adjusted person, the process of talking it out was enough in itself to help her recover quickly from her temporary neurotic state, and she was able to face the real problems confronting her and her young man. The soldiers and the girl were both in acute distress yet found relief quickly.

On the other hand, another case might be compared with that of the person with a hip dislocation. An intelligent and successful businessman in his forties had had an early marriage which had ended in divorce. One of us had known him personally and had had no idea there was anything bothering him. But at one meeting at the home of mutual friends, the subject of psychiatry and analysis had come up. And, as we were to learn later, he had shortly afterward consulted a psychiatrist who had recommended analysis for him.

To put it briefly, he had become an extremely lonely man, unable to form any close relationships with others, especially of the kind that might lead to marriage, though he considered marriage desirable. His fears and suspicions of other people had reached the point where he would refuse invitations he wanted to accept, would walk or take taxis rather than ride in public conveyances close to other people, and found it increasingly difficult to have friendly dealings with his business associates.

"My analysis has taken five years, but it's worth it," he could report later. "I can't tell you how different, how much better, my life has been since I no longer feel the way I used to . . . as though I was living in enemy territory and had to be constantly on guard."

As these cases help to indicate, the type of therapy needed depends upon many things—on the individual and how deep-rooted his problems are and also on the goal. In some cases, a cure will be rapid, since the aim is to eliminate just one or a few symptoms, as when, for example, an otherwise well-adjusted person has developed a recent tendency to insomnia. In other cases, a basic change in attitudes is essential. Only a qualified professional, after personal contact with and evaluation of an individual, can validly suggest the type of treatment that would be most suitable.

But the point is this: Unresolved emotional problems are the basis for much mental anguish and for much physical torment. That fact is very clear today. And society's attitudes have changed, too; there is no longer any shame (there never should have been) in having an emotional problem and in seeking help for it. Help is increasingly available, and effective, and quite often relatively inexpensive. Few people, if any, would not be willing to spend the time and money to be cured of tuberculosis or to have an operation to remove a cancerous growth. Surely, it is worthwhile to invest the same amount of time and money to overcome a crippling emotional illness.

It is important to emphasize that such an illness—even when the person suffering from it feels that he can take it—can have serious effects on others, especially spouse and children. Also, it is hardly wise to put off getting help in order to save money, since delay usually increases the amount of treatment needed.

It is true, of course, that some people just do not have the money for psychiatric treatment. Yet there are clinics at large hospitals and medical schools, and mental hygiene clinics operated by various social agencies, which often can provide therapy you might not otherwise be able to afford. Your family physician usually can provide information about such clinics. In special instances, the following organizations may be helpful:

American Association of Marriage Counselors, 270 Park Avenue, New York, N.Y. 10017.

The National Council on Family Relations, 5757 Drexel Avenue, Chicago, Ill. 60637. (This service agency publishes a monthly journal, *Marriage and Family Relations.*)

Alcoholics Anonymous (National), Box 459, Grand Central Annex, New York, N.Y. 10017.

The National Committee on Alcoholism, 2 East 103 Street, New York, N.Y. 10029

The National Save-A-Life League, 505 Fifth Avenue, New York, N.Y. 10017 (This organization offers help to people who consider suicide a way out of their difficulties.)

In addition, you may have use for the following Directory of Mental Health Agencies:

A Directory of Mental Health Agencies *

Federal Agencies
Children's Bureau, U.S. Department of Health, Education and Welfare, Washington, D.C. 20201.

* Address a letter to the "Director" of any of the organizations listed, together with your request for information or help. The title of the organization will tell you the type of work it engages in.

Exceptional Children and Youth, Office of Education, U.S. Department of Health, Education and Welfare, Washington, D.C. 20202.

National Institute of Mental Health, U.S. Department of Health, Education and Welfare, Bethesda, Md. 20014.

Office of Vocational Rehabilitation, U.S. Department of Health, Education and Welfare, Washington, D.C. 20201.

National Organizations (Private)

American Occupational Therapy Association, 250 W. 57 St., New York, N.Y. 10019.

American Psychiatric Association, 1700 18th St., N.W., Washington, D.C. 20009.

American Psychoanalytic Association, 1 E. 57 St., New York, N.Y. 10022.

American Psychological Association, 1333 Sixteenth St., N.W., Washington, D.C. 20036.

National Association for Mental Health, 10 Columbus Circle, New York, N.Y. 10019.

National Association for Retarded Children, 386 Park Ave. S., New York, N.Y. 10016.

National Association of Social Workers, 2 Park Ave., New York, N.Y. 10016.

National Council on Family Relations, 1219 Woodcliff Drive, Madison, N.Y. 07940.

State Mental Health Associations

Alabama Association for Mental Health, Box 3283, 901 18th St., South Birmingham, Ala. 35205.

Arizona Association for Mental Health, 15 W. Thomas Road, Phoenix, Ariz. 85013.

Mental Health Society of Northern California, 2015 Steiner St., San Francisco, Calif. 94115.

Southern California Society for Mental Hygiene, 3067 W. 7 St., Los Angeles, Calif. 90005.

Connecticut Association for Mental Health, 956 Chapel St., New Haven, Conn. 06510.

Mental Health Association of Delaware, 1404 Franklin St., Wilmington, Del. 19806.

Florida Association for Mental Health, 122 Wall St., Orlando, Fla. 32801.

Georgia Association for Mental Health, 502 Kempner Bldg., 41 Exchange Place, Atlanta, Ga. 30303.

Idaho Mental Health Association, 615 S. 20 Ave., Caldwell, Idaho 83605.

Illinois Association for Mental Health, 123 W. Madison St., Chicago, Ill. 62060.

Indiana Association for Mental Health, 615 N. Alabama, Indianapolis, Ind. 46204.

Iowa Association for Mental Health, 528 Flynn Bldg., Des Moines, Ia. 50309.

Kansas Association for Mental Health, 10th & Van Buren, Topeka, Kan. 66612.

Kentucky Association for Mental Health, c/o *The Courier-Journal*, Louisville, Ky.

Louisiana Association for Mental Health, 816 Hibernia Bank Bldg., New Orleans, La. 70112.

Mental Hygiene Society of Maryland, 317 E. 25 St., Baltimore, Md. 21218.

Massachusetts Association for Mental Health, 41 Mt. Vernon St., Boston, Mass.

Michigan Society for Mental Health, Room 645, 153 E. Elizabeth St., Detroit, Mich. 48128.

Citizens Mental Health Association of Minnesota, 309 E. Franklin Ave., Minneapolis, Minn. 55404.

Missouri Association for Mental Hygiene, 1210 E. University St., Springfield, Mo. 65804.

Montana Society for Mental Hygiene, 315 Spruce St., Anaconda, Mont. 59711.

New Jersey Association for Mental Health, 240 W. Front St., Plainfield, N.J. 07060.

New York State Society for Mental Health, 105 E. 22 St., New York, N.Y. 10010.

North Carolina Mental Hygiene Society, Box 2599, Raleigh, N.C. 27602.

North Dakota Mental Health Association, 1006 9th St., Bismarck, N.D. 58501.

Ohio Mental Health Association, 83 So. High St., Columbus, O. 43215.

Mental Health Association of Oregon, 429 Park Bldg., Portland, Ore.

Pennsylvania Mental Health, Inc., 1 North 13th St., Philadelphia, Pa. 19107.

Rhode Island Society for Mental Hygiene, 100 No. Main St., Providence, R.I. 02903.

South Carolina Mental & Social Hygiene Society, Charleston County Health Department, Charleston, S.C.

South Dakota Mental Health Association, 827 S. Dakota Ave., Sioux Falls, S.D. 57104.

Tennessee Mental Hygiene Association, c/o Dr. Joe Johnson, Interstate Bldg., Chattanooga, Tenn. 37402.

Texas Society for Mental Health, 2410 San Antonio St., Austin, Texas. 78705.

Utah Association for Mental Health, 112 So. State St., Salt Lake City, Utah 84111.

Vermont Association for Mental Health, c/o Mr. James Young, Department of Social Welfare, Montpelier, Vt. 05602.

Virginia Association for Mental Health, 1105 W. Franklin St., Richmond, Va. 23220.

Washington Association for Mental Health, 408 Seaboard Bldg., Seattle. Wash. 98101.

Wisconsin Association for Mental Health, 119 E. Washington Ave., Madison, Wisc. 53703.

34

PREVENTIVE PSYCHIATRY

FAMILY DOCTORS and pediatricians are often asked by prospective parents and actual parents: "How can we guarantee that our children will grow up free of emotional illness?" This is a logical question in an age when we can guarantee protection against polio and many other serious or unpleasant diseases. Unfortunately, we don't have vaccines to prevent development of abnormal personalities, neuroses, and psychoses. Some doctors even take a completely negative attitude; they feel that there is not enough knowledge to give any valid advice on prevention of mental disorder. However, most physicians, psychologists, and child educators believe that there are useful guidelines.

We believe that a child has a better chance to develop the type of normal personality we have outlined previously if certain guidelines are followed. And we go along with the thinking of those psychiatrists who believe that if there are any hereditary or familial tendencies to emotional breakdowns, the individual with a sturdy personality can fight them off or, if afflicted, will have a better chance of recovery.

We believe that of overriding importance are the basic attitudes of mother and father. When parents are loving and relaxed, there is usually a good future for a child. Even babies sense love, poise, and acceptance in their parents, especially the mother. The mother's voice and touch are appreciated by the baby at an early age. If they are loving, warm, positive, the baby has a good start.

When a mother is loving, eager to have her child grow into a happy, resourceful human being, and has realistic hopes for him, the child's upbringing and future are likely to be soundly based. Even though mistakes almost certainly will be made, they will be offset by a strong "bank balance" of loving, normal, good care.

Because the first year of life, even the earliest days and weeks, are important, planning during pregnancy is important. It is often helpful for new parents to take a course in baby care. If a rooming-in arrangement —one in which the baby can be close to the mother (and shared by the father)—can be arranged in your particular hospital, we think it a good idea. Sometimes, a little extra pressure on the obstetrician may make this possible.

We think breast feeding brings mother and child into a close, warm emotional relationship. However, if it is not feasible, the mother should cuddle the child closely so that bottle feeding has much the same overall physical feel for the baby as breast nursing.

If circumcision is desired, it should be arranged in the hospital before taking the baby home. Later in life, this minor operation may have major emotional importance.

Prolonged separation from parents, especially from the mother, in the first year of life (and later, too) can be the basis for later psychological problems. Separations should be avoided if at all possible. When unavoidable because of illness, divorce or death, a parent substitute should be introduced as soon as possible. The substitute should have the qualities of a good mother or father. Introduction of the baby to the new person should be made gradually because even a grandparent may rank as a total stranger to a child.

After breast or bottle feeding has been settled upon, there should be a decision about demand versus scheduled feeding. We favor letting the baby's hunger set the schedule rather than having the clock prevail. However, that does not mean that the mother must be a slave to every first whimper from a baby. Infants *are* capable of tolerating some minor frustrations.

Teething sometimes may be traumatic. Extra cuddling and affection at this time can be helpful. In some cases, the doctor may need to determine whether dental intervention may be required.

The baby with frequent and severe colic has a hard time, as do the parents. Many pediatricians would be glad to prescribe paregoric or other suitable medicine for relief of the colicky pain but are afraid that the parents may feel that they are "doping" the baby. If your baby is colicky, have a good talk with your doctor about providing relief.

Weaning is an important event for the baby. Weaning should be gradual and, if possible, at a time when the parents, particularly the mother, can spend extra time with the child. If in doubt about the technique, go over the details with the baby's doctor.

The baby should be introduced cautiously to water, whether it is for bathing, hairwashing, or actual swimming. Children vary enormously in their fears about the feel and look of water.

During the period of toddling and early walking—when the child begins to explore his room and his "world"—parents need to encourage his curiosity while protecting him from danger. Wise parents, building a secure emotional life for the child, will avoid the constant repetition of "No, no." They will try as much as possible to hide dangerous articles, provide reasonably safe play areas, safeguard beds, shield electrical outlets, put gates on stairways, etc.

To satisfy a child's natural curiosity and desires, a play space should be provided with a "messy area" where there will be opportunity to experiment with wet clay, sand, and paper.

A friendly puppy or kitten may prove a great asset at this stage of life.

Eating habits worry too many parents needlessly. If you stay relaxed, you will find that the child will settle down to an adequate diet. If not, rather than become a nagging parent, discuss diet with your doctor.

Toilet training. The handling of toilet training can be an important determinant of personality. During World War II, Navy doctors were so impressed by the relaxed behavior of Okinawan civilians under bombardment that they studied the personality backgrounds of these people. The significant factor seemed to be that the Okinawan child was permitted to set his own pace for toilet training. Children vary in the development of brain areas and nerve pathways involved in the complex reflexes required for urination and bladder control. Our advice is to consult your child's doctor; he knows at what pace the child is developing and can make a good estimate of the date when toilet training should be started.

Talking. There is big variation in the time when children begin to talk. Don't worry because a neighbor's or relative's child may talk at a very early age, earlier than your own child. But if you are getting nervous about your child's timetable, discuss this with your doctor.

"Abnormal" curiosity. A child is curious about everything. That includes genitals, feces, urine as well as more acceptable objects in the unfolding world around him. Let him explore. Don't shame him. If he gets too messy, distract him gently.

Social experiences. Introduce your child to other children gradually. Do it at play places, at home, in playgrounds. This is especially important for an only child.

Nursery school. One of us wrote some years ago that if he had to make a choice because of limited tuition funds between nursery school and college for a child, he would choose nursery school. He was thinking of a really good nursery school with trained, sympathetic teachers who supplement the efforts of parents in the important years between age 3 and 6.

Identification with parents. Many psychiatrists believe that in the 3- to 6-year age period, a struggle goes on in the inner, unconscious minds of children and that it has important bearings on later emotional health. At this time, the boy struggles unconsciously to supplant his father in his mother's affections, and gradually to identify with the father; the girl undergoes a similar reverse situation. This "oedipal conflict" may help determine how a boy or girl will feel later in life about the male or female role.

During this important period, parents should not make favorites of children, should be careful not to appear to be seductive, should exclude the child from the marital bed, and should exercise care that the child has no opportunity to view their sexual activities. It is best not to take baths together nor to share the bathroom with children at this age.

Vacations. Separation from home during vacations can be a positive or negative influence depending upon the child's readiness for the experience. Overnight camp is a big dislocation for a young child and should be undertaken with caution. And remember that a vacation with grandparents may seem natural to you but a child may view them as strangers.

Movies and TV. Parents should guard against making babysitters out of TV programs or movies. No one really knows how much influence these media are having on the emotional development of our children. But it surely seems sensible for parents to select programs carefully for the very young child.

Birth of a new baby. A child may fear displacement when a new baby arrives. It is a challenge to parents to make the child feel even more loved and to give him a sense of participation in the care of the new arrival. Parents should consider nursery school or other activities for the child long before the baby is born to challenge his place.

Beginning of school. This is a big event in the emotional life of a child, especially for one who has not gone to nursery school. Extra love, support, and praise should be given him as he makes this big adjustment. The parents should become part of the school life through visits, parent-teacher activities, etc.

Some experts on child rearing believe that personality is relatively fixed by the time a child starts school. We disagree, even though we believe strongly that the early years are highly important. We believe that personality is constantly developing and changing as life proceeds, and that only death marks the end of personality and emotional change for a human being.

From the beginning of school until puberty there is a quieter period in the emotional life, the so-called latency period, when the child undergoes fewer upheavals and is usually highly receptive to education at school and at home. This is the calm before the storm. Then come puberty, adolescence, and the teen-age years.

Until adolescence, there will be no doubt of a child's dependence on the parents. Now, however, the situation becomes ambivalent. The child lives at home but begins to feel the powerful biological and social drives that will transform him into an adult.

During these stormy years, personality will be molded by the outcome of explorations and reactions to

Dating and petting experiences
For the girl, menstruation (treated elsewhere in this book); for the boy, growth of sex organs and the occurrence of wet dreams
Masturbation
Homosexual feelings, activities, and fantasies
Sex drives toward the opposite sex
Acceptance or rejection by classmates of both sexes
Athletics and other school activities
Scholastic achievement
Some degree of rebelliousness with parents, teachers, police
Experimentation with drugs, cigarettes, alcohol
Part-time jobs and summer activities
Handling of money, budgeting, use of own or family car

Surely, we haven't listed all the possible critical factors of the lively teen years. We can only hope that these and other problems will be discussed by parents and children, because their resolution in a positive, healthy way will do much to prevent mental illness. We suggest that parents and children read the wise book by Haim Ginott, *Between Parent and Teenager.* When parents and teen-agers cannot achieve open discussion and communication, they should find a mature, sympathetic person who can provide guidance (and referee misunderstandings and quarrels). A teacher, clergyman, doctor, relative, or school counselor may be just such a person. A visit to a psychiatrist may be needed in some cases when personality problems become severe—for example, when a child wants to drop out of school, begins to use drugs regularly, exhibits cravings for alcohol.

Nineteen is the last teen year but hardly the end of emotional strains and growth. There follows the period when major decisions must be made about career and marriage. Surely, almost every expert on personality would agree that a rewarding job in which the individual is happy is great insurance for mental health. This, of course, is a good argument for obtaining the right education to open up a wider choice of career possibilities.

A secure, happy marriage can be a bulwark against emotional problems. We deal with marriage later. Let us stress that marriage is so important that the decision to enter into it should be based on mature judgment, not entirely on romance. Remember that more and more marriage counselors are helping people before marriage with advice about possible suitability and compatibility and by giving them realistic previews of problems to be faced.

Marriage can help assure a healthy mental and emotional life if there are true love, acceptance of each other's good and weak points by the mates, and a happy, fulfilling sexual life. Marriage should continue to grow as a creative experience and not settle into "dullsville."

Because marriage is so important in preventing emotional problems, at the first sign of significant marital trouble there should be a talk with a marriage counselor. Sometimes a single session will work wonders. (See page 327 for further discussion of marriage.)

Pregnancy and the arrival of children. Pregnancy can set off emotional problems. We have a section on pregnancy. The coming of the first child and then of later children expectably changes the quality of marriage. It should deepen ties. But each partner needs to realize that the other, deep down, wants and needs reassurance that a child hasn't usurped all love.

If pregnancies and the coming of children go well, what then can threaten the emotional stability of adults? Here are several situations that cause tension and sometimes serious emotional disturbances:

Loss of job or business reverse. We have known people who have lost fortunes and made them again. Nothing disturbs their inner conviction that they will succeed in their work. On the other hand, we have seen emotional disturbances develop at the threat of a change of job or a small temporary reverse in a man's business venture. Such disturbances call for a talk with your doctor or other counselor.

Menopause. This is a dramatic, emotion-charged event for some women. See our special discussion about its emotional component (page 618).

Sex in the later years. More and more, medical science recognizes the need of older people, and their ability, to continue sexual activity into very old age. Even many individuals with heart disease and other ailments can enjoy sexual activity. Sex deprivation, especially in an older man, may cause depression. Here again, a talk with a sympathetic physician will prove helpful.

Security. We live in a competitive society which really has little mercy for the person who doesn't provide for himself and his family. Social security benefits are inadequate. It is reassuring—and a good preventive of mental tension—to work out early in life a program of disability, retirement, and life insurance which will provide for the family. This doesn't mean that you have to become so worried that you become "insurance poor." There are low-cost, term insurance policies which young people can afford. And almost everyone belongs to at least one organization that offers inexpensive group insurance.

Retirement. What happens at retirement will probably reflect the sum total of your personality growth during your lifetime. Some people enjoy retirement; others abhor it. Talk at length to your doctor about your emotional as well as physical needs in the retirement period. A change of location may be beneficial emotionally for some people, not for others. If you need part-time work to keep you cheerful, remember that you usually get this more readily in your home location where you are known.

Sickness and operations. We live longer and so are more subject to chronic illnesses. Often, these illnesses can be well controlled. But the very fact that an illness exists, even when controllable, can lead to feelings of despair or depression. Be sure you talk openly of your feelings about an illness to your doctor. And be open, too, with your spouse and friends.

If you need an operation, you have every right to discuss with the doctor just what is involved, what will be done, how long a period of recuperation will be necessary, what the fee will be for operation, and what other expenses will be involved.

And remember that almost everyone has some gloomy days after a major surgical procedure, but there come the happy days when the body overcomes the stresses of surgery and anesthesia.

Fatal illness. Some people think that awareness of a fatal illness must lead to emotional depression. This is not necessarily so. Most people take the fact well. There may be forlorn moments as the situation is first accepted as reality. Most depressions come from misunderstandings, such as that cancer will inevitably produce unbearable pain or will so destroy the body that other humans will shrink from contact. If a diagnosis of cancer causes great anxiety or frank depression, a long talk with your doctor, or with a psychiatrist your doctor can arrange for you to see, can be most helpful.

We have seen people who have had a good, rich emotional life grow to even greater appreciation of life as they faced their last days during a known fatal illness.

PART FIVE

Family Preventive Care

35

HEALTHY ADJUSTMENT IN MARRIAGE

MARRIAGE HAS been described as the "incredible entanglement of two people." If incredible, such entanglement has proved to be the most suitable and durable means by which most men and women achieve emotional gratification.

A merger involving two personalities, each with his and her own individuality and distinctive familial background and standards, is not and never has been uncomplicated.

You may hear it said that the American family is heading for collapse. But such ominous predictions have long been made. Early in the century, some writers seemed to think that horse and buggy reins had been the ties that had bound the family together and "the citizen, shaken loose from his safe domestic base by much streetcar straphanging, takes to socialism and drinking. The matron, without the steadying discipline of having to get home in time to feed the horse, gads and grows extravagant."

If marriage and the family today face changes and problems, they have always done so. Every generation has its problems of progress. The Victorian era—patriarchal, well ordered, and romanticized ever since—lasted only half a century and constitutes a small part of our heritage.

Perhaps, as sociologists point out, if there is an American norm, it is the frontier tradition of breaking away from the Establishment at an early age, and young families today resemble the pioneers who fought the wilderness. They fight a new kind of wilderness, not geographic, but psychological and moral. They are almost constantly on the move, with jobs taking them from one city to another, one region to another. They "do it themselves"; household help virtually does not exist any longer nor the handyman for hire nor the quickly available, reasonably priced serviceman.

With disruption of many once-fixed values, with the moving about that does not allow the continuity that can be a stabilizing influence for children, young parents must and do compensate, working harder at understanding their children than any parents before. Perhaps in reaction to having been brought up on standards of material success, young couples today often consider material success of relatively small importance as contrasted with working for something of greater social significance. They try to be of service; young fathers carry petitions; young mothers attend lectures on social problems; they teach their children to think in terms of service to humanity.

And if the American family, as Phyllis McGinley has put it, "seems threatened—by the impact of violence and war, by frequent divorce, changing sexual attitudes and a general atmosphere of wariness toward established religion—it is also protected by this fresh concern for the rights of human beings."

Still, marriage is a highly personal situation, exposing the partners to the most private and intimate of contacts. Personalities and character structures are of prime importance in this most important contract of adult humans. It is upon these factors that the success or failure of the marriage depends.

When difficulty arises in a marriage, when there is discontent, frustration or discord, physical and psychic symptoms may follow. *Preventive medicine has become increasingly aware that many health problems are precipitated by marital problems.*

While there is no such thing as a blueprint for a happy marriage, it is wise, before entering marriage, to be aware of the factors that are most likely to lead to successful marriage and those that may foredoom a marriage. Out of scientific studies which have investigated many thousands of marriages to determine reasons for success and failure, experts in the field have arrived at some guidelines.

CULTURAL BACKGROUND. Generally, people feel more at home with others who have had similar childhoods and have similar customs, manners, and tastes. Certainly, marriages between people of different races, religions, and economic and social classes can be successful. But it is only realistic to recognize that such marriages must overcome extra problems, not necessarily insoluble but real enough—problems caused not only by social disapproval but by the number of adjustments that must be made. For example, a rural Southern boy and a city-bred Northern girl may find it quite difficult to arrive at a way of living that makes them both happy and comfortable.

EDUCATIONAL LEVEL. Not only the actual learning experiences but the experiences of being with others and the opening up of interests which schooling provides can be of importance in marital adjustments. It is usually helpful to a marriage when both partners have roughly the same amount of education.

ECONOMIC AND JOB STATUS.   More important than the size of a man's income is the job he has, not alone the salary he gets from it but the satisfaction; the challenge it offers him; the fulfillment he gets from working at it; the possibilities it holds for the future, either in itself or in other opportunities to which it may lead. Generally, today, the more educational preparation he has had for his work, the more rewarding— not only in immediate financial return but in other ways—it is likely to be, and the better candidate he is for marriage.

NUMBER OF FRIENDS.   Generally, men and women who have had many friends of each sex before marriage are likely to be the types who will make satisfactory mates.

MEMBERSHIP IN ORGANIZATIONS.   It may be a good sign if an individual is a member of a social, labor, or other club or organization, indicating that he accepts, and is accepted by, a large group of people.

EMOTIONAL ADJUSTMENT.   Obviously, people who are emotionally well-adjusted have the best chance for happiness in life and for making the many adjustments required in marriage. Some authorities list the following characteristics which should be considered before marriage and advise that at least two of the good characteristics should be present:

GOOD	BAD
Optimistic personality	Pessimistic personality
Cooperativeness	Dominating personality
Consideration and sympathy	Inconsiderate and unsympathetic
Some degree of emotional dependence	Too self-sufficient emotionally; too much narcissism or self-love
	Dependent personality; too strong an attachment to parents

NEUROTIC MARRIAGES

What do most people seek when they marry? Happiness, of course— but other things, too. Some marry for security; some for love; some for prestige or social gain; some because it is time to marry, to be grown-up, or to have children and family. There are other conscious, and socially acceptable, reasons. But if, without realizing it, people marry for buried neurotic reasons, a marriage is not likely to be successful. For example, some men marry women not really as wives but as mothers; and some women seek fathers in their spouses rather than husbands. Some people seek mates who will serve as both father and mother, the omnipotent decision-making parents of early childhood.

Some unhappiness is to be expected in every marriage, but when the unhappiness is constant and pervading, outweighing the pleasure and satisfaction that should be expected of marriage, the marriage is neurotic. It is sometimes possible for a neurotic marriage to seem to go along fairly well but it is so precariously balanced that any new factor may tip the scales. That is especially likely when a child is born, for then the neurotic partner may find the situation intolerable, regarding the child as a competitor.

It is helpful to understand that the neurotic factors an adult brings into marriage are likely to have had origins in childhood. Thus, the son of a domineering father who made all the decisions may have a desire to avoid adult responsibility and may well seek a wife who will make the family decisions. If he finds such a wife, his marriage may be far from blissful but not an outright obvious failure. But if the wife, like he, is a decision avoider, there can be chaos as each waits for the other to move.

Many factors in childhood may—though they certainly do not necessarily always—lead to difficulties in marriage. They include sibling (brother or sister) rivalry, favoritism, too demanding or too indulgent parents, parental discord and divorce, uncertain parental discipline, overprotectiveness.

It is helpful to understand the influence of such factors both in terms of choosing a marriage partner and, later, if there should be difficulty. Such understanding may in itself help a little to ease the problem, and it may permit proper help to be sought to save the marriage.

INSIGHTS FROM SOME RECENT STUDIES

With researchers today investigating every facet of the husband-wife relationship—many of the studies are sponsored by the National Institute of Mental Health because of recognition that marital conflict is a major health problem—new insights are constantly being turned up. It should be emphasized that they are insights, not definitive conclusions. It is difficult to reach definitive conclusions in areas as complex as marriage. But the insights are worth noting.

Thus, research studies at Harvard, the University of Michigan, and other major institutions suggest that when husband and wife are equally mature and motivated, they can get along as well—even though they do not have similar backgrounds, attitudes, interests, and personalities—as couples who do have such similarities. And, conversely, when a couple is unable to adjust and to grow with the marriage, it does not matter how great the initial similarities were.

Unrealistic marriage expectations, many studies show, are the chief source of marital unhappiness. Among couples asked to rate themselves on a happiness scale, those who scored themselves happiest turned out to be playing roles in marriage which they had expected to play and which their spouses expected them to play. Those who expected their spouses to act like a favorite TV or movie star, or like Dad or Mom, were in trouble. This is not surprising, of course, but some studies also reveal that some young people, even among those who plan seriously for marriage, have expectations that seem reasonable but aren't really realistic for them.

Thus, many young people tell researchers that when they marry, the wife will not work; she will go to college; it is more important for her to be an interesting and entertaining companion than a good housekeeper or cook. But the fact is that many wives must work, are unable to go to college, or fail when they do go. And study after study shows that most men, whatever they may say to the contrary, much prefer having a wife who is neat and efficient around the house than one who is brilliant and a witty conversationalist but leaves dust on the furniture or dirty dishes in the sink.

As one investigator has pointed out, the trend toward "equality" between the sexes in marriage, without any clear division of labor and authority—as there was when the wife was expected to be exclusively a homemaker and the husband a breadwinner—creates "great potential for conflict and disillusionment." Under any circumstances, "boys and girls are bound to differ in some areas of role expectation." How they are able to modify these expectations when the honeymoon aura is over, and human weaknesses are revealed, is vital to the marriage.

In describing how the health of a marriage can deteriorate when there is insufficient, or no, adjustment, Dr. Richard H. Klemer, of the Department of Psychiatry at the University of Washington, Seattle, says: "Although it may not be intentional or even conscious, one partner or the other begins to have something less than complete acceptance for his mate. If it begins with the wife, the husband soon senses this change of attitude and begins to protect himself, again perhaps only half-consciously. In turn, the wife protects herself against the husband's slightly changed attitude. . . . Then she protects herself further, and so forth. This goes on till the partners arrive at a state of complete hostility—or worse, apathy—in their efforts to protect their own ego against their mate's disillusionment."

It is this that Dr. Klemer calls the "modern marriage disease." It can be prevented and checked when husband and wife realize that some expectations have to be modified and proceed to modify them as soon as possible.

There is no marriage that does not require adjustment. Obviously, a mature person who acts on the basis of reason, not just emotion, will have much less trouble adjusting to marriage than a person who may be physically adult but is still a child emotionally.

Marriage can be an exacting business. It was once thought that personality development virtually stopped at the age of five; now it is recognized that personality development can continue all through life. If it does continue, a marriage is likely to be a happy one.

After devoting many years to marriage studies at Harvard Medical School's Laboratory of Community Psychiatry, Dr. Rhona Rapoport finds that getting married is exacting because it involves a "critical transition from one social role to another." It calls for changes in behavior and social relationships between the individuals and entails "personality change of a more or less enduring nature."

Dr. Rapoport goes on to note: "Major social-role relationships are inherently disrupting. As an individual's social role changes, his image of himself is affected, the way in which others expect him to behave changes. And his legitimate expectations for the behavior of others alter. As all this goes on, the individual may grow and develop under the impact of the stimuli or he may find them so burdensome and distressing that his functioning is impaired, in extreme cases involving symptoms of emotional disturbance."

Everything does not have to be mutually satisfactory in a happy marriage. Studies reveal that in most marriages that are happy, several phases of marital life are not what the partners would have liked. If adaptability and the maturity that makes it possible are essential, so is motivation. With strong motivation, the desire to make a marriage work, adaptability may be furthered.

The Harvard and other studies suggest that what happens in the engagement period before marriage often indicates how a marriage will go. Couples best able to adjust to each other during the engagement period have least trouble moving happily from the freedom of single life to the demands as well as opportunities of marriage and family life. This is a good reason for a fairly long, relaxed period of courtship.

A LOOK AT LATE MARRIAGE DISSOLUTIONS

The number of long-standing marriages terminating in divorce has been growing. In Georgia, for example, Dr. Alfred A. Messer of Emory University found that, in 1953, 9 percent of divorces involved couples whose marriages had lasted 20 years or more; by 1966, the rate had gone up to 11 percent. A sampling of divorces in Fulton County, Georgia, in 1967 showed 14 percent to have taken place after 20 years of marriage. Nationwide data for 1963 revealed that 24 percent of divorcing couples had been married more than 15 years, indicating that the problem is not localized.

As the result of his investigations, Dr. Messer advances several reasons for these "20-year fractures." For one thing, divorces are now more socially acceptable, and more people can afford them. Also, more women now are able to work and are no longer financially dependent on their husbands. Divorce laws, too, in many states are more lenient than in the past.

But one major reason, Dr. Messer believes, is that partners do not get to know each other well enough before marriage to be sure they can form a new identity as a pair. Also, child orientation is overemphasized in many families; the children become the nucleus around which all activities revolve, leaving little time or emotion for a husband-wife relationship.

Most couples attempt to make up in marriage for traits they think are lacking in their own personalities, says Dr. Messer. Unlikes attract and likes repel. The man who is shy and silent is often happier with a vivacious wife. The frail woman likes to have a strong and vigorous husband. In a child-oriented family, the parents may begin to look more and more to their children for this type of gratification. The woman may cook and dress more for her children than for her husband, and the man may prefer to be with his children rather than with his wife.

When the children leave, there is a void, and the husband and wife may feel that their needs are not satisfied by each other. In every family, there should be a balance between adult-oriented and child-oriented needs, says Dr. Messer. In our "century of the child," the pendulum seems to have swung a bit far toward the child side. There is need for more "adult time," more second-honeymoon activities for the husband and wife to balance their role as parents.

TWO TYPES OF MARRIAGE

As individuals, different people live by different standards. Couples do, too. And in understanding successful and unsuccessful marriage, it's important to understand that what connotes success to one couple may mean failure to another. For example, some couples take pride and obtain considerable gratification in participating in community cultural life. For them, this constitutes an extension of their good marriage. To other couples, with different tastes, that same involvement may seem to be a means of escape from an inadequate marriage. When a couple believe their marriage is happy, it may well be happy to them even if outsiders question the fact.

But sociologists have recognized that if some objective criteria could be found, they might help to give married people fresh insights into their relationships.

After studying 437 men and women, Dr. John Cuber, professor of sociology at Ohio State University, has concluded that marriages can be divided into two basic types. One, called *utilitarian*, serves primarily as a means to such familiar ends as establishing a home, having children, furthering a career, or enjoyment of wealth and prestige. The other, called *intrinsic*, makes such considerations second in importance to the intimate relationship of the partners.

All marriages do not fall neatly into one or the other category or remain constant. One category is not necessarily better than the other; each type of marriage reflects a different philosophy and serves different needs. But the categories and their patterns provide a basis for psychologists to determine how well a marriage is functioning and may help people, as Dr. Cuber notes, to "discard the idea of a perfect marriage and be spared the frustration of measuring their lives by impossible standards."

While a utilitarian couple may look upon marriage as a means to comfort and security, and while they may have only minor sexual feelings for one another, they do get along. And while the intrinsic couple find great pleasure in each other, enjoying differences as well as samenesses, revealing their secret thoughts and feelings to each other without embarrassment, yielding to the limits of intimacy and fulfilling their sexual natures, this type of bond, ideal as it may seem, sometimes leaves no room for the outside world to enter. And when external pressures invade, as they invariably do, the marriage can be in jeopardy. The utilitarian marriage, which thrives on outside interests, may have a greater chance for longevity.

As a follow-up to the Cuber theory and in an effort to see what early signs might provide a preview of what will happen to couples, investigators at the National Institute of Mental Health worked with volunteer couples who had been married just three months and were of comparable age and social background. After extensive interviews and detailed questionnaires, the couples were given a color matching test to take together to determine how they handled conflict.

Some couples virtually went into combat; others argued much like lawyers; some refused to argue and gave in almost immediately. There were also some who listened carefully to each other's point of view and eventually agreed to disagree. The latter couples maintained their faith in themselves and their relationship, and it is these couples who develop intrinsic marriages. Those who seemed to concede too quickly may find themselves in a utilitarian marriage or even in a devitalized marriage in which the partners start out with high hopes and settle into a life of apathy and disappointment.

Becoming familiar with marriage patterns may enable couples to understand the real nature of their relationship and may help them move toward the relationship they want.

COURTSHIP

Thus marriage, important to society, very important to the individuals involved, with considerable impact on both emotional and physical health, is a complex relationship, one not yet, and possibly never likely to be, scientifically blocked out, with definitive pretests to guide young people before they enter into it.

Not for one moment do we suggest here that a young couple contemplating marriage can depend upon any set of tests or rules to determine whether theirs will be a happy marriage. But certainly some exploration and stock-taking are in order before entering into such a significant contract.

However much the heart races at the sight of the beloved, do not rush into marriage. Give yourself and your potential future mate a chance to know each other.

Face up to the fact that you should not marry anyone with the idea in the back of your mind of reforming him or her. Remember you are marrying an adult with fairly well fixed habits and tastes. If you marry for what your partner is, not for what he or she may become, it will save you a lot of disillusionment. Use the time before marriage to discuss and try to reach basic understandings on all important matters. Should the wife work? For how long? Are the husband's earnings adequate for both to live on? Who will manage the family income? How many children? How should they best be brought up? These are examples of questions that have to be faced at some time and may best be faced before marriage.

Some additional questions may serve as a helpful guide:

*Do you really enjoy spending most of your leisure time together?
 Do you both enjoy the same friends?
 Do you have compatible tastes in books, movies, art, sports, other activities?
 Do your feelings and tastes about the kind of home you hope to have match reasonably well?

*Do you agree on whether or not to have children and on their upbring-
ing?

Does the prospective husband like to putter around the house, build and
fix things, do gardening? Does the prospective wife like to cook, sew?

*Do you both have the same basic philosophy about life and your goals
in life, the nonmaterial as well as material? Do you have the same
religion or agree on attitudes toward religion?

*Do you like or share each other's attitudes toward parents? And are you
in agreement on ways to deal with them?

*Will you be likely, as best you can determine now after serious thought,
to love each other when you are old?

Any couple who might answer "yes" to every question would be a
rare one. You should not expect, nor desire, a mate who is a mere carbon
copy of yourself. Disagreement on minor matters makes for stimulating
conversation. Basic antagonisms, however, are another matter and introduce risk into marriage.

Certain questions are more important than others. There should be a
positive "yes" to the questions that are starred. About the seventh question: Religious disagreements have been found to play a small part in
disturbing a marriage. These differences tend to be worked out satisfactorily during the courtship. After marriage, the problem is usually
centered on the religious upbringing of children. The eighth question
involves inlaws, who have been the cause of many marital upsets. The
courtship period is the ideal time to get to know them and make every
attempt to like and be liked.

The courtship period goes through several stages. Usually it has been
preceded by "dating"—a time when the opposite sex is met at dances,
school, clubs, and gatherings of various types. Dating should be constructive, a time for meeting different kinds of people and for enjoyment, but
also for thoughtful exploration and understanding of members of the
opposite sex.

Courtship may be said to begin with "keeping company," when, after
something "clicks" between two people, other dating falls off. "Going
steady" usually follows; the attachment has become stronger. Private
understanding is a succeeding phase for many couples. They have
exchanged avowals of love. Each has, if possible, been introduced to the
other's family.

Engagement is the final test before marriage. It should be the time for
free, honest, and practical talk, for getting to know one another at deeper
levels, for real understanding of each other's personality defects and for
deciding about compatibility. For the average couple, one year has been
suggested as a minimum engagement period. There is no ironclad rule;
some couples need more time than others to get thoroughly acquainted

or have had more time to do so prior to becoming engaged. But whirl-wind courtship should be avoided; too often it leads to divorce.

LOVE AND INFATUATION

There is a decided difference. A strong sexual desire is often mistaken for love. If it is not accompanied by other strong feelings, this is infatuation. In adolescence, infatuation is called "puppy love." Both in adolescence and later, infatuation is usually outgrown.

While an adequate definition of love has troubled poets and philosophers from time immemorial, for the practical purposes of successful marriage you can ask yourself these questions:

Do you feel a sense of oneness, each with the other? That is, do you consider the other person a part of yourself?

Do you feel you can trust the other person implicitly? Does he or she give you a sense of security?

Are you deeply concerned about his or her welfare? Do you try in all ways to make the other person happy?

Have you found that, after being apart from the other person for a period of time, you still feel the same strong emotional attachment?

Do you find that the longer you know each other the greater grows the desire to stay together and you do not grow bored as time goes by?

These questions, if answered glibly, will mean nothing. But if, after serious thought, you can say "yes" to all of them, you may safely say that you are in love. You will have noticed that they are concerned with true companionship. Physical attraction is not enough to guarantee a happy marriage. Sex is of basic importance in marriage. It is, one might say, the foundation upon which the house must be built; it is not the whole house.

MARRIAGE AGE

There is, of course, no one best age for marriage. Ideally, perhaps, marriage should be entered into when maturity, both physical and mental, has been reached. Maturity varies from one person to another, although experts place the usual age in the 22 to 30 range. This has been found to be the age range during which most successful marriages are formed, with the husband generally from four to seven years older than the wife. There are exceptions, of course. In many happy marriages, the wife is older. The important consideration is that the couple be emotionally stable and mentally mature enough to handle the stresses and strains of marriage.

Determination to make a marriage successful is a major weapon in doing so. There will need to be tolerance, understanding, and good humor. Neither partner can expect the other to give in on all points, to make all the sacrifices. Marriage is a mutual undertaking. When sacrifices have to be made, as they invariably must be, they should be made without resentment, with the larger view in mind—happiness for both partners.

It has been said of a successful marriage that it represents the real success in life, and that it is better to fail in all else and succeed at home than to have success in all else and fail at home.

Married love can be the most rewarding human experience. If we were to define it in its simplest terms, we would say it has three parts: sexual attraction; a deep feeling of companionship; and a desire for parenthood. The first two are essential; the third is valuable for emotional fulfillment and complete, enduring happiness.

36

SEXUAL ADJUSTMENT IN MARRIAGE

DESPITE MARRIAGE manuals, the Kinsey and other reports, and the so-called sexual revolution, medical authorities estimate that at least half of all married couples today still suffer from serious sexual problems. How unfortunate it is that the sex act, with its potential of deep and rewarding intimacy, should be clouded by fear, shame, ignorance, and misconceptions.

Perhaps some sexual anthropologist of a future century, upon analyzing the Pill, the drive-in, the works of some of our best-selling novelists, the Tween-Bra, and all the myriad other artifacts of the Great Sexual Revolution, will conclude that ours may have been an era in which there was some change in morality but not necessarily in sexual enlightenment and fulfillment.

Parents may think that young people today know as much as, if not more than, they should about sex; and many young people may smile in superior manner at any notion that they need education in such matters. Yet from the questions still asked by newly married couples, as well as by long-married ones, physicians are aware that much ignorance and misinformation remain. Both young and old couples often ask whether their sexual relations are "all right." They would like to have the boundaries of normal relationships defined, and they are concerned with problems of frigidity and impotence.

It is a good thing that questions are being asked, that hopefully fewer couples refuse to discuss sex matters. Yet there remain many people who believe that to put any significant emphasis on sex education is a mistake. They muster many arguments, even such as the one of a young married woman who declared: "I'm sorry Bill and I ever read that book about sex in marriage. It just made him feel guilty because he can't live up to what it says a man should do to satisfy his wife; and I feel guilty because I'm upsetting him. I'd rather be ignorant than become self-conscious trying to follow a blueprint."

It is true that some books dealing with sex education have been written in a way that tends to remove all spontaneity from this delicate relationship. Because matters of sex technique and skill were so long taboo, some writers have gone to the other extreme, exaggerating their importance and neglecting other aspects.

Yet physical attraction and intuition are not enough to enable people to solve the problems that may give rise to, or result from, an unsatisfactory sexual relationship. Not rules nor elaborate detailing of techniques can solve such problems; only a better understanding of sex in all its aspects may do that.

THE PURPOSES OF SEX

You notice that we use the plural, "purposes," rather than the singular. From the biological standpoint, the purpose of sexual intercourse is simple enough: reproduction. Of late, there has been some tendency to pass over this aspect of the sexual act, perhaps because it was once considered the only real purpose of intercourse. Although much has been written about men and women who want children because they think they should have them, or to prove they can have them, or for any of a number of neurotic reasons, most people who find life worth living want to pass on the gift of life, to create a new life with the beloved partner.

But sexual intercourse is much more. It is even more than an expression of love in the most intimate manner; it is certainly even more than giving and receiving pleasure.

As one discerning physician has written recently: "Because we use words to distinguish sex from love, we fail to understand that in human experience no such sharp division exists. As individuals we have integrity, a word that comes from the Latin *integer*, meaning whole or entire. We are whole; we are not 'minds' and 'bodies'; we are one. And as whole human beings our experiencing of sex and love ultimately must become one experience. We call love spiritual but it is also physical—in the embrace of man and woman, mother and child, friend and friend. We call sex physical but it is also spiritual—in the communication of tenderness, respect, solicitude, and, of course, love.

"When I think of love and sex in relation to marriage I think of the Greek myth of Antaeus, who was the son of Gaea, the earth goddess. In combat, whenever Antaeus was flung to the ground he arose more powerful than ever, for he drew strength from his contact with his mother Earth. And when a man and woman in love meet in the sexual embrace, each, like Antaeus, hopes to arise stronger than before, to go his individual way. In day-to-day living, the man who is diminished by a world that forces him to compromise or accept defeat finds total acceptance in the arms of the woman who loves him. And the woman who feels diminished by niggardly chores and obligations (and may still regard herself as the subordinate sex) receives heartfelt homage from the man who loves and desires her. With sex and with love the man restores her integrity and she restores his. And both have been nourished by sexual pleasure, which they seek as roots seek water—because without it their marriage will wither and die.

"As a physician, not a poet, as a man who speaks with some knowledge of flesh and blood reality, I know that when the act of sex is truly an act of love it unites two committed human beings, obliterating their painful awareness of being alone and lonely. And the pleasure of the embrace, together with the certainty that tomorrow they will embrace again, gives them new strength to stand alone."

SATISFACTORY SEXUAL RELATIONS

It would be possible to write almost interminably on this subject from a theoretical standpoint. But this is neither practical nor necessary. Sexual intercourse, which can lead to great happiness or great misery, is not a complete mystery to any person. When there are problems, it is usually because there are certain gaps in knowledge and understanding. And what we shall try to do here is to close those gaps, gaps that have been narrowed by the efforts of many physicians who, through tactful inquiry, have sought to help patients in whom they suspected that sexual maladjustment, even though not mentioned by the patients, might well be a source of psychological and psychosomatic problems.

We do not feel that it is within our province to take moral stands but rather to state problems and questions that most commonly concern husbands and wives and to try to provide information on the basis of established knowledge, dismissing the misconceptions and myths that even today prevail.

Is it necessary to read extensively on the subject of sex, to study many manuals about it? Some books can be helpful, but much more important for a successful sexual relationship than encyclopedic knowledge is a striving for mutual enjoyment rather than emulation of the practices of others per se, or an attempt to follow some rule in a book. Generally, the fewer idealized goals that a husband and wife set for themselves to attain, the more likely they are to achieve sexual happiness.

Should a couple have sexual intercourse prior to marriage to determine whether they are compatible? Whether or not to have premarital relations is a matter for each couple to decide. However, it seems naive to us to believe that one can successfully "test" so subtle and delicate a matter. A satisfactory sexual adjustment is seldom achieved at once; much more often, it is developed gradually.

Does the size of the respective organs of man and woman play an important part in the success of their relationship? Many men have worried unduly because they feared they were too small; many women have worried because they thought they were too large to give pleasure or so small as to make intercourse painful. Except in rare instances, relative size of genital organs is no problem because of the possibility of using techniques that will minimize any difficulties. It is worth noting that the vagina is greatly expandable; in fact, it has been established that at one stage of sexual excitement, it balloons so that if intromission occurs at the proper time, any vagina can accommodate any penis.

Can earlier-in-life masturbation affect ability to have successful sexual relations? Any harmful effects of masturbation are due to fears and guilts associated with it. Physically, no damage is done. Almost everyone has practiced some form of masturbation; 92 percent of all men interviewed by Dr. Kinsey recalled having practiced it at some time; 88 percent of unmarried men practiced it between ages 12 and 20, and some 50 percent did at age 50. The practice among females is scarcely less general, although it is often incomplete or only partially conscious.

Does youthful petting inhibit later satisfactory sexual relations? It is usual for young people to engage in some form of lovemaking which stops short of intercourse. It is a common way for them to discover, or demonstrate, their physical attraction for each other. Petting that is prolonged or habitual and involves great self-restraint to stop short of actual intercourse may have a temporarily bad effect. For example, if a girl has been accustomed to being on guard against letting herself go too far, she may have some difficulty, when first married, in relaxing and enjoying the sexual act. But, in general, petting is good preparation for full sexuality.

Is earlier sexual experience with others helpful or harmful in establishing successful relations with one's spouse? Premarital experience is certainly not necessary. Ideally, experience in the art of lovemaking should be obtained with one's chosen mate. It is often distressing to the other partner, especially a man, if the spouse has been intimate with someone else. But since modern civilization makes it difficult or even imposisble for people to marry until long after they reach maturity, premarital sex experiences do occur. We think it important to realize that loving someone as he or she *is* involves understanding that even past relationships have contributed to creating the person one loves.

Does an earlier homosexual experience mean that a person cannot have normal sexual relations? Studies have shown that many men and an appreciable number of women have had some sort of homosexual experience which did not interfere with normal sexual relations later. However, we feel that anyone who is concerned about such an experience should discuss it frankly with a doctor or competent counselor, since homosexuality is a complicated problem.

Is the wedding night crucial in establishing satisfactory sexual relations? It can be. The bride may be tense and overwrought, especially if the wedding was a large one. She requires great consideration from the groom, who is usually nervous himself. While there have been instances in which the shock of the wedding night experience has produced lasting damage to a girl's attitude toward sex, we are inclined to believe that such danger is less great now than in the past when many brides had no concept of the nature of intercourse. While a husband may find it difficult to avoid causing his bride some physical discomfort at this time, his tenderness is likely to be sufficient to compensate.

The bride should, if possible, select a wedding date far removed from her menstrual period. Also, the couple should not add a long journey to the stressful (even though happy) wedding day. It is best to stay at a place near the wedding reception. If there must be a tiring journey with arrival late at night, perhaps the sexual consummation will be happier if delayed until both have had a restful sleep.

Some wedding night difficulties can be avoided if the bride has had a preliminary medical examination. In some virgins, the hymen, the membrane at the opening of the vagina, may not rupture easily, and this makes intercourse painful or impossible. In such cases, it may be removed by a physician, a procedure so minor that it hardly is worth calling an operation. The hymen also can be stretched, according to medical directions, prior to marriage.

Before the wedding night, the marriage partners should discuss birth control with each other. Also, your doctor or marriage counselor will answer questions about contraceptive methods.

If the husband is considerate, will the bride enjoy intercourse? Some women derive no more pleasure from it than from any intimate caress. Sexual desire sometimes develops slowly in women. They may not reach sexual maturity until they have been married for some time. The awakening may be gradual or may take place suddenly.

Women tend to be less quickly and spontaneously aroused than men. Both partners should understand this. A woman should not feel that her husband is oversexed or "crude" if he desires intercourse because he has seen her partially undressed or because she has kissed him affectionately. A man should not consider himself rejected or decide that his wife is cold if she fails to be aroused so readily.

Many women need a warming-up period, both to feel desire and to be physically ready for intercourse. When a woman is sufficiently aroused, her vagina is well lubricated and naturally receptive to insertion of the penis. Many women respond best to lovemaking that begins with verbal expressions of affection, kisses, and gentle caresses and proceeds to stimulation of the breasts, the nipples, the clitoris (the small projection outside the vagina, which is composed of erectile tissue similar to the penis), and the vagina itself. Each husband should learn to know the degree to which his wife is excited by caresses of different parts of the body.

If the husband is skillful, will a wife always achieve sexual satisfaction? Even under the most favorable circumstances, some women do not experience an orgasm, or climax. Some experience an orgasm only after they have been married for some time. Some experience it only occasionally, perhaps only at certain periods of the month, as their desire may be of a cyclical nature, peaking before, during, or after the menstrual period. In men, the orgasm is clearly defined; in women it may be vague or diffuse. Its intensity varies. It may center in the clitoris or may appear to involve the internal portion of the vagina, or a woman may experience both types of orgasm.

Often, failure to achieve orgasm does not prevent a woman from having pleasure from the sexual act; failure does not necessarily make her tense and frustrated; this, too, varies in individual women.

It is important for a man to help his wife experience the sexual satisfaction he enjoys. Men often reach climax more rapidly than women. This can usually be compensated for by making certain that the woman is highly stimulated before actual intercourse begins. While many couples find it particularly satisfying to reach orgasm simultaneously, others see no objection to having the woman reach it first. Generally, a woman's desire fades rather slowly after orgasm, whereas that of a man tends to vanish rapidly.

It is not unusual, especially if a man is young or greatly excited, for him occasionally to have an orgasm almost immediately upon beginning the sexual act; this is called *premature ejaculation*. However, if it occurs habitually, he should consult a doctor. Often premature ejaculation is due to early, furtive, hurried sex experiences. As a result, a man may not have learned to enjoy a leisurely sexual pace and to adapt to his partner's needs. Yet it is frequently possible for such a man, with the help of his wife, to overcome the problem, by approaching sex more leisurely.

We would like to note, too, that premature ejaculation has varied meanings. In one medical center, a man may be considered a premature ejaculator if he cannot sustain the sex act for 30 seconds; elsewhere the standard may be a minute. Some physicians suggest that more realistically a man may be considered to have a premature ejaculation problem when he cannot control his sexual processes long enough to satisfy his partner in at least half of their attempts.

Is there excessive concern about orgasm? Often, there is. There is much more to the sexual relationship than this "end point" release. But when couples become concerned with this one goal above all others, they may do everything but enjoy themselves. The whole lovemaking process should be enjoyed. And for some people who have had problems, concentration on the pleasures of caresses, without thought of climax, can help unblock sexual response.

What causes frigidity in a woman? As we have indicated, failure to have orgasm does not necessarily mean a woman is frigid. Doctors speak of true frigidity as the inability to derive pleasure from sexual relations. This may be caused by insufficient lubrication or lack of adequate stimulation. Frigidity also may stem from psychological factors, conscious or unconscious feelings of guilt, inferiority, or fears, such as fear of pregnancy, of growing up, of surrendering to a man.

Women sometimes suffer from sexual self-consciousness because society has demanded sexual purity of them before marriage and suddenly demands whole-hearted participation in marriage. Some women find it difficult to make the transition. Yet the potential is there. "The sexual potential of a woman is not less but far greater," observes Mrs. Virginia Johnson who, with Dr. William Masters, conducted pioneering laboratory studies of human sexual response, "for, unlike a man, she can immediately go on to another orgasmic experience."

When a woman is frigid, her understanding, coupled with her husband's, of possible reasons and their joint efforts to relax and to approach sex leisurely and lovingly sometimes may be enough to solve the problem. When it is not, professional help often may do so.

What is impotence and what causes it? By impotence doctors mean the inability of a man to have an erection. It does not mean sterility, which is inability to have children. Impotence can be, but rarely is, due to physical causes. Often, it is due to psychological difficulties such as hostility to women, guilt, and fears—for example, the fear of contracting a venereal disease or of being sexually inferior. Some men are able to have intercourse only with women they do not respect; they are impotent with a woman they admire or love. This may be due to their subconscious classification of women as either madonnas or good mothers with whom intercourse is forbidden or harlots with whom it is permissible. This stems from an idea that sex is wicked or from overveneration of the mother. Psychiatric help may be needed to solve such problems.

But many chronic cases of impotence start from a commonplace cause. It's natural for every man to have occasional episodes of impotence, usually the result of fatigue, preoccupation, or alcohol. Some men, especially those over 40, worry unduly about such an episode and develop a "fear of failure" cycle. It is the fear, not the aging, that leads to their chronic impotence.

What if a husband wishes sexual relations when the wife is not in the mood? Assuming that she is not disturbed by unsettled problems outside the bedroom and that she is not withholding sex as a kind of punishment, the fortunate fact is that a wife can participate in sex as a loving partner even if she is not in the mood. Often, the fact that she is giving pleasure to her husband is enough to change her mood, to transform passive acceptance into active desire. Certainly, there are times when illness or extreme fatigue prevent this, and an understanding husband will wait for a more favorable time.

Should sexual preferences be discussed between husband and wife? In as many as 90 percent of sexually unhappy marriages, some investigators have found, there has been a barrier of silence. The wife has never told her husband the things that are sexually meaningful for her, that help her develop her sexual feelings. She has never told her husband the things she wishes he would do. It is essential for wives and husbands to learn to say: This is what I like and don't like, what I want and don't want.

How often should one have intercourse? There is no proper frequency for sex. Sexual satisfaction is much more a matter of quality than quantity. Appetites vary. If there is any suggestion it is that frequency of intercourse should be as spontaneous as any other aspect of sex, and no rule should be followed.

Statistics compiled by various investigators indicate that the average is about twice a week, more often in young or newly wedded couples, less often in older ones. But so many factors—temperament, opportunity, fatigue, compatibility—are involved that such figures mean little to any individual. The best guide, we suggest, is: If both partners feel well, if coitus does not cause discomfort or fatigue, and if it is followed by physical and emotional relaxation, there is no need to worry about overdoing. Repeated failure to obtain satisfaction after experiencing orgasm indicates some problem, which should be discussed with your physician or a trained counselor.

While there usually is some decline in desire to have intercourse as middle age is reached, some women reach the height of sexual vigor quite late in life, even after they have passed the menopause, and some men remain sexually vigorous into old age.

Should there be intercourse during the menstrual period? This is a matter for each couple to decide. Coitus may cause the wife some discomfort, especially if she has "cramps" during her period, but it will do no physical harm to either husband or wife.

Coitus does not "consume" one's potency, and abstention does not increase virility. However, sexual relations regularly several times a day may decrease the amount of sperm a man produces, thus reducing chances of having a child. "Too much" sexual activity does not cause insanity; neither does too little, although distressing emotional tension may result from frustration. Lack of interest or too much interest in sex is an indication of difficulties that require expert help. Occasionally such difficulties are of a physical nature; mostly, however, they spring from psychological problems.

On this score, we want to warn you: *Never* take any medicine, pill, injection, or anything else to increase or decrease sexual desire unless a competent physician has discovered a physical condition that requires it. "Potency pills" containing hormones can be dangerous. Aphrodisiacs such as cantharides ("Spanish fly") are actually poisonous irritants. Alcohol does not increase desire, although it may seem to do so because it releases inhibitions. A tense or shy person occasionally may find it easier to relax after a glass or two of wine or some other alcoholic beverage. But anyone who remains dependent on an artificial aid will probably find some form of psychotherapy a wiser way of overcoming repressions. Too much alcohol eventually decreases sexual potency, as it does health in general.

A well-balanced diet, enough rest, and general care of the body, as discussed elsewhere in this book, are essential to your health, of which your sexual health is an important part. It is obviously hazardous to try to decrease sexual desire by exhausting yourself or eating so little as to feel generally below par. Let us add that there are no special foods that increase or decrease potency. When abstinence is necessary, keeping busy and avoiding erotic stimulation as much as possible may relieve sexual tensions.

Is intercourse ever dangerous or harmful? It is dangerous when either partner has a venereal disease. Intercourse, as well as other forms of close contact, should be avoided during contagious illness of any type. Certain noncontagious diseases make intercourse unadvisable or even dangerous. Anyone who is not in good health should discuss this matter frankly with his or her physician, who will be able to decide whether or not coitus is permissible.

However, we want to make the point that it is often possible to prevent undue strain or overexertion for one or both partners by using certain positions during intercourse. We know of couples who have abandoned sexual relations because the wife could not tolerate the weight of her husband, or the activity was too much for the husband's heart. They had the misconception that it was not "nice" or "right" or "normal" to use positions for coitus that would overcome their difficulties.

While most people in our culture assume one position for intercourse, this is only a matter of custom. There is absolutely no reason to consider that any position is the right or normal one if another is desirable because of health, relative size, or individual preference.

POSITIONS FOR INTERCOURSE

One is face-to-face; another is that in which the man faces forward while the woman turns her back; and there are variations of these basic positions. The purposes of different positions are to increase pleasure and to prevent hygienic dangers or injuries. Also, a person who has heart disease or another serious illness may want to use positions that require the least amount of physical exertion, e.g., the side positions.

MAN ABOVE WOMAN. In this position—considered the standard one in our Western culture—the woman lies on her back, with thighs spread so there is room between her legs for the man's thighs. By bending her legs, she allows for deeper penetration. The man lies upon his partner's abdomen, supporting his knees and elbows on the bed as much as possible so he is less of a burden. If the woman holds her thighs together after entry, it will help in cases where the penis may be small or the vagina large. It will also increase friction against the clitoris. With thighs tight together, the woman can prevent the penis from entering too deeply, if this is needed to prevent pain.

If the vagina is large, this technique may be helpful: The woman lifts her thighs high enough to encircle the man's neck with her legs or to rest her feet on his shoulders. Thus her body is almost at right angles, with her shoulders flat and her torso lifted as vertically as possible.

WOMAN OVER MAN. The woman can kneel over the man and let herself down gently until the penis is inserted. The advantage of this position is that she has full control of the movements and can quicken or slow down as she pleases. She can also adjust herself to the penis by bending forward so full contact with the clitoris is made. Properly used, this position can result in sexual delight. It is helpful if the man is tired. A possible disadvantage is that it requires a good deal of exertion by the woman while the man is relatively passive. It is not recommended if the vaginal passage is unusually short. And it is not recommended if the man is sick or convalescing, since it is likely to be more stimulating than the following side position.

LYING ON SIDE, FACE TO FACE. The partners lie on their sides, facing each other. The woman raises her upper thigh and rests it on the man's upper thigh. This is excellent for those who wish coitus during pregnancy as there is little pressure on the woman's abdomen. For couples who wish to relax, this side attitude will be appealing and restful.

REAR ENTRY. This method is also recommended for pregnant women or in any other case where deep penetration and weight on the abdomen are not desirable. The woman, usually in a kneeling stance, has her back to the man. The man enters the vagina from behind. This position does not give the woman as much pleasure as some others since the clitoris is not touched by the penis. The man can compensate for this by fondling the clitoris (and the breasts) with his hands.

WHAT ARE ABNORMAL SEX PRACTICES BETWEEN A MAN AND A WOMAN?

A couple are sexually normal in the broadest sense if each derives the greatest pleasure from insertion of the male genital organ into that of the female. But this does not mean that experimentation to obtain satisfaction by other means is abnormal. For example, there is certainly nothing abnormal for a man who reaches climax rapidly, before his wife does, to make it possible for her to achieve climax by manual manipulation. There is nothing abnormal about any caress, in the foreplay before coitus, that both partners find pleasurable.

The oral zone—mouth, lips, and tongue—is, to a greater or lesser degree, a sexual one. Some couples find the genital kiss important for fullest sexual satisfaction. This does not constitute abnormality.

We have described sexual deviations earlier (page 348). In doing so, we noted that mature people usually carry with them some holdovers from childhood. These may lead to problems in marriage if they happen seriously to conflict with those of a partner—if, for example, a man derives pleasure from seeing his wife's body but she feels distaste for exposing her body. Such differences often can be resolved provided both partners approach sex matters open-mindedly and intelligently and not with indignation or shame.

In some cases, however, it may be impossible to reconcile maladjustment without trained assistance. The following are some examples. You will find additional discussion of these problems on page 350. Of course, we are not referring to people who have a trace of the following characteristics but rather to extreme cases.

NARCISSISM. Women (or, a little less often, men) who have this problem can love only themselves. If their partners love them, they have that much in common—love of the same person. But the partner usually, and rightly, wants more than that. A successful marriage, including successful sex relations, is usually impossible as long as one partner remains extremely narcissistic.

MASOCHISM AND SADISM. There are marriages in which the husband or wife seems to enjoy being dominated, even badly treated, by the other partner, while the partner enjoys treating the spouse badly. But things seldom work out so neatly, and even when they do, they don't constitute happiness.

EXCESSIVE SEXUALITY (NYMPHOMANIA AND SATYRISM). We do not refer to instances in which one partner is more highly sexed than the other. Consideration, based upon love, will find ways to bridge such differences under ordinary circumstances. But compulsive sexuality that cannot be satisfied has roots that love cannot reach. Fortunately, this condition is rare.

PROMISCUITY. A truly promiscuous person has coitus as readily with one person as another, with no wish for real intimacy in the sexual act. This is not the same as infidelity, although the two may overlap. Promiscuity is more serious; infidelity is more common and leads to many unhappy marriages. Actually, both infidelity and promiscuity, while they may indicate something wrong in an individual, may be indications as well of something wrong in a marriage. We wish every husband and wife faced with the problem of infidelity would not be satisfied with simply blaming the "other man" or "other woman" but would honestly face the question, "What is wrong with yourself, your spouse, or your marriage?"

REPRESSION. People are said to be sexually repressed when they have pushed the normal sex instinct so far below the surface of consciousness that they feel indifference, distaste, or even repugnance for sex. There are, of course, degrees of repression and, in mild cases, it may melt away in the warmth of love. But in extreme cases it may make happiness in marriage impossible.

THE UNRESOLVED "OEDIPUS COMPLEX." A man seeking his mother when he chooses a wife, or a woman wanting a husband to take the place of her father, will not find what they seek. Sometimes a degree of happiness may be possible for a "little girl" wife who needs to be mothered. But there will be no true happiness in the marriage because such people cannot be good spouses and certainly not good parents.

HELP FOR FAILING MARRIAGES

Some sex problems are due to ignorance or misinformation and often clear up readily in the light of truth. Others are more complicated. If you need information which we have not provided, or if you have any worries about yourself, your spouse, or any aspect of your marriage, be sure to talk things over with a trained person.

We suggest that you talk to your physician first if that is possible. Not all physicians are expert in sexual and marital matters, but more and more today are taking an interest and attending special postgraduate courses in this area. Sometimes, the physician may be able to provide guidance and advice that will be enough to help you settle a problem with the aid of your spouse. When your physician feels that specialized knowledge and experience are required, he can direct you to the proper person—a psychiatrist or a marriage counselor.

Marriage counselors are relatively new. They concern themselves with every aspect of marital and premarital problems. There are a bewildering number of professional counseling services in most communities. If your own physician is unable to advise you on finding the right specialist, the heads of departments of psychiatry and gynecology at any medical school usually can make informed local referrals.

To find a qualified marriage counselor, you can write to the national referral service of the American Association of Marriage Counselors, which is directed by Dr. Edward Rydman, Suite 104, 3603 Lemmon Ave., Dallas, Tex. 75219. The Family Service Association of America at 44 East 23rd Street, New York, N.Y. 10010, can direct you to social workers throughout the country who do marital and sex counseling. The National Council on Family Relations, 1219 University Ave., S.E., Minneapolis, Minn. 55414, can provide a directory of its members. The American Institute of Family Relations, 5287 Sunset Blvd., Los Angeles, Calif. 90027, maintains a large staff of qualified counselors in the Los Angeles area and also can recommend qualified people in many other parts of the country. Harold I. Lief, M.D., Director of the Marriage Council of Philadelphia, Pa. (4025 Chestnut St.), has been a pioneer in educating the medical profession to the importance of sex in the lives of their patients.

There are many kinds of troubled marriages and many sources of help. Help is worth seeking. Not every marriage in trouble can be saved; not every one should be. But even some of those which seem most likely to founder, to be most hopeless, can be saved with almost surprising ease once an expert sits down with a couple, helps them explore their problems on a realistic basis they may not have been able to find on their own, and helps them set up channels of communication between them which may well be all they need to be able to work out a solution.

If yours is a sex problem, don't be ashamed to ask for help. It isn't easy, nor may it even be necessary, to solve every problem that can be involved in achieving sexual fulfillment in marriage. You may find that you have been worrying unduly about a problem so minor that it has assumed significance only because of your worry. You may find that you have difficulties that can be solved with relative ease before they congeal and perhaps lead to further difficulties.

But even when a sex problem is not one that can be solved easily, it is worth solving. A satisfying sexual relationship is part of every truly happy marriage. It can be achieved by any physically and emotionally healthy man and wife who care for each other.

This word about psychiatric treatment when it is needed for marital problems: Modern psychiatry recognizes that the fragmenting forces in marriage are much like those in any human interaction. Jealousies, fears, anxieties, tensions are universal. Within the intimacy of marriage, however, such emotions can all too easily reach intolerable levels. Seldom is a marriage in trouble through the sole fault of one partner. Both partners —and a third factor, the marriage itself—usually need therapy.

In recognition of this, modern psychiatric treatment for marital trouble primarily seeks to treat both partners. There are several commonly used forms of treatment: successive therapy of husband and wife; concurrent therapy, i.e., simultaneous treatment of both partners by the same therapist but at different times; conjoint therapy, i.e., simultaneous treatment of both partners in joint sessions; collaborative therapy, i.e., with a separate therapist for each partner; group therapy of various types; and family therapy oriented mainly toward the parental relationship.

In marital therapy, there is opportunity for both husband and wife to learn alternative patterns of behavior to replace those which have caused distress. With successful treatment, children are likely to benefit significantly. And it should be added that, as the two partners themselves learn to give and receive more positively and adequately in their marriage relationship, they may also increase their capacities for obtaining rich emotional and other rewards from interactions with the world at large.

37

─────────────────────────────

TOWARD HEALTHY PARENTHOOD

THE STRATEGY

WHEN MOST young couples marry, they are not immediately interested in having children. Rather, their primary concern is with each other. They have established their own little private world; they wish to explore it, savor living in it.

Over a period of many months after marriage, the two partners become more deeply cognizant of each other, of each other's interests, of compatibilities, of differences. Today, quite likely, each will have a job, and each will enjoy some measure of freedom within a pattern the couple jointly set up. This is the period during which they will be establishing a foundation for the family unit.

Most married couples want and expect to have children. When should they have them? Let us assume you wish advice about that. If we were to be asked for it, we would probably suggest that you wait a few months or a year before embarking on the venture of having a child. It might be longer. This would depend upon you—how long you have known each other prior to marriage, how many rough edges there are (and there always are some) to be smoothed down, and how old you are.

A woman does not have to be young to have her first child in safety. But it is nice to be young enough to enjoy one's grandchildren. How long to wait depends upon the time, too, you need to get your home settled and to be financially prepared, at least reasonably so, for the baby. At the same time, it is true that people generally tend to become somewhat less fertile as they grow older. If they wait too long, it may be difficult to have children exactly when they wish to have them or to have as many as they would like.

If you live in a moderate climate or have modern conveniences, there is no need to be concerned about a special season of the year that might be best for the baby to be born in. If the climate is severe, it would be better to have mild weather during the baby's first few months to give him a good start and to simplify things for the mother.

How should children be spaced? There is no magic interval but we would suggest that when your first child is two or three years old, you might well consider having a second. Usually a child is in a comparatively "settled" state at age 2 or 3, and this is a good time to add a brother or sister. How you space your children, of course, depends too upon income and health. It would not be wise to have a second child, any more than the first, before you are physically, emotionally, and economically ready. Being an only child for a while will not hurt your first born. Having tired, worried, harassed parents might.

How many children should you have? There is no standard answer, of course. As many as you want and can afford—afford physically and emotionally as well as financially. Large families are nice; so are small ones. Quality is important—more so, we believe, than quantity. You will do best, we think, to keep an open mind about the number of children you will have. Your ideas may change; having each child is a unique experience; all of us change with experience; this is natural and to be expected.

Why not, you may say, let nature decide the number of children and the spacing? Nature works wonders, but on a large scale, without particular concern for the individual. Nature, for example, sets up an ecological balance; it produces organisms with their own niches; it makes some that are useful to man (those, for instance, that we need for cheese) but others that are capable of killing people; it balances organisms against each other, species against each other. Nature made men and women to have children, many children, so that at least some might survive the hazards nature puts in the way. Since man has eliminated many of these hazards now, has developed means for preventing malnutrition and means for conquering and even preventing many of the diseases of childhood which once took a huge toll, it is not necessary to have many children in order for a few to survive.

In ancient days, unwanted babies were left out to die. Civilization stopped that practice and is now increasingly concerned with not permitting unwanted children to perish emotionally and spiritually.

Major religions, and recently even governments expressing the desire of peoples, have recognized the need for and wisdom of controlling nature's lavish manner of providing children. Birth control, they agree, is desirable, even necessary.

Many methods of birth control are now available. Conception can be avoided by mechanical and chemical means, and also by the calendar or rhythm method, the latter approved by the Roman Catholic Church.

BIRTH CONTROL METHODS

THE CONDOM. A thin flexible sheath worn over the penis to prevent entrance of sperm into the vagina, the condom is effective as a birth preventive as well as protection against disease. Since the condom has been under the control of the U.S. Food and Drug Administration as a medical material, its quality has been improved. There is little danger it will break during intercourse.

But it is important to buy condoms at a good pharmacy and to select recognized brands. To be absolutely certain, a condom should be tested before use. An inflated condom can be placed under water; if there is a leak, bubbles of air will appear.

Some men dislike the condom because they feel it lessens sensation during intercourse; others find it satisfactory. It should be in place before the penis is inserted into the vagina. Donning it just before orgasm is risky, since some sperm may leak out before ejaculation actually takes place. The condom should be worn so there is loose space at the tip to provide room for the ejaculated semen. Usually, it is advisable to lubricate the outer surface of the device with K-Y jelly or some other bland lubricant before intercourse in order to facilitate entry.

Unless the condom is forbidden by religious precepts, it can be a useful preventive of pregnancy while a woman is learning to use another contraceptive method.

THE PESSARY. This device, worn by a woman, prevents sperm from entering the uterus or prevents the fertilized egg from embedding itself in the uterine wall.

The type that covers the cervix or mouth of the uterus is called a diaphragm and is an excellent method for preventing conception. It is made of soft rubber with a rim bound by a flexible metal spring. Some time before the sexual act, the diaphragm is coated with a vaginal contraceptive jelly, inside and out, and inserted. Properly placed, it lies across the opening of the uterus and will remain there until withdrawn.

When a diaphragm is left in place eight hours after intercourse, no douche is needed, although a plain warm-water douche may be taken for the sake of daintiness. When a diaphragm has been carefully fitted by a physician, when directions for its use are followed exactly, and when it is regularly inspected for holes or tears by holding it up to the light and stretching it gently, it should be reliable and comfortable. There may, however, be some risk of impregnation while a woman is first learning to use the diaphragm method and, during this period, perhaps for several weeks, the husband may do well to employ the condom, until the wife feels certain about the method and has returned to her physician for a recheck of technique.

Another type of pessary is the intrauterine device, or IUD, which is in increasing use. IUD's, of which there are many varieties, are made of metal and plastic in varied shapes—rings, coils, loops. All, when properly inserted into the uterus, discourage conception. None is 100 percent effective; no method is; but according to some reports, a properly fitted and used IUD may be as much as 98.5 percent effective. All IUD's permit fertility to return as soon as they are removed. A minority of women find that their device tends to be ejected; sometimes, when this happens with one type, another type will remain in place. Also in a minority of women an intrauterine device may cause bleeding.

No one is quite certain how IUD's achieve their effect. Somehow, the presence of the device within the uterus either prevents sperm and ovum from meeting, or prevents the egg from implanting itself within the uterus.

THE RHYTHM METHOD. This is a method of periodic abstinence based on the fact that women are able to conceive during only part of each month. During her fertile years, a woman ovulates, or releases an egg cell from an ovary, about once a month. Leaving the ovary, the egg travels down a fallopian tube toward the womb. If a sperm unites with the egg, conception occurs. For about two weeks after ovulation, the lining of the womb, its tissues built up through an enriched supply of blood, is ready to nest and nourish the fertilized egg. If conception does not occur, the unused, built-up tissue breaks down and is discharged in the process known as menstruation. While the time varies somewhat among women, menstruation generally occurs fourteen days after ovulation.

A woman's safe period averages about twenty days long, starting ten days prior to menstruation and lasting until about ten days after menstruation begins. Usually, conception can occur only when intercourse takes place during the middle days of the menstrual cycle, the period four or five days before to four or five days after ovulation.

Since the safe period varies according to the menstrual cycle, each woman must determine it for herself. Some women can tell when ovulation occurs because at that time, midway between periods, they experience intermenstrual pain, a peculiar, sudden, spasmodic sensation opposite one of the ovaries, followed by a heavy feeling in the lower abdomen which may last several hours. If they are alert for it, most women will observe an unusual mucous secretion at that time. These indications are helpful in determining the exact day of ovulation. Much more accurate, however, is a rise in temperature, which occurs at this time, usually between 0.6° and 0.8°F. To determine the period of ovulation, you should keep a temperature chart for no less than three months, taking your temperature for five minutes every morning after awakening, while still in bed.

In even the most regular women, illness or an emotional upset may hasten or delay ovulation. When this happens, calculations will be in error. Because of this possibility, the rhythm method cannot be considered as reliable as the condom or pessary. It has the disadvantage, too, of limiting days for coitus. One of its advantages is that it depends upon both partners; it is a joint responsibility. And because it does not depend upon an artificial device, it is morally and ethically acceptable to Roman Catholics and members of certain other religious denominations.

For complete safety—when, for example, pregnancy could seriously threaten health or life—we feel that all couples whose religious beliefs permit should use both the condom and the diaphragm-contraceptive-cream or IUD methods and should avoid intercourse on the days when conception might take place.

THE ORAL CONTRACEPTIVE PILL. The pill is a means of preventing ovulation, or egg release, thus making conception impossible. It became available as the result of the development of certain chemicals that behave in a woman's body like the hormones that control the reproductive cycle.

The pill is highly effective in avoiding conception when used exactly as directed. As an example, one type requires that a woman take the first dose on the fifth day of her menstrual cycle and continue a daily dose for twenty consecutive days. One to three days after she has taken the last tablet, menstruation begins and the count starts again.

The pill is considered reasonably safe in terms of health. In a small minority of women, it produces undesirable side effects. If you are considering using this method of preventing pregnancy, *you should do so under the close supervision of your doctor, who will prescribe the tablets, warn you of possible side effects, and help you to be prepared to cope with them.*

OTHER METHODS OF BIRTH CONTROL. These consist of douches, suppositories, jellies and creams, and coitus interruptus, all of them unsatisfactory in varying degree.

Douches are intended to wash out or kill the sperm before conception can occur. Since it is usually impossible to wash all sperm from the vagina, emphasis is placed on killing them by chemical means. Often, sperm have already reached the uterus before a woman has a chance to wash out the seminal fluid. By then it may be too late. Women may find it disturbing to douche immediately after intercourse, a time when they may want most to relax. As we have noted previously, in most women sexual feelings do not end abruptly and they want, and need, some relaxation and affection after coitus.

We advise avoiding use of advertised douches containing chemicals such as creosol or hypochlorite. Except on a doctor's prescription, we think it best not to use anything except a little salt or vinegar in a douche. So-called feminine hygiene douches are not effective for contraception and are not necessary for cleanliness.

Suppositories are capsules made of gelatin or cocoa butter which contain a sperm-destroying chemical ingredient. A suppository, when inserted in the vagina a few minutes prior to intercourse, is melted by body heat. The melted greasy base coats the opening of the uterus and forms a barrier to sperm while the chemical kills the sperm. Although sound in principle, the suppository has not been found to be completely reliable. Sometimes it does not melt properly prior to ejaculation or when melted does not completely cover the mouth of the womb.

Jellies and creams work on the same principle as suppositories. Inserted into the vagina with a special applicator, they are intended to block the opening into the uterus and destroy sperm. Since they are already in semifluid form, they have an advantage over the suppository in not having to melt before the crucial moment. Tests on some jellies and creams have been promising. Your doctor will know if physicians conclusively demonstrate in the future that these methods are reliable.

Coitus interruptus consists of withdrawing the penis from the vagina just prior to ejaculation. One of the oldest methods of birth control, mentioned in the Bible in the story of Onan who "spilled his seed upon the ground," it is still widely practiced.

We do not recommend it for several reasons. Even if successfully practiced, it is not an adequate safeguard since sperm may leak out before actual ejaculation. It can cause tension and strain, placing heavy responsibility upon the man, who finds it no easy matter to exercise control while highly excited. He may become irritable, emotionally disturbed, and have guilt feelings if he fails. The wife's concern lest he should fail to withdraw at the proper moment is a source of fear, tension, and emotional difficulties for her as well. Coitus interruptus does not permit development of the full love and tenderness that come when intercourse is completed with sexual organs united.

The contraceptive techniques we have described here are the most common, but others exist. Every couple must decide which, if any, to use—and should discuss the subject with their doctor or a qualified person at a birth control clinic or family planning agency. Most large cities and many smaller ones have such services. Or you may write to Planned Parenthood–World Population, 515 Madison Avenue, New York, N.Y. 10023, for information.

ABORTION

Generally, abortions have been illegal except when essential for safety or health. When performed illegally, they have been subject to no controls. Those who performed them, including so-called doctors, often have been fly-by-night individuals with little or no medical knowledge, working under conditions not completely sanitary, trusting to luck that nothing would go wrong that could be traced to them.

The death toll from illegal abortions has been tragically high, and the toll in illness and injury even higher. No accurate figures are available because so few cases have been reported. Sterility may result from an abortion, unreported and performed years earlier, and the abortion may not be suspected as the cause even by the victim herself. Some drugstores have carried on a lucrative under-the-counter business in drugs "guaranteed" to produce abortion. These are useless or dangerous drugs, and it has not been easy to obtain much information about their effects.

Fortunately, there has been a trend recently to liberalization of abortion laws in some states. While some people feel that destroying embryonic human life is never justified—and we respect the religious, ethical or moral grounds on which they base their opinions—we do not agree with them, and we are sure they will respect our viewpoint as we respect theirs. Our conviction is that the life of a mother should not be sacrificed or endangered, with all that means to her present children and possibly her future children, to maintain the life of an unborn infant whose survival chances often are slim.

This places great responsibility upon physicians who must decide whether or not an abortion is necessary. In some cases, the decision may not be difficult. In a tubal or ectopic pregnancy, for example, the embryo develops outside the uterus, in the fallopian tube which leads into it from the ovary. Fortunately, this is a rare condition. Such embryos cannot survive; they die in one way or another, sometimes bursting through the tube. At that point, the danger to the mother's life is great. Therefore tubal pregnancy is considered a clear-cut reason for terminating pregnancy by removing the embryo rather than waiting for it to die, thus endangering the mother's life.

Most cases are not so clear-cut. The doctor's decision may be a difficult one. But in many other circumstances doctors are used to, are forced to, make difficult decisions. They must do their best to decide wisely.

One important reason for a woman to have a complete medical checkup *prior* to pregnancy is that in most cases it will indicate whether or not she can safely have a baby, avoiding need for a difficult decision —for her and for her doctor—after she has conceived.

DISEASES THAT MAY MAKE PREGNANCY DANGEROUS

Heart disease
Kidney disease, especially Bright's disease and chronic pyelonephritis
High blood pressure
Diabetes
Tuberculosis
Venereal disease

They are dangerous if uncontrolled. Some can be cured completely. Others can be controlled so as not to necessarily endanger the life of mother or baby. Even heart disease in many instances does not pose too serious a risk if proper care is taken. But only a physician, after thorough examination, can validly decide whether pregnancy will be harmful or dangerous in an individual case.

However much a woman with a serious disease not yet brought under good control may wish to become pregnant, it may be reckless for her to do so if her physician advises against it. If she survives the pregnancy, she may not have the health and strength to properly care for her baby.

ADOPTION

Most couples who are unable to have children of their own for any reason—the health of the mother or a problem of infertility, which we will discuss next—need not be childless. Responsible agencies in the field of adoption today eliminate virtually all risk when a couple wishes to adopt a child. Such agencies obtain information about the real parents, examine and test the child, try to match child and adoptive parents as far as possible. Of course, there may be risk when one obtains a baby through unofficial sources.

If you or your physician do not know of any responsible adoption agency, The Child Welfare League of America, 44 East 23rd St., New York, N.Y. 10010, can provide a list of approved agencies. Discuss your feelings about the problems of adoption freely with representatives of the agency handling the adoption. This will help to avoid reservations in the love you give your adopted child and the love and enjoyment you can expect to receive.

CAUSES OF CHILDLESSNESS

Miscarriages

Although she may conceive readily enough, a woman may lose her child early in pregnancy. Some women repeatedly experience such miscarriages, or spontaneous abortions. Any one or more of several reasons may account for this: emotional disturbance, general poor health, malnutrition, acute illness including infection, glandular disorder. Often, these conditions are comparatively easy to cure.

Many miscarriages may be avoided by refraining from sexual intercourse during the days on which the woman's menstrual periods would occur if she were not pregnant. Sometimes a week's rest in bed at these periods, especially during the early months of pregnancy, may save the baby. Rest during the week or so corresponding to the time in pregnancy of a previous miscarriage often is helpful.

There is no need to be discouraged by a miscarriage, especially if it is your first pregnancy. It has been estimated that one of every six married women in the United States under the age of 35 has had at least one miscarriage, and the figure might well be much higher if it were possible to determine how many "late" menstrual periods were actually early miscarriages.

Reduced Fertility

Few people are really sterile, without reproductive power at all. Many who consider themselves sterile have reduced fertility, but can reproduce and often do so at some point—to their own surprise.

Infertility, or reduced fertility, has many possible causes. Often, emotional factors are involved. You may know at least one couple who adopted a child when one of their own seemed impossible, and shortly afterward conceived a child. Why this happens is not thoroughly understood: It may be the result of reduced tension when, after many efforts, hope is given up and a child is adopted; it may be that the act of mothering has a beneficial effect on a woman's glandular system.

Physicians usually can determine a man's or woman's fertility level. A man may produce few or many sperm; they may have long or short life-spans; they may be highly motile or not motile enough to make the journey to the egg. A woman's secretions may be injurious to sperm; her fallopian tubes may be narrow; or her uterus may be incapable of forming tissues needed for the egg after fertilization. Many other factors may influence fertility. Fortunately, most of them can be corrected today, though it often takes time and the skills of specialists to achieve correction.

If you are childless and want a baby, give yourself the best possible chance of conceiving one. This means having intercourse at a time when it is most likely to lead to conception. Study the rhythm method of birth control described earlier—and use it in *reverse*. Some couples who consider themselves infertile happen never actually to have had intercourse at the appropriate time.

Upon completion of the sexual act, it may be helpful for the woman to elevate her legs and keep them elevated for a short time, as a means of helping the semen to reach and be retained in the inner portion of the vagina. No douches of any kind should be used.

Some men fail to produce an adequate number of sperm if they have intercourse too frequently. Therefore, it often helps for an infertile couple to refrain from coitus for a week before the day of ovulation, and on that day to have intercourse both in the morning and at night.

Try following these suggestions before you become convinced you have a difficult infertility problem. If you still do not succeed in having a baby, both of you should consult a physician or a fertility clinic which he may recommend. It was once believed that inevitably the wife was at fault in childlessness. It is now known that quite often the trouble may lie with the husband. And it is also known that frequently when both partners seek help, minor treatment for both may raise their joint fertility level enough to assure success where even major treatment for one or the other may fail. (Planned Parenthood–World Population, 515 Madison Ave., New York, N.Y. 10023, can recommend clinics and private physicians specializing in the treatment of infertility.)

Don't simply blame yourself or your spouse for your childlessness. Find out what the trouble is. It may be readily correctable. Sometimes it may be correctable with some difficulty—but correctable.

And if your condition cannot be corrected, take thought of that vow you made, "for better or worse." It will not be for worse if, having acted intelligently, sought the reason for failure, found it, determined that it could not be overcome, you go on, knowing you have done all you could, to philosophically and lovingly join in adopting a child to love as your own.

PREPARING FOR PREGNANCY

Every single day of pregnancy is important for the baby. Yet in every pregnancy there is a period of weeks when the mother does not know she has conceived. At any time in this country more than three million women are pregnant but almost one million of them are not yet aware of it.

At the time a woman notices her first skipped period, her baby is likely to have been developing for about two weeks. Early development is rapid. Even within a month after conception, the baby's heart, kidneys, brain, liver, digestive tract, arms, legs, eyes, and ears have begun to form. Before the fourth week, the heart is already beating. And yet in the early weeks, when so much is going on within her to form her baby, the mother-to-be is unaware.

There is only one way she can contribute to protecting her child from the start—by being in the best possible condition prior to pregnancy. That requires nothing very special but it does put added emphasis on the usual, simple rules for good health, since now they are being observed for the benefit of two people.

Like anybody else, a mother-to-be should have regular periodic medical checkups. If the physician finds that all is well during such examinations, that reassurance adds to mental ease. If a condition is found that needs correction, it is all to the good that it is found and corrected early when it almost invariably is easier to correct.

Good nutrition, vital for everyone, is certainly so for the woman who is looking forward to having a child. Maintaining proper weight is advisable. A daily quota of exercise—beyond housework which, of course, provides activity—is important. To go walking, swimming, bicycling, gardening—doing something beyond the daily round of household chores —is good exercise, provides change of pace, and is beneficial for both body and mind.

Preventive medicine in terms of mother and child will be at its best when every woman is examined prior to every conception, whereas now usually only those with special problems seek such attention. The fact is that while maternal mortality has steadily declined, infant mortality is still too high. Forty years ago, about 65 mothers died for every 10,000 births in the United States; today there are less than 4 deaths for each 10,000 deliveries. In the University of Chicago's Lying-In Hospital, only 13 mothers died during a 9-year period in which 34,000 deliveries took place, and only 6 of them died from conditions due to pregnancy and childbirth. Much has been done to make pregnancy and childbirth safer and more comfortable for the mother.

The need now is for ways and means to diminish infant mortality and for measures to actively promote the good health of the growing fetus. It is highly desirable to carefully prepare the maternal soil each time, before the seed is implanted. During a preconception health inventory, adequacy of diet can be checked, any systemic disease can be detected and treated, any endocrine imbalance can be corrected—and such measures should do more to insure a healthy child than when carried out after conception.

Pregnancy is not a disease state. It is a healthy condition. And any woman who enters it in good health can expect to find it pleasurable.

PREGNANCY BEGINS

Conception occurs when one of the 300 million or more spermatozoa in the teaspoonful of semen a healthy man ejaculates reaches an egg cell which, if the woman has ovulated, may be waiting in one of the two fallopian tubes.

Sperm cells face hazards, beginning in the vagina whose acid secretions kill millions. But many escape, swimming up through the vagina by means of their whiplike tails. Those with sufficient energy proceed through the cervical canal into the uterus, and on into the fallopian tubes. There is only a short period, about two days, when the egg cell is in the right place and in the right condition to be fertilized. Average sperm can retain their potency for only about 48 hours within the woman's reproductive tract except in rare instances. But if all goes well, if the act of intercourse occurs at or near the time of ovulation and the sperm are normally active, the chances are that a male cell will reach the egg, penetrate it, and in that moment a new life is created.

The moment fertilization occurs—with the union of one sperm cell and one egg cell—all the characteristics the child is to inherit are determined. The question of whether the baby will be blond or brunet, blue-eyed or brown-eyed is settled. So is sex. Whether a baby is to be boy or girl depends entirely upon the sperm cell.

Will you have twins or triplets? This, too, is determined at the time of fertilization. Multiple births tend to occur more frequently in some families than in others. On the average, the chance of having twins is one in 88; for triplets, it is one in 6,000; and for quadruplets, one in 500,000.

Very quickly after fertilization, the egg begins to divide. Five to seven days later, the embryo, still tiny but made up now of many cells formed by division, travels to the wall of the uterus where it attaches itself. At this stage, it grows rapidly. By about the twenty-eighth day after conception, the embryo is large enough to be seen without a microscope.

KNOWING WHEN YOU'RE PREGNANT

At this stage, the average woman is aware of, or suspects, the existence of her baby. Some women know even earlier. A few women insist they know immediately after conception; perhaps they do. But most women have to wait for some signs and symptoms to appear.

Often a woman's first clue to her pregnancy comes when she observes that her breasts are enlarging, the nipples becoming larger and darker in color, and new and tiny blood vessels are forming on the breasts. There may be new sensations of tingling and fullness.

Another early symptom may be an overpowering drowsiness, which is not related to fatigue but is a simple, acute sleepiness. Some women awaken early in the morning. Others feel suddenly dizzy. There may be a feeling of pressure in the bladder and increased desire to urinate.

The best-known indication of pregnancy is a missed menstrual period. However, menses are sometimes delayed or absent for reasons other than pregnancy, and in rare instances women menstruate for several months after conception. So the presence or absence of menstruation is not a reliable indication. Indeed, all of the symptoms we have just noted can be due to other causes. They may sometimes develop because of purely emotional factors such as fear of, or hope of, having a baby.

Medical Diagnosis of Pregnancy

In arriving at an early diagnosis of pregnancy, the doctor is guided, as in most other diagnoses, by symptoms the patient reports. If she experiences all the symptoms just mentioned, he can be fairly certain she is pregnant. His training allows him to evaluate some symptoms and indications better than she can. For example, he can tell a great deal by examination of the breasts.

By about the tenth week, the physician can detect pregnancy with a fair degree of accuracy by pressing the abdomen in the right place and feeling the slight enlargement produced by the swollen uterus. He can also detect a bluish hue in tissues at the entrance to the vagina and he can feel that the cervix, or mouth of the womb, is softer than in the nonpregnant state.

By the beginning of the fifth month or even a few weeks earlier, an x-ray will reveal the baby's bones, its movements can be felt, and its heartbeat is detectable.

Laboratory Tests

Tests have been developed which allow, in at least 95 percent of all cases, determination of pregnancy within two weeks after the first missed menstrual period. If you have any reason for wanting to be certain immediately, it is simple to have such a test made. The best-known is the A-Z, or Aschheim-Zondek, test named for the two doctors who developed it. For the test, a small quantity of urine voided by a woman in the morning is injected into a mouse or rabbit. If she is pregnant, certain definite changes take place in the animal.

A more recently developed test uses a urine sample and a particular type of female toad. If the woman is pregnant, the toad will put out a large number of eggs within about 18 hours.

Doctors often use another method of testing in which certain female hormones are administered; if the woman does not menstruate within a certain number of days or hours (depending upon the hormone used), the likelihood of pregnancy is about 95 percent.

THE COURSE OF PREGNANCY

In broad outline, you get an idea from the following chart of how pregnancy progresses, what happens to baby and mother after conception takes place. Incidentally, physicians use the word *embryo* in talking about an unborn baby in early stages, the word *fetus* later on.

The chart, of course, provides only a general idea of the course of pregnancy. You will want to know more and your physician will provide information. Indeed, all the facts we present here are designed not to replace the information your doctor will provide but to serve as background for his information. We would like to emphasize, too, that there are usually several good ways to handle this or that situation which may arise during pregnancy. Knowing you, your doctor will pick the one that may be particularly effective and practical for you. If you have confidence in your physician, you should follow his advice. If you don't have confidence, you should get another doctor.

WHY PRENATAL CARE

Although pregnancy is a healthy condition, as we have said, every pregnant woman should consult a physician as soon as she thinks she is pregnant. Prenatal care has much to offer in the prevention of possible complications.

The work of many hundreds of research scientists is constantly adding to our knowledge of what happens in detail during the nine months of pregnancy. From their pioneering studies come new means of understanding, detecting, and treating many factors which may affect the mother-to-be or her unborn child. Physicians can make these new developments and safeguards available to the women who seek prenatal care.

As just one example of newer insights: It was once thought that if a pregnant woman was in reasonably good health, her baby would be properly nourished because he would take what he needed from her system. It now appears that what she eats every day is vitally important to her child, and if her diet is deficient there may be permanent effects on the child. Protein, especially animal protein, is most important. A protein deficiency in the mother's diet can harm the baby's nervous system. There is a better chance, too, of delivery at term—and without toxemia—when the mother has a balanced diet.

Out of a study with 50,000 expectant mothers and their babies conducted by the National Institute of Neurological Disease and Blindness recently has come evidence that malnutrition in a pregnant woman may

END OF MONTH NO.	THE BABY	THE MOTHER
1	The embryo, now past the microscopic stage, is visible as a tiny piece of tissue.	May be sleepy in early evening. Often must get up to urinate during the night. Breasts may be larger, the pigmented areas darker. Nausea and vomiting may occur.
2	Is now a little over 1" long, with face formed, limbs partly formed. Has the definite appearance of an infant now.	Nausea and vomiting may persist. Breasts continue to enlarge, blood supply to them increases, and bluish veins appear.
3	Now weighs one ounce, is 3" long, with limbs, fingers, toes, ears fully formed. Sex is clear. Nails begin to appear.	Abdomen may show some enlargement. Tissue at entrance to vagina is bluish. There may be food cravings, emotional upsets.
4	About 8" long, weighs nearly 8 oz. Movements can be felt by mother; heart sounds can usually be heard, bones detected by x-ray. Eyebrows and lashes are formed. Skin is pinker, covered with fine hair.	Nausea and vomiting and drowsiness are over. Begins to feel unusually well, energetic, with sense of distinct well-being.
5	About 12" long, weighs one pound, has hair on head.	
6	Now 14" long, weighs nearly 2 pounds. Skin is wrinkled and fetus has an "old man" appearance. Not likely to survive if born at this stage.	Pink or silvery white lines, called striae, may appear on abdomen and breasts.
7	Weighs about 3 pounds, is 16" long, has more fat under the skin. In a boy, testicles are in the scrotum.	
8	About 18" long, weight about 5 pounds. A good chance to survive if born now.	Breathing may become a little difficult. Baby is pushing the diaphragm up, causing shortness of breath.
9	Average length about 20", weight about 7 pounds.	Increased desire to urinate may return, especially at night. Baby's kicking may cause some discomfort. Experiences much shifting and moving about of the baby.
At birth	Head is as large around as shoulders are across. Infant is less wrinkled, almost smooth, and covered with cheeselike material.	

endanger the mental development of her unborn child. The study found, for example, that when children were followed up at the age of four years, those born to mothers on protein-deficient diets during pregnancy had IQ's 16 points below the average of those born to women on more normal diets.

There are women who may remind you that years ago it was customary to have babies without any medical attention, and that is true. But the reduction in maternal and infant deaths in recent years proves that medical care during pregnancy and delivery benefits both mother and child. Even during a normal, uneventful, uncomplicated pregnancy, a doctor's advice and guidance are invaluable. He supervises diet, the amount and kind of activity, many other aspects of day-to-day life, and knows how to alleviate most effectively, and safely, most of the discomforts that might otherwise bother a woman during pregnancy. Prenatal care increasingly now provides a firm foundation for the most healthy and comfortable pregnancy, the best and safest delivery.

We suggest that, if possible, you put yourself in the hands of a specialist, a well-trained obstetrician, and follow his advice, not a neighbor's. Your doctor can usually recommend a good obstetrician. If you cannot afford a private doctor, find out about clinics at the nearest hospital. The best and most highly paid obstetricians usually contribute some of their time to clinic patients. If you live in a rural area, your general practitioner may be very skilled in obstetrics. Knowing the responsibilities they have, general practitioners or family physicians in rural areas often take special postgraduate courses in obstetrics.

A Special Note about Unmarried Mothers

Every prospective mother has the right to, as well as need for, good care for herself and her unborn child. This is fully as true for the mother who is unfortunate enough to bear a child out of wedlock. Many tragedies might be avoided if these girls, often very young, made use of (and, in many cases, even realized the existence of) good care available in most communities. The Salvation Army and other agencies sponsored by various religious denominations provide, or help the girl to find, a physician or hospital clinic. They offer advice and guidance as well. So do other organizations such as the Florence Crittendon Homes Association, Inc. There are about fifty branches of this association in various parts of the country, with headquarters at 608 S. Dearborn Street, Chicago, Ill. 60605. Information also can be obtained by writing the National Association on Service to Unmarried Parents, 44 East 23rd St., New York, N.Y. 10010, or the Children's Bureau, Social Security Agency, U.S. Department of Health, Education and Welfare, Washington, D.C. 20201.

YOUR FIRST VISIT TO THE DOCTOR

Your physician will probably take considerable pains in your first visit to get a thorough medical history. He will need to know what, if any, diseases or surgical operations you may have had. He will question you about previous pregnancies, if any. Your family history will give him some idea of your chances of having twins or triplets. Answer his questions as best you can and don't hesitate to admit that you don't know something or can't remember. He will appreciate the fact that you are flustered, not scatterbrained.

He will weigh and examine you. If this is your first internal pelvic examination, you may be tense and embarrassed. Your doctor will understand and try to minimize your discomfort and embarrassment. He will drape you in sheets as completely as possible and proceed in a straightforward, objective manner. If you are tense, you may find that breathing in and out hard, with your mouth open, tends to relax muscles and make the examination less uncomfortable.

Your doctor will examine you from head to toe, listening to your heart, measuring your blood pressure, checking your breasts, examining your abdomen. At about the tenth week, he may be able to detect the baby's presence as he feels the abdomen. He is almost certain to be able to do so by the fourth to fifth month when he can also probably hear the baby's heartbeat which differs from the mother's in being nearly twice as fast.

In the vaginal or pelvic examination, your doctor will determine the size and shape of the uterus, whether it is normal or turned (retroverted). If it is turned, he will prescribe exercises to return it to proper position. The examination will also reveal whether there are any growths in the uterus or any disease or abnormality. The doctor will also probably take your pelvic measurements so he can decide whether the hard bony structure through which the baby must pass at birth is large enough. If it is small, or otherwise abnormal, he will consider the possibility of a cesarean or abdominal delivery.

Also, in your visit, your doctor will test your urine, mainly to determine whether it is free of sugar and albumin. Sugar may be an indication of diabetes; albumin sometimes signifies kidney disorder. He will test your blood, routinely, for syphilis and for anemia. He will also type the blood to see which group you are in—A, B, AB, or O—since you may need a blood transfusion at some point in pregnancy or possibly at delivery. Whether or not you are Rh-negative will also be determined, and the doctor may wish you to have a chest x-ray taken, if you have not had one recently, to make certain there is no tuberculosis of the lungs.

Thus, the first examination is important. It will probably be followed by routine monthly visits during the first five or six months of pregnancy and, after that, visits every three weeks and then every two.

TALK THINGS OVER

During your visits, by all means ask any questions, voice any doubts that occur to you. In any case, your physician will give you advice about your life as a pregnant woman and he will try to dispel your fears. But he can do a much better job of reassuring and informing you if you let him know what is on your mind.

Don't be self-conscious about asking questions; don't have any fears the doctor may think them silly. He would much rather answer the "silliest" question than have you worry needlessly. And no question that bothers a patient and that she discusses with her physician is silly.

When Will Your Baby Be Born?

This, of course, is one of the first things you will want to know. The period of gestation—the time the fetus spends in the uterus—differs considerably from species to species. The human baby requires nine months, the opossum eleven days, the elephant nearly two years. In humans, the gestation period also varies, probably influenced by the length of the mother's menstrual cycle. On the average, pregnancy lasts 280 days, which means that a fairly high percentage of women will have their babies a week or two before or after this date.

It is sometimes difficult to determine the exact date when the baby was conceived. Your doctor will make a rapid calculation when you tell him the time of your last menstrual period and give you a date when you may expect your baby. If, for example, your last period was November 16, he will advise you to expect the child about August 23. This is how he does it: He adds seven days to the date of the last menstrual period, and then counts back three months.

CARING FOR YOURSELF TO CARE FOR YOUR BABY

Taking good care of yourself is the best way to take care of your unborn baby. You need not worry that things which happen in everyday life, and so are not rare in pregnancy—a fright, a craving, an emotional experience—will harm the baby. Nor will an accidental bump in the abdomen or sleeping on your stomach or in any other position hurt him. He is well protected inside your womb.

There are many old wives' tales modern medicine can dismiss—such as that a mole on a child may be due to a mother's craving for strawberries, or a child's buck teeth developed because his mother was frightened by a horse. In some ways, however, we do know that the fetus in the womb is subject to outside influences. Physicians have noticed that if a woman is exceptionally tense during pregnancy, full of irritations and complaints, her unborn child may be unusually active. In more specific fashion, a pregnant woman's diet and general health will have an important bearing on her baby's physical condition. The pregnant woman must be on guard against some specific illnesses and conditions, such as those that follow.

GERMAN MEASLES. While any serious disease or complication of pregnancy can be dangerous to both baby and mother, one disease, German measles, is mild in its effects on the mother but can seriously affect the unborn child, especially if the disease is contracted during the first three months of pregnancy. Some babies whose mothers have had German measles are born with cataracts, deaf-mutism, heart disease, or mental retardation.

Fortunately, today, there is an effective vaccine against German measles. If you have never had German measles, have not been vaccinated, and are exposed to someone with the disease, notify your doctor at once. He may want to give you an injection of gamma globulin that can reduce your risk of contracting the disease.

SELF-MEDICATION. During pregnancy especially, you should never take any medication except what your doctor prescribes for you, and in the precise dose. It has become clear that some medications may have what are called teratogenetic effects—that is, they may affect the unborn baby adversely when taken at certain times during pregnancy when certain structures of the baby are being formed. This is a subject of intensive research today. Every physician keeps up with the work and makes use of new knowledge in his practice. So, in your very first visit to him, let your physician know what, if any, medication you have been taking, and let him counsel you on whether to continue taking it or, if necessary, perhaps use something else. This is not a scare matter. Actually, growing knowledge about teratogenetic effects promises to reduce the incidence of birth defects.

VENEREAL DISEASES. Even though it is possible for a woman to experience only minor symptoms from venereal disease, the effect on the baby can be tragic. Syphilis is particularly dangerous. Unless women with the disease are treated in its earliest stages, nearly half deliver stillborn or infected babies. The babies who survive are likely to be physically or mentally defective. There is no excuse for so handicapping a child, since early syphilis can be cured in about a week by injection of large doses of penicillin (see page 657).

Gonorrhea is less dangerous to the unborn baby but inflicts damage while the baby is actually being born, as it passes through the birth canal. Germs responsible for gonorrhea may, if they enter the baby's eyes, cause blindness. Routine use of silver nitrate in the eyes of all newborn babies has prevented this disaster in most deliveries. But there is no excuse for running the slightest risk, since gonorrhea, too, can be readily cured (see page 580).

MISCARRIAGE. If you have never had a miscarriage, your doctor will probably tell you not to worry about it. He may suggest that you refrain from intercourse during the days when your first three menstrual periods would occur if you were not pregnant. He may also suggest that you take things fairly easy during those days.

If you have had a miscarriage, he will probably suggest additional precautions on those dates, and especially at about the time your previous miscarriage occurred. Women who have had repeated miscarriages may have problems that can be solved only on an individual basis; and for this, an obstetrician may need help from a specialist in another field, such as an endocrinologist.

Remember that most women do not miscarry easily or often. It is, in fact, astonishing what most women can endure without miscarrying. So don't worry about it. It is desirable for you to be familiar with this and other possible complications of pregnancy which we discuss later in this chapter—but they are the exception, not the rule, and modern science can cope with them.

WHAT CAN YOU DO DURING PREGNANCY?

The chances are that your life need not be materially different now that you are pregnant. Your appearance need not be unattractive, and your activities will not be much restricted. If you enjoy your work, or must work for financial reasons, you may well be able to continue if your job is not too strenuous or physically exhausting. If your health is good, your doctor may even approve your continuing to work until the eighth month. Many women feel that working keeps their mind off "symptoms." Others feel that work is too tiring.

Your other activities may not need to change a great deal. Many doctors feel that a pregnant woman can safely engage in such sports as golf, riding, tennis, and dancing as long as she does not become overtired. Some doctor feels that it is helpful to engage in only mild forms of exercise during the early stages of pregnancy when the risk of miscarriage is greatest. They recommend walking, housework, a normal social life for the healthy pregnant woman.

There is no reason why a pregnant woman cannot drive a car or take motor trips as long as her figure does not become too cumbersome. If you go on a long trip, do make it a point to stop every 90 minutes and get out and move around for a few minutes; this reduces danger of blood clotting in the veins. In all forms of travel, obey the cardinal rule: don't overtire yourself. If you have a tendency to motion sickness, it may be wise to avoid boat or plane trips.

Always consult your doctor before undertaking anything new or any time you are in doubt.

Keep occupied. Try to get some fresh air and exercise daily—but don't overdo. Get as much sleep as you need.

Instead of being a time of boredom, full of real or imaginary indispositions, pregnancy can be a time when a woman can develop new skills or reestablish those she gave up after marriage.

CLOTHING

It's possible for a woman today to dress attractively in clothes that conceal pregnancy during the early stages and avoid an ungainly look later. About the only taboo so far as clothing is concerned is that it not be too tight or uncomfortable in any way. Round garters constrict leg blood vessels; wear a garter belt instead. Wear comfortable, safe shoes. Because the extra weight you carry is localized, it will shift your center of gravity, and high heels will not support you properly during the last months of pregnancy.

Some physicians recommend a maternity corset after the fourth month; others leave it up to the patient. Such a corset is not designed to disguise your figure; rather, it is a sling to support the abdomen, and can be helpful in relieving back strain and fatigue. Most women are more comfortable when they wear a firm brassiere that supports but does not flatten the breasts. However, whether or not you wear a corset or brassiere usually makes little difference in the way you feel or look after you have had your baby. Recovery of a youthful, prepregnancy figure depends primarily on muscle tone and on how much weight was gained.

PERSONAL HYGIENE

There is no reason why you should not bathe the entire body. Tub baths are sometimes forbidden in the last months of pregnancy because of the danger of infection. Shower or sponge baths are always safe.

424 / Family Preventive Care

Douches are unnecessary. Never take a douche during pregnancy unless your doctor recommends it.

Some physicians recommend rubbing lanolin or cocoa butter into the nipples in the last months of pregnancy as a means of helping to soften them and prevent cracks during the nursing period. Most obstetricians, however, consider this unnecessary and advocate simply ordinary cleanliness.

ALCOHOL AND TOBACCO

Most doctors permit their obstetrical patients to drink alcoholic beverages occasionally and in moderation. Until recently, they had the same attitude about smoking. But with new information on the effects of smoking, many physicians now advise their pregnant patients to stop altogether. We suggest that now is the time to stop smoking. If you cannot give up the habit, it is important at least that you smoke only moderately for the sake of both your baby (the baby's heart beats faster when the mother smokes) and you. There is a real possibility of toxic effects on the developing fetus.

SEXUAL RELATIONS

With the exception of certain days of the month when it may increase the risk of miscarriage, sexual intercourse is safe during the first seven to eight months of pregnancy. Moderation is essential. Intercourse is not considered safe during the last six weeks, since bacteria are forced into the mouth of the womb during coitus, and if labor should begin early, the organisms might cause a dangerous infection.

Sexual desire in women during pregnancy is not predictable. In some, it may be heightened; in others, decreased. Don't worry about it. Whether or not you have an orgasm will make no difference to your baby. You may find, especially as pregnancy progresses, that you prefer some position other than the one you usually use.

EMOTIONAL REACTIONS

You may find that you are emotionally on edge early in pregnancy. You may be unusually irritable and sensitive, easily upset, likely to cry if anyone speaks crossly to you. The demands and fretfulness of your other children may seem almost too much to bear.

Try to take this in stride. It's not anybody's fault. Our bodies and emotions are influenced by hormones. During pregnancy, some hormones are in increased supply in the body, others in decreased supply, and this temporary imbalance may lead to exaggerated emotional reactions. After the first few months, if you are a reasonably stable person, you will recover your calm disposition. But pregnancy can be a strain and occasionally in very unstable individuals may lead to severe nervous reactions. If you are at all concerned about this, consult your doctor, who will reassure or advise you.

DIET AND WEIGHT

Excess weight puts a strain on everyone, especially a pregnant woman. You will be more comfortable if you carry no excess fat in addition to carrying your baby. And it is certainly easier to avoid gaining fat than losing it. Many women fail to regain trim figures after pregnancy because it is so difficult to get rid of extra pounds after the baby has arrived.

If you have been of normal weight, 20 pounds is a good amount to gain in pregnancy. If you have been underweight, your doctor may decide this is a good time to pick up extra pounds. If you have been too heavy, he may actually advise a reducing diet.

It is not necessary, as many women rationalize when they overindulge, to "eat for two." Eat for one—enough, not too much, watching quality as well as amount. Most of your calories should come from meats and other proteins, green vegetables, and fruits. Starches, fats, and sugars —bread, rice, potatoes, spaghetti, butter, and desserts—should usually be restricted. Many nutrition experts believe that a pregnant woman needs one and one-half times as much protein as a nonpregnant one, to supply demands of fetal and maternal growth and tissue replacement. Fruits and vegetables are valuable for their mineral and vitamin content.

Your doctor may prescribe extra iron to avoid anemia. He may urge you to drink milk because of its calcium content, suggesting skim milk if you need to watch your weight. This contains as much calcium as whole milk.

Drink plenty of fluid, at least eight glasses a day. This can be anything liquid—milk, coffee, tea, fruit juices, soups. Avoid fattening beverages such as soft drinks. You need plenty of fluid to flush the kidneys and bladder frequently; this greatly reduces risk of infection in the urinary tract. You may have heard of women who become puffy in appearance because they retain an unusual amount of water. This is not due to fluid they have been drinking but indicates something is wrong, and it requires immediate attention of the doctor. He may be able to control it simply by reducing or eliminating salt intake. But it may be more serious.

426 / Family Preventive Care

You may experience cravings for certain foods—pickles, candy, lobster, almost any food. Don't be upset if you have an intense desire for something you were never interested in before. If it's edible, it will do no harm to eat it. Also, it won't hurt you or the baby if you don't eat it. At any rate, the capricious yearning will pass.

COMMON NUISANCE PROBLEMS

NAUSEA. While many theories have been advanced about what causes nausea and vomiting in pregnancy, the most likely relates the problem to the hormone changes in pregnancy. Seldom does the symptom persist beyond the third month. And it's not inevitable; more than one third of women escape it completely.

There are many ways to prevent or minimize "morning sickness," so called because the nausea and vomiting usually, but not always, appear in the morning. Avoid excessive fatigue. Eating often helps, so try five or six small meals rather than three large ones. Have some dry crackers, a thermos of weak tea, or whatever appeals to you, on your bedside table, ready for you to eat before you get up. Lie still afterward for a while.

Although you need fluids, they may not stay down on an empty stomach. So eat dry foods first, sipping fluids in small quantities.

Rest after eating. Lie down for 20 minutes or so after even a small meal. Avoid sights and smells that seem nauseating to you. Even if you used to like cigarettes, they may disturb you now.

HEARTBURN. Heartburn has nothing to do with the heart but is caused by stomach acid sneaking up into the esophagus. Avoiding greasy or fried foods often helps; so, too, does omitting gas-forming foods such as cucumbers and cabbage. Try to eliminate desserts and rich foods, too. Heartburn sometimes can be prevented by taking a tablespoonful of cream half an hour before a meal. You may find relief after taking a level teaspoonful of milk of magnesia. It works far better than bicarbonate of soda, or baking soda, which many doctors do not recommend during pregnancy.

CONSTIPATION. Most women are no more likely to have constipation during pregnancy than before. If it should develop, it can be corrected by diet. Avoid irritating bran, however. Fruits, including the time-honored prunes, and vegetables are much better. A coarse cereal like oatmeal is also good. Cold fruit juice or a glass or two of cold water before breakfast is helpful. A mild laxative such as milk of magnesia is not harmful, but don't get into the habit of taking laxatives and never take any really strong laxative without consulting your doctor. Remember, too many people worry about bowel movements; it isn't necessary to have one every day; try to be relaxed and casual, as well as regular. (See Constipation, page 226.)

TOOTH DECAY.   Put no stock in the old and false saying: a tooth for every child. If you experience an unusual degree of tooth decay, the baby isn't at fault; it may well be overindulgence in sweets or inadequate diet. See your dentist so your teeth will be in good shape while you are pregnant; this is important because it eliminates any possibility of infection arising from tooth decay.

DIZZINESS.   In pregnancy, as at other times, if you stand in one place for a long period, your blood tends to pool in the legs, reducing circulation to the brain. This can lead to dizziness and even fainting. If you feel dizziness coming on, sit or lie down at once. Late in pregnancy, some women get dizzy when lying on their back. This is the result of the heavy uterus pressing on part of a big vein, the vena cava. The dizziness disappears if you roll on your side or sit up.

FATIGUE.   If, early in pregnancy, you experience this, frequent short rests are a help. In extreme cases, anemia may cause excessive fatigue. During your regular checkups, your doctor can make blood tests to see if you are anemic and, if so, correct the anemia.

SHORTNESS OF BREATH.   This may be caused by growing pressure of the baby. If it becomes so severe, at any time during your pregnancy, that you cannot climb a short flight of stairs without discomfort, be sure to see your doctor about it. If a mild case interferes with your sleep, propping up your head and shoulders with several pillows so that you are half-sitting and half-lying will bring relief.

LEG CRAMPS.   If you get these, it may be because you've been over-enthusiastic about drinking milk. Milk is necessary but too much may build up excess phosphorus in the system. Your doctor may prescribe some aluminum antacids to counteract the phosphorus.

VARICOSE VEINS.   As suggested earlier, avoid round garters or anything that restricts the circulation in your legs. Get off your feet as often as you can, and avoid standing in one position for any length of time. If the veins are marked or troublesome, your doctor may recommend elastic stockings or bandages or may treat them more actively.

BACKACHE.   As pregnancy progresses, the body's center of gravity shifts forward. Many women then stand in a swayback position which puts strain on the back and legs. Try to stand with your seat tucked under. It sometimes helps if you straighten your back along a wall or lie flat on the floor and push your back down so it touches the floor. A maternity girdle can help ease the strain on back muscles. Low-heeled shoes will give you better balance and help the back.

HEMORRHOIDS. These may appear or become exaggerated during pregnancy. Your doctor can help you. See page 593 for suggestions.

SWELLING OF FEET AND ANKLES. If the swelling does not disappear after you have taken extra rest and remained off your feet for a day or two, your doctor should be consulted. The swelling may indicate that something needs medical attention.

DANGER SIGNALS

Like anybody else, a pregnant woman can develop some illness during the course of her pregnancy. Because you have both your baby and yourself to consider, it is most important that you be familiar with the danger signals we discussed elsewhere (see page 29). There are a few conditions to which pregnant women are more than usually susceptible, and there are some, such as miscarriage and complications of childbirth, which the rest of us are spared.

CYSTITIS AND PYELITIS. Cystitis is a bladder infection which may lead to appearance of bacteria, pus, and sometimes blood in the urine. Symptoms include a desire to urinate often and pain and burning sensations on urination. The infection responds quickly to sulfa drugs and antibiotics and drinking of large amounts of fluid. It should be treated immediately to avoid pyelitis.

Pyelitis, an infection of the kidney, can be serious if not treated. Fortunately, sulfa drugs and antibiotics are effective. The symptoms are chills and fever, back pain in the region of the kidneys, and sometimes frequent urination and pain on urination.

ECTOPIC (TUBAL) PREGNANCY. When a fertilized ovum does not reach the uterus but instead burrows into a fallopian tube, the pregnancy is called ectopic. Because the tube is small, the egg is likely to burst through it after reaching a certain size. This is called a ruptured ectopic pregnancy. The tube may also abort the fetus by pushing it out. The symptoms are vaginal bleeding and severe pain on one side. Usually surgery is required to remove the damaged tube and stop the hemorrhage. With prompt surgery, mortality is greatly reduced. Removal of one tube does not prevent a woman from becoming pregnant again.

Since bleeding can indicate an ectopic pregnancy, a miscarriage, or premature labor, it is vital to report it immediately to your doctor. Delay in seeing your doctor for even the slightest amount of bleeding can endanger your life or that of your baby. He can often prevent a threatened miscarriage.

TOXEMIAS AND ECLAMPSIA. Fortunately, these are rare conditions. Little is known about their cause. Eclampsia is the more serious. While there is no specific medication to cure eclampsia, careful medical management has saved many women with this condition. Actually, prompt attention to the symptoms of toxemia will usually prevent eclampsia. Treatment varies in individual cases but usually includes regulation of salt intake and rest.

If you observe any of the following danger signals of toxemia, notify your doctor immediately (and do so even if you feel well):

Puffiness about the face and hands
Persistent vomiting
Severe, persistent headache
Vision disturbances (blurring, dimness, spots before the eyes)
Very rapid weight gain

The doctor has means of detecting toxemias in early stages, even before symptoms appear, by taking your blood pressure and examining your urine, which is why you should have these tests made and cooperate with him wholeheartedly even if he gives you instructions that seem unduly cautious to you. These illnesses are usually associated with the last three months of pregnancy and are more common in women pregnant for the first time. Serious trouble is prevented by good care.

PLACENTA PREVIA AND PREMATURE SEPARATION OF THE PLACENTA. These, too, are rare complications. Little is known of causes. Both occur in the last three months of pregnancy and are accompanied by vaginal bleeding.

In placenta previa, the placenta, or afterbirth, is not positioned normally. Instead of being attached high up on the uterine wall, it is attached near the cervix. If some of the placental tissue is torn by the expansion of the cervix, which is the mouth of the uterus, pain and premature labor will result. The bleeding that occurs may be serious for the baby.

Premature separation is caused by a hemorrhage just below the placenta's point of attachment. A blood clot forms and loosens the placenta from its mooring.

In both conditions, immediate medical care is needed. Fortunately, the danger to the mother has been greatly reduced by use of blood transfusions. With immediate care it is often possible to save the baby as well, sometimes by cesarean section.

Note: If, after reading about possible complications, you feel abashed about pregnancy, there is no need for dismay. Complications are the exception, not the rule. For example, the danger from placenta previa and premature separation of the placenta is no more than about 1 in 200. Now that you know about the complications that are possible, you will run even less risk. You will be prepared to cooperate with your doctor and avoid even the slightest danger by either preventing a complication or, in the unlikely event one occurs, by taking care of it promptly.

PREPARING FOR CHILDBIRTH

Long before your baby is due to arrive, you will have made arrangements for delivery. Undoubtedly, you will have your baby in a hospital. Home deliveries were once the rule. Today, they are rare. In the hospital, everything is available and ready, even in the event of the most unlikely complication. You will be more comfortable in a hospital and receive better care than is possible at home. However, if you and your doctor decide for home delivery, be sure to follow his instructions carefully.

You may have opportunity to use the rooming-in system which some hospitals provide. We think it is an excellent system. Many of us believe that the act of birth is something of a shock for the baby. Suddenly, after comfortable existence in the womb, he is forced to adapt to many new stimuli—light, air, drafts, hunger, pain. Rooming-in eases the transition for him. With rooming-in, the baby shares his mother's room, from a day or so after birth until leaving the hospital. The crib is arranged so the mother can reach the child without getting out of bed. She helps care for, change, dress, feed, and comfort him. It seems likely that this makes the baby happier than he would be in a nursery; the mother, too, profits from the intimacy, and the father comes to feel at home with the child.

Of course, the system has certain penalties for the mother. She does not have the vacation she probably needs. But we feel, as do many mothers, that the advantages outweigh the disadvantages, provided the added expense is not a problem.

If your hospital does not provide rooming-in, there is no need to worry. If the birth was normal, as almost all births are, you will be in the hospital less than a week. Every three or four hours, your baby will be brought to you for feeding, by breast or bottle. In the rooming-in system, feeding is on demand. But once you are home, you (with your doctor's advice) can decide on your baby's routine for feeding.

CHILDBIRTH PAIN.   If this is your first pregnancy, you can hardly fail to think about the pain connected with having a child. How bad, you wonder, will it really be? From what some women may have told you, you may well imagine it to be a nightmare of an experience. Others may well tell you they felt nothing. Still others may indicate that it was unpleasant but perfectly bearable. Where does the truth lie? Don't hesitate to talk this over with your physician. One thing is certain: fear and tension aggravate pain, especially labor pain, and pain will be much less intense if the patient can relax.

NATURAL CHILDBIRTH.   Some years ago, an English physician, Grantly Dick Read, worked out a method called natural childbirth. Women in primitive countries usually have their babies with little difficulty. They may stop working in the field to have a baby, then almost immediately return to work. Why, Dr. Read wondered, couldn't civilized women be just as well off?

To make this possible, he developed a method of helping the prospective mother, from earliest stages of pregnancy, both emotionally and physically. Emotional preparation consists of ridding a woman of all her fears and teaching her exactly what happens during pregnancy and at each stage of delivery. She knows just what to do to keep the pain at a minimum. For physical preparation, she does exercises to limber up muscles she will use in delivering the baby.

During her entire pregnancy, she has the support of her doctor and his staff. During labor, someone is with her throughout—her doctor, a nurse, or her husband—to massage her back, tell her what to do, and give her warm support and encouragement. Anesthetics are available if she needs them.

Doctors who use this method or an adaptation of it report that nearly half their patients do not want an anesthetic during labor. Some require it at the final moment of delivery. Women who have had babies this way usually are enthusiastic. They find it satisfying to be conscious throughout delivery, thrilling to know the exact moment they have given birth, and to see and touch the baby the instant he is born. Without doubt, it is a beautiful experience.

Natural childbirth requires a great deal of time from doctors and nursing staff who must be well trained and convinced of its advantages.

If you have a choice and decide to use this system, be sure you are making your own decision. Don't do it because you think you should. There are arguments against as well as for it. As one woman has put it: "I'm not a primitive woman—and, under the best of circumstances,

I doubt that I could do a day's work in the fields." It is true that most of us are not used to hard physical work of any kind, and childbirth is work, which is why it is called labor.

Whether or not you elect natural childbirth, you can benefit from one of Dr. Read's principles: that if you know exactly what happens when a baby is born, you will have less fear and quite possibly none at all, and this will help greatly in making childbirth less painful and more rewarding. That is why we are going to tell you exactly what happens.

ANESTHESIA

Most doctors use some form of anesthetic, or analgesic, or both, during childbirth. An analgesic lessens the sense of pain; aspirin, for example, is a mild analgesic.

Anesthesia and analgesia have their virtues and their faults. In skilled hands, the faults can be minimized or even avoided. That is why an experienced doctor is needed during childbirth. Many doctors use analgesics early in labor to help the mother relax and doze between pains. Most use an anesthetic at the time of delivery.

Your doctor will choose the method of pain relief most suitable for you. Have confidence in him. But by all means talk things over with him before delivery, so your mind will be at ease. While you are in labor, let him know if your pain becomes too intense so he can relieve it.

WHEN LABOR BEGINS

Usually, you will become aware of labor through one or more of these signs:

1. "Show," or the passage of blood-tinged mucus, usually only a small amount, from the vagina
2. "Breaking of the bag"—rupture of the membranes which may be indicated either by a gush of water from the vagina or by slow leakage
3. Labor pains

The first two signs are usually unmistakable. Call your doctor if either occurs.

Labor pains can be more difficult to identify for a woman having her first child. She may be fooled by "false labor" which consists of contractions of the uterus at irregular intervals, with or without pain.

It may help you to identify true labor pains if you remember the following:

The pain itself: It may be slight but usually, unlike an ordinary twinge, it increases to a peak, then fades. It is cramplike at the beginning, when it seems to be in the small of the back. In a few hours it moves around to the front.

Regularity: Even at the beginning, true labor pains are usually spaced regularly, with pain-free periods in between.

Uterus contraction: True labor pain is accompanied by contraction of the uterus, and you can feel the contraction by putting your hand on the abdomen.

Even so, it may be difficult to distinguish between true and false labor contractions at first. If either of the other two signs of labor appear, there is no longer any doubt. Otherwise, it is best to wait, in the case of a first baby, until the interval between contractions has grown shorter and they have become more intense. Your doctor has probably told you to call him when the contractions come at 10- to 15-minute intervals. Even then he may want you to wait a while so your stay in hospital will not be too long. Don't worry if the membranes rupture before labor contractions appear. Any stories you may have heard about difficulties of "dry labor" are untrue. In fact, such labors often are easier.

INDUCED LABOR. If your doctor feels it necessary to start or speed up your labor—for example, if the baby is overdue and quite large—he can rupture the membranes easily. Labor usually occurs shortly afterward. He may also speed labor by giving you an enema or a medicine such as castor oil. But never attempt to speed labor yourself.

THE STAGES OF LABOR

DILATION. You can look upon the uterus as a kind of large rubber-like bottle with a small neck about half an inch long which is almost closed. For birth, the neck must stretch to about a four-inch diameter to make room for the baby to pass. At a certain time, the muscular walls of the uterus begin to contract and force the baby downward, and gradually the neck—actually, the cervix—stretches until there is room for the baby to go through.

It's while this is happening that labor contractions are felt. At first, they are far apart and brief. As labor progresses, they occur more often, last longer, are more intense. At its worst, labor contraction is an intense, grinding type of pain. Fortunately, the peak of pain is brief, and there is a blessed interval between contractions during which the mother can relax. Being sufficiently relaxed to take advantage of these respites makes a big difference to a woman in labor.

Another reason for relaxing is that this helps the cervix to dilate more quickly. If you are restless during this stage of labor, it may help to walk around a little. Sometimes, breathing through the mouth, panting like a puppy, helps to relieve tension during a contraction and thus lessens its intensity. Experiment, during the first, mild contractions, to see what makes *you* feel best.

EXPULSION. Once the cervix is fully dilated or open, the baby must be pushed through this narrow birth canal. Now the mother can help by holding her breath and bearing down as though she were having a bowel movement. Even though the doctor gives her a whiff of gas to lessen the pain, she is usually conscious enough to bear down.

The doctor may use instruments to help. Many routinely use "low forceps" at the last moment to guide the baby's head through more readily and gently; this is entirely safe for the baby.

An episiotomy may be performed, too. There is a strip of tissue, the perineum, between vagina and rectum. In the final moment of birth, the baby's head stretches the tissue, which may rip. Although the tear may be slight and will heal readily, many doctors prefer to prevent this by cutting the tissues, making a neat cut instead of taking the chance of a possibly jagged tear. It is sewn up as soon as the baby is born. The stitches are absorbed and do not have to be removed. The mother is anesthetized for an episiotomy.

THE AFTERBIRTH. The third stage of childbirth consists of the expulsion of the placenta, or afterbirth. This is virtually painless.

DURATION OF LABOR. The three stages of labor vary considerably in duration. A woman having her first child may be in labor as long as 15 or 16 hours, though a labor of 3 hours is not uncommon. For subsequent labors, 8 to 10 hours is about average. Long labors are usually less painful in a way. The pains are likely to be at greater intervals or of shorter duration and intensity. The dilation period of labor is the longest; the expulsion period usually lasts about 90 minutes for a first child, 30 minutes for subsequent children. The third period lasts about 15 minutes.

CHILDBIRTH COMPLICATIONS

BREECH BABIES. Most babies are born head first, the easiest way. In about 4 out of 100 births, however, the child may emerge feet first. This makes little, if any, difference to the mother, but is not as easy for the baby. One baby in a hundred will lie crosswise in the womb, in the transverse position. In this case, the doctor prefers to reach in and turn the baby to a more favorable position.

By x-ray and manual examination, the doctor will know the baby's position before birth begins and will be prepared for the type of delivery he faces.

FORCEPS (HIGH). In rare instances, it may be necessary, for safety of mother and child, to hasten delivery before the head has appeared in the opening of the birth canal. For example, the journey may be slow because the mother is in poor condition and cannot expel the baby properly, or the baby may appear to be in danger if it is not born quickly. The doctor will then reach into the birth canal and draw the baby out with forceps.

CESAREAN DELIVERY. If, for any reason, the baby cannot be born through the vagina—because the mother is ill, or her pelvic structure is too small—an operation can be used to effect delivery through the abdomen. This is called a cesarean delivery or cesarean section. Women need have little fear of such an operation. Many doctors prefer to deliver subsequent babies this way if a woman has had one baby by cesarean section, but it is possible for her to have other babies normally in some cases. The chief danger lies in the possibility that the wound from the first incision may open during a subsequent hard labor.

Although quite safe, a cesarean is still a major surgical procedure. Few doctors perform it without a very good reason. It is certainly not to be recommended because it is less painful than a normal vaginal delivery.

DIFFICULT LABOR AND PRECIPITATE LABOR. Labor may be difficult or prolonged if the pelvis is narrow or the mother is so weak that her contractions are not forceful enough to expel the baby. The obstetrician then will use instruments or operate. A mother need not worry about whether her labor is unduly slow. The doctor will know and will take any necessary measures.

Precipitate labor, or spontaneous birth, is something mothers often ask about. Can a baby come with little or no warning? This rarely happens, especially in the case of a first child, yet babies have been born with as little as one labor pain. While this may seem desirable, it has disadvantages. Tissues may stretch so rapidly that a severe tear results; and, of course, the baby may be born before the doctor can get there. Because of the possibility of precipitate labor, doctors urge mothers not to eat if they feel they are starting in labor, since this could lead to vomiting while under anesthesia.

AFTER THE DELIVERY

Once the baby has been expelled, the doctor holds him upside down, removes any mucus from the respiratory tract, and the baby gasps and cries. The doctor then clamps the umbilical cord in two places and cuts between the two clamps. The stump of the cord, about two inches long, is bandaged. The baby's eyes are treated with silver nitrate solution to prevent infection. A nurse then wraps the baby warmly and places him in a crib while the doctor gives his attention again to the mother.

He sews up the episiotomy incision while waiting for the afterbirth. If necessary, he can help her expel the afterbirth, which he examines carefully to make certain none remains in the uterus.

Again, the doctor turns to the baby. He weighs, measures, examines, and places identification marks on the infant. During the examination, he will discover any abnormalities if present. If they are minor, they can be easily corrected at this early stage. Partial or complete correction of many others is simplified if they are attended to early.

About 7 births of every 100 are premature. The degree of prematurity may be so slight that it makes little difference. However, a baby born very prematurely requires great care. Fortunately, it is now possible to reproduce very closely the conditions inside the mother's womb. A premature infant can be provided with proper temperature, humidity, freedom from germs, and easily digested food. The larger the premature baby, the better his chances. Doctors consider any baby weighing less than five and a half pounds as premature. This is an arbitrary figure, but there has to be some dividing line. Don't worry unduly if your baby falls just a bit under the dividing line or even a pound or more and is regarded as premature. It just means he will get extra care.

As soon as the baby is ready, the nurse takes him to the nursery. The mother is wheeled back to her bed when the doctor is certain she, too, is all right. If she has been lightly anesthetized, she will probably be hungry within a few hours after her delivery and may eat a fairly substantial meal.

CONVALESCENCE. Many women say that the sense of well-being after having a baby is an incomparable experience. Once they were treated like invalids, scarcely allowed to stir for weeks. But this has changed. Physicians now generally like to see their patients up and about for part of the time during the first few days after delivery. They find that bowels and bladder function better, there is less danger of infection and clots in veins, and strength returns more rapidly.

"Afterpains" may occur during the first day or two after childbirth. These are due to contractions of the uterus, which is rapidly returning to original size. They are similar to menstrual cramps and, though usually not troublesome, can be relieved by aspirin or similar medication.

There is a vaginal discharge, called lochia, which is sometimes incorrectly referred to as menstruation. It is bright red for the first few days, then fades until it is yellowish white on about the tenth day. If it continues beyond the fourth week or recurs, the patient is probably overexerting and should see her doctor.

Occasionally, a woman has a chill soon after delivery. This may be a nervous or emotional reaction. Quite likely, the nervous system is more sensitive at this time.

A mother may wonder why her baby is brought to her to nurse about 12 hours after birth, before she has any milk. One reason is that the thin fluid she secretes, called colostrum, contains substances valuable to the child. Also, both mother and child need experience in the art of nursing. If it is at all possible, we hope you will nurse your baby at least for a time. If your nipples become sore, your doctor can prescribe ointments or a nipple shield to help them.

Your bowels may be sluggish after childbirth, so your doctor will probably prescribe oil or a mild cathartic.

It will probably make no difference to your figure whether or not your abdomen is bandaged; some doctors recommend this while others do not.

Your appetite will probably be good and you will be allowed a hearty diet. Rest is important.

AFTER-CHILDBIRTH BLUES. Within the first week after giving birth, many mothers experience a feeling of sadness. Women often speak of this as "childbirth blues." A woman may not be able to explain why she has this feeling. She may cry and yet laugh through her tears.

Doctors estimate that as many as 60 percent of women may have a short period of feeling blue. It may occur in the hospital from the third to fifth day after delivery or sometimes at home even a month after the child's birth. In most cases, these feelings are temporary, and disappear after a night's sleep, a good cry, or a discussion with the physician.

Several factors are believed to be involved in childbirth blues. At birth, sudden changes occur in hormone production which can affect emotions. At birth and during the next few days, a mother may lose as much as 20 pounds, and so there may be some reaction as internal organs, especially the uterus, readjust abruptly after the stretching that occurred gradually during the months of pregnancy.

There are psychological changes, too. During pregnancy, labor and birth, a woman gets close attention. During the first days after birth, mother and baby are cared for by nurses. As attention decreases, a mother may realize the responsibility of caring for her child and so may experience some anxiety.

Actually, many doctors believe there may be less opportunity for childbirth blues to develop today because women leave the hospital sooner and become involved in their home routines.

Many women overcome the blues by themselves or with reassurance from their doctor. In some cases, a doctor may prescribe medication to help.

When a mother experiences blues at home several weeks after leaving the hospital, it may be because of a feeling that she is unable to cope with her family and care for the baby. In that case, she may need help and should consult with her doctor.

An expectant mother can often help to avoid childbirth blues by preparing for the birth and care of her baby. Actually, an understanding of the birth process, as we have described it, will do much to relieve anxiety. A mother-to-be can learn in advance about caring for her new-born baby. More and more hospitals and social agencies today provide courses in childbirth and child care. With some planning in advance, it may be possible to arrange for a practical nurse or relatives to help at home during the first few weeks after delivery while strength is fully regained.

Going Home. Next to the feeling you experienced after your baby was born, there is probably nothing so wonderful as the way you feel when you, your husband, and your baby leave the hospital together. Since serious complications seldom develop after childbirth, most mothers leave the hospital within about a week, sometimes less. Even though this is half or a third the time that mothers used to stay, you may become impatient and want to go home even earlier. But take your doctor's advice about that, no matter how impatient you feel. He knows how strong or weak you are, and how much you will be doing when you get home.

There may be moments, once there, when you feel overwhelmed. There will be problems to overcome—there always are. But as every woman knows, they're worth the effort, for there is no substitute for a woman, and for her husband as well, for the fulfillment that comes with having a family.

38

GENETIC PROBLEMS AND COUNSELING

In his new classic of modern biology, *The Person in the Womb*, Dr. N. J. Berrill makes this declaration: "If a human right exists at all, it is the right to be born with normal body and mind, with the prospect of developing further to fulfillment. If this is to be denied, then life and conscience are mockery and a chance should be made for another throw of the ovarian dice."

The human reproduction process is, in a way, a game of chance. The odds are favorable. Miraculously complex as they are, the genes that are carried by egg and sperm and join randomly are dependable on the whole. But there are losers in the game. Of every 50 babies, about one is born with some degree of abnormality inherited from its parents. These weaknesses, several hundred of them serious enough to be considered diseases (diabetes, for example), are determined by the genes.

This has always been so, but less and less now does it have to remain so. The biological revolution of recent years has been enabling scientists to probe the mysteries of the human cell and increasingly to understand and even to begin to predict the workings of the genes. And it now appears that man can have some control over the game and may be able to transcend hereditary limitations.

An example of how this is now beginning to be achieved: In Chicago recently, a newly married woman sought help from a physician who is among the pioneers in genetic counseling, putting to him a haunting question: "If I have children, will they be mentally retarded?" She herself was the only one of four children who was normal; her three younger sisters were affected by a genetic disorder known as Down's syndrome or mongolism.

After taking a thorough family history, the physician and his colleagues made a microscopic study of the woman's chromosomes—the tiny bundles within her cells that contain the genes, or hereditary units. From the analysis, the prediction could be made that there was a 30 percent chance that a child born to her would also have Down's syndrome. The woman decided to take the chance and return to the physician when she was three and a half months pregnant.

Under local anesthesia, a small amount of fluid was removed from the sac surrounding her unborn child, and analysis of the chromosomes in the cells of the fluid showed that the child would be a boy—with Down's syndrome.

The woman chose to have an abortion. Three months later she became pregnant again. This time analysis of the baby's chromosomes revealed a girl who in all likelihood would be perfectly healthy. Later, the birth of a healthy child confirmed the prognosis.

Genetic counseling is still in its infancy. But it is a lusty infancy as a small but growing group of medical experts work to answer the vitally important question, "Can we have normal children?" brought to them by many worried men and women—married couples whose first child was abnormal, engaged couples with a family history of birth defects.

Up to now, a genetic counselor's answer could only be given in terms of risks or odds. Given the family backgrounds of the couple and the nature of the defect that might develop in a child of theirs, the counselor could only say that the odds are 3 to 1 or 5 to 1 or something else that a healthy child could be expected. This has provided at least some measure of guidance, some reasonable, rather than fanciful and often hopelessly pessimistic, indication of what hope there was.

Now counseling is beginning to move beyond. Many defects now can be detected in the cells of potential parents and in the cells of a child in the womb. Treatments have been developed to modify or correct the effects of some abnormal genes.

KINDS OF DEFECTS

Virtually everyone is born with some type of birth defect. Some of us are color-blind; some slightly pigeon-toed; some are less well-coordinated than others; almost everybody has a mole or small birthmark of some kind. These are minor and nondisabling defects. A serious defect is one that may produce either disfigurement, a physical or mental handicap, shortening of life, or early death.

The reasons for many serious defects still remain unknown. But there has been encouraging progress in recent years in establishing the causes and mechanisms of some and in detecting the defects early and greatly minimizing their consequences.

More than 40 inborn errors of metabolism have been detected thus far, and there are now specific tests to find some of these very early in infancy. For example, there is phenylketonuria, also known as PKU. Once this was the unsuspected reason for many cases of mental retardation. Now it is known that a baby with PKU, because of an inborn error of metabolism, is unable to properly dispose of a substance present naturally in some foods. The substance builds up in the body and leads to retardation. Now there is a simple test which can detect the inborn error almost immediately after birth. And with special diet, retardation can be avoided.

As another example, Wilson's disease, which may lead to severe mental degeneration, also stems from a hereditary error, this time in the handling of copper by the body. Wilson's disease usually becomes apparent only in adolescence and later. It is associated with a deficiency of a substance called ceruloplasmin. Today, even as early as three months of age, a relative lack of ceruloplasmin can be determined by a blood test and, with diet and medication, symptoms can be prevented from appearing.

THE ENZYME DEFECTS

Enzymes are special substances needed to stimulate virtually all the important chemical reactions that go on in the body. We discuss them here because inherited defects in enzyme systems have been found to be responsible for many disorders. And it is suspected that many still-mysterious disorders will be traced eventually to enzyme problems.

Generally, there are three ways in which an inherited enzyme defect can result in an abnormality. There may accumulate in the body a material that would otherwise be acted upon by a properly functioning enzyme, and this material, accumulating in excess, may be toxic or poisonous. Disease may also arise from lack of a product that can be produced only with the aid of the enzyme. Or a defective enzyme may lead to production of an abnormal material.

There are generally five means of treating such disorders:

1. Reduced intake in the diet of a material that may otherwise accumulate because of an enzyme deficiency. An example of this is the low phenylalanine diet used for infants with PKU.
2. Administration of the product that should have been made by the enzyme. Use of thyroxin for treating some types of cretinism is an example.
3. In rare cases, a missing enzyme may be provided. The use of coagulation factors in treating bleeding disorders is an example.

4. Medication may be used to block the injurious effects of an enzyme deficiency. An example is the use, in gout, of allopurinol to inhibit the formation of uric acid.
5. A defect may be corrected or compensated for by physiological manipulation. For example, blood-letting can be used to remove the excess iron in the blood characteristic of a disease called hemochromatosis.

THE INHERITANCE MECHANISM

Genetics—the study of heredity and transmission of characteristics—began, as you probably know, with Gregor Mendel, a nineteenth-century Austrian monk and botanist. While cross-breeding garden peas, Mendel discovered that traits in one or another parent plant might not be apparent in a direct offspring plant but then would become apparent in a later generation, and Mendel went on to discover that this happened in ways that allowed prediction.

Thus, when a white-flowered plant was crossed with a purple-flowered plant, all offspring were purple-flowering. But then when two purple-flowering offspring were crossed, three-quarters of their offspring continued to be purple-flowering but one-quarter had white flowers. The hereditary material, later to be called the "gene," never was lost. It was to become clear that each plant—and each human—inherits two sets of genes, one from each parent. One gene may be dominant and the other recessive.

Thus, in man, whether we will have brown eyes or blue is settled at conception. If the genes governing eye color are both programmed for blue, we will have blue eyes, but if either is programmed for brown, our eyes will be brown. Brown eyes are dominant over blue; blue eyes are a recessive trait.

As another example, when two brown-haired parents have a child with red hair, it may turn out that the mother's mother had red hair. The maternal grandmother had inherited both genes of red hair, none for brown, but had married a man with brown hair, and the gene for brown is dominant over the one for red hair. And so all the children, receiving one gene for brown and one for red, had brown hair. But the daughter married a man who also had brown hair but carried the gene for red, and so each of the children of this marriage had one chance in four of getting the red hair gene from each parent, and one child did.

Genes are carried on chromosomes. Every normal person has a complement of 46 chromosomes, paired in 23 sets, per cell. The germ cells—egg and sperm—are the exceptions; they have only one of each pair of chromosomes, a total of 23. When they unite to produce a new baby, the proper number, 46, results, and both parents give the child inherited traits.

After egg and sperm unite, repeated cell division occurs. Each cell of the embryo—skin, liver, nerve, bone, etc.—will have 46 chromosomes. But the egg and sperm cells remain the exceptions. As they mature, their chromosomes are reduced from 46 to 23 by a process called reduction division. And during this process, some switching occurs, with a piece of one chromosome taking the place of its partner's piece. This "crossing over" makes for tremendous variety among individuals.

MUTATIONS

Less commonly, variety among individuals is produced by mutation—a mistake a chromosome may make when it starts to copy itself. The mistake is repeated in future generations. Thus, Queen Victoria of England passed on to some of her children the gene for the bleeding condition hemophilia. Two of her daughters passed it on to their sons, heirs to the Spanish and Russian thrones. And other descendants were affected.

Some mutations can be good while others are bad. Rust-resistant wheat is an example of the good; insecticide-resistant pests of the bad.

AND THE ENVIRONMENT

Actually, whatever the genetic endowment of a child, his development is also determined by environment. And from the earliest stage of development, beginning even immediately after conception, the environment is never exactly the same for any two humans. Even if two children had exactly the same genetic material, slight differences in the environment would affect the material in different ways.

The fact is that since both heredity and environment interact in every human being, the question of which is more important has no real significance. According to some authorities, about 20 percent of birth defects are caused by faulty genes, about 20 percent by environment, and the other 60 percent probably by a combination of the two.

Here, before proceeding further with hereditary influences and genetic counseling, we think it is important to look briefly at the growing knowledge of environmental factors and some practical things that prospective parents can do to favorably influence them. Environmental factors that act on the baby include not only those in his immediate surroundings in the uterus but those in the mother's environment as well. Thus such defects as cataracts of the eyes, congenital deafness, abnormal heart function, and mental deficiency may stem from a virus infection to which the mother is exposed and which she develops—German measles, for example—early in pregnancy.

As experience with the drug thalidomide all too tragically demonstrated among children born without arms or legs to mothers who had taken it, another type of environmental cause of birth defects is chemical in nature. And the thalidomide cases have had a salutary effect in that they have focused very special attention and special research on the possible effects of many medications which perhaps, taken freely in the past, may have accounted for many seemingly mysterious cases of birth defects.

WHAT PARENTS CAN DO ABOUT ENVIRONMENTAL FACTORS

These are among the practical things that prospective parents can do to help assure that environmental factors are favorable for the birth of a healthy child:

1. Every woman should see her physician immediately when she believes that she may be pregnant and should then take only medicines he prescribes. Pep pills, reducing pills, sleeping pills, tranquilizers, and pain killers are all medicines, and their effect on the fetus early in pregnancy may be harmful. Actually, since the possible effects of indiscriminate, long-term use of many medicines still remain to be determined, a rule against constant self-medication is healthy for anyone of either sex—and especially so for women of childbearing age.

2. Since virus diseases such as German measles may lead to birth defects, prospective mothers should obtain as much protection as possible in the form of vaccines. They should make a special effort to avoid exposure as much as possible to other infectious diseases, especially early in pregnancy, for which no vaccines are yet available.

3. Except in emergency, abdominal x-rays should be avoided during the early weeks of pregnancy, and for that reason any physician who may be consulted for any reason should be told when a woman is pregnant.

4. Excessive smoking during pregnancy should be avoided. Studies indicate that the more cigarettes a pregnant woman smokes, the less her baby is likely to weigh. The reduction in weight caused by smoking may be especially critical for a small baby, under five and a half pounds, in terms of survival.

5. Prenatal care is of great importance. For one thing, premature babies are more prone to defects. Medical help should be used to reduce the risk of prematurity. Medical advice about diet, and medical help to correct any problems that may interfere with appetite and good nutrition,

should be used as a means of maintaining a good growth environment for the unborn baby.

6. Actually, since diet affects growth, often in ways not yet fully understood, it is important for girls to acquire proper eating habits early in life. These are conducive not only to their own but to their children's good health.

HOW GENETIC COUNSELORS WORK

Many couples seeking counseling have already had an abnormal child and want to know the risk that a second also will be abnormal. Some have strange misconceptions. Thus, one woman was convinced that her child had been born mongoloid because she had gone horseback riding during pregnancy; another believed that climbing too many stairs had caused her child to be deformed. One dividend from counseling in many cases is enlightenment about the actual factors in defects; this helps to remove a burden of needless guilt feelings from parents.

The counselor's first task is to determine if a family's problem really is hereditary. Many birth defects—such as cerebral palsy, some heart conditions, and ailments caused by German measles—are not genetic in origin. In the case of mongolism and other disorders due to genetic abnormalities, laboratory testing may be required. But often the counselor can get much valuable information through taking detailed family histories of both parents, extending if possible back to their grandparents. If a hereditary defect is established, the counselor calculates the odds that the defect might occur in a child, making use of the genetic laws first formulated by Mendel.

A defect may be either recessive or dominant. If it is recessive, then both parents must contribute a defective gene for the defect to occur in a child. Thus, in the case of parents who have had one child afflicted with PKU, the counselor can advise that they stand a 25 percent chance of having another baby with PKU. If an ailment can be passed along by a single dominant gene, then the odds change. When one parent carries the flawed gene, the counselor puts the chances of an abnormal child at 50 percent.

As an example of how genetic counseling works for people who seek help before marriage, a man and his fiancee are concerned about the possibility that their children may suffer from deafness. Both partners have normal hearing but the man's mother was born deaf as was a maternal uncle.

The counselor studies the family histories, building pedigree diagrams. He finds no history of deafness in the woman's family. And he finds that the deaf members of the man's family suffer from a type of deafness that is inherited as a recessive trait.

The counselor then reports his conclusions: For this couple, as is happily most often true in genetic matters, normality is dominant over abnormality. Since both partners have normal hearing, both must have at least one of the dominant normal-hearing genes. Moreover, both the woman's genes are probably normal, since there is no deafness in her family. Thus any child they will have will almost certainly have normal hearing, since he will receive one dominant normal-hearing gene from his mother.

It is still necessary for the counselor to hedge—to say "almost certainly" rather than certainly. Because it is always possible that somewhere in the woman's family background there is the recessive deafness gene. She may have inherited it, in which case she has one normal and one abnormal gene. Her fiance has probably inherited the abnormal gene from his family. And if she, in fact, did carry an abnormal gene, then any child would stand a 25 percent chance of receiving a double dose of the undesirable gene and would be born deaf.

There is a tradition among genetic counselors that the patient should make the decision about whether or not to have a child, possibly in consultation with the family physician, while the counselor simply presents the odds. Yet many counselors privately admit that their own attitudes often influence the decision.

As one put it: "It makes a difference how you state the odds. Do you tell a couple they have a 75 percent chance of having a healthy baby or a 25 percent chance of having an abnormal one? Do you let them get to the point of saying, 'Doctor, what would you do?' Or do you steer them away from it? When a couple is utterly confused, unable to make a sober judgment, you have to help them. Does that mean I'm playing at being God? I don't think so—I hope not. I don't know what else I can do."

Dr. F. C. Fraser, Director of the Department of Medical Genetics at Montreal Children's Hospital, has written:

"I am sometimes asked whether I tell couples that they should, or should not, have any more babies, and indeed the parents may ask the question directly. I used to say that this is something that the parents must decide for themselves, and the counselor should only provide facts and help clarify issues. Of course, it *is* something that the parents must decide for themselves, and the counselor should never say, 'Thou shalt not . . .' Nevertheless, the longer I follow the families I have counselled, and the more counselling problems I see, the more willing I become in certain cases to slant my counselling in a directive way. When parents ask whether they should have another baby, I sometimes do say that although this is something they will have to decide for themselves, if I were in their situation, I think I would not take a chance—or would, as the case may be."

One of the most exciting medical frontiers today is the intrauterine diagnosis of genetic defects. Currently, in the case of about 30 defects, it is possible to spot the specific enzyme deficiency by examining samples of cells from the amniotic fluid, the liquid in which the developing fetus floats. The 30 include cystic fibrosis and galactosemia, the inability to properly handle a substance found in milk, which leads to mental retardation.

The procedure for obtaining the fluid, usually carried out between the twelfth and fourteenth week of pregnancy, is called amniocentesis. A hollow needle is introduced through the mother's abdomen and into the womb, and a sample is withdrawn.

Ultimately, a major value of amniocentesis will be realized when birth defects, having been detected in an unborn child, will be correctable. Currently, amniocentesis—which carries a small risk of damage to mother or child—can relieve parents' minds or confirm their fears. In the latter case, there is the decision, sometimes agonizing, to be faced: to let the abnormal fetus come to birth or abort it. Abortions based on such diagnoses are being performed in some hospitals. More probably will be performed as rigid, antiquated abortion laws are repealed.

Genetic counseling must also consider other medical developments. Some birth defects, once fatal or crippling, now can be treated with considerable success. With use of a new blood plasma product, hemophiliacs today can lead relatively normal lives. Surgery and speech therapy overcome cleft lip and palate defects and their effects. Prosthetic devices replace missing limbs. A pituitary hormone can add inches for congenital dwarfs. For birth defects that affect metabolism, it is often essential that treatment begin soon after birth, even sometimes before any obvious symptoms appear, as a way to avoid permanent damage. Tests that can detect some of these diseases have been devised, and others will be forthcoming.

HOW TO FIND A COUNSELOR

Only a small fraction of all the families deserving genetic advice are receiving it now. To some extent, this is because the advice is not sought; people are not aware of the availability or value. But it is also true that there is need for additional genetic counseling facilities. Training for physicians who intend to specialize in genetics requires two years in most programs. But more genetic counseling on the part of physicians who are not genetic specialists is being urged.

Actually, there has been a great increase in the number of facilities since 1951 when less than a dozen genetic counselors were available in the whole country. There are now 157 genetic units in the United States. The cost of such counseling varies considerably, from no charge at all in some places to several hundred dollars in others. The field is expected to grow rapidly as more medical schools include comprehensive genetics courses in their curricula.

Your own physician may be able to refer you to a genetics counseling facility. And information on the location of counseling units is available at the National Foundation–March of Dimes, 800 Second Ave., New York, N.Y. 10017.

39

PREVENTIVE MEDICINE FOR CHILDREN

ALMOST EVERYONE is aware, because of the work of men like Freud, that early influences in an individual's life have deep and lasting effects on mental and emotional characteristics. Few people, however, recognize the equally important truth: that early influences have similar determining effects on the body and physical health of the adult.

Until recently, as Dr. Rene Dubos of Rockefeller University has pointed out, the small stature of the Japanese was attributed to genetic constitution. But contemporary teen-agers in Japan are as tall as American teen-agers, not because of any change in inheritance but because Japanese postwar ways of life have been radically changed. Similarly, children born and raised on Israeli kibbutzim are often so tall that they tower over their parents who migrated from central Europe's ghettos.

"Wherever in the world social groups adopt the ways of Western civilization," Dr. Dubos points out, "children grow faster, achieve sexual maturity earlier and develop into taller adults. Menstruation begins three years earlier than it did 100 years ago. Teen-age boys are now too big for the armor of medieval knights."

One of the world's most distinguished scientists, Dr. Dubos has conducted repeated laboratory experiments with many animal species which show the lasting effects of early influences in the physical sphere and the mental—how, at critical stages in early development, nutrition deprivation, minor infectious processes, and behavioral disturbances can have lifelong stunting effects.

When, for example, female mice, either during pregnancy or in the nursing period, receive a slightly deficient diet, not only are the offspring unusually small at the time of weaning; they remain small for the rest of their lives even though they get optimum diets after weaning.

The mechanisms by which early influences produce such lasting effects are not fully understood. But there are working hypotheses. One suggests that hormonal development may be affected, and, in fact, reduction of the size of the thymus gland has been observed. Another hypothesis is that with stunting at an early age, there is a reduction of efficiency in utilization of food.

All of this, far from being alarming, should be reassuring. Much can be done today not only to safeguard a child's health but to help the child to realize full potentials. Making use of available knowledge, you can give your baby a good start in life. You can do this, as we noted earlier, by good prenatal care. And you can do this, as we will now discuss, by what you provide and do for the child from the moment you leave the hospital after childbirth.

YOUR BABY'S DOCTOR

Decide who is going to look after your baby's health before you leave the hospital. Will your family doctor take over, or are you going to have a pediatrician or "baby doctor"?

Your baby has had a thorough examination in the hospital. For the first six months, he should be seen by a doctor regularly. Decide who that doctor will be; the physician who took care of your pregnancy can help you in this. And, having decided, follow through on the doctor's advice. What we discuss in this chapter can be helpful to you; it can supplement but cannot take the place of the physician who will be concerned with your baby's welfare.

THE QUESTION OF CIRCUMCISION

It is wise to consider ahead of time the question of circumcision if your baby turns out to be a boy. Circumcision consists in cutting off the "sleeve" of skin (foreskin) covering the penis, because this skin may encourage the collection of a cheeselike substance (smegma) that can cause irritation or infection. It is a simple procedure in little babies.

You may wish to have it done for religious reasons, or you may prefer to wait and see whether the doctor recommends it. If your doctor thinks it should be done, have it done early, as soon as he suggests; it will disturb you and the baby more if done later. Always have this minor operation performed by a qualified person—that is, someone of whom your doctor approves.

IMMUNIZATION

It should go without saying that every child deserves to be immunized against the dangerous diseases for which protective inoculations are now easily available. And yet, even now, every year in this country many hundreds of lives are lost because of such preventable diseases as smallpox, diphtheria, tetanus, and measles. Your family doctor or pediatrician can provide these injections. They are also available free, or at very little cost, so lack of money must not keep any child from having protection. Any hospital, public health department, court or health officer can provide information about this.

Beginning at about the age of two months, your baby's physician will want to undertake an inoculation program. Today, in addition to such protective shots as those for diphtheria, whooping cough, tetanus, smallpox, and typhoid fever, which have been available for many years, there are equally valuable newer ones—basic new triumphs of preventive medicine—including inoculations for polio, mumps, measles, and German measles.

Still others are under development and new methods of administering vaccines, of combining many of them, for the convenience of child and parents are constantly being worked out. Your physician, aware of this and following the guidance of official bodies such as the American Academy of Pediatrics, will make available the latest and most effective and convenient inoculation program. By all means, follow his advice.

A HEALTHY ATTITUDE TOWARD YOUR BABY

All babies, of course, are not alike. They differ in personality and inherent qualities; they differ in appearance. Some are big-boned; some, delicately boned. Some are especially sensitive to sound. Some are lusty; some are subdued. Some eat and sleep a great deal; some do not.

Still, the environment—the way a baby is cared for and the surroundings in which he lives—will make a huge difference. Beyond a difference in physical health and growth, it can determine, for example, whether or not a high-strung baby becomes "nervous" or a stolid one becomes lethargic, even backward. Your child's environment is also going to affect his intelligence, which is not some fixed quality he is born with but a potential that can be encouraged to develop. How you care for your baby and the stimulation you provide in the all-important first months and years of life will help determine how well he will use his mind later and adapt to life's changing situations.

Since babies are individuals, all cannot be treated exactly alike. But all have the same basic needs for security and affection and for a loving, relaxed atmosphere if they are to develop their full potentials.

These are some of the things you can do to help create such an atmosphere:

1. Love your baby, of course; you do without our telling you to. But go beyond that: show the baby you love him. Soft words of affection and cuddling are not extravagances; they are needs of an infant. They help make him feel his new world is a pleasant place to be in.

2. Thoroughly enjoy your baby, now and at every stage of his development. Don't wait for him to do things you can be proud of. Take pleasure in him now.

3. Forget any worries about spoiling him. He doesn't need discipline as an infant; he will probably be better off without it. Comfort him when he cries. You will soon learn to tell whether he just wants attention, and when he can get along without it if you can't spare the time. The baby who gets too little attention is often more demanding than the one who gets his share.

4. Don't try to train him, either. He will develop good habits with the proper encouragement—as far as eating, sleeping, and amusing himself are concerned. Don't try to toilet-train him during his first year.

5. Don't be concerned about his being fragile. He isn't fragile, either physically or emotionally. He won't be harmed for life if you are human enough to be occasionally preoccupied or irritable or overattentive. It's his basic security that counts.

6. A baby ideally needs two parents. Although the mother is vitally important to him, his father should be a part of the baby's world from the beginning, not just a visitor who plays with him for a few minutes a day. Too often, fathers gradually take on the role of dispensers of disciplines and "treats" rather than of parents.

7. If you should become concerned about your baby's development, your best source of information is his doctor or the clinic. They will tell you whether your child is as big or strong as he should be at his age. While it is natural to discuss such things with relatives and friends, take their well-intentioned but often not-well-informed opinions lightly.

You will want to be alert, between visits to the doctor or clinic, for any signs or symptoms that may indicate all is not going well. We tell you on page 468 how to determine whether or not your baby is ill.

If your baby is sick, don't give him any medicine or treatment. Don't try to make him eat. If he isn't vomiting or having diarrhea, let him have his milk as usual. If he is, don't offer any food, but try to get him to take a little boiled water frequently, unless he vomits it, in which case wait an hour or two before trying again. Keep him quiet and let him sleep as much as possible. Don't let him cry if something like rocking will soothe him. And, of course, send for the doctor immediately.

BREAST OR BOTTLE. There is much to be said for breast feeding. It has its advantages for mother and baby. It does have some disadvantages for the mother.

Breast milk is easily digestible; nature made it for the baby. It contains virtually everything necessary during the first months of life. Babies who are breast-fed seem to have a partial or temporary immunity to certain diseases. The act of nursing also helps to satisfy emotional needs.

For the mother, nursing contracts the muscles of the uterus, aiding its rapid return to normal. It makes her feel close to the baby, satisfying her emotional needs. It is less expensive, and it will not ruin her figure. Nursing mothers need not gain weight even though they eat well and drink a quart of milk a day (skimmed milk is far less fattening and will do exactly as well). If the mother does not gain, and if she wears a good supporting brassiere, the appearance of her breasts will not be appreciably altered. Nursing does not interfere with her health. It may be tiring, as exercise is, but not harmful. If she becomes overtired, she is under par in some other way and should see her doctor.

Nursing does restrict a mother's freedom. She can't go away for days at a time. It is difficult to nurse a baby and go out to work, although it is possible. If, for example, she returns to work when her baby is two months old and on a four-hour schedule, she may be able to manage things so she need miss only one feeding, which may be given in a bottle.

The main disadvantage in nursing lies in the feeling some women have about it. If you feel a real revulsion toward nursing, not just an objection on the ground that it may be a nuisance, don't force yourself to nurse. Or try it and stop if it disturbs you. Don't blame yourself; you are not going to be an "unnatural" mother. While nursing is better for the baby than bottle feeding, there is not enough difference for you to get upset. Cuddle your baby and give him plenty of affection while you give him his bottle.

SCHEDULE. Much has been said in favor of demand feeding; much, too, in favor of a rigid schedule. Those who favor the latter emphasize that the average baby requires a sufficient amount of milk at four-hour intervals to satisfy his hunger and grow properly—and this is a great convenience to the mother who will know just when to feed him. While this is true, it fails to take into sufficient account the fact that all babies are not the average baby. No two have the same appetite; some are hungry sooner than others, or eat less at each feeding and need to be fed more often; some want to sleep longer at a stretch than others.

We believe it is important to satisfy a baby's hunger and thirst when they arise. This will not spoil the baby; on the contrary, it will make him less demanding if he is happy and satisfied.

It is worth remembering that when you follow the self-demand method you are working toward a schedule. Both self-demand and rigid time-table methods have the same objective: to give the baby enough to eat and establish a routine that helps the mother find time for everything else she must do. Often, they arrive at this objective in about the same length of time. Mothers who follow a fixed schedule usually modify it sensibly, so in the long run it comes close to the demand method. For example, they feed the baby early if he is crying rather than let him wear himself out and fall asleep exhausted. Similarly, many mothers on the self-demand method will wake the baby if he happens to be sleeping about four hours after his last feeding; they know he will be glad to eat and that he is bound to awaken soon in any case and want food just when his mother is busy with something else.

Whichever system you follow, remember that you are working toward a goal. Some infants do well on a four-hour schedule from the beginning, while others won't be able to wait that long, or won't be regular at all for several months. It is wise to feed babies who weigh less than seven pounds more often than once every four hours—every three hours at least.

Be flexible about the 2:00 A.M. feeding. Babies sleep through the night as soon as they are able to go that long without food, so don't deprive your child of that feeding in the hope of speeding the time when you won't be disturbed at night. It helps to be flexible about the feeding that precedes the night one, too. That is, put it off till you go to bed if the baby is sleeping, so he won't be likely to awaken quite as early for his next one.

PHYSICAL NEEDS

On the average, a baby will gain seven ounces a week during the first three months of life; then about four ounces a week (less regularly) until the age of six months; and (still less regularly) about two ounces a week until nine months. But this, it must be remembered, is average; each baby has his own rate of growth. If your baby fails to gain properly, your doctor will find out what needs to be done—perhaps supplementary feeding if you are nursing, perhaps a change of formula.

How the Average Child Develops

At 2 years of age, the average child weighs 28 pounds and is 34 to 35 inches tall. He has about 16 teeth. He sleeps about 14 to 16 hours of the 24. He has been able to walk, "holding on," since he was about 12 months old and by himself since he was 18 months old. Now he can run, after a fashion, as well as walk. The dozen words he could say when he was 18 months old have increased to 200, and he uses them in phrases or short sentences. He has a fair degree of bowel and bladder control in the daytime (girls do better at night than do boys).

At 3, the child has passed through a certain amount of turmoil manifesting itself in temper tantrums, negativism, and so on, and is in a relatively stable period. He has all his "baby" teeth (20), speaks in sentences (short), practically dresses and toilets himself, and even "helps" around the house. His daily diet might consist of 1/3 cup juice, 1/2 cup stewed or fresh fruit, 1/2 cup cereal, about 1/2 cup meat, 1 baked potato, 1/2 cup vegetable (cooked and raw), 1 egg, 2–3 pieces of toast, 3 teaspoonsful of butter or margarine, 2 small cookies or some other dessert such as junket, and between a pint and quart of milk.

For the average child, the years from 4 to 7 mark a transition from dependence of babyhood and beginning of the independent school years. Outdoor activity increases, too.

Between 4 and 5, a child develops more self-reliant eating habits; he should be encouraged to eat a variety of foods. Between 4 and 7, his legs and arms grow proportionately more than the rest of the body and become more slender. On the average, there is a gain in height of 2-1/2 to 3 inches a year. At 5, the average height for both boys and girls will be about 43 inches; by 7, the average for boys is 49 inches and 48 for girls. On the average, a 5-year-old boy will weigh about 41 pounds and a girl, 40. At 6, the average for boys is 48 pounds, and for girls 46; and at 7, about 54 pounds for boys and 52 for girls.

At 5, a child needs only one or two naps a week if any, and by 6 seldom takes any at all. Usually, between 4 and 7, he will sleep 11 hours a night.

During the 4-to-7-year period, posture becomes more erect; muscular coordination increases; writing, however, can still be difficult. Between 6 and 7, the average child learns to print.

As they enter school, children more frequently are exposed to infections, and colds and nose-and-throat episodes are frequent. Generally, after the first grade, fewer diseases occur.

Age 7 to 12

There is steady but gradual growth during these years. And this is a period during which sexual development begins. Many girls enter puberty between 10 and 12; most boys, not until 13.

The slowest growth years are those from 7 to 10. At 8, boys average 51 inches, girls 50. Growth for both continues at about 2 inches annually until the tenth year. At that point, many girls have a spurt and are taller at 12 than some boys of the same age. At 12, boys average 59 and girls 60 inches.

Weight gain is slow and steady. At 8, an average boy weighs 60 pounds, a girl 58. Both gain about 6 pounds annually until the tenth year, when girls start to gain faster than boys. By 12, girls average 88 pounds, boys 84.

At about 10, as girls begin their preadolescent growth spurt, their hands and feet may be first to grow. Soon hips broaden, pelvis widens, and breasts enlarge. Pubic hair appears between 10 and 12 and some girls begin menstruation. At this age, boys begin to lose fat and move ahead of girls in muscle strength.

Between 7 and 8, a child tends to become more graceful in movement and develops greater manipulative skill. Boys now tend to enjoy team sports such as baseball; girls play hopscotch and skip rope. At 8 and 9, children show improved coordination, and both manual dexterity and coordination continue to improve from 10 to 12. Now, for boys, skill in sports is important.

Between 7 and 12, permanent teeth are replacing baby teeth, and by 12 or 13 the child usually has 28 of his full set of 32 permanent teeth.

Children from 7 to 12 need 2,100 to 2,400 calories a day. Well-balanced meals are important. During this same age span, the child develops increased resistance to fatigue and usually sleeps about 10 hours a night.

The Adolescent Years

Each child has a kind of biological clock of his own which determines the time of sexual maturity. Generally, this will be between 11 and 15 for girls, between 13 and 16 for boys. Adolescence begins as the pituitary gland secretes hormones which spur the final growth spurt and also stimulate the sex glands to secrete sex hormones. In a girl, the ovaries enlarge and there are such physical changes as breast enlargement and pubic hair, most of them begun by the thirteenth year. When the ovaries begin to release egg cells, the menstrual cycle begins.

In a boy, between 13 and 16, pubic and underarm hair appears and the voice begins to deepen as the larynx enlarges. Between 16 and 18 facial hair appears. Usually between 12 and 13, the testes, scrotum, and penis enlarge and sperm cell production begins.

Girls generally reach their peak height at about 12. At 13, boys are about 61 inches and girls about 62. Between 13 and the end of growth, boys add about 10 or 11 inches. A girl's growth slows after 13, and between 13 and 17 she usually adds about 4 inches.

At 13, boys weigh about 93 pounds and girls 99. Between 13 and 17, boys gain about 50 pounds and girls about 35. In the teen-age years, fatigue is common; both sexes are prone to acne as hormone production increases and the skin is affected. Between 17 and 20, the wisdom teeth, the last permanent teeth, appear.

If teen-agers sometimes appear clumsy, it is because they are still adjusting to their growing bodies. Muscle strength and endurance increase greatly in boys during adolescence. Because of their growth and vigorous activity, adolescents, particularly boys, have greater nutritional needs. Girls may require 2,600 calories daily, boys 3,200.

YOUR CHILD

We want to make it very clear that we have been talking in terms of "the average child." Really, this is a mythical child, a statistical child, not any one real child. Your child is an individual and it would be remarkable if he or she happened to be average in every detail. More likely, your child will be above average in some respects, below in others, and may even alternate between the two at various periods.

GROWTH.   You might like, and we think it a good idea, to keep a running record of the weight and height of your child and the arrival of teeth so your doctor will know whether the rate of development is within normal limits. Leave that up to him and don't worry about it yourself. Your child should never be made to feel uncomfortable about his or her physical development.

SLEEP.   If your child has had a good start in life, sleep should not be a major problem. Some difficulties undoubtedly will arise at some time. If they do, don't decide your youngster is being willfully bad; try to determine and eliminate the cause of trouble. For example, at some point your child may be afraid of the dark, usually because someone, not necessarily you, has frightened him. A dim light, or a door left open just a bit will often help dispel the fear. Children usually go to sleep more readily if the evening meal is simple and they are not too stimulated at bedtime.

EATING.   At some time or other, most babies fail to eat as well as their mothers would wish. If the mother becomes tense and begs the child to eat, he may be balky. If she punishes him, it may make him hate mealtimes. We advise mothers to place food before their children and remove it if they don't eat it, with the result that they are ready for it by the next meal. But this simple method does not always work. It may be necessary to use ingenuity and imagination to make certain a child is getting enough to eat.

If a child is a poor eater, the mother should calmly try to discover the circumstances under which he eats best. Often being alone so he is not distracted helps. Sometimes he does well with very small portions, or food that is easily chewed, or food that is easy to manipulate, or some foods he likes; other foods should be gradually and tactfully added.

Don't worry excessively about a child's eating. Children do not starve themselves. Studies have demonstrated that even very small children who are allowed to freely choose their foods select a reasonably well balanced diet; they do not eat ice cream and candy only.

Remember that feeding problems are often problems involving something other than, or in addition to, eating. It is best to discover what the other problems are and solve them, but if you can't, a general atmosphere of love and relaxation will help.

Your child grows and changes, and at one time may eat (or sleep) well; at another he may not. Most children eat less in hot weather, in teething periods, and during the second year of life.

Remember this, too, about feeding: The chubby child is not necessarily the healthiest child, although there has long been a misconception that this is the case. Recently, data from animal experiments indicate that the number of fat cells may be programmed early in life and an increase in the number of such cells will make the animal permanently obese so that it is exceedingly difficult to take off and keep off weight later in life. If these data prove to be true in the human, then early childhood may be a critical period in determining whether or not an individual will be obese later in life. With this in mind, it would seem best to feed a child healthily, moderately, and definitely not to merely make him chubby.

EMOTIONAL DEVELOPMENT

Physicians and many parents understand children's actions and attitudes better today than was true forty or fifty years ago. We know, from studies of human emotions, that much of what even adults do is the result of complicated feelings, some of which we are not consciously aware of. We know that the development of generally reasonable behavior comes only with growing up physically, and so we expect children to be governed by their feelings rather than by reason or logic.

We know that glib judgments that a child is "good" or "bad" are useless. It is far more important to realize that a child's emotional development, along with his physical and intellectual development, does not march smoothly down a broad highway, nicely in step. Children have their "bad" periods—for example, at about two and a half when they suddenly seem to become tense, fearful and contrary. Then perhaps, just as suddenly, they become "good" at three.

Periods of equilibrium are, of course, easier than those of uneven development, but both are part of growth. The suddenly balky child at two and a half is the same child as at two, and equally deserving of love.

We don't want to give the impression that parents need never be concerned about children's behavior. But we do want to emphasize that difficulties are part of growth and should be regarded as challenges to you to find ways to help and support a child as he weathers the squalls. Don't be a "fair-weather" parent who loves a child only when things are going well.

DISCIPLINE

Many American parents in the 1920's and 1930's, in a reaction to the stern, authoritarian ways of the old European families, adopted an excessively permissive attitude with their children. In some homes, youngsters were almost under no restraint at all. More recently, many conscientious parents have wondered whether there wasn't some good in the old-fashioned tough discipline.

In our opinion, neither extreme is good. Letting a child "do anything" does not really help the child; it may do harm. On the other hand, his spirit should not be curbed nor his natural curiosity and energies squelched. Dr. Arnold Gesell, a distinguished specialist in children's development, calls this modern attitude "informed permissiveness." Parents who adopt this attitude try to understand what they can reasonably expect from their children, always keeping in mind age and basic personality. They keep their demands on their children within reason, so they can guide them consistently and in kindly ways, and still let them grow at their own pace and within their own limits.

Authoritative versus Authoritarian

Actually, there is a considerable difference between parents who are authoritarian and those who are authoritative. And they tend to produce quite different kinds of offspring.

Authoritarian parents, suggests Dr. Diana Baumrind, of the University of California Psychology Department, are detached and controlling, and their children often turn out to be discontented, withdrawn, and distrustful.

Authoritative parents, on the other hand, are controlling and demanding, but also very warm, rational, and responsive. Their children are the most self-reliant, self-controlled, and explorative, according to a long-term study Dr. Baumrind and her colleagues have conducted.

Permissive parents, who make few demands of their children and rarely try to control them, produce the least self-reliant, explorative, and self-controlled children, the Baumrind research indicates.

Successful parents, according to the study, recognize their own special rights as adults as well as the child's individual interests and special ways. "The mother," Dr. Baumrind notes, "does not base her decisions on group consensus or on the individual child's desires, and neither does she regard herself as infallible or divinely inspired."

During the first six years of a child's life, "exercise of power is a legitimate right of the parents." By early adolescence, however, a child "can see clearly many alternatives to parental directives, and a parent must be able to defend rationally, as she would to an adult, a directive with which the adolescent disagrees. . . . The adolescent cannot be forced physically to obey over any period of time."

Gentle Threats

As they try to discover more and more about human behavior in general and in particular child behavior and the influence of training upon it, psychologists report interesting findings. Often, these cannot be considered definitive, clearly established; for that, there must be many repetitions of the experiments and confirmation of the findings by many workers. But sometimes a finding is of a type that, even though not definitively established as valid, is provocative, worth thought, and possibly even worth trial by parents.

One of these is a finding that if you want to instill values in children, speak softly and carry a *small* stick. Big sticks may control behavior but *small sticks change attitudes*. This thesis comes from Dr. Elliot Aronson, a University of Texas psychologist, who induced children to turn their back on toys they really liked and to decide they didn't like them after all. The technique used was request, followed by a mild threat—which meant that the child had to build his own internal justifications for not playing with the toys in order to comply with the request.

Dr. Aronson and his colleagues first spent days playing with the children and building rapport. Then, picking out a favorite toy of each child in one group, an experimenter said, "If you play with this toy, I will be a little cross with you." The experimenter then left the room. In another group, the children were more severely threatened with possible loss of all the toys plus the friendship of the experimenters. The results were quite startling. Very few children under mild threat played with the interdicted toy. But many of the severely threatened did. And two months later the first group still ignored the toy. That the effect lasted for 60 days is "absolutely phenomenal," Dr. Aronson says, and it indicates a long-term attitude change. He sees no reason why the same effect would not work when dealing with more important values.

Preventing Self-devaluation

There have always been self-devaluative individuals, those who have a feeling of being unacceptable to themselves. Today, it is being recognized that self-devaluation poses a serious threat to emotional health and even physical health. It begins in childhood, is internalized during adolescence, and reaches its full devastative power in adulthood. Bitterly painful, it can sap a person's joy in living and dilute his incentive for active life-participation. Parents can do much to avoid self-devaluation for their children.

All of us have met adults who are influenced by severe self-devaluation. They can be recognized through the manifestation of one or several symptoms: depressed mood; hopelessness and futility expressed in speech and manner; fatigue, low interest level, and difficulty in concentrating; and, in severe cases, chronic sleep disturbance, motor retardation, loss of appetite and weight, and suicidal thoughts or attempts.

It appears that self-devaluation takes root in the potent emotional atmosphere of childhood when conditions are such that parental influences can combine with a child's receptive, immature personality to produce a self-devaluating response.

Our society itself, because of the emphasis on achievement and the discredit heaped on failure or departure from "norms," is devaluative. Yet an adult who has not been molded in a self-devaluative pattern in childhood has a far better chance of taking in stride any devaluative influences of society and of living a happy and useful life.

What makes a child self-devaluative, a victim of self-unacceptance? A primary source is parental belittling—and this, often, in ways that do not seem obviously belittling.

The fact is that in our culture behavior is evaluated within a kind of moralizing, good-bad framework. The framework provides unrealistic standards for conduct, characterizes conduct as either good or bad, and is not flexible enough for understanding and dealing with children. For example, if a preschool child is abnormally docile, if he withdraws from active play to avoid getting his clothing dirty, he may be labeled good. On the other hand, a normally aggressive or negativistic child may be called bad.

Unless they are aware of the lack of validity and the danger of this good-bad framework, parents use it in controlling behavior. It is usually not enough for many parents to say, "No," firmly to a child's immature behavior which affects the rights of parents or others; somehow, they feel they must say, "No, you naughty child." They use other berating words, such as "bad," "ridiculous," "stupid," "silly." They may say, "I'm ashamed of you." Subjected to such beratings, children may begin to use them on themselves, growing up to be dissatisfied with and even ashamed of themselves.

There is a danger, too, in using guilt to control a child. Some parents may allow a child, for example, to destroy a toy, or hurt a brother or sister, and, after the deed, give the child a shaming lecture or series of lectures, telling him of their disgust with him, of how sorry he should be for what he has done. But under the influence of such guilt feelings, a child, instead of learning self-control, may learn to think of himself in a devaluated way.

Some parents often use unfavorable comparison of a child with another child or with their own behavior and achievements as children. The child may begin to internalize this unfavorable comparison and go on comparing himself unfavorably with parents, sibling, or others, becoming convinced that he is wanting in some respects.

However complex this may make discipline seem to be, any loving, mature parent, through knowledge of the risks, can avoid methods that produce self-devaluating attitudes in a child. And it should be remembered that none of us is perfect, and it is not an occasional blow-up, an isolated instance of a guilt-producing lecture or unfortunate comparison that is likely to do harm, but rather a repeated pattern.

Some Guides for Discipline

During a child's first year, he is absolutely dependent for everything, and we consider it unwise to put any responsibility on him for either his cleanliness or safety. Babies and toddlers are not being willful when they are eager to explore. We need to help and encourage them as much as possible in their explorations and not frustrate them every time they go for an appealing object.

Starting in the second year, a child should be taught that certain things must be avoided. A firm "No" is certainly in order when he plays near the stove, climbs on a table, or starts for a sharp knife. However, it is best to prohibit as little as possible and to remove dangerous temptations. As much as possible, breakable items, sharp-edged furniture, and other treasured or potentially hazardous items should be temporarily removed. Often, by the time a child is three, he is ready to accept a certain, definite amount of discipline for his own safety and that of other people.

To determine whether you may be demanding too much of a child, try to count the number of times a day you and the other adults in the household say "No," or exert pressure in another manner. If you discover that the child is exposed to an almost continuous chorus of negatives, you can be reasonably certain that discipline is too strict. Try to find ways to assume more responsibility or to make it easier for your child to do so.

Your child does not "need" to be punished. Provided there is a good relationship between parents and children, most difficulties can be resolved without resort to punishments. Consider how a good nursery-school teacher or camp counselor is able to handle many children, usually without punishment. Of course, parents have other things to attend to besides their children, and a punishment often seems like a shortcut. We don't suggest you should never punish a child. If, for example, your firm

"No" fails to stop him from reaching for a forbidden, dangerous object, a slap on the hand will probably stop him, and in most cases will cause him little more than momentary discomfort. Children usually have a good sense of fair play and know when punishment has been deserved and can accept it in good spirit.

Of course, none of us invariably does what he knows he should. You will sometimes act impulsively, without careful consideration of the situation, perhaps because you are tired. Don't worry too much about that. Children are resilient. Tell your child honestly that you acted unfairly because you didn't understand. The child will forgive and forget the punishment.

We do want to emphasize that punishments often are two-edged swords, doing more harm than good. It is extremely difficult to find an "ideal" punishment that will accomplish what you want without causing any harm. Nagging, threatening, or shaming a child can have a very bad effect. Never punish him for things that are not his fault, for acting like a child rather than an adult. Most important, whatever disciplinary measures you use, make it clear that the child has not lost your love.

Let Children Express Their Emotions

Children tend to express their emotions in undiluted fashion. They say "I love you," "I hate you," or "I'll kill him dead," when we would say "That's nice of you," "I wish you wouldn't do that," or "I'd like him to go away."

If a child tells you "I hate you," don't be shocked. Take it in stride, perhaps making a noncommittal remark such as that everyone feels like that sometimes. As soon as the child's frustration is over, you can count on him being in a loving mood again. But if you are horrified, the child will feel guilty and repress his reactions. It is natural to have feelings of hostility. Accepting this makes it easier for children and adults to feel and express their affections and love more fully.

While children should be allowed and even encouraged to act out and talk out their natural hostilities rather than repress them, they should not be allowed to hurt people physically. Children seldom know how far they should let their emotions go. We parents must show them. We think children want us to show them. When they go too far, they often seem to welcome being restrained by a firm word or even by being removed physically from the situation.

Toilet Training

Toilet training *is* important. Some authorities believe that there is a connection between physical and mental health of adults and the way they were toilet trained.

Many parents try to train too early and strictly, often with feelings of revulsion and shame on their own part. Children then may be conditioned toward being unsure, worried about dirt, or ashamed of parts of their bodies. Frequently, the child of a mother who takes toilet training too seriously discovers that he can upset or delight her by failure or success—and so what should be a simple physiological function becomes a source of power or shame.

On the other hand, children who receive toilet training when they are ready for it, who are not pushed too hard and not punished or shamed when they fail, have a better chance to realize the full potentialities of their personalities.

We would like to urge parents to remember that a child, if left to himself, will stop wetting and soiling when he is ready to do so. Parents will, we think, do best if they let nature take its course, with just a little encouragement and guidance. Parents can, for example, make occasional suggestions about use of the potty when the child is really ready to understand what is meant, or remind a child that it is a good idea to go to the bathroom before he becomes so engrossed in something that he won't take the trouble.

Toilet training should, we think, be avoided in the first year for all children and in the second year for most children. If you do insist upon trying early, you should be prepared for many failures; and when there are failures, you should be prepared to be nonchalant and willing to start over again.

Doctors often encounter parents who are so upset about soiled diapers that it seems almost necessary to encourage them to go ahead and try premature toilet training. But this is regretful because the child is being required to assume a burden the parents should be willing to carry. Talk the matter of toilet training over with your doctor. If he sees that you appreciate the value of being in no rush, he will undoubtedly encourage you to wait until the child is ready.

Thumbsucking

Almost all children suck their thumbs at times—when they are going to sleep or are frightened or lonely. Babies also suck their thumbs or fingers when hungry and when teething. The best way to handle thumbsucking is to regard it as a harmless way for a child to obtain satisfaction or reassurance—and to forget about it. If your child seems to thumbsuck excessively, don't immediately worry about his face being distorted or his teeth injured. These things almost never happen if sucking stops before the second teeth appear. But do think about possible reasons why he requires this kind of satisfaction. Often your doctor can help you discover them. Usually thumbsucking indicates that a child is, in some way, being deprived of all the affection he wants or that he needs the solace of his thumb in situations that make him feel nervous and tense. Babies are less likely to suck their thumbs very much if they are breast-fed (which requires harder sucking than bottle feeding), if they are bottle-fed and the holes in the nipples are not too large, if they are allowed to drink their fill, and if they are allowed to progress from breast to bottle to cup at their own speed.

Older children who still suck their thumbs do so out of needs other than an urge to suck. They may suck when bored, tired, very sleepy, or when they have been scolded, or are lonely or tense. Usually, children stop thumbsucking by the age of four or five. If your child is older and you are fairly certain that the habit is simply lingering, you can generally find a way to help the child give it up. For example, if thumbsucking is associated with twisting a blanket, you might suggest that the child cuddle a doll instead. But don't make an issue of it.

Interest in Sex

You can be certain that sooner or later a child will be interested in the sex organs, where babies come from, even in sexual intercourse. If your relationship with him is a good one, he will ask questions just as freely as he asks why grass is green. They may not be easy questions to answer, but do your best to answer them truthfully.

The fact is that telling the truth is simpler in the long run. Children don't mind deception about Santa Claus, mainly because there is fun in the deception and no tension about it in their parents. Deceptions about the stork, however, are likely to create problems. It is often hard for parents to explain later why they told the stork story. It is easier to answer truthfully the simple questions small children ask than to take on the complicated ones they think of later.

Tell the truth and you and the child get off to a good start. You need not go into details. That is more than the child usually can understand. Tell the truth simply and without baffling, meaningless analogies about birds and bees.

The first thing children usually want to know, sometimes when they are no more than two years old, is where babies come from. The answer can be simply that they grow inside their mothers. Then, or sometime later, a child is likely to ask how the baby got there, and an adequate answer can be that "It grew from a little seed that was there all the time." When, as is likely, the child wants to know how the baby got out, the answer can be "Through a special opening that mothers have." And when the child asks whether daddies have anything to do with it, it can be said that the father's seed is needed, too.

It may be necessary to repeat all or part of this information frequently.

But that does not mean that you should add more facts than the child demands. Small children rarely expect explicit information about the sexual act or the actual mechanism of birth. When they are older and do want to know, explain simply in your own words. If you feel you can't do this, tell your child you will read to him about it. Many excellent books on birth in animals and human beings are available, and your librarian can suggest several.

Give your child truthful answers about the sex organs, too. Sometimes, it may be necessary to volunteer a little information, since children are not always able to make their curiosity, or concern, known to their parents. The fact that a boy has a penis, and a girl does not, often is a source of worry to both of them. The girl may feel deprived; the boy may fear something can happen to him so he will be like the girl. If often pays to take the lead and avoid such problems by explaining that boys and girls are made differently because they are going to be different when they grow up; a girl is going to be a mother, a boy a father.

While false modesty is to be avoided, most experts in child psychology advise parents not to expose their naked bodies to children, even very young ones. Adults and children should not take baths together. It may disturb children to be reminded so vividly of the physical differences between themselves and their parents.

It is important to take precautions so that children do not witness or hear the sexual act; they are likely to mistake passion for violence and to become frightened by seeing or listening to ardent lovemaking.

Be sure to remember that sex is more than reproduction. Nothing you can tell a child about the "facts of life" can be as important to him as seeing and realizing for himself what a good relationship between a man and a woman means in terms of tenderness, respect, and loyalty. It has been said that the greatest sex education in the home comes when a child sees his father pat his mother lovingly.

Masturbation

Take it as a virtual certainty that your child will masturbate. Babies play with their genitals as naturally as they play with their toes. Unless their attention becomes riveted on this area—because of an irritation or because of the attitude of parents—no bad habits result. At various stages of development, both boys and girls play with their own genitals, and those of other children, out of natural curiosity. It is also, of course, a source of pleasure, but that is no reason to worry about it. Think of masturbation as we suggested you think of thumbsucking. When indulged in excessively, masturbation, too, indicates that the child has an emotional problem. It is a sign, rather than cause, of "nervousness."

Ignoring excessive masturbation is not the answer. A child so engrossed may be having trouble making friends or may have other worries. He may also be worried about masturbating so much. If one of his parents talks it over with him openly and calmly, offering reassurance that masturbation is something all children do and that in itself it is not harmful, the conversation can accomplish more than nervously ignoring the whole subject.

Stammering, Nail Biting, Tics, Other Habits

Children, as we have indicated earlier, go through periods of increased tensions in their development. These vary with age, home situation, the child's temperament and manifest themselves, too, in various ways.

Some babies rock violently or bang their heads against the crib. An older child may bite his nails, make grimaces, blink his eyes, or twitch his lips. Simply trying to use the new words he is learning so rapidly may make him stammer.

Don't nag, scold, or shame the child. This will simply increase his tensions and establish the habit more firmly. Ignore these symptoms and try to find and eliminate their cause. Usually, time will help. And you often can help in simple ways. For example, if you listen closely to a stammering child, he may relax because he doesn't think he has to try so hard to get his ideas across. If you play at "manicuring" a child's nails, you may make it easier for him to stop biting them. If tensions persist, describe them fully to the child's doctor.

Jealousy

Once it was thought that having siblings—that is, brothers and sisters —made every child happy. Then opinion shifted to the other extreme and we heard so much about sibling rivalry that it sometimes seemed that every personality problem could be traced to the effect brothers and sisters have on each other. There is some truth to both viewpoints.

It's important, we think, for parents to remember that jealousy is painful, and pain can have bad effects. It may take great ingenuity to avoid causing any more jealousy than is necessary, but it is worth it. You can't prevent jealousy entirely, and you certainly should not make children conceal it. But you can help your children to overcome it.

With the arrival of a second child, the first must share the limelight and must adjust to that. Make it as easy for him as you can without neglecting the rights of the second child. For example, it won't harm the new baby if you avoid talking about him constantly in front of the older child, and it certainly won't harm him if you show you love them both.

Let your children know that they are not alike and you wouldn't want them to be; that you love them as they are. Let them realize that your love is so elastic it will always "go round" with room for one more.

Unexpressed love does little good for a child. Parents should show their love. Ask yourself whether you have had the time—and patience—to show your love every day. True love is given freely without asking anything from the child. Remember that you can praise and pet a child without pampering and overprotecting him. Give your child plenty of praise, encouragement, and affection.

RECOGNIZING SICKNESS IN CHILDREN

Early recognition that a child is sick means a better chance of (1) reducing the seriousness of the disease itself, (2) avoiding complications, and (3) sometimes preventing fatal consequences.

Of course, infants are unable to tell us that they are sick. Children under three can't be relied upon too definitely for announcements of symptoms of illness. And even older children may become so frightened or drowsy from illness that they do not tell us early enough that they do not feel well.

How can you recognize illness in babies and young children? Don't rely completely on a list of symptoms and signs. Actually, a mother usually can tell as soon as a doctor that a child is not feeling right. She senses that he is not eating well or is unusually irritable. She may notice that expected spitting-up of milk has turned into real vomiting. She may notice that a child is drowsy at a time of day when he is usually alert. The child's mother knows his cry, too. There are cries of hunger, of loneliness, and of fright; these are different from the cry that accompanies pain. There may be an obvious explanation for a pain cry—for example, an open safety pin in a diaper. More likely, it is caused by colic, which is frequent in infants. If the pained type of crying continues, take the child's temperature. If the temperature is elevated, notify your doctor. Even if the temperature is normal and the crying does not subside in the next hour, it is best to tell your doctor.

Severe diarrhea is another sign of illness, as is also the appearance of bloody or black bowel movements.

Unconsciousness, stiff neck, and convulsions, of course, are such important signs of potentially serious illness that your doctor should be told about them immediately. If he is not available, take your child to the hospital with which your doctor is associated so an intern or resident can start treatment until your own doctor can be located.

Cough is more unusual in infants than in adults and therefore is an important indication of illness. Difficult, rapid, or labored breathing is also a potentially serious symptom. Hoarseness, or a hoarse quality in a baby's cry, may be an indication of impending croup or diphtheria, and should always be reported to your doctor.

When babies and small children get sick, their illness usually manifests itself quickly with fever. The best way to make certain a child has a fever is to take his temperature. When babies are even moderately sick, temperature often goes quite high. A temperature of 102° to 104°F in a child may not mean serious illness. In a sick adult, such a fever would generally be much more important.

COLDS

Children are usually more susceptible to colds than adults. It isn't a cold itself that need worry you, but what a cold may lead to, and every mother should be on guard to prevent the complications.

There is no certain way of avoiding colds, but there are things you can do to reduce the frequency of a child's colds. He should not be allowed to get overtired. A well-balanced diet will help increase a child's general health and to some extent help improve his resistance; it will certainly not guarantee that he will not get a cold, but if he does get a cold it will help prevent complications.

Try to keep a child away from other people, both adults and children, who have colds. If a mother gets a cold, she should mention it to the baby's doctor and ask him about the need for any special precautions. Wash your hands often with soap and water and once again before handling the baby.

If your child is under two years of age and has a cold, put him to bed and make sure he is kept warm in every part of his body. With older children, it is not necessary to confine them to bed unless they are feverish. See to it that the room is free of drafts. You can get ventilation by opening a window in another room.

For a sick child with fever, it's important to make certain he gets adequate amounts of fluid. Encourage him to drink small quantities frequently. Because fever makes a child perspire, he loses body fluids and may become "dried out," lowering resistance to germs still more. To prevent this, give a sufficient volume of fluids so that the child urinates normal amounts. An adequate urine output will be indicated by a light-yellow color instead of a dark-brownish color, which usually signifies insufficient fluid. In addition to milk and water, try fruit juices and carbonated drinks; grapefruit and melons are good sources of extra fluid.

If you think you should give your child nose drops, ask your doctor first. Nose drops and antihistamine pills have no curative effect whatever. They simply ease symptoms. But always let your doctor decide whether any medicine should be used and what kind it should be.

There are two simple measures you can use to relieve a mucus-plugged nose in an infant. First, loosen the mucus by putting in the nostrils a few drops of sterile saline solution. You can make the solution by adding a teaspoonful of salt to a pint of boiling water and *then cooling to body temperature*. Next, after a few minutes, suck out the mucus with a rubber-tipped bulb. Second, try increasing the humidity of the air the infant breathes. An electric humidifier is a worthwhile investment, helpful for all the family's colds. A fair substitute is to keep one or more pans of hot water on a radiator.

It's very important to realize that a cold paves the way for other germs called "secondary invaders." These are germs like the pneumococcus and especially the streptococcus.

STREPTOCOCCAL INFECTIONS

The streptococcal germ can cause sore throat, tonsillitis, sinusitis, middle ear infection, and indirectly rheumatic fever and kidney disease (nephritis). Rheumatic fever or nephritis may follow a week or so after strep infection. This does not mean that most, or even many, strep infections lead to these illnesses. But by guarding against strep infections, the chances of getting these more serious diseases can be significantly decreased.

The first step in protecting your child against strep is to follow the measures outlined for preventing colds.

A fever that develops when a cold seems to be ending suggests a potentially serious complication until proved otherwise by the doctor. Some of the complications are described below. Quick treatment by the doctor will promptly suppress strep infection and will almost always prevent its complications.

Sore Throats, Swollen Neck Glands, Tonsillitis, Sinusitis, and Middle Ear Infections

These may be caused by the streptococcus although most sore throats, swollen glands, and severe upper respiratory infections in childhood are caused by viruses. *Tonsillitis* produces a high fever which lasts several days. The child may vomit and have headaches, and his throat may become so sore that he can barely swallow. A doctor is needed. The first thing to do if the child complains of sore throat is to put him to bed. Don't expect overnight recovery. It takes a while for tonsillitis to be cured.

The tonsils are located at the back of the mouth and are composed of lymphoid tissue. They are like the lymph nodes and have the same purpose: to trap and destroy germs. Yet sometimes they become overloaded by a heavy invasion of germs and, instead of destroying the germs, the tonsils themselves are overwhelmed and infected.

Should tonsils be removed? Once they were, almost routinely. Now doctors feel they should not be taken out except when there is good medical reason. Removal of tonsils will not decrease the frequency of respiratory infections. If they must be removed, the operation should be performed at a good hospital. Some family doctors and pediatricians are skilled in tonsil removal; if they are not, they will arrange for a throat specialist to carry out the operation.

ADENOIDS.   These can be regarded as small "tonsils" located in the part of the throat behind the nasal passages. When they enlarge they can block the outlet from the nose so much that the affected child breathes chiefly through the mouth. Also, enlarged adenoids may block the eustachian tubes which connect the middle part of the ear with the back of the throat. This may lead to pain or a sense of pressure in the ears. It may also cause infections in the middle ear and occasionally interfere with hearing.

Adenoids may be removed along with tonsils. Not infrequently, only the adenoids need removal. Recurrent middle ear infections and hearing loss associated with enlarged adenoids are conditions treated by removal of the adenoids.

MIDDLE EAR INFECTIONS.   Germs from colds, sore throats, infected adenoids and tonsils may travel through the eustachian tubes that lead to the middle part of the ear. Middle ear infections are usually quite painful, and even a young child will point with distress toward his ear as the area where he knows something is wrong. A discharge from the ear is occasionally the first sign. Fever, vomiting, headaches, and drowsiness may accompany middle ear infections. A doctor should be notified at once, or the child should be taken to the hospital if a doctor is not available. The middle ear contains important parts of the hearing apparatus. Also, since the middle ear connects with the mastoid cells, uncontrolled infection can lead to the complication of mastoid bone infection. The brain is not far from the middle ear. Neglected middle ear and mastoid infections have sometimes led to devastating brain infections. Before the advent of sulfa medicines and antibiotics, middle ear infections and their complications were serious problems. Now, if a doctor is notified early enough, he can stop these infections with suitable antibiotics. Rarely now do eardrums have to be incised to drain pus, and mastoid operations have become a rarity.

SINUSITIS.   The sinuses—the air-filled cavities in the bones around the nose—are subject to infections, less so in children than in adults. A tiny opening connects each sinus with the inside of the nose. During a cold,

472 / Family Preventive Care

infection may spread to the sinuses, which will get clogged with pus. The pus drips out from the back of the nose into the throat, causing a "drip" which may make the child cough when he lies down. In more severe sinusitis, the child will have fever and headache. Redness and swelling of the inner parts of the eyelids, the portions near the nose, may be signs of a serious form of sinusitis (ethmoiditis). The doctor can do many things, such as using nose packs, suction, and medication, to relieve sinusitis.

Scarlet Fever

This is an infection by a strep germ that happens to produce a special poison (scarlet fever toxin) which causes a scarlet-colored rash. Not all strep germs cause scarlet fever, and not everyone is susceptible to the rash-producing poison. Thus, if such a strep infection occurs in a family of three children, one child may get scarlet fever because he cannot resist the poison; a second may develop only strep sore throat; and the third may carry the germ without being sickened at all by it and may be able to pass it on to others.

As scarlet fever sets in, the child feels tired, restless, and irritable. Then he develops fever and sore throat, and begins to vomit. His skin feels hot and dry. After a day or so, bright red spots break out, starting in the body creases such as the armpits. The rash spreads to the neck, the chest, and the back. It may later cover the entire body and, from a distance, it may look like a uniform coat of redness except for the skin around the mouth which remains pale. But the tongue will be inflamed, a blazing bright red. After about two weeks, peeling of the skin occurs.

Medicines such as penicillin may shorten the course of the disease and are also tried in the hope of preventing complications like ear infections, swollen neck glands, and nephritis. Not only have antibiotics reduced the dangers of scarlet fever, but the disease itself has become less severe in recent years for reasons still not understood. For both these reasons, the complications that used to follow scarlet fever are much less common now, although the disease is still not to be taken lightly.

Rheumatic Fever

This serious disease (see also Heart Diseases, page 585) most often afflicts children between 5 and 15 years of age. It is responsible for heart disease in 2 percent of American schoolchildren.

Rheumatic fever is a delayed result of a streptococcal infection such as a strep sore throat, scarlet fever, tonsillitis, or middle ear infection. The infection may still be present when rheumatic fever strikes but more often has disappeared before the rheumatic fever becomes evident. A well-developed case of rheumatic fever may affect many parts of the body, the most important being the heart. The best way for a doctor to reduce the threat of rheumatic fever is to treat children with strep infections promptly and effectively.

The early signs of the disease usually begin 10 to 14 days after the strep infection and consist of fever ranging between 101° and 103°F, irritability, striking pallor, moderate weight loss, and poor appetite.

More specific symptoms then appear. The joints are tender to the touch and they hurt when moved. Redness and swelling of the joints occur. Several joints—knees, ankles, wrists, elbows—may be involved at once or in succession. This severe condition is quite different from the vague, fleeting muscle and tendon pains often called "growing pains."

The heart may become damaged, causing a weak and rapid pulse, shortness of breath, and a puffy face. Often, blood vessels in the nose are weakened, and the nose begins to bleed. Sometimes, rashes may appear.

A special type of rheumatic fever is chorea, also known as St. Vitus' dance. This most often affects children between the ages of 6 and 11, especially girls. A rash caused by the fever may appear on the body. Hard little ball-like swellings (nodules) may be seen or felt under the skin at the elbow, knee, and wrist joints, as well as along the spine. The brain is temporarily affected, causing involuntary twitching or writhing movements which make the child so clumsy he drops things and writes illegibly. Fortunately, chorea clears up and doesn't cause epilepsy or serious brain trouble.

Most people with rheumatic fever do not have all the various symptoms. At least 50 percent of people who have chronic (long-standing) rheumatic heart disease that is discovered when they are grown, never knew they had rheumatic fever when they were children. Careful questioning by doctors sometimes reveals that at some period in the past such a person suffered from repeated nosebleeds, mild joint pains, "growing pains," or perhaps a period of months when he was not feeling up to par. The important lesson from this is to try to spot the mild cases in childhood and to take appropriate steps to prevent attacks from occurring again and again.

PREVENTION OF RHEUMATIC FEVER.   The key to prevention is the recognition of strep infections, especially when they cause sore throat or tonsillitis. Early diagnosis by a doctor and prompt treatment with penicillin or another antibiotic are most important.

When a person has had rheumatic fever once, everything possible must be done to prevent repeated attacks because of the damage they may do to the heart. With proper care, most people who have rheumatic fever will recover. With careful management, they can avoid further attacks by avoiding strep infections.

By use of antibiotics or sulfa medicines, the strep infections which cause recurrences can usually be controlled. Any child with rheumatic fever or who has recovered from an attack should remain under the care of a doctor or a heart clinic so that recurrences of this potentially serious disease can be prevented. If this is done, these patients can lead fully normal lives.

Heart Murmurs

Murmurs may be caused by changes in the heart valves and by blood leaking from scarred valves which do not close properly. The idea of a murmur usually frightens parents. Yet the fact is that there are innocent murmurs which mean absolutely nothing. There are other murmurs which do not come from heart conditions associated with rheumatic fever. And sometimes a heart only very slightly affected by rheumatic fever may produce a loud murmur.

It is up to the physician and not the parents to decide when the heart is healed and when a child may start playing and doing things that normal children do. If there is any doubt, as there sometimes may be, consultation with a heart specialist (a cardiologist) should be arranged.

Years ago when less was known about rheumatic fever and such excellent laboratory tests as we have now were not available, physicians used to advise a good deal of bed rest or very little activity for people with heart murmurs. These people may have had mild rheumatic fever. The bad psychological effect of such needless restriction was worse than a mild impairment of the heart.

If your child has had mild rheumatic fever, don't coddle him or make him feel in any way that he is an invalid and different from other children. See that he obtains plenty of rest, sunshine and fresh air, and a good, nourishing diet. This you should do for any child to build up his resistance to germ diseases, but with the child who has had rheumatic fever take special care. If he has had a severe illness and must have his activities restricted, teach him not to overexert himself, but otherwise to think and act like other children. The prevention of further streptococcal infections is the prime measure, and your doctor can help advise you about this.

See your doctor for regular checkups of your children. If a child should have undiscovered rheumatic fever, the doctor can help you take proper precautionary steps against repeated attacks.

WHOOPING COUGH

Whooping cough begins much like an ordinary cold, with running nose and perhaps a little dry cough. Days may go by with nothing further appearing. A mother may think the child is well again and send him back to school. But then he feels chilled, begins to vomit, his temperature goes up, and the coughing spells become longer. Soon he is coughing a great deal, eight to ten times without catching his breath. When he finally does get his breath, there is a long noisy intake of breath, which is where the whoop comes in. *This* cough, please note, does not appear until the second week, so you need not be unduly alarmed any time your child has a cough right after catching cold.

The three major indications of whooping cough are (1) the long coughing spells, at night as well as during the day, (2) the whoop, and (3) vomiting. The average case lasts about six weeks—two weeks coming, two running, two going away. In deciding whether a cough that has gone on for a long time is whooping cough, the doctor may need to do some laboratory tests.

Especially for infants, whooping cough can be dangerous because it paves the way for pneumonia. During the first two weeks, it's very contagious. Be careful to see it is not spread to other children or adults in the household who have not been immunized. Temporary protection for the latter can be obtained with a special type of gamma globulin shot. A booster dose of immunizing vaccine can be given to those previously immunized.

While most cases are mild enough to be cared for at home, severe ones, especially in infants, require hospital care. Treatment involves bed rest. The room should be well ventilated. Conditions that provoke coughing—such as smoke, dust, activity, sudden temperature changes—should be avoided. Small, frequent feedings help. Be certain to call your doctor when you suspect whooping cough.

Remember, whooping cough can be prevented by immunization in early infancy.

MEASLES

Measles, a virus-caused disease, is very contagious. It starts with cold-like symptoms—sneezing, coughing, temperature elevation. The eyes are sensitive to light and become pink from inflammation. Both the eyes and face look puffy. After a few days, a characteristic rash appears; the spots are pink and may show first behind the ears, on the forehead or the cheeks, and then spread downward. Usually the spots itch when the fever is at its highest point. The rash begins to fade after two or three days. By then, the child feels better.

Once, measles was considered a mild disease. It was thought that every child should get it and be done with it. We know now that measles can be a serious disease because of the complications. It sometimes produces convulsions which can be extremely worrisome. It may lead to ear infections and pneumonia. Death does not occur often—1 in 10,000 cases—but any death, or serious complication from a disease that is now preventable is, indeed, a tragedy. And measles complications include encephalitis, brain damage, and mental retardation.

Today, measles vaccine is available, notably effective in providing long-term, quite probably lifelong, immunity. By all means, have your children protected.

Measles may pave the way for invasion by other germs, and so only the minimum number of people required to care for the child should be allowed in his room. Adults may infect the child with germs of other diseases. The child with measles should be kept in bed and given plenty of fluids. If light bothers his eyes, protect them with an eye shade or visor and, of course, avoid glare. The sensitivity to light (photophobia) will clear up without any permanent effects on the eyes.

GERMAN MEASLES

This, too, is a virus disease which begins with coldlike symptoms, a little fever, and sore throat. Then comes the rash in the form of rosy-colored spots that spread over the entire body. At first the rash looks like a measles rash, then like scarlet fever. The lymph nodes behind the ears and in the neck become swollen.

German measles is contagious. The rash lasts about two or three days. In children, the disease is usually mild, without complications. The real threat comes when an expectant mother develops it early in pregnancy. Then, there is serious risk that her child will be born deformed. If a pregnant woman, especially in the early months of pregnancy, who has not had German measles is exposed to the disease, this becomes an emergency. She should notify her doctor at once; he may advise immediate injections of gamma globulin in the hope it may increase her resistance to the disease.

Fortunately, another significant advance in preventive medicine is the development of a vaccine effective in providing immunity to German measles.

MUMPS

Mumps, a virus disease, leads to swelling of the parotid gland beneath the ear. This is a gland that secretes saliva. The virus may attack the gland on one side of the face first, then sometimes the gland on the other. Less often, other salivary glands under the jaw may be affected.

In adult males, mumps can be a painful illness because it can attack the testicles. Although painful, mumps involving the testicles rarely leads to sterility or impotence, so the fear of that is generally unwarranted. Nevertheless, if the father or any young male in the household has not had mumps, he should consult his doctor about protective measures. If mumps vaccine is given in time, it can usually prevent the illness. Second attacks of mumps are possible, but the first occurrence almost always gives lifelong immunity.

Let your doctor decide whether the illness is mumps and not some other disease that may imitate it. For example, an infection of lymph nodes by bacteria may look like mumps, but the treatment is quite different. Mumps is treated by bed rest until fever and swelling have cleared.

CHICKENPOX

Chickenpox is a virus disease, a very highly contagious one and therefore very common. First, pimples appear, usually starting on the chest. The pimples become blisters which dry into scabs. The main danger is that the blisters itch and may become infected by scratching. To ease the child's itching, place him in a cold starch bath. There should be two handfuls of starch in the tub. Because you will be unable to prevent a certain amount of scratching, keep your child's hands clean by washing them several times a day, and keep his nails cut short. The scabs are not infectious.

Call the doctor if the child appears really sick or has a fever. This is mainly a precaution to rule out smallpox or other serious diseases. Most cases of chickenpox are mild and require no special treatment except bed rest and plenty of fluids during the feverish stage. The child should remain in bed during the acute period and away from other children until about a week after the blisters first appear. Once the scabs are gone, it is not necessary to isolate him.

ROSEOLA INFANTUM

This is a fairly common fever-producing disease in children during the first three years of life. It is worth considering when a child has a fever, is irritable and drowsy, and has no other diagnostic signs such as a rash. In roseola infantum, strangely enough, a flat, reddish rash does appear, after three or four days of fever—and at that point, the disease is ended; the fever and other symptoms disappear quickly. This contrasts with illnesses such as measles, scarlet fever, and chickenpox, in which the rash heralds the beginning of the most intense phase of illness.

Roseola infantum yields without treatment. It is presumed to be a virus disease. There is no specific treatment for it. Fortunately, one attack appears to provide immunity for life.

DIPHTHERIA

Happily, this disease has been almost completely eradicated in the United States through immunizaton. Once it killed 25 percent of its victims and left incapacitated many of those who survived.

Every child should be immunized early and completely against diphtheria. If there is doubt about the completeness of the immunization, the Schick test can be used. The doctor injects into the skin a small amount of the poison secreted by the diphtheria germ. If protection is complete, the test will be negative; that is, no reddened, blistered area will appear on the skin. If the test is positive, the child must be further immunized until a negative test result is obtained.

Diphtheria is caused by a bacillus type of germ which usually grows on the tonsils and in the throat. It can infect nose and larynx. When the disease develops, the throat becomes sore and swollen, and a grayish membrane may cover the tissue. This membrane may get so large that it, plus the swelling, can obstruct breathing. This is one reason why diphtheria needs immediate medical attention, usually in a specialized contagious-disease unit of a hospital. Another reason for the high fatality rate of the disease is the powerful poison given off by growing diphtheria germs. It is absorbed into the body and affects the heart and other vital organs. It may paralyze nerves that control swallowing or breathing.

Fortunately, a powerful antitoxin is available. It can be injected to neutralize the poison. However, antitoxin must be given before the child has been ill more than three days. After that, the mortality rate is high despite use of large quantities of antitoxin.

Diphtheria usually provides plenty of warning that something serious is going on. There will be fever, prostration, vomiting, as well as sore throat. Sometimes, bloody mucus appears in one or both nostrils. The doctor should be notified at once if diphtheria is suspected.

DIARRHEA IN CHILDREN

Once diarrhea ranked as the leading cause of death in infants. The reasons included contaminated water and milk; poor sanitation and refrigeration which encouraged germ growth; inadequate knowledge about infant feeding and therapy. Exposed to harmful organisms at a time in life when their immunity was low, countless young children died of intestinal infections which doctors then could not combat.

Today, the situation has changed so greatly that we are apt to forget that diarrhea still is a serious threat to the health of infants and young children. With good medical care, virtually every child affected by diarrhea can get well. The important need is for parents to understand danger signals so treatment can be started early enough.

If a child develops severe diarrhea—for example, watery stools passed more than once an hour—call your doctor without delay. If he cannot be reached, take the child to the hospital. Less severe diarrhea usually can be cared for at home, especially if it has been caused by foods or a formula that does not agree with the child. But if bacterial infection is setting in, the diarrhea may progress to the point of bloody stools, requiring immediate medical help.

Assuming that the diarrhea is mild, no vomiting accompanies it, and you cannot reach your doctor, this is what you should do:

1. Discontinue the usual formula or foods. Don't worry about the child starving; he will benefit from resting of the inflamed disgestive system.
2. Stop any medicines until you talk to the doctor, because paregoric, patent medicines, and other medicines may make the child worse.
3. For infants, you can prepare the usual formula and dilute it with water to half-strength or you can use half-strength diluted skim milk. Offer it to the baby in small amounts frequently.
4. For an older child, a diet consisting of dilute skim milk, clear broth, ginger ale, weak tea with sugar, puddings or gelatin dessert, crackers or toast is appropriate in any mild diarrhea.

But if mild diarrhea is accompanied by vomiting and you cannot reach your doctor, somewhat sterner measures are needed in the diet.

For babies change to the following formula as a temporary measure: 1 quart of boiled water, 2 tablespoons of sugar or Karo syrup, and 1 level teaspoonful of salt (be sure to use no more salt than this).

Offer the same thing to an older child. If, as is likely, he refuses the water-sugar-salt formula, substitute any clear liquid—water, weak tea, ginger ale, etc. *But note:* The child needs salt which is not present in plain water or such drinks. Add the salt in the proportion of a level teaspoonful to a quart—that is, 1/4 level teaspoonful of salt to 1/2 pint of liquid.

Remember that these restricted diets are meant only as temporary measures—to be used until the doctor can be reached, and, at any event, no longer than 24 hours.

Dehydration

Dehydration means that the body is dried up from loss of vital fluids. This is the greatest threat to the life of a child with diarrhea. The loose, watery stools drain out water plus valuable chemicals from the body—chemicals such as sodium and potassium which are essential for regulating the body's fluid and acid-base balances. If diarrhea continues unchecked, severe illness or even death may result from the ensuing dehydration and the acidosis that goes with it. Dehydration may show itself by (1) decrease in amount of urine and a dark yellow or light brown appearance of the urine; (2) loss of the usual elastic quality of the skin; (3) sunken eyeballs; (4) rapid breathing; (5) drowsiness or even unconsciousness.

In severe cases accompanied by vomiting, the physician will have to replace the fluid and the sodium and other chemicals by injections into the child's veins. Such injections have often saved the lives of desperately sick infants.

CROUP

This is a narrowing of the air passage through the larynx, the voice box in the neck where the vocal cords are located. If the narrowing is great, air cannot reach the lungs and the child begins to choke. The narrowing is caused by spasm, or involuntary contraction, and swelling of the larynx, which may be the result of some infections or a severe allergy. Most often a virus infection is at fault. Fortunately, while terribly frightening to both child and parents, croup is rarely fatal. It usually comes in spasms, generally precipitated at night. The mild fever and apparently healthy look of the child between spasms, and the fact that a child has been immunized against diphtheria, usually make it certain that the illness is croup. However, always notify the doctor when the child develops a hoarse, croupy voice or cough, or seems to be having spasms of difficult breathing.

Occasionally, a severe croup attack may represent an emergency before the doctor can be summoned. The spasm can be relieved by placing the child in a place where there is cool moist air. Hospitals are equipped with special apparatus to provide this cool moist air, but at home, warm, moist air can be an adequate substitute. A croup tent can be improvised by boiling water in a kettle or pan on an electric hot plate under a blanket which is placed over the child and a parent. *A parent or other adult must always sit with a child during treatment.* The reason is important to know: More children have been burned to death during treatment for croup than have died of the disease itself. Keep the steam going until the spasm has been relaxed. Allow the child to rest. Plenty of clear fluids should be given.

If a croup tent can't be improvised, or your druggist can't rush over a good water vaporizer, fill the bathtub with steaming hot water, or turn the shower on and keep the hot water running. Close the bathroom window and the door so the room becomes saturated with moist air. *Sit in the bathroom with the child,* never taking a chance for even a second that the child can be trusted not to fall into the scalding water. Even an older child who starts a paroxysm of croup may become so breathless and frightened that he doesn't know what he is doing.

Croup attacks often tend to recur on two or three successive nights. Ask your doctor what to do to prevent the recurrences. He may leave medication that will help shorten a recurrence if it cannot be prevented.

Note: If an attack doesn't respond to the above measures in 20 minutes, or if high fever is present, the situation is a serious emergency. If you cannot reach your doctor, rush the child to a hospital.

MENINGITIS

This is a serious disease because it affects the coverings of the brain and spinal cord. It may be caused by different varieties of bacteria. Until the advent of sulfa medicines and antibiotics, meningitis was one of the most fearsome diseases. Now, if treated early, it can usually be cured. Also, when epidemics threaten, medicines can be given to prevent spread. There are no successful vaccinations against the common forms of meningitis.

The typical meningitis attack produces high fever, severe headache, convulsions, violent vomiting, and drowsiness or complete unconsciousness. There may be a skin rash. The neck and back muscles may become stiffened and painful. The brain, eyes, or ears may be permanently damaged.

A doctor should be notified immediately or the child rushed to a hospital if the doctor cannot be reached, so treatment can be started before he is located.

Meningitis is highly contagious, so those who have the disease must be isolated. Parents who must be in contact with a child suffering this disease must be treated by their doctor. To prevent further spread, they should follow their doctor's orders carefully about cleaning the room and the belongings of the meningitis patient.

CONVULSIONS

Convulsions may indicate onset of serious disease such as meningitis, but this is not necessarily true even when there is high fever. So potentially serious, however, is the combination of convulsions and fever that medical attention must be obtained without delay. Fortunately, many cases turn out to be meningismus—false or simulated meningitis. For example, during pneumonia and other illnesses, there may be enough irritation of the brain to set off convulsions. However, as soon as the pneumonia or other infection is brought under control, the convulsions disappear. Convulsions without fever may indicate epilepsy (see page 575).

WORMS

A good reason for considering worm infections—more properly called intestinal parasites—at this point is that parents often blame them for children's convulsions. Actually, convulsions are never caused by worms.

The chief worm infections of children are transmitted from humans to humans rather than from animals.

Three main types of worms affect children in the United States. These are the long round worm, *Ascaris;* the tiny, threadlike pinworm, also called seatworm; and the hookworm, midway between the other two in size. These three cause many more infections than either the tapeworm, or the trichina worm which infests pork. While children often are less susceptible to trichinosis than adults, they too should be given only thoroughly cooked pork or pork products.

Roundworm Infection

Resembling earthworms, roundworms may sometimes be seen in bowel movements or in a child's bed. Occasionally, one may be vomited. The worm should be saved to show to the doctor.

Roundworms may make a child irritable, restless at night. He will probably develop an erratic or poor appetite and may not gain weight. He may tire easily.

The worms can be eliminated by special medicines which must be administered under a doctor's care. Do not try to treat worms by getting medication at the drugstore. Children have died from overdosage of such medications. Also, only a doctor knows how to judge when the treatment has been completely effective. Unless all eggs and worms are killed or expelled, the sickness will return.

Hookworm Infection

This parasite, which infects children in the southern states, enters the body through the skin, usually when a child walks barefooted in infected soil. The worm then travels via the blood into the lungs and gets into the air passages, from which it enters the esophagus when coughing occurs. After arriving in the intestine via the esophagus and stomach, it takes up permanent residence in the small intestine, and discharges many eggs into the feces. It breeds at a lively rate. Being parasites, the worms live off the infected person's food and body, taking valuable protein and blood-building materials. This is why anemia is a chief symptom of severe hookworm infestation. The child usually looks and acts rundown and listless.

Hookworm disease is diagnosed by examination of the stools for the characteristic worm eggs. Treatment is effective when administered by a physician or health officer. A good preventive is a pair of shoes or sneakers. While there may be a problem in getting some children to give up the pleasures of walking barefoot, they would cooperate in wearing shoes or at least sneakers if they were educated by parents, teachers, and doctors about the dangers of hookworm disease.

Pinworm Infection

This is the most common worm infection in children. The medical term for it is oxyuriasis. Pinworm infections occur in the intestine. The tiny worms, less than half an inch long, do not debilitate a child as a heavy roundworm or hookworm infestation will. But they cause trouble by their habit of coming out around the rectal area during sleep. They irritate this area, leading to painful scratching and restless sleep. Occasionally, in a girl, pinworms may migrate into the vaginal opening and cause intense itching and distress. You may be able to locate pinworms with a flashlight and remove them with a swab of cotton on an applicator rod. Put them in a bottle for the doctor to see, or burn them if the pinworm diagnosis has already been made. Do not treat pinworm infections yourself. Let the doctor prescribe treatment. He will also decide what to do about other family members. He will also advise you about disinfection of bedclothes and other materials that may be harboring pinworm eggs.

HEAD LICE

The medical name for head lice, or nits, is pediculosis capitis. The head louse is a tiny insect which inhabits the scalp and sucks blood. Almost always, lice affect only the back portion of the scalp. Lice eggs are called nits. They are contained in silvery oval-shaped envelopes which are attached to the shafts of hairs. They can be seen when plentiful and are just large enough to be combed out by a fine steel comb.

When lice bite the scalp, they cause itching. The resulting scratching produces scalp infections with inflammation of the lymph nodes of the neck.

The condition can be diagnosed definitely by a doctor or nurse who can recognize the characteristic nits. Schoolchildren are particularly susceptible to head lice, but anyone, rich or poor, of any age, may contract pediculosis.

Once, laborious treatments were required; heads often were shaved. Now effective agents such as benzyl benzoate may be prescribed and the hair need not be cut or shaved. It is important not to make a child with head lice feel self-conscious. Avoid letting him know the diagnosis; the problem can be passed off as "dermatitis" or a "scalp infection."

INTUSSUSCEPTION

This is an intestinal obstruction, a much less common illness than many we have mentioned. But it happens often enough for you to be on guard against it, because unless it is recognized within a few days of onset, it may be fatal.

Intussusception results from telescoping of a part of the intestine into the section ahead of it. It may occur when the intestine is partially filled with roundworms but usually there is no obvious cause. The child appears healthy. Then paroxysms of abdominal pain set in, with vomiting and restlessness. Within 12 to 24 hours, bloody mucus is passed by rectum instead of the usual fecal matter. On the second day, there may be fever as high as 106° to 108°F.

Death can occur within two to four days after onset unless the condition is relieved. The diagnosis may be confirmed by a barium enema x-ray test. Actually, this examination in itself frequently reduces the intussusception and may completely correct the telescoping. Treatment by surgery cures the condition.

POSTURAL ABNORMALITIES

Special attention should be given to posture in children because failure to attend to any difficulties and defects can result in permanent deformity.

When we speak of poor posture in children, we don't mean that they should have the good posture characteristic of healthy adults. Children are not built to sit or stand like adults. When they are under nine years of age, they are not large or strong enough to hold in their stomachs without straining. Odd foot positions and many other postural peculiarities in children are phases of physical development and will pass with maturity. But we are concerned about children's posture when it is unusual or poor by childhood standards.

Poor posture is a broad term; it covers minor as well as potentially serious problems. It can be caused by weakness, disease, or deformity involving muscles, bones, or joints. Some examples include rickets, Pott's disease, congenital dislocation of the hip, flat feet, and scoliosis (curvature of the spine).

Poor posture may also stem from defective vision or hearing. For example, a nearsighted or hard-of-hearing child is apt to thrust his head forward to see or hear better. As a result, his shoulders and back may be thrown out of line. Clothing that is too small or even too heavy may prevent a child from standing straight. A bed or chair that prevents a child from lying or sitting properly can also be responsible for poor posture. Finally, but no less important, emotional factors may cause postural problems. A shy, unhappy child who feels inferior may slump. Emotional problems, especially in adolescence, have contributed to many cases of curvature of the spine.

We wish it were possible to persuade all parents and teachers never to scold or nag a child about his posture. It is obviously cruel as well as useless to keep telling a child with a physical weakness or disease to stand up straight and to walk properly. It is also likely to do harm if the child's poor posture is due to emotional difficulties.

Regular physical examination will determine whether or not a child has a real posture problem and will usually reveal any condition likely to cause postural problems in the future. If you are concerned about your child's posture, don't wait for his regular examination to fall due. Consult a doctor as soon as possible. Taken in time, corrective measures can usually prevent difficulties and even deformities. If special exercises are needed, they should be supervised or at least initiated by a doctor or some other person with special training.

SKIN DISEASES IN CHILDHOOD

Both the infant and the young child are subject to many minor and even some serious skin diseases. Most of these, such as impetigo, scabies, and fungus infections of the skin, we have previously discussed under preventive body care (see pages 162–185). The more serious diseases, such as eczema and psoriasis, are taken up in separate sections, since they affect adults as well as children (see Index).

Children are peculiarly susceptible to ringworm of the scalp. While adults frequently are affected by fungus infections of the smooth skin, such as athlete's foot, ringworm infection of the scalp is rare in adults. It is a stubborn infection in children and often one schoolchild infects another. The disease is recognized chiefly by the bald patches when the fungus destroys hairs which fall out. The itching and scratching may lead to irritations which may be confused with bacterial infections. However, if a doctor is given a chance, he can diagnose the ringworm by special methods. One is to use an ultraviolet lamp which causes the fungi to fluoresce in the dark, allowing them to be seen in the hair. Also, the doctor will confirm his suspicions by finding the characteristic spores of the fungi. This is done by treating some infected hairs with chemicals and examining them under a microscope.

Treatment can be effective but requires patience on the part of doctor, child, and parent.

Petechial Rash

Infants and children often have rashes which are not serious. But one type, while rare, indicates a potentially dangerous disease. This is called petechial rash and is caused by bleeding under the skin. If your child has a rash, you can determine whether or not it is of this type by pressing one or more of the spots between your thumbs. If it does not blanch, that is, if the color still remains, call a doctor immediately.

ADOLESCENCE

Adolescence is a tempestuous phase of human development. In our first decade of life, we are children; in our third, we become adults; somewhere in between, adolescence is initiated by the physiological event of puberty, which has a profound influence not only through the physical changes it brings but also through its impact on social interests, behavior, and emotional life.

The adolescent is trying to discover himself and to move from dependent childhood to independence. He brings to this time of life his psychological characteristics and whole personality configuration, of course, but no matter how fine and healthy, they are now under tremendous stress. Emotional conflicts are triggered because the still immature adolescent has not yet succeeded in mastering his now-increased instinctual drives; he experiences strong urges for immediate expression of both sexual and aggressive impulses.

Society does not help him. It flaunts attractions of adult sex before him, caters to his whims in entertainment, but then prolongs his dependence far into the teens and even into the twenties, insisting that long years of education and training must precede marriage and family. Teenagers have much to contend with, not alone their own inner churnings but the contradictions and confusions of the world they live in.

Preventive medicine is vitally concerned with the adolescent years. In this period, we face the greatest danger from certain illnesses, such as tuberculosis. The development of the sex organs is a natural event but not without problems. Emotional illness must be guarded against, including schizophrenia, which often chooses its victims from this age group (see page 645).

Every generation frets about adolescents who, seemingly, will go to the devil in no time at all unless they listen to their elders. Adolescents have rarely listened in the past; most have managed to come through all right. But more will come through with less difficulty if we understand the problems associated with this phase of life—problems, of course, for parents as well as the younger generation.

This is a time for parental self-examination. It is important for parents to determine whether their responses to their teen-ager's behavior are really justifiable, or whether they are responses to their own anxieties. They may exert inappropriate pressures on their adolescent sons and daughters to adopt certain social customs, prepare for certain careers, go to certain schools, behave in a certain manner. It is certainly not easy for parents who have devoted themselves to caring for a child for 15 or 16 years to realize that he is no longer a baby but is now seeking to become what he must become, an independent, self-reliant human being.

So adolescence is trying for both parents and teen-agers. Given understanding on both sides, controversies in the home will be reduced to reasonable proportions. They are not likely to be eliminated completely. Emotionally, the "birth" of an adult is scarcely less of an event than the actual, physical birth of a baby. But it is fully as rewarding.

If parents make an effort to remember their own stormy adolescence, and if adolescents make an effort to understand parents' anxieties and dilemmas—and if they can talk freely to each other and even joke a bit about their respective problems—tensions will be markedly reduced.

PROBLEMS OF ADOLESCENTS

Physically, many boys and girls are ready for mating by the time they are 13 to 15; they are sexually mature. But they are not ready for marriage, with all its responsibilities. Aside from difficulties they would have in establishing and supporting a home, they are not yet emotionally adult. They long to be grown-up but in some ways are still attached to childhood.

Independence and sex constitute two of the main problems adolescents must face. They must break away from old ways of living within a familiar framework. They must resolve the problem of what to do about sexual desires—and, despite all they may read or be told, they must do the resolving themselves. They must develop not so much a workable theory of sex but a workable means of handling their new reactions, sensations, and emotions.

As if this were not burden enough, the picture may be complicated by a number of factors. For example, shortly before, or in early, adolescence, youngsters go through a period of preferring members of their own sex. Girls may avoid boys, developing "crushes" on other girls. Boys look down on girls, become devoted to a chum. This is a natural phase. It is naturally followed by interest in members of the opposite sex.

But these phases follow no precise timetable. Ages of youngsters in a group—a school grade, for example—vary. Some may have started school earlier than others; some, unusually bright, may be as much as two years younger than many of their perfectly normal classmates. A normal child may also, for any of many possible reasons, be older than others in his group. Boys are usually about two years older than girls when maturity arrives. The age of maturity varies considerably, too, among individuals. And emotional development does not always proceed at the same pace.

It can be expected, then, that some young people will be out of step. They will be attracted to members of the opposite sex which the crowd still disdains, or prefer members of their own sex while their friends have advanced to dating and flirting. This is disturbing to them. Not wanting to be on the outside, they try to be like the majority, and may rush through, or even miss, an important phase of emotional development or remain in it too long.

Social contact is virtually essential during this period. Young people sometimes have difficulties here, because of many barriers, including those of race, creed, color, social position. Such barriers should not be allowed to exist. They do, however, and parents can make a significant contribution to the welfare of their own children and the community by doing everything possible to tear them down.

No less difficult for a young person than achieving a sense of balance about sex is achieving one regarding independence. "Parents are the greatest problem of adolescence," some young people say. In a sense, this is true. Even under the best of circumstances, it is not easy for a young person to develop a new attitude toward the man and woman he has regarded as "father" and "mother" and whom he now must look upon as people as well as parents. If, as so often happens, he swings back and forth between extremes, it is as painful to him as it is to parents.

It is helpful if parents can understand the problems and the pain of adolescence—and the promise as well. As the adolescent tries to move toward adulthood, he must find new values and a new role for himself in the world. It is easy to dismiss his idealism and his criticisms of his parents' generation as mere naiveté or youthful rebellion. Yet it is much more: It is part of his search for values and role—and, let us recognize, it is such repudiation of the past that has always been the driving force for the progress made by each new generation.

PROBLEMS OF PARENTS

Parents, meanwhile, are suddenly now required to face the fact that the child is becoming an adult. This means growing independence, possibly leaving home for school, job, or marriage. Particularly in small families, the loneliness they see ahead may overwhelm parents. It is often tempting to try to prevent the child from becoming really adult—from "growing up too fast"—in the hope he will stay at home. It is no easy matter for anyone to face the fact that, with children becoming mature, middle age is here. Nor is it easy to pass the reins to another at just the right time and gracefully.

Parents, even the most mature and realistic, face problems at this period. They know their help is needed; their children, however intelligent and well-balanced, still lack experience. Almost daily, parents hear or read about a tragic accident to a teen-ager, ruined health, a marriage of necessity, cases of rape, homosexuality, insanity. It is hardly a wonder that parents cannot sit back passively and let children court disaster. But if they exert undue authority, the result may only be rebellion. How much should they tell their children? Long ago, they told them the facts of life—normal life and its reproduction. But now how much should they tell them about life's uglier aspects? These problems for parents are complicated because they occur along with many other problems, for other things are happening, too—perhaps an illness in the family, need for the father to change jobs, etc. There is not always all the time needed, as one parent has put it, "to give your calmest consideration to this teen-ager who has become a will-o'-the-wisp and slips through your fingers just when you want to do your best."

Always, there will be problems and emotional stresses for both parents and children during this period. It is important not to exaggerate them, to give them the best thought and effort we can, and to realize that time and nature, which create the problems, also help to solve many of them.

THE HEALTH OF ADOLESCENTS

All the problems adolescents must face—and we will discuss them as we go along—can be easier for them to handle if they have a basically healthy and well-nourished body. If anything, nutrition at this time is more important than ever. In a period of active growth, of strenuous physical activity, of mental and emotional stresses, there is need for plenty of protein for developing muscles and body tissue, minerals for bone growth, vitamins for general health, energy-rich foods to keep the metabolic fires burning properly.

Foods for Adolescents

On their own, teen-agers often eat poorly balanced meals. They go for the quick hamburger, the malted, and French fries. Girls often take up food fads and try crash diets. Some of this behavior must be tolerated by wise parents. If the mother provides a balanced diet at home, there will be no great harm if her teen-ager gulps French fries and malteds. Remember, too: adolescent appetites are often enormous. A teen-ager may eat more than his parents.

For a balanced diet, adolescents, like everybody else, need proteins, minerals, vitamins, and iron. Protein foods include meat, fish, eggs, and milk. They may be expensive but they are vital for healthy growth. Two good sources of protein should be served at all meals. For example, for breakfast, an egg and large glass of milk, or bacon or a slice of ham instead of the egg. For lunch, there should be meat or fish or a dish containing cheese, plus a large glass of milk. At the evening meal, the main course should consist of fish, meat, eggs, or cheese, with another glass of milk. Between meals, milk should be taken to make a total of four glasses a day.

We emphasize milk because, in addition to supplying protein, it is an excellent source of the minerals calcium and phosphorus, which are required for bone building. If adolescents won't drink enough milk as such, it can be provided in other ways, such as in soups and desserts. It can be flavored with chocolate or vanilla. Skimmed (fat-free) milk is better for adolescents who are overweight; it provides the valuable protein and minerals without weight-adding fat.

Vitamins should be provided via fruits and vegetables; both green and yellow vegetables should be included. Liver, an excellent source of all the B vitamins, should be eaten once a week. A daily addition of vitamin A and vitamin D is helpful during the period of active growth. Some margarine is fortified with vitamin A, and some milk with vitamin D. Ask your doctor about the need, if any, based on your teen-ager's regular dietary pattern, for multivitamin capsules.

Extra iron is needed to build rich red blood for growing young people. Girls who are beginning to menstruate may require additional iron to replace what is lost in the menstrual blood. The following foods are rich in iron: meat, especially liver, heart, kidneys; leafy green vegetables; egg yolk; whole grain and enriched bread and cereal; potatoes; oysters;

dried fruits, peas, and beans. Your doctor can also prescribe supplements of iron in capsule form if needed.

Adolescents also need carbohydrates—plenty of bread and starches—to maintain or gain weight.

Mothers will recognize that this diet is similar in many ways to what they were advised to eat during pregnancy. The extra proteins, minerals, and vitamins are needed for the growing teen-ager just as they are for the growing fetus. The main difference is that the adolescent needs plenty of supplementary carbohydrate and fat to provide energy for his active life.

Overweight and Underweight

Underweight, to the point of impaired physical well-being, is not an important problem among American teen-agers. Many tend to be thin, but relatively few are so underweight that they are unusually subject to serious illness. The average, healthy teen-ager, especially when going through a period of rapid growth, has a rangy, spare appearance despite the fact that he eats large quantities.

Overweight, however, is a more serious problem, physically and emotionally, and may have long-range consequences. The overweight adult quite often was an overweight adolescent. The potentially harmful effects of obesity on health are becoming better known. In addition, obese boys and girls are often teased by playmates or left out because they are unattractive. This may lead them to eat still more to console themselves, creating a vicious cycle that becomes difficult to break.

Getting young people to gain or lose weight requires tact. Each parent has to consider the individual child. However, we can make several general suggestions—which, incidentally, apply not only to health matters but to others in which the parents must exert authority.

Don't use ridicule; prevent others in the family from doing so if you possibly can. Ridicule is cruel; adolescents are especially sensitive to and affected detrimentally by it.

Don't nag. This defeats its purpose, especially with adolescents who are usually impatient.

Give the problem special consideration from the standpoint of the particular child. Consider the suggestions on gaining and losing weight made elsewhere in this book (see Index) and evaluate them from the standpoint of which is most likely to work best for him or her.

Use an authority your child will recognize. Teen-agers often are inclined to think their parents know less than they actually do, just as they were inclined, as children, to think their parents knew everything. The word of a doctor or health authority is useful reinforcement.

Adolescents, despite their rebelliousness, often accept something that is presented calmly and firmly. They respond to a certain amount of authority. So save your authority for the things that are really important.

IDEAL WEIGHTS IN BOYS AND GIRLS

HEIGHT (INCHES)	Boys AGE 14	15	16	17	18	19	HEIGHT (INCHES)	Girls AGE 14	15	16	17	18
54	72						55	78				
55	74						56	83				
56	78	80					57	88	92			
57	83	83					58	93	96	101		
58	86	87					59	96	100	103	104	
59	90	90	90				60	101	105	108	109	111
60	94	95	96				61	105	108	112	113	116
61	99	100	103	106			62	109	113	115	117	118
62	103	104	107	111	116		63	112	116	117	119	120
63	108	110	113	118	123	127	64	117	119	120	122	123
64	113	115	117	121	126	130	65	121	122	123	125	126
65	118	120	122	127	131	134	66	124	124	125	128	130
66	122	125	128	132	136	139	67	130	131	133	133	135
67	128	130	134	136	139	142	68	133	135	136	138	138
68	134	134	137	141	143	147	69	135	137	138	140	142
69	137	139	143	146	149	152	70	136	138	140	142	144
70	143	144	145	148	151	155	71	138	140	142	144	145
71	148	150	151	152	154	159						
72		153	155	156	158	163						
73		157	160	162	164	167						
74		160	164	168	170	171						

From American Child Health Association.

Skin Troubles During Adolescence

Adolescents are very likely to develop acne and other skin problems. Be sure to read the section on acne. Always consult a doctor if an adolescent suffers from severe acne. It is important to make every effort to bring severe acne under control before it leaves lasting effects.

Frequent boils may be a sign of diabetes. Diabetes not infrequently occurs during the teen years as well as earlier and later in life. Recurrent boils, or a carbuncle, are sufficient reason to consult a physician.

Freckles can be a source of concern for young people. There is no way you can remove them safely at home. But they can be prevented from getting worse through reduced exposure to the sun or use of protective ointments or lotions. Mothers can be helpful, when freckles are really unsightly, by providing a disguise in the form of face powder or "Covermark." Very disfiguring cases should be referred to a specialist in skin diseases who may try "peeling" treatment. Make it a point to cheer up a freckler by pointing out the fact that these spots usually fade with the passing years. And, again, don't permit freckles to be made a target for family jokes.

Awkwardness

Young people often seem unable to handle their rapidly growing bodies gracefully. Their clumsiness is not due to carelessness or willfulness, as some parents believe. Helping young people to understand their problem, instead of complaining about it, prevents them from becoming self-conscious, which only adds to the awkwardness.

SPECIAL PROBLEMS OF GIRLS

Breasts

Some adolescent girls are shy about, or even ashamed of, their breast development. They may even try to walk, shoulders hunched forward, to conceal their bosoms. Mothers should encourage them to be proud of their developing womanhood. They can help, too, by choosing clothes suitable to the girl's new figure, making allowance for the fact that the girl's preferences are important.

In addition to emphasizing that breast development is normal at puberty, mothers should explain that, shortly before or during menstruation, some tenderness and swelling are apt to occur and should cause no concern.

Body Hair

An adolescent girl may develop excess hair over the thighs and legs or under the arms. Facial hair sometimes becomes disfiguring. Parents should take this seriously, since it can be important to a sensitive young girl. Bleaching is usually enough to keep excess hair from being prominent. If neither this nor shaving seems satisfactory for unsightly facial hair, your daughter may want to have it permanently removed. This can be dangerous if attempted by anyone but an expert. Read our discussion of excess hair on page 166. If an expert is not available or is too expensive, use all your tact to convince your daughter to wait rather than risk infection and scarring.

Menstruation

Menstruation usually begins at 12 to 14 years of age but may start as early as 10 or as late as 18. Maturing early or late often runs in a family,

However, if a girl's menstrual periods begin at 10 or earlier, or if they have not started by 17, a doctor should be consulted. A doctor also should be consulted if the characteristic changes of puberty—development of breasts, pubic hair, and so on—occur unusually early or late. This may be due to a glandular disorder that can be corrected, and the child usually needs help with the emotional problems which are apt to arise under such circumstances.

In the average woman, menstruation occurs every 28 days, but the cycle varies considerably in different women. However, each woman has a fairly definite cycle, which should be reasonably well established by the end of the first year after onset of menstruation, or the menarche, as this is called.

Although menstruation is a normal physiological event, many people, consciously or unconsciously, regard it as an illness, and instill fears about it into young girls. In other instances, girls reach puberty without knowing there is such a thing, so their first menstrual period is a severe emotional shock. All girls, and boys as well, should be told about menstruation before they and their friends reach the age of puberty—preferably by their mothers.

Exactly when children should be told about menstruation is not simple to define. Parents, as we have already indicated, should not give children information they cannot understand or have no interest in. On the other hand, children should not get the impression that menstruation is, as they often put it, "a dirty secret" which has been kept from them. The opportunities for privacy, the possibility of a child's learning about menstruation in other ways, and similar factors must help determine the age at which each child should be told. The important thing is the mother's attitude.

Mothers should realize that menstruation is not a sickness, not something to be ashamed of, not to be called "the curse" or to be made to seem mysterious or shameful. They should explain to adolescent daughters that some women experience discomfort or "cramps" in the lower abdomen, usually at the onset of a period, and that menstruation may be a "nuisance" for the first day or so, especially if flow is profuse. However, it should cause no real difficulty. Girls should be able to go to school, walk, dance, play ordinary games and, if the weather is warm and the flow not profuse, go swimming. If a girl tires or chills easily, she should avoid swimming and the more strenuous sports during her menstrual period. She should not be goaded into overdoing things by a mother who is overly anxious to emphasize that menstruation is normal. Girls should be told that menstrual disorders do occur but are usually of a minor nature, and that a doctor can almost always cure them, or at least help them a great deal.

Should a pad or tampon be used? Either is safe from a health standpoint. The choice depends on the individual. If flow is profuse, pads may be required to absorb it. Most virgins can use small-size tampons, and certainly no mother should imply that a girl who uses a tampon is not "nice." Abnormalities of menstruation are described later (page 620).

Feminine Hygiene

Aside from ordinary washing and bathing, there is no necessity for "feminine hygiene." Baths or showers may be taken during menstruation, although very hot or very cold ones should be avoided. Women who prefer not to bathe during their periods should wash the outer genital area with warm water and soap at least once a day.

If strong odors occur, or if there is a discharge from the vagina between periods, be sure to see a doctor or consult a hospital clinic. These odors and discharges usually stem from an infection, which should be attended to. Douching is seldom necessary. If you believe you need vaginal douches, ask your doctor about it.

SPECIAL PROBLEMS FOR BOYS

Boys usually reach puberty about two years later than girls—that is, between 14 and 16 on the average, although some mature as early as 12 and others as late as 20. If a boy matures at an unusually early age, a doctor should be consulted. We think it especially important for a doctor to be consulted if a boy matures late. Boys are apt to be concerned about their virility if they mature late. There may be a glandular difficulty which requires treatment. But even if nothing is wrong, a doctor's reassurance can help prevent emotional problems.

Boys grow rapidly during this period, and their appetites often become enormous. Hair appears on the face and the pubic region, the genitals enlarge, and the boy is able to have erections and ejaculations. Nocturnal emissions ("wet dreams") start.

Nocturnal Emissions

This is nature's way of indicating a boy is maturing. It is also nature's way of relieving sexual tension.

The fluid, discharged at night, usually accompanied by a sexual dream, contains spermatozoa. This event should not be, as it too often is, a cause for shame, pride or concern. It is a natural part of adolescence about which boys should be informed in advance. Parents should not comment upon finding seminal stains on bedclothes or pajamas.

Masturbation

This is a problem for both sexes although it is usually regarded as a special one where boys are concerned. It is a problem in the sense that almost every individual has been faced with the desire to masturbate and must work out his or her own solution to the question. It is also a problem in the sense that sexual desire is not all physical but encompasses desire for intimacy with a member of the opposite sex, and this intimacy cannot exist during masturbation except in fantasy form. These are the only real problems of masturbation. Others, although not real, have caused countless heartaches and tragedies.

Masturbation is not harmful and fear is unnecessary. It never causes physical or mental sickness. Guilt is unnecessary because a very large percentage of boys and girls have practiced some form of masturbation during their growing years and often into adult life. Fear and guilt can cause emotional problems that can mar a child's future. Don't inflict them on your children in order to prevent the "evil" of masturbation. There is no such evil—and you couldn't prevent it if there were.

If a boy or girl becomes addicted to masturbation—practicing it, say, daily—the problem is an emotional one which should be discussed with a doctor or counselor. The masturbation is a sign, not a cause, of the emotional difficulty.

Homosexual Practices

Many girls and boys indulge in some form of homosexual play with a companion or companions. Usually this is harmless and stops as the boy or girl matures. But it is at this time that an older, confirmed homosexual may exert unfortunate influence. If such a situation has arisen, parents need a great deal of skill and tact; in many cases, they would be wise to discuss the problem with a trained counselor.

Such situations are less likely to arise if boys and girls know the facts about homosexuality. Most young people pick up some information on this subject; usually it is misinformation. This may cause them needless worry about whether they themselves are "queer," or it may make a homosexual seem sophisticated, wicked, and fascinating. Understanding what homosexuality actually is will serve as a protection for healthy adolescents.

Every young person should know that a preference for members of one's own sex is natural in late childhood or early adolescence and that it may overlap, but only for a short time, the development of interest in the other sex. A normal adolescent then grows up emotionally, finding the opposite sex attractive. A man or woman who has not progressed in this way can be regarded as emotionally immature, retarded, or ill, however intellectually brilliant he or she may be.

It is not necessary to give a child a lecture on this subject. It is much better to make the points as opportunities present themselves. We know that some parents have difficulty doing this. We urge that you honestly face the question of whether you are one who has such difficulty. Do you feel awkward or embarrassed about discussing masturbation, nocturnal emissions, or any other subject with your children? Does your own early training make you act as though you thought some things were wicked when you know they really are not? If so, if you have any doubts, you will do your children the most good by first facing your own situation. If you have doubts, discussion with your doctor, a marriage counselor, or someone in the field of child guidance will either increase your confidence or help you decide that it would be best to let the doctor or some other trained person discuss these matters with your children.

HEALTHY SEXUAL ATTITUDES FOR CHILDREN

As parents, we are not likely to exert great influence on what our children do about sex through direct suggestions or commands. Undoubtedly, their attitudes will be influenced by the example we set in our pattern of living and the maturity and love displayed in the home. What other roles do we have—potentially effective roles—in helping them to develop healthy sexual attitudes?

We can stand in the background, unobtrusively observing, so we can be ready to help when necessary. We can make the home an attractive and welcome place for our children's friends. Allowing them freedom and privacy in and around the home will help them work out normal sex urges. Restrictions and suspicions will only drive them into secretive relationships which may end in disaster.

Is a child becoming friendly with someone who may not be suitable —perhaps too old, too sophisticated, or in some other way not the right type? Don't step in and order that the friendship be terminated. Rather, invite the friend into the home. Then, when you raise questions with your child later, he or she will know you are not just talking without knowing the person.

There is no one simple answer to the question of petting and sex relations for the adolescent. It depends to a great extent on the religious and cultural background of the family and the personality and maturity of the individual. An attitude we commend to your thoughtful consideration is one expressed by Dr. John Levy, a psychiatrist, who wrote, in a book * co-authored with Ruth Munroe, Ph.D.:

* Levy, John, and Munroe, Ruth, *The Happy Family.* New York, Knopf, 1938.

"Advising children about their sex life is a highly personal and individualized problem. You cannot recommend the same behavior for all of them indiscriminately. I rather hope that my own daughter will pet or neck, or whatever the proper term may be, preferably with boys she knows well and likes, and only with her contemporaries. Love-making of this type is a healthy preparation for marriage. I hope that she will not have intercourse or end up merely a technical virgin. Quite aside from any moral implications, such a step is risky. . . . If she does have a complete relationship, though, I most earnestly hope that she will know what she is about, that she will not go into an affair because she happens to be tight, or thinks it's 'the thing' or wants to prove that she can carry it off. These are my hopes. They are based on my observation of the kind of behaviour least likely to cause trouble in our particular social group. But she may order her life quite differently and be none the worse for it. If she is neither afraid of sex nor bamboozled by its glamour I shall be very content."

Note these points made by Dr. Levy, which are applicable equally to boys and girls: Adolescent lovemaking should be with friends of approximately the same age. A certain amount of petting and necking is good as a preparation for the fuller, richer love of marriage. If the young person prefers some other way, accept the decision with the hope it will be a realistic one and will not cause unhappiness.

As parents, we cannot live our children's lives; we cannot order or predetermine their lives. Above all, however, we can be close enough to our children so they will always know they can turn to us for honest, sympathetic guidance—and also for help—if there should be trouble, even pregnancy or a venereal disease. If all young people could feel this way about their parents, how very many tragedies could be avoided!

HOW PARENTS CAN HELP IN OTHER WAYS

With adolescence comes an upsurge of growth and emotions and aggressions that cannot be stopped. Nor would any intelligent, sensitive parent want to stop it. It is a vital force. We can hope to guide it constructively; never should we dam it up.

Parents who show sympathetic understanding can expect not only an immediately happier home life than would otherwise be possible but the reward, too, of love and respect from their children in later years.

If we parents find our adolescent children's behavior seemingly outlandish, we can do well to recall our own behavior as adolescents. Did we resent the authority of our parents? If we are honest, we must admit we did. We can then understand why our children object to strict rules.

If we remember our daydreams and grandiose plans—and is there any one of us who did not have them?—we will hear out tolerantly, not derisively, our children's plans to remake the world or to become artists, writers, composers, or explorers when we think they should enter the family business.

We can think of the adolescent as half-child and half-adult, and if we do, we may more easily "weather" the storms and be able to be gentle and firm rather than threatening and authoritarian. We would do well to consider, too, as Dr. Benjamin Weininger, a psychiatrist, has suggested, that adolescents often have the correct attitude toward living. They are intense about life, and idealistic, and hopeful they can play a part in making life better for everyone. They may not be very practical in their attempts to achieve ideals but their outlook on life is worth respect.

As parents, our job is to help the adolescent child reach maturity, social as well as sexual maturity. We have talked about the sexual aspect. What can we do to help in the attainment of social maturity?

As much as possible, we should give him or her a sense of place and participation in the family. We can, and should, discuss—or at the very least, explain—family decisions.

We can acquaint him or her with details of the family budget, providing a true picture of what things cost in terms of parents' outlay of time and energy. We can let him see for himself that his share is reasonable, not the result of an arbitrary decision. We can help to build a sense of adult responsibility about financial matters by giving a child a regular allowance, once a week for younger children, and then, at 16 and over, once a month. It may be helpful, too, to provide older children with personal checking accounts; they realize then that they are being treated as responsible individuals.

We can do everything possible to enable our adolescent boy or girl to have friends. We should not be overly strict, insisting that every acquaintance be "desirable." For a child who has previously been well adjusted, there is less danger from "bad" companions during adolescence than from being kept apart from contemporaries.

We can give the adolescent opportunities to be away from home. Younger children can first go to camp or to visit relatives. Then we can let them visit friends. And we can allow older and more mature children to take jobs away from home during summer vacations. These breaks from home life provide valuable training in self-confidence. They also help reduce tensions adolescents generate in their rebellion against home rules. They soon learn that there are rules everywhere.

We can let the child think about and decide on his or her own career. We can show our appreciation of the importance of this by trying to get expert guidance for the child. We can discuss his or her aptitudes with high school teachers, and we can invite into our homes friends and acquaintances who will describe their own careers in the arts, professions, and business.

We can let a daughter, if she wants to enter a profession rather than marry at the same age as her mother did, work it out her own way. We can avoid adding to social pressures that often make a girl marry before she is ready. A girl who feels shy or inadequate won't have her problems solved by marriage; marriage doesn't solve emotional problems and may only add to them. Similarly, we can let a son who may want to forgo a lucrative family business for the lesser financial return of teaching follow his interests. If he comes back to the business later, it will be from realistic desire and not with resentment at having been forced into something.

And we can help our children to learn to know us not just as parents but as human beings—as individuals who make mistakes but want to do our best for our children because we love them. And we can remember that it is far better to show our love than it is to talk about it.

40

HOME ACCIDENTS AND
THEIR PREVENTION

THE MODERN home is becoming one of the most dangerous spots on earth because of technological advances which have paid little attention to personal safety. So a recent study on home accidents, made for the World Health Organization, concluded.

The home is being turned, according to the study, into a "complicated workshop filled with technically advanced machinery . . . so complex as to be well beyond the understanding of the persons who have to use it." Electrical erasers, circular power saws and attachments, and can openers are just a few examples of advances in electrical power use which introduce increased hazards. "Machines for the pulping and shredding of vegetables and mechanical vegetable peelers are presenting increasing hazards to the family in the kitchen, and guarding them is frequently inadequate. The cheaper and less well-designed spin dryers and power wringers are also dangerous. It is relatively easy and cheap to construct guards on all these machines and it will become increasingly necessary to impose industrial safety standards on the manufacture of these implements—in effect, make them foolproof."

All of this may be true—and certainly there is room for making all types of equipment safer, including many potentially hazardous devices used in the home. But the fact is that the home long has been a dangerous place.

Accidents rank fourth as a cause of death in this country. More children, aged 1 to 14, die of accidents than of the next half-dozen causes of death combined. Yearly, for persons of all ages, accidents in the home cause more deaths than tuberculosis, diphtheria, polio, syphilis, rheumatic fever, appendicitis, and homicide combined.

501

If the scores of thousands of deaths and millions of injuries annually from highway accidents constitute a national catastrophe and a scandal, so we think does the toll from accidents in the home. Medical science has made great strides in conquering many diseases, but there has been virtually no reduction in the death rate from accidents.

But this has to be added: No physician or safety expert or anybody else can do as much to prevent accidents in the home as the parent aware of the threat they pose, of what the specific hazards are, and of what measures, often quite simple, can be used to reduce or remove the hazards.

FALLS

In recent years, the death toll from accidental injuries in the home has been running at an annual rate of 28,500, and falls in and about the home take about 10,000 lives; they also injure nearly 7 million each year. Currently, 3 million people in this country have an impairment of back, limb, or other part of the body that resulted from an accidental fall.

One startling recent finding, not previously well-recognized, is the frequency with which babies, before they walk, fall from high places. Studying 536 infants in two groups—urban clinic patients and suburban private practice patients—a team of investigators at the Northwestern University School of Medicine, Chicago, found a combined incidence of 47.5 percent first falls from cribs, adult beds, and dressing tables. Among the urban group, 77 percent of the infants fell at least once during their first year, mostly from adult beds. Among the suburban group, 30 percent fell during the first year, often from dressing tables. Almost all falls resulted in head injuries. If this average incidence of falls holds true nationally, then 1,750,000 infants annually sustain at least one fall before they are a year old.

The Northwestern researchers urge a national campaign to alert mothers to the dangers of infant falls, noting that most of the falls occur at about the average age of seven and a half months when infants begin to roll from prone to supine position and begin to sit up, pull themselves up to standing position, and climb. If parents are prepared for these activities, they can be on guard against leaving babies unattended even briefly on beds and tables.

Much can be done to eliminate other factors involved in the falls of children and adults. A house with poor lighting will have more accidents than one with proper illumination for entrances, staircases, and rooms. There is always a direct relationship between the state of repair of stairs and railings in a house and the number of sprains or broken bones sustained by people living there. All such danger spots should be corrected immediately. Lights in hallways and over staircases should be large enough to illuminate the entire area; economizing here is poor economy. Railings should be in sufficiently good condition to keep children from falling through and should provide adequate handholds for adults, especially the elderly, for whom fractured bones are serious matters. Loose steps or slippery and worn steps should be repaired or replaced. In cold weather, icy or slippery steps should be scraped and, if necessary, protected by sprinkling with ashes or sand.

Tripping hazards, such as unanchored small throwrugs, should be eliminated. Highly polished floors can be a serious hazard. When floors are waxed, the wax should be rubbed in thoroughly; this tends to harden wax globules and convert them into tiny beadlike particles which provide better traction. Since repeated waxing can fill in spaces between the particles, making the surface slippery, it's a good idea to remove all wax after every fourth or fifth waxing and start with a fresh layer.

Use a rubber mat in the bathroom to prevent slips.

When children are learning to walk, cover or remove sharp-edged furniture. Keep low stools, and other objects that can trip children or adults, away from passageways.

It's a good idea to cover stairs with carpeting or rubber safety treads, and by all means keep them clear of mops, baskets, toys, and other odd items.

Make electric light switches available for each room so that people walking from one room to another will be able to light their way. It is often desirable, especially when there are children or elderly people in the home, to keep a night light on, especially near the bathroom.

Provide abrasive strips for the tub or shower to assure firm footing. Use stair gates to block toddlers from access to stairs. And an untippable stepping stool that will not move while you're using it can give you easy —and safe—access to top-shelf items.

FIRE

Three of every four Americans who are killed in fires lose their lives either in their own home or in that of a friend. For every one who dies, many are seriously injured. There is a residential fire in the United States every 57 seconds. To protect your family and property, fire prevention is essential. It requires good housekeeping and constant attention in certain major areas:

MATCHES AND SMOKING. Keep matches and lighters out of the reach of children. Place good-sized, deep ashtrays in every room. Use only the type of ashtray that will keep cigarettes from falling out. Check or wet down ashtrays before emptying them into wastebaskets. When smoking in a chair, put out your cigarette or cigar at the first feeling of drowsiness. Make it a rule never to smoke in bed, while lying on a sofa, or reclining in a chair that invites sleep. And before going to bed, make certain no pipe, cigar, or cigarette has been left burning anywhere.

Remember that smoking and careless placement of matches constitute the greatest fire hazard in the home.

ELECTRICITY. Electric wiring and appliances are the No. 2 cause of home fires. Overloaded circuits, "octopus" outlets, wrong amp fuses, forgotten irons, frayed wiring—all are dangerous.

Use the right size fuse, usually 15 amperes, for your circuits. Don't use a penny for "convenience" when a fuse blows and don't substitute a larger amp fuse. A fuse is a safety valve for an electric circuit; if the fuse has greater capacity than the circuit and so will not burn out when the circuit is overloaded (and, of course, a penny will not burn out), then fire may occur somewhere in the circuit, perhaps in a wall.

Don't overload your wall outlets. If you need more places to plug in lamps or appliances, call in an electrician.

See that your TV antenna is rigged so it cannot fall across a power line, and have it equipped with a lightning arrestor. Also, keep an air space behind and around your TV set. Unless you really know your business, don't try to make any internal repairs to a TV set, even if it is disconnected. A set builds up a heavy charge of static electricity that can give you a dangerous jolt even when the plug is out.

Buy irons and electrical cooking appliances that have heat-limit controls. And be fussy about making certain that irons are turned off after use and before leaving the house.

Never procrastinate about repairing a frayed electric cord. Check appliances, or have them checked regularly to make certain they are in good operating condition.

THE STOVE. Do not light a gas stove or gas oven if there is a distinct odor of gas. Open a window. If the odor persists, call a repairman.

Never keep a coal or gas stove or a gas grate burning unless there are vents or flues to take away the gases. Keep a window partly open. And if you leave the kitchen, turn off the gas, even if this strikes you as inconvenient.

Remember, pots that boil over may put out flames, creating a risk of gas explosion.

Almost every cook sooner or later is confronted with a grease fire, perhaps while broiling meat too close to the flames. Keep equipment, such as sand and fire extinguisher, at hand to put out such fires. If you have no fire extinguisher, use plain baking soda or salt. Water is ineffective and sometimes dangerous for oil or grease fires.

And teach children to keep away from the stove. Many burns and scalds would be avoided if children, as a rule, were kept out of the kitchen when hot foods were being prepared.

CLEANING FLUIDS. If you must keep flammable liquids around the house, store them in tightly closed metal containers (never glass), in a cool, well-ventilated place away from anything else that might catch fire.

Use cleaning fluids only in a well-ventilated place, making certain there is no open flame, lighted tobacco, or electric spark nearby.

Keep such liquids where children can't get to them.

Never use kerosene or any other cleaning fluid to start a fire in the furnace, wood stove, or fireplace.

CHRISTMAS TREES. These are special fire hazards. As a tree dries out, it becomes a potential torch which can be set off by a cigarette, candle flame, or a short circuit in a string of lights.

You might consider buying a fire-retardant synthetic tree. Or buy your tree as late before Christmas as possible, get rid of it as soon afterward as you can, and in the meantime keep its base in a pan of water. Use only flameproofed materials for decoration. Avoid candles; use only lights approved by one of the major fire-testing laboratories.

HEATING. Between them, heating and cooking accidents are responsible for about 40 percent of home fire deaths.

Defective heating equipment can cause death from both fire and carbon monoxide gas poisoning. All flues and chimneys should be inspected on a regular basis, and any cracked or corroded sections should be repaired or replaced.

All furnace and heating appliances should be inspected by qualified personnel to make certain they are in proper adjustment and good condition. Proper adjustment assures complete burning of fuel and avoids dangerous amounts of carbon monoxide in the flue gases. A good time to have your heating system inspected and serviced is every fall before cold weather arrives.

And if you use your fireplace, make certain there is a spark screen in front of it and that the rug is far enough away for safety.

IF FIRE STRIKES. Heat and smoke, not fire itself, kill most victims. Air moving through a building can be hot enough in five minutes to ignite floors, doors, walls far from where the flames are. So get everybody out immediately; then call the fire department; and never, no matter how

506 / *Family Preventive Care*

great the temptation or how small the risk may seem to be, go back inside for valuable papers or anything else; you may not get out alive.

Make it a habit to sleep with bedroom doors closed; this helps retard fire. And in case of a blaze, do not open the door unless absolutely necessary.

Be ready with emergency items such as rope cr other means of escape from bedrooms. If yours is a two-story house and a typical one, it has only one stairway, which may be blocked by flames.

HOME FIRE DRILLS.   If your child were to awake tonight to see smoke and flames creeping into his bedroom, what would he do? Unless properly trained, most likely he would hide, as do most children, under the bed or in a closet or rush out into a smoke-filled hallway. Instead, he should have gone out of a window if that were at all possible.

Any parent would be distressed if a child's school did not have regular fire drills, yet few parents have ever had a fire drill at home where a fire is 200 times more likely to occur. Fire authorities urge that every family set up a regular home fire drill program.

Begin by making everyone understand the danger of home fires and the importance of drills. Explain that the major danger is not the flames but the deadly gases and smoke; that fire can build up toxic gases in minutes which then rise quickly to upper floors. Underscore the absolute need to get to fresh air and out quickly, with every second counting.

Emphasize that no one should stop to dress or look for belongings but should be concerned only with saving himself.

Plan a fire signal—perhaps a whistle or shout. Assign family members to assist small children or invalid or elderly members.

Draw a chart of every room, and plan escape routes from each room. Each bedroom should have two planned escape routes—normally a hall or stairway and, if this is blocked, an alternate which probably would be a window leading to a roof or porch or a folding ladder that can be dropped from a window.

Fire drills should be conducted from bedrooms.

ELECTRICAL BURNS AND SHOCKS

These are becoming more frequent with use of power tools and appliances in profusion. As already noted, promptly replace worn cords, cover exposed wires, and replace faulty equipment.

Protect children by shielding electrical outlets.

Ground all electrical equipment with ground fault devices.

Under no circumstances use electrical products outdoors when grass or earth is damp unless the equipment has been specifically designed and approved for such use.

SPECIAL HAZARDS—ROOM BY ROOM

Fires, falls, and electrical burns and shocks are the chief dangers but there are many others to watch for. Each room has its special hazards. For example:

KITCHEN. Keep sharp knives, lye, ammonia, acids, insect and rodent poisons, and every other caustic or poisonous substance out of children's reach. All, especially lye, have killed or seriously injured a great many children.

Keep the children out of the kitchen except when they are being watched.

During food preparation, you need light to prevent accidental cuts. Asbestos pads, tongs, and large holders for hot pots and pans can prevent burns and scalds.

Be careful with hot fat or grease. If fire occurs, do not pour on water because water will spatter the fire. Use sand, dirt or ashes, if available, to put the fire out. Small fires can be extinguished by pouring salt or baking soda on them, or they may be smothered with heavy wet clothes or asbestos pads. If the amount of fat on fire is large and the flames high, pull all inflammable material away and guard against spread of the fire by pouring water over the areas the flames threaten to reach.

Have your gas range and electric refrigerator checked once a year. This service is sometimes provided free by a utility company.

BATHROOM. A rubber mat can prevent slips in the tub. Have good lighting. Soap needs a sturdy holder.

Never place electric equipment of any type, especially electric heaters, in the bathroom where they may fall into the tub. The safest rule is to warm the bathroom with the electric heater first, then disconnect the heater while the baby or anyone else is in the tub. Do not touch an electric socket, switch, or appliance while standing in the water; you can be electrocuted, since water helps current flow through the body.

Keep all medical supplies where children cannot reach them.

CELLAR. As already noted, have your heating system checked by a competent serviceman before cold weather arrives.

The cellar is often a play area, especially in winter. Try to separate heating equipment from children's play space. You can put up a wall inexpensively with a few 2" x 4" wood studs and some pressed board partitions. Until your children are old enough to be trusted alone for an hour or more, never let them go to the cellar alone.

Avoid clutter. Clearly defined areas should be set aside for tools, equipment, screens, and other paraphernalia.

The cellar, including the stairs, should be as well lighted as any other room. There should be at least one sturdy railing for the cellar stairs.

LIVING ROOM.   As already suggested, have a screen covering the entire fireplace. Fasten window curtains, etc., so they cannot blow near the fireplace.

You can use various means, including rubber mason-jar rings sewn on the undersides, to anchor rugs. Make certain there are no long electric light cords to trip over, no open sockets where young children can get to them.

BEDROOM.   Observe the precautions about fire and electrical hazards already listed. Don't smoke in bed or sleep with a heating pad turned on. If there are young children, have bars or safety catches on windows. Make certain the paint on anything they might chew on is not poisonous. Keep any objects a baby might swallow or hurt himself with out of reach. The sides of cribs should have extensions, because standard cribs are not high enough.

THE MENACE OF CHILDHOOD POISONING

"Beware—poison is some other name" is an apt slogan recently adopted by the National Planning Council. Each year now, more than one million cases of poisoning (85 percent of them among young children) occur in the United States, leading to thousands of deaths and a great deal of sickness and suffering.

Actually, the death figure given—which is sometimes put at 3,000 annually—is much too low, many authorities believe. Many more children die each year because of accidental ingestion of or exposure to toxic chemicals in household agents and drugs, but the correct diagnosis is not made because incriminating evidence is not detected or recognized. Not infrequently, for example, symptoms from irritation of the central nervous system and obvious convulsions lead to the diagnosis of viral encephalitis.

"Poisoning," says Dr. Jay M. Arena, President of the American Association of Poison Control Centers, "is now the most common medical emergency among young children that exists in pediatrics."

No mother, of course, deliberately goes shopping for poisons, but she buys several every time she goes to market. She uses them whenever she cleans house, polishes the furniture, washes dishes, paints, cleans spots off clothes. Often she is not aware of the dangers of these products due to failure to pay attention to the labels. Naturally curious children are tempted to investigate the more than 250,000 products and myriad medicines available and often present in the home.

In a careful investigation into the precise circumstances surrounding child poisoning tragedies and near-tragedies, the Children's Hospital Medical Center, Boston, made some discoveries which all parents should keep in mind:

Most poisonings involve children big enough to walk but not over three years of age.

The most dangerous time of day is during the hour just before the evening meal.

The unpleasant taste of a potential poison has little deterrent value. Toddlers will swallow virtually anything.

Parents tempt disaster when they underestimate a young child's ingenuity or overestimate his ability to obey orders. Every day, dozens of children poison themselves by getting medicine out of safety-cap bottles —bottles they are told never to touch but which are left within reach.

Reports from the nation's 535 poison control centers indicate that, after aspirin, the products most commonly involved in childhood poisonings are insecticides, bleaches, detergents and cleaning agents, furniture polish, kerosene, vitamin and iron pills and syrups, disinfectants, strong acids and alkalis, and laxatives.

As Dr. Arena notes, 75 percent of all poisonings in small children are with in-sight drugs or household agents, which means that three out of four poisonings are due to carelessness or negligence and could be prevented by one very simple action—putting all medicines and chemical agents out of sight and reach of children. The formula is simple enough —Poison, child: store one, save the other.

There is certainly need for other measures. A federal law requires that hazardous household products bear information to protect users and warn against accidental ingestion by children, and vigorous enforcement and education of the public to its significance can help. Industry can and should develop and use increasingly effective safety closures and containers for medicines and poisonous agents, for while some children may circumvent such measures, there will be many who are unable to get a safety cap off. Any medicines administered to a child should be administered on a serious basis, not as a game, and parents should not themselves take medication in the presence of small children.

IF A POISONING OCCURS

More and more now, physicians and official medical bodies such as the American Academy of Pediatrics advise that every home should always have on hand two items for emergencies. One is a 1-ounce bottle of syrup of ipecac and the other an inexpensive can of activated charcoal. The ipecac efficiently induces vomiting. The charcoal, which is mixed with water to make a souplike substance, absorbs any poison in the stomach after vomiting occurs.

With these available, you can immediately call a physician, hospital, or poison control center if poisoning occurs. Even if you are not certain exactly what the child has swallowed, they can give you instructions over the phone which may involve use of one or both of these items. Used immediately and properly, they may avoid fatality, serious illness, and even need for hospitalization, stomach pumping, and other drastic measures.

It seems to be human nature not to like to think of accidents when all is going well. But since we can't immunize against accidents, we have to give some thought to their prevention. Perhaps the easiest way to play safe is to organize a home safety council and make its meetings pleasant occasions and a kind of game for the children. Perhaps once a month, the family can sit down and discuss safety rules, any new hazards that may have developed, any accidents that may have occurred.

We suggest that husbands can play a major role in accident prevention in the home. Men know the technical side of dangerous equipment. They should take major responsibility for checking electrical apparatus, furnace, gas connections, and similar equipment. Their wives could then educate the children in accident prevention.

If youngsters are given prizes for observing safety rules, and special prizes for new suggestions, plus a treat, say, of ice cream, when the home "safety council" meets, they will look forward to the meetings. In this way, their interest in obeying good safety rules and in making new ones will be strengthened at an early age.

PART SIX

Disease Scenarios

In this part of our book we tell you about a number of diseases—some potential killers, others disablers, some just nuisances. You may be puzzled by our approach and by use of some words new to you in discussions about your health. For example, you will find mentioned scenario, *also* primary, secondary, *and even* tertiary prevention *of disease.*

We use the word scenario *because it conveys the idea of the dynamic picture the physician can foresee for the course of a disease after he completes his questioning to understand the patient's symptoms, his physical examination, and his study of x-ray and laboratory reports. Sometimes, there can be no valid scenario until the physician sees the patient in several return visits. For example, two patients may have high blood pressure. Mr. One has a pressure reading of 164 over 98; so does Mr. Two. But in subsequent measurements of blood pressure, Mr. One's has settled down to 150 over 86 whereas Mr. Two's has gone to 190 over 110. Mr. One has no signs and symptoms, whereas Mr. Two shows a small hemorrhage in his retina and slight enlargement of the heart. The physician will see very different scenarios or possible future courses for these two patients, and his preventive treatments will be much more active for Mr. Two than for Mr. One.*

By primary *prevention, we mean measures that can be used to prevent a disease completely. A good example would be the use of the Sabin vaccine to keep polio from developing. By* secondary *prevention, we mean the use of measures to keep a disease that is already present from progressing. For example, for a patient with a definite ulcer of the duodenum, the physician can foresee and wants to avoid a scenario in which hemorrhage, perforation, or scarring and obstruction may take place; so he institutes diet and medical therapy as part of a secondary prevention program.*

We may be the first to employ the word tertiary *for preventive medicine. Our concept is that when every type of secondary prevention may fail, there is still a chance of providing new health for the patient in a special way—that is, by giving him a new organ to replace the destroyed organ. For that, however, the patient's general health must not become so undermined that the new organ would be of little use. For example, suppose every effort has failed to stop the ravages of nephritis (Bright's disease); the kidneys have failed; the patient is in uremic poisoning. If the physician institutes* tertiary *preventive measures at this time to avoid damage to the heart and brain and eyes, then at a suitable time he can save the patient with a kidney transplant. In the future, this type of tertiary prevention may become very common as transplants or mechan-*

ical replacements for heart, lungs, liver, pancreas, and other important organs become routinely feasible.

For your convenience, the diseases are arranged in alphabetic sequence and thus the order in which they are presented has nothing to do with their frequency or seriousness.

ADDISON'S DISEASE

The adrenal glands, small bodies sitting astride the kidneys, are essential to life because of the important hormones—adrenaline, hydrocortisone, aldosterone, and many others—they secrete. Any disease process that attacks the adrenal glands may produce a serious problem—adrenal insufficiency or Addison's disease.

Years ago most cases of Addison's disease stemmed from invasion of the adrenals by tuberculosis. Now the majority are due to shrinkage and withering away of the gland (atrophy) without known cause. Tuberculosis still causes some cases. In a very few instances, metastatic cancer, syphilis, or fungal infection is the cause.

A patient with Addison's disease is weak, tires easily, has nausea and vomiting with generally poor appetite, and usually experiences bouts of diarrhea. The patient is irritable and has fainting spells. The skin turns dark and the dark color is especially prominent in body creases, over the buttocks, in the nipples, and in any recent scars. Black freckles may appear on the tongue. The doctor finds low blood pressure, small heart, scant hair in armpits and pubic area. Laboratory tests show low blood concentration, reduced concentration of sodium in the blood, and reduced levels of adrenal corticoid hormones.

Before modern replacement therapy for missing hormones became available, Addison patients had a grim outlook, usually dying within a few years or even months. Now the outlook for them is decidedly favorable. With expert medical treatment and their own wholehearted cooperation, many can lead essentially normal lives.

Cortisone or cortisol is the keystone of therapy. The hormone is administered by mouth. To help raise the abnormally low level of sodium in blood, large amounts of salt may be used or a corticosteroid hormone, DOCA, may be given since it helps regulate salt exchange. Addison patients do well on a diet high in protein and carbohydrate, especially if they take many small meals a day rather than the usual three larger ones.

Addison patients must still guard against infections and any unusually severe stresses such as prolonged swimming in cold water. They need careful attention during pregnancy and surgery. An Addison patient needs to discuss stress hazards thoroughly with his physician just as a diabetic, through discussion with his physician, learns what he needs to know about his disease. For example, an Addison patient who understands his tendency to lose too much salt from the blood will be careful after profuse sweating to replace losses.

Since most cases now involve atrophy of the adrenal cortex from unknown cause, primary prevention is not yet possible. For the tubercular type of Addison's disease, primary prevention, of course, is the same as for tuberculosis (page 659). Secondary prevention, too, in a case resulting from tuberculosis requires intensive treatment of the tuberculosis.

AGING

You may be surprised to find aging included in our list of diseases. Doctors really do not know whether or not aging is a disease or a natural phenomenon. The scientific study of aging (gerontology) and of diseases of the aged (geriatrics) is still in its infancy. It may be many years before scientists learn enough about aging mechanisms to answer the question of whether aging is normal or abnormal.

In the meantime, most of us assume that aging is part of the divine or natural scheme of life. In our country, when a person is not afflicted with a grave disease, he still rarely lives beyond age 100, and usually 110 seems to be the limit, although there are reports from India and Siberia of some people living as long as 150 years.

So-called normal aging brings changes in many parts of the body. The skin becomes less firm and elastic and develops wrinkles; vital organs such as heart, kidneys, and brain lose some of their cells so they have less reserve capacity; bones tend to thin out and lose strength and resilience; the endocrine (including the sex) glands tend to become less active. In women, the ovaries stop functioning, the uterus decreases in size, and the vagina tends to lose its softness and elasticity. In the male, the prostate gland enlarges. Fortunately, the muscles hold up rather well throughout life if exercised adequately.

Despite the many changes, there still is adequate function left to sustain a good life in almost all aged people. However, the man of 85 should recognize that his heart cannot respond as quickly to sudden demands and the brain is not quite as finely tuned an instrument as it was in younger years. Older people learn to adapt by cutting down physical demands, reading more carefully, paying closer attention to names when being introduced.

Few people live to 100 or 110. Atherosclerosis (especially its effect on the heart) and cancer are the deadly enemies of the aged. High blood pressure, diabetes, kidney diseases, tuberculosis, emphysema, pneumonia, accidents, and liver disease also claim too many victims. Many of these diseases are preventable or curable, and it is a pity that so many older persons succumb unnecessarily. This book has been written in the hope that the information it provides, especially the stress on prevention of disease and disability, will bring many more people into the older years free of illness and able to enjoy living. We suggest that everyone read the sections on the illnesses just mentioned.

There seems little point to living to advanced age if one is chronically disabled or handicapped. Every effort should be made to keep the eyes in good condition, hearing at its best, and to avoid the unpleasantness of hernia, backache, and other nonfatal but annoying and sometimes disabling conditions.

The skin should be kept in good shape and the hair as lustrous as possible (see our chapter on skin and hair). Some older men feel happier with a hairpiece, some when they dye their hair; many women tint hair, some use wigs to make their hair seem more abundant. If these supplements to nature add to happiness, why not use them?

There are some medical conditions that make a person age prematurely. Among these are hypothyroidism (low function of the thyroid gland), pernicious anemia, and a vitamin deficiency called pellagra. At your regular medical checkups, your doctor can watch for onset of any of these and correct them if they occur.

DIET. The aging person should eat the well-balanced diet we have advocated in Chapter 6. Many older people feel better when they take a multivitamin tablet or capsule daily. If this produces indigestion, ask your doctor to prescribe a diet that will provide the extra vitamins. Old people do better, whenever possible, taking small meals at frequent intervals rather than depending upon one or two large meals a day.

WEIGHT. The older person does best to be on the thin side. This can be achieved by regulating intake of calories and by using regular exercise. (See page 65 on weight reduction.)

EXERCISE. One of the truly important aids to vigorous healthy old age is regular daily exercise. Brisk walking is one of the best exercises. Swimming is another. But the choices are limitless. Simply check your kind of exercise, what you enjoy most, with your doctor to determine that it falls within the capacity of your heart and lungs. And reread Chapter 8 on exercise.

HEALTHY EMOTIONAL LIFE. Good physical condition is necessary for a good emotional life in old age because it is a rare person who can be happy when constantly bothered by chronic illness or pain. On the other hand, good physical condition does not guarantee emotional health. It is such a pity to find elderly people whose bodies are in good shape but who are mentally depressed, lonely, or dispirited from empty hours. Retirement from work is always a serious change and should be discussed with your doctor. If you are a "doer" and not a "sitter," it may be necessary for you to find a new job, full or part time; or if you prefer not to work or cannot find employment you like, then as a doer you need vigorous activities and work hobbies.

COMPANIONSHIP. This is very important, and as friends and relatives move away or die, new human contacts should be sought in church groups, clubs, and social groups for older citizens. For those who do not work, the day can still be full if there are friends and relatives to visit, books to read, movies and television to see, radio to listen to—and time for exercise. Each season has its appropriate sports, and there is much enjoyment to be found in viewing them on television or in person.

SEX. Part of healthy emotional life of old age is sex. Good medical thinking today recommends that people continue sexual activity until they die. The enjoyments and also the health benefits of an active sex life are set forth in detail and persuasively by Dr. David Reuben in his book, *Everything You Always Wanted to Know about Sex* (David McKay, Publisher, 750 Third Ave., New York, N.Y. 10017).

SURGERY IN THE AGED. With the great advances in surgery and anesthesia, even the very elderly today can be operated on safely. There is no need for an older person to be disabled by a hernia for fear of the surgery involved. And the same applies to cataracts and many other conditions that require surgery for correction.

YOUR PHYSICIAN. The older person needs a good, understanding physician to help him with the more numerous illnesses and minor annoyances to be expected with aging. Also, as friends and relatives die, the doctor becomes a needed friend.

What of so-called *rejuvenation operations* and other methods purporting to stop or even reverse aging? As far as medical science can determine, there is no validity to the claims for any of these methods: e.g., transplantation of animal glands, injections of novocaine.

We are very much in the early infancy of biological and medical research into aging. It is entirely possible that some "Peter Pan" substance may yet be found to keep us young longer. We have to learn why the white rat rarely lives more than three years, a dog no more than twenty, and man seldom more than one hundred. Possibly out of such research, with animals as well as man, will come new knowledge to provide clues to longer, youthful life. Until then, we can only learn how to prevent the diseases and ravages of the years so we may enjoy to the full a near century of life.

Note: Problems of the later years— e.g., retirement, change of location, hospitalization for surgery, choice of physician—are discussed in additional detail in a book by one of us: *The Complete Medical Guide,* by Benjamin F. Miller, M.D., published by Simon & Schuster, 630 Fifth Ave., New York, N.Y. 10020.

ALLERGY

With all the talk about it, one might assume that nearly all Americans are allergic. This is not true, but allergic ailments are common enough if one considers all the people who have hay fever, asthma, hives, and sensitivity reactions to medicines, pets, foods, cosmetics, and industrial substances.

The term *allergy* means altered reaction. A person with allergy has become sensitive to a specific substance which is perfectly harmless to the nonallergic population. The word *specific* is a key one because an allergic individual may have a violent attack of asthma, for example, when exposed to cat dander but may be perfectly comfortable with dogs, hamsters, canaries, or other pets.

The offending substance is called an allergen and is protein in nature or has the capacity to combine with protein in the body. Thus a person may be sensitive to such proteins as those in milk, egg white, or lobster but be able to take fats, such as butter, and starches and cane sugar in any amount without symptoms. When a person becomes allergic to a nonprotein substance such as iodine or penicillin, it is believed that the offending substance is itself a partial allergen and becomes a complete one when taken into the body where it combines with a protein.

It is also believed that in the allergic person's body, a specific allergen is regarded as an enemy; the body produces an antibody to combat it; allergen and antibody interact and in the course of doing so, a chemical, histamine, is released and accounts for swelling and other local tissue changes. Thus, the medicines called antihistamines work in some allergies by neutralizing the histamine.

Aside from asthma, which we have treated separately (page 537), allergies rarely cause death or serious disability. They are nuisances, and most allergy sufferers would qualify that by calling them "damned nuisances." The allergic reaction rarely damages tissues; for example, we know one patient who has had 50 years of hay fever yet, between "seasons," has perfectly healthy-looking nasal and eye tissues.

Allergens hit their body "target organs" in different ways. Airborne or inhalational allergens strike the nose and bronchi and lungs; food allergens are absorbed through the intestine and distributed to various parts of the body, frequently showing their effects on the skin; contact allergens affect skin, lips, eyes; allergenic medicines also may affect the skin. Some persons have physical allergies, developing typical allergic responses to sunlight, heat, cold, or humidity.

The symptoms of allergy depend upon the target or shock organ affected. If it is the nose, there may be congestion, watery discharge, and sneezing, as in hay fever; if the skin is the target, there may be rash, hives, or eczema; if the bronchial tubes are the target, there is the wheezing of bronchial asthma.

Allergies affect both sexes and may appear at any age. There is a strong hereditary factor. One patient with severe hay fever has a son of 21 who had asthma from age 6 to 14 and has had almost no attacks since, as the result of avoiding cats; and a daughter who had hay fever for several years as a child and then "outgrew" it; the remaining child has not been allergic.

It is important for any person with allergy, or with even a family history of allergy, to mention the fact to any doctor or nurse who is treating him. An allergic or potentially allergic person usually will not be given penicillin or certain other medicines known to commonly produce allergic reactions unless the medication is absolutely necessary.

Hay Fever

Chief among airborne allergic diseases is hay fever. Curiously, it has nothing to do with hay but is caused by pollens of trees, plants, and weeds. The typical case is seasonal except in a few parts of the South where there may be pollen in the air all year. In the northern United States there is spring hay fever caused by pollens of trees and grasses, and the summer-autumn variety caused usually by ragweed pollen.

The symptoms, which develop when pollen contacts nose and eyes, include congestion of the nose, watery discharge, tickling and irritation, and sneezing. The eyes are irritated and reddened, and tears flow. Some hay-feverites have a daily cycle, awakening with symptoms in the early morning, experiencing relief from late morning until late afternoon, then becoming discomfited again. Some patients notice that symptoms are affected by environmental factors such as humidity, heat or cold, strong sunlight, or wind. One patient, very sensitive to high humidity, noted severe aggravation of symptoms whenever he took a hot bath. He improved greatly by changing to sponge baths. Air conditioning helped his attacks, too, by reducing humidity as well as by filtering out pollen and dust.

Usually, the symptoms and their seasonal nature are all that are needed for diagnosis. In addition, the doctor tests for sensitivity to a large variety of allergens, by injection or scratching them into the skin. These tests help determine the substance or substances to which the patient should be desensitized.

The outlook for hay fever is varied. At best, there may be only minor symptoms easily controlled by filtering air in the bedroom and perhaps by occasional use of one of the medicines employed for hay fever. At worst, there may be severe symptoms which prevent enjoyable living and working for weeks; danger of sinus blockage with headaches, middle ear pressure, or infection (especially in children); development of nasal polyps; and appearance of asthma. Most cases fall between, with several weeks of annoying symptoms during which the victim is uncomfortable and unable to work or live at his usual productive level. With most patients, the end of the season brings an end to all symptoms, and the malady may be forgotten until the next season comes around. Doctors often warn hay-feverites to avoid, at all times, house dust, fumes, heavy tobacco smoke, etc., because these may set off a hay-feverlike attack between seasons or aggravate attacks during the season.

Effective treatment will frequently prevent the formation of the little benign cystic tumors in the nose called polyps. Also, such therapy will help prevent development of asthma.

One form of preventive treatment is to avoid the allergen. People who can afford it, or whose work is not dependent on a special locale, may go to an area in the United States or abroad where the particular sensitizing pollen does not occur. While this is not possible for most people, many can take their two- to four-week vacation at places away from the pollen or where the humidity and other atmospheric factors are pleasant and helpful.

Another form of prevention is to remove the pollens. There are effective filters for ventilating and air conditioning units; also, there is a special device which precipitates out pollen. Your doctor or a specialist in allergy (allergist) will tell you where you can purchase these and what rooms to use them in. For homeowners who can afford it, a central unit that filters out pollens and controls humidity makes life comfortable; sometimes the cost of such a unit is not greater than the loss of time from work or the expense of distant vacations. Those who do not have such methods of removing pollens sometimes prevent serious attacks by going to an air conditioned movie, theater, or restaurant when they feel symptoms coming on.

Desensitization treatment is often effective. For this, the doctor administers small, gradually increasing amounts of the offending allergen by injection before the season starts in order to build up tolerance. Even after the season has started, desensitization treatment may sometimes help symptoms, at least to some extent.

Various medications are available to help provide relief. Decongestants, such as ephedrine or Propadrine, can be taken internally or in nose drop form. Many antihistamines are available. Some cause drowsiness or other unpleasant reactions, and it may be necessary for your doctor to try several before finding one that is most suitable for you. If your antihistamine causes drowsiness, use it only before bedtime—certainly not when driving or working with anything dangerous. A good combination is a decongestant during the day, an antihistamine in the evening and at bedtime. There are also helpful eye drops. To be effective, both nose and eye drops must reach the entire irritated area; ask your doctor or the pharmacist exactly how to apply them. Steroids, or cortisone-like medications, can be helpful when applied locally or taken by mouth. Doctors hesitate to give steroids internally for a relatively mild disease such as hay fever because of the possibly dangerous side effects of such medications.

Surgery may be useful. Sometimes, there is obstruction to breathing because of a deviated nasal septum or the presence of polyps. At present, there is little need for electrical or chemical cautery of the nasal membranes, but occasionally cautery may prove helpful.

Other Inhalant Allergies

Symptoms similar to those of hay fever may be caused by many allergens other than pollens. Such allergy is called inhalational allergy, perennial hay fever, or perennial allergic rhinitis. House dust is a common cause. House dust is not simple dirt or dust or sand but has been described as a mixture of "cotton, bits of wool, feathers, animal hair, pesticide, powder, insect scales, mites, shreds of kapok, shreds of cellulose, and other

foreign material, and colonies of mold (mildew) and bacteria."

Other causes of year-round hay fever include hair and dander of pets, horses, goats; wool; feathers; cottonseed (from mattresses and furniture stuffing); pyrethrum powder; flaxseed; orris root; and such miscellaneous items as gums and resins, soybean, glue, castor bean, flour, jute, hemp, sisal, coffee, and sawdust. There are still others which doctor and patient may have to track down in individual cases.

Desensitization to these allergens is more difficult than to pollens. Therefore, avoidance or removal of an offending substance becomes important and is usually fairly easy if there is clear-cut recognition of a single allergen. For example, the person who sneezes only in the presence of a cat can have another pet. Avoidance of house dust is more difficult, but the doctor will discuss various ways to reduce it in the home. As for medicines, those helpful for pollen allergy may be used.

Food Allergy

Some people notice that ingestion of a certain food causes hives, nasal congestion and sneezing, or asthma. Others trace to a particular food such symptoms as abdominal discomfort, nausea, cramps, belching, and diarrhea. Some people experience migraine headaches after eating particular foods such as chocolate.

When there is a clear association between particular foods and symptoms, diagnosis presents no problems. But when the symptoms are those of indigestion, it may be more difficult to be certain that a true food allergy is involved. In such cases, the doctor relies not only on the patient's account but does skin tests with allergens prepared from egg, milk, and many other foods. Also, he has the patient keep a diary of food intake and symptoms. Then, in some cases, the doctor puts the patient on a basic nonallergenic diet and adds suspected offending foods one at a time to establish which produces symptoms.

Food allergy is rarely a serious disease. When milk is the offender in a child or adolescent, care must be taken to include in the diet other foods which can provide the minerals and protein of this important dietary constituent. The best way to treat food allergy is to avoid the troublesome foodstuff. This may sound simple but there are dozens of foods that contain eggs and milk, for example; and the purchaser may not realize this or he may have to eat in restaurants where food preparation is not under his control. Thus people who are allergic to common foods should learn the long list of dishes that may contain such foods. Complete lists are provided in *All About Allergy* by M. C. Harris, M.D., and N. Shure, M.D. (Prentice-Hall, Inc., Englewood Cliffs, N.J., Publisher, 1969). This 368-page book contains much of value to persons whose allergies are not readily controlled or whose doctors want them to read extensively about their ailment.

Can a person allergic to food be desensitized? The method is not easy. It consists of taking very small amounts of the offending food by mouth until resistance to it is finally built up.

Medicine-Induced Allergy

Any medicine may have more than just a primary effect. For example, an antihistamine may provide some relief for hay fever; that is its primary action. But it may have a secondary effect, drowsiness. In addition, it may have unexpected bizarre actions, producing varied symptoms, sometimes including hives, skin rashes, hay fever, or asthma.

The most feared reaction from administration of a medicine is the allergic condition known as anaphylaxis or anaphylactic shock, in which the patient develops itching, hives, runny nose, and asthmatic breathing, sometimes followed by pallor, cold sweats, low blood pressure, stupor, or coma, and in some cases, death may occur. In some cases of anaphylaxis, there may be only hives with or without swelling of the throat and larynx; this reaction is called angioedema.

Another allergic reaction to medicines and serums is the delayed or serum sickness type. It occurs five to ten days after the sensitizing substance is used and involves itching, hives, and joint pains. In addition to hives, medicines may sometimes produce other skin reactions including eczema. Other adverse reactions to medications which are considered by some experts to be allergic are untoward effects on blood platelets leading to hemorrhages into the skin, depression of blood cell production in bone marrow, and liver reactions.

Almost any medication, even aspirin, may produce allergic reactions either mild or severe in some people. But there are certain compounds noted for allergic potential. Of these, penicillin is one of the most notable offenders. Five to ten percent of patients receiving penicillin have allergic reactions; indeed, ten percent of all adverse reactions to medicines in the United States are due to penicillin.

Sometimes a first injection of penicillin causes allergic symptoms, even fatal anaphylaxis. How did the individual become sensitized? Very likely through unsuspected previous exposure to penicillin contained in milk from a treated cow, or penicillin contaminating a vaccine, or from other "hidden" contact. It is not easy to test for sensitivity to penicillin (though promising tests now appear to be in the offing). Most doctors use penicillin only when absolutely necessary and there is no history of previous reaction to its use. Also, doctors are doubly careful if the person is known to be allergic to other substances or has a strong family history of allergy. Allergy to penicillin is another *good reason why people should not try to pressure doctors to give them a shot of penicillin for a cold or slight fever.*

Many other medicines can cause allergic reactions. The list includes such agents as aspirin, sulfa compounds, tetracyclines and other antibiotics, insulin, antitoxins, local anesthetics such as procaine, some of the tranquilizers, mercury, and arsenic. In some cases, a person seemingly allergic to a medicine may actually be reacting to milk sugar used as a filler for the tablet or a dye used to color a pill.

An important preventive measure for anyone with sensitivity to a medicine is to carry a card or bracelet indicating so, and also to announce the fact to every doctor or nurse who has occasion to take care of him. And when such a person is in a hospital, there should be a sign on or near his bed or in the room stating sensitivity to a given medicine.

A person experiencing a severe allergic or other adverse reaction to a medicine should be promptly treated by a doctor or go to an emergency room in a hospital. It is not enough to rely on an antihistamine, which may be useful for a mild reaction.

Skin Allergy

HIVES. A hive is a raised, blister-like area containing fluid, white in color but surrounded by a reddened area. It usually itches intensely.

An acute attack of hives—also known as urticaria, giant hives, angioedema, angioneurotic edema, and nettle rash—may be caused by allergenic foods, medicines, or serums. There are also physical causes such as sunlight, heat, cold, and pressure on the skin.

When hives are accompanied by edema or water-logging and swelling of throat and laryngeal tissues, there may be danger to life. Treatment is effective. In addition to the same medicines used for hay fever, the doctor may prescribe soothing creams, lotions, or baths for the itching skin. Sometimes a strong laxative helps shorten an attack induced by food by hastening its elimination from the intestine.

People subject to recurrent severe hives should be prepared to act to prevent an attack from progressing to the point of interfering with breathing. They should learn from their doctors how to handle an emergency and should carry the necessary materials with them at all times.

There seems to be a strong emotional component in some cases of recurrent hives. Patient and doctor should discuss life-style and tensions and consider whether a session with a psychotherapist might be helpful.

ECZEMA. Eczema, also called atopic dermatitis, is manifested by a rash of "weeping" blisters. Later, the area may become dry and scaly. Eczema occurs most frequently in the bends of elbows and knees and on the face and neck. It is common in children, many of whom also have hay fever and allergic asthma. The condition can be stubborn, especially in adults. Some children benefit when an allergenic food is found and removed from the diet.

Usual medicines for allergy are not very helpful for eczema. Treatment is directed toward stopping the itching, since scratching aggravates the rash.

Two possible complications are of concern: adults may develop cataracts in the eyes after many years; both children and adults with eczema may have severe reactions to smallpox vaccination. The doctor knows how to prevent and handle these complications.

CONTACT DERMATITIS. In this type of allergy, which occurs upon direct contact with an offending substance, the reaction is almost always localized in the skin. There is usually a rash which clears rapidly when the offending agent is removed.

To test for this type of allergy, suspected offending substances are placed on the skin and covered with bandages. After one to three days, the sites are inspected to determine whether any of the substances has produced a small rash typical of the patient's allergic reaction.

Poison ivy, poison oak, and poison sumac are well-known contact allergens. The reactions produced by their oils can be disabling in particularly sensitive people, especially if the eyes or face are affected. Sometimes the oils can be washed off with strong laundry soap. Antihistamine is helpful, plus application of soothing creams or lotions to affected skin areas. In severe cases, steroid medicines are given.

As we have noted earlier, hair dyes and hair curling preparations should be tested for allergic sensitivity before use.

Dozens upon dozens of substances can cause local allergic reactions when applied to the skin. The best preventive measure is to stop wearing or using an offending item if it can be identified. Often, the patient may suspect what it is; in other cases, the doctor can help identify it. Here, according to site, are some common contact allergens:

Scalp: Lotions, tonics, pomades, soap, hair dyes and rinses, wave sets, shampoos, patent dandruff removers, hair brush bristles, plastic combs, bathing caps, massage brushes, hair nets, hair pins and curlers, toupees, wigs. *Note:* Dermatitis produced by substances used on the scalp may appear predominantly and sometimes even exclusively on eyelids, neck, ears, face, even the hands.

Forehead: Hat bands, linings or other hat materials; massage creams; suntan lotions and other cosmetics; hair nets; celluloid visors; helmets; dye.

Eyelids: Mascara, eyebrow pencil, eyelash curlers. Also substances used elsewhere such as cosmetics, soaps, hand lotions, face powders, nail polishes and lacquers. The eyelids may be affected, too, by insect sprays, nasal sprays, perfumes, airborne pollens, clothing dust, furs, gloves, fabrics, dyed clothing.

Face: Cosmetics; any material that may be transferred by the hands or may be airborne; substances used on face, scalp, or hands; shaving soaps and creams; after-shaving and other lotions.

Ears: Earrings, various plastics and

metals, perfumes, hair dye, shampoo, lacquers, eyeglass frames, ear phones, ear plugs, bathing caps.

Nose: Spectacle frames, nose drops, nasal ointments, sprays, perfumes, handkerchiefs, paper tissue.

Lips and mouth: Lipsticks, mouthwashes, toothpastes, throat lozenges and patent medicines, toothpicks, cigarettes, cigars, pipes, foods, candies, denture materials.

Neck: Collars, scarves, neckties, dress labels, fur, fur dyes, materials used on the scalp, necklaces, perfumes, hair cosmetics and other hair preparations, nail lacquers, cosmetics for the face.

Chest: Clothing materials and dyes.

Underarm areas: Antiperspirants, deodorants, depilatories, dress shields, shaving materials, dyed materials, perfumes.

Hands and forearms: Soaps, cleansers, plants, gloves, rings, bracelets, topical medications, and virtually any object which may be touched or worn.

Trunk: Clothing, sanitary belts, suspensory underwear, nightclothes, bathing materials, soaps, perfumes, bath salts, massage creams.

Anal area: Rectal suppositories, douches, enema substances, intestinal parasites, ingested foods, topical medications, underwear, sanitary napkins, toilet paper, toilet seats.

Vaginal area: Douches, contraceptive jellies, suppositories, sanitary napkins, perfumes, deodorants, pessaries.

Penis and scrotal area: Condoms, prophylactic agents, fabric finishes and dyes in undergarments, pajamas.

Legs: Materials and dyes of clothes; coins and other metallic objects carried in trouser pockets; garters.

Feet: Shoes, socks, shoe polishes, galoshes, fur linings, ankle bracelets, medications, rubbers, cements, pastes.

Occupational Allergy

It appears that about one percent of all workers develop an allergy, usually of the skin. When the allergenic substance is volatile and inhaled, asthmatic symptoms may develop. Men seem more susceptible to occupational allergy than women, possibly because women tend to clean their skin more thoroughly. Cuts, abrasions, and rashes may predispose to occupational allergies.

There is virtually no end to substances that can produce occupational allergies. Some are natural substances such as wool and foodstuffs; some are highly complex new chemical molecules coming from the expanding chemical industry. Laundry workers get sensitized to detergents (as do housewives). Printers are exposed to allergenic dyes, gum arabic, and metals. In other occupations dusts from grains, plastics, and wood can afflict nose or lungs; fumes from metals and liquids can do the same.

In the textile industry, workers may be exposed to countless dyes to which they may become sensitized. And the fixative for dyes contains chromium, a chemical that is often allergenic. Wool and other materials may be offenders.

The cosmetics industry is a source of many allergenic substances. Not only workers in plants but salespeople who demonstrate cosmetics in stores may develop allergies to them.

The health professions have their allergies. Pharmacists may become sensitized to medicines they handle in filling prescriptions. Nurses may become allergic to penicillin and other antibiotics as well as lotions, creams, and antiseptics. Dentists and their assistants may handle procaine which is noted for producing skin allergy.

Physiotherapists may become sensitized to chemicals in creams and lotions they use.

There is virtually no occupation in which some substance capable of producing sensitivity in some people cannot be found. Workers should know of the dangers and be taught how to avoid sensitizing contact with notably allergenic materials. Skin creams and other protectants may be helpful. Protective clothing and gloves may be required. For protection against volatile materials and dust, ventilation must be adequate, and in some situations masks may be necessary.

Desensitization in some cases may provide relief. Medications used for skin allergies and hay fever may prove helpful, too.

Insect Allergy

The sting or bite of many insects —including wasps, bees, hornets, yellow jackets, and ants—can set off allergic reactions, and in some instances, these can even be fatal. Allergic reactions also may be produced by various flies, mosquitoes, fleas, bedbugs, and kissing bugs.

Among 2,606 persons who registered with the American Academy of Allergy in its search for people with insect allergies, the type of allergic responses varied from local swellings to generalized reactions involving the whole body. Of the generalized reactions, 630 were life-threatening; many patients experienced unconsciousness, severe breathing difficulty, throat swelling—in effect, anaphylactic shock for which prompt emergency measures were needed to prevent death.

We are not alarmists and have no wish to frighten people away from enjoying outdoor life. However, insect bites can be dangerous. Fortunately,

there are preventive measures. Those who know they are sensitive to bees, etc., should carry cards indicating so, and should also be trained by their family doctor or an allergist in the use of a special kit available for emergencies. Also, there is effective desensitization treatment for those allergic to bee, wasp, and other stings.

It makes good sense for anyone who is allergic in any way and who receives a bite by a bee, wasp, hornet, or yellow jacket to discuss with his doctor the advisability of carrying an emergency kit on the assumption that since he is allergic to other things, he might become so to these insects from a second sting.

In terms of general sanitation and comfort as well as for protection against bites, foods should be covered when camping or cooking outdoors, and patios and other areas should be treated with insect repellent. Sensitive people should consider wearing white clothes which are less likely to attract bees than gay colors. Also long sleeves and trousers will reduce danger of contact with stinging insects.

If you are ever confronted with a person suffering a severe reaction to an insect sting or bite, and if an emergency kit with adrenaline and antihistamine is not available, you can do some good by placing a tourniquet between bitten or stung area and the heart, applying ice to the inflamed area, and rushing the victim to the nearest doctor or hospital.

Emotions and Allergy

You may ask how emotions can have any effect in the reaction between an allergen and an antibody. Yet, asthma has been found to have a significant psychosomatic component. While the relationship is not so clear in other allergic states, many patients with hay fever or hives find that their symptoms become worse when emotional problems are bothering them. Doctors understand this and welcome having patients discuss any relationships they have observed between emotions and symptoms, and are glad to discuss too how psychological states may be improved.

AMEBIASIS (AMEBIC DYSENTERY, AMEBIC LIVER DISEASE)

Most of us think of amebic infections as problems only in tropical and subtropical countries. Yet they occur in every part of the United States, affecting as much as 5 percent of the population, according to some estimates. They are more common in the rural South where some experts believe as much as 40 percent of the population may be affected.

Amebiasis is basically a disease of the large intestine caused by a protozoan organism, *Entameba histolytica.* The organism develops in the large intestine after gaining entrance in the form of a cyst which the victim ingests. Food and drink contaminated by infected fecal matter are responsible for infection. Usually, in this country, the source is a food handler who may have no symptoms or only very mild ones, and whose unclean hands transmit the disease. In some countries, water is infected, or human feces may be allowed to contaminate food-growing areas; in some parts of the world, human feces are used as fertilizer.

Since amebic infection can cause great pain and disability from diarrhea—and may lead to death if the infection spreads from intestine to other parts of the body—it is important to understand basic facts about its transmission. With this knowledge, primary preventive measures can be used.

Where dependable, clean water is not available and the traveler or camper must rely on questionable supplies or use wells, streams or lakes, water must be boiled for ten minutes or treated with special chemical disinfectants. All fruits and vegetables should be washed and scrubbed. In suspect areas, travelers should eat only cooked foods and use only milk known to be pasteurized.

You may be asking, "Why all this fuss about a disease I have hardly heard about?" Consider this one fact about amebiasis: in some forms, it has a fatality rate of 40 percent. Your life, if you become infected, is only as good as a 6 to 4 bet; not very good odds. In addition, if an acute attack is survived, there may be serious, chronic complications. Fortunately, treatment has been improving, and today, when the best available treatment is applied promptly and vigorously, the fatality rate can be reduced to less than 5 percent.

How is the disease recognized? In the tropics, it will usually start as full-blown amebic dysentery, with up to 25 bowel movements a day, and with stools often containing blood and bits of mucus. The patient may feel slightly feverish and will soon be weakened by the abdominal distress and dehydration. In this country and other temperate zone countries, there is rarely such extreme diarrhea; and the combination of abdominal distress, diarrhea alternating with constipation, fatigue, slight fever, and vague aches and pains throughout the body may be passed off as "colitis," "irritable colon," or "upset stomach." In some persons, symptoms are so mild that they do not see a doctor for treatment and unknowingly become carriers of the amebic organisms.

Another problem in diagnosing the disease arises from the increasing numbers of Americans who take short winter vacations in semitropical and tropical countries. If a vacationer develops diarrhea and other intestinal symptoms, he is not eager to consult a doctor in a strange country. He also does not want to interrupt his brief holiday. So he doses himself with Lomotil, paregoric, or anything else he has brought along for "tourists' diarrhea." When he returns home, he plunges into work. Thus, the diagnosis of amebiasis may be missed, and the best time to treat it lost; later, there may be dangerous spread of infection in the body, making for treatment problems.

To be sure, most cases of diarrhea during vacations are the relatively harmless tourists' diarrhea. But we strongly advise anyone who develops diarrhea in a semitropical or tropical country to tell his physician about it promptly upon return home or, if the stay is to be more than the usual brief vacation, to consult a local doctor (you can usually find a competent physician by calling the nearest American consul and asking for the name of his doctor).

When there are symptoms suggestive of amebiasis, your physician will rarely start treatment until a precise diagnosis is made. That means finding the amebic organisms in the stool. Unfortunately, locating the organisms is not always simple; and some physicians who have devoted themselves to the study of this disease will not exclude the diagnosis of amebiasis until six stools, including one passed after a saline purge, have been judged negative by a competent diagnostic laboratory.

When the diagnosis of amebiasis has been established, the doctor starts treatment to clear up symptoms and also to eradicate the disease completely. He knows that complete cure is necessary to prevent spread into the liver where abscesses may develop and dangerous generalized infection may be triggered. Also, the doctor knows that without complete cure, the patient may be freed of symptoms and yet remain a carrier who is a danger to his family and others.

Usually, there is very good response to emetine, chloroquine, and other medications used in treatment of this disease. Since emetine may have dangerous effects on the heart, it is generally administered with the patient in bed either at home or in hospital.

Sometimes, medications alone do not cure amebic abscesses of the liver, and surgical drainage may be needed to eliminate the pus.

ANEMIAS

Blood normally contains 5 million red cells per cubic millimeter. These cells are packed with hemoglobin. Hemoglobin has a great affinity for oxygen and combines with it in the lungs and transports it to all tissues of the body. On the average, each 100 cubic centimeters of blood contains 15 grams of hemoglobin, so that, roughly, there is 1/2 ounce of hemoglobin for 3-1/2 ounces of blood. Anemia is present when either the number of red blood cells or the amount of hemoglobin in them is reduced below normal values.

There are many types of anemia but some symptoms are common to all types. With mild anemia, there is lack of pep and easy fatigability. With somewhat more severe anemia, there may be shortness of breath on exertion, some pounding of the heart, a more rapid pulse rate then usual. With very severe anemia, there may be fainting spells, dizziness, headaches, ringing in the ears, loss of appetite, and sometimes swelling of the ankles. It is only with moderate or severe, not mild, anemia that a patient looks pale, and usually the pallor can be detected best in the palms of the hands and the fingernails.

Since anemia reduces the ability of the blood to transport oxygen, it will intensify ailments in which there already is difficulty in obtaining sufficient oxygen. For example, the patient with heart failure cannot circulate blood properly; anemia adds an extra burden for the failing heart. When arteries of the heart are narrowed and the heart muscles receive through them only marginal supplies of oxygen, the extra stress of anemia may cause appearance of heart pain (angina pectoris). In patients with acute or chronic lung disease, such as pneumonia or emphysema, severe anemia may turn a hopeful situation into a disastrous one by depriving the body of vital supplies of oxygen.

Even mild anemia can be detected by determination of red cell count and hemoglobin content, using just a drop of blood from a finger or from an ear lobe.

Iron-Deficiency Anemia

Hemoglobin includes an iron-containing pigment, and iron-deficiency anemia is common. Most often it is the result of chronic loss of blood. In the female, a common reason is excess menstrual flow. In the male, a common cause is slow bleeding from a peptic ulcer. In both sexes, hemorrhoids (piles) may lead to anemia. There are many other possible causes such as hiatus hernia, large doses of aspirin or other salicylates, tumors of stomach or intestines which may bleed, hookworm infestation. Failure to ingest enough iron in the diet—as when a person lives on coffee and doughnuts or goes on a prolonged fad diet—can produce iron-deficiency anemia.

Because there is so little iron in the body, it takes only a regular small loss of blood, especially if iron intake in the diet is limited, to produce this type of anemia. Frequently, gastrointestinal blood loss will not even make the stool appear bloody, black, or tarry and will be detectable only by special chemical tests on the stool.

For treatment, the physician may prescribe an iron preparation to be taken by mouth or may inject an iron compound into the muscles.

The balanced, nutritious diet we talk about in Chapter 6 should provide enough iron for primary prevention of iron-deficiency anemia unless there is chronic loss of blood. There is no need to take advertised remedies to provide extra iron for "tired blood." If there is blood loss which is producing anemia, it's important not only that the anemia be corrected but that the underlying cause be found and corrected.

Pernicious Anemia

For red blood cell manufacture in the bone marrow, vitamin B_{12} is needed. The vitamin is present in adequate amounts in any balanced diet. But for absorption by the body, B_{12} requires the presence in the stomach of a substance called "intrinsic factor." In pernicious anemia, intrinsic factor is lacking or operates inadequately. Vitamin B_{12} absorption is then inadequate, and in such patients the vitamin must be administered by injection.

In addition to the common signs for all anemias, pernicious anemia manifests itself in a red and sore tongue, difficulty in swallowing, a pale lemon skin color. In about 10 percent of patients, there are symptoms from spinal cord changes such as numbness and tingling in the lower extremities ("pins and needles" sensations) and unsteady gait. Sometimes the fingers are affected by numbness and tingling. Memory may be affected, and sometimes even psychotic states may be induced.

The nervous system changes are referred to as "combined system disease" or "posterolateral sclerosis." It is important that they be recognized for what they are, especially when they occur before anemia becomes manifest. If treated early, by vitamin B_{12} injections, the changes may be reversed completely; if neglected and treated too late, complete reversal may not be possible.

The diagnosis of pernicious anemia is made through the characteristic appearance of the blood cells, examination of a bone marrow sample obtained by simple needle puncture, a finding of acid deficiency in stomach juice, and by other laboratory tests. It is important that the diagnosis of pernicious anemia be unequivocal because this condition requires lifelong care. If correctly diagnosed and treated, the outlook for pernicious anemia today is excellent. Blood returns to normal. The patient feels well. Once blood values return to normal, usually just a single injection of vitamin B_{12} per month suffices for good health.

There is no primary prevention for ordinary pernicious anemia. But there are other conditions that lead to vita-

min B_{12} deficiency and to an anemia that resembles the pernicious type. They include destruction or removal of the stomach, regional ileitis, removal of the ileum (the lower portion of the small intestine), and fish tapeworm disease. When anemia stems from these conditions, primary prevention is possible. Fish tapeworm disease can be avoided by eating only well-cooked fish. When the stomach or ileum is destroyed or removed, injections of vitamin B_{12} can be given regularly to prevent the anemia from developing.

Hemolytic Anemia

In this type of anemia, red blood cells are destroyed. Hemolytic anemia may be congenital or acquired, acute or chronic. In addition to symptoms common to other anemias such as fatigue and shortness of breath, hemolytic anemia usually produces some degree of jaundice because the destroyed red cells release their hemoglobin which is converted into jaundice pigments.

Sometimes an acute form of hemolytic anemia appears suddenly, with chills, fever, nausea, vomiting, abdominal pain. The cause may be a medicine to which the patient is sensitive, bacterial or malarial infection, metastatic cancer, or Hodgkin's disease. If the basic cause can be removed (e.g., an offending medicine) or cured (e.g., malaria), the outlook is good. Usually the situation calls for prompt hospitalization. In the hospital, with injections of fluids, transfusions of packed red cells, and use of corticosteroid medicines, the patient makes a good recovery.

Some hemolytic anemias are chronic and may last for years. If neglected, they may lead to development of gallstones and in some cases leg ulcers. The spleen is enlarged. When the spleen is surgically removed, about 90 percent of patients benefit. If gallstones have already formed, a separate operation may be required to remove them.

Another form of hemolytic anemia affects the black race. This is sickle-cell anemia, so called because the ordinarily round red blood cells become sickle-shaped under certain conditions. This is a serious, sometimes fatal illness. It produces recurrent attacks of fever with pain in the legs, arms, and abdomen. For severe pain attacks, hospitalization may be required to provide relief.

There is no primary prevention. When, however, both partners in a marriage know they carry the sickle-cell trait, they may wish to have genetic counseling to determine the risk in having children.

Sickle-cell anemia occurs in about 1 of 500 American black people whereas the sickle-cell trait occurs in about 1 in 11. With sickle-cell trait, there is no anemia and health is usually good unless there is exposure to special stress. People with the trait may suffer when deprived of oxygen at high altitudes or when there is heart disease, acute alcoholism, surgical shock, or inadequate anesthesia; then they may develop severe, even fatal conditions in the blood vessels of lungs and brain.

Sickle-cell hemoglobin disease is an anemia that closely resembles sickle-cell disease but has a more favorable outlook. It occurs in 1 of 1,500 American blacks. Many patients live to age 70 and beyond. When complications occur, they are apt to be infarctions of blood vessels of lungs or spleen, bleeding from the kidney, or eye problems (retinal detachment or hemor-

rhages into the rear fluid compartment of the eye, the vitreous).

Hemolytic anemia other than sickle-cell may result from transfusion of mismatched blood, which should be preventable with today's knowledge and techniques for blood grouping. It may also result from Rh incompatibility (see page 562). In addition, this type of anemia may be produced by some industrial poisons (such as benzol, aniline, TNT), and sometimes by such substances as sulfonamide medications, quinine, lead, snake venom, castor and fava beans. Outcome will depend on severity of the anemia and on how quickly the cause can be determined and eliminated, as well as on prompt treatment with fluids, transfusions, and corticosteroid medications.

Another hereditary type of hemolytic anemia is thalassemia, which is subdivided into major and minor categories. Thalassemia major is also called Cooley's anemia and Mediterranean anemia. It is found in people with ancestry tracing to northern Africa, southern Europe, and such Asian areas as Iran, Iraq, Indonesia, Thailand, and southern China. It is a serious disease which starts in early life. In addition to the usual symptoms of anemia plus the jaundice of the hemolytic type, there is enlargement of liver and spleen. During the course of it, there may develop leg ulcers, gallstones, and a type of heart failure that is resistant to therapy.

In thalassemia minor, the anemia is mild and the outlook very good. Lifespan is normal. Usually no treatment is needed except possibly in pregnancy when blood transfusion may be used to keep the blood hemoglobin level at a safe point for the sake of mother and child.

There are many other types of anemia, relatively rare, in which some slight abnormality of chemical structure of hemoglobin is the basic fault. Usually, when such anemias are suspected, study by a specialist in blood diseases, a hematologist, is needed.

Other types of hemolytic anemia which usually require attention of a blood specialist for diagnosis and follow-up are autoimmune hemolytic anemia, ovalocytosis, paroxysmal nocturnal hemoglobinuria, and primaquine-sensitive hemolytic anemia. The latter disease, which occurs in 10 to 15 percent of black males and 1 to 2 percent of black females, involves an unusual sensitivity to certain medications and chemicals; it usually clears up as soon as the offending substances are eliminated.

Aplastic Anemia

Since blood cells are manufactured in the bone marrow, anemia may result when the marrow is damaged and becomes sluggish or fails to function at all. In this type of anemia, not only are red blood cells reduced in numbers; so, too, are the white cells. Resistance to infections is thus reduced, too. Blood platelet count drops as well, and thus there may be bleeding.

When aplastic anemia is severe, the outlook is grave. The mortality rate may go as high as 50 percent. With good treatment, the remaining 50 percent sometimes do quite well and, fortunately, in some cases, the disease clears up spontaneously.

Aplastic anemia may be a result of sensitivity or toxic reaction to many medications and chemicals, including chloromycetin, Butazolidin, Mesantoin, benzene, hair dyes, volatile solvents, and insecticides. Irradiation in large doses also may be responsible.

At the first suggestion of aplastic anemia, a physician will stop all medications and search, too, for possible exposure to toxic materials.

Diagnosis is made on the basis of changes in blood cells and the appearance of bone marrow in a sample obtained by puncture of the sternum, or breastbone.

In some patients with aplastic anemia, a thymoma, or tumor of the thymus gland, is found; removal of the tumor is sometimes done but without guarantee that this will be helpful. Sometimes the spleen is enlarged and removal of the spleen may be considered.

Transfusions may be used. And recently there have been reports of promising results with the use of compounds related to the male sex hormone, testosterone. These compounds appear to have a stimulating effect on the bone marrow.

What of replacement of diseased bone marrow by transplantation as a tertiary preventive measure? This appears to be a likely future measure as more experience is gained in the whole field of tissue and organ transplantation.

Miscellaneous Anemias

There is a group of anemias that are secondary to various diseases. For them, prevention, either primary or secondary, depends upon diagnosis and successful treatment of the underlying disease.

For example, the anemia associated with low thyroid function (myxedema) yields to thyroid treatment; anemia associated with the presence of intestinal parasites yields when the parasites are eliminated by appropriate treatment; anemia associated with lead poisoning yields when the poisoning is properly treated; anemia accompanying chronic infection clears when the infection is found and cured. Anemias associated with cirrhosis of the liver and with advanced kidney disease (uremia) have outlooks similar to those for the basic diseases, as does the anemia that may occur with cancer.

Special Note: It should be apparent that there are anemias that are easy to diagnose and treat, and others that are obscure and require highly skilled diagnosis and treatment. Certainly, no patient who suspects he or she may have anemia should undertake self-treatment, which may only delay proper diagnosis and adequate treatment.

Some anemias are readily recognized by the family physician and can be successfully treated by him to prevent development of serious consequences. But there is complete justification for the family doctor, when diagnosis is not absolutely certain, to send the patient to a blood specialist. Sometimes, this may mean a journey of considerable distance to a large medical center or hospital equipped with special laboratories in which the modern hematologist does his diagnostic studies and can pin down even anemia of the most obscure type. Such a journey is worth any inconvenience.

APPENDICITIS

Prevention can be an important factor in overcoming the risks of appendicitis. The appendix is a hollow, 2-1/2- to 3-inch structure located at the juncture of the large and small intestines. It serves no known purpose in humans. Not a lot is known about what causes the appendix to become inflamed ex-

cept that some cases have been associated with obstruction of the appendix by hard fecal material or, rarely, worms.

Once inflamed, the appendix can cause serious trouble if it ruptures and spreads pus through the abdomen (peritonitis). Preventive measures aim at removing the appendix before it has a chance to rupture. Primary prevention may be considered to be the removal of a normal appendix before it has a chance even to become inflamed. Secondary prevention involves removal of an inflamed appendix before it can rupture. Tertiary prevention is treatment of the complications of a ruptured appendix.

Primary prevention is sometimes exercised by a surgeon when he removes the appendix in the course of doing other surgery in the abdomen such as removing the gallbladder or performing a hysterectomy. This adds little time to the operation and virtually none to the postoperative recovery period. The patient should make careful note of whether the surgeon states that he removed the appendix incidental to another operation, for this may be meaningful at a future time when abdominal pain is a diagnostic problem.

A more complex question is whether a person who plans to be away from civilization for a period of time should have his appendix removed as a prophylactic precaution. With modern means of communication and travel, this is probably not necessary unless the person will be extremely isolated (as on a Pacific island or in an unexplored jungle area).

The best secondary preventive measure is prompt diagnosis and treatment of an inflamed but still unruptured appendix. The problem here is that the initial symptoms of appendicitis may be mimicked by so many other conditions—pneumonia with abdominal pain, gallbladder disease, ruptured ovarian follicle, tubal pregnancy, or just plain gastroenteritis—that the diagnosis of appendicitis can tax the most astute physician.

The symptoms usually are nausea, abdominal pain, loss of appetite, and sometimes fever, constipation or diarrhea. Typically, the pain of appendicitis will become most severe in the lower right side of the abdomen where the appendix is usually located. Since the appendix in some individuals may be located in an unusual position, pain may localize elsewhere.

Careful history-taking and physical examination with close attention to where the pain is located are the most useful diagnostic measures. As noted, the pain of appendicitis is typically very localized; to pinpoint it further, a rectal or vaginal examination is of value. Suggestive clues such as increased white blood cell count, fever, and failure of symptoms to subside help confirm the diagnosis. Treatment is surgical removal, and with good anesthesia and modern surgical techniques, the risk of surgery is virtually zero, while problems encountered after an appendix ruptures are formidable.

After removal of an intact inflamed appendix, the patient is usually out of bed next day and home from the hospital in five to seven days. Further convalescence is ordinarily uneventful. Even those suffering from other ailments such as heart disease usually come through the surgery and anesthesia very well.

In contrast, a ruptured appendix calls for intravenous feeding, antibiotics, strict bed rest sometimes for several days before surgery can even be performed. Recovery from surgery may involve several weeks of hospitalization because, even with antibiotics, peritonitis is still a difficult and dangerous medical problem. There are still 15,000 to 20,000 deaths a year in this country from appendicitis and its complications.

Naturally, it is of the utmost importance to reduce the possibility that an inflamed appendix will rupture. Therefore, if symptoms are equivocal after 8 to 12 hours of observation, the physician will be inclined to operate rather than risk rupture.

The patient's role in preventing rupture is important. Delay in diagnosis or improper treatment greatly increases the risk. The guidelines are simple:

1. Do not treat any abdominal pain lasting for 3 to 4 hours with cathartics, enemas or local heat. Laxatives and enemas increase contractions in the large intestine and cause pressure to develop in the appendix, increasing the chance of rupture. With each dose of laxative, the risk of rupture and death increases greatly. Local heat may obscure symptoms and may also hasten rupture.

2. Consult a physician as soon as possible.

3. Do not eat or drink anything.

Recurrent attacks of acute appendicitis are uncommon but can occur. Chronic appendicitis—that is, appendicitis causing pain for weeks or months—does not occur; this type of pain is indicative of other medical or surgical problems.

ARTHRITIS

When a joint (or several joints) in the body becomes swollen, stiff, and painful, a person is said to have arthritis. The term "arthritis" merely describes a group of symptoms, much as fever means only elevated body temperature. To determine what the scenario —proper treatment and outlook—is for an individual patient, the physician must differentiate among a number of diseases that can produce arthritic symptoms.

Rheumatoid arthritis, a chronic disease of unknown cause, is one. Osteoarthritis, produced by "wear and tear" in the joints, is another. Gout, an inherited disorder of metabolism in which uric acid in excessive amounts appears in blood and tissues, produces arthritic symptoms. There is infectious arthritis which results from infection of a joint by bacteria such as those involved in tuberculosis or gonorrhea. Arthritis, too, may be associated with ulcerative colitis, urethral infections, rheumatic fever, and lupus erythematosus.

We will discuss here the three most common types of arthritis: rheumatoid, osteoarthritis, and gouty arthritis.

Rheumatoid arthritis is really a systemic illness that manifests itself primarily by joint pain and inflammation, usually leading to deformities. Infrequently other organs, such as the lung, may be damaged as well. Rheumatoid arthritis (RA) does not seem to be related to rheumatic fever, with which it may be confused. The latter is predominantly a disease of young people, which may affect the heart, and commonly is associated with episodes of nondeforming joint pain.

Many people with RA have at first only nonspecific symptoms such as fever, chills, poor appetite, and a general rundown feeling. Finally, when the joints become stiff, sore, and painful, they consult a physician. RA usually begins between the ages of 20 and 40. It most frequently affects the joints of the fingers, wrists, knees, ankles, and toes, alone or in combination, although all joints may be involved. One hallmark of the disease is that usually both sides of the body are affected; that is, both hands or both ankles, for example, are involved at the same time. The joints may be stiffer and more sore in the morning than after exercise. In some cases, small hard nodules may appear under the skin, especially in pressure areas. In many instances, the hand affected by RA begins to deviate outward (toward the little finger).

To confirm the diagnosis, x-ray studies may reveal characteristic changes of bones and joints. Blood tests may be used, including one for an unusual protein that appears in the blood of patients with RA, although it may sometimes be related to other diseases.

Once RA is diagnosed, the physician can envision two possible scenarios for the disease. In one form of RA, there is severe joint inflammation, with pain, swelling, fairly rapidly developing deformities. Fever and prostration often accompany this type of RA; and if the disease is untreated, not only may there be rapid development of deformities, but the deformities may become crippling.

In the second and more common type, the arthritic pains and swelling are not as severe and disabling, and there may be intervals during which few, if any, symptoms are experienced. However, gradually over many years and often after several attacks of more severe joint pain, the joints may become deformed and impaired.

Although medical science is learning more and more about rheumatoid arthritis, much remains to be revealed about the cause. The latest findings seem to indicate that an unusual type of bacterium or virus may cause the disease.

Meanwhile, lacking means of primary prevention, the physician must rely on methods of secondary and tertiary prevention to counter the ill effects of RA—joint deformity and disability. For secondary prevention, a many-pronged approach is used. Bed rest is important for acutely inflamed joints. In severe cases, this may mean hospitalization. In less severe cases, adequate sleep and avoidance not only of excessive fatigue but also of coldness and dampness may serve.

It's important, too, that inflamed joints be maintained in nondeforming positions. Swollen, inflamed joints are most comfortable when slightly bent, but if they freeze in this position they become of limited usefulness. Therefore every effort must be made to keep the joints extended or straight. This may require that splints and braces be worn at night and, in some cases, during the day as well. It may also call for use of a nonsagging mattress with a small pillow under the head to help keep the back straight; chairs with firm seats and straight backs; avoidance of tightly drawn sheets; use of cane or crutch to avoid excess weight on sensitive joints; and proper shoes with straight last.

Exercise is important as part of the program to keep joints from stiffening. Special exercises may be needed to increase or maintain muscle power or to relieve any deformities that may have begun to develop.

Local heat—from heating pad, lamp, etc.—helps relieve muscle spasm and pain. Pain-relieving medications also are essential for the arthritic. Among the most effective for RA is aspirin, because in addition to its effect on pain it has a valuable anti-inflammatory effect. Frequently, large doses

of aspirin are needed around the clock. In an occasional patient, aspirin will cause bleeding in the stomach or intestine or may even help produce a peptic ulcer. Such patients may obtain relief of pain from a medicine such as Tylenol.

Indocin and Butazolidin are other antiinflammatory pain relievers that may be used along with, or in place of, aspirin. These agents may sometimes produce peptic ulcers so, as a precaution against this, the physician will advise that they be taken with meals or with liquid antacids. Narcotics should be avoided because of the risk of addiction.

Gold salts and certain compounds for malaria are occasionally of value in RA. Their side effects, however, may be drawbacks to their use.

Steroid compounds provide the most dramatic relief because their potent anti-inflammatory properties lead to rapid suppression of joint pain and swelling. They may be used for acute disabling attacks or when all other medicines fail to produce adequate results. Steroids, however, do not cure RA. They have such side effects as bone brittleness, weight gain, ulcer formation, diabetes, and others. Therefore, the physician must weigh carefully the risks involved in using steroids as against the danger of joint deformity from inadequate treatment. In less severe cases, or where only one or two joints are inflamed, injection of steroids directly into a joint may bring long-lasting relief.

Surgery now is used with increasing frequency—to remove overgrown tissue in a joint, to loosen any tendons or ligaments that may be distorting a joint, or to replace a severely diseased joint with a prosthesis or artificial joint.

Since RA in most cases is a long-term disease posing the threat of deformity and disability, the patient must be under close medical supervision and, much like the diabetic, must learn to adjust his life to his disease. This means meticulous attention to posture, fatigue, exercise, etc. It may mean consultations with orthopedist, physical therapist, or an internist specializing in joint diseases.

Too often, arthritics are preyed upon by makers of quack medicines and quack healers who promote quick "cures." The "cures" range from drug concoctions that are either completely ineffective or have dangerous side effects to mysterious devices that emit "magic" rays. One feature of RA that favors the quacks is the occurrence of spontaneous remissions—periods of freedom from symptoms—which the unscrupulous seize upon as testimonials to the effectiveness of their "medicines" and manipulations.

Unhappily, we know of many patients who have developed severe arthritic disability while being "treated" by quacks and who thereafter required very long periods of hospitalization to correct the joint deformities which, with proper care, might have been avoided.

The role of climate in RA is still poorly understood. The disease is one of temperate zones, particularly cold damp areas. Many patients get relief from warm, dry climates, but the physical and emotional relaxation that usually accompanies trips to these areas undoubtedly plays some part in the relief obtained. On the other hand, when moving to a southern climate introduces emotional upset and economic worries, the arthritic problems may be magnified.

Osteoarthritis, sometimes referred to as degenerative joint disease, is arthritis associated with "wear and tear" in the joints. It does not usually develop before middle age except when a joint has been injured or when joints have been subjected to much stress and overuse, as in the finger joints of some pianists.

Degenerative joint disease (DJD) is an uncomfortable but not very severe disease. Unlike RA, it produces no constitutional symptoms such as fever and weight loss. In some cases, however, it may cause joint disability.

The joints usually affected are the weight-bearing ones such as hips, spine, knees, and ankles. Frequently swellings of small finger joints are seen. Affected joints may "creak" and grate on movement. Typically, and in contrast to RA, pain is increased by exercise and relieved by rest.

An essential element of primary prevention is the avoidance of excessive weight gain, which adds to the burden and wear and tear of weight-bearing joints. Secondary preventive measures are directed at reducing the strain on affected joints by weight reduction, use of back braces, abdominal support for sagging abdomen (to take strain off the back), neck braces, and adequate rest. Pain-relieving medication and local heat applications are useful. Steroid injections of affected joints may be used in some cases.

Usually these measures work very well. In cases not adequately helped by them, the arthritis may cause distortion of joint structure and may necessitate such tertiary measures as replacement of a joint by a metal prosthesis or surgical removal of restricting diseased tissue.

In some cases of DJD, bony overgrowths may cause pressure on nerves. When this happens in the neck region —a common site for DJD—it may cause pain and weakness in the hands and fingers. Surgical removal of the bony spurs is the only effective treatment.

Gout is a disease thought lightly of by all except those who suffer from it. Books are replete with cartoons of obese aristocrats suffering from painful gouty toe, and the implication is that "high living"—overindulgence in food and drink and lack of gainful work—is responsible for the disease.

In reality, gout is an inherited ailment related to abnormal metabolism of certain important compounds, called purines, in foods. As a result of the abnormal metabolism, an increased level of a purine breakdown product, uric acid, builds up in blood and body tissues. When excess uric acid is deposited in joints it may lead to inflammatory reaction by the joint tissues. This produces severe pain, swelling, and stiffness. The joints usually affected are those of the lower extremities, particularly the great toe, but any other joint in the body can be involved. The arthritis of gout can be severe and disabling if untreated and may lead to permanent deformity. Also, changes leading to impairment of vital organs such as the kidney may occur.

Not everyone with gout develops the chief clinical symptom of arthritis; by far the great majority of cases are without symptoms. People in sedentary work are more likely than manual laborers to have clinical gout.

The physician suspects gout particularly when a middle-aged man (gouty arthritis is predominantly a disease of men) complains of pain and swelling in one or occasionally two joints which are extremely sensitive to the slightest pressure. He will confirm the suspicion by a test which measures the amount of uric acid in the blood.

The outlook is for recurrent arthritic attacks involving great pain and leading to joint deformity unless adequate treatment is instituted, in which case the patient can be free of all symptoms of the disease.

The physician will perform tests to evaluate the function of the kidneys, because uric acid can cause kidney stones and in other ways can damage the kidneys. Kidney failure is a dreaded complication of gout and fortunately an uncommon one that can be prevented. The physician also will be alert for high blood pressure and heart disease, since, for unknown reasons, many people with gout also have these ailments. Finally, he may ask blood relatives to have their uric acid levels checked, since gout is an inherited disorder.

Because it is well known that stress or injury to joints can precipitate an attack of gouty arthritis, the obese patient will be advised to reduce weight. Tight shoes should be avoided and so, too, any form of stress or injury to joints.

Many excellent medicines are available to relieve the agony of gouty arthritis once an attack has begun. One of these, colchicine, is particularly effective and can stop an attack usually within 24 hours. For individuals who can predict when they are about to have an attack—through warmth and tingling in the joint—colchicine may be taken to prevent the attack. Some physicians recommend use of the drug in small daily doses to prevent acute flare-ups or reduce their severity. With a decrease in frequency and severity of acute attacks of gout, the risk of joint damage is decreased.

Several medicines are available to promote excretion of uric acid via the kidneys, thus reducing the amount in the tissues. The preparations are taken regularly, and it is important that fluid intake be high so that uric acid does not precipitate in the kidneys but is washed away.

A recent addition to the treatment of gout, useful in prevention of adverse effects, is a medicine called allopurinol. This compound is extremely interesting because it blocks the enzyme that converts certain compounds into uric acid. Therefore, uric acid is not formed and there is no danger of it depositing anywhere in the body. Allopurinol, therefore, almost may be called a means of primary prevention. The compound also stimulates the breakdown and excretion of uric acid deposits that may already have accumulated in the body. The medicine has few side effects. Allopurinol may make obsolete many older drugs used for secondary prevention (i.e., those that promote uric acid excretion through the kidneys).

In occasional patients, certain foods may precipitate gout attacks. In most cases, however, it is no longer considered necessary to ban many "rich" foods from the diet (those which have high purine content), with the possible exceptions of such items as sweetbreads, anchovies, liver, and kidney. More important in dietary control of gout is high fluid intake to minimize any uric acid precipitation in the kidneys.

Tertiary measures—for removal of uric acid deposits already damaging joints or kidneys—are actually effected through use of the medicines already mentioned.

ASTHMA

Air reaches the lungs through the bronchial tubes which branch off from the windpipe (trachea) and become smaller and smaller as they penetrate the depths of the lungs. Obstruction to passage of air in the tubes, especially the smaller ones, causes difficult breathing, often of a wheezing character, which is called asthmatic.

Asthmatic breathing may occur in many conditions that interfere with free passage of air through the bronchi, such as infection of the bronchi, obstruction by an inhaled foreign body, pressure from an enlarged thyroid gland, lung congestion from a failing heart. Here, however, we are discussing the disease bronchial asthma, rather than the symptom of asthmatic breathing.

Bronchial asthma is an allergic disease but since it has special characteristics we are treating it separately from other allergic disorders. For example, asthma may cause permanent, even fatal, lung damage whereas most allergies do not severely damage their target organs. Also there appears to be a stronger psychological factor in many cases of asthma than in other allergies, enough stronger so that asthma is considered a psychosomatic as well as allergic disorder. We suggest that since asthma is allergic, the reader may benefit by reading our section on allergy.

The bronchial tubes have muscular, elastic walls and soft, delicate linings containing many mucus-producing cells. In asthma, depending upon severity, there may be constriction of the tubes, swelling of the linings, and overproduction of mucus, and plugs of mucus may harden and block air passage.

An asthmatic attack may be so mild that a patient feels only a slight heaviness in breathing, or it may be so severe that the patient strains virtually every muscle of his upper body

538 / *Disease Scenarios*

as he attempts to get air in and out of the blocked bronchi. His breathing may be loud and wheezing, his lips blue from poor oxygenation of his blood, and his face may have the agonized look of someone suffocating. Most attacks are moderate ones, last a few hours, then clear. Between attacks, the patient breathes normally. After a severe attack, there may be some soreness of chest muscles from the labored breathing.

In typical asthma, all smaller bronchi are involved, and the doctor ascertains that there is general involvement by listening to the breathing through his stethoscope. This is important because if there is only some one localized area of difficult breathing, it would suggest another cause, such as localized obstruction, perhaps by an inhaled object.

Very often, a patient knows that he is sensitive to pollen or a pet or a certain food. This helps in diagnosis. The physician can perform sensitivity tests for various common allergens. True bronchial asthma almost always responds to certain medications, and the relief provided by these constitutes still another aid in diagnosis.

Not all cases of asthma are clearly allergic. There are asthma patients who seem to be reacting to infections of their bronchi or sinuses. Some physicians believe that such patients are sensitive to allergens in bacteria or viruses (intrinsic asthma). Other doctors believe that there is an extrinsic allergen which is not apparent and that the infection only intensifies symptoms. The conflict is hard to resolve because it is difficult to desensitize patients to the many bacteria and viruses that inhabit and infect the respiratory tract and sinuses.

There is also a type of asthma which seems to be entirely emotional. Yet, many allergists believe that in such cases there is a basic sensitivity to some allergen such as house dust and that emotional tensions act as a trigger or intensifier of symptoms.

All of this must be considered by the physician when he diagnoses asthma and the outlook for the patient. If attacks are definitely related to an inhalational allergen such as ragweed or cat dander, then the physician knows the outlook is good. The patient will either avoid the allergen or be desensitized to it. And if avoidance or desensitization is not 100 percent productive, the patient will do well with one of the medicines used for treating asthma. Similarly, a patient with a strong emotional component can be helped greatly by psychotherapy.

For the patient with frequent attacks without clear-cut cause, there are several possibilities: (1) The patient may do very well on the medications to be discussed shortly and with the help of other preventive measures. (2) The patient may not respond well to treatment, may experience almost constant breathing difficulty, and severity may be great enough to endanger the lungs through slow development of emphysema. (3) In addition to the outlook described in (2), the patient may experience repeated bronchial infections not easily controlled with antibiotics. (4) The patient may have frequent, extremely severe attacks. During such attacks, called status asthmaticus, the patient becomes blue from lack of oxygen, exhausted from straining to breathe, and seems on the verge of death. Fortunately, with modern asthma therapy, death is rare but intensive care in a hospital is required.

Almost all available medicines of use in asthma may be tried on a patient experiencing frequent attacks to determine which is most helpful. Adrenaline may be given by injection or inhalation and a related compound, ephedrine, may be administered by mouth. Aminophylline is often helpful and may be given in rectal suppositories or by injection into a vein.

Antihistamines do not help the asthma patient and may even be harmful in drying up the mucus which needs to be kept loose. For loosening phlegm, iodide is a standard medication; another is glycerol guaiacolate. Steam inhalation and high water intake help keep the mucus thin enough so it will not plug the bronchi.

Corticosteroids — cortisone - like agents—are often helpful for moderate and severe asthma but must be used with great respect for their possible dangerous side effects. They can be given in short courses to stop an attack or over longer periods to prevent recurrences. Since introduction of corticosteroids, many asthmatics are leading happier, more productive lives but must cooperate fully with their doctors in frequent checkups to observe the effects of these potent medications.

There are general protective measures useful in all types of bronchial asthma which help to reduce the intensity and frequency of symptoms.

Dress. The head, hands, and feet should be well protected against chilling in cold weather. Men and boys do well to wear mufflers, hats, lined gloves, wool socks; women and girls should keep heads covered, wear warm scarves, lined gloves, and flesh-colored lisle understockings beneath their nylons.

Ventilation. Damp or excessively chilled air in the bedroom on cold nights should be avoided. Bedroom windows should be kept closed, with a door ajar into an adjoining room with window open. Parched, dry air in the home should be avoided. An electric humidifier is valuable. Short of that, pans or trays of water can be kept on radiators.

Food. Eat moderately, slowly, never after 7:00 P.M. If possible, the major meal should come at midday rather than in the evening. A 30-minute rest period after dinner and supper is advisable. Overtaxing the digestion with excessive food encourages asthma.

Tobacco. The patient with bronchial asthma should never smoke.

Drink. Cocktails before dinner may provide relaxation and enjoyment. But drinking after dinner, late in the evening, may interfere with digestion, lead to abdominal distention, wakefulness, and asthma.

Constipation. It is important for the asthmatic to avoid this, by drinking no less than six glasses of water daily and eating a fair share of fruits and vegetables (see page 226).

Chemical odors. Asthmatic attacks may be triggered or aggravated by such fumes as those from fresh varnishes and paints, moth balls, and dry-cleaning fluids.

Exertion. Excessive fatigue, mental or physical, from work or play, should be avoided.

Patients who are subject to frequent bronchial infections should ask their doctor about taking antibiotics on a prophylactic basis during the months when they tend to get such infections. If there is obvious sinus infection, it should be treated.

When asthma is severe enough to make the doctor worry about possible development of emphysema, the patient should learn exercises which have helped many asthmatics improve exchange of air. The exercises given below take patience. It may be necessary for the patient to receive instruction in them from a specialist in asthma.

The primary purpose of these breathing exercises is to teach the asthmatic to exhale completely, letting stale air out of the lower part of the lungs, making room for fresh air to enter and fill the lungs. The exercises also tend to build up breathing muscles and increase their power. They assist, too, in loosening up muscles of shoulders, upper chest, and abdominal wall.

1. To develop abdominal or diaphragmatic breathing, lie on the back with knees drawn up. Place the hands on the upper abdomen, exhale, and let the hands sink in and contract the abdominal muscles. Then take a short breath, relax the abdominal muscles, making certain the upper part of the chest does not move during the process.

2. Also for abdominal breathing, sit on a firm bed or hard chair with the back supported. Place hands over lower ribs and, while breathing out or exhaling, contract the abdominal muscles. At the end of the exhaling, squeeze the ribs to push out any remaining air. Next, relax the abdomen and take a short breath while the lower ribs move out.

3. Breathing with the lips held close together is valuable since the greater effort required to let air out exercises the diaphragm, abdominal muscles, and lower rib muscles. For variety, you can achieve the same purpose by blowing bits of paper across a table, blowing bubbles in water through a straw, and even by whistling or humming.

4. Sit with feet apart and arms hanging down loosely, bend the body forward until the head is at knee level —at the same time breathing out, keeping abdominal muscles contracted. Then sit up and inhale.

5. To loosen shoulders, stand with feet apart and circle both arms so they cross each other in front of the face.

6. As a relaxing exercise, sit on a chair, shrug your shoulders quickly, then relax them, letting the arms hang down, and head, shoulders, and back sag.

After you have worked for a time with these exercises, you can add others which are more advanced.

1. Lie back on a firm bed with knees drawn up, arms limp at the sides. Exhale as you rise and bend forward to place the head between the knees. Inhale as you slowly sink back to the starting position. Rest for a moment and breathe out quickly, using abdominal muscles. Inhale before resuming the exercise. Rest, breathing normally and allowing only the upper part of the abdomen and lower portion of the rib cage to move.

2. Stand with feet apart and arms elevated almost to top-of-head level, with fists clenched, and elbows well back. Bend shoulders and neck to one side, with the corresponding arm going to side of body in direction of bend. Use fist of opposite arm to help push head down. Repeat in opposite direction. Do three times in each direction.

3. Sit with feet well apart. With right hand over ribs on right side, bend to right, breathing out and pushing hand into ribs. Inhale while resuming original position. Do the same in the opposite direction. Repeat about half a dozen times.

4. Stand with back, shoulders, and head braced against a wall, with feet about six inches in front of body. While exhaling, bend down slowly—

first head, then shoulders and back, with arms hanging limply. Inhale while resuming erect position—first body, then shoulders, then head.

5. Stand with feet apart and, while inhaling, lift arms above head. Bend slowly over to right as far as possible, while exhaling. While bending, twist body counterclockwise so arms are eventually outside the right foot. During bending, exhale slowly, contracting muscles of the abdomen. Raise body and turn back to normal position while inhaling. Repeat in opposite direction. Do this about four times in each direction.

These exercises have the additional value of making it easier for an asthmatic patient to breathe during an actual attack.

Until the advent of modern medications, patients with disabling asthma often were advised to move to the Southwest or southern California. But a move can be a serious matter and may involve increased emotional tension, which can negate any gain from better climate. If circumstances are favorable, a change may indeed be helpful. Usually, it is advisable that at least a year's trial be made for a child or wife before the father/husband gives up his job and makes the move. For the wage earner, it is best to get a leave of absence to make sure the new location is truly helpful. In the new locale, the patient should obtain advice from a specialist in asthma or allergy about where it may be best to live. In the greater Los Angeles area, for example, there are locations where asthmatics do well and other areas where they do not improve.

When an asthma patient finds that an attack is not yielding to the usual medication, or that attacks are getting more severe and prolonged, he should notify his doctor. The change may signal status asthmaticus.

An asthmatic who becomes depressed by his illness—and people vary greatly in their reaction to labored breathing—should receive psychotherapy if he wishes it. With such therapy, some asthmatics are aided in adopting a more cheerful attitude, and some find that psychotherapy helps reduce severity and frequency of attacks.

PRIMARY PREVENTION. Effective desensitization to pollens that cause hay fever helps to reduce the risk of developing asthmatic reactions to these substances. So, too, avoidance of food allergens that may produce allergic upsets for a given individual. Some allergists suggest that, as a precaution, children of allergic parents should not be given eggs and other commonly allergenic foods during the first year of life and should not be exposed to wool. Also, each new food should be introduced in small quantity and increased slowly in amount. It is believed that a child can build up tolerance for small amounts of new foods but might be made allergic by sudden introduction of large amounts.

LOW BACK PAIN

Some physicians believe that almost every American over the age of 40 experiences some degree of pain in the lower back.

The lower part of the spinal column does not have the support of the rib cage as does the upper part. The spine is made up of vertebrae. Between the bodies of the vertebral bones are disks which act as shock absorbers. Ligaments bind the bones together. And, finally, muscles of the lower back and of the abdomen as well are designed to give the spinal column support.

Young people who are vigorous in sports and physical activities rarely are troubled by backache unless there is a direct injury. It is usually the person who gradually has lost physical fitness, whose supporting muscles have weakened, who has put on excess poundage, and who has developed poor posture, who is a candidate for low back pain.

Many persons erroneously ascribe backache to "kidney trouble" and waste money on medicines to "flush" the kidneys. Similarly, the uterus has been blamed by many women for their backache. Only rarely is a malpositioned womb the cause.

Acute Low Back Pain

This may be produced by a fall, blow, lifting a heavy weight, pushing a car, shoveling snow, etc., or there may appear to be no cause. The pain is usually severe and there is difficulty in walking and standing. Most acute attacks yield completely, or show decided improvement, after a few days of complete rest in bed with a very firm mattress, preferably with a bed board under it (the board should be about six inches smaller than the mattress so sheets can be tucked in, and so no one will bump against it). Aspirin is helpful, but the doctor may prescribe a stronger pain reliever such as Darvon, Demerol, or codeine. Many muscle-relaxant medications are advocated for relief of the muscle spasm which contributes so much to pain. It is doubtful that they live up to their claims. Muscle spasm will be helped by warm, moist packs which should be changed frequently to maintain warmth (and should not be scalding

hot, since excessive heat can induce muscle spasm). A bath in comfortably warm water is helpful if there is no problem about getting into and out of the bath. A soothing way to apply warmth to the back is to have the patient sit on a stool or waterproof chair set in the bathtub; place a large towel over the shoulders and upper back; and have the shower trickle comfortably warm water onto the towel and down to the painful area in the low back. When done for 15 to 20 minutes at a time several times a day, this can be very helpful.

If an attack of low back pain is so severe that there is inability to sleep, or if there is urgency about shortening the attack, then a short stay in a hospital may be helpful. In the hospital, strong pain relievers can be given by injection; this helps not only to reduce suffering but to stop muscle spasm. The hospital's specialist in backache (an orthopedist) will usually arrange for traction apparatus.

After an attack has ended, it may still be necessary for the patient to wear a supportive corset or brace which should be prescribed by the doctor. Its fit also should be checked by him. After a time, it will usually be found that the brace may be needed only when traveling or during periods of extra stress.

If complete healing does not occur, the doctor will need to investigate the back in the same way as described below for chronic backache.

Chronic Low Back Pain

This is the condition that makes life miserable part or all of the time for millions of people. Yet it is, in almost every instance, unnecessary and preventable.

First, there should be a commonsense review of causes. The typist who sits with poor posture in a rickety chair with an air conditioner blowing on her back will get relief by eliminating these three predisposing factors. The mother with a busy schedule of work and with children to lift may need to lie down for a short time every three or four hours, or to take a relaxing bath in the middle of the day. We remember a young mother who weighed 96 pounds and had a miserable backache. She had been carrying around her 22-pound child frequently because the child was fretful from prolonged teething. The cure was evident.

A backache sufferer must sleep on a firm hard mattress, as mentioned earlier. Also, the car seat should be firm or a backrest should be used. At home, a hard chair that provides back support should be used in place of a soft, well-worn upholstered chair.

Wobbly feet put a strain on the back, and women in particular should wear comfortable, strong shoes with reasonable heels when working and walking.

Some backaches are aggravated by a cold bed and strong drafts from windows. An electric blanket is a good investment. The bedroom should be kept warm enough for comfort, and drafts and streams of cold air from windows should be avoided. In winter, enough air will leak in around most windows to provide ventilation.

Weekend backache occurs in people who lead sedentary lives throughout the week and then plunge into excessive activity on weekends.

Obesity with its constant pull on the back can also be the reason for back pain.

Part of a commonsense inventory of possible causes should include noting whether backaches come on after sexual intercourse. If so, a change to an easier position (see page 398) may help until the back has been reconditioned.

If the preceding suggested investigation fails to turn up an obvious cause which, when corrected, relieves the pain, then the basis for the pain is most likely muscle weakness and/or imbalance, or excess emotional tension, or a combination of the two.

However, before going in for a program of strengthening muscles that support the back or trying to reduce nervous tension, there should be a complete checkup of the back by your doctor or an orthopedist or other back specialist (some internists and general practitioners are skilled in examining and treating backs). It is possible that some organic problem is causing the back pain—e.g., arthritis, a spine infection, a muscle or nerve disease, a tumor.

Once it is established that there is no organic cause, then attention can be focused on achieving good physical fitness. This means discussing with the doctor how to achieve optimum weight and good posture. Then a program of general exercise should be agreed upon, and also a set of exercises to strengthen the lower back. Usually, the doctor prescribes a few basic exercises which strengthen not only the back muscles but also the large muscles of the abdominal wall. He may also give instruction in how to relax certain muscles which may be too tense and are constantly pulling on the lower back. Such muscles may even be located in back of the thighs—for example, the hamstrings which you can feel behind the knees.

If nervous tension is contributing to the backache, emotional problems should be freely ventilated with the doctor. If the problems warrant, a visit to a psychotherapist is surely worth the effort if it will prevent days, months, and even years of nagging back pain.

During the period of reconditioning, the doctor will prescribe a pain reliever, relaxing warm applications or warm baths, and possibly a tranquilizer to help quiet nervous tensions. Use of a brace or corset may be helpful until muscles are strengthened sufficiently so they act again as nature's own brace and support.

Our chapters on exercise, diet, and mental health contain material that you may well find helpful in preventing backache if you are reaching the susceptible age.

BONE DISEASES

Osteoporosis and Osteomalacia

Beginning at about age 50, it is not unusual for people to note a slight diminution of height every few years. It is well known, too, that bones tend to become more brittle and to be more prone to fracture as we pass from the middle years to the later years.

Both the slight height reduction and tendency to bone brittleness result from a process called osteoporosis (literally, softening of the bones) which occurs with aging. Bones that are osteoporotic contain the same individual minerals and proteins but they are less dense than younger bones. Hence, they are more likely to be compressed (resulting in height loss) or broken. While x-rays do not invariably reveal the presence of osteoporosis, it is not uncommon for the condition to be first identified on a routine x-ray film. One rather common x-ray finding in osteoporosis is compression and fracture of a vertebra which may cause mild back pain but does not endanger the spinal cord.

Osteoporosis is not limited to the later years. Other causes which a physician must consider include:

1. Steroid medications which may produce osteoporotic changes even in very young patients when administered for prolonged periods.
2. Lack of stress. Bones begin to weaken when they are not subjected to normal stresses such as those exerted by muscles and by the pull of gravity. Astronauts, as the result of exposure to gravity-free environment, have shown early changes of osteoporosis. More commonly, such changes may stem from immobilization because of illness or the casting of a fractured bone. Osteoporosis also may become apparent after a stroke when muscles in a limb fall into disuse.
3. A diet low in calcium and protein. These are the basic building blocks of bone, and a diet deficient in them will eventually lead to weakening of bones.
4. Cancer, when it spreads to bone, weakens the intrinsic structure.
5. Menopause apparently hastens the development of osteoporosis, and many women past the menopause exhibit bone changes (see page 618).

What can be done to prevent osteoporosis and to treat it should it occur?

Prolonged immobilization should be avoided. If it cannot be, exercises to maintain muscle tone and stress on bone are of value. Almost every hospital today has a physical therapist to administer such exercises as a precaution. Orthopedists instruct patients with casts to manipulate and exercise the muscles as much as possible while a fractured extremity is immobilized.

A well-balanced diet helps those with osteoporosis from nutritional deficiencies. Calcium supplementation may be helpful in some cases. Currently, too, dietary supplementation with fluoride is being investigated and may prove to be of value. Estrogen therapy for postmenopausal women may be very helpful (see Menopause, page 618).

A program of regular physical activity as approved by a physician, especially after retirement from work, coupled with good nutrition, avoidance of undue physical stress, and reasonable precautions against accidents represents a well-balanced approach to the prevention of osteoporosis.

Softening of bones in children (rickets) has largely been eradicated through vitamin D supplementation in the diet. A somewhat comparable condition in adults, called osteomalacia, may be the result of poor calcium absorption or excess calcium loss. Usually, the basic cause of osteomalacia is an intestinal disorder such as chronic diarrhea or malabsorption, or a kidney disorder, and the basic cause requires treatment.

Osteomyelitis

With modern treatment, bone infection (osteomyelitis) no longer is the disabling disorder it so often was in the past. But every physician approaching a bone infection does so with respect, realizing that it may still be no easy infection to cure completely.

Infection of bone is often difficult to drain—and this is a primary treatment of any localized infection. Also, since most bones have a relatively poor blood supply, natural body defenses against infection, which are circulated by the blood, have a more difficult time reaching a trouble area.

Bone infection may result from injury to a bone, such as a compound fracture, or the entrance of a foreign body, or from spread of infection from elsewhere in the body. If acute bone infection is not treated effectively, the infection may become chronic. With chronic osteomyelitis, the bone is weakened and made more subject to fracture, pus may be discharged chronically through the skin, the body's reserves are drained by the constant need to fight the infection, and there may be considerable pain and discomfort.

For these reasons, any attack of severe bone pain and fever—usually it occurs in a child or young adult—needs quick evaluation and therapy. An effort will be made to identify the causative organisms and select an antibiotic suitable for combatting them. In addition, surgery to drain the infected area may be required.

Surgery is often an indispensable adjunct to antibiotic treatment in cases of chronic bone infection. Dead and dying tissue which serve as the nidus, or nest, for continuing infection must be removed. Occasionally it is difficult to remove all the infected or dead tissue located in and around the bone, and repeated surgery may be required. In some instances, chronic osteomyelitis may be present for years, with alternating periods of quiescence and activity, and intensive therapy is needed to effect a cure.

When bone has been severely weakened by chronic infection, it may be necessary to provide support for it with plates and pins or bone grafts in order to avoid repeated fractures and to allow normal function.

Scoliosis

Scoliosis means abnormal curvature of the spine. A minor degree of it is present in a large proportion of all people, in whom it is usually barely noticeable and does not interfere with posture and function.

Two important causes of severe scoliosis in the past—polio and tuberculosis—have been minimized in recent years. Polio may lead to scoliosis if muscles on one side of the body are weakened to a greater extent than on the other side. When this occurs, the stronger muscles pull harder on the spine than the weaker ones, leading to curvature. Tuberculosis may affect the spine, leading to an imbalance of the bony spinal column.

Scoliosis may be the result of a congenital defect, such as absence of half of a vertebra. It may develop for unknown reasons, usually between the ages of 5 and 15, and most often in girls. Sometimes, unequal leg length or faulty function of a hip joint can unbalance the spine, leading to curvature.

Scoliosis can progress rapidly, particularly the type that affects young girls. Therefore, it should be brought to a physician's attention as soon as possible. The physician is most concerned about whether the curvature is progressing, and if so how fast.

If the cause of the scoliosis is unequal leg length, treatment may require nothing more than use of a shoe lift for the shorter leg. Most cases of scoliosis are minor and require little if any treatment. But when treatment is needed, it should be supervised by a specialist in bone problems, an orthopedist.

X-ray studies of the spine with careful measurement of the degree of curvature is an important step in evaluation of the scoliosis. If the scoliosis is of the type which, if unchecked, may progress to become a serious deformity, it may not only interfere with normal posture and gait but also lead eventually to compromising of lung function, since the chest wall on one side may be compressed.

Treatment should be begun without delay. The further the spine is deformed, the longer corrective measures will be needed. Recent advances have made treatment of scoliosis more effective and less inconvenient as well. The Milwaukee brace, a device designed to gradually reposition the curved spine, is particularly effective. It is essential that an experienced technician measure and fit the brace and an orthopedist supervise the wearing. Another method of treatment is to cast the spine so as to gently nudge it into normal position. Most children adapt readily to several months of treatment with brace or cast. Surgery may be avoided in this way.

With age, the spinal column becomes less pliable and bracing or casting may be insufficient to correct a deformity. Several surgical procedures are of value. One of the most outstanding is the insertion of special rods, called Harrington rods, in the back muscles, one on either side of and connected to the spinal column. One rod pushes up on the shortened side of the spine while the other pulls the longer side. Once the spine is correctly aligned, surgical fusion of bones of the spine secures the alignment.

Fractures

Fractures of bone are not uncommon occurrences today, with accident rates on the highway and in the home increasing, and with people living longer and becoming more subject to osteoporosis. Primary prevention requires accident prevention at home, on the job, on the road. It also involves prevention and treatment of osteoporosis.

The seriousness of any fracture depends upon the particular bone involved, the extent of damage to the bone, and also whether or not adjacent structures are injured. An important preventive first-aid principle for fractures or suspected fractures (soreness, swelling, and severe pain on motion at the site of the injury) is immediate immobilization of the limb with splints so fractured bone ends do not move farther out of place and damage adjacent structures.

One of the first things a doctor does in examining a suspected fractured limb is to feel for arterial pulses farther down the extremity from the fractured site. Sometimes bone may compress or tear an artery. Absence of pulses is an indication that treatment must be started immediately to reduce the compression or stop the bleeding. Sometimes a great deal of blood may be lost from a fracture, especially a hip fracture.

X-rays help assess the location and severity of a fracture. Testing the extremity for intactness of sensation will indicate whether there has been any injury to nerves.

Bones can be broken and the ends may still remain aligned. This is called *simple* fracture. Alternatively, the ends may be misaligned. If broken edges of bone pierce the skin, the fracture is called *compound* and is more serious, since the risk of infection is increased.

Treatment is directed at realigning broken pieces and securing the alignment so the ends can grow together. Bone misalignment interferes with natural muscular balance and can impair limb function.

Realignment often can be achieved by closed manipulation and application of a cast. Sometimes, however, as in many fractures of hip, forearm, and upper arm, extra support may be needed to insure that the bone knits together. Such support may be provided by operative placement of plates and screws or nails, or occasionally by bone grafts.

Simple fractures can often be treated by a general practitioner. But most fractures should be evaluated and treated by an orthopedist, who will decide on the need for operative or nonoperative measures.

Bone requires six or more weeks to heal, and during this time proper alignment is maintained by a plaster cast. Although the fractured bone must be immobilized if it is to heal properly, muscles that normally move the immobilized part must be kept limber and strong. Special exercises achieve this.

Doctors also pay close attention to the cast itself, making certain it is neither too snug nor too loose. Too tight a fit can lead to compression of the blood supply to the extremity. Fingertips and toes are left uncovered by a cast so the physician can judge the status of blood supply from skin color. Too loose a fit of the cast can allow movement of the fractured bone and misalignment. X-rays after application of the cast can be used to check proper alignment.

As mentioned earlier, prolonged immobilization weakens bone and muscle. Therefore, return to normal functioning as soon as possible is encouraged.

BREAST DISEASES

The breast is an important part of the female reproductive system. And, like internal reproductive organs, it is dependent to an extent on the level of hormone activity. This is exemplified by changes in size and consistency of breast tissue during the menstrual cycle and during pregnancy as hormonal levels change.

The breast is made up of glandular tissue arranged in a complicated pattern of lobes. The milk ducts lead into the nipple at the approximate center of the lobes.

The breast is subject to a number of disorders that are difficult to differentiate by physical examination alone, since they most commonly take the form of a lump or mass. The lump may be a benign growth, a cyst, or a cancer. Since primary prevention for any of these conditions is limited, early detection of a lump and identification of its nature are an important preventive measure.

Self-examination of the breasts at least once a month, at the end of the menstrual cycle (after the monthly flow) when the breasts are normally soft, is an excellent means of early detection. Women who feel that they cannot adequately perform self-examination can make arrangements with their doctor for a brief monthly examination. The technique of self-examination is described on page 559.

Of course, examination of the breast is an important part of a regular physical examination. In many cases, when a mass is found, the physician can determine if it is benign through history and examination. Among other things, he will consider the age of the patient; breast cancer is rare below age 20 and quite uncommon until the 40's. Any pain and fluctuation in size of the lump usually indicate that the cause is benign cystic change of glandular tissue. Some women are prone to recurrent breast cysts, a condition referred to as chronic cystic mastitis or benign cystic disease (see below). Nipple discharge, with or without a lump, is almost always indicative of a benign growth. The physician also will consider the consistency of the mass, whether it is well demarcated, and whether there are skin changes over the area.

In most cases, when there is any doubt as to the nature of the suspicious mass, the physician will remove it for microscopic examination. This will resolve doubts and fears of both doctor and patient. The surgery is minor even though it is usually done under general anesthesia.

Mammography—special x-ray study —is usually reserved for special situations. Mammography is often more accurate than physical examination but less accurate than biopsy. A skilled radiologist is needed to read these x-rays. Newer radiological techniques promise to make the x-rays easier to read and may help to make the test more feasible for screening purposes. Mammography often helps in cases where the physician feels that the lump is not cancerous but would like additional supportive evidence. It is also employed when many cysts are present in a breast, making it difficult to detect a new mass. Mammography often is helpful when a lump is difficult to feel and outline clearly, or when there is persistent pain in one breast. It is often used routinely for women who have a strong family history of breast cancer or who have had a cancer removed from one breast, since they may have a higher-than-average risk of developing breast cancer.

Many women between the ages of 30 and 50 have benign cystic disease of the breast. The condition is characterized by dilatation and cyst formation in the glandular tissue, perhaps connected with estrogen secretion. There does not seem to be any relationship between cystic disease and cancer development, but many physicians will not prescribe estrogen-containing medications (such as birth control pills) for women with cystic disease, because there is a tendency with such medications for the cysts to become larger and more numerous, making cancer more difficult to detect.

The most common lump in the breast of a woman less than age 30 is a fibroadenoma. This is usually an isolated and well-demarcated lump. It may grow to large size and cause pain. Treatment is removal of the mass to make certain that it is not cancerous.

Early detection and prompt treatment are vital for winning out over cancer of the breast. If the cancer is removed before it has spread to local lymph tissue, the five-year cure rate is 75 to 90 percent; e.g., 75 to 90 percent of patients are alive and well at the end of five years. If removed after such spread, the cure rate is in the 50 percent range. At present, the recommended treatment is radical mastectomy—removal of all breast tissue and adjacent lymph nodes. Most women withstand the surgery well. There are often emotional upsets because of the psychological significance of the breast, and the patient may require counseling. There are many prosthetic devices—artificial breasts—to conceal deformity.

If cancer has spread, much still can be done to prolong life and make the patient comfortable. Radiotherapy can be of value and is often used after surgery as an aid to effecting a cure. Hormone treatment is sometimes helpful for those with metastases (cancer growths spread elsewhere) that are causing discomfort. In some cases, removal of the ovaries and/or the adrenal glands may be called for as a means of producing hormonal changes that may be helpful. The decision on suitable treatment for the individual patient is often difficult, and the physician caring for the patient may require the advice of a specialist, usually a surgeon with extensive experience with this disease.

Women who develop cancer in one breast will sometimes develop cancer in the other. Also, women with a strong family history of breast cancer are at higher risk. Therefore, they should have more frequent examinations by their physician along with mammography studies.

Simple mastectomy—removal of the breast tissue without removal of the lymph nodes as in radical mastectomy—is rarely employed for cancer. It sometimes may be used, however, for cystic mastitis after repeated biopsies of cysts over several years because the physician fears he may miss a possible hidden cancer.

At present, there is intensive and, in the opinion of many experts, highly promising research into many aspects of cancer—causes, new detection methods, and new methods of treatment.

Men rarely get breast cancer, but it is nevertheless a possibility. Any breast lump in a man should be biopsied.

See the section on cancer concerning the question of removal of breasts as a means of primary prevention of cancer.

For some women, breast size is a matter of concern. Exercises can help tone muscles adjacent to breast tissue and may help to make the breasts appear larger. Augmentation mammoplasty is an operation in which material, sometimes silicone, is added to the breasts, to increase their size. It is not a minor operation and should be performed only by an experienced plastic surgeon after thorough discussion of the pros and cons. Surgery is available for the removal of excess breast tissue and the correction of pendulous breasts.

CHRONIC BRONCHITIS AND EMPHYSEMA

Most people are aware of the serious problem of cancer of the lung. But the major single cause of disability of pulmonary origin in the United States is not lung cancer but emphysema. In and of itself, emphysema causes a significant number of deaths each year. In addition it is often a contributing factor to deaths occurring after surgery, deaths from heart disease, from other lung diseases, and from many other disorders.

Emphysema and chronic bronchitis are ailments for which preventive medicine has particular relevance for two reasons:

1. They take a long time to develop into destructive, disabling diseases. In part, this is due to the tremendous reserve possessed by the lungs. There often has to be 50 to 75 percent deterioration of lung function before such symptoms as shortness of breath and wheezing become manifest.

2. Many factors are known to predispose to emphysema and bronchitis. Chief among them is cigarette smoking. It is rare for the disorders to occur among those who have never smoked cigarettes, and often severity of disease is directly related to the number of cigarettes smoked.

Recent evidence indicates that cigarette smoking for even a short period affects health adversely. It has been shown, for example, that adolescents, with not many years of smoking behind them, have increased respiratory problems such as cough and colds, and take more sick leave than nonsmokers. There is also experimental evidence of the harmful effects of smoking in animals in which lung changes mimicking those of human chronic bronchitis and emphysema have been produced by exposure to cigarette smoke.

Air pollution and exposure to industrial fumes of certain types increase the severity of respiratory symptoms. It is well known that patients with chronic bronchitis and emphysema can become severely ill when there are high levels of air pollution.

Recently, an inherited defect in the production of a certain enzyme has been detected in some patients with emphysema. It is particularly common among those who are seriously affected by the disorder at a younger age than most. The finding may have important implications. If a simple screening test can be developed to disclose the enzyme defect, individuals particularly susceptible to emphysema could be identified and firmly counseled against smoking and against jobs in industries that would expose them to irritating fumes, dusts, or excessive smog.

At present, advice for primary prevention is limited to the admonition: "If you don't smoke, don't start, and if you do, stop as soon as possible."

Detection of emphysema and chronic bronchitis is complicated by the insidious nature of these diseases. They may take a long time to produce symptoms, and by the time they do, much damage has been done. There are certain clues, however, that make the physician suspicious that a patient may be showing early signs of chronic bronchitis or emphysema. One is a history of chronic "cigarette cough," usually worse in the morning on arising and frequently productive of sputum. Another is a history of frequent respiratory infections which are severe and take long to resolve. There are other possible clues: on physical examination, the physician may detect some wheezing after forced expiration or may find an increase in chest diameter ("barrel chest"). Not everyone with such symptoms and signs necessarily has emphysema or chronic bronchitis, but the physician may suspect that this is the likely diagnosis if there is no past history of asthma, other lung or heart disease, and if there is a smoking history of ten or more years' duration. By making use of certain simple lung function tests (spirography), the physician can confirm the diagnosis.

While chest x-rays may not reveal emphysema until the disease is well along, the routine yearly or semiannual physical checkup is the time for detection of symptoms and signs that indicate that emphysema may be present —and with early detection, appropriate measures can be taken to prevent worsening. All too often it is severe shortness of breath or severe respiratory infection that brings the emphysema patient to the doctor for the first time—at a point when much damage may already have been done.

Are chronic bronchitis and emphysema different diseases? When lung tissue is examined under the microscope, a distinction can be made. But during life, the distinction is hazy because the two problems so often coexist. For this reason, they are frequently described together under the name of "chronic obstructive lung disease" (COLD) or "chronic obstructive pulmonary emphysema" (COPE). The word "obstructive," which appears in both names, refers to the changes that occur in the air passages (the bronchi and bronchioles) which conduct air to the lung areas where oxygen is exchanged for carbon dioxide.

The bronchi and bronchioles serve as a first line of defense against infection. They have special cells that destroy invading organisms. They also have cells that produce mucus to trap foreign material. The mucus is washed up to the throat where it is swallowed or eliminated through the mouth and nose. Cigarette smoke impairs these mechanisms and particularly hampers proper elimination of mucus from the bronchi and bronchioles. As a result, chronic infection sets in, destroying or weakening and narrowing the bronchioles. Retained mucus acts to narrow the air passages, too, making cough less efficient, and leading to further mucus retention and narrowing of bronchioles.

As a result of this obstruction and distortion of lung architecture, a greater force is required to expel air. This puts abnormal strain on the walls of the alveoli, where oxygen and carbon dioxide are exchanged. If a balloon is inflated to moderate size and immediately deflated, it will return to original size and shape. But if left overdistended for a few hours, it will develop wrinkles. So it is with the alveoli: abnormally high and prolonged pressure overdistends and finally disrupts them. Moreover, unnaturally high pressure in the lungs tends to compress blood routes to the lungs, further impairing oxygen–carbon dioxide exchange. In emphysema, the patient must produce positive pressure to force air through the narrowed and compressed bronchi and bronchioles; in effect, he must squeeze air from his chest.

The stage of mucus collection and chronic inflammation is called chronic bronchitis; the stage in which alveoli are destroyed is called emphysema. During the chronic bronchitis phase, the patient may have persistent cough and sputum production; it is when the alveoli become compromised that shortness of breath sets in. In certain instances, chronic bronchitis does not go on to produce emphysema, but this is the exception rather than the rule. Similarly, some individuals suffer from emphysema predominantly with little or none of the changes of chronic bronchitis.

Senile emphysema is a term that refers to a normal aging process in which the normal elasticity of the lung is somewhat diminished. By itself, this causes little or no difficulty. However, it does make the problems of chronic bronchitis and emphysema more severe.

The complete scenario for obstructive lung disease is one that a physician can visualize easily enough but it is one that, as we have already suggested, is not readily apparent to the patient in its early phases. In the beginning, there may be persistent cough and repeated respiratory infections, sometimes complicated by pneumonia. Gradually, infections become more severe and disabling for longer periods as the disease process progresses. It may take ten years or more before the symptoms of cough and sputum production trouble the patient.

Shortness of breath and wheezing will sooner or later become evident, progressively limiting activity. But these indications may take as few as five years or as many as thirty years to develop. In cases of pure emphysema, they may not be preceded by the hypersecretion of mucus and repeated infections that are the hallmarks of chronic bronchitis.

Later in the disease, heart failure may develop because of the strain on the heart which must try to pump blood through the vessels of the diseased lungs.

The earlier that secondary preventive measures are instituted, the better. Among the most important of these measures are elimination of cigarette smoking and avoidance of irritating fumes. The latter may require staying indoors on days of severe pollution and installation of air filtering devices in the home.

Colds and minor respiratory infections will be treated vigorously to try to avoid serious lung infection. In some instances, antibiotic treatment will be needed continuously. Flu shots will also be given prophylactically.

Exercises may be prescribed for developing muscles ordinarily not used for breathing. These muscles can help increase breathing effectiveness.

Great pains will be taken to drain mucus from the lungs because trapped secretions are an excellent medium for bacterial growth and infection. Methods of promoting drainage of mucus through positioning of the body have been shown to be of value.

Special medicines that help liquefy thick secretions or help keep bronchioles open are often employed. In some cases, periodic treatment with machines that push air into the lungs (intermittent positive-pressure breathing, or IPPB) to help open collapsed areas in order to drain mucous collections or prevent their formation is extremely valuable. IPPB is an important therapeutic aid and is used extensively in-hospital to deliver medications that help keep air passages open in acutely ill bronchitis or emphysema patients.

Surgeons and anesthesiologists are particularly concerned about emphysema because there is a tendency, during anesthesia and in the postoperative period, not to breathe as deeply and efficiently as normal. IPPB treatments and special medications may be started before surgery to get the lungs into optimum condition.

Obstructive lung disease is a serious problem, but far from a hopeless one. With vigorously used secondary preventive measures, patients can feel better and much can be done to prevent or retard progression of the disease.

Milder forms of chronic bronchitis and emphysema can be handled by the general practitioner or internist. More advanced cases should be under the care of specialists and specialty clinics which have been and are being established at most hospitals. Special equipment and specially trained personnel are needed to treat emphysema, to instruct the patient in how to treat himself, how to prevent worsening of symptoms, and when to recognize that symptoms may require more intensive care than can be given at home.

Chronic bronchitis and emphysema at present call for long-term care, initially perhaps by a specialty clinic, then later by more routine means. Your physician is best able to evaluate when specialty care is needed.

Emotional support for patients with any chronic ailment is an essential element in proper therapy. Emphysema clinics provide this by offering the opportunity to meet other people with the same disability as well as by the encouragement offered by the trained personnel administering treatments and teaching the patient how to live with the disorder.

It can be expected that with optimum therapy only severe or moderately severe cases of emphysema will need periods of hospitalization.

Tertiary prevention also holds some promise for the future. Lung transplants or the removal of severely diseased sections of the lung may prove beneficial. At present, surgery is considered only in cases where air collects in one section of a lung, forming cyst-like structures which may compress remaining lung areas or which may rupture and cause pneumothorax (air collection between chest wall and lung).

BRUCELLOSIS (UNDULANT FEVER)

Brucellosis is so named because it results from infection by germs of the *Brucella* genus of organisms. It is also called undulant fever because the fever it produces tends to undulate in waves rather than stay constant. Swine and cattle transmit it. There is one form, called Malta fever, transmitted by goats.

The disease comes on slowly, with fever, chills, and sweats. There may be joint and muscle pain and enlargement of the lymph nodes of the neck and armpits. The fever comes and goes. It is generally highest at night. It may last for years if the disease is not diagnosed early and treated vigorously.

Absolute diagnosis is made by finding brucella organisms in the blood, urine, cerebrospinal fluid, bile, and tissues. If the organisms cannot be found, then less absolute diagnostic tests include blood serum agglutination, skin tests, and examination of the number and type of white blood cells. Sometimes diagnosis is very difficult and may rest on the response to treatment.

A person ill with brucellosis rarely affects another person, in contrast to animals which readily transmit the disease from one to another. Also, brucellosis of the abortus type, which causes spontaneous abortions in cattle, does not cause loss of the baby in human pregnancies.

The outlook, or scenario, for this disease is very good in terms of mortality but not always so happy in terms of chronicity and debility. However, when diagnosis is made early and treatment started with antibiotics such as streptomycin, the tetracyclines, and chloromycetin, about 75 percent of patients can expect to be cured in three to six months, and most of the remainder will be well within a year.

There can be serious complications arising as a result of neglect or inadequate treatment. They include infection of a joint, heart infection, meningitis, and encephalitis.

Primary prevention depends upon understanding how the disease is spread from infected animals to humans. Infected fluids, secretions, and tissues of an animal may transmit the germs through an abrasion of the skin. This is how meat handlers, farmers, and veterinarians usually become infected. The other chief mode of transmission is through infected cow's or goat's milk.

Thus, primary prevention requires using gloves to handle infected or potentially infected swine, cattle, and goats, and frequent washing of hands and arms. Workers in the meat industry should learn all details of protection from the company physician or nurse or their own private physician. For avoiding transmission through milk, there is one absolute rule: use only pasteurized milk and milk products. It is a wise farmer who refuses to use his own milk unless he has the facilities for home pasteurization; otherwise, he does better to purchase milk at a store after it has left the farm and been commercially pasteurized.

Another important preventive measure is increased testing of susceptible animals for the disease, and destruction or segregation of the infected ones. Young calves can be vaccinated against *Brucella* germs.

BURSITIS

A bursa is a thin sac or pouch located around a joint. It contains a small amount of lubricating fluid and aids in making joint motion smooth and gliding. This delicate structure is subject to both acute and chronic inflammation. Rarely, it may be infected by fungi, tuberculosis organisms, or syphilis spirochetes.

Inflammation of a bursa may be traceable sometimes to a general body disorder such as gout. By far the most common cause, however, is excessive or improper use of the adjacent joint. The bursas deep in the shoulder are most commonly affected, but almost any bursa in any joint in the body may become inflamed, and some of these inflammatory conditions have earned special names such as "tennis elbow" and "housemaid's knee."

In an acute attack of bursa inflammation (bursitis), there is great pain when any effort is made to move the joint. The joint area is tender, warm, and often boggy. Muscles in the area are tense and spastic. The bursa may contain enough fluid to be felt or seen as an enlarged sac.

Complete rest for the joint—in a sling or on pillows—is a primary part of treatment. Of course, this is easy for a doctor to recommend but often difficult for a patient to agree to. A worker wants to earn a living; an athlete wants to get back into the lineup the next day; a ballet dancer with painful bursitis of hip or knee wants to perform as soon as possible.

So the physician seldom can use the simple, conservative method for treating acute bursitis. That method consists of rest for several days; aspirin for relief of pain, usually with some codeine, Darvon, or Demerol added; and alternating cold and warm compresses to determine whether cold or warmth provides most relief (usually dry heat is not helpful in the acute phase of bursitis). These measures are followed, as soon as acute pain subsides, with gentle exercise for the joint to prevent formation of adhesions which may lead to chronic disability.

The patient, however, usually demands quick relief. He has heard of "miracles" from injection or manipulation of the joint, or use of x-ray or diathermy. So the family physician—or the orthopedic or other specialist he may refer the patient to—will generally attempt to relieve pain and disability by reaching the inflamed bursa with a needle, under local anesthesia, to drain the fluid and instill a small volume of corticosteroid solution. Sometimes, drainage of fluid coupled with the local anesthetic produces almost immediate relief. Usually, it takes longer for the corticosteroid to act. Sometimes, unfortunately, insertion of the needle exacerbates the inflammation, and the acute pain becomes truly hellish. One of us who is subject to frequent attacks of bursitis has known the ecstasy when an acutely inflamed bursa yields up its pain to successful needling—and also the agony when the procedure results in intensification of pain and spasm.

For bursitis deep in the shoulder area, x-ray treatment may prove helpful. But many doctors dislike using x-rays, especially in young people, for a condition that is almost certain to clear up with conservative treatment.

Manipulation of the joint under local anesthesia is sometimes tried in the acute stage, but it should be done only by a specialist experienced in the use of this potentially dangerous technique, which may cause major exacerbation of an already terribly painful problem.

Some doctors prescribe phenylbutazone by mouth for five days and sometimes get gratifying relief of acute bursitis.

Chronic Bursitis

Sometimes, an acute bursitis fails to clear completely and becomes chronic, or the chronic condition may develop gradually. In either case, there is pain upon prolonged or strenuous use of the joint. Movement of the joint may become limited. There may be flare-ups similar to attacks of acute bursitis.

Usually, the chronic condition clears up in one to two years, and this period generally can be shortened with adequate therapeutic and preventive measures. Physiotherapy—use of heat followed by special exercises —may be of value. Corticosteroids taken by mouth are sometimes helpful. Also, corticosteroids may be injected into the affected areas. X-ray, needling of the bursa, injection of procaine, and joint manipulation usually are not effective for chronic, low-grade types of bursitis.

Patients with chronic bursitis should become detectives, ferreting out their particular causes of trouble. For example, a typist noticed that her attacks of shoulder bursitis developed in late spring, and she could trace them to the fact that the air conditioning was turned on then and she worked directly in the path of the cold air stream. Another person found that his attacks decreased markedly when he gave up being a fresh-air enthusiast in winter and kept his bedroom windows almost completely closed. Some persons must modify their work or sports activities to prevent the pain of chronic bursitis.

Sometimes in chronic bursitis, if pain and disability justify it, surgery may be used to remove deposits of calcium material which collect in some chronically inflamed bursas, or to eliminate any adhesions that may be present.

A *frozen shoulder* is the result of long-standing shoulder bursitis which has not been treated properly or has been unusually resistant to treatment. The pain and spasm lead to disuse of the shoulder joint and atrophy, or wasting away, of muscle, bone, and joint substance. Adhesions, too, may form around the joint. In time, the shoulder becomes immobile or "frozen." However, with physiotherapy, even such a shoulder may be made to develop good function again.

CANCER

Cancer is second among killer diseases, coming after heart disease. Yet it is the most dreaded of ailments. Much of the dread stems from lack of sound information—for cancer is curable in at least half of the people it attacks. With modern methods of combatting both infection and pain, there is no basis for the fear that inevitably cancer must be agonizing and that the cancer patient will undergo some mysterious, horrifying decomposition.

There are other reassuring features of cancer. It is rarely inherited; children with parents or other relatives who have had cancer need not fear that they must develop the disease. Cancer is not contagious, not even in its terminal phase. Any number of doctors and nurses who specialize in treatment and care of cancer patients remain free of the disease. And intensive research in the field of cancer gives us good reason to hope that treatments will constantly improve and that cures for various types of cancer will be forthcoming.

Cancer involves abnormal growth. Under normal circumstances, body tissues grow in orderly fashion not only in infancy and childhood but throughout life when new tissue grows to replace injured tissue. Anyone who has seen the orderly, beautiful way in which nature restores the skin to healthy intactness after numerous abrasions, small cuts, and minor wounds can appreciate the need for and efficacy of orderly growth.

Sometimes, however, tissue grows abnormally. The growth is purposeless and disorderly. If the growth is confined to an organ without becoming invasive elsewhere, it is called a benign tumor rather than a cancer. Such a growth may become harmful only through its size and the pressure it may put on nearby nerves or organs. If free to grow, some benign tumors reach enormous size. One of us once saw an ovarian cystic tumor weighing 30 pounds removed from a woman whose total weight was 95 pounds. Benign goiters of the thyroid gland in days past were sometimes carried hanging down in a wheelbarrow by the victims.

But the true cancer is a destructive, malignant growth. It can destroy the tissue in which it originates, eroding it, or eating into a vital blood vessel, causing severe or fatal hemorrhage. Equally bad is its tendency to spread to far removed parts of the body (metastasis) through lymph vessels or veins. There are even special tendencies for metastatic spread: breast cancer into the lymph nodes of the armpit; prostate cancer into bones; stomach cancer to the liver.

Always cancer starts in one tissue or organ; it never begins as a generalized, body-wide disease. This makes possible prevention of spread if it is detected early enough. Some experts believe that cancer may take as long as seven years to grow large enough in a given organ or tissue to become obvious as a small, visible lump. Unfortunately for detection purposes, cancers tend to be painless in their early stages.

Cancers are of several types. Carcinoma is a cancer of the outer part of the body (such as skin, lip, breast, tongue) or of the innermost part of the body (such as stomach or colon). Sarcoma is a cancer of in-between tissues (such as muscles and bones). A teratoma is a mixture of these types. A hamartoma is an overgrowth of cells in an organ which does not progress and is now considered more a congenital abnormality than a tumor or cancer.

Because cancer starts in a single organ rather than diffusely, there have been some daring suggestions about primary prevention. Quite seriously, some distinguished surgeons have discussed the possibility of prophylactically removing organs that are common cancer sites. Why not, they suggest, remove the uterus after childbearing when it is no longer needed, or the breasts, or the prostate? From a straight surgical viewpoint, the decision would rest on the dangers and disability of operation versus the danger of the cancer.

But surely other considerations enter in. Removal of the breasts is a great emotional shock for a woman. The danger of operation, while small, cannot be overlooked. And, too, this danger comes for a relatively young woman, for if prophylactic surgery is to be meaningful it would have to be performed when a woman is entering the time of life when cancer becomes a possibility. Thus, at 40 years, she may be exposed to the danger, discomfort, and psychological hazards of the operation, whereas even if she is destined to get cancer, it may not strike until she is 55 and she has a good chance of getting years of relief or even complete cure from surgery performed at that time.

Prophylactic removal of the uterus after the childbearing years might seem more desirable if it were not for the Pap test, which makes it possible to detect precancerous lesions in the uterus and thus institute surgery that will be curative. And for men, prostate removal is a major operation with some risk of mortality and danger of impotence, which a younger man would not want to face. At present, then, primary preventive surgery does not seem a practical answer.

There are more practical methods possible for primary prevention of cancer even though we realize from the frequency of the disease that these are far from sufficient. First, as we have noted earlier, cessation of smoking can save thousands of lives otherwise doomed to be lost from cancer. And an appreciable additional number can be saved from cancers of lip, tongue, larynx, and possibly stomach and urinary bladder.

Then there are the precancerous lesions which can be removed before they have a chance to become malignant. They include leukoplakia (white patches) on tongue and lips; senile changes in the vagina; skin lesions such as moles which begin to enlarge; certain polyps of the colon and rectum. These precancers can be detected by the type of regular checkup we have described earlier in this book.

There are cancers that follow heavy exposure of the skin to sun and wind —the so-called sailor's and farmer's cancers—which can be prevented by covering the skin and shading the face.

Radiation can lead to cancer. There is much less danger from diagnostic than from therapeutic x-ray or other irradiation. But every exposure to radiation should be entered in your medical record and shown to your doctor and dentist whenever they suggest x-rays. Workers in the radiation industries should know every safety precaution.

Some chemicals can cause cancer, and workers handling them should learn the safety rules as a means of primary prevention. Historically, it is interesting that one of the first chemically induced cancers to be noticed by doctors was in chimney sweeps whose contact with the tarry material in the chimneys led to cancers of the scrotum. Chromate chemicals today can cause lung cancer; aniline dyes can cause bladder cancer; asbestos can lead to cancers of the outer lining of the lungs or the intestinal cavity.

Some 500 chemicals have been found to cause cancers in experimental animals. One of these, which was widely used as an artificial sweetener, cyclamate, was restricted after animal experiments produced cancers and led to fear that humans using it in large quantities over long periods might develop cancer.

An additional reason for prevention of chronic liver disease (page 611) is the tendency of this disease to allow cancer to be superimposed. Patients with ulcerative colitis need careful scrutiny because of their higher risk of developing cancer of the diseased colon.

Secondary Prevention

Once cancer is found, much can be done to prevent it from becoming a fatal illness. As we have indicated, cancer can be a curable disease.

When the doctor discovers a lump in a breast or sees a suspicious sore on a lip, he must make a definitive diagnosis. Usually this is possible only through removal of part or all of the suspicious area (biopsy) so a pathologist can examine it microscopically as well as grossly.

If the diagnosis is cancer, then the physician considers the outlook for the patient in terms of localization versus metastasis or spread. If there has been spreading, the outlook is much less hopeful than if the cancer is still confined to the area of origin. For example, a breast cancer which has not spread to lymph nodes in the armpit offers a 70 percent or better chance for cure. If there has been a single metastasis, the chance for cure may drop to 50 percent. If there have been several metastases, the likelihood of living five years may drop to about 25 percent. Similarly, for example, a kidney cancer that has spread to a bone has a much more ominous outlook than one that is still confined to the kidney. With metastasis, treatment usually depends upon radiation and chemicals, often less likely to provide permanent cure than when a surgeon can remove an entire intact growth at its primary site.

Thus, early detection is the key to effective secondary prevention in cancer. Cancer in early stages rarely makes its presence known by such general symptoms as fever or loss of weight. It does, however, often provide local signals such as a painless lump in the breast or bleeding in stomach or rectum.

Cardinal signs of cancer are lumps or sores that do not heal; bleeding from any part of the body when there is no obvious explanation for the bleeding; chronic hoarseness; chronic cough; unexplained stomach or intestinal symptoms such as constipation, diarrhea, nausea, vomiting, "indigestion"; unexplained pain; jaundice; impaired vision; convulsions; possibly headache. If such indications appear, do not wait for your next checkup but see your doctor at once.

Your regular medical checkup is another important means for early detection of cancer. Your doctor will examine larynx, rectum and sigmoid colon, and usually your lungs.

For women, additional preventive measures are important. Early breast and uterine cancers are readily curable. Therefore, women should arrange with their doctors to have regular Pap smears of the uterine cervix. This is a simple, painless test which requires only a few minutes and involves only taking a smear through the vagina so cells can be examined under the microscope. It should be done regularly, as often as your physician, or the gynecologist to whom he refers you, may suggest.

Regarding the breasts, we feel that most women should learn to examine them once each month. If that makes them unduly nervous, then they should set up a schedule of regular examinations by the doctor.

Self-examination is a simple process. Immediately after the menstrual period when the breasts are normally soft, look into a mirror and raise both arms over your head so that the sides of the breasts are visible. Study your breasts carefully, noting whether one looks higher than the other or whether one seems larger than it was the previous month. Also, check for any slight depressions or dimpling of the skin over the breast.

Next, using the right hand on the left breast and vice versa, push the breast back gently against your chest and feel for any small lumps.

Then, feel the armpits for any swelling.

The best time to make this examination is in the morning. If you decide that something may be wrong, you have all day to reach your doctor, if only to get his reassurance. Not every lump in the breast means cancer. Many lumps are harmless formations due to glandular functioning. Let your doctor decide what they are. Fortunately, he can now use a special type of x-ray study for breast cancer, a technique called mammography (see page 548).

If cancer should be diagnosed, your doctor will suggest whether surgery or radiation is the best therapy. Most surgeons do cancer surgery. Only a few surgeons restrict themselves to cancer work alone. In our largest cities there are hospitals that specialize in treating cancer patients. Let your doctor advise you.

Surgery for removal of the cancerous area may be followed by a course of x-ray or other radiation to try to kill any cancer cells that might be lying beyond the area the surgeon has excised.

There are cancers of the brain. Understandably, because of fear of disease that affects our brain and the fear about cancer, people don't like to hear the phrase "cancer of the brain." So we speak in the medical profession of gliomas and astrocytomas and the lay person talks about brain tumor. There are many types of growths that affect the brain, everything from circumscribed, completely benign tumors to the dreaded cancerous glioma. Once a space-occupying lesion in the brain is diagnosed, the doctor sees the outlook in terms of the information provided by special x-rays and radiation scan tests that determine location and size of the tumor. A repeat of these observations provides information about the rate of growth of the mass. A malignant growth usually grows faster than a benign one. In most cases, there must be operation—and there is that moment of prayer when the surgeon reaches the growth and learns whether it is benign or cancerous. If cancerous, the situation is more ominous than in other organs where the surgeon usually can excise the cancer and surrounding suspicious tissue. There are limitations in the brain because death or massive paralysis might be the result of too extensive surgery.

Striking advances have been made in the treatment of some cancers for which there was once very little hope. For choriocarcinoma of the uterus, for example, treatment with methotrexate and actinomycin D now is producing long-term remission in nearly 75 percent of patients; and many children with Wilms' tumor, a cancer of the kidney, are responding to actinomycin D. These results provide hope that increasingly effective chemical agents will be found for other cancers.

RADICAL SURGERY FOR SECONDARY PREVENTION. There is some division of opinion among surgeons about how far to go in removing widespread cancer. Most surgeons try to get the primary growth and adjacent lymph nodes. A school of more radical surgeons believes that even important organs should be sacrificed if permanent cure may be possible with extensive surgery.

For example, if cancer of the uterus has invaded the adjacent urinary bladder, more conservative surgeons would feel that the spreading cancer has already invaded other body areas and only palliation by radiation and chemical treatment is feasible. A radical surgeon, however, might hope that the cancer had invaded only organs in the pelvic area and might remove the uterus and bladder, and implant the ureters (which ordinarily connect bladder and kidney) into the colon to permit urine to drain into the fecal stream.

Or suppose a cancer of the colon has been found to have spread to the liver. On the chance that there has been no spread beyond this, a radical surgeon might remove the cancer in the colon and then operate on the liver to remove all cancerous nodules there that he can see. Obviously, the rate of cure of widespread cancers by surgery is not high, but radical surgeons reason that even one life in a dozen saved is worth the gamble and effort.

When a patient has to decide about radical surgery, he should discuss the problem openly with his family doctor, who can be objective and weigh the pros and cons.

ENDOCRINE GLAND SURGERY FOR SECONDARY PREVENTION. The growth of some cancers is influenced by certain of the endocrine glands. For example, in the spread of prostate cancer, hormones of the testicles play a role. It has been found that the painful metastases of prostate cancer to bone can be relieved for long periods by removal of the testicles. This is not as drastic as it sounds, since prostate cancer patients have reached an age when the "eunuchizing" effects of testicle removal will be minimal.

When breast cancer gets out of control and spreads to bones and other parts of the body, an endocrine gland operation may help to extend life for months and even years. The operation may be on either the ovaries, adrenal glands, or pituitary gland in the brain. The age of the patient, the duration of the cancer, and the location of the metastases will be considered before the decision as to which operation to use is made.

Tertiary Prevention

Perhaps not too far distant is the day when organ transplantation becomes fully practical. Then cancers that are destroying such vital organs as the liver and the pancreas may be removed entirely, and the missing organ will be replaced by a transplant from a cadaver.

Cancer Phobia

Cancer is such a dreaded disease that, understandably, many people have an irrational fear of it. The realistic fear that everyone has of this disease should be allayed by the sensible, scientific approach to prevention presented in this book. If strong fear of cancer persists, the phobia should be discussed with your doctor. He can help you overcome it. If not, then he may wish you to have a talk with a psychotherapist.

CEREBRAL PALSY

Cerebral palsy (CP) ranks as the most common cause of crippling of children in the United States. Almost one quarter of a million persons are afflicted. Too often people associate the abnormalities of movement and muscular control, which are the outstanding features of CP, with mental retardation and lifelong dependency on others. But the majority of CP victims are not mentally retarded and are capable, with special training, of becoming self-sufficient.

Cerebral palsy is not an inherited disorder, or a contagious one, or a progressive one. Cerebral refers to the brain, and palsy to muscular weakness. So the name implies that it is a condition of muscular weakness or disability resulting from brain damage. The brain damage may occur before, during, or shortly after birth for many different reasons. (Brain damage in adulthood leading to disability is not considered CP.)

The nature and extent of disability will, of course, depend on the amount of brain damage. There are three ways in which the muscles may be affected: in the *spastic* variety of CP, muscles are stiff and tight, and weakness is profound; in the *athetoid* form, muscles contract without apparent reason, leading to uncontrolled grimaces and limb movements; in the *ataxic* form, talking and other movements are poorly coordinated. Along with these difficulties there may be hearing and sight impairment, speech disturbance, poor ability to learn, convulsions, emotional problems, and sometimes, unfortunately, mental retardation. Despite these handicaps, however, modern training methods offer more hope than ever before for even the most severe form of CP.

Primary prevention of CP begins with good antenatal (prenatal) care. German measles and other infections early in pregnancy may damage the brain of the developing child. Vaccination against German measles—before a girl reaches childbearing age or, in the case of an adult woman, when there is little likelihood of immediate pregnancy—is an important preventive measure. Other infections during pregnancy are often hard to detect, and the physician cannot always predict whether or not they will harm the baby. The preventive approach is limited to recommending adequate protection against diseases for which vaccines are available and avoiding unnecessary exposure to others.

Another known, and now preventable, cause of potential brain damage to children is Rh incompatibility. Detecting this blood problem is now part of routine antenatal care. The use of special techniques—such as intrauterine blood transfusion for the fetus and delivery by cesarian section if necessary before severe damage occurs —can prevent brain and other organ harm.

A recent development promises to eliminate the hazard of Rh incompatibility. It is well known that the first child does not suffer harmful effects from Rh incompatibility; the succeeding children are at risk. This is because it takes time for the mother to become sensitized to the Rh factor. A new medication, called Rhogram, when given to the mother within 48 hours after birth of the first child, prevents development of sensitization to the Rh factor and eliminates risk for succeeding children. To prevent sensitization from ever developing, the medication must be given after each subsequent pregnancy.

Premature infants are more likely than others to be afflicted with CP. Among factors in the mother which predispose toward premature birth are cigarette smoking, infection of the kidney and bladder, and a history of having borne previous premature infants. Good prenatal and obstetrical care can greatly decrease the risk of prematurity.

No one has yet clearly defined exactly how much of an effect good nutrition may have in preventing birth defects. There is little doubt that extreme malnutrition in the mother can have serious consequences for her child. There are more subtle forms of malnutrition—involving deficiency of a vitamin or a mineral—which may predispose to the birth of a handicapped child. Most obstetricians today stress the importance of good diet for the mother and instruct their patients in sound eating habits.

Diseases present in a pregnant woman can significantly influence the health of her child. They can, and should, be detected and treated even before a woman becomes pregnant. Failing that, their early detection and treatment during pregnancy can be helpful in avoiding handicaps for the child.

By getting a chance to know a patient long before delivery, throughout her pregnancy, an obstetrician can anticipate and be prepared for any problems that may arise at the time of birth. Good obstetrical and anesthetic care during labor and delivery are important in preventing brain damage. Improper use of forceps and techniques to hasten labor and delivery can cause brain damage in the infant. General anesthesia, narcotics, sedatives, and obstetrical complications have some potential for depressing the breathing center of the newborn, with the risk that insufficient oxygen may reach the brain, resulting in damage there. Many obstetricians prefer to have an anesthesiologist present at delivery to administer the anesthetic for the mother and to evaluate and treat any respiratory difficulties that may arise in the infant.

Similarly, pediatric care during the first months of life helps in primary prevention, particularly in the area of prompt detection and treatment of an infection such as meningitis, which is a common cause of brain damage in the early period after birth.

Unfortunately, in about 40 percent of cases it is not possible to detect or prevent causes of brain damage. For example, some errors of metabolism—either hereditary or arising spontaneously—are difficult to detect immediately at birth and treat adequately.

Radiation is probably a somewhat exaggerated hazard. Nevertheless, every physician will attempt to keep radiation exposure to a minimum during pregnancy, because of harmful effects demonstrated in animal studies and because the effects in humans of x-rays, except in very large doses, are still not clearly established. Occasionally, x-ray study may be required to detect disease; at such times, there should be no hesitancy about its use.

Secondary preventive measures are most effective when applied early. Early detection and proper evaluation of CP may require study by a neurologist and other specialists who are most often readily available at a children's hospital.

The aim of secondary prevention is to keep emotional difficulties from arising as a result of handicap and to train the CP patient and his or her family to utilize to the fullest their abilities to overcome physical and personality problems.

A child with CP needs individual evaluation and a program of therapy most appropriate for him. The program—to prevent loss of the child's potential for maturation and independence—may include medicines, various forms of counseling, physical therapy, and special training.

There are medicines to help control the seizures which may afflict some of those with CP. Other medications help minimize uncontrolled movements; still others aid learning ability and may help bring about a more positive attitude toward life and work. Antibiotics are available as needed to help combat infections to which defective body systems are prone.

Vocational counselors, social workers, and psychologists are just a few of the professional people whose special training enables them to assess the mental and physical assets of a child with CP and advise the best way to maximize these assets. It is often difficult to gain insight into the real capabilities of children with CP because of difficulties of communication resulting from speech and hearing impairment, depression, and withdrawal. Help in overcoming such difficulties is increasingly available now at centers dealing with the problems of CP.

Physical therapists can help to correct deformities and to educate muscles to perform such important functions as walking, eating, and dressing. Speech therapists, occupational therapists, and sympathetic teachers are other members of the team. In many areas now, special schools and special classes are available to train children with CP.

Employment is an important part of every adult's life. Training for jobs—if necessary, for jobs under special, favorable conditions such as those to be found in sheltered workshops—is helping many with CP. Today, it is being recognized increasingly that the handicapped are often punctual, dependable, even outstanding workers. Employment often gives new meaning to the life of a CP victim because it establishes goals and makes the patient feel more independent and self-sufficient, important factors in the maturation of anyone's personality.

Those CP victims who are mentally retarded often function well in employment where there are simple repetitive tasks to perform. They may derive tremendous satisfaction from jobs that nobody else is willing to perform.

It is surprising what the handicapped can achieve with training and encouragement. Ambition to achieve is an important attitude to be inculcated in a child with CP. If the ambition is not fostered, even the best training and physical development program may be of little avail.

Bob is now 25 years old. From birth, CP affected the muscles of the right side of his body. At several months of age, he was evaluated at a children's hospital and seemed to be developing normally except for his right-sided weakness. He learned slowly, however, and his parents were guided by physicians, physical therapists, and other specialists on what to expect, how to help him develop, and how to prevent muscle deformities through daily exercises. He went to a school for the handicapped and received intensive help in speech and in feeding and clothing himself. He was found, in evaluations by a psychologist and vocational counselor, to have some aptitude for mathematics and was enrolled in an accounting course.

It took him longer than average to complete his training, but he did become an accountant, now holds a job, and goes to school at night with the hope of becoming a certified public accountant.

Families of children with CP are under great strain. Parents unconsciously may feel guilty about the birth of a child with CP. This can be a tremendous emotional burden, and help from a doctor, social worker, psychologist, or psychiatrist can do much to alleviate it. Cerebral palsy never resulted from bad thoughts, quarrels, lack of willingness to have a child, or even attempted abortion.

A family may hinder, rather than help, development of a child with CP through overprotection. Like other children, the CP child must learn through experience. Encouraging a CP child to do things, rather than doing everything for him, will get him over many hurdles and help him to achieve a certain degree of self-confidence. For example, climbing stairs may seem well-nigh impossible at first to some CP children and their families. Yet if the child is not allowed to try and try again until he learns to manage stair climbing, he will be at a disadvantage.

Setting realistic goals for a youngster with CP is important for his mental development and eventual ability to care for himself. A realistic but optimistic view about what can be done is most helpful. It is best when goals are set collaboratively by professionals, family, and the child himself.

An optimistic view is justified. The outlook for the person with CP is much brighter than it has ever been, and further gains seem most likely.

CLUBFOOT AND CONGENITAL HIP DISLOCATION

For anyone, and for a child in particular, an abnormality in gait such as a limp or "waddle" can be a physical and emotional handicap. Preventive medicine is aimed at early diagnosis of conditions that can lead to such handicaps in order that they may be corrected quickly and effectively.

Clubfoot is a readily distinguishable condition which can produce abnormal gait. A less obvious one is congenital dislocation of the hip, which is present from birth but, unless specifically looked for, not apparent until a child begins to walk. Both conditions are completely correctable in well over 90 percent of cases if diagnosis is made early and correct treatment begun immediately.

The primary causes of clubfoot and congenital hip dislocation are unknown. Some investigators believe they may be caused by the position of the fetus in the womb; others attribute them to muscle imbalance, while still others consider them the results of abnormal bone development arising from unknown, but possibly inherited, factors.

In clubfoot, or talipes, the foot is turned inward and upward and the heel is drawn up. The defect is usually noticed soon after birth, and this is the time to begin treatment. In almost all instances, the treatment will be carried out by an M.D. who specializes in orthopedics.

Mild cases, in which the foot can be moved into normal position by a physician or parent, often can be corrected by simple exercises. In such cases, some authorities do not even refer to the deformity as clubfoot. More severe cases, especially when bony abnormalities are present, require use of a plaster cast, with weekly changes to progressively align the foot properly. Several months of such treatment may be needed, but the prognosis for complete correction is very good.

If clubfoot is not corrected early, adequate treatment becomes more difficult as bones and muscles develop in improper alignment, and surgery will be needed.

When clubfoot is present in an infant, a preventively minded physician will look for other conditions that may be more likely to be present, such as congenital hip dislocation and abnormalities of the nervous system. He may order x-rays of the hips and back, or may refer the patient to a neurologist for thorough evaluation.

Congenital hip dislocation involves an abnormality of the hip socket, or the head of the femur (thigh bone), or the tissues that hold the hip in place. The physician will be particularly alert for dislocation if there is a family history of the disorder or if there are musculoskeletal disorders, such as clubfoot, present. Dislocation is more common in girls than in boys.

To detect the presence of hip dislocation, the physician will examine the infant's legs for any evidence of unevenness in length or position. He will flex the hip, then slowly spread the thighs; with this maneuver, he can determine whether the hip dislocates and then pops back into place. X-rays will be taken to confirm the diagnosis.

In milder cases, double diapering for several weeks may suffice to correct the dislocation. In other instances, the use of casts for several weeks will solve the problem. The earlier treatment is begun, the less time is needed in a cast. Unfortunately, in some cases, hip dislocation is not detected until the child begins to walk, when a peculiar waddling gait may be noticed. Treatment at this stage may require several weeks of traction or even surgical correction.

In addition to gait abnormality, there is a tendency for an untreated dislocated joint to undergo severe arthritic changes which will require major surgical correction procedures in later years. Early treatment, thus, constitutes excellent preventive medicine, helping the child immediately and avoiding future trouble.

COMMON COLD

Actually, some medical authorities would like to ban the common cold from medical terminology. Their preference: upper respiratory infection (URI). For most of us, under any name, it will remain the same nuisance ailment it always has been.

It's now known to be caused by a vast assortment of agents: rhinoviruses (some 30 different types); echoviruses; adenoviruses; coxsackie viruses; influenza and parainfluenza viruses; and even by some organisms, called pleuropneumonia-like (PPLO), which aren't viruses at all. It's this great diversity of causative agents that may explain the frequent recurrence of colds in many individuals.

Usually a cold has a simple life history or scenario which is depicted with some accuracy by the old adage: "Three days acoming, three days astaying, three days agoing."

The symptoms, of course, are well known: nasal stuffiness, watery discharge, sneezing, redness of the outer soft part of the nose, slight harshness or sometimes frank soreness of the throat. There may also be general malaise, possibly some headache and muscle soreness, and a sense of feverishness but usually no real fever.

For the preventively minded physician, a cold is a real challenge. Can it be prevented? This is an especially important matter for patients with lung or heart disease, particularly if there is serious impairment of pulmonary or cardiac reserves. Colds also can be more than mere nuisances for patients with severe diabetes and kidney and liver ailments.

Prevention

Prevention of a cold involves maintenance of optimum health. It also requires avoidance of sources of contamination—which means, if feasible, staying away from close contact with infected people at home, at work, in public conveyances. It means, too, if feasible, avoiding crowds during the high cold-incidence months—in the United States, September–October, January–February, April–May. A person sneezing nearby can be spewing millions of infective agents at you.

None of this is easy. But research now has established fairly clearly that such factors as chilling and drafts, once considered important, are not really important at all in causing colds. Until an effective vaccine against colds becomes available, avoidance of carriers remains a prime means of prevention. And difficult as this may be, it can be of special importance for people with the diseases mentioned earlier. They should, at least, discuss the risks with their doctors.

Secondary preventive measures, for cold complications, are available. If you have a severe cold accompanied by fever, suggesting that secondary bacterial infection may be setting in, your physician may prescribe an antibiotic to bring the secondary infection under quick control. If, with your cold, you develop severe headache over the sinus areas, with high fever and purulent discharge from the nose and down into the throat, pointing toward a frank infection of the sinuses, there may be need to get the sinuses draining freely, and your doctor may advise a visit to a nose and throat specialist. Similarly, ringing in the ears accompanied by a feeling that the ears are clogged may suggest the start of a middle ear infection. In that case, it may be advisable for an ear specialist to shrink the eustachian tubes which have become swollen and inflamed because of the cold.

Such complications are not very common.

Treatment

Usually, if you have a heavy cold but are otherwise in good general health, the doctor can make you feel more comfortable and probably can shorten the course of the cold by a few days. He may prescribe a nasal decongestant, which will allow you to breathe more comfortably and will also permit the nasal tissues to fight the cold agents more effectively. Nose drops—for example, three drops of 0.25 percent Neo-Synephrine in each nostril every two or three hours—can help, especially if prescribed along with an internal medication such as Propadrine, a vasoconstrictor. An antihistamine may be prescribed—with some reservation, because people vary greatly in response to antihistamines. (One of us once tried 16 different antihistamines for a personal bout of nasal

congestion before finding one that relieved symptoms without causing unpleasant side reactions.)

Also of value: aspirin, two tablets every four hours, and on a regular schedule rather than just when you feel aches or feverish. Buffered forms are suitable, too.

No medication in a gargle has been found to be directly useful against cold agents. But when the throat is sore, gentle warm gargling does provide some relief and does bring more blood to the throat tissues to help combat the viruses. A teaspoonful of table salt added to a pint of warm, not hot, water makes a good gargling fluid.

People who have serious diseases—of heart, lungs, liver, for example—which requires them to be under constant treatment should immediately notify their doctor when a cold starts. A preventively minded physician may deem it wise to actually hospitalize some patients for whom a cold might precipitate a severe attack of heart or lung failure.

VITAMIN C FOR COLDS. Some people, including physicians and research scientists, believe that large amounts of vitamin C (ascorbic acid) may shorten and reduce the severity of a cold or even prevent colds. Acceptable conclusive evidence from large-scale scientific study is not available.

But since vitamin C for short periods in the high doses suggested is not toxic, there seems to be no reason why it should not be tried by those who believe it helps. One group of supporters for this treatment say that its success depends upon using the vitamin several times a day for at least three days, beginning at the very onset of the cold, in the amount of 1,000 milligrams a day.

Some believe that much larger doses are needed. One regimen calls for starting—within the first 24 hours of any visible indication of a cold, and the sooner the better—with doses of 600 or 625 milligrams of vitamin C every three hours (three 200-milligram tablets or two and one-half 250-milligram tablets). Both before bed and upon awakening in the morning, the dosage is increased to 750 milligrams. After three to four days, the dosage is reduced to 375 to 400 milligrams every three hours. After several more days, another cut is made—to 200 to 250 milligrams every three hours. And after another few days, the dosage is reduced to 200 milligrams every four to six hours. Overall, the vitamin, which is relatively inexpensive, is used for 10 to 12 days.

See your doctor before trying Vitamin C for treatment, or for its possible use in *prevention* of colds. Perhaps your "frequent colds" may be allergic symptoms and need a different preventive therapy.

CUSHING'S SYNDROME (ADRENAL CORTICAL HYPERFUNCTION)

The hormones produced by the adrenal glands, as we have noted under Addison's disease, are vital. In Cushing's syndrome, there is overproduction of the hormones and the patient suffers from too much of a good thing.

In most cases, Cushing's syndrome results from a diffuse, benign enlargement of the outer portions (cortices) of both adrenal glands. In a smaller number, about 15 percent, there is a single, benign tumor in one of the glands which produces the oversupply of hormones. In about 5 percent of cases, there is cancerous enlargement of the cortex of one of the glands.

Typically, a patient with Cushing's syndrome has a rounded face ("moonface") and a pad of fat in the upper part of the back referred to as a "buffalo hump." There is usually obesity with protuberant abdomen but thin legs. Purplish lines appear in the skin of the abdomen, thighs, and breasts. The skin bruises easily. Excess hair appears on the face. Backache, headache, and acne are common. Women have little or no menstrual flow; men develop impotence.

The doctor finds high blood pressure, a high blood sugar level, and often sugar in the urine suggesting the presence of diabetes-like illness. X-rays show thinning of bones. Other special tests may be used to confirm the diagnosis especially when the disease occurs in mild form without all the characteristic findings.

There is no primary prevention. Secondary prevention of disability and death requires early diagnosis and vigorous treatment.

In working up the diagnosis, the physician will try to determine whether the changes in the adrenal glands originate there or may be secondary to overactivity of the pituitary gland at the base of the brain. The pituitary produces a hormone that stimulates activity of the adrenal cortex. Sometimes, diffuse enlargement of the adrenal cortices results from overstimulation by the pituitary. When this is the case, usually there is a tumor of the pituitary gland which can be detected by x-ray. When the pituitary is the cause of the adrenal gland trouble, the condition is called Cushing's disease rather than Cushing's syndrome.

Treatment consists of surgical removal of part of the adrenal gland tissue when there is diffuse enlargement, or removal of the tumor when it is the cause. Only rarely is a cancer of the adrenals found and removed before it has spread to the rest of the body; fortunately, this is an infrequent cause of Cushing's syndrome.

When the pituitary gland is involved, irradiation of this gland may be tried alone to observe the effect on the adrenals. Sometimes, adrenal surgery must be combined with pituitary irradiation. Rarely, there will be a large pituitary gland tumor that must be surgically removed.

Sometimes so much of the adrenal cortex tissue must be removed that the patient goes from hormone overproduction to underproduction and is then like a patient with Addison's disease and requires similar treatment (page 513).

IATROGENIC CUSHING'S SYNDROME. This formidable name means simply that medical therapy has produced some of the symptoms of Cushing's syndrome. For example, when cortisone, cortisol, and related steroids are given for a long time in the treatment of asthma, sarcoidosis, and other diseases, a patient may develop "moonface" or some of the other symptoms of Cushing's syndrome. This is undesirable and the physician who prescribes corticosteroid medication warns the patient to notify him whenever any strange symptoms are noted so he can take appropriate measures to reverse the changes.

DIABETES

Diabetes affects an estimated four million Americans. It is a chronic ailment for which there is good treatment but no known cure. It is a formidable disease because of the possible complications. Fortunately, much can be done now in areas of both primary and secondary prevention.

In diabetes, something is wrong with the body's ability to use (or metabolize) sugar. In a typical, overt case of diabetes, the level of sugar in the blood will be too high and sugar (glucose) will "spill over" from the blood into the urine. On the other hand, in many cases of diabetes, the defect in sugar utilization will become apparent only with a glucose tolerance test. In this test, blood sugar is first determined after several hours of fasting and then again at intervals after the patient is given three and one-half ounces of glucose solution to drink. By studying the curve drawn between the measurements at various times, the doctor can detect a diabetic tendency. If the test is positive and the patient as yet has no symptoms of diabetes, he is said to have preclinical or chemical diabetes.

What causes the defect in the body's use of sugar? Insulin is the sugar-regulating hormone produced by the islets of Langerhans in the pancreas. Insufficient insulin production may be the problem, or the body may be resistant to the effect of insulin.

It is now known that there are two quite different types of diabetes. One, the juvenile type, affects children, adolescents, and young adults and involves a definite lack of insulin secretion. The other, maturity-onset, tends to occur in middle life; in this type insulin production is adequate, but for reasons that are still not clear the body does not properly respond to the insulin.

Major symptoms of diabetes include increased thirst and urination (in some children, bed-wetting may be due to diabetes); loss of weight, sometimes with increased appetite and excessive food intake; fatigue; weakness; itching of genitals and rectum; decreased resistance to infections such as boils and carbuncles and to general infections such as tuberculosis.

There is a tendency in diabetics toward atherosclerosis of heart, leg, and brain arteries. Sometimes diabetes may announce itself by poor leg circulation, angina pectoris, or a frank heart attack.

Is primary prevention possible? There is considerable evidence now that diabetes is more common in the obese and sedentary. It may be possible in some cases to reduce the likelihood of diabetes through weight reduction and sensible exercise (see our chapters on these subjects). Diabetes is inherited, and if there is a history of diabetes in the families of both partners in a marriage, they may wish genetic counseling before deciding on whether to conceive or adopt children.

Secondary preventive measures today can be effective in controlling symptoms of diabetes and reducing the risk of serious complications. In addition to insulin, which is of major value for young diabetics, there are now various oral preparations presumably useful for maturity-onset diabetes. But good preventive medicine for diabetes involves much more than medication alone.

Choice of doctor is of great importance. The patient must have complete confidence in the physician, since few diseases require more close cooperation between patient and doctor. The diabetic who does well with his disease is the one who can accept the discipline which the disease necessitates. Most doctors treat diabetes and there are some who specialize com-

pletely in its treatment. A young diabetic with severe disease who may be difficult to regulate may well do best under the care, constant or consultative, of a specialist.

The diabetic patient must come to know his disease. He must understand, for example, that sugar is a vital body fuel and a quickly utilized one, and there is only a limited reserve of sugar for the blood in the liver. When the reserve is exhausted, blood sugar can be replenished only slowly from the general pool of chemicals such as protein. Thus excessive exercise can bring a diabetic's blood sugar to dangerously low levels since he does not have the normal action of insulin to regulate it. A good diabetic patient gets to know that before sports or heavier-than-usual exertion he must take in extra food, and possibly some extra insulin to help the body utilize it. Diabetic patients who know their disease control it so well that some of them have become champion athletes.

On the other hand, physicians know all too well the unpleasant outlook for the patient who will not learn the relationship between food intake, energy output, and insulin requirements. There can be serious, even fatal complications. Too little sugar-producing food coupled with too much insulin leads to a hypoglycemic reaction in which blood sugar goes too low.

Insulin and oral medicines for diabetes are always used in connection with a diet in which the doctor has allocated definite amounts of sugar. Because the doctor knows how important the diet-exercise-medication relationship is, he often starts treatment for a moderately severe or severe diabetic in the hospital. There, with the patient not confined to bed but approximating his usual daily exercise routine, blood sugar level can be tested frequently as can sugar in the urine. Since there are several types of insulin —fast-acting, slow-acting, and intermediate—the doctor can determine which one or which combination is best suited for the individual patient. In the hospital, too, a skilled dietitian can teach the patient and family how to translate the physician's prescription for sugar-protein-fat content of the daily diet into food equivalents. Today, doctors rarely expect diabetic patients to actually weigh their food but find it satisfactory to have a dietitian teach them simple methods of measuring out what is being prescribed in terms of cups, average portions, slices of bread, etc.

Two undesirable reactions are possible if the food-exercise-insulin ratio is wrong. With too much insulin in relation to food intake or expended energy, blood sugar falls and symptoms of hunger, shakiness, muscular tremor, and lightheadedness follow. At this point, the blood sugar must be increased by eating sugar, candy, orange juice or other concentrated sweets, or by use of special medicines. If the reaction is severe and relief is not provided, dreaded insulin shock or coma may result. The patient loses consciousness and, if not treated soon, may suffer brain damage and even death.

To prevent this reaction, the patient must train himself to take extra food if he indulges in extra exercise. On the other hand, if he misses a meal, he must reduce the amount of insulin taken. Also, he should carry with him concentrated sweets such as candy for use in the event he senses an insulin overdosage reaction. It is also important that a diabetic carry with him identification—preferably, both a bracelet with the notice "I am a dia-betic," and a card indicating that he is on insulin, the type and dosage, and also that if he is found dazed or unconscious, he should be taken to the nearest hospital or doctor.

The other reaction develops when too much food is taken, or too little insulin, or there is less than the usual amount of physical activity, or there is the stress of an infection. Then, sugar is not burned at the usual rate, builds up in the blood, and appears in the urine. This is the setting for diabetic acidosis, another dreaded complication which may lead to coma and death. With acidosis, the victim develops great thirst, dry skin and tongue, deep breathing, frequently nausea and vomiting with abdominal cramps and back pain. If untreated, acidosis can lead to death within a day—an event all the more tragic since treatment for diabetic acidosis is so effective that almost every victim can be saved if it is given in time.

How can diabetic acidosis be prevented? Diabetics must avoid eating sprees. They must also watch for conditions that can require extra amounts of insulin to avoid acidosis—e.g., colds and other infections, surgery, dental extractions. The dentist always should know when he is treating a diabetic. One of the worst things for any diabetic is to become alcoholic. During heavy drinking, a diabetic neglects his routine, forgets to take insulin, opening the way for acidosis and coma. At the same time, if he develops coma, it may be mistaken for drunkenness, and emergency medical treatment for the coma may be neglected until too late.

Diabetics should avoid, as much as possible, people who have colds, fevers, sore throats, flu, pneumonia. When an epidemic of respiratory infection occurs in the neighborhood or community, it's a good idea to avoid crowded places. A diabetic should avoid getting chilled and rain-soaked.

The diabetic patient should always remember that insulin is a natural substance secreted by the pancreas. Therefore, its repeated injection is not habit-forming or anything like taking a drug. There should be no shame in administering insulin when traveling and visiting people. The patient should learn from the doctor exactly how to measure insulin into a syringe, the type to purchase, how and where to give the injection, and how to vary the injection site so that no one area of skin is used too much. He should also learn how to test his urine for sugar; this can be done simply enough with a special strip of paper.

DIABETES IN LATER LIFE. Maturity-onset diabetes, which most commonly sets in at age 50 or later, though it may occur earlier, is generally less severe than juvenile diabetes and rarely leads to acidosis. The symptoms are the same for both types.

Maturity-onset diabetes often can be controlled without medication. The doctor usually will try, unless the case is very severe, to treat the patient with a low-sugar diet. He will also try to bring weight down to normal or even somewhat below the accepted normal. If diet and weight reduction do not have the desired effect on symptoms and blood and urinary sugar, the doctor then will generally prescribe one of the oral hypoglycemic medicines rather than insulin.

Medicines taken by mouth are not usually effective in replacing insulin in younger diabetics but do work well in maturity-onset diabetes. The medicines include Orinase, Dymelor, DBI, and Diabinese. Sometimes oral agents are supplemented with small amounts of insulin. If acidosis should occur, it will usually not yield simply to more of the oral medicines but will require use of insulin. The oral medicines act on body chemistry in ways different from insulin. Currently, their long-term effects on the atherosclerotic aspects of diabetes are being evaluated. There is worry that one or more of these oral medicines may not be as helpful as insulin. Every diabetic on oral medication should review the situation with his doctor; a consultation with a specialist in diabetes may be recommended and should be accepted by the patient.

As the population lives longer, more and more people develop maturity-onset diabetes, from which the main threat is atherosclerosis. What can be done to prevent the ravages of arterial disease in the diabetic? Most doctors would recommend that the diabetic follow the advice we have given elsewhere (page 587) about prevention of atherosclerosis. The diabetic, we think, would do well to keep his weight down to normal levels, get regular exercise, emphasize foods containing unsaturated fatty acids and low in cholesterol, avoid cigarette smoking, reduce emotional tensions, and make sure blood pressure is normal (and if not, seek treatment to bring it down to normal levels).

PREGNANCY. Pregnancy is not an easy time for the diabetic patient. It puts greater stress on the prospective mother's diabetic condition and increases risk for the baby. Fortunately, these facts are now well recognized by obstetricians and by physicians who care for diabetics.

The key to prevention of many complications during pregnancy lies in close cooperation between obstetrician and other physician and the pregnant woman. She may need very frequent visits to the doctors to regulate insulin dosage. Insulin requirements change during pregnancy.

Babies of diabetic mothers are at higher risk than other babies. Usually, a pregnant diabetic will be admitted to the hospital several weeks before the expected delivery time so her diabetes can be kept under rigid control before delivery and the decision can be made about possible need for delivery by cesarean section. After delivery, the mother needs to be watched carefully for changing insulin requirement.

Babies born of diabetic mothers have tended to have more congenital defects than those of nondiabetic mothers. This may be the result of inadequate control of the diabetes in the early months of pregnancy. It is another reason why a prospective diabetic mother should notify her doctor the moment she suspects she may be pregnant. Then she should work out an absolutely clear arrangement: Will he or the obstetrician take the responsibility for control of the diabetes throughout pregnancy?

FOOT CARE. The leg arteries of diabetics are especially prone to hardening, narrowing, and thrombosis. The resulting poor circulation increases dangers of infection. Infection, in turn, can lead to ulcers and, in extreme cases, gangrene. Even an ingrown toenail or corn may be a threat for the diabetic. Ideally, the diabetic patient should go regularly to a foot specialist, a podiatrist, for preventive care for the feet. The diabetic patient who cannot afford this should give extra study to our section on care of the feet (page 285). If an infection develops, there should be no delay in seeing a doctor or podiatrist.

TERTIARY PREVENTION. Perhaps someday it will become possible to transplant a normal pancreas to the diabetic who suffers from deficient secretion of insulin. As a surgical feat, pancreas transplantation presents no great problems. It is the body's tendency to reject the transplant that is the big problem—here as with other transplants—that must be solved.

We have described the most common problems of the diabetic patient. Unfortunately, there are additional difficulties which some diabetics may experience, and which they should recognize and discuss promptly with the doctor. Impotence may afflict the male. He should feel no shame in mentioning this to his doctor; if necessary, he should discuss the problem with a psychotherapist. Some diabetics may develop neuralgias; any unusual shooting pains or pins-and-needles sensations should be mentioned to the doctor. Swelling of the ankles may be an indication of a kidney complication of diabetes, called Kimmelstiel-Wilson syndrome, and should be reported promptly to the doctor.

All that we have written and admonished may seem so forbidding that a diabetic may ask, "Is life worth living?" We can assure him that it is. Many people with diabetes have distinguished themselves in sports, in industry, in the arts. They accept their disease—and the extra discipline needed to live successfully with it. As one wise physician has observed, the way to long life is to get a chronic disease and learn to live with it.

DIZZINESS AND MÉNIÈRE'S DISEASE

Almost everyone has experienced the sensation of dizziness as the result of whirling around too fast or too long or perhaps while looking down from a great height. This mild sensation is considerably different from the severe attacks of dizziness (vertigo) which bring a person to a doctor. With true vertigo, the patient feels that he is being whirled about or that everything around him is whirling; in addition, he feels nauseated and may vomit; he is pale and sweaty; he tries to stay in one position because movement makes the symptoms worse.

There are many possible causes for this type of dizziness, since the sense of balance involves the labyrinth of the inner ear, areas of the brain, and the eyes. Thus, infections in or around the inner ear may lead to severe dizziness as can hemorrhage into the labyrinth. Medicines such as quinine, salicylates, and streptomycin may sometimes set off vertigo by their effect on the labyrinth, and so may alcoholic indulgence. General infections such as influenza may cause dizziness which may last long after the acute general infection has passed. Motion sickness is a frequent cause.

Brain tumors, lesions of blood vessels in various parts of the brain, brain infections, and multiple sclerosis have been known to set off attacks of vertigo.

Paralysis of a muscle that moves the eyeball may lead to dizzy spells. First attempts to wear bifocals may do so.

Prevention of such types of dizziness usually depends on treatment for the underlying disease or removal of the offending medication.

PSEUDOVERTIGO. Some patients experience sensations of lightheadedness, swaying, spots in front of the eyes, or dimming of vision and mistakenly term this dizziness. Some have dizzy feelings without the complete complex of symptoms of vertigo. Such sensations constitute pseudovertigo. They are apt to occur in high blood pressure, anemia, emphysema, and in elderly persons with atherosclerosis (particularly after a warm bath). Sometimes they occur with change of posture in a debilitated individual, a convalescent person, or someone who is in extremely poor physical condition.

MÉNIÈRE'S DISEASE. This disease is marked by attacks of severe true whirling dizziness with nausea, vomiting, sweating, and pallor. In addition, there may be hearing impairment and ringing in the ears (tinnitus). Attacks last from a few minutes to several hours. Sometimes, an attack develops so suddenly that the victim is thrown to the ground. Usually, however, the patient senses an attack coming and has time to sit or lie down.

Ménière's disease involves a little understood faulty functioning of the labyrinth of the inner ear. The course may vary. Sometimes the vertigo attacks stop but the hearing impairment and tinnitus continue. Or the vertigo may stop only when the deafness is complete.

Since the exact cause is unknown, primary prevention as yet is not possible. For secondary prevention, one important measure is ventilation of emotional tensions. First, the patient may have emotional problems which help to trigger attacks. And, second, the fear of sudden disabling attacks of dizziness is enough to make even a well-adjusted person nervous and apprehensive.

Many medications are used to treat or help prevent attacks; no one is effective for all patients. They include Diamox, Diuril, nicotinic acid, Benadryl, and Dramamine. For a severe prolonged attack, it may be necessary to inject atropine or Benadryl. Some physicians prescribe a low-salt diet and restricted fluid intake along with ammonium chloride.

In severe, unyielding cases involving one ear, surgical treatment may be considered. If useful hearing in that ear is lacking, electrical coagulation of the labyrinth may be used. Recently, excellent results have been reported from use of ultrasound to selectively destroy the labyrinth while preserving hearing.

DENTAL PROBLEMS AND DIZZINESS. Some doctors and dentists believe that attacks resembling those of Ménière's disease may be caused in some cases by faulty bite resulting from poor alignment of the teeth. Such misalignment may cause the socket of the jawbone to impinge on ear structures. To correct the alignment and bite requires long, expensive dental treatment which must be done by a specialist in such work. Your doctor or dentist can arrange a consultation if there is a possibility that dental bite may be causing attacks of dizziness.

EPILEPSY

Many terms in medicine are carryovers from times when knowledge about underlying causes of disease was limited. Often, diseases were named on the basis of their dominant symptom. Many years were required to show that several disorders may produce the same symptom. This is true, for example, of heart failure and anemia; it is also true of epilepsy.

The dominant symptom in epilepsy is the recurrent seizure, for which there can be many causes. All seizures, however, have in common a change from orderly activity of cells in a part of or in the whole brain to brief, intense, uncoordinated overactivity. Since the brain provides the ultimate control for all body activities, sensations, and motions, this uncontrolled hyperactivity is manifested by changes in body movements or perception.

The activity of brain cells can be detected by the minute amounts of electrical energy they generate. An instrument called the electroencephalograph (EEG) records the average electrical activity of the cells of the brain.

There are three major classifications of seizures. The best known and most common is the *grand mal* type produced when almost all cells in the brain fire rapidly and without coordination. It is manifested by a groan or cry followed by a fall and violent twitching or contorting which may last one to five minutes. Thereafter, the patient may sleep heavily for several hours; on the other hand, he may get up immediately and experience some confusion for a time, or in some cases may even feel fine right away.

Another type of seizure, called *Jacksonian*, may start in one part of the body and spread gradually to become a grand mal convulsion. This type is indicative of a single overactive area of the brain from which seizure activity may spread to the entire brain.

Petit mal seizures are characterized by a fixed "blank stare" lasting only a few seconds, sometimes accompanied by twitching movements but without falling. In fact, these "absences," as they are sometimes called, are so brief that they may go undetected as the patient resumes his preseizure activity without giving any evidence of a lapse. Petit mal seizures occur mainly in children; they are rare after puberty. They should not, however, be ignored because they seem innocuous. About half of petit mal patients sooner or later have a grand mal seizure.

About one third of adults who have seizures have the psychomotor type. A psychomotor seizure may be difficult to detect because it is characterized by inappropriate but seemingly purposeful activity without the obvious changes found in grand mal epilepsy. The patient may suddenly seem withdrawn; he may rhythmically pluck at his clothing, hear or smell things that are not present, smack his lips. Such a person should not be restrained; he or she may become angry and difficult to manage. The seizure usually lasts only for a few moments.

Sometimes a seizure is preceded by a warning, or "aura," that gives the patient notice of an oncoming attack. It may take the form of hearing unusual sounds, seeing strange lights, feeling nauseated or just restless and irritable.

There are many possible causes of seizures, not all of them known as yet. The known include brain injury at birth or later in life, brain tumor, infection, disturbances produced by toxic substances such as lead, fever (usually in children only), insufficient flow of blood to the head as may occur during a heart attack or as the result of a blood clot in a vessel supplying the brain, and metabolic causes such as low blood sugar or low blood calcium.

There are also the seizures of unknown cause, the so-called idiopathic epilepsy. Idiopathic epilepsy is not inherited. Recent research, however, indicates that there may be an inherited susceptibility, and that the susceptibility in some cases may lead to seizures while in others a seizure is never experienced.

Epilepsy merely refers to recurrent seizures; it does not indicate the cause.

And it is important for the physician to determine, if possible, the cause because of the implications for treatment.

Anyone who has had a seizure should seek medical help without delay. He should be accompanied, if possible, by someone who has observed the entire seizure or the immediate preseizure or postseizure interval.

In most cases, especially for persons under 20, diagnostic evaluation includes a general physical examination, neurological testing, EEG, head x-rays, and spinal tap. All of these procedures may be carried out in the doctor's office or in a hospital on an outpatient basis. People who have seizures for the first time after age 20 will frequently need special x-ray and blood tests, since there is a greater likelihood of finding a specific cause, while most cases of seizures in people under 20 fall into the "unknown cause" category.

In almost all cases now, potent medicines are available to prevent recurrences of seizures. These agents do not cure but they serve the important function of helping to prevent hyperactivity of susceptible brain cells. Usually with the proper medicine in the proper dosage, side effects are few.

It is essential, for secondary prevention, that antiseizure medicines be taken steadily. Stopping them abruptly may increase the tendency to seizures. It may require several weeks or months to achieve the proper balance of medications needed to keep seizures under control. Once this is achieved, and after several months then of regular observation by the physician to make certain that all is going well, visits to the physician should be continued at suitable intervals, which may vary, depending upon the patient, from monthly to semiannually.

Since there is a decreasing tendency to seizures with age, it is possible in some cases to discontinue medications after two to three seizure-free years.

In some cases, certain stimuli—such as blinking lights, fatigue, or repeated deep breathing—may precipitate a seizure. Of course, every effort should be made to avoid these stimuli.

When, of course, there is a known cause for seizures, it often is remediable. And with the cause eliminated —by correction of low blood sugar or calcium, for example—no further treatment is required.

The outlook now in cases of seizures of unknown cause is almost uniformly a bright one. Thanks to medicines available today, most epileptics can lead a normal life without restrictions as to type of employment, driving, or sports, so long as their seizures are being kept under good control. It is advisable, though, to avoid extreme fatigue.

Although there have been intensive educational campaigns about epilepsy, too many people still remain woefully ignorant about the disorder and wrongly think that epileptics are "possessed" or mentally retarded and unfit for work. The fact is that many men of recognized genius—Napoleon, Alfred Nobel, de Maupassant, for example—have been epileptics. Studies have established that epileptics are trustworthy employees in every business field, with almost no loss of time or accidental injury to be expected from their epilepsy. Disability policies in many businesses no longer make distinctions between the epileptic and nonepileptic.

Epileptics can and should marry and have children.

At times, epileptics or their families may need vocational counseling or advice on how to cope with the reactions of others to epilepsy. Such advice may be obtained from social workers, psychologists, and, of course, the physician.

It is an important part of preventive medicine for parents of an epileptic child to be counseled. Parents may worry a great deal about the possible physical and psychological repercussions of the disorder. Actually, children are most likely to have problems when their activities are unduly restricted, when they are treated as invalids, when their disorder is not discussed with them at a level appropriate to their understanding, or when they are constantly fretted over and made nervous.

Preventive medicine also calls for the patient with epilepsy to carry identification. It may be a pin or bracelet with instructions to examine the patient's pocket or wallet, where a diagnosis card and medications may be kept. This helps to assure prompt and proper treatment of a seizure.

As part of the preventive approach, in the case of a patient subject to grand mal seizures, the physician may advise that members of the family and perhaps others be instructed in how to handle a seizure.

At the beginning of an attack, the patient should be lowered to the floor, or if that is not possible, any hard objects should be removed from his path.

A folded handkerchief, a roll of paper, or some similar object—one too big to be swallowed—should be placed between the teeth on one side of the mouth. The purpose is to prevent tongue biting or possible breaking of teeth. Do not try to force the mouth open; wait for it to relax momentarily; and keep fingers out.

There should be no attempt to force liquids down the patient's throat or to move him during a convulsion. When the attack is over, make sure that he rests quietly until consciousness is fully regained. There is no need to rush him to a hospital unless he has a series of seizures.

Prevention in some cases may involve surgical removal of a focal area in the brain that can be shown to be a source of cell hyperactivity that triggers seizures which cannot be managed by medicines. Such surgery is uncommon because (1) medications are usually effective, and (2) it is unusual to isolate such a focal area.

GALLBLADDER DISEASE

The gallbladder, which is located in the upper right part of the abdomen under the liver, is a pear-shaped sac that stores bile coming from the liver. It holds an ounce or two and discharges the bile through the gallbladder duct (cystic duct) into the common bile duct, from which it enters the intestine at the level of the duodenum. Bile is discharged when food, especially greasy food, leaves the stomach; it helps in digestion. The gallbladder is not an essential organ; when it is removed, the liver supplies bile directly to the intestine.

Most common gallbladder diseases are associated with the presence of stones in the gallbladder. Most gallstones are a mixture of cholesterol, bile pigments, and calcium carbonate. Since they contain cholesterol, a logical question is whether there is any connection between the level of blood cholesterol and the risk of getting a stone. Such a relationship has not been shown.

The stones frequently contain so little calcium that they do not show up on ordinary x-ray films and must be detected by special x-ray studies after a radiopaque dyestuff is taken by mouth or administered via a vein.

Stones manifest themselves in different ways. When a stone passes out of the gallbladder and becomes lodged in the common bile duct, there may be an acute attack of agonizing pain, gallbladder colic. Frequently, symptoms include nausea and vomiting, fever, increased white blood count, and jaundice. Sometimes, the stone causes no pain, sitting in the common bile duct and blocking free passage of bile and producing yellow jaundice as the bile pigments back up into the bloodstream.

In making a diagnosis of an acute gallstone attack, the doctor realizes that he is dealing with a potentially serious scenario. If the flow of bile is not restored, there can be liver damage from back-pressure or from infection which usually sets in. So if the stone is not passed in a day or two, an operation is performed to remove it; frequently, the gallbladder will be removed at the same time if the patient is in good condition, because almost always the gallbladder contains more stones and may also be infected. If the patient is seriously ill, the surgeon may remove only the stone and wait until a later date to remove the gallbladder.

Chronic presence of gallstones is a common finding. It is estimated that 32 percent of women and 16 percent of men at 40 years of age have stones in their gallbladder. The numbers increase after age 40, and also with obesity. There is some truth in the aphorism that gallbladder disease is a disease of those who are "female, fat, and forty."

Some people with gallstones never have symptoms; others may have dyspepsia, with abdominal gas, belching, nausea, and dull pain in the upper abdomen, all made worse by large or fatty meals. Many of these people learn to avoid fatty foods, especially greasy ones.

The usual scenario for chronic gallstones (chronic cholecystitis) calls for continuance of the above symptoms and the risk of colic when a stone passes out of the gallbladder. Then, as already noted, the stone may become lodged in the common bile duct and create a serious situation. Usually, with chronic stones, there are chronic inflammation and infection of the gallbladder.

Since stones may spell trouble, it is usual for the gallbladder to be removed if the patient is a good surgical risk (free of disabling heart or lung disease, etc.). Surgical removal relieves all symptoms. It also eliminates the possibility of cancer of the gallbladder which is more frequently found in stone-containing than in normal gallbladders.

When the decision is to operate—and the family doctor may properly want a consultation with a specialist in gallbladder diseases—then a good and experienced surgeon should be found even if it means traveling to a medical center. Gallbladder removal is a major surgical procedure. Since nature sometimes provides different duct and artery arrangements in the gallbladder area, an experienced surgeon is desirable.

Is the situation hopeless for the person who is a bad surgical risk or who decides for one reason or another not to have the operation? Medical treatment is less satisfactory than surgery but will prove helpful. The doctor will advise a "no grease" diet which is more generous than the low-fat diet popular in the past; special medicines may be used to quiet gallbladder spasms; and Decholin may be taken by mouth to encourage flow of bile from the gallbladder. Of course, medical treatment may not keep a gallstone from moving out to block the common bile duct and thus create a surgical emergency at a time in life when a patient may be less able to withstand surgery than when stones were diagnosed originally.

Occasionally chronic gallbladder disease may exist when no stones can be detected by even the most detailed x-ray studies. The gallbladder may seem to empty in sluggish fashion. Symptoms may be annoying and resemble the indigestion produced by chronic gallstones. One would think that removal of the gallbladder should produce relief. But experienced surgeons have learned that often symptoms may persist after surgery. Probably the symptoms arise from the stomach, intestines, or liver. In any event, few surgeons will advise gallbladder removal unless stones can be demonstrated.

An acute infection of the gallbladder is a serious matter. The doctor is immediately alert when the patient has an attack of upper right abdominal pain with tenderness of the gallbladder and spasm. Prostration, nausea, vomiting, and fever occur. The white blood count is elevated. The best to be hoped for is that within 24 hours there will be evidence of clearing of the infection. In that case, nonsurgical treatment may be chosen with the idea that three to six months later the diseased gallbladder can be removed under more favorable circumstances.

But if the infection persists or even gets worse, then the doctor foresees the possibility that the gallbladder may rupture, spreading pus, bile, and gallstones into the delicate abdominal (peritoneal) cavity. This is an ominous situation requiring immediate surgery. Another possibility is that the gallbladder may form a large abscess, which either may become walled off and will require surgical drainage or may rupture into the stomach or intestine. All of these are serious situations, but perhaps a bit less serious than before antibiotics were available to fight the inevitable spreading infection.

Another ominous possibility is that the gallbladder may become gangrenous and spew infection into the delicate, important ducts and blood vessels near it, or send the infection into the vital liver. All of these situations call for immediate, skillful surgical help. Frequently, the infection may be so bad or the patient so sick, or both, that all the surgeon can do is drain the gallbladder. Later, when infection has been cleared and the patient returned to good health, the diseased gallbladder can be removed.

Is there any primary prevention for gallbladder disease? Obviously, sex or age of anyone "female, fat, and forty" cannot be changed. But something can be done about the fat; it is important to maintain normal weight, as we detail in Chapter 7.

Since it may give rise to potentially serious problems as the result of stones and infection, and occasionally may be the site for cancer, why shouldn't the gallbladder be removed routinely early in life before troubles may begin to set in after age 40? A gallbladder removal is a major surgical procedure —and so, as with any other, there is a slight but definite mortality risk even when the operation is performed by the best of surgeons. It is also an uncomfortable procedure which requires several weeks before full recovery. And major surgery is not inexpensive. So we take a calculated risk, with the expectation that if gallbladder disease does develop, modern secondary preventive measures will prove successful, as, indeed, they do in about 99 percent of otherwise healthy individuals.

GONORRHEA AND OTHER VENEREAL DISEASES

Gonorrhea—also commonly known as clap, strain, gleet, and by a dozen other names—is a dangerous disease. It is dangerous because it can produce serious, painful derangements of various organs of the body, and because these complications are not sufficiently widely known and feared.

It is dangerous for other reasons. In women, initial signs of infection may not be apparent and the disease process may be allowed to progress. Many people, too, have the impression that, since treatment in most cases is easy and effective, gonorrhea is no worse than a cold. But inadequate treatment may do no more than suppress symptoms without eradicating the disease.

Currently, with more than two million new cases of gonorrhea each year in the United States, the disease is reaching epidemic proportions, particularly among teen-agers.

It is caused by a germ usually transmitted through sexual intercourse. In very rare cases, it may be transmitted by contaminated materials such as washcloths and personal articles. Most cases of such indirect transmission, however, are in young girls. Another mode of indirect transmission is to newborn babies. If gonococcal germs get into the eyes of a newborn during passage through an infected birth canal, blindness can result. Fortunately, almost all states now require doctors to place a mild disinfectant, capable of killing gonococci, in the eyes of all babies at birth as a preventive measure.

The measures for primary prevention are much the same as those for syphilis (page 657). On the community level, children and adults must be educated to the dangers of the disease, how it is acquired and spread, signs and symptoms, and where to go for treatment. Many cities and states have programs aimed at seeking out and treating, confidentially, the contacts of known infected individuals. This is a vitally important preventive technique for any communicable disease. On a personal level, primary prevention includes avoidance of illicit sexual contact. An effective means of preventing infection involves use of a condom and washing of the genitals with warm, soapy water after intercourse.

In men, the first symptom of infection is usually a whitish discharge from the penis, with or without burning on urination, beginning three to seven days after exposure. In women, there may be a whitish vaginal discharge and burning on urination, but often symptoms may be quite mild and even entirely absent.

There are no special blood tests for gonorrhea and because several other diseases may cause similar symptoms, the diagnosis of gonorrhea has to be made by examination of the discharge under a microscope to detect the gonococcal organism. Actually, because discharge may not be present in women and because gonorrhea may lead to serious complications, a history of sexual relations with an infected person is usually sufficient reason for instituting treatment.

In some cases, the gonococcal organism can infect glands associated with the internal genital tract. In men, the infection may affect the prostate or the epididymis (a structure located alongside the testicle), causing severe discomfort. Infertility can result. In women, infection may affect the fallopian tubes leading from ovaries to uterus, sometimes with spillover into the abdominal cavity, causing fever, severe abdominal pain, and peritonitis. Symptoms may be so severe that emergency surgery is sometimes performed in order to make certain that they are not due to appendicitis or other life-threatening disorders. Antibiotics, although they take time to work, are effective, but in severe cases hospitalization may be needed.

Generally, the outlook is good after adequate treatment. But in some cases, particularly those with repeated infection, there is a possibility, despite adequate treatment, of scar formation at the site of infection. In men, such scarring narrows the urethra and may obstruct flow of urine. Repeated dilatation of the urethra or even surgery may be required to prevent scar tissue from closing the channel.

Women run a higher risk of infertility from repeated episodes of gonorrhea because the fallopian tubes may become chronically infected and scarred, and an egg discharged from an ovary each month cannot pass normally and arrive at the uterus. Abscesses also may form internally, requiring surgical drainage.

Other complications of gonorrhea may include arthritis and pleuritis.

For secondary prevention, the physician will use antibiotic treatment and, in severe cases, bed rest. Follow-up of the patient for several weeks is needed to make certain that there is no further evidence of disease and that there is no other venereal disease. In about 2 percent of cases, syphilis may be acquired at the same time as gonorrhea, and treatment is needed for this. To make certain that syphilis has not been missed, a blood test will be done. Reappearance of symptoms after several months is almost always due to reinfection, for *infection with gonorrhea does not confer immunity.*

The physician must report confidentially a case of gonorrhea to the local public health department for its records and to enable the department to try to trace contacts and stop spread of the infection.

A physician—and not any "man doctor" or other quack—is the only one capable of effective treatment of gonorrhea because he is alert to the many problems we have discussed. Of particular concern of late is the emergence of strains of gonococcal organisms that are resistant to usual treatment and are more virulent as well. This is another reason for treatment by a physician, who may apply other measures when usual ones fail.

Tertiary preventive measures are directed at correcting sterility problems in women and preventing complete destruction of the usual route of urine passage in men. Several medical centers do the very delicate surgery that may correct scarring of fallopian tubes responsible for sterility, though such surgery is not always successful. In men, periodic dilatation of the urethra by a urologist can prevent strictures from worsening.

Other Venereal Diseases

There are three other less common venereal diseases: chancroid, lymphogranuloma venereum, and granuloma inguinale. They are also transmitted during sexual intercourse. With the exception of lymphogranuloma venereum, which can lead to narrowing and stricture of the rectum, they do not usually produce long-term, late complications as syphilis (see page 657) and gonorrhea may.

The three diseases, although caused by different organisms, produce sores on the genitals, and swollen and painful lymph nodes in the groin. If neglected, the sores can enlarge and cause discomfort and deformity. Treatment with antibiotics is available. One danger is that the disorders may mask syphilis or gonorrhea which may be present. Preventive measures are the same as for gonorrhea.

HEADACHE (INCLUDING MIGRAINE)

Headache is virtually a universal ailment. It is a rare person who goes through life without from time to time experiencing a headache—piercing, throbbing, pounding, splitting, or just dull. Many people recognize the "why" of their headaches and feel confident that when the overwork, mental tension, eyestrain, fever, cold, or poor ventilation is relieved, the headache will pass.

Usually, headache is a symptom of life's stresses and strains. But it also can be a warning sign of serious illness. How does one know whether a headache is a minor matter or a serious signal? Usually, commonsense observation reveals the cause. It sometimes helps to note in writing the time of day, duration, location of headaches, and any other symptoms such as vomiting and fever that may accompany them.

Headaches are common in the premenstrual period for some women. Headaches in the morning, especially upon awakening, may reflect poor ventilation in the bedroom. Carbon monoxide can produce headaches, and sometimes running the car briefly in a closed garage just long enough to warm the engine may produce a headache. Or a gas heater with a defective burner or flue may do it. Head pain after meals may be due to allergy to a food such as milk or chocolate. Too much alcohol, of course, can produce headache. Headaches that occur outdoors may be results of excessive glare or smog. Pain just above the eyes or over the cheeks may result from sinus infection. Medicines of almost all types on occasion may produce headache, especially tranquilizers, sleeping pills, pain relievers, and appetite suppressants. In children, Monday morning headaches may reflect fear or dislike of school.

Once you have a definite clue to what may be causing repeated headaches for you, you can see if removing or avoiding the suspected cause makes any real difference. For example, if you relate headaches to some specific food such as chocolate, you can first remove it from the diet; then you can try to incur the headache by taking the food.

Headaches associated with infections are easy to diagnose. The common cold and mild sore throats with fever usually bring headache with them. So do more serious infectious diseases such as influenza, strep sore throat, scarlet fever, pneumonia. Headache accompanies acute sinusitis. When headache is accompanied by fever and stiff neck, meningitis is a possibility and the doctor should be notified immediately.

When headaches get worse, come every day, wake the patient during the night, or are accompanied by vomiting or other symptoms, a thorough medical checkup is in order. Also, if headache comes on after a fall or injury to the head, the doctor should be notified at once because the headache may signal hemorrhage around the brain.

In pregnancy, unexpected onset of headache should be reported at once to the doctor because it may be a symptom of a potentially serious complication, toxemia of pregnancy.

There are many serious causes of headache. Among them are brain tumor, impending stroke, severe anemia, glaucoma, lead poisoning, high blood pressure, uremia, low blood sugar due to a tumor of the pancreas, congestive heart failure by itself or secondary to chronic emphysema.

TENSION HEADACHE. Of all chronic headaches, tension and migraine headaches account for about 90 percent, and the tension, or nervous, type is by far more common, accounting for an estimated seven of every ten headaches.

When a job demands a fixed head position (for example, driving against bright headlights), we often set the muscles of our neck, jaw, and scalp in pain-causing postures. We commonly do the same as a part of a reaction against psychological pressures. Tension headache victims, one physician observes, "symbolically carry a great weight on their shoulders." Upon feeling anxious, they set scalp and neck muscles and develop headache. Some researchers have established that the degree of muscle tension they can measure with instruments is directly related to the patient's degree of anxiety.

Can tension headaches be prevented? Mild tranquilizers have been used with some degree of success, but these medicines are stopgap measures since they do not change the underlying situation. Many authorities believe that simple psychotherapy—just talking out problems with a family physician—can help.

One distinguished headache specialist and researcher has reported finding that two thirds of tension headache victims can help themselves if they seriously try to cut down on the number of things ordinarily done in one day, plan regular periods of rest and relaxation, and end overconcern about things being "just so." Some physicians urge patients to keep a daily activity record and analyze it to see under what conditions the headaches recur. The objective is to show the patient how to live headache-free within his emotional and physical capacity.

What will relieve the pain of tension headaches? In mild cases, aspirin is still the most practical and useful relief. But no analgesic alone or sedative alone does much good for more severe, persistent pain. Studies indicate that either an analgesic or sedative will provide only 50 to 60 percent improvement. A double-pronged approach is needed for effective treatment: the pain threshhold must be raised, achievable with an analgesic; tension must be reduced at least somewhat, achievable with a sedative. Gentle massage of neck muscles and applications of moist, warm compresses to the back of the neck are helpful, too.

MIGRAINE. Also known as "sick headache," migraine affects about 5 percent of the population. It is more common in women than in men, generally starts between the ages of 10 and 20, and sometimes disappears after 50.

In 8 to 10 percent of cases, visual disturbances precede migraine headache: blind spots occur, or zigzag lines or flashes or spots of light are seen. At migraine's peak, many victims experience nausea and vomiting.

What causes migraine is still uncertain. Theories range from allergy to gland disturbances. Many studies show that personality and stress are also factors. The migraine sufferer is apt to be a perfectionist, with a rigid personality, wedded to exact schedules. That is why some migraine patients get their headaches only on weekends when they do not have their precise daily work schedule to follow.

Fortunately, there are potent medicines for treating the attacks. Since the sufferer usually knows in advance from premonitory symptoms that a headache is coming on, the headache sometimes can be averted by taking ergotamine tartrate or ergotamine tartrate combined with caffeine or phenobarbital or both, then relaxing for a while in a warm bath, and resting in a darkened room.

When an attack comes on, an injection of ergotamine tartrate will usually stop the headache within an hour. Ergotamine tartrate plus caffeine (Cafergot) can be taken by mouth or by rectal suppository, the latter being particularly useful when there is vomiting. The important thing with medication by mouth is to take it immediately if an attack is sensed and to use it to the limit the doctor permits, so as to build up its concentration in the body quickly but without exceeding the toxic limit.

Another medicine is available for use between attacks as a means of trying to reduce their frequency. It is called methysergide maleate (Sansert). In occasional patients, however, it has been found to have profoundly toxic effects, and any patient who uses it should keep in touch with his doctor to report any unusual symptoms and to have checkups on a schedule the doctor advocates.

Should migraine sufferers have psychotherapy? We believe they should start with a frank discussion of emotional problems with their own doctor. If the problems seem too complex to be resolved without expert help, then by all means there should be a visit to a psychotherapist to let him decide on the possible need and value of psychotherapy.

HISTAMINIC CEPHALALGIA. This is also called atypical migraine, Horton's headache, Sluder's neuralgia, cluster headache, vidian neuralgia, facial neuralgia, etc.

This headache can be one-sided like migraine. Pain is usually severe and is accompanied by redness of the eye, free flow of tears, stuffy or running nose, swelling of the temporal arteries on the affected side. The headache usually affects males, tends to come on during sleep, and frequently subsides in less than an hour.

It is called histaminic cephalalgia or histamine headache because it can be reproduced in the susceptible patient by injection of histamine, and this serves as a diagnostic test.

An acute attack can be shortened by injection of ergotamine tartrate. For prevention, methysergide maleate has been used with the precautions previously noted. Also, a desensitization technique may be tried. It involves injection of an initial small dose of histamine, followed by increasing amounts until a preventive maintenance level is found.

HEART DISEASES

Heart diseases constitute the major threat to life in the United States and most countries of the Western world. In our country alone, they cause nearly one million deaths yearly. Most of the deaths are due to one type of heart disease which affects the coronary arteries, the vessels that carry blood directly to the heart muscle.

It is a curious fact that despite the vast amount of heart disease, the heart muscle itself rarely is directly diseased. Viral or bacterial invasions are uncommon. There are virtually no cases of cancer of the heart.

The heart consists of four chambers —two atria and two ventricles. The atria receive blood returning from the body and from the lungs; the ventricles pump out blood to the lungs and to the body. There are four sets of valves to control direction of blood flow.

The valves are subject to disease. If they become damaged by disease and fail to close properly, there is interference with proper blood flow, and this may cause enlargement of heart chambers and damage to the chamber walls.

RHEUMATIC FEVER. Rheumatic fever is a disease that may produce heart valve damage. Once the disease was greatly feared; today, thanks to both primary and secondary preventive measures, it has become less ominous.

Most often, rheumatic fever afflicts children between 5 and 15 years of age. It usually follows a streptococcal infection such as strep sore throat, scarlet fever, tonsillitis, or middle ear infection. Early signs, which usually begin 10 to 14 days after the streptococcal infection, consist of fever of 101° to 103°F, irritability, pallor, poor appetite, and moderate weight loss. More specific symptoms then appear —pain in the joints, which are tender to the touch and hurt when moved. Redness and swelling of the joints occur.

The joints are never crippled. The acute phase of the disease passes in a matter of some weeks or months, but some subtle mark may be left on one or more of the valves of the heart.

Rheumatic fever frequently recurs and adds further injury to the heart. It may be many years before the heart valve damage begins to manifest itself clearly.

Weakened heart valves are also susceptible to a special type of infection. Bacteria that get into the bloodstream may settle on the damaged valves and chew them up over a period of several months. This condition is known as *subacute bacterial endocarditis*. Until the discovery of penicillin, it was almost invariably fatal. A recovered case of subacute bacterial endocarditis would be reported in medical journals as an example of the fact that every rule has its exception. Today, with penicillin and other antibiotics, the outlook is entirely different.

What can be done to prevent rheumatic fever and its subsequent damage to the heart? Many practical measures are now available. It's important, of course, to protect anyone, especially a child or teen-ager, from someone who has a sore throat, especially one that is definitely streptococcal. There should be no visits to the sick person until the doctor has given the all-clear. The person with strep throat should be isolated and should use paper plates, which can be disposed of.

Quick, effective treatment of strep sore throats with modern medicines has become an effective primary preventive of rheumatic fever. Remember that any sore throat accompanied by a temperature of over 101°F or by nausea, vomiting or other signs of severe illness requires a doctor's attention.

When a person has had rheumatic fever once, everything possible must be done to prevent him from getting repeated attacks, because of the damage they may do to the heart. By constant use of antibiotics or sulfa medicines, the strep infections which cause the recurrences can usually be controlled. Any child with rheumatic fever, or who has recovered from one attack, should remain under the care of a doctor or a heart clinic so that recurrences can be prevented.

What if the valves have become seriously damaged, enough to threaten heart failure and death in a matter of months or years? Tertiary prevention, in the form of modern heart surgery, today is effective. Almost every type of valvular heart disease caused by rheumatic fever can now be helped by great advances in open-heart surgery. In this form of surgery, with a heart-lung machine taking over the functions of heart and lungs, blood can be temporarily bypassed around the heart and the surgeon can work within the heart, seeing exactly what he is doing.

We have mentioned the fearful complication of bacterial endocarditis. If it develops, cures today are often possible through use of massive doses of penicillin or other antibiotics.

Actually, much can be done to prevent development of endocarditis. The disease is usually caused by another type of streptococcal organism which is present in the mouth. Prevention of subacute bacterial endocarditis depends upon preventing entrance of these bacteria into the bloodstream, which can carry them to a damaged heart valve. How can this be achieved? The person with rheumatic fever should never have a tooth extracted or any dental work done on the gums without the dentist being notified about the rheumatic fever. An injection of antibiotic before the dental work will protect the heart valves. All infections in a patient with chronic rheumatic heart disease should be reported to the doctor without delay before bacteria attack the injured valve or valves.

CONGENITAL HEART DISEASE. Most forms of congenital heart disease—disease present at birth—are recognized early in the child's life by routine physical examination. Some manifest themselves unmistakably, as when a baby has a distinctive blue color.

Today the serious forms of congenital heart disease can be prevented from incapacitating or killing a child. With open-heart surgery, it is now possible to repair defects, sometimes to the point where a completely normal life becomes possible. The important thing for parents to do is to locate, with the help of their physician, a medical center or hospital where there is an experienced heart surgeon to perform the required operation. This may mean traveling many miles from home, but it is surely worth the effort and expense.

There are two forms of congenital heart disease which sometimes may give no trouble early in life. One is coarctation of the aorta—a narrowing of the main artery leaving the heart. The other is patent ductus arteriosus, in which an embryonic arterial connection does not disappear as it normally should. Some people take the attitude that with either of these disorders it is all right to wait until the patient develops symptoms. By then, however, it may be too late. It is good preventive medicine to take the sur-geon's advice on when an operation should be performed.

SYPHILITIC HEART DISEASE. Before the advent of antibiotics, syphilis often caused severe heart disease many years after the primary infection. One of the triumphs of secondary prevention has been the recognition of this danger and the intensive treatment of early syphilis with penicillin or other antibiotics so as to completely eradicate the infection. As we have advised elsewhere, anyone with a syphilitic lesion should, no matter how small or painless the lesion is, undergo complete therapy until cured, in order to avoid late effects on the heart (as well as on the brain and other parts of the body).

CORONARY ARTERY DISEASE. In terms of numbers afflicted and deaths caused, by far the most important form of heart disease is coronary artery disease in which the arteries supplying nutrients to the heart muscle itself become clogged by deposits on their walls (atherosclerosis). We have already discussed some of the means of preventing this disease in other sections of this book dealing with diet, exercise, and smoking.

Doctors speak of high-risk factors in coronary artery disease. They mean that in addition to any basic risk which may be imposed by heredity, a given individual can add to the risk of developing the disease by (a) wrong diet, (b) obesity, (c) smoking of cigarettes, (d) lack of regular exercise, (e) poor control of diabetes if present, (f) high levels of blood cholesterol and neutral fats, (g) poor control of gout if present, (h) uncontrolled high blood pressure, and (i) possibly excessive emotional stress, especially in some job situations which involve deadlines.

It is highly unlikely that all of these factors would be present for any one individual but if they should be, he would have 25 or more times the likelihood of getting a heart attack from coronary artery disease than another person. Even if only a few are operative in an individual—e.g., heavy smoking, high cholesterol, high blood pressure—the risk gets high.

Just think of this: Something can be done about almost every one of these factors. They don't have to inevitably add to risk.

Cholesterol, when elevated, can be brought down to normal by proper diet, weight control, and exercise. If necessary, medicines can be added to reduce the cholesterol level. We have indicated elsewhere how weight can be controlled, how to achieve proper diet, and exercises you can use.

See the sections on high blood pressure and gout for information about how these diseases can be controlled. In the area of diseases that contribute to coronary artery atherosclerosis, diabetes is a big problem. But if a patient eliminates other high-risk factors, he should have a good chance of escaping a heart attack, especially with good control of the diabetes.

Anyone can stop smoking if he has motivation. We have offered advice in Chapter 11 on motivation and breaking the habit. Surely, a habit that brings risk of heart attack, cancer, and emphysema deserves to be eliminated.

We are inclined to believe that emotional stress increases the risk of coronary artery disease. Suggestions for achieving a relaxed type of living are offered on page 100, and on what to do about anxieties and nervous compulsive habits in earlier chapters.

HEART ATTACKS. Suppose a heart attack occurs. The immediate problem, of course, is to get the patient through it. A severe attack is a real emergency. Ideally, the person should be transported by ambulance with a doctor or skilled attendant giving him oxygen and other emergency treatment on the way. Equally important, he should be taken to a hospital equipped with a coronary care unit—a special section where he can be constantly monitored with special instruments and is under the constant observation and care of skilled nursing personnel.

The fact is that a heart attack, even a very severe one, today is not a hopeless situation—provided the patient gets immediate, expert care. More and more patients who reach the hospital before death today are being kept from dying. A big problem that remains to be solved is getting more heart attack victims more quickly to the hospital, and efforts are now being made to solve the problem with specially equipped ambulances kept moving about under radio direction and even equipped to provide some of the care previously available only in hospitals.

After a heart attack, there are two major areas of secondary prevention —to prevent another attack and, of great importance, to prevent the patient from becoming an unnecessary invalid, a cardiac neurotic.

There is still a widely prevalent misconception that a heart attack, if it doesn't kill, must invariably incapacitate; that a patient can never be the same again afterward; that his life must be limited; that he cannot work again; that he cannot enjoy a normal sex life again. All of this is bunkum.

Consider, among others, Dwight Eisenhower and Lyndon Johnson, both of whom held the most difficult job in the world after having suffered severe heart attacks. There is no reason whatever why victims of heart attacks cannot expect to resume most jobs, except perhaps jobs involving the heaviest type of physical labor. And they can expect to carry on a satisfactory sex life.

What about preventing another heart attack? All risk factors mentioned earlier should be reduced to the zero point or as close to that as possible. Should anticoagulants be used as an aid? The idea is that such medications help to keep blood from clotting—and, commonly, it is when a clot happens to lodge in a narrowed coronary artery, shutting off circulation to a portion of the heart muscle fed by that artery, that a heart attack occurs. Medical experts still do not agree upon the value of routine use of anticoagulants. Your doctor—and if he is not a heart specialist, he may wisely request a consultation—will decide on the need for long-term anticoagulant therapy on the basis of severity of the attack, family history of heart trouble, the risk factors you have, and your reactions to a trial run with anticoagulant treatment.

Another important preventive measure is exercise. This may seem strange to those of you who remember when people, after a heart attack, were told not even to climb a few stairs. Medical thinking has changed radically on this point. Many heart specialists now put their patients through a graded program of exercise after a heart attack until they reach the point where they are jogging and running. The idea is to exercise the heart sufficiently to encourage the development of new blood vessels to take over the function of the diseased vessel or vessels. Exercise after a heart attack has another important value: its psycholog-ical effect on the patient, who can hardly consider himself a cardiac cripple if he runs a mile each day, or swims, or jogs several miles. Of course, such exercise programs must be supervised by the doctor, who can tell by the electrocardiogram or other tests whether a program is exactly suited to an individual patient.

ANGINA PECTORIS. Coronary artery disease may manifest itself only by attacks of pain without frank heart attack. Angina pectoris means, literally, breast pain. It is a common manifestation of coronary artery disease, usually occurring after physical exertion, although it may sometimes be set off by emotional stress.

The pain, which occurs over the heart and frequently spreads down the left arm (and sometimes into the jaw, teeth, and other parts of the body), arises because the heart muscle is not receiving adequate amounts of oxygen to meet the needs of exertion or stress.

Any vigorous muscle becomes painful when deprived of adequate oxygen. You can prove this to yourself by using the muscles of your hand and forearm to squeeze a ball vigorously and rapidly. Soon you will develop fatigue, and when you keep up the squeezing, there will be enough pain to make you want to stop.

Obviously, primary prevention of angina pectoris is exactly the same as for coronary artery disease.

Secondary prevention requires some detective work on the part of the patient. Some patients quickly learn to avoid the particular situations that set off attacks for them. For example, walking briskly on level ground may be nonsymptomatic, whereas the slightest climb may cause the pain. What may be possible in good weather may become pain-provoking in cold or damp weather or when a wind is blowing. Sometimes covering the face with a muffler prevents the attacks. A rest of 30 minutes after a heavy meal may be beneficial. Ideally, all meals should be small and well-spaced.

Most patients with angina experience a reduction or disappearance of symptoms if they lose substantial amounts of weight.

Patients learn to use nitroglycerin to relieve the attacks and also to prevent them. For example, if sexual intercourse sets off an attack, the pain can often be avoided by taking a nitroglycerin tablet five or so minutes before starting activity. The same is true for other situations that cause trouble.

When angina reaches the point of causing incapacitation, there is the possibility of tertiary prevention by means of surgery. Many types of operations have been developed and performed successfully. In some, arteries from areas near the heart are brought over and attached to the heart muscle to increase the blood supply. In other procedures, a diseased coronary artery may be reamed of clogging deposits, or if there is a localized area of narrowing it may be bypassed with a vein graft.

Heart transplantation is another possibility for the future, although many surgeons now are increasingly convinced that even when it becomes feasible, when the rejection phenomenon is licked, it will be needed only rarely as surgical methods of treating diseased coronary arteries and making other repairs improve further.

A WORD ABOUT INNOCENT HEART MURMURS. The heart valves are delicate structures and respond to all sorts of stimuli which may not be basically harmful. Some valvular murmurs do indicate organic disease of the heart, but many are not associated with true organic disease. These latter murmurs —the functional or innocent—may be present intermittently or constantly. It is a pity to have a person with a harmless murmur consider himself a heart victim. To prevent this, it is desirable for anyone with a questionable murmur to have a complete checkup by a heart specialist.

HEMOPHILIA AND RELATED DISEASES

Hemophilia and other "bleeder diseases" result from defects in the mechanism by which blood normally clots. The clotting mechanism is one of the most delicate, complex, and wondrous in the body.

To form a blood clot, the red cells must be enmeshed in thin tough threads of a protein, fibrin. These threads are produced when thrombin, fibrinogen, and calcium ions interact. In addition, at least ten other factors are required in the chain or "cascade" of chemical interactions needed to produce the final, normal, firm, retractive clot. One of the key factors in the chain is found in tiny blood platelets and is released when clotting is required.

If blood could talk it might be heard complaining: "In all the rushing around within arteries, veins, and heart, I must remain perfectly fluid because a clot can cause great—even fatal—damage by blocking my flow to heart, brain, eyes, and other vital organs. However, the moment I begin to escape from the blood vessels because of a cut, tear, crushing injury, or a surgeon's incision, then I'm expected to know immediately how and where to form a beneficial, restraining, lifesaving clot out of the thirteen factors contained in me. It's a wonder I don't get mixed up more often than I do and that there aren't many more bleeders than the relatively few who have hemophilia and related clotting disorders."

Deficiency or absence of a blood factor can lead to a bleeder disease—e.g., hemophilia, which is caused by lack of factor VIII. Also, if there are too few platelets in the blood, there may be bleeding disease such as described under Purpura.

Hemophilia

This disease is well known because it affected royal families in Europe, apparently transmitted by the famous Queen Victoria of England. When it appeared in young Alexis, born in 1904 and heir apparent to the throne of czarist Russia, there was consternation. Czar Nicholas and his Czarina, Alexandra, had only the one son. Alexandra believed beyond doubt that only the "mad monk" Rasputin had the ability to check Alexis' attacks of bleeding and thus came under the influence of this enigmatic "holy man." In this strange way, Rasputin was able to attain great power over the royal family and swayed their decisions, especially during World War I. Some historians believe that hemophilia thus may have played a considerable role in determining the destiny of Imperial Russia and the subsequent Communist Revolution.

One of the striking facts about hemophilia is that it occurs only in the male and must be transmitted through the child's mother. Because it is such a potentially serious disease, it not only makes problems for the sick male but can create a guilt complex in the mother.

Usually the disease is suspected when it is noticed that a boy bleeds easily from the nose, intestinal tract, or kidneys. Also, upon mild injury, swellings may appear, produced by oozing of blood deep under the skin or in the muscles. There may be bleeding into the joints. There is rarely any bleeding into the skin itself, so this bleeder disease is not characterized by black and blue spots as is *purpura*. In severe cases, bleeding may persist for days, causing huge accumulations of blood (hematomas). Tooth extractions and surgical incisions can cause serious bleeding. Fortunately, there are mild cases of the disease which become apparent only when there is delayed clotting after a tooth extraction or surgery.

Before the era of modern treatment, hemophilia had an ominous prognosis. There could be disabling, even fatal hemorrhages. Bleeding into joints caused deformities, restricting movement; permanent injury was common. Young children could start to bleed after a slight fall or as the result of a game. Young Alexis, heir to the Russian throne, was guarded—and often carried—by two stalwart men whose permanent assignment was to prevent falls and games that were too active.

Fortunately, today, the outlook is much better for the hemophiliac. Knowledge of blood factors has pinpointed factor VIII as the culprit in this disease. The factor is present in fresh frozen blood plasma and also in concentrates from plasma. It tends to disappear rapidly from whole blood, so that transfusions are not very helpful. The thawed plasma or a concentrate can be injected as soon as bleeding is observed and will in almost all instances control the hemorrhaging. Thus it is even possible for patients to be prepared by this replacement

592 / *Disease Scenarios*

therapy so they can undergo tooth extractions and surgery.

Why not give plasma or plasma concentrates regularly each day, the way insulin is given to diabetics? At the moment, to control severe hemophilia to the point that blood would clot normally would require two intravenous injections daily at a cost of about $18,000 a year. But it is hoped that cheaper supplies may become available.

Sooner or later the hemophiliac child learns that his ominous illness has been passed to him through his mother. This may lead to hostile feelings which he represses and feels guilty about. The physician should encourage an open relationship with the patient so that all emotional problems get ventilated. As we said earlier, the mother may become depressed by her guilty feelings about genetic passage of the disease and may require some preventive or therapeutic psychotherapy.

Families known to carry hemophilia or those in which it appears to have arisen spontaneously should have genetic counseling (page 439).

Bleeding Diseases Related to Hemophilia

VASCULAR HEMOPHILIA (also called von Willebrand's disease and pseudo-hemophilia). In this disease, the prolonged bleeding resembles that found in true or "classical" hemophilia. Because it is inherited differently—as a dominant gene in both sexes—both male and female children are·susceptible. It tends to cause excessive bleeding from the nose and from minor cuts in the skin as well as after mouth or throat surgery. Menstruation may be excessive. Strangely, vascular hemophilia patients not only can deliver children without marked bleeding but also undergo major abdominal surgery without hemorrhagic complications.

The outlook is relatively good because the disease becomes less severe as the patient grows older. Also, the bleeding is usually controllable by administration of fresh frozen plasma, after it has thawed.

This blood disease is being recognized more frequently. Parents and patients should have genetic counseling because of the strong hereditary tendency.

OTHER RELATED DISEASES. There are several other diseases in which bleeding is the prominent feature. One is hemophilia B, which is also called Christmas disease because it was first observed in a patient by that name; it results from deficiency of factor XI. Others include hemophilia C, acquired fibrinogen deficiency, and acquired prothrombin-complex disorders (e.g., from vitamin K deficiency, severe liver disease, and other diseases).

Hereditary hemorrhagic telangiectasis is a disease marked by easy bleeding in which there is a weakness of the small veins, especially in the skin of the face and upper extremities and the linings of the nose, mouth, and intestines. This disease is inherited as a dominant trait.

When the diagnosis of any bleeder disease is not clear-cut, the family doctor will need the help of a hematologist, who specializes in blood diseases and has the laboratory facilities to make the special studies needed for a precise determination.

Therapeutic Bleeder Diseases

In some situations when clotting has become dangerous—as when clots form in veins or there has been a heart attack from a clot in a coronary artery —the doctor may wish to interfere with the normal clotting of the blood to prevent the clot from enlarging. This can be done by injections of heparin under the skin or by use of tablets of Dicumarol. The doctor checks carefully on the individual patient's clotting ability and knows the range of dosage for achieving beneficial effects without leading to hemorrhage. Yet sometimes too much of the anticlotting agents may be used, and bleeding occurs. Any patient receiving anticlotting or anticoagulant treatment should immediately report the mildest unexplained bleeding to his doctor. He should also carry a statement or wear a tag indicating that he is receiving anticoagulant therapy; this is of special importance in the event of an accident that requires surgery at a time when the patient is dazed or unconscious and cannot tell the surgeon that his blood will not clot properly. Once the fact that anticoagulant treatment is being used is known, the effects of heparin or Dicumarol can be neutralized by special medication so that the blood is brought quickly back to normal clotting capacity.

HEMORRHOIDS

Hemorrhoids are an extremely common human ailment. Also known as piles, they are dilated and engorged veins inside or just outside the rectum. What causes these veins to distend and enlarge in the first place is not completely understood. But several thoughts go through a doctor's mind when he encounters a patient with hemorrhoids. Some authorities believe that there is a family tendency toward weakening of veins in certain parts of the body; and in taking the patient's history, the doctor may well find that family members are all hemorrhoid sufferers and in many instances are also afflicted with varicose veins.

The physician also knows that anything that causes increased pressure in the larger veins into which the veins from the rectum drain can aggravate existing hemorrhoids. Most commonly such pressure results from straining at stool because of chronic constipation, hard stools, or diarrhea. It may also occur with straining at urination, as in a person with prostate disease. Other factors may be:

Tumors in the intestine or abdomen which cause pressure on hemorrhoidal veins with resultant worsening of hemorrhoids.

Disease of the liver, particularly cirrhosis: in this case, blood channels in the liver are partially obstructed and, since much of the blood returning to the heart from the intestines flows through the liver, a back pressure develops in these veins.

Inefficient working of the heart, as in heart failure: then the heart is unable to handle all the blood returning from the veins in the body, and venous pressure becomes elevated.

Pregnancy—for the pregnant womb presses on the veins draining blood from the rectum; hemorrhoids of pregnancy almost always subside within three to six months after delivery, without treatment.

Treatment of hemorrhoids varies, depending upon the age of the patient and how severe and recurrent the problem is. In mild cases, regulation of bowel habits so as to avoid constipation and hard stools, with help from low-roughage food, stool softeners, and plenty of fluids, will provide relief. More severe or resistant cases may be treated by surgery or by injection therapy, an office procedure in which the affected veins are injected with a solution that causes them to harden and become obliterated (usually providing only temporary relief). Surgery is preferable.

In any event, before treatment is instituted, a physical examination to seek any of the causes of increased venous pressure discussed above will be performed. In patients over 40, in those with recurrent problems, and in those with hemorrhoids resistant to conservative treatment, a sigmoidoscope examination and usually a barium enema are performed in order to make certain that no tumor is present.

Treatment of hemorrhoids is important because it constitutes secondary prevention. Hemorrhoids can produce complications. They may bleed, sometimes producing a small loss of blood over an extended period that can lead to anemia. They may thrombose, leading to a painful, temporarily disabling condition. They may protrude (prolapse). As a result of prolonged local irritation, infection or tiny cracks (fissures) in the perianal area may appear and produce a great deal of pain.

Whenever hemorrhoids are troublesome, a doctor should be consulted. Emergency measures for use until medical treatment is secured may consist of sitz baths and a soothing suppository (e.g., Anusol).

Preparations claiming to cure hemorrhoids may be advertised, but the only real "cure" is surgery or, rarely, injection therapy. Often, advertised preparations contain medication that relieves symptoms only. They are potentially dangerous, because over a period of time there may be allergic reactions to their ingredients and because treatment of symptoms alone can delay the diagnosis of underlying problems related to the hemorrhoids.

HERNIA

Hernia, or rupture, is one of the most common human afflictions. Rupture is an inaccurate term because a hernia is really a weakness or defect, not a tear, in tissue supporting an organ. Because of this weakness, the contained organ may protrude some or all of the time.

Hernias may be found in many parts of the body. By far the most common is the inguinal hernia, so called because of its location in the groin area. A variant form of groin hernia is the femoral hernia. Other common types include the umbilical hernia in which the navel protrudes, the hernia that may follow surgery when a scar heals poorly, and internal hernias which produce no external bulges but permit organs to enter areas of the body where they ordinarily are not found.

Inguinal hernias occur in about 5 percent of the total population. Men are five times more prone to them than are women. The probable reason for the higher incidence in men is that during early development in the womb, the testicles migrate through the lower abdominal wall to their position in the scrotum. A cord attaches each testicle to the internal organs and passes through the aperture in the abdominal wall. In some cases, the wall fails to shut tightly around the cord, leaving this area weak. The weakness may not become apparent until adulthood, when constant or vigorous straining such as caused by lifting heavy objects may force the intestines to bulge out through the weak area. In some instances, natural weakening of muscle and fibrous tissue with age progressively allows underlying organs to bulge through a weakened area.

The physician cannot always tell in advance who is at risk. Many vigorous individuals never get hernias even though they may perform heavy work daily, while men in sedentary occupations may be afflicted.

It is known that prolonged increase in abdominal pressure is an important precipitating cause of hernia. Pressure is exerted against the abdominal wall not only by lifting but also by coughing, sneezing, straining at stool, straining to pass urine (as in prostate disease), or partial intestinal obstruction from a tumor. It is for this reason that many patients with chronic bronchitis have inguinal hernias from constant coughing. This is also why most surgeons, prior to repairing a hernia, will evaluate the large intestine and genitourinary tract (by x-ray and digital or sigmoidoscope examination). If abnormal conditions in either are uncorrected, there is a greater risk of hernia recurrence.

Obesity also increases the recurrence rate and the risk of postoperative complication because of increased pressure on the abdominal wall.

For primary prevention, make use of the following guidelines:

1. Get used to doing any heavy work gradually so muscles become adjusted to increased strain.
2. When lifting heavy weights, face them, keep the feet close to them, and spread the feet twelve inches apart. When lifting from the floor, keep the knees bent, and rise slowly, using leg rather than back muscles.
3. As much as possible, carry loads on the shoulders rather than hips.
4. Don't reach too high for packages.
5. Try to have someone help with unusually heavy lifting.
6. Use mechanical aids to lifting whenever possible.

The most common indication of a hernia is a bulge in the groin that may disappear with change in position or may be reduced by hand. A hernia may become painful as the intestine slides in and out. Sometimes a hernia may become so severe that the intestine extends downward into the scrotum.

A hernia can be diagnosed without the bulge being present when the physician feels the tightness of the tissues surrounding the area where the cord passes through the abdominal wall. Weakness will become apparent, too, when the patient is asked to strain.

Once diagnosed, a hernia should be corrected by surgery fairly promptly. The operation is not a serious one. In older patients or those who, because of the coexistence of another ailment, may present a high anesthetic risk, the repair may be safely carried out under local anesthesia.

Babies should have hernias repaired within a month or so of diagnosis, even though newborn.

Surgery is the only way to correct a hernia satisfactorily and in all but very rare cases is the recommended treatment. Injection therapy has been found to be useless and trusses are expensive, inconvenient, uncomfortable—and, most important, trusses do not prevent a hernia from expanding nor eliminate the possibility of the intestine becoming trapped and strangulated in a hernia defect. Strangulation is the most dangerous complication of hernias and is the reason why prompt surgical repair is recommended. Strangulation means that blood supply is cut off to a loop of intestine which has become trapped in a hernia. This results in gangrene of the strangulated segment of bowel and carries a risk of mortality even if surgery is performed rapidly. Strangulation is a surgical emergency, and any time pain arises in an untreated hernia a doctor should be consulted promptly.

The femoral hernia is a variant of groin hernia that occurs in the upper thigh below the groin. It is more frequent in females and carries the same risks and the same recommendations for prevention and treatment as the inguinal hernia.

Umbilical hernia is found mostly in children. It results from weakness of tissue in the area where the umbilical cord exits from the body. Many infants have protrusions around the navel for the first several months of life. Many of these hernias disappear within a year or two and there is no need for alarm during this period, because strangulation does not occur. Strapping the skin with adhesive tape does not increase the likelihood that the defect will close over. If by 3 or 4 years of age, the hernia is still present, surgery should be performed. The operation is relatively minor.

In the adult, umbilical hernias are usually found in obese individuals and are aggravated by the previously mentioned causes of increased abdominal pressure. Surgery should be performed, since strangulation is a possibility.

The most common internal hernia is the hiatal; it is a defect in the diaphragm which separates the chest from the abdominal cavity. A part of the stomach may enter the chest cavity through this defect, either intermit-tently or constantly, and lead to poor drainage of food and gastric juices.

Symptoms of hiatal hernia are heartburn, regurgitation, burning pain back of the breastbone, which is worse after eating and with lifting or stooping. Sometimes, the pain may resemble the anginal chest pain associated with heart disease. In many cases, however, there are no symptoms.

Diagnosis is made by x-ray. Secondary preventive measures include weight loss to reduce upward pressure from the abdomen and avoidance of overeating and of carbonated beverages. Antacids are helpful. So is elevation of the head of the bed.

Hiatal hernia rarely causes serious complications and most patients respond favorably to the measures outlined. If these measures should fail, however, or if an ulcer should develop in the hernia, then surgery is the definitive mode of therapy. This is major surgery which entails opening the abdomen and chest.

In infants hiatal hernias may threaten life, because often much of the intestine enters the chest cavity, compressing the lungs and causing respiratory distress. Emergency surgery is vital here.

HIGH BLOOD PRESSURE (HYPERTENSION)

High blood pressure, or hypertension, which affects at least 17 million Americans, is a disease capable of disabling and killing if uncontrolled. Today, almost invariably, it can be brought under effective control and prevented from progressing.

There is much loose talk about hypertension, ranging from the old wives' tale that it stems from red meat to the idea that blood pressure should be 100 plus your age, a misconception that has led some people to worry needlessly that their pressure is too low and caused others to refuse treatment for very real hypertension.

Blood pressure, as we have noted in the discussion in Chapter 3, to which you may wish to refer, is measured as two pressures: the systolic, which is the pressure when the heartbeat occurs; and the lower diastolic, the pressure between beats.

The idea that pressure should be 100 plus your age refers only to the systolic pressure—and this is a fairly good but not foolproof index for systolic pressure in adults. But it is the diastolic pressure which is more significant.

On the average, when recorded in a relaxed person, normal systolic pressure is around 120; normal diastolic, around 80. But pressures somewhat above and below these values also are considered normal. For example, a blood pressure of 140/90 is within the normal range whereas 150/95 is a little high.

Let your doctor interpret your blood pressure measurements. He has been trained, both in medical school and in postgraduate education, to understand what the figures mean and how much they may vary in the normal individual.

Almost every human being at some time or other shows a temporary increase of pressure over normal range. But it is only true sustained high blood pressure that is of concern. Some people show an increase of pressure purely out of nervousness, realized or not, when measurements are taken—and it is for this reason that many physicians take pressure measurements several times during a visit, making an effort to have the patient feel relaxed.

When an elevation is found after repeated measurements during a checkup visit, especially when it is relatively mild and there are no symptoms or signs, the physician may suggest that it be checked again in a few weeks.

Suppose that in several successive visits, your blood pressure consistently registers 160/105. What does the physician do? First, he will consider many pertinent factors: family history, since hypertension tends to run in families; emotional state (perhaps some job or marital worry is bothering you and influencing pressure); your weight, since obesity can elevate pressure and influence the course of hypertension. He will also consider other factors: color, since American Negroes have hypertension more commonly than whites and are more susceptible to the effects of pressure elevation; sex, since hypertension tends to run a milder course in women than in men.

Diagnosis Within a Diagnosis

Now the physician proceeds to a diagnosis within a diagnosis. He is reasonably certain that you have hypertension. He wants now to estimate how long you have had it. This is important because if the same mild elevation has persisted for ten years, it is not rapidly progressive in type; but if six months ago your pressure was normal, even this mild elevation may signal that another rise may well occur during the next six months and that this is an active, progressive type of hypertension.

So at this point the physician may drive you almost out of your mind trying to get you to recall every time in your life you had your pressure taken —perhaps in a hospital for minor surgery, during an employment or insurance examination. Since you may not have many of these records, he may make notes for follow-up letters. One of our patients, a 26-year-old woman with markedly elevated pressure, was finally able to recall that during an employment examination the examiner had remarked that she should see her family doctor because her pressure was somewhat elevated and she also had sugar in her urine. Several weeks later, when her family doctor followed through, her pressure and urine both were normal. Yet the employment examination incident now provided a clue to the fact that her hypertension was due to an adrenal gland tumor which can produce both high blood pressure and diabetes. She was cured permanently by removal of a benign tumor from one adrenal gland.

In addition to questions about previous pressure readings, the physician will ask questions to elicit any information that might indicate there has been some effect of the hypertension on eyes, brain, heart, kidneys. And when he proceeds to physical examination, he will focus on these areas. He may put drops in your eyes to dilate the pupils so he can get a good look at the retina. If the small arteries in the eyes are normal, he can be reasonably sure that the blood pressure has been only modestly elevated or that if high it has been present only briefly.

He will study the heart to determine if it has been enlarged as the result of hypertension. Usually he will need an x-ray for this, and he may also want an electrocardiogram to determine the state of the heart arteries.

He will study the kidneys, listening with his stethoscope over the kidney areas, trying to locate any sound that may suggest an abnormality in the kidney arteries as a possible cause of the hypertension. He may order a urine examination as a check on any possibility of kidney disease as a cause.

The careful physician will make blood pressure measurements in the legs as well as arms and compare them, because there is one type of hypertension produced by narrowing of the aorta, the big artery coming out of the heart, in which pressure is elevated only in the upper part of the body.

Usually, too, there will be a careful check for any indications of possible mild stroke in the past or hardening of brain arteries.

This completes the first general survey—and you may be staggered at this point. Why so much trouble?

As you probably have concluded, quite correctly, the diagnosis of hypertension establishes only that pressure is above normal limits, but not the cause.

The Types of Hypertension

Hypertension can be divided into two broad categories. In about 15 percent of all cases, a definite cause can be found—and very often corrected once and for all. The remaining 85 percent of cases are classed as essential hypertension, which simply means that thus far medical science has not been able to establish causes.

One definite cause of hypertension, as we have suggested earlier, is a narrowing of the aorta (known as coarctation of the aorta). This type of hypertension is completely curable by surgical operation which eliminates the narrowing.

An adrenal gland tumor, called a pheochromocytoma, can elevate pressure. It is usually benign, seldom spreads to other parts of the body, but produces large quantities of hormones that raise pressure. It, too, is curable by surgery.

Kidney diseases or obstruction to normal blood flow in a kidney artery may cause the kidney to release a substance, renin, which leads to pressure elevation. When an artery is obstructed, surgery often can eliminate the obstruction and cure the hypertension. If kidney disease can be eliminated, blood pressure may be reduced. But if the pressure cannot be reduced this way, the situation is not at all hopeless, for the blood pressure can be brought down with medication. And this is equally true for the large numbers of people with essential hypertension.

Until the advent of modern treatment, beginning about 1950, the course of essential hypertension depended upon type and severity. Patients with stabilized, relatively mild elevations usually did well for ten or twenty years, some even longer. Those with the fulminating type called "malignant" or "accelerated," rarely survived more than two years, most of them dying from kidney failure because of intense damage to the small blood vessels of the kidney. Patients with moderate degrees of essential hypertension usually died eventually of heart failure, coronary artery disease, stroke, or kidney disease.

Now the outlook has been changed radically by availability of many effective medications for blood pressure control.

It is possible now to lower even the most elevated pressure and, in many instances, return the pressure completely to normal. When pressure is lowered, the strain is taken off the heart muscle, which no longer must work so hard to pump out blood against the resistance caused by pressure elevation. Enlarged hearts return to normal size, and any signs or symptoms of heart failure often improve or disappear completely. Moreover, when pressure is lowered, any deterioration of the kidneys is arrested and the threat of strokes is greatly diminished.

It has been said that high blood pressure multiplied by time equals hardening of the arteries. Hopefully, as more patients with hypertension are treated early, they will not develop hardening of the arteries of the brain, the heart, the legs, and other areas.

Already, a particularly dramatic double effect of treatment has been noted in connection with malignant hypertension. First came the saving of the lives of patients having this once deadly disease. And now, happily, it is becoming difficult to find patients with malignant hypertension because early treatment for moderate and mild hypertension is preventing development of the malignant type.

Today, many different antihypertensive drugs are available. They range from mild to potent. There are many of each type. They can be used singly or in combination. If one drug or combination doesn't work for a particular patient, another can be found that almost certainly will. If undesirable side effects occur, they can be eliminated by either a reduction in dosage or a switch to another medication.

Give your physician every possible cooperation, and time, to find the right medicine or combination of medicines for you if you require treatment for hypertension.

HODGKIN'S DISEASE

Is Hodgkin's disease a cancer? This is not an easy question to answer because the basic cells of the lesions produced by the disease do not look like typical cancer cells. However, because of many facts about the disease —its start in a single organ system, its enlargement there, its tendency to metastasize or spread in a malignant way, and its responsiveness now to anticancer therapy—it is considered to be in the cancer constellation.

The disease does not appear to be hereditary. It attacks young adults and occurs in all races. It begins with enlargement of lymph nodes, the tiny catch basins in the drainage system of the body which normally trap poisons and infections and send out lymphocytes to fight them. The disease comes and goes, producing fever, weight loss, itching, excessive sweating, fatigue.

Frequently, enlarged, firm, but painless lymph nodes are seen in the neck, armpits, and groin. Usually these lead the patient to seek medical help. Sometimes only internal lymph nodes are enlarged, leading to such symptoms as difficulty in breathing as the enlarged nodes press on the tubes carrying air to the lungs.

Until about a decade ago, Hodgkin's disease had a reputation as a hopelessly fatal ailment. The youthfulness of its victims intensified the horror with which it was regarded. Today, the outlook is dramatically changed. Methods for primary prevention still remain to be found, but secondary prevention is on solid ground.

We recall two patients who exemplify opposite ends of the spectrum of malignancy of this disease. One, a young physician, developed enlarged lymph nodes in the neck. His was diagnosed as Hodgkin's disease of an active variety. Within six months, the disease spread to other lymph nodes and invaded bones, bone marrow, lungs, and kidneys. Death came shortly. This patient was seen many years ago. At the same time, we saw a recurrence of the disease after 17 years in a patient who originally had the mildest form of it with only local involvement in the lymph nodes of the groin. His first symptoms appeared when he was 30; he is still alive and active at age 66. Both the original node enlargement and the recurrence in the neck were treated with great success.

Today, Hodgkin's disease, in terms of potential seriousness, is classified according to the following scheme: Stage I, with single diseased lymph node; Stage II, with two or more discrete abnormal nodes limited to one part of the body; Stage III, with involvement of lymph nodes in various parts of the body; Stage IV, with involvement of bone marrow and bones, kidneys, lungs, brain, liver, and other internal organs.

Until very recently it was thought that only patients in Stages I and II had any good chance for long survival after radiation treatment. Now much more aggressive radiation treatment than ever used before is prolonging lives for patients with Stages III and IV disease—and, it is hoped, may even lead to cures. Patients with Stage IV disease may also benefit from more aggressive types of treatment today using special anticancer medicines.

New ways of applying radiation for Hodgkin's patients make use of specialized equipment and highly trained personnel. It may be necessary for a patient to travel some distance to a medical center where such treatment is available. But such effort is surely worthwhile.

An important question the doctor faces when he makes a diagnosis of Hodgkin's disease is what will happen to the patient when he learns of the diagnosis, since most people still believe the disease is invariably fatal in a short time. Or should the patient learn of the diagnosis?

The patient cannot be told he has nothing to worry about. He will know from the radiation or the chemotherapy that something serious has been diagnosed. However, the doctor can mercifully use the term "lymphoma," which encompasses Hodgkin's disease. We know of one patient who went for a number of years very happily with the diagnosis, "You have a disease of your lymph nodes called a lymphoma; yours is relatively mild and should respond well to radiation treatment." However, when he had a recurrence, another physician remarked, "You know you have a cancer of the lymph nodes, but I think we can get it under control." The patient then became depressed, wanted to sell his established business and retire at an early age—and even had suicidal thoughts. Fortunately, the family doctor learned of the unfortunate remark of the later physician, spent time with the patient, and finally convinced him of the wisdom of seeing a psychotherapist. After several visits with the therapist, the patient became convinced that many physicians do not believe lymphomas are necessarily cancerous, and also was able to consider calmly and rationally the fact that, regardless of the name, he had done remarkably well for years after his first enlarged nodes had appeared, so why not reasonably hope for and expect that he would do as well after the recurrence.

Anybody with Hodgkin's disease should have a doctor with whom he can speak frankly and at length about his fears. If the family doctor or the radiologist or other specialist cannot take on this responsibility, then the patient should be referred to a psychotherapist.

KIDNEY DISEASE

The work of the kidneys in purifying the blood and regulating body water and salt content has been explained earlier in this book. Serious damage to these important organs can endanger life. When kidney function is seriously impaired, uremia (which literally means "urine in the blood") sets in as a potentially fatal end result.

After the kidneys produce urine, they must pass it through two sets of tubes to the outside: the ureters leading to the urinary bladder, and the urethra leading from the bladder to the exterior. Anything that prevents normal flow of urine through these tubes can produce back-pressure which may destroy kidney function; usually such back-pressure is also accompanied by infection. Such a situation can stem, for example, from an untreated enlarged prostate gland in the older man.

Purification of blood in the kidney is carried out by two million delicate filters. They must be free of disease if they are to function properly. Also, blood vessels designed to feed into the filters must be healthy, for the filters cannot do a thorough purification job if inadequate amounts of blood reach them.

Not only may the kidneys be damaged by intrinsic diseases of their own; others may affect them. For example, high blood pressure may injure kidney blood vessels, and prevention or control of high blood pressure is an important measure for prevention of kidney disease. This is also true for atherosclerosis which can affect important blood vessels supplying the kidneys and thus render them inoperative. Diabetes, too, may do serious damage to the kidneys. And control of both atherosclerosis and diabetes is important for kidney health.

There are other diseases, less common, which if uncontrolled can have serious effects on the kidneys. They include overactivity of the parathyroid glands (hyperparathyroidism), subacute bacterial endocarditis, gout, disseminated lupus erythematosus, and sarcoidosis. Excessive intake of vitamin D may also affect the kidneys adversely.

You may be surprised that we have not thus far used the term Bright's disease, which to many people is synonymous with kidney disease. We have done this purposely as a means of indicating that very much has been learned about the varieties of kidney disease and damage since the time of Dr. Richard Bright more than a century ago. We want to impress on you that if your doctor wishes consultations with specialists in both internal medicine and urology when the diagnosis of kidney disease is not absolutely clear, he is justified even if it means sending you to a distant medical center. Effective treatment, based on clear diagnosis of any kidney disorder, is worth a great deal to you.

The term "Bright's disease" is no longer adequate because it is too inclusive. Physicians today use more specific terms, such as glomerulonephritis, nephrosis, and pyelonephritis, instead. These three major diseases affecting the kidneys will be described separately. It should be mentioned that these diseases, as well as some others, reveal their presence by certain changes in the urine. That is why a careful doctor always includes a complete urine study as part of his examination. He may also want to culture the urine for bacteria to make certain that no silent infection of the kidneys or of the passages leading from them will escape attention.

GLOMERULONEPHRITIS. Acute glomerulonephritis is a disease of children and young adults, though about 5 percent of cases do occur in persons over age 50. Contrary to the belief that this is always a serious, fatal disease, 95 percent of cases in children, and a good percentage of those in adults, clear completely. The misconception has to do with chronic glomerulonephritis which, as we shall see, tends to be more relentless.

Acute glomerulonephritis almost always follows a streptococcal infection, usually a strep sore throat, developing 10 to 14 days afterward. Of the many dozens of types of strep bacteria, only a few, notably Type 12, cause nephritis. Even a severe strep infection of the skin, such as erysipelas, rarely causes kidney infection. However, scarlet fever—a form of strep sore throat with a rash—may lead to nephritis.

In a typical attack of glomerulonephritis, the patient's face and eyelids become puffy. Urine may be scant and may appear bloody, brown, or have the look of coffee with cream. There may be headache, fever, shortness of breath, and tenderness in the flanks. The doctor usually finds some increase in blood pressure. He also makes the diagnosis by characteristic findings in urine and blood.

Once the diagnosis is clear, the

doctor has a solid statistical base for the outlook. He knows that 95 percent of cases in children will go to complete healing in a matter of weeks or months. Of the remainder, a small number will have such overwhelming disease that nothing can save them except the methods we discuss later under tertiary prevention, and even these may not help because of the ferocity of the attack. Fortunately, most of those who do not heal will go into a latent or subacute phase of the disease. Those with latent disease will not have symptoms but will show changes in urine and eventually will develop chronic nephritis and uremia. A rare one will go from latent stage to healing. The latent period may last for months or years.

In the subacute stage, the patient may have all or many of the symptoms of nephrosis (to be described), and this stage is often called the "nephrotic stage" of glomerulonephritis. Eventually, the subacute stage ends, but unfortunately what the patient and family may interpret to be healing is not that at all. Now the patient enters the advanced or even terminal stage of chronic nephritis. We recall one patient who entered the nephrotic stage at age 25; this lasted 10 years; then he went into the dry, chronic phase; finally, he became terminally uremic at age 53 and was considered then for kidney transplantation.

Patients with the latent or chronic form of nephritis pass albumin in their urine. This is why a test for albumin is carried out at medical checkups, insurance examinations, and examinations for the armed forces and special occupations. In the latent and chronic phases, there may be no symptoms, so diagnosis has to be made by careful examination of the urine for albumin and for red blood cells and casts (cylinders that take the form of kidney tubules and indicate kidney disease to the trained eye).

Eventually, most people with latent nephritis move into the chronic phase, and slowly over months and even many years move toward the serious uremic stage. During the chronic phase, there may be headaches, weakness from anemia, some shortness of breath, intermittent swelling of the ankles—or there may be no symptoms at all. During this stage, the doctor relies mostly on laboratory tests to tell him the degree of function of the kidneys. He knows that when kidney function falls to about 10 percent of normal, uremia will soon follow.

What about primary prevention of glomerulonephritis? Surely, the key to it lies in avoiding strep sore throats and scarlet fever. People with sore throats, fevers, or colds should be avoided as much as possible. If it is necessary to care for anyone with such problems, the doctor should be queried about isolation procedures and the advisability for taking prophylactic antibiotic treatment.

When a person has sore throat and fever, the doctor should be notified immediately. It is believed that prompt eradication of strep sore throat decreases the chances of subsequent nephritis. People with sore throats, colds, and fevers do well to keep warm and, when returning to normal activities, to avoid getting chilled. In many cases of chronic nephritis, patients are unable to recall any acute preceding illness; there may have been a slight sore throat which went unnoticed or untreated.

In the latent and chronic stages of nephritis, secondary prevention depends upon avoidance of strep throat, and the foregoing precautions should be observed. Also, nephritis patients should be especially careful in late fall and winter months, when colds and sore throats are prevalent, to avoid crowded places as well as individual cases of upper respiratory infection. In this type of kidney disease, it is also desirable to avoid excess stress for the body. For example, exercise should not be carried to the point of fatigue; swimming should not be carried on to the point of chilly sensations; sunburn should be avoided —and, so too, dampness and cold.

NEPHROSIS. Nephrosis may be a disease by itself with its own special scenario, or it may be a stage of glomerulonephritis. The type of nephrosis that is called "true, lipoid nephrosis" occurs almost entirely in children. It is marked by edema, or water-logging, so pronounced that the child seems swollen like a balloon. The accumulation of water under the skin is painless. Fluid also may accumulate in the abdomen, which appears distended.

That these symptoms are the result of kidney disease is clear when the urine is examined. It contains large amounts of albumin and, in addition, fatty casts and other fatty bodies, some of which give the appearance of maltese crosses when examined under a microscope with polarized light. The blood serum contains a high concentration of fat but albumin tends to be abnormally low because of the large amount excreted in urine. However, in contrast to chronic glomerulonephritis, nephrosis does not permanently damage the kidneys.

Before the introduction of modern treatment, children with nephrosis were disabled for periods of up to ten years, lying in bed with their huge swellings. They were prone to bacterial infections. All children need large amounts of protein in the diet for growth; children with nephrosis had to have special high-protein diets to help replace the large amounts lost in the urine. Sodium (salt) had to be restricted to keep the edema under partial control. If these nephrotic children survived, then eventually the edema disappeared completely and they returned to complete normalcy.

Today, the scenario is much more pleasant for the patient with true nephrosis. Infections can be controlled by antibiotics and edema by steroid hormones. It does, however, take special skill to regulate steroid dosage, and it may be desirable to have the child treated at first in a large hospital or medical center which has a specialist in this disease.

Unfortunately, about 50 percent of children who seem at first to have true nephrosis lose kidney function and turn out to have chronic glomerulonephritis.

In adults there are occasional cases of true nephrosis which clear completely without damage to the kidneys. But most adult nephrotics unfortunately are undergoing a stage of glomerulonephritis and will eventually lose kidney function.

PYELITIS AND PYELONEPHRITIS. Pyelitis is an infection of the part of the kidney that collects the urine after it has been discharged from the special filtering units, the nephrons. Pyelonephritis indicates that infection has affected the nephrons, too. Because it is probably impossible to have an infection of the kidney without some invasion of the nephrons, the more modern approach is to classify the kidney infections as acute and chronic pyelonephritis.

An acute attack begins suddenly

with fever and chills. Frequently, headache, nausea and vomiting, and a feeling of being very sick are early symptoms. Along with pain and tenderness in the flanks over the kidneys, the patient usually develops an urgent need to pass urine, and passage is frequent and burning. The urine may look cloudy. The doctor finds pus cells in the urine and may even detect bacteria through the microscope; if not, a culture of the urine will prove positive for one or more types of bacteria, frequently of the gram-negative variety. One or both kidneys may be affected.

Usually, an acute attack of pyelonephritis can be terminated, with the antibiotics and other medicines available now, within a week or two. The outlook is very favorable if there is no anatomical abnormality that interferes with free passage of urine. But the doctor knows how easy it is to mistake apparent cure for complete cure. If cure is not complete, infection may hide in the kidneys and lead to chronic pyelonephritis. In that case, there will be relapses, with fever and kidney pain, possibly a continuous feeling of being rundown. One end result of chronic pyelonephritis may be destruction of the kidneys and uremia. Another may be high blood pressure, which can be a factor in heart failure, heart attack, and stroke.

Because of the serious nature of chronic kidney infections, the doctor makes every effort to clear an acute attack completely. This is why he insists that a patient, no matter how well he or she may feel, return for examinations and urine cultures and perhaps remain on antibacterial medications for some months. Also, since the doctor knows that kidney infections frequently are associated with anatomical abnormalities in the path-

ways for urine excretion, he may want special x-rays or even urological examinations of bladder, ureters, and kidney to detect any stones or narrowings and, in older men, any prostate enlargement.

Pregnancy may foster the development of acute pyelonephritis because the enlarging womb may press on the ureters leading from the kidneys. Knowing this, doctors carefully watch the urine during pregnancy for any evidence of infection.

Symptomless urinary infection is known to exist and, if untreated, may lead eventually to serious kidney disease. Thus, it is desirable to have the urine checked by culture for bacteria at periodic physical examinations.

CYSTITIS. This is infection of the urinary bladder. Since the bladder is so closely related to the kidneys, cystitis is considered here.

An acute attack is similar to an acute attack of pyelonephritis except that the pain and tenderness tend to be low in the abdomen, and sometimes when the attack starts it is accompanied by frankly bloody urine.

It is essential to eradicate cystitis completely because there is danger of infection spreading through the urinary tract to the kidneys, producing pyelonephritis.

Polyps, stones, or narrowing of the urethra can impede normal flow of urine and cause repeated attacks of bladder infection. When cystitis recurs or becomes chronic, the doctor may want a urologist to examine the bladder and urinary tract.

KIDNEY STONES. Stones constitute a fairly common problem. They are deposits of mineral or organic substances which may vary in size from tiny "pebbles" to a staghorn stone (calculus) which may be large enough to fill the entire pelvis of a kidney.

Kidney stones usually develop when too much of a substance formed in the kidney appears in the urine or when the urine is either too acid or too alkaline to hold some substance in solution. Infection, too, may act as a primary focus around which material can precipitate from solution to form a stone.

Thus, one important primary preventive measure against kidney stones is keeping the kidneys free of infection. Another is keeping the urine dilute by drinking adequate amounts of fluid, especially during hot weather or when engaging in work or sports that lead to heavy sweating. People subject to such dehydration or who have a family history of kidney stone formation may be advised to keep the urine dilute during the night hours by setting the alarm for the midpoint of the sleep period so they can wake then to drink a large glassful of water.

Some disorders are sometimes accompanied by kidney stone formation. Thus, gout may lead to the deposition of uric acid stones in the kidneys, and tumor or overactivity of the parathyroid glands may cause so much calcium and phosphorus to appear in the urine that they settle out and form stones. It is important that such disorders be treated without delay as a means of preventing stone damage to the kidneys.

Some kidney stones may remain silent for years, and may in fact never cause symptoms or trouble. Others start to pass out of the kidneys and, in so doing, cause severe pain and tenderness over the kidney area, frequent and painful urination, blood in the urine, fever, and chills and prostration. Small stones may get through and be eliminated in the urine. Larger ones, however, may become impacted in the kidney, ureter, or bladder and may have to be removed surgically. A kidney stone, if it blocks passage of urine, can cause back-pressure and infection and may eventually lead to kidney destruction.

It is worth noting here that when a patient must be kept in recumbent position for an extended period—because of a major fracture, for example—there is some risk that the bones will give off extra mineral which may form kidney stones. The alert physician, realizing this, can do much to prevent this by increasing fluid intake and the flow of dilute urine, reducing mineral content of the diet, and using certain medicines to reduce absorption of minerals from the intestine.

Because of the many ways kidney stones may form and their potential danger, they call for special blood and urine studies and x-ray and urological examination of the entire uninary tract. This constitutes good secondary prevention, because once the nature of the stone or stones is clarified, it may be possible to prevent further formation by use of special diets or medicines. Anyone who has experienced a renal colic—one of the worst of pains—or who has undergone kidney surgery would agree on the importance of prevention.

UREMIA. This is the end result of destructive diseases of the kidneys. Usually, it sets in only after some years because kidney diseases tend to progress slowly and the kidneys have a large functional reserve. Uremia often does not develop until 90 percent or more of kidney function has been lost.

During the pre-uremic phase, the doctor can check on progression of disease by special tests of kidney function.

When uremia appears, fatigue, malaise, and nausea may be among the manifestations. There may be need to pass urine one or more times during the night. There may be pallor, and the skin may take on a slight lemon color. As uremia deepens, there may be vomiting, itching, an odor of urine on the breath. In addition, there may be signs and symptoms of failing heart or high blood pressure. Toward the end, black and blue spots and a whitish deposit of urea may appear on the skin. Coma follows; then, death.

Until the advent of dialysis and kidney transplantation, all the doctor could do was to treat symptoms and modify diet to try to slow down the relentless course of chronic uremia. Now, tertiary preventive measures may save patients from the final stage of uremia.

One measure, dialysis, purifies blood of the toxic materials which the diseased kidneys cannot excrete. This is achieved by passing the patient's blood through a machine which allows the poisonous substances to wash out. Since the kidneys are practically functionless, this process must be repeated once a week or more often. Dialysis has required a stay in a hospital and skilled personnel. Now simpler and cheaper machines are being built so that purification of the blood can be carried out by certain patients at home.

Since a person can live perfectly well with one good functioning kidney, there have been many attempts to transplant good kidneys. The kidneys have been taken from cadavers soon after death; many have been donated by living relatives of patients. In more than two thousand kidney transplants, not one donor has died as a result of the surgery to remove the donated

kidney. Many patients, who previously would have died of uremia, are now alive and carrying on happy, useful lives. Some have even undergone pregnancies and borne normal children. Indeed, this might well be called the era of "Lazarus surgery," recalling the miracle of Jesus in raising Lazarus from the grave.

LEPROSY (HANSEN'S DISEASE)

Leprosy has a far worse reputation than it deserves. It is not a disease that is easily spread, contrary to the injunctions of the Holy Bible. In fact, leprosy is only communicated from one person to another by intimate contact extending over a period of years.

Although found mostly in tropical and subtropical countries, leprosy does occur rarely in various parts of the United States. Its cause is a germ called Hansen's bacillus, and the disease is often referred to as Hansen's disease.

It may show itself in minimal form —with only a patch or two on the skin, pale, slightly raised, without nerve sensation. As it progresses, it involves more and more nerves, causing neuritis, thickening of nerves under the skin, and many areas in which sensation is lost. Thickening and corrugation of the skin of the nose and face may make the patient look somewhat like a lion. If untreated, the disease is usually fatal in 10 to 20 years.

Depending upon the nature of the skin involvement, doctors usually classify the disease into two main types: tuberculoid and lepromatous. The former sometimes stops spontaneously.

Both types yield to modern therapy.

Usually, the diagnosis can be made by finding the causative Hansen's bacillus in scrapings of the affected areas or by biopsy of an affected nerve. However, in some instances, the diagnosis is difficult in early stages of the disease when changes are minimal. Then it may be necessary for the patient to be examined by U.S. Public Health doctors who specialize in diagnosis and treatment of this disease. The diagnosis of leprosy is still more horrifying than cancer to many people, so no doctor wishes even to mention the diagnosis until it has been established without any doubt.

Years ago, when he had to make a diagnosis of leprosy, the doctor could only visualize a sorry outcome: slow, progressive deterioration of the patient in a leprosarium where he was kept isolated. Now the picture has so changed that some doctors do not even isolate the patient from his family. Other doctors prefer hospitalization until the disease is obviously under complete control—in a hospital such as the U.S. Public Health Service Hospital at Carville, Louisiana. Here excellent, free medical service is provided by experts on the disease; the patient can have visitors, and is often permitted to take trips to visit his family when his recovery warrants.

Modern medicines for leprosy are of the sulfone group and include Avlosulfon (DDS), Promin, Sulphetrone, Diasone, diphenylthiourea (DPT). Some are injected; some are taken by mouth. The medicines are fairly toxic and must be given under careful medical supervision so that any sensitivity or toxic reactions may be noted. Unfortunately, treatment is slow. Many months may be required, and in some resistant cases as much as eight years of treatment may be needed.

Once the disease has been completely arrested or cured, there may be the problem of bringing the patient back to normal life and gainful work. He may feel stigmatized, afraid to mix freely with others. Many patients and their spouses benefit by discussions with a psychotherapist.

When any unsightly lesions have been left by the disease, they can and should be treated by corrective plastic surgery before the patient returns to home or work.

LEUKEMIA

The leukemias are considered to be forms of cancer. In these diseases, there are vast increases in numbers of white blood cells. The cells reproduce rapidly, showing many immature forms. They become invasive, spreading to many parts of the body other than the blood. Both rapid cell proliferation and invasiveness are typical of cancer.

The leukemias can be divided into three major categories: (1) acute leukemias; (2) chronic myelocytic leukemia; and (3) chronic lymphocytic leukemia.

It is natural that a cancer arising in cells circulating throughout the body should sound fearsome. And the fact is that at one time patients who developed acute leukemia had a life expectancy of only a few months. Now, however, as we shall see, there is a much more optimistic side to the leukemia problem than would have been possible to relate even just a few years ago.

Is there any means of primary prevention for either acute or chronic leukemia? It is known that some cases of leukemia are the result of over-exposure to radiation. Everyone should heed the precautions we have stressed elsewhere in this book about having too many x-rays or other radiation. And with growing use of radioactive materials in industry, it is important for workers to know and follow all the safety rules.

ACUTE LEUKEMIA. In a full-blown case, an adult patient will tell the doctor of weakness, fever, black and blue spots. There may be lymph node swellings in the neck, armpits, and groin. Unusual bleeding may have occurred after a tooth was pulled. There may be pain over the breastbone. The patient may feel swelling of liver and spleen in the upper abdomen. In a child, parents will have noted that the child is listless, quickly tired, doesn't eat well.

Any or all of these indications will lead the doctor to examine the blood. He will usually find that the white cells are greatly increased in numbers. But in about one third of patients the white count may be below normal, though the blood smear will show immature, abnormal white cells. In fact, in about 20 percent of patients, the smear will show Auer bodies, which are red-staining rods in some of the white cells; this is virtually full proof of acute leukemia. Also, in many patients, blood platelets will be low (explaining the increased tendency to bleeding), and there may be anemia, since leukemia damages bone marrow where red cells are produced.

Thus, confirmation of the diagnosis is not difficult for acute leukemia. And the doctor then views the outlook with misgivings.

A patient with acute leukemia is apt to be a child who does not under-stand why he feels so sick. Treatment may require that the child be transported long distances to a medical center. Repeated transfusions may be needed. As the disease goes on, there may be periods of bleeding into the skin, pain in the joints, severe infection.

When special medical treatment for acute leukemia first began, victims rarely survived more than a few weeks. Now remissions are being obtained in as many as 93 percent of cases; median survival time is in excess of 36 months; worldwide records list more than 150 patients who have survived five years or longer thus far. Most encouraging, survival time has doubled in just the past three years.

Among medications used to treat acute leukemia are folic acid antagonists, corticosteroids, and purine antagonists. Combinations—such as 6-mercaptopurine, methotrexate, and prednisone—are used. New compounds are being added to the existing ones: L-asparaginase, vincristine, and cytosine arabinoside.

It may not seem like much of a therapeutic achievement to add five years to the life, of, say, a three-year-old. Yet this may bring some happiness to child and parents. And it keeps the child alive to satisfy the doctor's as well as parents' hope that in the meantime research may produce a new, completely effective cure for this sad disease.

Another problem the physician must face when a child has acute leukemia is the great psychological trauma for the family. Some specialists in leukemia have become excellent psychotherapists in the course of their work with parents. Others prefer to send families back to their family physician, who can decide on whether a psychotherapist is needed. Some parents have solved their emotional problems by working to supply better care and improved research facilities for leukemia children.

CHRONIC MYELOCYTIC LEUKEMIA (CML). In this disease, there is proliferation of a granulocytic type of white blood cell. Eventually, the vast numbers of these cells spread into the spleen and many other parts of the body.

Symptoms are quite similar to those of acute leukemia: pallor, weakness, fever, black and blue spots, tenderness over the breastbone. There may be abdominal discomfort from gross enlargement of the spleen. The diagnosis is confirmed by the blood smear, which shows characteristic changes, and by biopsy of bone marrow.

Once the diagnosis is established, the doctor can usually foresee that treatment will help to extend life for at least some years. Patients with chronic leukemia are adults. Four or five years of added life can be meaningful in themselves, and there is the hope that research will produce more effective therapy for CML.

Current treatment makes use of chemical agents such as Myleran, x-ray, or injection of radioactive phosphorus. All symptoms and signs may disappear in response to treatment. When there is a recurrence, the same type of treatment or a variant may bring it under control. Unfortunately, patients with this type of chronic leukemia are subject to a "blast crisis" —a complication which may arrive three or four years after first treatment of the disease. In blast crisis, the CML becomes more malignant and appears more like acute leukemia.

A patient with CML should be encouraged to live and work as normally as possible. With treatment, his symptoms can be counteracted for some years—perhaps even, in some cases, for ten years or more. And there is hope, increasingly justified with each passing year, not only of new additions to treatment that may improve the outlook but even of cure at some point in the future. A patient with CML should be watched for mental depression and should be offered psychotherapy (whether it is called that or not) by his family doctor or by a psychotherapist.

CHRONIC LYMPHOCYTIC LEUKEMIA. We are happy to report that patients with this form of leukemia have lived 15 years or longer with minimal or no symptoms.

This is the form that may be detected in a routine checkup when the white blood cell count is found to be excessive. Especially in the older age group, the disease tends to be benign. In younger adults, CLL may produce some weakness, pallor, enlargement of lymph nodes in the neck, armpits, and groin. Diagnosis is made by blood smear study and bone marrow biopsy. Some experts do not treat this type of leukemia even if the white blood cell count goes to ten times normal values unless there are definite symptoms.

There is an effective medication called chlorambucil for CLL so the physician feels that if things change for the worse—if anemia develops, bleeding occurs because of reduced blood platelets, or enlarged lymph nodes produce pressure—he can readily control the situation. If, as sometimes happens, chlorambucil becomes less effective, there are other chemicals that may be used, such as TEM and Cytoxan. Corticosteroids, too, are helpful. And heavy doses of irradiation are being found useful in prolonging lives and well-being of CLL patients.

When a physician hears the diagnosis, leukemia, he almost automatically prays that it is the chronic lymphocytic type. Psychotherapy may be desirable here as with other types because just the name leukemia strikes terror.

What of tertiary prevention? Someday it may become possible to kill all leukemia cells with massive radiation or use chemical agents to destroy the bone marrow's ability to produce white cells. Then the patient would be kept alive by transplantation of bone marrow from a healthy donor.

LIVER DISEASE

Among the most vital organs in the body, the liver is located in the upper right abdomen. It manufactures and excretes bile and does the many other jobs described in Chapter 21. As stated there, this organ has tremendous powers of regeneration, which is fortunate since it is so essential to so many major chemical reactions in the body. A diseased liver becomes a serious handicap to health.

What damages this organ? How do we recognize that it is damaged? And how can such damage be prevented?

Viruses are prime enemies; also, toxic materials such as alcohol, carbon tetrachloride, and other solvents including one in glue (which makes teen-age glue-sniffing so dangerous). On occasion, even certain otherwise-valuable medications—including the antibiotic Chloromycetin, the potent tranquilizing agent Thorazine, and the arthritis medication Butazolidin—may cause liver trouble. Bacteria, amoebas, and larger parasites such as worms attack the liver. So do cancers.

Widespread liver disease usually manifests itself by jaundice, the yellowing of the skin and whites of the eyes. Jaundice usually indicates that either most liver cells are not functioning properly (intrinsic jaundice) or the outlet for bile flow is blocked by a gallstone or tumor (extrinsic jaundice). Sometimes there is so much destruction of red blood cells that the liver cannot dispose of the jaundice pigments from the cells fast enough and hemolytic jaundice results.

Acute liver disease generally is accompanied by exhaustion, nausea, loss of appetite, and tenderness over the liver itself. When a tender, inflamed liver is affected by additional inflammation or even the ingestion of a big meal or some back-pressure from a weak heart, the resulting pain is among the most miserable in human experience. Patients soon learn to eat sparing, small meals, limit exercise or rest completely just before the times liver pain is to be expected.

Jaundice may or may not accompany chronic liver disease. There is usually some pain around the liver area, and fatigue. Often there is swelling of the abdomen by fluid (ascites) caused by back-pressure on veins produced by a scarred and damaged liver. Also, because of such back-pressure, enlarged veins in the esophagus and stomach may bleed (varices), hemorrhoids may develop, and ankles and legs may become swollen with fluid accumulations. Slow loss of blood from internal varicose veins may lead to anemia, which adds to the weakness and tiredness produced by chronic liver disease.

Among signs of chronic liver disease which alert a doctor when he makes his physical examination are a characteristic redness of the palms of the hands and a red streaking on the skin which takes the shape of spider marks.

When a doctor sees a patient with any of these indications, he is immediately alert because of the vital nature of the liver and the tendency of some liver diseases to become fatal. The doctor knows well that the large reserve of the organ is not limitless—as many alcoholics like to think. (One of our patients drank a full quart of whiskey daily for ten years before showing the signs of chronic liver disease.)

Faced with a patient with liver disease, the preventively minded physician is likely to think how much wiser it would have been for the patient to have prevented the life-threatening problem—perhaps simply by better washing of hands to ward off acute viral disease, joining Alcoholics Anonymous, refraining from glue-sniffing, or refusing to dose himself with antibiotics indiscriminately.

But the physician has the patient there in front of him, with all the indications of acute liver disease rather than chronic or cancerous. How does he determine the outlook? First, he must find out more.

Often he may learn all he needs to know with a few shrewd questions. Did the patient have a recent blood transfusion? That may indicate serum hepatitis. A trip abroad may point to infectious hepatitis. A course of treatment with some medicine known to have potential for damaging the liver may indicate a sensitivity-to-medicine type of liver disease.

There are many laboratory and x-ray tests a physician can use to determine the type and degree of liver disease. Knowing the nature of the acute liver problem, he can foresee the future for the patient and move in with secondary preventive measures.

VIRAL LIVER DISEASE. There are two types of viral liver disease. Infectious hepatitis (IH) is caused by a virus which enters the system via the mouth. It is spread by fecal contamination and tends to be epidemic in crowded places such as military bases and camps and mental hospitals. It is also more prevalent in countries with poor sanitation.

Serum hepatitis (SH) is caused by a similar virus but one that is found in blood and tissues, not in the feces. It is spread by contaminated blood transfusions or when people, usually drug addicts, use the same contaminated needle and syringe.

Most cases of viral liver disease are relatively mild. Occasionally, there is overwhelming disease. But generally complete recovery is the rule and the doctor institutes secondary preventive measures to provide as much rest as possible for liver cells and to spare them from any further toxicity. Thus, he prescribes complete bed rest during acute symptoms and a nourishing diet (and if the patient cannot eat, supplementation by intravenous feeding). Liver toxins such as alcohol and medications such as those mentioned earlier and others including barbiturate sleeping pills, morphine, and sulfonamides are forbidden. Cortisone or related compounds may be given when the patient's situation is deteriorating.

Primary prevention is much to be desired. For IH, remember Moses' injunction to the Jews to wash the hands before every act of eating; in modern times, this means employing a good soap or detergent with warm water for a thorough cleaning of hands and fingernails. In countries with poor sanitation, one should forswear all foods that are not thoroughly cooked and served hot. For SH, there should be care that any surgery required is carried out in an accredited hospital so there will be a high-quality blood bank if transfusion is needed. Another protection: when you have blood drawn for a test, insist that it be done with a new, disposable needle. If you must inject drugs, use your own needle and syringe exclusively.

Suppose the course of IH or SH is unfavorable and it appears that the patient will die—can the doctor use tertiary prevention, employing a liver transplant from a cadaver? Probably not—because the patient's resistance may well be so low he could not withstand the massive surgery, and the transplanted liver would probably be destroyed by the liver virus circulating in the patient's blood.

OTHER ACUTE LIVER DISEASES. As we have indicated, some people become hypersensitive to certain medications. Among common and valuable agents that can cause liver disease must be listed even penicillin and the sulfa medicines. Fortunately, because the liver has so much reserve and because doctors are alert to the toxic effects of medicines on the liver, fatality is rare. Once the diagnosis is established, treatment is much the same as for viral infections of the liver—rest for the patient and his liver, good nutrition.

Essentially the same treatment is used for toxic liver diseases. The doctor may establish that a patient uses carbon tetrachloride, chloroform, phosphorus, arsenicals, or special metals, any of which may damage the liver. Once the offending material is avoided and treatment instituted, chances for recovery are high. After recovery, a preventively minded physician will consider, with the patient, the risks in his job and may discuss

them with the industrial physician at the patient's place of work to see if the poisonous contact can be eradicated or, failing that, if the patient can be given another job without exposure to what is, for him, a serious troublemaking material.

CHRONIC LIVER DISEASE. This whole classification is virtually filled by the type of disease called cirrhosis of the liver. The term means hardening of the liver. Leading causes are alcoholism and malnutrition (especially vitamin B deficiency). Less often, cirrhosis may be a result of infectious or other types of acute liver disease, congenital syphilis, and certain tropical diseases such as schistosomiasis.

This disease lasts for years as a rule, becoming progressively more severe. There are dangerous episodes from internal bleeding or from piling up of fluid in the abdominal cavity. Finally, the liver fails completely and the patient goes into liver coma and dies.

When a physician diagnoses cirrhosis of the liver, he foresees the long, difficult years ahead for the patient. The condition cannot be reversed. It can be slowed down; occasionally, it can be stopped from progressing. Generally, it is relentless unless every secondary preventive measure available is put to use.

First, the underlying destructive influence must be found and eliminated. Use of alcohol must be stopped—and this means alcohol in any form. So-called gin drinker's liver can be caused by any form of alcoholic beverage, not just gin. In France, wine as well as absinthe drinkers may develop cirrhosis.

Malnutrition must be overcome. Vitamin supplements are in order. It must be remembered that the chronic alcoholic rarely takes a proper diet and hurts his liver both through malnutrition and alcohol toxicity. Some extra protein in the diet of the liver patient is desirable.

It undoubtedly is not easy for a patient with a liver damaged by alcohol to stop drinking. The reason for doing so, however, is urgent. He should read our chapter on alcoholism and have a thorough discussion with his doctor. If necessary, psychotherapy should be started. We recommend joining Alcoholics Anonymous.

When symptoms of water retention such as ascites and leg swellings appear, these can usually be prevented from progressing by (a) low-salt diet, (b) diuretic pills or injections, (c) withdrawal of abdominal fluid by special needle if it does not yield to the medical regimen.

It is a very serious matter when back-pressure from a scarred liver leads to development of internal varicose veins. There may be a large fatal hemorrhage. A patient who has this problem should always know what hospital to go to immediately bleeding starts. He should not wait to try to reach the doctor, who can be notified by the hospital or by relatives. Once hemorrhaging has been stopped, the doctor will evaluate with surgeons the possibility that a surgical procedure might be used to attack the varicose veins in the esophagus or stomach directly or to change the circulation in the liver so back-pressure is reduced. Such procedures help in a small number of patients and must be performed by a highly experienced surgeon who is usually to be found in a major medical center.

Patients with chronic liver disease should not strain at stool, since this increases pressure and may induce hemorrhage. They should follow our directions for preventing constipation (page 227).

Blood-streaked or brownish vomitus or blood-streaked or black (tarry) stools should alert the patient to internal bleeding and the need to get to the designated hospital.

If a patient with chronic liver disease notices that he is getting unduly drowsy or that he has a muscle tremor or a flapping of the hands, he should notify his doctor. These may be signs of impending liver coma, a serious complication. There are means of preventing its progress which usually require hospitalization. Prompt action is necessary.

Most patients with chronic liver disease suffer from anemia for which iron can be prescribed. Some have bleeding tendencies which may be helped by use of vitamin K.

In chronic liver disease, obesity adds stress for the liver. See our chapter on weight control. It is worth noting that some physicians believe that primary prevention of liver disease is helped by prevention of obesity.

What of tertiary prevention? Liver transplants have been tried. They are technically feasible even though difficult operations. But the success rate to date has been low because of rejection of the liver graft. Liver transplantation in the future may become a feasible measure as progress is made in combatting the rejection phenomenon.

LOW BLOOD PRESSURE (HYPOTENSION)

In most instances, as one medical authority puts it, low blood pressure is a cause for congratulations. Rarely does it indicate illness of any kind.

If you were to measure the blood pressures of a thousand healthy young or middle-aged persons, you would find that the majority have systolic pressure of about 120, but others would have pressures ranging up to 140 and down to 100, and some would have pressures in the 90's. In other words, you would be finding what statisticians call a normal biological distribution curve. And if you did the same in terms of height, you would get the same type of curve.

Certainly, you wouldn't call abnormal any person whose height might be only five feet two. Why then should a person with lower-than-average blood pressure worry about abnormality? Note that we say "lower-than-average" not "lower-than-normal." Too often anxiety arises because of a misconception that the blood pressure is lower than normal when in reality it is only lower than average.

People with blood pressures on the low side have a very good life expectancy, and a physician is always happy when his checkup reveals blood pressure in the lower range. Even when a patient may complain of fatigue or nervousness, the physician knows that there is almost no chance that the symptoms are caused by low pressure. He will generally find an emotional cause.

Usually, when the systolic pressure persistently registers 90 or lower, the doctor will check for certain organic problems that do cause low pressure. He considers the possibility of low adrenal gland function such as is found in Addison's disease (see page 513), or low thyroid gland function, or low pituitary gland function. Occasionally, blockage of free flow of blood through the final outlet valve of the heart will lead to low blood pressure; this condition is called stenosis of the aortic valve. Sometimes, persons with chronic infections—tuberculosis, for example—may have low blood pressure. In organic diseases, low blood pressure will revert to its usual level for the individual when the underlying problem is treated adequately.

Organic causes for low blood pressure are comparatively rare. Too often, people consider themselves sick or turn themselves into invalids because a doctor or nurse has told them, without adequate explanation, that their blood pressure is low. Instead of celebrating the possession of a healthy, lower-than-average pressure, they develop unwarranted fears and symptoms.

We have been discussing chronic low blood pressure. There are acute and intermittent low blood pressure states that deserve description.

Severe hemorrhaging from an artery or large vein may lead to shock, which is always accompanied by low blood pressure. Similarly, shock may arise from collisions, burns, falls, and other accidents and will reduce blood pressure. An intense emotional experience may cause a fall in pressure and may result in fainting, since the pressure becomes so low that blood is not propelled adequately to the brain.

There is a form of low blood pressure which may develop when a person changes position from lying down to standing up. This is called postural or orthostatic low blood pressure. It may be accompanied by weakness, pallor, lightheadedness, fainting sensations, or partial blacking out. It may follow a long illness in which the patient has been lying flat in bed all or most of the time. Certain medicines used in the treatment of high blood pressure may, in some instances, cause postural hypotension.

Pooling of blood in the lower extremities because of a severe varicose vein condition also can produce postural hypotension. So, too, can standing rigidly at attention for prolonged periods without moving the leg muscles, as some healthy young soldiers have discovered. People with nervous system diseases or with very flabby muscles may develop postural hypotension. Another cause is chronic anxiety and emotional tension. A surgical operation called sympathectomy, in which certain nerves are cut, may also be followed by postural low blood pressure.

Intermittent attacks of low blood pressure may be caused by irritation of the carotid sinuses. These are areas in the large artery of the neck containing sensitive nerve endings that help control blood pressure. In persons whose carotid sinuses become sensitive, undue pressure over areas in the neck—such as that produced by a tight collar—may set off an attack of low blood pressure sufficient to cause fainting. Sudden turning or raising of the head may also do this. Many patients learn what pressure and motions to avoid. Also, there is quite good preventive treatment provided by such medicines as ephedrine and phenobarbital. In very severe cases, nerves in the carotid sinuses may have to be surgically severed. Some patients develop their attacks as the result of emotional tension, and the attacks may be prevented when they receive help from their own doctor or a psychotherapist for their emotional problems.

MALARIA

Malaria is one of the oldest and most widespread diseases of mankind. In recent decades, with the use of newer medications, malaria has been virtually eradicated from the United States. But the disease is still common in many parts of Asia, Africa, and Europe. And with increasing United States involvement in southeast Asia in the 1960's, the number of malaria cases reported in this country increased significantly from 71 cases in 1959 to almost 3,000 in 1968.

The rising malaria incidence has implications for preventive medicine at both individual and community levels.

The disease is caused by an organism that parasitizes the red blood cells. It can be transmitted only via the blood and, in nature, the mosquito does the transmitting. The mosquito bites an infected person, ingests some of his blood and, with it, malaria organisms. The organisms pass through a stage of their life cycle within the mosquito. When the mosquito then bites a noninfected individual, it deposits some of the malaria organisms in his blood.

Malaria organisms can live and reproduce only in a certain species of mosquito called *Anopheles*. Where there is no *Anopheles* mosquito, there is no malaria. Malaria eradication in the United States, where the disease was not uncommon through the mid-1930's, depended first of all upon eliminating *Anopheles* from its breeding places—mainly in warm Southern regions—through swamp drainage, use of DDT, and other measures. With action against the mosquito, and with the discovery of effective medications to treat malaria, the number of cases dropped sharply, and there was no longer a pool of infected individuals serving as sources for transmission of the disease. With the recent upsurge of malaria, it has become important to identify and treat infected individuals in order to prevent malaria spread.

A significant potential source of malaria transmission in the United States is blood transfusion. To guard against this, blood banks do not accept donations from servicemen or other people who have been in areas where malaria is present until there has been a lapse of two years. After two years, even inadequately treated malaria will disappear from the body in most cases.

United States physicians, too, have become more alert to the possibility of malaria today in servicemen or civilians returning from areas of the world where the disease is common. A history of recurrent episodic fever—or sometimes just lingering fatigue, headache, and loss of appetite—will prompt them to send a blood specimen to a laboratory. With special staining, any malaria-causing organisms in the red blood cells can be detected.

It is important to note here that narcotic addicts risk malaria when they use unsterilized needles.

Although malaria rarely causes death, it is a serious, disabling disease, producing uncomfortable periodic fever, chills, and loss of vigor. Several medications are available for treatment, and complete cure can be effected in most cases quickly and with a minimum of discomfort. No quarantine or isolation for the malaria victim is necessary.

A major medical problem arises in areas where malaria is common, for curing one episode of it in an individual does not provide protection against reinfection. It is for this reason that United States servicemen in malarious countries are regularly given low doses of medicines that keep the malaria organism from entering the bloodstream and producing symptoms.

However, the organism may still invade the liver without causing symptoms. Any evidence of actual malaria infection requires more intensive treatment with other medications capable of eliminating the organism from the body completely. These medications are not used routinely because of potential side effects.

Malaria may develop after a person has left a malarious region. When it does, it is usually in a person who has received low-dosage medications to keep the malaria organisms from entering the bloodstream—but while this has been achieved, the organisms have penetrated the liver. Symptoms appear usually only after the suppressive medications have been stopped for several days or weeks. Prompt treatment should be given.

One problem in treatment has been the development of strains of malaria organisms that are resistant to newer medications. When such organisms are involved, quinine therapy may be required. Several new compounds also are being developed to treat such organisms.

Danger of death from malaria arises only when there has been acute infection by a certain malaria strain—falciparium malaria. For such infection, immediate and complete therapy is essential and requires immediate hospitalization and consultation with specialists in malaria treatment.

Not long ago, an American woman, while vacationing in Central America, was in an automobile accident. In the hospital, she required blood transfusions. Soon afterward, she returned to the United States for further treatment. Within two weeks, she began to have recurrent fever and chills, and her condition became grave. Her doctor, suspicious of the presence of a tropical disease because of her recent travels, ordered blood smears for malaria. The organisms were detected and treatment was immediately begun with antimalarial medications. The patient made a complete recovery.

The source of her malarial infection was most likely the blood transfusions, although mosquito transmission is a possibility.

We mention this case here to illustrate the need for awareness of the possibility of malaria in travelers in this day when increasing numbers of us travel far and wide. While it may not always be possible to avoid infection by the use of such measures as insect repellents and mosquito netting when traveling, awareness of the possibility of infection can lead, should symptoms develop, to prompt diagnosis and treatment.

MENOPAUSE

How much more fortunate women would be—and men and, indeed, whole families—if the menopause had not been nicknamed "change of life." There is no undesirable change of living that must occur with the menopause; in fact, many women today find life more satisfactory after menopause.

Surely, the menopause represents a change—an alteration not in life-style, however, but simply in ability to conceive and bear children. And since most women already have borne or adopted the children they have wanted, they can and usually do welcome the change to inability to conceive. Why, then, the undesirable aura that surrounded menopause in the past and continues to do so needlessly now?

The menopause does bring with it, in most instances, some immediate symptoms and some delayed ones. They can be unpleasant. The characteristic ones are hot flashes which may be accompanied by chilly and sweating feelings. Some women experience muscle and joint aches; some get dizzy spells; others become anxious and uneasy and the emotional upset may bring with it palpitations, faintness, and overbreathing.

Actually, some women sail through the menopausal years without a single unpleasant reaction and without need for medication. Fortunately, for the others, all of the symptoms now can be prevented.

What is nature doing during the menopause? The ovaries where eggs mature are ending their functioning. Usually, menopause occurs between the ages of 45 and 50, but it is not unusual for it to start earlier or later. If the ovaries must be removed surgically earlier in life, then an artificial menopause is created—and that, too, can be prevented from becoming distressing.

With the drying up of the ovaries, their output of hormones, estrogens, declines. When, at puberty, estrogenic hormones were poured out by the ovaries, breasts developed, pubic hair appeared, the uterus and vagina grew, and feminine contours were shaped. Now, at menopause, as hormone production declines, there is some reversal of what happened at puberty. The hair loses gloss; the skin is less resilient; the womb shrinks; the vaginal lining loses its velvety touch. These changes—and hot flashes and other immediate symptoms—are caused by reduction in the usual amounts of estrogen.

So, the answer for prevention is simple: supply the deficient estrogen. And this is precisely what a doctor can do if you give him a chance. He has available a number of preparations, natural and synthetic, to replace estrogens and abolish hot flashes and other unpleasant symptoms. If the symptoms are very severe and do not yield readily to his treatment, the family physician may want the patient to see a specialist for additional suggestions about treatment. He will recommend either an expert in women's problems, a gynecologist, or a specialist in hormones, an endocrinologist.

During the menopause, of course, monthly flow begins to diminish and usually, after a year or two of irregularity, ceases. Treatment with estrogen may regularize the flow somewhat but is not intended to interfere with natural termination of menstruation.

The hot flashes and other acute symptoms that may accompany menopause disappear in the course of a few years. But other effects of menopause may persist for the rest of a woman's life, a fact not sufficiently recognized in preventive medicine in the past. As a result, many women have suffered needlessly from premature aging, uncomfortable vaginal itching, greater tendency to bladder infections. One of the severest complications has been thinning of the bones, especially those of the spine. This condition, called osteoporosis, can cause pain and disability.

Why not give estrogens for the late changes as well as for the hot flashes and other immediate symptoms of menopause? This question has been debated by the medical profession. There has been some fear that continued use of estrogens might cause cancer. We do not believe that this is so, nor do leading authorities. In their book on medical treatment,* which

* Goodman, Louis, and Gilman, Alfred, *Pharmacological Basis of Therapeutics.* New York: Macmillan, 1965.

other physicians often call "The Bible," Drs. Goodman and Gilman note: "Attempts to induce malignant tumors in most animals with estrogen have been unsuccessful, and no evidence of a carcinogenic [cancer-producing] action has emerged from extensive use in man. It has been stated that in the 25 years since diethylstilbestrol was first widely used, not a single malignant tumor has been ascribable to estrogen. Curiously, it may turn out that replacement therapy after the menopause may, by preventing the atrophies and attendant changes, actually reduce the incidence of malignant tumors in older women."

The Gilman-Goodman statement is surely a reassuring one, especially as it touches upon the possibility that estrogen usage may even decrease the chances for cancer.

There may be an occasional doctor left who wants to pass off the menopause as nothing more than an emotional experience which can be controlled by reassurance and sedatives such as phenobarbital. But most physicians now realize that estrogen therapy is the answer to most of the troubles of the menopause.

Some additional matters deserve mention:

The thinning of bones which follows menopause requires use of extra calcium and vitamin D in addition to use of estrogen for full protection.

There is also the important question of how to combat and prevent the emotional problems that menopause brings for many women. Since the menopause marks the end of the childbearing period, it becomes frightening to some women who have not had children or to those who see themselves as useful only when they are producing babies. Some go into deep depression. Women who fear the menopause or who notice that they are feeling low or having crying spells should act quickly to prevent later serious emotional problems. A frank, open talk with the family doctor is advisable. He can judge whether he can handle the situation or whether it requires help of a psychiatrist or other psychotherapist. Sometimes, just one session with an expert in emotional problems will give a troubled woman a clearer perspective which will carry her through the stresses of her menopause.

Also, women who are troubled about their reactions to approaching or imminent menopause should talk openly to husbands and friends. If her doctor isn't the warm type sympathetic to emotional problems, then a woman might try her clergyman, who will know of a psychotherapist if one is required or will have a list of mental health agencies in the community or a nearby one. It is important to avoid letting emotional tensions and depressed moods build up to the point where they may precipitate a serious "nervous breakdown."

After menopause, women begin to become as susceptible to atherosclerosis and heart attacks as men. Do read what we have written about how to prevent the ravages of aging on the vascular system, artery linings, and heart.

Two myths about the menopause still are prevalent. One is that at that point a woman should no longer expect to have an active sexual life. The other, a corollary, is that at that point she becomes less desirable sexually. Both are total myths. Women can and should continue active sexual lives; indeed, many enjoy sexual activity more after being freed of fear of unwanted pregnancy. (Birth control measures should be continued beyond the last menstrual period, usually for a year or more; your doctor can advise you about this.)

MENSTRUAL DISORDERS AND FIBROIDS

Fibroids

The uterus has two layers. The inner lining undergoes monthly changes and, if no pregnancy occurs, is shed. If an egg is fertilized, the lining receives the egg and eventually forms the placenta and other membranes that surround and nourish the fetus.

The outer layer of the uterus, which makes up the bulk of the organ in nonpregnant women, consists of thick, involuntary muscle. At the time of childbirth labor, the muscle undergoes rhythmic contractions which result in birth of the child. The muscle also may contract irregularly during menstruation, accounting for the cramps sometimes associated with menstrual flow. Tumors that develop from this muscular layer are rather common *and are known best by the name "fibroid."* Although the word fibroid implies that the tumor is derived from fibrous tissue, it is actually an overgrowth of muscle and medically it is referred to as a myoma.

Myomas are almost always benign. They may grow inside the muscle layer of the uterus, near or distant from the lining, or they may grow on stalks attached to the uterus. Myomas may cause symptoms when they become large enough to press on the lining of the uterus or on adjacent structures. Pain is not common; more often, myomas may cause varied menstrual disorders. In some cases, they may so distort the normal uterine shape that implantation of the fertilized egg is difficult and so there may be infertility or miscarriage. Sometimes, myomas may interfere with labor or delivery.

Fortunately, most myomas do not cause any symptoms or problems and are usually only detectable on pelvic examination. The growths are usually readily distinguishable from other tumors. When there is any doubt about their nature, Pap smears, x-ray films taken after instillation of a dye into the uterus to outline it clearly, or dilatation and curettage can make the diagnosis certain.

Upon finding myomas, the physician will want to perform regular pelvic examinations in order to assess their rate of growth and detect any new ones. With this information, he can be guided in determining if and when surgical removal of the myomas may be advisable. For example, myomas reaching a certain size can cause childbirth difficulties, and the physician may recommend their removal prior to pregnancy.

Most women who develop myomas are in their thirties and forties. Often the growths enlarge under the influence of estrogen. When estrogen secretion diminishes after menopause, they tend to get smaller and sometimes disappear entirely. For this reason, it may be advisable in some cases to delay a decision about surgery until after menopause; at that point, it may not be needed. Some physicians will not prescribe estrogen-containing medications (such as birth control pills) to women with myomas; others may do so but only with the condition that frequent examinations be performed to assess any changes in sizes of the myomas.

The only cure for myomas is surgical removal. However, occasionally, a D and C (dilatation of the uterus and curettage of the inner wall) will correct menstrual abnormalities which may be caused by myomas. Removal, therefore, may be delayed or avoided. There are many reasons, however, to remove myomas—for example, if they cause pain by pressure on adjacent bowel or bladder, if they will interfere with pregnancy, if they twist on their stalks or enlarge rapidly, if they cause persistent menstrual irregularities, or if they produce uncontrolled bleeding.

Most women past childbearing age who need to have surgery for myomas will be advised to have the uterus removed at the same time. This does not add much to the surgical procedure or to postoperative discomfort and, of course, is absolutely curative. Since the ovaries, the source of female hormones, can be left intact when the uterus is removed, there will be little if any interference with sexual desire and enjoyment or with secondary sexual traits. Some surgeons favor removing ovaries along with uterus as a preventive measure against the development of ovarian tumors in the future. After removal of the ovaries, they prescribe female hormones to make up for the deficits.

It should be noted that there is no specific test for myomas. The diagnosis depends upon the doctor's skill in performing pelvic examination. Any decision to operate should usually be confirmed by a specialist in gynecology, even if this means that you have to travel a good distance for the confirmatory consultation.

Menstrual Disorders

Menstrual disorders are extremely common. Irregular flow, excess flow, pain, and absence of menstruation are not diseases in themselves but rather are symptoms that something is wrong. They are most often caused by abnormalities in the uterus itself or by imbalance in the delicate hormonal pattern that regulates menstruation. In turn, the hormonal balance is very sensitive to a multitude of factors such as emotions, changes in other body hormone levels, fatigue, and almost any illness (physical or mental).

The physician will try to determine what the underlying disturbance might be and then institute corrective measures. A careful history and pelvic examination are often helpful for diagnosis. There are also many diagnostic tests and procedures to determine hormone levels and their interrelationships, including the following:

a. *Basal body temperature.* Body temperature fluctuates in response to hormone changes. In particular, in the normal menstrual cycle, after progesterone appears and just before ovulation (or egg-release) occurs, the temperature falls slightly. It then rises by about a degree after ovulation. Taking body temperature in a resting state (usually on awaking in the morning) with a special thermometer is useful in determining if ovulation occurs and also if normal hormone fluctuation takes place.

b. *Vaginal smears.* The cells and the mucus in the vagina undergo changes in appearance and consistency when hormone levels change. Vaginal smears thus can provide helpful information.

c. *Blood and urine tests.* These assays for hormone levels are more accurate than most other tests. They do, however, take time to carry out, require careful attention to details of collection, and are expensive.

d. *Dilatation and curettage (D and C).* In this examination, which is performed under anesthesia, the cervix is widened and the uterine lining is scraped gently to get a representative sample of cells which may then be examined for abnormalities. Indications of hormone levels may be obtained from examination of the glandular structure of the uterine lining.

e. *Endometrial biopsy.* This is usually an office procedure. A small piece of the uterine lining (the endometrium) is removed for microscopic examination. At the same time, a small flexible metal rod passed into the uterus can be of value in outlining the interior of the uterus to detect abnormalities.

f. *Hormone administration.* Menstruation results from an interaction of several hormones. It is possible to determine the relative lack of one or more of the hormones by measuring the response of the uterus to test administration, by mouth or by injection, of the hormones. The yardstick of measurement may simply be the onset of menstruation, or it may be necessary to perform a D and C in order to assess the response of the uterine lining more directly. Most often, hormone administration is used to control various menstrual irregularities which may result from hormone imbalance. In women with menstrual irregularities, proper administration of hormones often may reset internal hormone production so it becomes normal.

Primary prevention for menstrual disorders requires regular periodic physical examinations to detect any still symptomless pelvic abnormalities and to evaluate the state of general health. Regular Pap smears for detecting cancer of the cervix or uterus before it can produce menstrual disturbances is, of course, a vital measure. It is also important for the physician to know the timing of his patient's cycles in health and disease. Therefore, every woman would do well to keep a record of her cycle length, amount of bleeding (number of pads used), and any associated symptoms.

Secondary preventive measures have to be tailored to the particular menstrual irregularity. The gynecologist is the specialist most familiar with such irregularities.

Amenorrhea means absence of menstruation. If it develops after a woman has had a history of menstruating, it is called *secondary amenorrhea* and the implications are much different than if menstruation had never begun (*primary amenorrhea*).

Secondary amenorrhea, of course, occurs with pregnancy and menopause. At other times, a common cause for it is an emotional upset—as, for example, when a teen-ager leaves home for the first time to go to college. A wide variety of physical conditions—including anemia, malnutrition, and serious illness—may also lead to temporary cessation of menstruation.

Primary amenorrhea often means that hormone production is deficient or that an anatomical abnormality is present. Careful discussion of menstrual, developmental, and emotional history often will delineate the underlying problem. Physical examination is helpful in finding anatomical abnormalities and evaluating the general state of health. Blood and urine tests may reveal general physical problems causing amenorrhea. Other tests, such as endometrial biopsy or hormone administration, may be used to determine if hormonal abnormalities are present. Establishing the cause of amenorrhea is often difficult but is essential to guide proper treatment.

Excessive bleeding during or between periods also can have varied causes, ranging from emotional difficulties to abnormalities of the lining of the uterus. Here again, the diagnostic approach emphasizes consideration of previous menstrual irregularities, emotional background, and any other physical ailments. Dilatation and curettage is particularly helpful in determining the presence of some of the most common causes of excessive flow such as nonspecific inflammations of the uterus, tumors, polyps, or cancer of the uterus. Analysis of the scrapings often indicates hormonal disturbance as well. D and C can be of particular value in emergencies when excessive bleeding has to be stopped quickly. It is also an essential part of the evaluation of postmenopausal bleeding because cancer of the uterus accounts for more than 30 percent of postmenopausal bleeding and can be accurately diagnosed by D and C.

Most often, excessive bleeding is due to a benign condition. The D and C not only is diagnostic but in well over one half of patients is curative as well. Most others can be helped by hormone therapy. Excessive bleeding over a period of several months can cause anemia, and dietary supplements of iron often will be prescribed to correct the anemia.

As an example of the value of careful diagnosis, a 55-year-old postmenopausal woman had been taking estrogen-containing medication. She began to note irregular spotting and consulted her physician. Frequently, estrogens can produce such spotting, but to be certain a D and C was per-

624 / *Disease Scenarios*

formed. The scrapings indicated that precancerous changes were taking place in the uterine lining, a hysterectomy was performed, and the patient has done very well. (A combination of surgery and radiation therapy provides a favorable outlook for uterine cancer that is detected fairly early.)

Many, if not most, women experience some degree of discomfort at the onset of their menstrual periods. Since individual reactions vary, it is sometimes difficult to draw a line between discomfort and pain that deserves to be called *dysmenorrhea*. For practical purposes, however, it can be said that a woman has dysmenorrhea if her menstrual cramps do not yield to aspirin or other mild pain-relieving medications, and if they keep her from engaging in her work or social activities.

Dysmenorrhea (pain with menstruation) may be caused by a wide variety of pelvic disorders which usually can be diagnosed on the basis of the patient's history and pelvic examination. Treatment is then directed at the underlying disorder, such as endometriosis, polyps, or myomas.

More usually, though, women with dysmenorrhea have no organic abnormalities. Full understanding of dysmenorrhea is still lacking. It seems to occur more often in unmarried women, and in many cases there is evidence of underlying emotional disorder. Treatment in such cases includes reassurance that no organic problem is present. Insight into emotional problems, whether provided by the gynecologist or a psychiatrist, can be beneficial. Mild pain relievers, sedatives, and antispasmodic medication may be helpful. In addition, hormone therapy can temporarily benefit painful menstruation.

Beginning four to seven days before menstruation, many women, particularly those in their thirties and forties, experience slight weight gain, stiffness in the extremities, sometimes headache, backache, diarrhea or constipation, anxiety, agitation, irritability, or even depression. Some experience only a few such symptoms to a mild degree; others suffer greatly from several or all. The condition that is called the "premenstrual tension syndrome" is poorly understood. Symptoms promptly subside with onset of menstruation. A notable feature is that there is almost invariably a four- to eight-pound weight gain due to fluid retention. It is thought that changes in hormone levels which occur toward the end of the menstrual cycle produce water retention and possibly temporary changes in the functioning of a variety of body organs.

The diagnosis is usually apparent to the physician after he hears a description of the timing and nature of the patient's complaints. Examination may reveal only some congestion of the uterus and water retention in the extremities (edema).

Treatment with diuretic medications which promote excretion of excess fluids is often effective in eliminating physical and psychological symptoms. Sometimes, tranquilizers are a useful aid to treatment, and occasionally psychiatric help is needed for particularly severe problems. Often, for prevention of the monthly upset, a physician will prescribe a diuretic and tranquilizer, and sometimes a low-salt diet, for use beginning ten days before the end of the cycle. Please note that diuretics, though very useful where indicated, are powerful and potentially dangerous medicines if abused, and should be taken according to the doctor's prescription only.

INFECTIOUS MONONUCLEOSIS

Infectious mononucleosis is a common ailment in teen-agers and young adults; it becomes rare after the age of 40. Despite its name, it is not highly infectious under ordinary circumstances, and most adults can attend a sick person without contracting the disease. Occasionally, it does occur in epidemics among young people living close together—soldiers in barracks, students in dormitories, etc.

Because it occurs so often among young people who do a lot of dating, it has been called the "kissing disease," which is regrettable since it is probably not spread this way and may be giving kissing a needlessly bad name. It is believed to be caused by a virus and to be spread via the air by discharges from infected throat passages.

In a typical case, symptoms include fever, sore throat, and swollen glands in the neck (the disease also has been called "glandular fever"). There may also be weakness, poor appetite, sore muscles. In many cases, the spleen (in the upper left portion of the abdomen under the ribs) is enlarged, soft, and tender. Frequently, the liver is involved, and jaundice appears in some cases.

The incubation period from time of contact to appearance of first symptoms may run 4 to 7 weeks. Usually, there is a period of discomfort of 3 to 6 days before the typical symptoms appear. The active period usually runs 5 to 20 days. Convalescence may last from weeks to months.

Doctors usually are not worried excessively about the outlook. The disease generally clears without residuals. Fatality or severe complication is rare. However, there are just enough instances of ruptured spleen, involvement of brain and nervous system with respiratory paralysis, hemolytic anemia, and obstruction of breathing by acute sore throat and swollen tonsils (or by the respiratory paralysis) so that doctors do not shrug off the malady. Students are usually kept in the college infirmary until symptoms pass. And young people eager to return to sports have to be warned that convalescence may be long and that some symptoms may recur when activity is started.

Diagnosis can be made with a high degree of certainty from (a) the symptoms, (b) the appearance of stained blood cells which show characteristic changes in the lymphocytes and monocytes, and (c) a test on blood serum (heterophil test) which shows positive reaction when the serum is mixed with sheep or beef red blood cells.

There is no available primary preventive measure except that it is best for teen-agers and young adults to keep away from a sick person with "mono" during the active period of the disease. No vaccination is available. For secondary prevention, there is little that can be done except to ensure an adequate period of bed rest and very gradual return to activity. Some doctors give corticosteroids in the hope they will shorten the course of the disease and length of convalescence; however, the consensus is that such treatment may make a patient feel better but does not speed recovery. Occasionally, sore throat and tonsillitis may be complicated by bacterial infection, and antibiotics may be used. Otherwise, there is no point to giving penicillin or other antibiotics, since infectious mononucleosis does not respond to them.

We know of a doctor who was

convalescing from the disease and was bouncing his child on his abdomen when he suddenly realized that his spleen had ruptured. A ruptured spleen is a surgical emergency, and the victim must be rushed to the hospital. Rupture may be prevented in patients with enlarged spleens if they avoid heavy lifting, contact sports, straining at stool, and pressure on the abdomen—precautions that should be continued for at least a week after the spleen has returned to normal size.

Another real emergency comes when breathing is obstructed; immediate hospitalization and treatment are required.

If purplish or black and blue spots appear on the skin, the doctor should be notified immediately because a rare case develops purpura (page 642). The same is true when the yellowness of jaundice appears, signifying that there is damage to the liver.

Occasionally sore throat may be so painful or the mouth and gums may become so inflamed that the sick person is better off in a hospital where soothing fluids may be used on the inflamed areas and pain relievers administered.

MOTION SICKNESS

Motion sickness is the overall term for such disturbances as *sea sickness, car sickness, airplane sickness, train sickness, space sickness,* etc. All result from overstimulation of the delicate system of canals in the inner ear which regulate the balancing mechanism of the body.

Certain types of motion cause this overstimulation in susceptible people. Also, because the nerve pathways involved in balance are involved in the process of focusing of the eyes, motion sickness may be brought on by an attempt to focus the eyes on rapidly moving objects, particularly when they are close up. Since nausea is the principal symptom of motion sickness, people with irritable stomachs and intestines may be more apt than others to develop the condition. Motion sickness is more likely to occur when the individual is in an enclosed space with poor ventilation, especially if there is any unpleasant odor from cooking, gasoline, etc.

There is a strong emotional factor in many cases of motion sickness. One of the authors was once a doctor on a ship and treated, for severe sea sickness, a woman who had developed her nausea in the taxi on the way to the boat! People who fear the separations involved in journeys or who have specific fears of plane, auto, or train accidents are particularly susceptible to motion sickness.

The primary symptom, nausea, comes in waves and recurs until, in many cases, it ends in vomiting. It may be preceded by cold sweats, sleepiness, yawning, pallor, excess salivation, and deep breathing. Some persons then develop dizziness, headache, weakness, inability to concentrate. While most persons soon adapt to the motion, there are some who do not and who may become seriously ill from continued vomiting and dehydration.

The potentially serious effects of motion sickness must be kept in mind by both patient and physician when a person convalescing from a serious illness, such as a heart attack or heart failure, plans on taking a long sea voyage or plane trip. This is also true for patients with diabetes, certain kidney and liver diseases, Addison's disease, and any other condition in which a severe upset of food intake or of the body's water and acid balance could have serious consequences.

Fortunately, there is effective prevention for motion sickness through use of general measures and special medicines. Good ventilation is one important measure. On a boat, anyone with a tendency toward motion sickness should try to be on deck as much as possible and, while there, should not look at the water but rather at some fixed object on deck. It may be best not to read until there has been good adaptation to the motion. Eating should be restricted to small, bland meals, and heavy use of alcohol and tobacco should be avoided. It is best not to chew gum because there is a tendency to swallow air. In planes, the susceptible person should choose a seat over the wings if possible, and keep the ventilator on. Some people find that small amounts of crème de menthe on ice provide relief.

Use of medicines to *prevent* attacks is important. It is much easier to prevent an attack than to treat it successfully once it is under way. Successful prevention depends upon using an adequate amount of medicine, taking it long enough before travel starts (usually 90 minutes) and continuing to take it on a regular schedule.

There are many effective medications. They include Dramamine and Benadryl, which are antihistamines and tend to produce some drowsiness. Phenobarbital is a good sedative for the apprehensive person and is often combined with scopolamine or atropine. Marezine and Bonine are also useful. Your doctor can judge which combination may be good for you because he can judge best whether the motion factor or an emotional factor may be the paramount influence. Obviously, too, the driver of a car cannot

be given the same medicine that might be useful for someone who can sleep on the back seat during the journey.

In addition to antimotion-sickness medications which are taken by mouth, it is best to carry rectal suppositories containing such medications for use when there is vomiting; medicine that is being vomited up cannot be helpful.

Travel is such an important part of our lives that a person who is seriously hampered by motion sickness should see his or her family physician for help in overcoming the problem. And if fear of travel is the basic problem, it can be most worthwhile to discuss it with the family physician and, if he suggests it, with a psychotherapist.

MULTIPLE SCLEROSIS

Multiple sclerosis (MS) is one of the most enigmatic diseases known to medicine.

It rarely begins before the late teens or after age 40. It affects only the nervous system (usually the spinal cord and sometimes the brain) and, through destruction of the covering tissues of the nerves, interferes with nervous impulse transmission. Since all sensations and movements are transmitted and coordinated through the nervous system, the disorder can have far-reaching consequences.

An important feature of MS lies in the body's ability to partially combat the changes taking place in the nerve tissue, thereby leading to partial restoration of function of the affected nerves. Unfortunately such remissions in the disease are succeeded by further episodes of destruction in the same or in a different site in the nervous system. The disease, then, is one of ups and downs, with remissions and exacerbations that last weeks or months or years. In fact, about 17 percent of MS patients experience complete spontaneous remission of the disease. But the progression of disability in most cases is unfortunately relentless.

The course of the disease and the extent and sites of nerve destruction and disability are largely unpredictable.

The cause of the disease is still not clearly established. There are some indications that an environmental factor, perhaps a virus, plays an important role. For example, the disease is much less common among inhabitants of tropical climates than among those living in temperate zones. However, a disease similar to MS has been artificially produced by injecting nervous system tissue from one animal into another, suggesting that an allergic reaction may be responsible.

Since the cause is still not clear, primary prevention is lacking.

MS can make itself known in any of a number of ways, depending upon what areas of the nervous system are affected. Most commonly, there is loss of sensation, loss of strength, and/or loss of coordination of a body part innervated by the affected nerves. Blindness and loss of bowel and bladder control are other possible symptoms.

Symptoms may develop quickly, on the one hand, or, on the other hand, they may appear slowly and insidiously. The diagnosis is strongly suspected when there is a history of transient deficiency of some function followed by almost complete recovery. For example, a woman, who had experienced at age 27 a sudden loss of vision in one eye with complete recovery after several weeks, began to notice when she was 30 years old that her legs hurt and tingled after walking. Over the next several days, she noted that her right leg was weak and numb. After three months, most of the symptoms disappeared, leaving only some weakness in the right leg.

Special tests may be needed to differentiate MS from many other disorders of the nervous system, including tumors, infections, emotional difficulties.

Secondary preventive measures are nonspecific. Effective specific treatment is not available yet. However, a relationship has been noted between onset or worsening of an attack and such factors as emotional upsets, excess fatigue, feverish illness, exposure to the sun, surgery, and pregnancy. Therefore, every effort should be made to avoid these stresses. There is considerable debate among physicians over the advisability of terminating pregnancy in a woman with MS.

A good diet is an important positive aspect of treatment and secondary prevention. Physical therapy to maintain a full range of motion in affected limbs and to keep muscles toned is needed during acute attacks. Physical therapy is also important when limbs have become disabled. Good skin care is needed to avoid pressure sores which may break down and become infected.

MS is a chronic disease. Patients must learn to live with it and within their limitations. Because the disease is *slowly* progressive, many people have been able to live many productive and happy years by avoiding fatigue and other factors that can make the disease worse.

Emotional support during times of discouragement, particularly during exacerbations of the disease, is vital. The patient's physician and family can play key roles here. There is always the hope that a remission will soon follow a flare-up of symptoms.

We know of many patients who have kept on earning livelihoods while afflicted with MS. One of them, a physician, a specialist in dermatology, was able to carry on with patient care for some years. Later, when there were considerable limitations on his activities, he concentrated on writing. He was helped by good diet, by plenty of rest, by his determination to provide for his family, and by his family's eagerness to help and lend emotional support in times of stress.

Many MS patients fall prey to "miracle cures"—ranging from special vitamin preparations to varied concoctions of medicines—which do nothing but raise false hopes. There is no known curative treatment for MS at present, although there is much research into the mysteries of this disease and good reason to hope that it may yield more effective treatment and, ultimately, cure and even measures for primary prevention.

MUSCLE DISORDERS

The more than 600 muscles in the body control such important functions as pumping blood, breathing, swallowing, digestion, and walking. All are dependent upon blood circulation to provide them with nutrients and oxygen and to remove waste products. All are under nervous system control.

Muscles themselves are not subject to many diseases. Usually, muscle abnormalities are due to disease of the nerves that control them (as in poliomyelitis, cerebral palsy, and multiple sclerosis); to a defect at the nerve-muscle junction (as in myasthenia gravis); or, uncommonly, to derangements of the total body economy (as in hyperthyroidism which may sometimes produce muscle weakness, or in cancer, or consequent to the toxic effects of a black widow spider bite).

Diseases of the muscles themselves are, generally, poorly understood. They have been classified, largely, according to the particular muscle groups affected and age of the patient at onset of the condition. Definitive cure is available for only a few muscle diseases. Yet it is important that a muscle condition be diagnosed and its severity assessed in order to permit suitable treatment.

Muscles react to a disease process in a limited number of ways: weakness, change in mass, or pain (cramps). Anyone who notes muscle weakness should see a physician as soon as possible. Neurologists and internists are the specialists in diagnosis and general treatment of muscle disorders; physical therapists (physicians and nurses) provide specific therapeutic exercises and measure changes in muscle power.

On the basis of a patient's history and physical examination, the physician usually can distinguish diseases of muscles themselves from other categories of disorders which may impair muscles. In equivocal cases, he may employ various tests. One aid to diagnosis is the electromyogram, which records the tiny electrical discharges from muscles. The discharge pattern often reveals whether weakness or pain results primarily from a muscle disease or a nerve disorder. There are blood and urine tests to detect the presence of distinctive muscle enzymes and protein; when muscles are diseased, their enzymes and protein leak out and appear in abnormally large amounts in the blood and urine. Muscle biopsy—the study of a small sample of muscle under the microscope —is of diagnostic value.

The most widely known group of muscle diseases are those classified as muscular dystrophy. The word dystrophy refers to abnormality of function and development. Muscular dystrophies are chronic diseases that gradually lead to wasting of voluntary muscles. The wasting may occur over a variable period—years or decades. Mind and sensation are not affected. Of the approximately 200,000 cases of MD in this country, two thirds are in children.

While the dystrophies have varying patterns, all are believed due to derangements of muscle metabolism possibly related to enzymes.

The Duchenne or pseudohypertrophic type affects young children. The calf muscles usually are affected first, becoming weak and also larger than normal as muscle tissue is replaced by fat. The condition, unfortunately, is progressive and frequently leads to death in late childhood or the early teens.

Most forms of MD, however, are more benign although potentially disabling. The facioscapulohumeral type usually is confined to the facial, neck, and shoulder muscles and begins during the teen years. There are limb girdle types which involve the pelvic muscles and begin in adulthood, and other types which involve eye muscles or small muscles of hands and legs. The rate of progression of muscle weakness in all but the pseudohypertrophic type is usually fairly slow, but there are variations from individual to individual.

The role of heredity in the pseudohypertrophic type is fairly well established. Only males are affected; females are carriers. Hereditary factors are probably important in the other types of dystrophy as well, but are not as clearly established. There is now active research to find ways to detect the carriers of faulty genes that may lead to dystrophy.

A family history of muscle disease —whether the affected have been uncles, cousins, or others—will be a clue for the neurologist to study the history in detail in order to determine whether having children is advisable. (Probably, a check of family history should become part of the premarital examination in order to evaluate the possibilities of hereditary illness. Currently, it is possible to take a sample of amniotic fluid during pregnancy and, in the case of some lethal or exceptionally disabling diseases, determine whether the fetus is affected. Therapeutic abortion then may be advised. This is not yet possible for muscular dystrophy but in the future may become one type of primary prevention.)

Since it has been shown that excess exposure to x-rays can produce harmful genetic mutation, a limited primary preventive measure is avoidance of all but essential x-ray studies. Most physicians are particularly wary of exposing women in the childbearing age to x-ray except when absolutely essential.

Early treatment is important to delay helplessness. Other muscle groups may be trained to take over the function of weakened muscles. Emotional problems for patient and family can be serious if neglected. Physical therapy, occupational training for jobs within the patient's capabilities, sympathetic advice from knowledgeable people, and opportunities to see how others have compensated for their disabilities can go a long way toward preventing loss of morale and physical deterioration. The

Muscular Dystrophy Association of America has chapters in many cities which work with patients and physicians, helping not only those with MD but with other muscular diseases as well.

For the patient with MD, attention to certain factors can help limit disability. Obesity should be avoided, since it puts greater strain on muscles. Periods of immobility, too, should be avoided; they have a tendency to accelerate progression of the disorder. Care must be taken to make certain that joints do not freeze in unnatural positions; splints at night and meticulous attention to position at all times can help prevent such freezing.

Like patients with many other chronic illnesses, those with MD are prone to fall prey to false hopes and suffer disillusionment when the hopes prove unjustified. Full information, factual and detailed, should be obtained from the physician.

A great deal of research seeking thorough understanding of the causes of MD, methods of prevention, and more effective means of treatment is under way.

It must be emphasized that muscle weakness does not invariably mean muscular dystrophy. There are other muscular disorders and they may be more readily controlled or even cured. Their diagnosis requires the acumen of a specialist in the field, since some are uncommon. For example, a 20-year-old man noticed that he was having increasing difficulty in climbing stairs. The weakness in his leg muscles progressed over a period of several weeks, and when he consulted a neurologist, weakness was also detected in muscles of the hip, neck, and shoulder. Although MD was feared, electromyography and muscle biopsy proved that he was suffering from an inflammatory disease, polymyositis. He was then treated with aspirin, steroid medication, and physiotherapy, and recovered within a few weeks with only mild residual weakness in the shoulders.

MYASTHENIA GRAVIS

Several Indian tribes in South America have long known that arrows dipped in the extract of a certain plant have the ability to paralyze. As early as the nineteenth century, the active ingredient in the extract was identified as curare. In the 1940's, curare found its way into routine anesthetic practice. By producing temporary muscular relaxation, it made the surgeon's job easier. In effect, curare induced temporary paralysis. It was then discovered that another compound called neostigmine could reverse the paralysis from curare.

Both curare and neostigmine are of importance in myasthenia gravis. This disease has long fascinated neurologists, for it causes muscular weakness but no change in muscle mass. Affected muscles fatigue easily on exertion, but they show relatively prompt, partial recovery after rest. It was thought that myasthenia gravis was a disorder of chemical interaction at the junction of nerve and muscle— the site where the nervous impulse directs the muscle to contract. Laboratory studies showed that curare exerts its paralyzing effect by deranging transmission of the nerve impulse to the muscle at this very same site.

The exact nature of the deranged transmission in myasthenia gravis still has not been fully elucidated; no one has ever isolated a curare-like substance from myasthenia patients. Yet, when the curare antagonist, neostigmine, is given to myasthenia patients, there is a remarkable return of strength to previously weakened muscles. In order to maintain the improvement, neostigmine has to be given every two or three hours. Nevertheless, it represents a major development in the treatment of myasthenia.

Myasthenia is high on a physician's list of possible diagnoses when a patient, usually between the ages of 20 and 40 and without a family history of muscle disease, begins to complain of easy fatigue, especially in the muscles of the face, eyelids, larynx, and throat. There may be drooping of the eyelids or swallowing difficulty. Weakness may also affect other muscles of the body and is particularly dangerous when it affects the breathing muscles.

The physician may elect to give the patient a test dose of neostigmine or a shorter-acting compound called Tensilon. One of the most dramatic phenomena to be seen in medical practice occurs when a patient with drooping eyelids, hands he cannot clench, and arms he cannot move because of excessive weakness suddenly comes to life within seconds after either of the compounds is administered.

In equivocal cases, a tiny dose of curare may be given to make certain of the diagnosis. Myasthenics are extremely sensitive to curare, and this tiny dose may produce transient, moderately severe weakness.

In a substantial number of myasthenic patients, the thymus gland is enlarged; sometimes a tumor is present in the gland. In some instances, removal of the thymus has a beneficial effect on the muscle weakness; occasionally it even cures myasthenia. Whether and when to remove the thymus is a delicate medical question. In the postoperative period, such patients, who may be temporarily paralyzed before recovery, require sophisticated respiratory care. During this time, the patient often needs assistance with a respirator. Clearly, the operation is one to be done only in a medical center familiar with the problems and equipped to handle them.

Medical therapy with neostigmine or a compound called Mestinon enables almost all myasthenics to lead near-normal lives. The disease tends to wax and wane in severity, and so the dose of medication may have to be adjusted from time to time. Myasthenia may be aggravated by respiratory infection, loss of sleep, menstruation, high carbohydrate meals, and intake of alcohol. It is important to have a regular physician (usually a neurologist) who can detect incipient change in severity of the disease and treat it accordingly and who will provide prompt care for respiratory infection.

Pregnancy is possible for the myasthenia patient. Although the child may be weak for a few weeks after birth, spontaneous recovery is the rule.

Sometimes severe swallowing difficulty or respiratory insufficiency may occur suddenly. For this reason, many physicians urge myasthenic patients to carry with them at all times both spare ampules of neostigmine and a card indicating the diagnosis and medication.

NARCOLEPSY (AND RELATED CONDITIONS)

Narcolepsy is a strange illness which causes its victims to fall asleep at inappropriate times. At any point during the waking hours, they may be seized by uncontrollable urges to sleep. They awake minutes or hours later, usually feeling refreshed. The sleep attacks may develop even in the midst of conversation; unfortunately, they may also occur while driving or operating potentially dangerous tools or machines.

The illness usually starts between the ages of 10 and 20, affects males more often than females, has no known cause, and usually tends to become milder or to disappear after age 50.

In many instances, sleep attacks are accompanied by another dramatic phenomenon—*cataplexy,* or unexpected paralysis. With cataplexy, the victim, while remaining fully conscious, may find his knees buckling, his head nodding, and his arms without any strength. Such an attack usually clears completely in a few minutes.

Less frequent are attacks of *sleep paralysis* in which, just before falling asleep or immediately upon awakening, the afflicted person cannot move his muscles, speak, or open his eyes. He usually experiences great anxiety even though realizing from previous attacks that he will recover completely in a few minutes. Sleep paralysis may occur in people with narcolepsy and in others who are free from it.

Another accompaniment of narcolepsy—less frequent than cataplexy—is *sleep hallucination* in which the individual has such vivid dreams that he feels he must act upon them; he may, for example, envision an intruder passing through his room and actually get up out of bed and search for him.

When narcolepsy, cataplexy, sleep paralysis, and sleep hallucination occur together, the afflicted person is said to have the *full narcolepsy syndrome.*

None of these four conditions, or any combination of them, does any damage to the brain. There is no association with epilepsy. Strangely, too, no matter how many attacks of narcoleptic sleep the patient has during the day he sleeps his usual quota at night.

Narcolepsy is not always readily diagnosed. The illness frequently begins during the student years when a young person may ascribe sleep attacks to dull lecturers, late dates, fatiguing athletics, heavy meals. When, however, attacks come on in the midst of dancing with an attractive date or while performing some delicate or dangerous manipulation, he should realize he needs medical help.

Fortunately, treatment with amphetamine, Meratran, and other medications which stimulate the central nervous system is often effective in preventing attacks. Also, taking a nap at a strategic time of day—at lunch hour or before or after the evening meal—may reduce the chances of an unwanted "nap."

People with narcolepsy should have a detailed talk with their physicians on dangers, if any, in their work and other activities. This may save injuries to patients and possibly to others.

Part of good secondary prevention is the understanding which the physician can provide that narcolepsy is a benign disorder. This can help reduce anxieties. Since the cause is still unknown, there is no primary prevention for narcolepsy.

PARKINSON'S DISEASE

The outlook for Parkinson's disease has changed, and is continuing to change radically. It is a disease of the brain that, if untreated, produces tremor, muscle weakness and rigidity, slow movements, loss of facial expression, stooped posture, a peculiar shuffling gait. It does not, however, cause any intellectual deterioration or changes in sensory ability.

The cause of most cases is unknown. A small percentage of cases, however, have been linked to a special form of encephalitis which reached near-epidemic proportions in Europe between 1918 and 1923. Some other cases have followed brain injury from such diverse causes as carbon monoxide poisoning and manganese poisoning. Brain tumors do not cause parkinsonism. Certain medications have side effects that mimic the symptoms of parkinsonism, but the symptoms disappear quickly after cessation of the medicine.

Primary prevention then is almost entirely lacking. The disease usually begins between the ages of 50 and 70 in an insidious manner. Most often, it starts with muscle stiffness and slowing of ability to perform one's usual activities, then progresses to a constant tremor in one hand, and gradually over a period of years affects both sides of the body. The constant tremor is one of the hallmarks of parkinsonism, which is also called shaking palsy. The tremor may affect hands, legs, tongue, lips. Immobility of facial muscles of expression ("mask-like faces"), muscle rigidity and weakness, and slurred speech progressively limit the victim's ability to carry on normal interactions with others. A peculiar feature of the disorder is that in times of crisis or with strong voluntary effort, all symptoms can be briefly overcome. Thus a patient may be able to jump up and run out of a burning building upon hearing "fire" only to have symptoms return when the crisis is past.

At present, unpleasant symptoms of parkinsonism can be alleviated with a variety of therapeutic agents, including antihistamine and antispasmodic compounds. In some cases, particularly younger patients with parkinsonism affecting only one side of the body, surgical destruction of certain brain structures has proved to be a highly successful form of therapy. This surgery is done by means of a small hole in the skull through which is inserted a special instrument guided very precisely to a specific brain area. The area is then destroyed by intense heat or cold (the patient feels no pain), and all symptoms may disappear. Why the surgery works has not been fully clarified, but certain pathways involved in involuntary muscle control are known to be destroyed.

Surgery for parkinsonism, of course, requires great skill. It has been a major advance in treatment of the disease. When done properly, it is not as traumatic or hazardous as most major surgical procedures, requires only a short postoperative convalescence, has a good success rate and, when successful, produces permanent abolition of symptoms. Still, because most people with parkinsonism are elderly and more likely to have other diseases as well, and because any surgery does entail some risk, surgical treatment for parkinsonism has not achieved widespread use.

Fortunately, a dramatic breakthrough is being made and promises to radically alter the course of parkinsonism. Advances in biochemistry have revealed the identity of certain compounds that act as mediators of nervous impulse transmission in the brain. Investigators have noted that certain of these mediator compounds appear to be deficient in patients with parkinsonism. And using a biochemically related compound called L-dopa (levodopa), they have achieved a considerable success rate in completely reversing disabling symptoms. Worldwide trials are now under way to more fully evaluate the efficacy and possible side effects of L-dopa.

Another agent, one recently developed and marketed as a preventive agent for influenza, called amantadine, has in several instances been shown to relieve parkinsonism symptoms.

These medications do not cure. They eliminate symptoms so long as they are taken—much as antihypertensive agents lower blood pressure as long as they are taken regularly.

Besides these agents, other measures are of use in helping patients cope with, and avoid progression of, any disability. They include physical measures such as massage and exercise of affected muscles to promote relaxation and alleviate joint and muscle aches and prevent freezing of joints. Important too is sufficient rest to compensate for the fatigue associated with the extra effort that parkinsonism patients may require for movement. The measures also include providing the patient with an understanding of the disease and what can be expected from treatment—and relief of anxiety, tension, and depression which have been shown to exacerbate symptoms.

Even in instances where medications are not very successful, these ancillary measures are helpful. It should be emphasized that parkinsonism progresses slowly and does not impair the mind, so a productive life can be carried on. Finally, surgical treatment, if it carries some small risk, is a relatively safe and often effective mode of treatment.

THE PNEUMONIAS

Most of us tend to regard pneumonia as a disease that has succumbed to modern medical developments. Yet, if we measure the success of medical advances in terms of eradicating disease, much remains to be done before the battle against the pneumonias can be considered successful.

At present, we are able to treat and *cure most cases* of pneumonia, but we are as yet unable to prevent pneumonia with the same success we have for such diseases as smallpox and typhoid. Moreover, pneumonia is still a potentially fatal or severely disabling disease in some instances. About 5 percent of all deaths in the productive years of life are due to pneumonia.

In speaking of pneumonia, we most often refer to an infectious disease caused by the pneumococcus organism (pneumococcal pneumonia). To be more precise, however, the word pneumonia refers to an inflammatory reaction of lung tissue produced by invading bacteria, viruses, or sometimes nonliving material. This inflammation leads to consolidation of areas of the lungs usually filled with air to permit oxygen and carbon dioxide exchange.

Pneumonias are usually classified as "lobar" or "broncho." Lobar pneumonia refers to the type in which a specific section or "lobe" of the lung is inflamed and consolidated. In bronchopneumonia, there is a more widespread, patchy process. A chest x-ray is usually needed to differentiate the two types.

However, since the same organism can cause either patchy or lobar infiltration, a more sensible classification is based on the actual cause. By far the great majority of pneumonias are caused by pneumococcal bacteria or by viruses or viral-like organisms. But many other organisms may cause pneumonia, including streptococci and the agents responsible for such diseases as tuberculosis and chickenpox. Pneumonia may also follow the aspiration of oily substances or stomach contents into the lungs, which occurs most frequently in unconscious persons.

Primary prevention of pneumonia is very much dependent upon the individual and the quality of his daily health care. Generally, the best preventive medicine for pneumonia as well as many other health problems rests upon maintaining good general health, good diet, adequate rest and relaxation. Current medical opinion is that pneumonias don't occur without loss of resistance either in the general body economy or in the lung itself. It is well known that pneumococcal bacteria as well as other potentially harmful organisms can be found in the mouth and throat of almost all of us at any time, but such organisms cause difficulty only under special circumstances.

Most commonly, it is the untreated or poorly treated cold that sets the stage for pneumonia. The infection in nose and throat lowers body reserves and infected secretions may drain into the lungs and overwhelm natural defenses. Typically, pneumococcal and most other bacterial pneumonias begin to cause symptoms three to four days after a cold begins. There is usually a fairly abrupt onset of high fever and chills, chest pain, blood-tinged sputum, and sometimes shortness of breath. Prompt consultation with a physician is then necessary to permit adequate treatment to be instituted. With prompt antibiotic therapy, symptoms resolve in one or two days and the patient is back to normal soon after.

In some cases, a bad cold may seem to linger and perhaps worsen, frequently becoming associated with fever and dry cough. This may indicate viral, or primary atypical, pneumonia which is sometimes referred to as "walking pneumonia." Usually the signs of pulmonary consolidation will evade detection by physical examination and are only apparent on chest x-ray. Viral pneumonia will take about two weeks to run its course. Antibiotics don't help. The most important part of treatment is adequate rest.

Early in the century, much was said about influenzal pneumonia. Many people died during the influenza epidemic of 1918, for example. But the influenza virus in most cases is not responsible for the pneumonia; usually it affects only the upper respiratory system. In reality, it is secondary infection by the pneumococcus or staphylococcus, capitalizing on the profound weakness that influenza causes, which produces the actual pneumonia and death.

There are many diseases and chronic conditions which may weaken body resistance and make a person more susceptible to pneumonia. They include malnutrition (often associated with alcoholism and drug addiction), pregnancy, diabetes, heart disease, chronic leukemia. Conditions that affect the lungs often decrease their ability to combat invading organisms. Examples are chronic bronchitis and emphysema, bronchiectasis, tuberculosis, chronic exposure to industrial fumes or dusts (such as coal dust), and cigarette smoking (which decreases ability of the lungs to wash away harmful substances). Sometimes lung cancer will partially obstruct a branch of the bronchial tree, leading to collection of secretions which may become infected.

People with such conditions, as well as other people—the elderly, the very young, and those recovering from surgery or any illness—should avoid contact with known cases of pneumonia, make every effort to avoid crowds, get adequate rest, and avoid as much as possible conditions (such as cold, damp, or rainy weather) that put stress on the body. They should also discuss vaccination against influenza with their physicians. Vaccines against pneumococcal pneumonia are being developed, and people in the high-risk groups mentioned should check with their physicians about availability of such vaccines.

A vaccine against one virus that has been shown to cause pneumonia is in use in the military. It was developed after it was noted that the close contact of recruits, coupled with the physical strain of basic training, made them more susceptible to this form of pneumonia. Use of the vaccine in the civilian population, however, is of limited value and not considered practical.

Prolonged exposure to certain dusts —such as those to be found in coal mining, cotton milling, and the asbestos industry—may cause lung disease. In large part, these special environmental conditions are checked by the federal government with the objective of keeping the level of irritants as low as possible. Recently, the chronic ingestion of mineral oil or daily use of oily nose drops has been found to cause a focus of chronic inflammation in the lungs. This results from inadvertent aspiration of the oily material. It usually produces few or no symptoms but may be detected on x-ray, be confused with cancer, and result in an operation to remove the suspicious area.

The outlook for pneumococcal pneumonia in most reasonably healthy individuals is for a quick (24 to 48 hour) resolution of most symptoms after appropriate antibiotic therapy is begun, with a return to feeling completely well in several days. Thinking preventively, the physician will perform certain tests to make certain that he is treating the right organism and that treatment is progressing satisfactorily. He will culture sputum and sometimes the blood before selecting an antibiotic. He may take blood counts and x-rays, will want to insure that the patient gets complete rest, oxygen if needed, and will be concerned about the spread of infection to others. If response to treatment is inadequate, a reevaluation will have to be made quickly to avoid further destruction of lung tissue. Finally, the physician will try to find any reason for the pneumonia—diabetes, a lung condition, etc. To carry out all these objectives efficiently and safely, hospitalization is necessary.

It is our opinion that hospitalization is important for all people with pneumonia except perhaps those with viral pneumonia which rarely causes complications and resolves spontaneously. For most cases, hospitalization will be for five to seven days, but it will be comforting to know that diagnosis and treatment have been thorough and accurate and that risk of spread of the disease has been minimized.

At the turn of the century, pneumonia was the No. 1 killer in the United States. Today it is No. 6. Once pneumonia was a killer of people in all age groups. Now, in the antibiotic era, it is fatal usually only in those with other debilitating diseases—for whom the risk of death can be as high as 40 percent. Pneumonia, thus, is still a disease to be taken seriously, to be avoided if at all possible, and to be treated promptly and vigorously when it occurs.

POLIOMYELITIS

Poliomyelitis is now a rare disease in the United States. Up to recent years, however, it was common, often reaching epidemic proportions, causing temporary and sometimes permanent disability in children and young adults. The reason for the dramatic change, of course, was introduction of first the Salk and then the Sabin polio vaccines. Virtual eradication of polio in the United States and in other countries practicing widespread vaccination is an example of what modern research combined with good public health practices aimed at primary prevention can achieve in a short period of time.

Primary prevention today begins with the routine care offered by the pediatrician during a child's first year of life. Up to the age of 6 months, an infant is protected from polio and many other diseases by the maternal antibodies transferred to him while in the womb. After this time, vaccination procedures begin.

The Sabin antipolio vaccine is an oral one which has been shown to be better than 90 percent effective in preventing poliomyelitis. It consists of a greatly weakened strain of polio virus that causes the body to manufacture antibodies against the virulent virus. A powerful immunity is built up after vaccination and is expected to remain with the individual for the rest of his life. The Sabin vaccine essentially has supplanted the Salk vaccine, which consists of killed polio virus. The Salk vaccine must be given by injection and calls forth a weaker immune response than the Sabin. For this reason, the Salk vaccine requires yearly booster shots. Three doses of the oral Sabin vaccine at about six-week intervals provide immunity.

The Sabin vaccine should not be administered when there are symptoms of an intestinal ailment (nausea, vomiting, diarrhea). This is because polio is primarily a disease of the gastrointestinal tract. The virulent form of the virus first invades the intestine and then may spread to the nervous system, where it causes nerve cell destruction and paralysis. Similarly, the weakened virus must invade the gastrointestinal tract before the body can develop immunity. If, however, an intestinal infection is present, it is unlikely that the weakened virus can establish a foothold. It should be emphasized that there is no danger that the weakened virus used in the vaccine will damage the nervous system. If intestinal symptoms develop shortly after administration of the vaccine, the doctor should be informed.

The presence of intestinal infection is the only reason why vaccination should be delayed. Every child should be vaccinated because virulent polio virus is still present in the general population.

Should adults be vaccinated? Probably not, since most have immunity to polio virus. It is undoubtedly wise for everyone up to age 20 to be immunized. Polio is very rare after age 20. It has been shown that most people have been infected with polio virus at some time during childhood even though there were only gastrointestinal symptoms; actually, it is the uncommon case when the polio virus moves on to invade the nervous system. In special situations, it is desirable that adults be vaccinated—for example, men entering the military or going abroad, particularly to a country where polio is still uncontrolled. Your doctor can supply further details.

In unimmunized people, polio often presents with fever, sore throat, aching muscles, and sometimes nausea, vomiting, headache and stiff neck. It is mainly a disease of the summer months. Polio is transmitted by the respiratory route but more commonly by the gastrointestinal. The virus is excreted in the feces, and flies and other insects may then transmit it. Even before vaccination became available, polio incidence was declining as the result of elimination of unsanitary conditions.

Most cases of polio do not involve paralysis; when paralysis does occur, it is usually not serious and frequently is only temporary. Should paralysis be a problem, death is now rare and up to 85 percent of the paralyzed can be rehabilitated as the result of advances in nursing care, physical medicine and rehabilitation, and treatment of respiratory problems.

PROSTATE GLAND ENLARGEMENT

The prostate gland serves to add a lubricating and nourishing fluid for the transport of sperm cells which pass through it on their way from the testicles to the urethra. The gland normally weighs two thirds of an ounce and is located at the neck of the urinary bladder.

At about age 50 in most men it begins to enlarge. After 60, 35 percent or more of men have some symptoms as the result of the enlargement. As the gland enlarges, it encroaches on the urethral tube carrying the urine from the bladder. In addition to causing symptoms, the enlargement puts a strain on the bladder which has the added burden of forcing the urine past the partial obstruction. This leads to enlargement of the bladder with some stasis or lessening of the flow of urine, and this may set the stage for urinary infection. An even more serious effect of obstruction may be a back-pressure of urine in the bladder sufficiently high to force urine into the ureters leading from the kidneys. Thus, in some cases of enlarged prostate gland, the kidneys are damaged by stretching (hydronephrosis) and may also be infected by the stagnant urine. An end result may be the loss of so much kidney function that uremia (page 606) develops or blood pressure may become elevated because of the kidney disease.

An enlarged prostate is benign and never becomes malignant because of enlargement. However, there have been some instances in which cancer of the prostate has arisen independently in the presence of benign enlargement of the gland.

Usually, one of the first symptoms of enlargement is the need to urinate one or more times during the night (nocturia). Then there may be difficulty in starting or stopping the urinary stream. The patient may notice that he dribbles urine instead of passing it in the usual forceful stream. Another symptom may be frequency of urination, with the patient noticing that he feels the urge to urinate again almost as soon as he thought he had finished urinating. Sometimes the symptoms are mild and the patient pays little attention to them. He may, nevertheless, develop symptoms of uremia (nausea, weakness, lassitude, etc.) or of high blood pressure (page 596).

The physician diagnoses the condition by examining the prostate with a gloved finger inserted into the rectum. Usually, there is obvious enlargement to twice—and quite frequently many more times—the size of the normal gland. However, the physician also recognizes that there may be an enlargement of a portion of the gland which cannot be felt through the rectum, and this enlargement also can be dangerous. The extent of enlargement also can be determined by passing a rubber catheter into the bladder after the patient has voided as much as he can to determine what "residual" urine may be present. If there is a large amount of urine left in the bladder, it is a sign of severe and long-standing obstruction. Through examination of urethra, bladder, and kidneys with special instruments and with x-rays, the physician obtains additional information on the nature and location of the obstruction and the state of the kidneys. Kidney function tests also help determine if the obstruction has injured the kidneys' functional capacities. The latter diagnostic procedures are usually carried out by a specialist, the urologist, who frequently takes over treatment of more severe cases. Milder cases often are taken care of by the family physician, who may occasionally want the urologist to check on the state of the prostate, bladder, kidneys, and urine.

The cause of benign enlargement of the prostate gland is not known. Therefore, there is no primary prevention.

Secondary prevention is enormously important for saving the bladder and the kidneys from damage. Once diagnostic tests are completed and evaluated, the physician can arrive at a picture of the problem and the probable future course. If symptoms are mild and do not distress the patient, and if there is no back-pressure of serious degree in the bladder and kidneys, he will probably adopt a conservative plan of treatment and a wait-and-see attitude rather than insist on immediate surgery. With medication to control infection, with regular sexual intercourse or prostate massages (through the rectum) to keep down congestion of the gland, and training in how to space intake of fluids, the patient may remain comfortable. Mild, warm tub baths with water circulating around the buttocks and lower abdomen are helpful.

If such treatment does not make the patient comfortable or fails to overcome the danger to bladder or kidneys, then surgical removal of the prostate becomes essential. This is a major operation but it has a high degree of safety when performed by an expert surgeon. There are, in fact, four types of operation, each approaching the gland in a different way. *Transurethral prostatectomy* means going through the urethral orifice and bladder and is the most commonly used; *suprapubic transvesical* goes through the lower abdomen and the bladder; *retropubic extravesical* avoids the bladder; and *perineal prostatectomy* goes into the area just forward of the rectum and close to the gland. The slight risk is virtually the same for all four operations. However, with the perineal approach there may be permanent impotence. The choice of the particular operation is usually left up to the surgeon, who should be informed about the sexual activity and desire for it by the patient.

In some instances, a patient is too sick or feeble to withstand operation and, instead, urine is drained via the bladder to the outside. However, with advances in modern surgery and anesthesia it is amazing how well even sick, weak, and very old patients survive prostatectomy.

PSORIASIS

Psoriasis is a chronic disease that affects skin, scalp, and nails. It is marked by the appearance of rather sharply defined reddened patches which become covered by thick silvery scales. The patches favor elbows, knees, scalp, groin, chest, lower back, and body folds. Fortunately, the face is rarely affected. There is itching in many instances, and in fact the name comes from the Greek *psora*, which means "to itch."

There is no parasite or germ involved. The disease is noncontagious. Its cause is still not clear, but it tends to run in families. Occasionally, it is accompanied by hypertrophic arthritis —the noncrippling wear-and-tear type which tends to produce knobby fingers. Psoriasis seems to be made worse when emotional tensions run high.

The disease comes and goes over many years and some victims have it for a lifetime beginning in young adulthood. It rarely afflicts children. Occasionally it may clear up completely.

Psoriasis may consist of only a few small patches which remain in the same place for years—as in one patient we have seen who has had patches over both elbows and some fingernail involvement for 30 years, but no other involvement. At the other extreme, psoriasis may affect the whole skin covering of the body, including the scalp.

Even in severest cases, there is no impairment of general health, no fever, no weight loss. But victims of severe psoriasis suffer mentally, often considering themselves lepers, feeling that they cannot go swimming or engage in other sports for which they need to wear abbreviated clothing. Worse still, some feel they should not enter into love relationships because of their disfigurement.

There is no real primary prevention for psoriasis, although it is true that people who live in sunny climes get psoriasis less frequently and in milder form. However, there is really good secondary prevention for almost every patient with psoriasis provided the patient will (a) find a doctor skilled in treatment and (b) really cooperate with the doctor.

Many patients benefit, some to the point of almost complete clearance, by tanning in sunshine. In areas lacking in regular sunshine, treatment may depend upon applying a suitable ointment prescribed by the doctor (or a skin specialist, a dermatologist, to whom he may refer the patient). Standard ointments contain coal tar chemicals or ammoniated mercury. Some also include corticosteroids. In addition to application of the ointment to affected areas, sunlamp treatment is used, with the dose increased daily until a proper tanning dose is achieved. This dose is maintained. The eyes, of course, are protected. And it is a good idea to stand when taking sunlamp treatments because of the risk of falling asleep and getting severely sunburned when seated or reclining.

A very severe acute case of psoriasis may well require care from a skin specialist who may want the patient in the hospital for a time.

In stubborn chronic cases, some doctors prescribe triamcinolone or other corticosteroids to be taken by mouth, with careful watch for untoward symptoms these powerful medications can evoke. Often, the corticosteroids get the lesions progressing toward healing, at which point ointment and sunlamp treatment may become effective.

Small resistant patches on prominent places sometimes can be made to disappear by injections directly into them of the corticosteroid medicines.

It is important that ointments remain in contact with psoriatic lesions for hours. This may be accomplished by applying a large Band-Aid or similar patch over the area after the ointment has been rubbed in. Plastic wrap of the household type may also be used.

Some persons with the severe, generalized chronic form of psoriasis find that they are greatly helped by entering a hospital or sanatorium which has facilities for ointment treatments and nurses and orderlies who are patient enough to carry out the doctor's orders for painstakingly covering every affected area. Usually, a week in a hospital or a sanatorium twice a year, combined with home treatment, will control even the most stubborn case.

As one experienced dermatologist puts it: "Treatment is more effective than most patients think. If it is to succeed, it requires more than a few minutes a day. Psoriasis yields more readily when the lesions are fresh. One tries to get rid of every trace with the expectation that, once cleared, the disease can be held thereafter in abeyance."

For lesions of the scalp, the doctor can prescribe helpful lotions or ointments. Little can be done for the nails; occasionally, mild doses of x-ray are tried.

People with psoriasis who are sensitive about their disease should talk to a psychotherapist unless their own doctor has the time and is a "natural psychiatrist," as many family doctors tend to be. Sensitive people with the disease should reach the point where they can talk freely about it with family, friends, roommates, fellow workers, and especially a prospective spouse. A psoriatic person in love should tell his or her sweetheart about the presence of the disease and about the disease itself: that it is completely noncontagious, does not interfere with health or procreation, and that there is some chance that it may be transmitted to offspring. When intimacy is contemplated, it is good to understand that psoriatic lesions do not affect either vagina or penis.

PURPURA

Purpura derives from the Latin word meaning "purple." In patients with the condition a prominent symptom is the appearance of purple spots in the skin. The spots are caused by bleeding into the skin and are similar to the "black and blue" marks that may appear in a small area of skin after a hard blow.

Purpura is no single disease entity. It is very often secondary to one of a long list of maladies or to use of medicines and chemicals. However, there is a special type of purpura without obvious cause which is called *primary* or *idiopathic* purpura. It is this type which we shall describe first.

PRIMARY PURPURA. The technical medical name for this condition is idiopathic thrombocytopenic purpura, which means that bleeding into the skin occurs as a result of a low count of platelets, which are elements in blood, but that the basic cause is unknown. The condition can be acute or chronic.

The acute type occurs mostly in young children. In addition to dark spots in the skin, there may be bleeding from the nose, in the intestines or stomach, and into the urine. The condition usually lasts a few weeks, then disappears by itself—permanently. This is the favorable outlook in at least three out of four cases. Some patients will require use of corticosteroids, and a small percentage will require surgical removal of the spleen.

In the chronic form of primary thrombocytopenic purpura, too, bleeding into the skin occurs, dark spots appear, and there is a history of easy bruising. In addition there may be nose bleeds and hemorrhages from the stomach and intestines, with bleeding into the urine from the kidneys and bladder. Hemorrhage into the brain is something the doctor fears as he projects the future for the patient with this disease, which can go on year after year, with only about 25 percent of chronic adult cases clearing spontaneously. Also, bleeding from gastrointestinal and urinary tracts occasionally may be fatal.

The diagnosis is made by excluding the many diseases that are accompanied by purpura and the many toxic substances that can cause this type of abnormal bleeding. In addition, the doctor finds that the platelet count in the blood is lower than normal, coagulation time is normal, bleeding time is prolonged, and clot retraction is abnormal. The bone marrow on biopsy shows typical findings of primary purpura. And when a tourniquet is placed on the upper arm to constrict the veins, many little black and blue spots (petechiae) appear below the tourniquet.

Many patients do well if they can avoid bruising in contact sports and other potentially traumatic situations, and can also avoid surgery and tooth extractions. They should be given the minimum number of medicines, because many medicines can cause purpura and add an extra burden for the patient who has the primary form. Usually these patients are treated with corticosteroids as the doctor plays for time to see if they have the form of the condition that may clear spontaneously.

If the disease continues for more than a year, or is especially severe and does not respond to the corticosteroid medicine, then the doctor advises removal of the spleen. This operation leads to a cure in up to 90 percent of patients with primary thrombocytopenic purpura.

Why does removal of the spleen, a nonvital organ, produce such dramatic cures? It is believed that the spleen in patients with this disease produces either harmful antibodies against the blood platelets or a substance that travels to the bone marrow and depresses production of platelets.

Thus, while there is no primary prevention as yet—since the cause of the condition is unknown—secondary prevention, with corticosteroids or spleen removal, is effective.

SECONDARY PURPURA. There are two kinds of secondary purpura. In one, blood platelet count is abnormally low; in the other, platelet count is normal but the small blood vessels are very fragile and allow easy bleeding into the skin and mucous membranes. In secondary thrombocytopenic (low platelet) purpura, the cause may be leukemia (often a first symptom of acute leukemia is purpura), aplastic anemia, tuberculosis, sarcoidosis, or such rare conditions as Gaucher's disease and lupus erythematosus. In an infant, this type of purpura is secondary often to blood poisoning (septicemia), congenital syphilis, or hemolytic disease of the newborn.

Many medications may on occasion cause secondary purpura. Among them are Sedormid, quinine, quinidine, sulfonamides, Diuril, Hydro-Diuril, Diabinese, Diamox, chloramphenicol, penicillin, meprobamate (Equanil and Miltown), streptomycin, salicylate, phenobarbital, digitoxin, Orinase. Chemicals that may also cause purpura include hair dyes, bismuth, gold salts, iodide, organic arsenicals (some of these are also used as medicines).

The other type of secondary purpura with normal platelet count is seen in such disorders as scurvy, severe blood poisoning, allergic purpura of the Henoch-Schonlein type, and as reactions to medicines and chemicals such as iodides, belladonna, atropine, quinine, phenacetin, salicylic acid, chloral hydrate, bismuth, and mercury.

With any type of secondary purpura, prevention of progressive disease depends upon the underlying disease. If the latter is cured, the purpura secondary to it will, of course, be resolved. If the disease is not cured, the purpura may come and go spontaneously or may yield to the use of corticosteroid medicines. When a medicine or chemical is the cause, stopping its use will end the purpura.

There is a form of purpura, fortunately rare, with a grim outlook. It usually strikes young adults and is almost always severely progressive. It is called *thrombotic thrombocytopenic purpura,* which means that in addition to the low platelet count and characteristic bleeding spots in the skin, small clots or thromboses form and block the flow of blood in vital organs. Often, in this type of purpura, hemo-

lytic anemia, jaundice, fever, drowsiness, and neurological signs of brain damage are seen.

SARCOIDOSIS (BOECK'S SARCOID)

Sarcoidosis is a long, chronic illness with great capacity for eventual healing though this may require as long as 8 to 10 years. It is found in all parts of the United States but is more often found in the Southeast, particularly in rural areas. It is about 15 times more frequent in black people than white and tends to be more severe in the former, too. It occurs most often between the ages of 20 and 40 years.

Its cause is unknown. It runs in some families but has never been shown to be transmissible even though it resembles tuberculosis in some respects. The sick person can live with spouse and children without danger to them.

The disease produces fleshy, painless, small lumps in skin, lymph nodes, and lungs. Under the microscope, these nodules resemble the early lesions of tuberculosis. Fortunately, they do not "caseate" and destroy tissue the way tuberculosis does. The nodules may become large or extensive enough to cause trouble by pressure on adjacent structures. Thus, for example, sarcoid lymph nodes in the chest may press on the bronchial tubes and cause coughing and infection.

The symptoms of sarcoidosis are highly variable. There may be weakness, malaise, loss of appetite, a run-down feeling. Fever is usually mild, although an occasional case may exhibit high temperatures. Although the disease most often occurs in skin, lungs, and lymph nodes, it can strike any place in the body: one form affects the eyes; another the parotid and other salivary glands; another may produce punched-out areas in the small bones of hands and feet. Frequently, the disease is found in the liver, but it rarely causes great damage there. Rarely it strikes kidneys, heart, and brain.

The diagnosis usually can be confirmed by a biopsy of the lesions in the skin or a lymph node. When no skin or lymph node lesions are available for biopsy, good results have been obtained by needle biopsy of the liver.

When the disease affects only the lungs, it may be mistaken at first for pulmonary tuberculosis until the doctor sees that the tuberculosis germ cannot be found and also that the sarcoid lesions do not respond to medications for tuberculosis. Diagnosis may be tricky when both sarcoidosis and tuberculosis of the lungs occur together.

Sometimes sarcoidosis is discovered by routine chest x-ray, and the lesions may be so extensive that doctors marvel that the patient has no fever or other symptoms.

There is no primary prevention for the disease. Once the diagnosis is made, the doctor works hard at secondary prevention. He knows that the disease has a great tendency to heal even though years may be required. He wants to prevent damage to lungs and other areas that may occur when diseased tissue gets an extensive foothold and scars other tissue or produces damage by pressure. He is also apprehensive lest damage occur to the eyes or about the face and nose, or in such vital organs as heart, kidneys, and lungs.

Treatment with corticosteroids— cortisone-like medicines—has revolutionized the outlook for patients with sarcoidosis. Before such therapy, only bed rest and good nutrition could be used. Many patients felt rundown or feverish year after year. Now, with careful attention to the dosage of corticosteroids, the physician is able to afford most sarcoid patients complete freedom to work and lead normal lives. He still wants them to avoid overfatigue. Also, because they are more susceptible than others to TB of the lungs, he instructs them in all means of primary prevention of TB given on page 660.

SCHIZOPHRENIA

Schizophrenia is one of the most widespread and devastating of illnesses. It accounts for more than half of mentally ill patients, who fill more than half the hospital beds in this country. According to some estimates, it affects two million people in the United States and Canada, and one of every 100 persons in the world today has, has had, or will have the disease. The 1 percent incidence seems to prevail in all societies, cultures, racial and ethnic types, and social classes.

Although it can develop at any time, even early in childhood, typically it overtakes people in the 16 to 30 age group. It also is called dementia praecox because it strikes such young victims.

In its advanced stages, it is easily recognized by anyone. The schizophrenic person may see visions which he is convinced are real; he may suffer from delusions that he can control other people, national destinies, the world; or he may be convinced that everyone is plotting to poison or kill him; he may be certain that he has strange diseases and may point to areas of his body where, he is convinced, worms are crawling; he may withdraw himself from others, not speak for weeks or months; he may endlessly repeat some act such as one patient who for days went about marching as a soldier.

Among schizophrenic patients we have known was a Boston businessman who spoke intelligently and convincingly about the national and international economic situation for a full hour—and then, when the baffled medical student was about to conclude that the patient was completely sane, observed virtually without a change of tone: "But, of course, you know that I am God and control all the banks in the world."

The big problem lies in recognizing the early stages of the disease, at a point when the sick person can be prevented from doing possible harm to himself and others, and when the illness can be treated most effectively. There is no blood or other test for this disease; it produces no overt physical indications. Only the person's words, attitudes, and behavior can provide clues to the diagnosis.

Usually, the first hint that schizophrenia is setting in will be something bizarre in behavior. For example, a person with average interest in religion may suddenly become deeply concerned with every ritual of his religion or may decide to adopt another quite foreign to his own tradition. Or a steady worker may lose one job after another with complaints that his bosses are out to get him. Or a previously good student may decide that he is not properly prepared and may refuse to take final examinations. Or a housewife may change from one butcher to another because she is con-

vinced that meat has been causing her to feel sick.

In a child with schizophrenia, there may be withdrawal, excessive temper tantrums, or antisocial acts such as setting fires. In some cases, a child may become afraid to eat or may insist upon having only one "safe" food.

Once you suspect that someone close to you is showing symptoms of schizophrenia, it is important not to discuss it with him but rather to contact your doctor immediately and describe to him what you have observed. Act promptly and decisively on his advice. If he advises hospitalization, even if that means legal commitment, you must act on the advice however distasteful it may be to you. The untreated schizophrenic person may become suicidal or may kill loved ones or endanger others by arson or other violent acts. More likely, the physician will suggest a consultation with a psychiatrist, and there should be no delay in accepting this recommendation.

Schizophrenia today is no longer hopeless. While it may not yet be curable, it is controllable—to the point where often the patient can function reasonably well at home and in a job. And the earlier treated, the more likely a satisfactory degree of control.

While secondary prevention—control of the disease once it appears, by measures we shall soon outline—is now possible, primary prevention is still elusive. The cause remains unknown.

There are two theories about schizophrenia. One, long-held, is that the disease is primarily psychological in nature, a matter of inadequate personality finally succumbing to some environmental stress. Stated very briefly, the theory suggests that the stage may be set for schizophrenia by a defective mother-child relationship or perhaps family-child relationship. The child's personality fails to develop normally. At some point, because of the personality deficiency, he may become schizophrenic when life introduces a critical situation.

The second theory is that schizophrenia is physical—basically, a disorder of body chemistry. The disorder produces a distortion of perception. Vision may be distorted; normal sounds may seem to blare in the ears; sense of smell may be affected; and there may be delusions and a loss of touch with the real world. As a result, changes occur in behavior. The victim may become mute and withdrawn, or feel persecuted, or become extravagant and silly.

Some investigators believe that both theories may be applicable. They conceive that schizophrenia may be a diagnosis that is not precise and that eventually it may be shown that several diseases of different causation are included in the present-day diagnosis of schizophrenia.

Meanwhile, the ranks of those who believe in the second theory—that body chemistry is involved—are growing. They include distinguished biologists, geneticists, and psychiatrists. Recently, many joined to establish the American Schizophrenia Foundation in New York, N. Y., aimed at intensification of biochemical research. They believe that although there is as yet no definitive proof of a biochemical factor, there is growing evidence in favor of such a factor and that, despite difficulties, it is in the biochemical search that hope lies, perhaps not too remotely, not only for curing schizophrenia but for preventing it as well.

In the past, electroshock and insulin shock treatment have been employed helpfully in some cases. The advent of potent tranquilizing agents has made a significant difference in the outlook for schizophrenia patients, particularly when they are treated early. At first these agents were thought to have only a calmative effect —but there is increasing evidence that they may have actual antischizophrenic activity. While they have not produced once-and-for-all cures, they have made it possible for many hospitalized patients to be released and, with continued medication under the supervision of family and other physicians, to take their place back in the home and the community. More and more now, these agents are being used to avoid the need for hospitalization.

One experimental treatment program, directly linked to the theory of biochemical origin of schizophrenia, makes use of niacin, or vitamin B_3, on the grounds that the schizophrenic person, because of a biochemical defect, has excessive need for this vitamin. Massive doses are used and according to reports by a small number of physicians who have employed the treatment, it is often helpful, particularly in early stages of schizophrenia. In more complicated cases, these physicians indicate, the vitamin treatment may need to be accompanied by use of tranquilizing and other medicines and by psychotherapy, and in very severe cases electroshock as well may be needed.

Thus, today, schizophrenia remains a very great problem, still one of the great mysteries of medicine. But while much remains to be done to fathom the mystery, schizophrenic patients and their families now have much to take comfort from. Under no circumstances should any illness, mental or physical, be a reason for shame. But we have still not escaped entirely from a misconceived aura of shame attached in the past to mental disorders. Thus, to many, it will be most welcome news that many distinguished scientists believe that schizophrenia has its roots in a physical aberration. Certainly, it is good news that research is intensive today and that many researchers foresee that, within a decade, there could emerge a clear biochemical understanding of schizophrenia and with it could come the means for making the disease not only a quickly remediable but also, quite likely, a preventable one.

And, meanwhile, there is this most important fact to go on: With treatment programs available right now, it is possible, especially when treatment is applied early and vigorously, to bring schizophrenia under control.

SCIATICA

The sciatic nerve is the longest and widest nerve in the body. Like many other nerves, it arises from the spinal cord at several levels, passes out through the special holes in the protective bony spine, and merges to form one nerve trunk. This trunk then courses down the back of the pelvis and thigh and branches just above the knee into two smaller divisions that travel down to the feet. The sciatic nerve carries pain sensation from most of the leg and innervates most of the leg muscles. The nerve's long course and large size make it rather vulnerable to pressure and injury.

Pressure, injury, and inflammation affecting the nerve are common causes of sciatica, a condition characterized by pain in the lower back and leg along the course of the sciatic nerve. In some cases, muscle weakness accompanies the pain. Sciatica can be mildly discomforting or severely disabling. It may be limited to thigh or buttock or extend to the feet. The pain is usually described as shooting down the leg. Typically, pressure on or stretching of the nerve (as on straight leg raising or walking) aggravates the pain. Sciatica usually lasts several days to weeks and may recur after a remission of several weeks to months if the causes of pressure or injury to the nerve are not corrected.

Confronted by sciatica, a doctor will seek out the source of pressure or injury—not always an easy search.

X-rays of hips, pelvis, sacroiliac joint, and lower spine help identify any anatomical abnormalities or severe arthritis which may be causing pressure on the nerve as it leaves the spine and travels down the back of the thigh. Injury to a nerve root inside the spine—from a slipped disk, for example—can be diagnosed with a special type of x-ray picture, a myelogram. In the vast majority of cases, it is a disk that proves to be the cause of sciatic pain.

Other sources of injury to the sciatic nerve include fractures of the pelvis, femur or lower spine, and dislocation of the hip—all readily diagnosed by x-ray. In some cases, inflammation of the sciatic nerve may arise for unknown reasons, produce all the symptoms of sciatica, and then disappear. In unusual instances, diabetes can produce sciatic nerve inflammation.

While the cause is being determined, the most effective treatment—bed rest for several days to weeks—will be instituted. Traction on the affected leg often reduces pain, as does mild heat. Sedatives and pain relievers may be beneficial.

In some cases, surgery to remove a slipped disk or arthritic bony prominence pressing on the nerve will be needed to prevent recurrences. In other cases, use of a back brace and firm mattress or bed board will suffice.

Sometimes people with sciatica consult chiropractors for treatment. Chiropractic manipulation of the back can be dangerous because it may cause a partially slipped disk to slip farther and cause more severe pressure, even increasing likelihood of permanent nerve damage.

Neurologists and orthopedists are the medical specialists most familiar with sciatica.

SENILITY

All of us hope that our last years will be golden ones, that our minds will remain sound, and that there will be no senile collapse into second childhood. Unfortunately, senility is the fate of some persons.

It is important to learn the symptoms, especially the early ones, of senility so that those forms of it that can be arrested or even reversed receive treatment as early as possible. Also, because the major cause of senile dementia is arteriosclerosis, or hardening, of arteries supplying blood and nourishment to the brain, we should early in life adopt the measures recommended earlier in this book to help prevent the development or intensification of arteriosclerosis. Thus, by age 25, each of us should be following a life-style that permits us to maintain normal weight, balanced diet, regular exercise, relaxed emotional attitudes, with cigarette smoking avoided, and with medical checkups carried out regularly. Such measures, begun early enough in life, may well save us from

becoming helplessly senile at age 65 or later.

Advanced senile dementia is easy to recognize—in the childish, babbling old person who is bewildered by almost any task and may even require help with eating and bathroom functions. The early stages of senility are more difficult to detect with certainty, and it is important to spot them in order to save a person from making unwise business decisions, unsound investments, a reckless marriage, an unwise change of will, or even committing immoral sexual acts.

Early senile changes may be manifested in swinging moods and displays of unwarranted anger, irritability, or laughter. There may be impairment of memory, and in early senility a person may begin to repeat words or actions. He may become stubborn and extremely rigid about daily routines. It is not unusual for a previously meticulous person to become slovenly. There is a great tendency for the individual to become self-centered. Not uncommon are delusions of persecution. Evidence of senile dementia may come from abnormal sexuality manifested, for example, in homosexual behavior or sexual approaches to children.

When signs of dementia appear, it is of vital importance for spouse, children or friends to arrange for a medical check. It is especially tragic when a curable form of dementia is neglected.

Senility may develop at a relatively early age—for example, in a person with low thyroid function. It may ruin the person's life and inflict great suffering on his family—and yet, when detected, the condition is completely curable with simple administration of thyroid hormone.

Other curable forms are those resulting from nutritional diseases such as pellagra; nutritional deficiencies that may accompany chronic alcoholism; pernicious anemia; syphilis affecting the brain; Cushing's disease; and chronic bromide usage. Occasionally, senile dementia follows injury to the brain and may be relieved by surgery to remove a collection of blood pressing on a brain area.

Not all forms of dementia caused by disease are at present curable, but enough are to warrant early medical intervention and search for a potentially curable cause.

The individual's physician, seeing him at regular checkups, is in a good position to observe any early signs of senility. Unfortunately, the individual experiencing dementia has no insight into his condition. The physician, spotting early signs, can notify responsible relatives and may be able to prescribe helpful treatment. In cases of progressive deterioration, care may be required in a special nursing home or in a hospital or institution with special facilities.

Care of a demented parent may be a serious problem—emotional as well as financial—for the children. If there are young grandchildren in the home, the effect on them of the presence of a senile grandparent must be considered. It may prove helpful to talk to a social worker experienced in dealing with the elderly, as well as to the family doctor.

If the decision is to keep the senile person at home, it is important to try to provide him with activities he is capable of carrying out so that he can gain some pride in participating. His routine should be kept as regular as possible. A night light in the bedroom can be an important aid in preventing confusion and fear about the dark.

A senile person may become excited when given barbiturate sleeping medicines. He is apt to do better with a medicine such as chloral hydrate. Also, the physician should be asked about the possible advisability of a mild tranquilizer for daytime use.

SINUSITIS—ACUTE AND CHRONIC

The sinuses are cavities or caves in the skull which help both to reduce the weight of the head and to make the voice more resonant. Their medical name, paranasal sinuses, suggests that they are intimately connected with the nose. In fact, all the sinuses connect through small openings (ostia) into the nasal passages. And the soft, moist mucous lining which coats the inside of the nose extends into the sinuses. The sinuses in the cheekbones are called maxillary sinuses; those above the bony orbit of the eyes are named the frontal sinuses; and there are others, the sphenoid and ethmoid, located more deeply in the skull. Normally, the soft, slippery secretion produced by the mucous lining of the sinuses silently drains away through the nasal passages.

Almost anything that can irritate, infect, or obstruct the interior of the nose can inflame the sinuses. That is why for primary prevention of sinus trouble it is important to treat colds early and properly (page 567), to do the same for nasal allergies (page 516), and to have the physician during periodic examinations check the nose to make certain that there is no blockage from a deviated septum, enlarged turbinate bone, or polyps. If a blockage is found, advice of a nose and throat specialist should be sought to learn if a corrective operation may be desirable.

People with colds should learn to blow their noses gently and without compressing the soft part of the nose —so as not to force infected material into the sinuses. All swimmers should note if the water, especially chlorinated water in a pool, irritates their noses; if so, they should discuss with their doctors the advisability of using nasal drops, antihistamines, or a nasal clamp. It is well for people who do much diving and find that their noses become irritated or that large amounts of mucus or pus are expelled afterward to discuss this with their doctors.

Workers in jobs that expose them to irritating smoke or fumes should learn how to minimize their exposure (page 149) as a means of reducing inflammation of the sinuses. One more reason, in addition to all the others, for abandoning the cigarette habit is that this will reduce irritation of the nasal passages and hence the risk of sinus trouble.

People with colds, sore throats, or tonsillitis should avoid airplane trips. If a trip is essential, the physician can help prevent sinus trouble by prescribing vasoconstrictor medicines and applications.

While nose drops and sprays are often prescribed for nasal and sinus problems, some people overuse or even habitually use them. This may actually complicate such problems. Nose drops or sprays should be employed only on your doctor's recommendation.

ACUTE SINUSITIS. When sinuses become infected—and it is rare for infection to be limited to just a single sinus —there are characteristic symptoms. The attack usually begins with fever, chills, headache, and a sick feeling. Often, there will be pain, tenderness, redness, and swelling over the affected sinuses. The nose may become congested, and often pus is discharged. In some cases, the teeth hurt when sinuses in the cheekbones are affected. These symptoms and the clouded appearance of the sinuses on x-ray examination and on transillumination (in which the doctor visualizes the maxillary and frontal sinuses by darkening the room and pressing a light up against the upper part of the bony orbit of the eyes and in the mouth) help in establishing the presence of acute sinusitis.

Once the diagnosis is made, the physician starts treatment designed to relieve symptoms and also to eradicate the infection completely and thus prevent development of chronic sinusitis. In addition to antibiotics to fight infection, he may prescribe vasoconstrictor medicines by mouth and in drop or spray form to promote drainage of pus from the sinuses. Steam inhalations are helpful. If pain is severe, medicines stronger than aspirin (such as Darvon, codeine, or Demerol) may be needed. If allergy is also present, antihistamines may be useful.

During acute infection, surgical drainage is rarely attempted. If, however, when infection has subsided, tests show mucus and pus blocking the maxillary sinuses, they may be washed out, since it is relatively easy to approach these particular sinuses through the nose.

Occasionally, infection of frontal or ethmoid sinuses leads to infection of bone around the eyes. In rare instances, frontal sinus infection may lead to the dreaded complication of meningitis or to a brain abscess. These possibilities are good reason for prompt, intensive treatment of every case of acute sinusitis, in addition to the desirability of such treatment for relieving symptoms and preventing chronic sinusitis.

CHRONIC SINUSITIS. The sinuses may become chronically infected, with thickening of the delicate linings and, in some instances, pus production. Common symptoms are congestion of the nose, cough, postnasal drip of mucus and mucopus. Headache is not nearly as prominent a symptom as is popularly believed. Chronic sinusitis is sometimes associated with bronchial asthma.

The modern tendency is to try to avoid direct surgical penetration of the sinuses to establish drainage or remove diseased lining membranes. Such operations are held in abeyance until more conservative measures have been given a chance. Allergic sensitivities will be explored and treated if found present. Pus from the sinuses can be cultured and the offending germ isolated so that antibiotics specific for it can be used. Drainage from the sinuses into the nose should be as free as possible; this may require minor surgery to remove polyps or correct a deviated septum or displaced turbinate bone. Sometimes cauterization of boggy turbinates helps to establish drainage. Infected teeth should be treated.

A frequent combination of cough, irritated nose and throat, and tension headaches should not lead to the assumption that chronic sinusitis is the problem. True chronic sinusitis can be unequivocally diagnosed by pus coming from the opening of a sinus plus the characteristic appearance of the sinus on x-ray and transillumination.

Is change of climate worthwhile for the chronic sinusitis patient? This is not an easy question to answer, especially in the very severe case. It should be borne in mind, however, that too

often a decision to move to a different climate is made hastily and the individual may exchange the "infective headaches" of sinusitis for the "emotional headaches" produced by loss of a satisfying job or relocation in an area far from friends and relatives. Such a step should be taken only with the advice of family doctor and nose and throat specialist, and only after a trial run of a year in the new climate. It is usually possible today, with modern antibiotic and other therapy, and with vacations in mild, dry climates at the height of the usual symptomatic sinusitis period, to make life bearable for most victims. Year-round climate control in house or apartment also may be very helpful and, even though expensive, may prove cheaper than moving an entire family to a distant state.

When drastic surgery is needed for chronically infected sinuses, it should be performed by a specialist in such operations. This may call for the individual to go to a medical center in a large city, an inconvenience but a most worthwhile one.

Some people with nasal allergy, either seasonal or year-round, notice recurrent sinus headaches whenever the nose is congested. This type of headache is believed to develop when congestion prevents free passage of air in and out of the sinuses. As a result, as air in a sinus or in several sinuses is absorbed into the blood, a vacuum is created, leading to pain.

This type of "vacuum" headache sometimes may be relieved with amazing rapidity by vasoconstrictive medicines taken by mouth or applied in the nose, or sometimes even applied by the physician directly at the location where the sinus channel enters the nose. One patient we know had frequent headaches of this type during the hay fever season. The pain was relieved dramatically when the doctor applied medication to shrink a particular area on a turbinate bone that pressed close to a sinus opening. Later, a minor corrective operation on this turbinate ended the recurrent headaches.

Sinus headaches related to allergies are generally best handled by the overall program for diagnosis and treatment of allergies discussed on page 516.

STROKE

Stroke, also known as apoplexy and cerebrovascular accident (CVA), involves injury to the brain and may be followed by such serious consequences as paralysis of one side of the body, loss of speech, impairment of memory, and even death. Until quite recently, strokes were regarded with such fatalism by physicians as well as laymen that little was done to prevent them or their end results. Now, fortunately, strokes are better understood, and with the understanding, areas of prevention have developed.

A stroke is the specific damage to the brain that results from injury to an artery either in the brain or leading to it. The artery damage deprives some of the brain of vital oxygen and other nutrients. So dependent is brain tissue upon oxygen that it may not survive complete loss of oxygen supply for more than five minutes or so.

In 60 percent of cases of stroke, blood flow to part of the brain is blocked by a clot in an artery (thrombosis); in 20 percent, the problem lies with a leaking or burst artery; in the remainder, flow is blocked by a clot coming from another area of the body and lodging in a brain artery (embolism), or there is some rare cause.

In almost every instance of blood clot blockage, the underlying cause is atherosclerosis or disease of the artery wall; and in hemorrhage, the underlying cause is atherosclerosis or a combination of atherosclerosis and high blood pressure. Emboli usually come from the heart, and among the causes is improper functioning of a chamber of the heart, leading to formation of a clot from which pieces may break away and clog a distant artery.

Since a stroke may result from an accident to an artery, large or small, anywhere in the brain or leading to the brain, the consequences can be quite varied. A stroke may block out a tiny area of the memory center, or it may deprive a large section of brain of oxygen, producing unconsciousness, paralysis, labored breathing—with death following soon thereafter.

One of the major developments that have opened up areas of prevention for stroke is the finding in recent decades that a significant number of strokes arise from damage to arteries outside the brain itself—in vessels in the neck leading to the brain and even in main arteries in the chest that supply the neck vessels and eventually the brain. These vessels are accessible to surgical exploration and repair.

Another significant development is the recognition that while a major stroke may seem to come on suddenly, the stroke process is not necessarily sudden and may even provide early warnings. In fact, three stages of stroke are now recognized: the impending stage (premonitory or transient ischemia); the developing stage (stroke-in-progress or transient ischemia with incomplete recovery); and completed stroke.

An *impending* stroke usually lasts

only a few moments. It may involve fainting, stumbling, numbness or paralysis of the fingers of one hand, or blurring of vision, seeing bright lights, loss of speech or memory, or some other indication that part of the brain has lost its vital blood supply.

Unfortunately, too often people, after recovering from these warning signals of stroke, do not recognize what they might be and pass them off as simply the results of fatigue, worry, or some other innocuous cause. Thus the opportunity to prevent the approaching stroke may be lost.

Any one or a combination of such symptoms should be the signal to notify your doctor or, if he is not available, to go to a hospital. A physician will know the serious portent unless there is some very definite other cause, such as overdosage of insulin in a diabetic, to explain the incident.

When he recognizes an impending stroke, the physician will probably need the help of a specialist in neurology to make a definite diagnosis. Special x-rays of the arteries leading to the brain may be taken. And if the cause of the symptoms appears to be a clot in an artery of the neck or other accessible spot, the decision as to whether an operation may be beneficial may require the combined skills of a neurologist and a surgeon who specializes in operations on arteries. Frequently, such a team of specialists can be found only in larger communities where there are medical schools or medical centers. In almost every state there is at least one medical school, and some large cities have more than one medical school.

If a definite clot is found, it may be decided to remove it or bypass it by constructing a new channel for the blood around the point of obstruction; or the decision may be against operation and to rely on anticoagulant medications to prevent the clot from causing a final stroke.

The *developing*, or stroke-in-progress, stage is recognized when there is progression of symptoms. For example, numbness in an arm may be followed by paralysis, or paralysis in a leg by weakness of the face, or headache and clouding of the mind by blurring of speech. This stage is an emergency. The patient should be hospitalized for confirmation of diagnosis and start of preventive treatment. Anticoagulants may be used and oxygen may be administered. At this stage, it may still be possible to use surgery to remove an accessible clot. While waiting for the ambulance and during the ride, the patient's legs should be elevated about two feet; his head should be kept from turning to right or left; he should be reassured; oxygen should be given if possible; a sedative or tranquilizer should be administered if he can swallow normally.

Unfortunately, too many developing strokes are not treated early enough. Some cannot be prevented by current methods and go on to the completed stroke stage. A typical victim of *completed* stroke may have paralysis of one side of the body with or without impairment of speech; there may be temporary loss of consciousness; the mind may be clouded and there may be regression to childish behavior such as crying and petty anger.

It has been learned that vigorous rehabilitation efforts can do much to overcome paralysis and speech impairment. Now, within two or three days after a stroke, or as soon as the patient is conscious, a program of exercises is started in bed, to be followed by out-of-bed and later out-of hospital exercises. Special braces for the leg may be helpful, and slings for a paralyzed arm. Speech therapy, if needed, is started early. It is necessary for patient and family to cooperate, understanding that progress may seem terribly slow, but progress will be made.

Once fullest possible recovery has been made from any stage of stroke, there needs to be a program of prevention of future strokes. Preventive measures include treatment of underlying disease—measures to prevent progression of atherosclerosis, measures to reduce high blood pressure, measures to treat a heart problem which may be causing emboli to be "thrown" to the arteries supplying the brain. And measures to combat atherosclerosis, high blood pressure, and diabetes are of vital importance as well in *primary* prevention of strokes. Since these three diseases underly most strokes, their effective control can do much to prevent strokes from ever happening.

SUICIDE

Suicide is a major problem. It now ranks among the ten leading causes of death. Each year in this country, there are 50,000 actual suicides and an estimated 400,000 attempted suicides. A completed suicide is a tragedy, but attempted suicides can be tragic, too, and for many others in addition to those directly involved—for families and friends.

Good preventive medicine is concerned with many aspects of the suicide problem—with preventing first attempts and repeated attempts, and with allaying fears, guilt feelings, and anxieties of others affected by actual or attempted suicides. It is important, we believe, for people who have been so affected not to bottle up their feelings but to obtain help by talking out their feelings with their doctor and, if necessary, in one or more sessions with a psychotherapist.

It is important for everyone, and certainly for family and friends of a suicide or attempted suicide, to know the facts about taking of one's own life. There are many misconceptions. Let us dispel the common ones and get at the basic truths.

Suicide knows no class bounds. It occurs among rich and poor, educated and uneducated. Professional people as well as nonprofessionals commit suicide. Indeed, the suicide rate among physicians, dentists, and lawyers, for example, is more than three times as high as among white-collar workers. And suicide occurs among all of the major religious groups in the United States.

There is no one simple cause or motive. People who are very sick physically, perhaps in the terminal stages of a fatal illness such as cancer, may take their own lives—but so may others who are depressed without being gravely ill physically.

Suicide is not necessarily the act of a crazed or insane person. Many people who commit suicide have seemed, right up to the event, to be perfectly normal. However, if they had been studied carefully, most psychiatrists believe, such people would have been found to have exhibited some neurotic or psychotic behavior before the event.

A suicidal tendency is not inherited. If there is a higher rate of suicide in some families, it may be because of a greater tendency toward depressive illness which may be inherited. Also, some experts believe that the fact that a suicide has occurred in a family may push some suggestible descendants in the same direction.

Weather and other meteorological or

climatological effects do not trigger suicide. Heat, cold, storms, humidity changes, barometric pressure, cold fronts, sun spots, phases of the moon, etc., have been studied and have never been shown, on a scientific basis, to influence suicidal behavior.

A particularly dangerous time for a suicidally inclined person is when he or she seems to be improving. It has been found that many suicides occur within 60 days after emotionally disturbed persons have left the hospital seemingly improved. And it is a fact that patients under a physician's care, even some undergoing psychiatric treatment, do still commit suicide.

Perhaps the most important misconception to be rid of is the one that holds that a person who talks about destroying himself or herself will not try suicide. This is at complete variance with the facts. Almost every suicide tries to tell someone in advance of his intention.

Besides noting, and reacting, to a spoken intention, how else can we spot the potential suicide?

Some insights come from an analysis of 21 cases of completed suicide. Of the 21, 20 had shown depressed moods; 18 had experienced insomnia; 16 had displayed retarded muscular movements; 15 had had feelings of worthlessness or guilt; 14 had exhibited anxiety or agitation; 13 had had weight losses; 9 had had fears of being victims of various types of sickness; and 6 had a specific and exaggerated fear of cancer. Seven of the 21 had attempted suicide previously, and 3 had known that a close family member had committed suicide.

The possibility of suicide may be suspected in a person who has frequent crying spells or who feels so depressed that he has difficulty with routine daily tasks, with sleeping, and

even with eating; who appears discouraged unduly, even hopeless, and self-deprecatory.

In a depressed person, high-risk signals include talk about suicide, family history of suicide, use of alcohol or drugs in excess. Risk is increased if he or she is unmarried and living alone.

As we have indicated, the most dangerous period for a depressed person is when he seems to be improving or when he has just left the hospital seemingly well enough to come home.

When suicidal tendencies are suspected in someone close to you, do not lose any time. Phone your doctor. If you can't reach him, try the Suicide Prevention Center if there is one in your community (if there is, you will find it listed in the phone book). If neither doctor nor prevention center is available, phone your local hospital and ask for the director's office. Also, your local health department will be of help. And your clergyman, too, will know how to obtain aid.

If you yourself feel an inclination to take your own life, do go immediately to your doctor. Talk frankly to him about your feelings. Don't hesitate to tell him about your suicidal drives. And if he isn't available, or if you feel you cannot talk to him, consult others suggested in the paragraph above. You need help; you deserve help; you can be helped; and help is available. We have many patients who thought they could not go on living but who have been helped to live happy, full lives.

We have been talking of one kind of suicide—in which a person intentionally ends his life by such means as poison or pills. But there are others, less obvious ways in which people destroy themselves and which should also be labeled as suicide. We are thinking of the patients who refuse to undergo examinations to ferret out possible diseases, or who refuse to follow prescriptions for treatment, for diet, for exercise. Aren't they committing suicide? And aren't many others—those who will die of cancer of the lung for failure to give up cigarettes, of heart disease for failure to make use of preventive measures, of breast cancer for failure to do something about a noticed lump? And those who will be killed in automobile accidents while driving under the influence of alcohol or drugs? Aren't they, too, suicidal?

These are the "secret suicides." We hope that there will be fewer of them among the readers of this book who consider the message of preventive medicine spelled out in these pages.

SYPHILIS

As part of many preemployment examinations, every hospital admission, and almost every premarital examination, a blood test is done for syphilis. When this screening test (called Wassermann test or VDRL) is negative, there is little concern unless findings on physical examination make the doctor suspicious.

When the test is positive, however, many questions are raised. The very first is, does the patient really have syphilis? Screening tests for syphilis not infrequently are falsely positive— that is, they are positive when patients do not have the disease and, indeed, may never have had it. Many conditions can cause the Wassermann test to be positive for long or short periods. To determine the true meaning of the test, the doctor will need to seek answers to such questions as:

Has there been a previous test for syphilis, and what were the results and treatment, if any?

Has there been sexual contact with a person who may have syphilis? (Syphilis is rarely if ever transmitted by means other than sexual contact.)

Are there suspicious sores on the body, particularly genitals, anal area, mouth?

Is there other evidence of syphilis?

Is the test still positive when repeated after several days?

Highly sensitive and specific blood tests can be carried out to confirm the diagnosis. In the course of his investigation, the physician is able to determine not only whether a person has syphilis but the stage of the disease and how best to treat it. Syphilis, if untreated, is a potentially fatal disease through its effects on the brain, heart, and/or blood vessels; but if treated early and adequately it is benign. The dangerously deceptive element in the disease is that initial symptoms disappear spontaneously without treatment, but the disease organisms remain in the body, taking ten to twenty years to cause lasting damage to various vital organs—and during this time the patient is free of symptoms.

Since it is easily diagnosed, deadly when untreated yet benign when treated, and treatment is quick, easy and safe, syphilis is a disease that dramatically illustrates the benefits of preventive medicine.

Primary prevention begins with awareness of the harmful nature of the disease, of its spread by sexual contact, and of its increasing incidence, particularly among teen-agers and young adults.

If contact is to occur with a partner who may have syphilis—and it should be remembered that the partner may have syphilis without displaying any signs of illness—then a condom should be worn and the genitals should be cleaned thoroughly with soap and water afterward. Large doses of penicillin immediately after contact have been effective in aborting syphilis but such treatment is usually not available.

Currently, a vaccine against syphilis is under development, but there are problems to be worked out.

Secondary prevention calls for treatment of syphilis before it affects vital organs.

In the primary stage of the disease, a sore develops (usually on the genitals) three to six weeks after contact with an infected individual. The sore resolves on its own without treatment. At this stage, blood tests may be negative. However, diagnosis can be made by microscopic examination of a specimen taken painlessly from the sore. Treatment then can be instituted with penicillin or another antibiotic, and blood tests are performed four times over the course of the next year to make certain treatment was adequate.

If untreated, syphilis next manifests itself, about three to six weeks later, with a rash (anywhere on the body), fever (sometimes), sore throat (sometimes), or other nonspecific symptoms. With or without treatment, these symptoms also will resolve. By this time, blood tests are usually positive, but the doctor will still take a smear from the rash and check microscopically for the presence of the syphilis organism. The disease is highly infectious at this stage. Treatment is with antibiotics, but now blood tests will be carried out for two years to check on treatment. Many doctors also will do a spinal tap to determine whether the brain or spinal cord has been infected. Adequate treatment will prevent adverse effects on the nervous system.

If untreated, syphilis next goes underground for many years, subtly and progressively destroying various organs of the body, indicating its presence only through a positive blood test (and late in the disease, this may become negative). Finally, when enough damage has been done to heart, brain, spinal cord, liver or other organs, the patient will seek medical advice. Treatment at this stage can arrest further damage to the body and often may repair to some extent the damage already done but cannot completely erase the ravages of the disease.

Because syphilis symptoms come and go and because the disease can affect virtually every organ of the body, the great physician Sir William Osler observed that "to know syphilis is to know medicine." For example, syphilis of the brain and spinal cord (neurosyphilis) can manifest itself as insanity, stroke, fleeting shooting pains throughout the body, or joint deformities. Syphilis affecting the arteries can manifest itself as congestive heart failure, angina, or even heart attack. Syphilis also can be transmitted to the fetus during pregnancy. An infected infant usually is very sick and may have deformities. This is why pregnant women should have a blood test for syphilis early in pregnancy. Treatment can prevent harm to the baby.

Treating syphilis prevents spread of the disease. When a case of syphilis is reported, it is then up to local health agencies to trace contacts of the patient so spread of the disease can be arrested.

It took many years of hard work by many researchers to learn of the intricacies of syphilis and discover means for adequate treatment and prevention. Despite great advances in diagnosis and treatment, however, cases may be undiagnosed until late in the disease and there are cases of inadequate treatment. It is with much chagrin that physicians view the rapid increase in incidence of syphilis in recent years and the blasé attitude that, since treatment is easy, why worry about prevention and elimination of the disease!

Syphilis is a sinister killer. It breeds on ignorance. It also breeds on shame. The health and happiness of too many families have been destroyed by false modesty and neglect. It is important that people remember that the doctor does not sit in moral judgment on syphilis or any other venereal disease. He is interested only in prevention and cure.

TUBERCULOSIS

Today the tuberculosis sanatorium in the mountains or desert is disappearing in fact as well as from the fiction in which it used to play a prominent role, as in the celebrated book of Thomas Mann, *The Magic Mountain*. But that does not mean that the disease itself has disappeared. Tuberculosis of the lungs (the form we are considering here) still affects a quarter-million Americans and kills up to 8,000 persons a year. Some experts estimate that there may be another 250,000 unrecognized cases in the country.

It is true that the days of TB as the "white plague" and "galloping consumption" are nearly over, at least in this country where the once terribly feared disease can be treated effectively with specific medicines.

Today, tuberculosis is more apt to attack older people rather than adolescents and young adults who were its prime targets a few decades ago.

One problem in prevention is the ability of the disease to exist in contagious form with minimum symptoms so that persons with active tuberculosis may expose healthy people to the germs.

Contrary to popular belief, the early symptoms are not fever, weight loss, coughing, and the spitting up of blood; these are usually apparent only when the disease has been affecting the lungs for a considerable period. We know of a case of a technician in a hospital who had a tuberculosis cavity in a lung for several months and yet appeared completely healthy to the doctors with whom she worked. In early stages of the disease, there may be only small changes in the lungs visible on x-ray examination— and no symptoms whatever. Doctors have learned that the stethoscope, which helps detect early changes in the heart, is almost useless in detecting the early stages of tuberculosis. When early symptoms do become apparent, they are apt to be subtle ones such as slight weakness, poor appetite, lack of pep, more colds and sore throats than usual; there may be some slight fever in the afternoon or evening.

The bacillus that causes tuberculosis produces a small area of infection in the lung, which is called a tubercle. Frequently, this occasions only a mild reaction in the lung, just enough to stir up the reparative, healing processes. In fact, during this period, the patient may not be conscious of being ill. Then the tubercle is walled off with scar tissue. The bacteria may be completely killed off or some may stay alive but inactive. The only evidence of such an inactive situation may be a small lesion of the lungs visible on x-ray or a positive skin test for tuberculosis called a "tuberculin reaction."

If the disease is not walled up, it can spread slowly through the lung, causing even large cavities.

Thus, a diagnosis of tuberculosis can mean anything from the mildest reaction to severe destruction of lung or lungs, and even spread of disease from lungs to larynx, brain, intestines, adrenal gland, etc. Fortunately, at every stage, no matter how severe the disease, treatment will almost always prove successful. The physician today, in contrast to the physician early in the century, tends to be optimistic when he diagnoses tuberculosis.

Nevertheless, he would like you to benefit from primary prevention—and never need treatment for TB. And TB lends itself well to primary prevention because it is spread in well-established ways. We know now that droplet infection in the air is an important mode of transmission, more important than direct contact, kissing, contamination of dishes or hands. Droplets get into the air as the result of coughing, sneezing, and talking and remain in the air for some time. When inhaled, they may start a new infection. Thus, a single person with tuberculosis may spread the disease not only within a family but in a classroom.

There is a vaccine for tuberculosis which is an aid to primary prevention. While it has not received general acceptance, it is used in special situations. It may be used when the disease is widespread in a particular area, for ward personnel in TB hospitals and in psychiatric institutions, and among American Indians, who are very susceptible to TB.

Some physicians use a mild course of treatment with the drug isoniazid (INH) for persons who have been exposed to tuberculosis and who show a positive tuberculin reaction, or for adolescents who develop a strongly positive tuberculin reaction. This treatment, truly of a primary preventive nature, is generally given for a period of one year.

There are other methods of primary prevention which anyone can make use of readily:

1. Have a yearly medical checkup which includes a tuberculin test or an x-ray picture of the chest, since the stethoscope alone cannot reveal early tuberculosis.

2. Visit a doctor or hospital clinic for an x-ray and examination if you have a cough, cold, or bronchitis that does not clear up in two or three weeks, if you are tired and listless, lose weight, have pains in your chest, "night sweats," a fever, or cough up blood or blood-streaked sputum.

3. Keep your resistance high by regular and adequate sleep, meals and relaxation. Be sure your diet is properly balanced, your work not too exhausting, and your home and place of work comfortably warm and free from dampness.

4. Use pasteurized milk only. TB germs from cattle may be transmitted to other parts of the body and then the lungs by unpasteurized milk, causing tuberculosis.

5. See to it that everyone in your household, including a boarder or servant, has a chest x-ray yearly.

6. Keep a good distance from people who cough, especially if they do not cover their mouth with a handkerchief or tissue. Make "covering a cough" a habit in your family.

7. Wash your hands before meals and after you have touched articles that are apt to be contaminated—for example, a bus or subway strap.

8. When applicable, follow the wise rule or suggest it: a checkup for tuberculosis should always precede marriage.

9. If there is a history of tuberculosis in your family, let your doctor know about it, and be especially careful about following these rules. TB is not inherited but does tend to appear more often in some families than in others.

10. If someone with whom you or any member of your household is in contact develops tuberculosis, be sure to have a checkup and x-ray immediately and again in six months. Don't get panicky about this. Exposure certainly does not mean that you have been infected. But do not ignore the possibility of danger. Why wait until you can smell smoke before you look to see whether the match is burning?

Once tuberculosis has been diagnosed because of routine x-ray check-up or suspicious symptoms, the doctor sets in motion secondary preventive measures to avoid major complications that can lead to permanent lung damage or damage to other parts of the body.

Some people think that with new modern medicines for TB treatment, patients after diagnosis of the disease simply walk around swallowing their pills. That is not the way it usually works out. The doctor wants to confirm the diagnosis in a hospital or sanatorium by actually finding the germs in the sputum or stomach washings. Also, he wants to have the patient at bed rest for some weeks or months until the best schedule of medications has been worked out. In mild cases, this can be done in six to eight weeks; in more severe cases, it may require up to six months.

Also, if a patient is to be treated at home where there are susceptible people, especially children, he must be willing to observe strict rules: cover coughs, avoid close contacts—if necessary, even remain within a demarcated area away from the children. The home atmosphere must be relaxing and conducive to healing. There must be facilities for preparation of a nourishing diet and for recreation. Otherwise, the patient is better off in a hospital or sanatorium. It is no longer necessary, thanks to modern methods of treatment, to send patients far from their home cities in search of mountain or desert air.

Secondary preventive measures for use in TB include three major medications and several others which may be used when necessary. The major ones are isoniazid, streptomycin and para-aminosalicylic acid (PAS). These are often used in sequence or in combination because the tubercle bacillus becomes resistant to any one of the medicines if it is used too long alone. Great skill is required to determine proper dosages, combinations and variations; that is why a family doctor is justified in having a specialist in tuberculosis see a patient early in treatment and at intervals thereafter to make certain that the best combination of the three medications is being administered.

Suppose all does not go as well as hoped for and medicines and rest do not provide the expected cure, or suppose that the disease has been discovered in such advanced form that it has destroyed part or all of one lung and threatens the other lung or other organs. Then surgery may be helpful. Today surgery, which involves removal of part or all of a lung, is highly successful. A person can live well with one healthy lung, and it is better to have a badly diseased lung removed before it leads to a hopeless outlook.

Advanced tuberculosis can be a most unpleasant disease—and yet, with modern methods of treatment, not a hopeless one. It may involve severe cough and production of large amounts of sputum. When large cavities are present, the patient may need to lie with head down to drain the copious sputum, and antibiotics such as penicillin may be required to combat infection by bacteria other than the tubercle bacillus. There may be severe night sweats, requiring frequent change of night clothes and bed linen. Worst of all, there may be a massive hemorrhage, a frightening experience though such hemorrhage rarely is fatal. When it occurs, it is essential to reassure the patient that he is not in danger. Unnecessary emotional distress coupled with loss of blood may lead to shock, which requires emergency treatment. Occasionally loss of blood itself may be severe enough to cause shock.

There are now prospects for tertiary prevention in the event that TB is discovered only after it has destroyed both lungs or because, in a rare instance, treatment has failed. Lung transplantation from a cadaver is technically feasible; and as methods for controlling transplant rejection are improved, this potentially lifesaving measure can be expected to find use.

ULCER OF STOMACH AND DUODENUM (PEPTIC ULCER)

Ulcer denotes any shallow erosion or open sore and may occur on the skin, on the tongue, in the large bowel, or in other areas of the body. For most people, however, the word "ulcer" means ulcer of stomach or duodenum, and this discussion is limited to such an ulcer, which is more specifically called peptic ulcer. The word "peptic" comes from the special enzyme, pepsin, in the stomach juice which helps digest protein.

Peptic ulcers generally occur in the end part of the stomach or in the duodenum. The latter is the first part of the small intestine into which food from the stomach empties. Also into the duodenum empty the digestive juices of the pancreas, and bile from the gallbladder and liver. The stomach secretes a strong acid, hydrochloric acid, which helps kill bacteria and also provides the acid medium required for action of pepsin. The stomach is muscular and produces strong wavelike or peristaltic movements which help churn food and eventually push food into the duodenum. The soft inner coating of the stomach contains cells that secrete hydrochloric acid and enzymes and also mucus. It is believed that the coating of mucus is very important in preventing the enzymes and acid from digesting the stomach itself.

When something goes wrong in the normal protective mechanism, the inner wall of the stomach or duodenum is eroded and a peptic ulcer develops. Peptic ulcers may vary from tiny open sores that are barely visible to large craters. A typical one could be one-half inch in diameter.

The typical symptom of ulcer is pain in the upper abdomen, which comes on one to four hours after eating and is relieved by foods or antacids. The pain comes and goes for about half an hour. Usually, for some weeks or months before this warning sign appears, the patient experiences frequent heartburn and belching. Also, there may be regular occurrence of "water brash," which is the feeling experienced when stomach juice regurgitates and mixes with saliva. There may be general abdominal malaise, diarrhea, nausea and vomiting.

On the basis of these symptoms, the doctor makes a tentative diagnosis of ulcer; he becomes somewhat more certain if the patient is male (ulcers are more frequent in men than in women) and if the patient's blood group is type O. Diagnosis is confirmed by barium meal fluoroscopy and x-ray of the stomach and duodenum and by removal of gastric juice for analysis. In most ulcer patients, gastric juice flow is increased and the fluid has increased acidity. In some instances, it is necessary to insert a special tube, the gastroscope, into the stomach to observe the ulcerated area and to remove a small piece for microscopic study (biopsy).

It should be noted that most true peptic ulcers occur in the duodenum. Some, of course, do occur in the stomach, but what looks like a stomach ulcer may sometimes be a cancer which has produced an area of ulceration. As we shall see, ulcers do not lead to cancer formation, as was once believed.

Since peptic ulcer is believed to be a psychosomatic illness, the doctor considers the patient's personality. People with typical ulcer personalities have been described as those "who have intense oral receptive tendencies with a strong wish to be taken care of and loved. They are tense and hard-driving, always in a hurry, self-sufficient, stubborn, critical, obstinate, overly conscientious, worrisome and emotional."

Peptic ulcer is sometimes termed the "executives' disease," "the malady of the Western world," and "the price of the rapid pace of urban living." In one study, while 78 ulcers were found among executives, only 24 were found among all other employees. It has been estimated that 18 million Americans have peptic ulcer.

Among other facts a physician may consider before making his final diagnosis: ulcer symptoms hit their peak in autumn and spring, and hemorrhage from ulcer is most frequent between September and January.

When a diagnosis of ulcer has been made, what scenarios can a physician envision? The most favorable is healing in weeks or months, but as the physician well knows, healing does not mean *cure*. Most ulcers tend to recur, and so the physician regards peptic ulcer as an ailment that will need a lifetime of watching even if there seems to have been a cure.

There are less favorable possibilities. An ulcer may perforate, boring through the wall of stomach or duodenum so that juices spill into the sensitive peritoneal cavity of the abdomen. If medical management is not adequate, then surgery is required to locate and repair the perforated area. An ulcer may hemorrhage. This occurs when a blood vessel is eroded and may be evidenced by vomiting of bloody or dark-brown stomach contents or by a stool that looks black and tarry or may even be frankly bloody. Many hemorrhages can be managed by medical treatment, but others require immediate surgery.

An ulcer may lead to obstruction —when it causes inflammation or scarring at the outlet of the stomach or in the narrow duodenum. Then food cannot pass, the stomach becomes dilated, and there is vomiting. Some cases can be relieved by medical therapy; others require corrective surgery.

As we have said, a true ulcer does not change to cancer no matter how many years it persists or how often it may heal and recur. However, when a supposed ulcer of the stomach does not heal readily, the doctor suspects that the area may be cancer masquerading as ulcer. While special x-ray studies and gastroscopy and examination of gastric juice may solve the problem of diagnosis, sometimes accurate diagnosis can be made only by examination of the area through surgery.

The doctor attempts to achieve healing and prevent perforation, hemorrhage and obstruction by a multipronged type of therapy. A special diet is used to help neutralize stomach acids, reduce their secretion, and cut down peristaltic movements of the stomach. The diet is bland and contains milk or milk and cream (or skim milk when fat content should be reduced). The patient is provided with a list of foods considered beneficial and of others presumed to be harmful. Antacids are prescribed—and must be taken precisely as directed for maximum benefit. Medicines to reduce stomach activity and flow of gastric juice may be prescribed; these are usually synthetic substances which have effects similar to belladonna and atropine. And for the particularly high-strung ulcer patient, a sedative or tranquilizer also may be prescribed.

What about alcohol, coffee, tea, and carbonated drinks? Most doctors would prefer to have these eliminated from the diet but are willing to compromise if they mean a great deal to the patient. The feeling is that it is better for the patient to have them in moderation than to become tense for lack of them. If alcohol is taken, it should be when there is food in the stomach. Black coffee and strong tea are undesirable. Both drinks should be weak and have as much milk or cream in them as possible, and they should be taken preferably only when there is food in the stomach. With carbonated drinks, if they must be used, it is best to let them stand for a while and to stir them until most of the gas has

been given off, thus minimizing gas distention of the stomach.

And smoking? Well, doctors are against smoking because of the known dangers to lungs and heart. And the ulcer patient may worsen his ulcer by smoking. But doctors are tolerant of the mild smoker who gets real relaxation from smoking. Smoking is an individual matter which should be settled by a particular patient and his physician.

Is psychotherapy required? This, too, is an individual matter. Some patients are under so much tension at home or at work that they realize their need for psychotherapy and press their doctors for it. Others work out emotional problems with the aid of their doctors, who often allow extra time for discussions at the periodic visits. Every ulcer patient should have plenty of sleep and, if possible, a rest period at noon or in the early afternoon. Some need to evaluate their work habits and do everything possible to make their existence less harried. Vacations, relaxing weekends, and hobbies are important.

A regimen of diet, medication, and relaxation of tension will heal many ulcers. It may have to be started in a hospital where the patient can receive intensive treatment free from the worries and tension of job and home. The doctor can best judge whether home or hospital treatment is most desirable.

If treatment does not bring about healing, the doctor thinks of the possibility of cancer, as mentioned earlier (duodenal ulcers, however, are almost never cancerous). Also, he may consider the possibility of two rare types of peptic ulcer—one resulting from tumor or overactivity of the parathyroid glands, the other from tumor of the pancreas (Zollinger-

Ellison syndrome). Both require surgery to correct the underlying cause, not for the ulcer itself.

For any type of ulcer, when secondary preventive measures do not work, surgery may be suggested. The physician is reluctant to suggest this unless he finds that medical treatment—with wholehearted cooperation of the patient—is inadequate. Surgery on the stomach or duodenum is major.

Several operations have been devised. In one, stomach contents are made to bypass the duodenum and go directly into the jejunum, the first half of the small intestine. There is some possibility that a new ulcer may form at the junction of stomach and jejunum. This operation has been improved by cutting the vagus nerve to the stomach in order to reduce the stomach acidity which the nerve stimulates.

Another surgical procedure removes all or part of the stomach, particularly the area that produces acid. After such a procedure some patients develop the "dumping syndrome," in which food traveling directly into the intestine sets off disagreeable symptoms.

The choice of operation is made in consultation between the doctor and a surgeon experienced in ulcer operations. The nature and location of the ulcer, age of the patient, presence of heart disease or other problems enter into the decision as to the best operation for an individual patient.

Surgeons are not eager to operate for ulcers unless the patient has cooperated in medical treatment. Only when it is certain that nonsurgical treatment has failed should surgery be considered; it should never be the lazy man's approach to ulcer therapy. Of course, the situation is different when complications such as perfora-

tion, bleeding or obstruction set in; then, surgery may be lifesaving.

Is tertiary prevention—through transplantation of stomach or duodenum—possible? It is doubtful that it would be successful even if rejection could be obviated, for the same ulcer personality might soon lead to ulcer formation in the donated organ.

Is primary prevention feasible? If all tense, hard-driving, compulsive people were placed on ulcer diets and medications, it might be, but the numbers would run into millions. Perhaps a reasonable compromise would be for those who fit the ulcer personality we described earlier and who have type O blood to have stomach juice tested for acidity. If the acidity is high, it might be desirable to use a modified ulcer diet and antacids and other medications to reduce acidity and stomach activity. Such people, too, might well review their emotional problems and work and home tensions with their doctors, and for many it might be advisable to have at least one session with a psychotherapist to decide whether simple rearrangements of life-style are enough or more extended psychotherapy is needed. No one knows whether such measures would provide primary prevention for peptic ulcer, but since they are certainly not harmful and could be helpful, they seem worth trying. And any gain in relaxing personality is surely beneficial for the individual and for spouse and children.

A final word about peptic ulcers in infants and children. By far, most ulcers occur in adults, but they may occur in babies and young children who, of course, have difficulty in locating sources of pain and describing symptoms. A pediatrician may consider possibility of an ulcer when a baby cries for no apparent reason.

Parents should report vomiting or passage of dark or tarry stools.

ULCERATIVE COLITIS

Diarrhea is a symptom associated with many disorders, including bacterial or viral infections, emotional disturbances, excessive activity of the thyroid gland, and various inflammatory diseases of the intestines. If unchecked, severe diarrhea can lead to dehydration; weight loss; depletion of vitamins, minerals and proteins; fatigue and incapacity to function efficiently. Confronted with a case of severe diarrhea, the physician will perform a careful investigation to determine its cause. If the patient is feverish and markedly weakened, hospitalization may be needed to prevent dehydration and emaciation.

To investigate possible infectious causes of diarrhea, stool and blood studies must be made. Various blood tests may be needed to detect metabolic causes. Special x-ray studies of the small and large bowel (upper GI series and barium enema) are used to check on intestinal abnormalities.

Another important diagnostic tool is sigmoidoscopy (rectal examination) and biopsy (removal) of a small piece of tissue from the rectum for microscopic examination. One cause of recurrent diarrhea that may be discovered by such investigation is ulcerative colitis.

Ulcerative colitis (UC) is a disorder characterized by inflammatory changes in the large intestine which can be seen on barium enema and frequently through sigmoidoscopy. The inflammatory changes make the intestine appear red, swollen, and in some areas ulcerated. Microscopic examination of a small piece of the bowel also shows up distinctive changes when UC is present.

It is important to remember that this disease has nothing whatever to do with ordinary "mucous colitis" or "irritable colon." While the latter produce diarrhea as a common complaint, with UC there are definite ulcerative changes in the lining of the bowel. Colitis or irritable colon responds well in most cases to antispasmodics, antidiarrheal agents, and antianxiety medications. UC, however, requires more vigorous and prolonged treatment.

UC is a disease of young adulthood and the middle years. Its cause is not completely understood, and so primary prevention as yet is not available. The scenario or outlook varies considerably. UC can be a life-threatening disorder characterized by bloody, uncontrolled diarrhea with as many as 15 to 30 bowel movements a day, with anemia, fever, emaciation, and prostration. At the other end of the spectrum, the disease may be characterized by bouts of diarrhea lasting one or two days and remissions of weeks to years. In almost all cases, however, the diarrhea is distinctively mucoid and bloody. The older the age of the patient at the onset of UC, the less severe the disorder.

Treatment of acute attacks includes rest, sedation, and good nutrition, using a low-residue diet (low in fruits, vegetables, whole-grain foods). Sulfonamides are often of value, and steroids (cortisone-like agents) are especially useful in severe cases.

Between attacks, secondary prevention calls for a low-residue diet and adequate rest. Frequently, flare-ups of the diarrhea are related to emotional upset, fatigue, and respiratory infection. Although some feel that UC is a psychosomatic disorder stemming from emotional conflicts, this is far from proven. It is well known, however, that patients with UC, perhaps because of the disabling nature of the disease, may have psychological maladjustments that in many cases resolve with cure of the disease. It is a fact, too, that in many cases, an emotional flare-up immediately precedes an episode of diarrhea—and for this reason, some physicians recommend psychiatric consultation and therapy when appropriate. In almost all cases, if emotional upsets can be avoided, attacks can be prevented.

Helpful in the treatment of severe ulcerative colitis and the prevention of some of the complications is the use of steroid enemas. Administration of steroids this way, instead of by mouth, helps to prevent occurrence of certain undesirable side effects of the powerful anti-inflammatory agents, such as weight gain, bone brittleness, and diabetes.

UC is a chronic disease and as such requires long-term medical care and supervision. During acute attacks, possible complications of bleeding, abscess formation, or perforation of the intestine may call for blood transfusion, antibiotic therapy, or surgery. For unknown reasons, arthritis can be a complication of UC and it requires treatment.

Carried out twice yearly, or more frequently in some cases, sigmoidoscopic examination or barium enema helps the physician assess whether the disease is getting better or worse, and in what way treatment should be altered. Such regular evaluations, as well as treatment of acute episodes, are usually done by a specialist in gastroenterology when one is available.

Unfortunately, cancer of the large bowel occurs more frequently and at a younger age in people with UC.

Early detection of cancer is another important reason for periodic evaluations by barium enema or sigmoidoscopy. The earlier cancer is detected, the better the outlook for cure.

The decision to remove a diseased large bowel (total colectomy) is a difficult one to make. Although it is the only certain cure for UC, it is a major surgical procedure and means the use afterward of an artificial opening, or anus in the abdominal wall. In most cases, total colectomy is not necessary.

The usual reason for total colectomy, which is now considered the only surgical procedure of merit for UC, is cancer, stricture from scarring of the bowel, or unresponsiveness to medical treatment. It is not a routine prophylactic measure. In rare cases, when there is an acute flare-up with devastating diarrhea and emaciation that cannot be brought under control with steroids, total colectomy can be lifesaving.

A society has been formed by those who have undergone total colectomy to provide psychological support for its members and to demonstrate to patients who have recently had to have the operation that it is still possible to lead a normal life.

VARICOSE VEINS

When internal pressure in a vein is higher than normal for a period of time, the vein tends to become wide, tortuous and elongated, and in medical terminology is said to be varicose. Two areas of the body where this happens with particular frequency are the rectum, in which case the condition is called hemorrhoids (see page 593), and the legs.

Normally, blood pressure in veins is quite low. From the head and upper trunk, blood flows back to the heart by gravity. From the lower extremities, it must flow "uphill," and this is achieved through the contractions of muscles during normal activity. The contractions "milk" the blood upward. In addition, the veins have valves which form floors of support for the blood as it moves toward the heart. If several valves in a vein are absent or fail to work efficiently, the weight of the column of blood becomes sufficient to distend the vein.

Valves may break down for a variety of reasons. Some individuals have an inherited tendency for valve weakness. Increased pressure in a vein resulting from obstruction of normal blood flow—the result of pregnancy, obesity, or abdominal tumors—can lead to poor valve functioning. Prolonged standing or sitting can increase pressure in veins and strain the valves. The superficial veins—those immediately beneath the skin in the legs—do not have support from surrounding muscles as do the deeper veins and are more likely than the latter to be distended by increased pressure. Another cause of varicosities may be thrombophlebitis (clot formation and inflammation) in a deeper vein, which may obstruct blood flow in that vessel so that the superficial veins have to handle more than their normal share of blood transport.

Primary prevention of varicose veins involves avoidance of prolonged standing or sitting; even taking no more than a five-minute break every hour or so can be helpful. Walking about or elevating the legs promotes the emptying of blood from the veins. During pregnancy, when increased venous pressure may be experienced for several months, elastic stockings and periods of leg elevation are of value. It is also important to avoid

tight shoes and tight garters that restrict circulation. Once varicosities begin to develop, such measures often can help keep them from developing further.

When the physician evaluates the patient with varicose veins, he will look for a possible cause of obstruction to blood flow—obesity or abdominal tumor, for example. If a cause is found, it will require treatment before therapy can be instituted for the varicosities.

The physician also will attempt to localize, by tests, those veins that have poorly functioning valves. One such test is performed this way: The leg is raised to drain blood from the veins, a tourniquet is applied on the thigh, the patient is asked to stand, and the tourniquet is removed. If blood drops quickly into the lower leg, it indicates incompetent valves. The physician's evaluation may also include x-raying of the veins after injection of a dye.

In addition to being unsightly, varicose veins may eventually cause dull nagging aches, pains, or cramps. Ankles may swell. There may be disturbances of skin nutrition, leading to discoloration and an increased tendency toward bruising, infection, and ulceration. Varicose ulcers are not easily cleared up, especially in the elderly and diabetic; they may refuse to yield to medication, requiring surgery, including skin grafting.

One fairly rare treatment is injection of a solution into the varicosed vein. The solution hardens the vein, and blood no longer flows through that vein but is rerouted to a healthier vein. Such treatment is safe in experienced hands, does not require hospitalization, and may be done in a single session. However, recurrence rate is high.

Surgery to remove damaged veins

and reroute blood to healthier vessels is effective. Such surgery, of course, while eliminating one or more varicose veins, will not prevent other valves from breaking down and other varicosities from developing where the tendency exists. Further surgery may be needed. But the use of the primary preventive measures mentioned earlier can be helpful in avoiding need for repeated surgery.

When there is a history of thrombophlebitis and indications of obstruction of deeper veins, surgical removal of superficial varicosities may not be of particular value. Many surgeons, however, do not agree. They believe that distended, poorly functioning veins may increase the load on properly functioning veins. They recommend removal of the varicosities in such cases.

INDEX

Disks, spinal, 188–89, 648
Dissociative neurosis, 347
Diuretics, menstruation and, 624
Divorce
   late, 382–83
   prevention, 400–402
Dizziness, 573–75
Dog bites, 304
L-dopa, 634–35
Dosage problems with medicines,
   38–41
Dosimeter, 153
Douches, 235
   birth control and, 407–8
Down's syndrome, 439–40
Dreaming in sleep, 92, 93
   medications and, 98
Drinking, 126–33. *See also* Alcohol.
Dromophobia, 345
Drugs, 134–42
   alcohol vs., 139–40
   allergy, 37, 520–21
   dosage problems, 38–41
   hashish, 137
   help for addicts, 142
   heroin, 139, 142
   interactions, 41–42
   LSD, 135–36
   marijuana, 136
   medicinal, 35–43. *See also*
      Medicines.
   narcotic, 139
   outdated, 41
   parents and, 141–42
   reasons for taking, 139–40
   reducing, 66–67
   sedative, 138–39
   sleep and, 98–99
   stimulant, 137–38
   suspected use, 140–41
   tranquilizers, 99, 359–60, 624,
      647
Drunkenness, 126. *See also* Alcohol.
Dubos, Dr. Rene, 449
Duchenne dystrophy, 630
Duodenum
   digestion and, 218–19
   ulcers of, 310, 662–66
Dura mater, 240
Dust
   house, allergy and, 519
   occupational hazard of, 149–50

Dwarfism, 267
Dyes
   aniline, bladder cancer and, 17
   hair, 183
Dysentery, amebic, 525–26
Dysmenorrhea, 624

Ear(s), 254–57
   anatomy, 254
   bones, 254, 256
   care, 254–55
   deafness, 256–57, 445–46
   drum, 254
   foreign objects in, 255
   infections, 254–55
   labyrinth, dizziness and, 574
   middle, 254, 255, 256
   ringing in, 574
   swimming and, 256
   wax, 255
Eating. *See also* Diet; Food.
   binges, 75
   children's, 457–58, 479
   overeating, 63
   underweight and, 78
   vacations and, 109
Eclampsia, 429
Eclipses, viewing of, 252
Ectopic pregnancy, 428–29
Eczema, 521–22
   depression and, 319
Edison, Thomas A., 94
Egg cell
   chromosomes and, 442–43
   contraception and, 406–7
   fertilization, 414
Eggs, white vs. brown, 57
Ejaculation, 233
   premature, 394
Elderly. *See* Aging.
Electric razors, 166
Electrical hazards
   burns and shocks, 506
   fires, 504
   on the job, 146
Electrocardiogram, 25
Electroencephalogram, 91–92
Electrolysis, 166–67
Electromyogram, 629
Electroshock therapy, 360
   depression and, 321

Executives, business (*cont.*)
    ulcers and, 663
Exercise, 80–90
    abdomen, back, and buttocks, 89–90
    age and, 83–84
    appetite and, 68
    asthma, 540–41
    basic principles, 85–86
    benefits, 80–81
    blood distribution and, 200–201
    calorie use, 67, 68
    cholesterol and, 82
    constipation and, 228
    eye, 248
    fatigue and, 81
    foot, 287–88
    health problems and, 81–82, 301
    heart disease and, 82–83, 86–87,
        203–4, 589
    muscles and, 195–96
    necessity of, 84
    opportunities for, 84–85
    pregnancy and, 422
    program, balanced, 86–88
    progression in activity, 86
    reducing and, 67–68
    relaxing, 327
    tension and, 81
    time, 85
    vacations and, 109
    warming up and cooling off, 88–89
Exhibitionism, 350
Exocrine glands, 259
Eye(s), 246–54
    blindness, 247–49, 250
    care, 247–49, 251–52
    cataracts, 250–51
    cleaning of, 251–52
    color, genetics and, 442
    conjunctivitis, 251
    crossed, 249
    drops, 252
    dyeing of hair and, 183
    exercises, 248
    glasses, 248
    glaucoma, 250
    gonorrhea and, 580–81
    infections, 51
    injury, 252
    lazy, 249–50
    lighting and, 146
    night blindness, 253

Eye(s) (*cont.*)
    strain, 252–53
    styes, 251
    sunlight and, 253
    television viewing and, 253–54

Facial nerve paralysis, 245
Fallopian tubes, 235, 269
    pregnancy of, 428–29
Falls in home, 502–3
Family therapy, psychological, 358
Farm workers, 147–49
Farsightedness, 247–48, 249
Fatigue
    anemia and, 205
    depression and, 320
    exercise and, 81
    heart and, 205
    monotony and, 103
    muscle twitching and, 196
    occupational safety and, 145
    pregnancy and, 427
    relaxation and, 100–113
    sleep and, 93
Fatness. *See* Overweight.
Fats
    cholesterol and, 50
    dietary, 64, 73–74
    digestion of, 218, 219, 221
    polyunsaturated, 50, 51
    saturated, 50, 51
Fear, 312, 314–15
    frustration and, 324
Feces. *See* Bowel movements.
Feet, 285–91
    anatomy, 285–86
    athlete's foot, 176, 289–90
    avoiding troubles, 290–91
    bones, 285, 286
    bunions, 289
    club, 565
    corns and calluses, 288
    diabetes and care of, 573
    early problems, 286
    exercises, 287–88
    flat, 287
    hammer toe, 290
    heel discomfort, 290
    ingrown toenails, 289
    myths about, 286–87
    shoes and, 286, 290–91

Occupation (*cont.*)
  lung disease and, 214–15
  marriage and, 379
  noise and vibration, 155
  overworking, 324–25
  poisons, 151–52
  radiation and, 153–54
  relaxation and, 104
  rest room sanitation, 146
  risk of disease and, 17
  rural problems, 147–49
  skin diseases, 150–51
  temperatures, abnormal, 154–55
Odor receptors, 257
Oedipus complex, 400
Office of Naval Research, 241
Oily hair, 180, 182
Oily skin, 165, 171
Ophthalmic ointment, 251
Ophthalmologist, 248
Ophthalmoscope, 22
Opium, 139
Organic foods, 56–57
Orgasm, 394, 395
Orthostatic low blood pressure,
  615
Osteoblasts, 187
Osteomalacia, 544–45
Osteomyelitis, 545
Osteoporosis, 544–45
Otosclerosis, 256
Ovaries, 235, 269, 406
  menopause and, 618
  uterus removal and, 621
Overdosage, medicinal, 38–39
Overweight, 59–77. *See also*
  Reducing.
  adolescents, 491–92
  breathing and, 59–60
  children, 77, 458
  dangers of ups and downs, 65
  definition of, 60
  disease susceptibility and, 60
  gallbladder and, 226
  glandular vs. ordinary, 62–63
  mortality and, 59
  pituitary and, 267
  pregnancy and, 425
  tests for, 62
Oviducts (fallopian tubes), 235, 269,
  428–29
Ovulation, 269–70, 406–7

Oxygen
  anemia and, 527
  muscles and, 195
  stroke and, 653
Oxytocin, 262, 267
Ozena, 212

Pacemaker, heart, 199
Pain, 30
  abdominal, 30
  appendicitis, 532
  chest, 21, 30, 101, 589–90
  childbirth, 431, 436–37
  depression and, 319
  low back, 541–44
  menstrual, 624
  reflex actions and, 243
  sciatica, 648
  ulcer, 662
Palpitation, 204
Panacea, or the Universal Medicine,
  115
Pancreas, 221, 260, 262–63, 271
  cancer of, smoking and, 119
  digestion and, 219
  enzymes, 219, 221
  insulin secretion, 219, 221, 262–63,
    569, 573
Pantophobia, 345
Papillae, dermal, 163
Para-aminosalicylic acid (PAS), 661
Paralysis
  facial nerve, 245
  hysterical, 346
  sleep, 633
  stroke and, 653, 654
Paranoia, 352, 353
Parasites
  intestinal (worms), 294–95, 482–83
  malarial, 616
Parasympathetic nervous system, 244
Parathormone, 262, 265
Parathyroid glands, 260, 262, 265
Parenthood, 403–438
  abortion and, 409–10
  adolescents and, 487, 489, 498–500
  adoption and, 410
  authoritarian vs. authoritative
    discipline, 459
  birth control and, 405–8
  childbirth and, 430–35

Reducing (*cont.*)
  talking about diet, 75
  wrinkles and, 167
Reflex actions, 243
Relaxation, 100–113
  achievement of, 103–4
  alcohol and, 127
  arthritis and, 100–101
  hobbies and, 104–5
  individuality in, 103–4
  muscle tension and, 326–27
  occupational safety and, 145
  sports and, 105–7
  vacations, 107–13
  values of, 101–3
REM (rapid eye movements), 92
Renin, 599
Rennin, 218
Reparative psychotherapy, 357–58
Repression, sexual, 400
Reproductive organs, 232–37
Respiratory system, 206–15. *See also*
    Lungs.
  anatomy, 206–11
  dust and disease of, 149–50
  mechanics of breathing, 210–11
  overweight and, 60
  preventive care, 212–15
  smoking and, 119–20
Rest. *See* Relaxation.
Rest room sanitation, 146
Retina, 22, 246
Retirement, emotional problems and,
    373–74
Rh incompatibility, cerebral palsy
    and, 562
Rheumatic fever, 20, 472–74, 585–87
Rheumatoid arthritis, 533–35
  relaxation and, 100–101
Rhythm method, 406–7
Ribs, 210
Rice polishings, 57
Rickets, 53
Ringworm, 176, 485–86
Risks, calculation of, 16–17
Rocky Mountain spotted fever, 298,
    303
Rooming-in system, 430
Roseola infantum, 477–78
Roundworm infection, 295, 482
Rupture, 594. *See also* Hernia.
Rural working problems, 147–49

Sabin polio vaccine, 638
Sadism, 351, 400
Safe period, 406
Safety
  home, 501–10
  occupational, 143–55
St. Anthony's fire, 178
St. Martin, Alexis, 222
St. Vitus' dance, 473
Salary satisfaction, 144
Saliva, 216–17, 476
Salk vaccine, 638
Sanitary pads, female, 235
Sansert, 584
Sarcoidosis, 644–45
Sarcoma. *See also* Cancer.
  definition of, 557
Sartorius, 193
Satyrism, 350, 400
Sauna baths, 68
Scabies, 176
Scalp, 164, 179–85. *See also* Hair.
  baldness, 184
  dandruff, 181–82
  infection, 182, 183, 483–86
  layers of, 240
  lice, 483–84
  number of hairs, 164
  psoriasis, 642
  ringworm, 485–86
Scanning, radioactive isotope, 25
Scarlet fever, 472
  nephritis and, 602, 603
Scenario, definition of, 512
Schick test, 478
Schizoid personality, 353
Schizophrenia, 352, 645–48
  chemical basis of, 647
Sciatica, 648–49
Scleroderma, 178
Sclerosis, multiple, 627–29
Scoliosis, 546
Scopolamine, 99
Scratches, infection and, 304
Screening, automated multiphasic,
    26–27
Scrotum, 233, 234
Scurvy, 53, 57
Sea sponge, 57
Seatworm, 482
Sebaceous glands, 164, 170, 171
Seborrhea, 181, 182